THIRD EDITION

W9-CDL-407

READINGS AND CASES IN INTERNATIONAL HUMAN RESOURCE MANAGEMENT

MARK MENDENHALL
UNIVERSITY OF TENNESSEE AT CHATTANOOGA

GARY ODDOU
UTAH STATE UNIVERSITY

 South-Western College Publishing
an International Thomson Publishing company I(T)P®

Cincinnati • Albany • Boston • Detroit • Johannesburg • London • Madrid • Melbourne • Mexico City
New York • Pacific Grove • San Francisco • Scottsdale • Singapore • Tokyo • Toronto

Team Director: Dave Shaut
Executive Editor: John Szilagyi
Developmental Editor: Theresa Curtis, Ohlinger Publishing Services
Marketing Manager: Joseph A. Sabatino
Production Editor: Tamborah E. Moore
Manufacturing Coordinator: Dana Began Schwartz
Internal Design: Rebecca Gray
Cover Design: Paul Neff Design, Cincinnati
Cover Photography: Copyright PhotoDisc
Production House: Rebecca Gray
Printer: Webcom

Printed in Canada
5 6 7 8 9 10

International Thomson Publishing Europe
Berkshire House
168-173 High Holborn
London, WC1V7AA, United Kingdom

International Thomson Editores
Seneca, 53
Colonia Polanco
11560 México D.F. México

Nelson ITP, Australia
102 Dodds Street
South Melbourne
Victoria 3205 Australia

International Thomson Publishing Asia
60 Alberta Street #15-01
Albert Complex
Singapore 189969

Nelson Canada
1120 Birchmount Road
Scarborough, Ontario
Canada M1K 5G4

International Thomson Publishing Japan
Hirakawa-cho Kyowa Building, 3F
2-2-1 Hirakawa-cho, Chiyoda-ku
Tokyo 102, Japan

International Thomson Publishing Southern Africa
Building 18, Constantia Square
138 Sixteenth Road, P.O. Box 2459
Halfway House, 1685 South Africa

You can request permission to use material from this text through the following phone and fax numbers: telephone: 1-800-730-2214   fax: 1-800-730-2215
Or you can visit our web site at http://www.thomsonrights.com

Library of Congress Cataloging-in-Publication Data
Readings and cases in international human resource management/ [edited by] Mark Mendenhall, Gary Oddou. — 3rd ed.
    p.   cm.
Includes bibliographical references.
ISBN 0-324-00634-9 (softcover : alk. paper)
1. Personnel management—Cross-cultural studies. 2. Intercultural communication—Case studies. 3. International business enterprises-culture—Cross-cultural studies. I. Mendenhall, Mark A. II. Oddou, Gary R.
HF5549.R3813 2000
658.3—dc21

This book is printed on acid-free paper.   99-27527

____Contributing Authors____

RAE ANDRE
Northeastern University
USA

BARBARA BAKHTARI
USA

SCHON BEECHLER
Columbia University
USA

ALLAN BIRD
California Polytechnic University, San Luis Obispo
USA

J. STEWART BLACK
University of Michigan
USA

MATT BLOOM
University of Notre Dame
USA

NAKIYE BOYACIGILLER
San Jose State University
USA

CHRIS BREWSTER
Cranfield School of Management
UNITED KINGDOM

MARK BUTLER
San Diego State University
USA

DIANNE CYR
Technical University of British Columbia
CANADA

SUE DAVISON
UN
KENYA

HELEN DE CIERI
University of Melbourne
AUSTRALIA

WILLIAM DAVIDSON
Mesa Consulting
USA

C. BROOKLYN DERR
University of Utah
USA

PETER DOWLING
University of Tasmania
AUSTRALIA

THOMAS D. DRETLER
COO of EduVentures, LLC
USA

ROBERT EDER
Portland State University
USA

EFRAT ELRON
Hebrew University
ISRAEL

GARETH EVANS
USA

CHRISTOPHE FALCOZ
L'Ecole de Management-Lyon
FRANCE

PEDRO FERREIRA
PARAGUAY

COLETTE FRAYNE
California Polytechnic University, San Luis Obispo
USA

J. MICHAEL GERINGER
California Polytechnic University, San Luis Obispo
USA

HAL GREGERSEN
Brigham Young University
USA

DONALD HAMBRICK
Columbia University
USA

MASAO HANAOKA
Daito Bunka University
JAPAN

ALAN HAWKINS
Brigham Young University
USA

MARTIN HILB
University of St. Gallen
SWITZERLAND

SUSAN E. JACKSON
Rutgers University
USA

MERRICK JONES
University of Manchester
UNITED KINGDOM

ROSABETH MOSS
KANTER
Harvard University
USA

RONIT KARK
Hebrew University
ISRAEL

ELLEN KOSSEK
*Michigan State
University*
USA

PETER LAWRENCE
*Loughborough
University*
UNITED KINGDOM

PAUL LEMIEUX
USA

LESLEY MAYNE
*Cranfield School of
Management*
UNITED KINGDOM

MARJORIE
McENTIRE
*Utah State Office of
Education*
USA

GLENN McEVOY
Utah State University
USA

MARK
MENDENHALL
*University of Tennessee,
Chattanooga*
USA

GEORGE T.
MILKOVICH
Cornell University
USA

TOMASZ
MROCZKOWSKI
American University
USA

GARY ODDOU
Utah State University
USA

ASBJORN OSLAND
George Fox University
USA

JOYCE OSLAND
University of Portland
USA

CYNTHIA OZEKI
*Michigan State
University*
USA

BARBARA PARKER
Seattle University
USA

J. BONNER RITCHIE
*Brigham Young
University*
USA

KAREN ROBERTS
*Michigan State
University*
USA

JENNIFER RONEY
University of Utah
USA

WILLIAM ROOF
USA

SYLVIE
ROUSSILLON
*L'Ecole de Management-
Lyon*
FRANCE

RANDALL S.
SCHULER
Rutgers University
USA

SCOTT SNELL
*Pennsylvania State
University*
USA

CHARLES SNOW
*Pennsylvania State
University*
USA

PAUL SPARROW
University of Sheffield
UNITED KINGDOM

GÜNTER K. STAHL
University of Bayreuth
GERMANY

SULLY TAYLOR
*Portland State
University*
USA

MARY TEAGARDEN
*The American Graduate
School of International
Management*
USA

OLGA TREGASKIS
*Cranfield School of
Management*
UNITED KINGDOM

ROSALIE TUNG
*Simon Fraser
University*
CANADA

WARNER
WOODWORTH
*Brigham Young
University*
USA

ALBERTO ZANZI
Suffolk University
USA

Contents

PART 4: MANAGEMENT DEVELOPMENT

PART 5: PERFORMANCE APPRAISAL AND COMPENSATION

PART 6: LABOR AND EMPLOYEE RELATIONS

Section 2:

Specialized Human Resource Topics in International Business

PART 7: CROSS-CULTURAL ISSUES IN PRODUCTIVITY AND QUALITY

PART 8: HUMAN RESOURCE ISSUES IN INTERNATIONAL JOINT VENTURES

PART 9: MANAGING EXPATRIATE ASSIGNMENTS

Preface

Welcome to the third edition of *Readings and Cases in International Human Resource Management.* If you are a long-time user of the text, we would like to take a moment to thank you for using the book in your teaching or consulting endeavors. We originally put this book together because we couldn't find one ourselves, and we wanted such a book to use in our classes. Since then, with your help, the book has evolved and become a standby for teachers of international management/HRM/OB. If you are a new adopter of the book, we would like to thank you, and we look forward to your comments concerning your experience in using the book. Feel free to contact us with your feedback.

In this third edition, we have kept the best of the previous editions and added new readings and cases that have the same type of "feel" as the old, "tried-and-true" ones. The format of the book has changed slightly; however, the conceptual groupings of each major section of the book have essentially remained the same. We were reluctant to tamper with a conceptual format that so many people liked.

Our field, however, is dynamic, and in order to be current we have updated most of the readings and some of the cases. However, a few of these readings and cases seemed to us to be classics. That is, the issues they address seem to transcend time (and copyright date!). We chose to keep these in the book, since we like to teach from them, and we know that most of you do, as well!

Our main objective for the book is simply this: to sensitize the reader to the complex human resource issues that exist in the international business environment. With this objective in mind, we have attempted to represent many parts of the world in the readings and cases. However, in doing so, we chose not to "force fit" something into the book for the sake of regional or geographic representation. We included what we, our reviewers, and our editors felt were quality readings and cases in the field of international human resource management.

AACSB, Creativity, and Course Design

Readings and Cases in International Human Resource Management can be used by instructors and consultants in many ways to enhance students' classroom experiences. If the instructor's preference is to teach a predominately case course, it can be used as a stand-alone text. Or, it can be used in tandem with a traditional principles textbook in order to provide outside readings and more substantial cases for the students.

Too, it can be used with other specialized books in the South-Western International Series (see below) or with other specialty books in the international management or international human resource areas:

- Dowling, P.J., Welch, D.E., & Schuler, R.S. (1999) *International Human Resource Management: Managing People in a Multinational Context* (3rd edition)

- Adler, N.J. (1997) *International Dimensions of Organizational Behavior* (3rd edition)

- Phatak, A. (1997) *International Management: Concepts and Cases*

The book can also be used as a stand-alone text and can be supplemented via lectures or other pedagogical strategies. However the book is used, students will find the complexities and details of international human resource problems fascinating, as we do.

Acknowledgments _____

We would like to thank all those who have contributed to this book. Many authors sent us cases, articles, and manuscripts in progress for possible inclusion in this edition. We only regret that we could not include all the materials offered to us. Many have given us input as to the best approach for this revision, and we are grateful to all of them.

We would like to thank Theresa Curtis for her incredible patience and expertise in seeing this project to its completion and John Szilagyi for his support for the project. And to our wives, Janet and Jane, we offer our gratitude for putting up with our international wanderings—without them, we would not be able to accomplish much, in our lives or our careers.

READINGS AND CASES IN INTERNATIONAL HUMAN RESOURCE MANAGEMENT

SECTION 1

Human Resource Management Functions in International Business

Part 1

THE CONTEXT OF INTERNATIONAL HUMAN RESOURCE MANAGEMENT

"Global Strategy" and Its Impact on Local Operations: Lessons from Gillette Singapore

Reading 1.1
Rosabeth Moss Kanter
Thomas D. Dretler

"Global" is among the most overused and least understood words in business today. The phrase "going global" is used to refer to everything from opening a firm's first international sales office to taking a trip outside the United States. Scott McNealy, CEO of Sun Microsystems, received almost full page coverage in the *New York Times* a few years ago just because he traveled personally to Southeast Asia. And the uses of "global" are often imprecise. One company with operations in Mexico and Brazil calls itself "global" when it is really "hemispheric." An Asian consumer products company has been pursuing what it calls "globalization" by moving from its Philippine and Hong Kong bases into Indonesia, Singapore, and Malaysia, a strategy that was at best regional. An increasingly global economy is clearly important to businesses today, and understanding of global strategy is a critical element in any leader's repertoire. Information technology and trade that link the world have made export markets a vital part of the sales growth plan for manufacturing and, increasingly, service companies of all sizes. Even companies with a low percentage of international sales have international suppliers, compete with international companies in their home markets, and must meet world class quality standards in order to hold their local business.[1]

Myths and Misunderstandings

What does global strategy really mean? Examination of the use of the words global and globalization by business executives and by the media

Source: R. Moss Kanter & T.D. Dretler. Reprinted with permission of Academy of Management, PO Box 3020, Briar Cliff Manor, NY 10510-8020. "Global Strategy and its Impact on Local Operations: Lessons from Gillette Singapore," R. Moss Kanter & T.D. Dretler, *Academy of Management Executive*, Vol. 12, No. 4 (1998). Reproduced by permission of the publisher via Copyright Clearance Center, Inc.

indicates the prevalence of six major myths or misunderstandings. Uncritical acceptance of these myths prevents companies from taking full advantage of global opportunities.

Myth #1: That global is synonymous with international, meaning simply having a presence in other countries whether or not there is any connection among activities across countries. Having a sales office, a factory, or a representative in other countries does not by itself make a company global, especially if country operations run independently, with few ties between them, and all power and influence resides at U.S. headquarters. Nortel's Turkish subsidiary, Netas, won Nortel's international quality award a few years ago; but few, if any, American and Canadian managers subsequently traveled to Turkey to learn best practices from Netas. Quaker Oats had a gem in its European pet food operations but sold the pet food division because of aspirations to be a beverage giant in the U.S.—and then later worried about insufficient international reach. Failing to include international outposts as key company resources prevents companies from crafting effective global strategies.

The second misunderstanding is the flip side of the first. If global implies something more than international activities, then it involves homogenization. Thus, **myth #2: That global strategy means doing everything the same way everywhere.** Coca-Cola is one of the world's great universal global brands, made with virtually a world formula and with a logo and brand identity known even in remote villages of underdeveloped countries. But the global product is handled very differently in each market. Local variations include different local bottling and distribution partners (such as the Coca-Cola-Schweppes joint ventures in the U.K. or the San Miguel partnership in the Philippines); different container sizes, different names ("Coca-Cola Light" instead of "Diet Coke" in Europe), and different product forms (fewer dispensing machines outside the U.S. means less demand for just the syrup).

The third confusion is about the identity of so-called global companies, as contained in **myth #3: That globalizing means becoming a stateless corporation with no national or community ties.** This myth is increasingly refuted by the rise of corporate citizenship. Indeed, one could argue that the more global the scope of business operations, the greater the need to make local connections in order to gain good will from customers, employees, and politicians who care about their local roots.[2] Companies must become insiders in all their markets in order to be globally effective—which is why Percy Barnevik, CEO of Asea Brown Boveri, prefers to call ABB a multilocal rather than a global company. At Kanter's suggestion, Novartis, the pharmaceutical giant created by the merger of Sandoz and Ciba, announced its new global identity with a day of local community service throughout the world. Becoming great local citizens can pay off within domestic as well as foreign markets. When entire blocks of businesses were burned and looted during the 1992 riots in Los Angeles, residents protected McDonald's stores because of community service projects such as the Ronald McDonald House for sick children.

A corollary is **myth #4: That globalization requires abandoning country images and values.** On the contrary, global products sometimes derive identity from their place or origin, like the famous Marlboro man, who once sold American culture as part of the cigarette. Indeed, country images can be so strong that some companies borrow ones that aren't even theirs to create an international brand, like Haagen-Daz ice cream, an American brand that suggests Scandinavia, or Au Bon Pain, an American chain of French bakery-style cafes that is exporting frozen French-style bread dough to Latin American from its Boston factory.

The process of globalization is also misunderstood by some companies. **Myth #5: That globalizing means tacking on acquisitions or alliances in other countries, without much integration or change.** Just because a company has a partner or even a subsidiary outside its home country doesn't make it global, unless there is some value-added in every market because of the international ties. Pharmacia & Upjohn, the troubled drugmaker, reportedly stumbled because it never melded its Swedish and American operations and cultures—nor those of the Italian company that Pharmacia had purchased before the merger. Without synergies, there is no global strategy. Similarly, it remains to be seen whether international airline agreements such as the Lufthansa/United Airlines alliance (now expanding to encompass SAS and Thai Air) confer more benefits than smooth transfers among flights. If all United does is to help travelers book a Lufthansa flight at its ticket counters and share lounges and frequent flyer points, United is no more global than it was before the alliance.

Finally, there is a common assumption that global strategy involves activities outside the home country, as in **myth #6: That to qualify as global, a strategy must involve sales or operations in another country.** Union Pacific Resources of Fort Worth, Texas, grew aggressively by pursuing what it calls a "home alone" strategy—concentrating on oil and gas exploration in the western United States while its competitors roam the world. But unlike myopic, parochial, domestic companies of the past, UPR scanned the world for opportunities, noted where its competition was strong, and considered all the areas in which it could best deploy new technology.[3] In short, global thinking is what's important for companies, not just counting international sales. That thought process, in turn, will expand opportunities in any market the company pursues.

If global strategy doesn't necessarily equate with international, universal, and unconnected to country identity, what does it mean? This is the question we sought to explore in our work with Gillette, especially in the Asia-Pacific region.

Global connotes holistic, integrated activity. Global strategy involves thinking in an integrated way about all aspects of a business— its suppliers, production sites, markets, and competition. It involves assessing every product or service from the perspective of both domestic and international market standards. It means embedding international perspectives in product formulations at the point of design, not as afterthoughts. It means meeting world standards even before seeking world markets and being world class even in local markets. It means deepening the company's understanding of local and cultural differences in order to become truly global.

Global success rests on the ability to listen and learn in locations far from the home base. Searching internationally for concepts as well as customers and suppliers can stimulate innovation and ease eventual entry into new markets. Consider how one Japanese auto company used an alliance with a car-leasing company in China to learn about use and repair of cars in that emerging market long before it considered manufacturing in China or even exporting its own cars there. International contacts suggest new ideas to bring to strategic discussions.

Global strategy involves focusing on areas of excellence against a backdrop of worldwide possibilities, determining the synergies that exist across markets and alliance partners as well as the differences that must be taken into account in various locations. What we discovered in the case of Gillette was that effective globalization required strong local integration across functions and divisions in every place the company operated.

The Gillette Company and Its International Organization ————

The Gillette Company is the world leader in male grooming products. Founded in 1901, the company has consistently led a category that includes blades and razors, shaving preparations, and electric shavers. Gillette also holds the number one position worldwide in various female grooming products such as wet shavers and hair epilation devices. The company is the world's top seller of writing instruments, correction products, toothbrushes and oral care appliances. Gillette's leadership in over 200 countries and territories is fueled by 50 manufacturing facilities in 24 nations.

Gillette has long demonstrated a commitment to international markets. Between 1905 and 1909, the company established manufacturing facilities in Canada, England, France, and Germany. By 1919, branch offices or companies were started in Copenhagen, Madrid, Milan, Istanbul, Calcutta, Sydney, Brussels, Geneva, Buenos Aires, Singapore, and Shanghai. Gillette's traditional multinational strategy was to market and distribute its latest and most technologically advanced products in only the world's most developed regions. Emerging markets were valued and deemed important to the company's continued growth, but the products available there may have been launched five, 10, or 15 years earlier in countries like the United States. This "Stone Age theory" according to Gillette CEO Alfred Zeien, survived until the late 1980s, when Gillette discovered that the forces of change had made such an approach obsolete. Beginning with the worldwide launch of Sensor in 1990, Gillette became one of the first truly global companies. Today, the latest and most technologically advanced Gillette products and manufacturing systems can be found almost anywhere in the world.[4]

To support Gillette's increasingly global focus, the company went through a restructuring in 1988, creating three principal divisions. The North Atlantic Group manufactures and markets the company's traditional shaving and personal care products in North America and Western Europe. The Diversified Group comprises the Stationery division's North Atlantic arm; as well as the Braun, Oral-B, and Jafra companies, each organized on a worldwide product line basis. The International Group produces and sells the company's Shaving, Personal Care, and Stationery products in all markets except North America and Western Europe.

The International Group is divided into three regions: Latin America; Africa, Middle East, and Eastern Europe (AMEE); and Asia-Pacific. Each area has a Group Vice President that oversees Gillette's sales of Shaving, Personal Care, and Stationery products in that region. The Asia-Pacific group markets are Japan, Hong Kong, China, Australia, Singapore, Korea, Indonesia, Thailand, Taiwan, Malaysia, the Philippines, New Zealand, South Pacific, South Korea, and Indochina.

Gillette's global strategy includes a clear understanding of local differences—that each market presents unique challenges, requirements, and opportunities. In the rapid growth Asia-Pacific region, for example, Gillette has used merger integration as a vehicle for developing a wholly integrated approach to individual markets. In Singapore, the acquisition of Parker Pen in 1993 triggered the establishment of a new organizational structure that has allowed Gillette to show one face to the customer and act as a single, integrated entity to suppliers in the region. While the integration reflects a global strategy, the ability to pull it off required a local sensitivity and orientation. Indeed, the story of Gillette Singapore's merger with Parker Pen illuminates the link between global strategy and local mastery. It demonstrates how managing local integration is key to unleashing the power of global brands.

Gillette Singapore and the Search for Global Integration in the Asia-Pacific Region

In the 1960s, Gillette established an Asia-Pacific manufacturing presence with a blades, toiletries, and liquid paper facility in Australia. In 1970, it added a small, old-style, double-edged blade plant in Malaysia. Over time, the company began constructing larger factories in areas such as the Philippines, Indonesia, and Thailand. By the early 1980s, Gillette had gradually put together Asian sales forces and an infrastructure in the region.

In June 1984, Gillette announced the $188.5 million purchase of Oral-B Laboratories, the leading marketer of toothbrushes in the United States. A profitable and well-managed company, Oral-B manufactured top-quality products that were distributed through many of the same channels that already existed within the Gillette network. As Gillette's technological expertise was in metals and other shaving-related raw materials, it saw no reason to disrupt the Palo Alto-based Oral-B operation with a heavy-handed management takeover. On the contrary, the value of the Oral-B acquisition was in benefiting from distribution channel synergies. Keeping Oral-B managers focused on a product-line basis was key to making the acquisition a success.

While the Oral-B management and reporting structure remained intact, managers at established Gillette operations in developing regions like Asia-Pacific were tapped to assist with sales and share with Oral-B such back-room services as finance and operations. This concept was a difficult one for many Gillette employees to accept. The Gillette Company culture was one where performance reigned supreme. Managers were pushed to set and consistently meet aggressive growth numbers in all of their markets. Gillette managers viewed the first Oral-B employees to arrive in Malaysia as nuisances and threats to their livelihoods. Gillette sales people were paid and evaluated relative to how much product they sold. As far as they were concerned, any time spent on Oral-B was lost on a Gillette-managed product. The company incentive structure was such that sales people had nothing to gain and everything to lose by helping Oral-B.

To remedy this situation, Corporate Controller Chuck Cramb introduced the concept of notional accounting. This double counting procedure allowed both Oral-B and Gillette managers to take credit for the same sales. Still, implementation of this concept was not easy. According to Norman Roberts, former Asia-Pacific Group VP and a champion of local integration, "Managers had to learn how to cooperate with people that they had no direct authority over."

Over the next several years, employees throughout Asia-Pacific became introduced to the notional accounting concept and the prospect of shared services. While each market was different, an initial display of resistance and turf-guarding was the norm. One issue that proved particularly disruptive in the company's effort to build cohesion was Gillette's strong shaving affiliation. In a company identified the world over for its shaving dominance, Oral-B managers couldn't help but feel like second class citizens. At the same time, managers on the shaving side were wary of spending their time on Oral-B for fear of losing ground on the core business. For headquarters, the challenge was to convince employees that Gillette was more than a shaving company. This was easier said than done. Still, despite the difficulties, Roberts felt strongly that a collaborative environment was necessary to take advantage of Gillette's established infrastructure in developing markets.

As Group VP, Roberts had the latitude to organize Asia-Pacific operations in a way that he felt would best maximize current and future performance. In 1992, he drafted and distributed to general managers in all AP markets a simple, one-page document called the Campus Charter. In it he wrote, "the campus concept is simply that in Asia-Pacific it is more efficient for the various divisions of the Gillette Company (Shaving, Stationery, Oral Care, Braun) to operate under the same roof sharing common services."

Essentially, the Campus Charter asked business unit managers to maintain their reporting autonomy while sharing support services such as finance, information technology, human resources, and, in some cases, sales. The new structure was designed to not only exploit synergies and avoid duplication but also to advance Gillette's global integration strategy by showing one face to the customer and allowing the company to act as a single entity to suppliers in developing markets.

In May 1993, Gillette acquired Parker Pen Holdings Limited of the U.K. for 285 million British pounds (equivalent to $460 million U.S. dollars on the date of purchase). Originally a division of a Wisconsin-based firm, Parker was sold to U.K. investors as part of $100 million management buyout in 1985. As a British company, it battled aggressively with Waterman, located just across the English Channel. When Gillette bought the French company in 1987, it was buoyed by Gillette's deep pockets and strong distribution network. Through Waterman, Gillette enjoyed a 21 percent share of the luxury segment of the world pen market. With the 1993 addition of Parker to the company's Paper Mate and Waterman brands, Gillette would own 40 percent of that market and become the clear worldwide leader in writing instruments.

Despite its strong market position, Parker maintained a close-knit and familial corporate culture. Perhaps because of its origins as a family-owned company, Parker had a flat organizational structure and prospered in an informal environment. It had a single-brand, high-end product line of which members of the company were extremely proud.

With the Parker Pen integration on the immediate horizon, Norman Roberts decided that now was the time for Asia-Pacific markets to embrace a full-fledged campus approach. Although already operating within a system of shared services and notional accounting, the prospect of physical relocation presented the opportunity for an organizational restructuring in the region.

The Four Lessons of Gillette Singapore _____

At the urging of Norman Roberts, Gillette Singapore would be the first Asia-Pacific market to fully integrate Parker Pen and establish formal campus operations. Gillette Singapore is the marketing and distribution arm for the Gillette Company in the 633-square-mile, Southeast Asian nation-state of Singapore. Originally established in 1919, Gillette's modern-day Singapore operation came into being during the mid-1970s. Consistently the most profitable market (on a per capita basis) in the Asia-Pacific region, Gillette Singapore's 1993 sales were nearly $9 million in an area containing only three million people. Gillette-managed businesses (Shaving, Oral Care, and Personal Care) accounted for 57 percent, 31 percent and less than 1 percent of profits respectively. Non-Gillette-managed Stationery was responsible for 12 percent of earnings. Braun (another non-Gillette-managed business) did not do business out of Gillette Singapore at the time.

The new organizational structure called for the current GM of Shaving and Personal Care in Singapore to assume the additional role of campus dean. In this capacity he would be responsible for overseeing all integration activities.

At the new Gillette Singapore campus, Shaving and Personal Care would be a division of nearly 20 people, including a 10-person sales force reporting directly to the GM. Also depending on this sales team would be the Oral Care division, which would have a staff of only four, along with a business manager. The Gillette Stationery division, naturally, would experience a complete shake-up. Formally a seven-person group that relied heavily on the Shaving sales force, this department would expand to over 20, in part because Parker's Singapore office housed its regional general management, as well. As a result, the Singapore Campus would contain a regional GM for Stationery in addition to a person in charge of the local operation. Under these people would be Marketing and Promotion departments, as well as an exclusive eight-person Singapore sales team. If the Stationery division was to be dominated by Parker people, the support functions would split right down the middle. The financial controllers of each office would be teamed up to head Finance. Under them would be clerks and various support staff numbering close to 20. Also greatly expanded would be the Materials Management office, whose five-person staff would triple and handle warehouse and other operations-related activities for the entire Campus. Initially there would be no Information Technology (IT) or Human Resources (HR) function but, once established, all four support areas (Finance, Materials Management, IT, and HR) would report directly to the campus dean.

The integration of Parker Pen and establishment of Campus operations in Singapore was both a tremendous challenge and an unqualified success. For Gillette headquarters in Boston, local integration of International Group operations was key to implementing its global corporate strategy. For those on the ground in Singapore, the experience provided several practical lessons that could be useful to other global players.

The Need for Integration Across Functions and Divisions

Tapping the power of global brands and the economies of global production requires greater integration across functions and divisions at the local level—and thus, strong local management. Even though Gillette was organized around worldwide or superregional product groups and functional groups, managers on the ground in various countries did not report to international bosses outside of their local territory, thus losing connection with their local base. The campus concept was born from the vision of showing one face to the customer. Without coordinated activities, the total effectiveness of Gillette's operations in Singapore would have been nothing more than the sum of its parts. Instead, the global synergies that Gillette sought were manifested through local relationships.

In Singapore, Personal care, Oral care—and eventually, the newest acquisition, Duracell—all benefited from Shaving's relationships and clout with local distribution channels. The new Stationery sales force—responsible for both Parker and Waterman stocks—also has considerably enhanced leverage. Indeed, when operational synergies are the motivation for an acquisition, the need for links between the combining organizations is high.[5] Housing all business units under one roof allows the relevant stakeholders—customers, suppliers, employees, and community members—to view Gillette Singapore as one company with one vision and one way of operating. Employees are better able to understand, exchange ideas with, and transfer into other divisions. The strong operational integration required by the campus creates a new and universally-accepted culture—one that can be consistently displayed to those outside the organization.[6] Besides the obvious benefits of cost-cutting, the Campus approach delivers bottom-line value by strengthening Gillette's brand identity in Singapore. Individual product lines are more easily associated with the Gillette name—thus elevating their perceived value in the marketplace. Like other successful integrators, Gillette understands that well conceived acquisitions ensure that valuable customers win too.[7] The emphasis on local integration in international markets is one reason the Gillette Company has developed such powerful global brands. Indeed, as the actual amount of resource sharing between two firms increases, and the years since the merger increase, so do performance benefits from the merger.[8]

The Need to Manage Change

Managing globalization means managing change, and handling a variety of human issues connected with local settings. Defining global strategy is a high-level corporate function that can be done for the whole corporation with a single plan. But operationalizing it means managing multiple changes in multiple places. Creating the Gillette Singapore Campus and integrating Parker Pen was identified by

Singapore managers as the most difficult change management challenge in recent memory. For all its strategic importance and global significance, successful integration was about dealing with people and managing resistance to change—and the nitty-gritty basics mattered.

For example, when the word got out that a new office location for the campus would have to be found, ex-Parker employees (who had been working at Parker headquarters on the east side of the island) threatened to quit if a new location was chosen in the west. Long-time Gillette employees, on the other hand, had grown accustomed to the west and were reluctant to commute the ten to twenty extra miles east. This posed a significant dilemma—especially since high-turnover at a target company has proved to be negatively correlated with successful integration.[9] Eventually, the Gillette Singapore GM plotted on a map the homes of every campus employee, then chose a new site on the side of the island inhabited by the greatest number of employees. When a new space in the east finally was found, employees and managers from all business units jockeyed for position regarding office space and transition responsibilities. While Gillette headquarters did have some standard guidelines regarding the size and type of office for various management levels, senior Asia-Pacific executives from different divisions lobbied the Gillette Singapore GM for extra space to house and support their particular business unit activities.

Furthermore, while the new structure was still being shaped, several managers tried to position themselves for greater power and authority in the new regime. Managers who weren't involved in the initial integration planning were particularly demanding and more likely to view the merger as a threat.[10] At Gillette, where the razor-and-blade division had long been dominant, the people not assigned to Shaving had power issues, and either wanted to change divisions or get some assurance (usually financial) that their contributions were valued. For those that weren't as vocal, it was by no means a sign of contentment. Individuals on both the Gillette and Parker sides were nervous about the proposed integration. For better or worse, they had established a routine in their old jobs; they knew what to expect and they knew what was expected of them. In the new environment, there would be new opportunities, challenges, and conditions. There also would be new rivalries and jealousies. Bringing together different units under one roof meant bringing together people with different wage scales and benefits packages. It didn't matter to an ex-Parker finance person in Singapore that his counterpart in Taiwan or Brussels or the United States was making the same money. He wanted to be paid on an equitable basis with the person sitting next to him. Indeed, the issue of pay-equity is critical—and successful acquirers will craft a new compensation system that fosters cooperation and the creation of a merged corporate culture.[11] That Gillette had historically paid higher salaries than Parker was no longer relevant. Parker had become part of

Gillette—and Parker people wanted to be paid the same money as their coworkers doing the same job.

The Need to Respect Local Cultures

Global processes must be tailored to local cultures. Many M&A experts in the U.S. have cited speed as a key element of successful integration. Two such experts write that "fast track integration ensures that anticipated gains are realized as soon as possible. Shaving one month off the integration timetable can generate millions of dollars for the bottom line of the combined organization."[12] Despite this widely held belief, Gillette wisely gave Singapore time to handle relationships and action steps in a way that was respectful of the norms and customs of the area.

Soon after the acquisition was announced in May 1993, the Gillette Singapore GM (a Singaporean in his mid thirties) paid a visit to the GM of Parker, a Chinese gentleman in his early sixties. As is customary in Asia, the two men discussed the merger in a pleasant, courteous manner. Although soon to be campus dean, and in many ways senior to his Parker counterpart, the younger GM was careful to lay out transition steps that would be amenable to the Parker side—and to defer to his elder in many subtle ways that would communicate the proper respect. Of course, the Parker GM and his employees had many questions about how the new organization would be shaped. In this part of the world, time was needed to feel out a new relationship. Various meetings and get-acquainted sessions were organized between Parker and Gillette over the next several months. Of course, time was important—but the Gillette Singapore GM knew that rushing things could have disastrous results. A December 1, 1993, joint reporting deadline was pushed back to March 1, 1994. Gillette could have demanded that Singapore move faster, but imposing one-size-fits-all policies without reevaluating for cultural appropriateness can be a costly mistake.[13] Even the Singapore Campus' eventual move-in date had cultural significance. In Chinese society, it is very important to choose an auspicious day for such a significant event. Both Gillette and Parker employees helped select a date in late February that they all felt was worthy of commemorating this organizational marriage. Recognizing that different cultures require different rules of conduct and administrative procedures, Gillette is able to solidify its presence around the globe.[14] Its sensitivity to local considerations improves the chances for global success.

The Need to Understand a Corporation's Culture

In global companies, business cultures can be even stronger than country cultures. During the Parker integration, Gillette Singapore's campus dean, a native of the area, was promoted and replaced by an American expatriate. The move was seen as positive by many, and the new GM was a powerful force in helping to bridge the cultural gap between the two organizations. Why was an American effective in this role? Because the integration issues had less to do with country culture and race than they did standard business practices and philosophies. Parker and Gillette were very different types of companies. Gillette was performance-driven, relatively centralized and formal, and promoted mass-market products throughout the world. Parker, on the other hand, was familial, informal, and identified itself as producer of a prestigious pen. Research has shown that some cultural problems associated with combining organizations are more amplified in domestic, rather than cross-national, settings.[15]

Indeed, the challenge in melding Parker and Gillette's operations in Singapore was not about country origin—in fact, the majority of employees on both sides were from Asia—but about corporate culture. For ex-Parker people, the Gillette Singapore campus was located not two miles from where they had previously worked. Former Parker employees even outnumbered Gillette staff in the new organization. The biggest adjustment was in combating the feelings of lost autonomy. Regardless of the circumstances, most cases show that people at the acquired company are likely to have higher anxiety levels than those at the buying firm.[16]

Despite Gillette's obvious sensitivities, several Parker employees likened their experiences to a new form of colonization—an imperialistic takeover that left no ambiguity between conqueror and conqueree. For Parker employees, the Gillette acquisition meant that they could no longer operate in the congenial atmosphere that many of them felt made the company unique. According to one particularly reluctant Gillette Singapore employee, "At the old Parker, coming to work was enjoyable and fun. After the move, I would wake up and say, 'Oh no, another day.'" Does his reaction suggest a heavy-handed takeover by Gillette? Probably not. What it does reflect, however, is the difficulty many people have adjusting to new business environments. The absorption of an organization characterized by very different value systems, expectations, and world views will tend to be associated with massive value destruction by acquired employees.[17] In fact, the Parker veteran said he spent several years working for the firm in Europe and enjoyed the experience just as much as he did in his home country of Singapore. For him and many others, stress and uneasiness about globalization comes not from entering new markets, but from integrating with other corporate cultures at home.

The Real Meaning of Global Strategy ————————————————

We initially began our exploration of Gillette's Asia-Pacific operations with an eye toward understanding how global strategy redefined country operations, reducing the power of countries as activities fell under international groups that managed them uniformly across wide geographic territories and attempted to wipe out local differences. In short, we too had been influenced by the prevalent myths and misunderstandings about globalization.

What we found instead when we examined global strategy in one of the world's most global companies was that local integration and local relationships became even more important as Gillette sought to gain the power of global brands. We saw that global strategy required a great deal of local coordination, across divisions and products as well as across functions. This local coordination, in turn, left room for incorporating local differences and variations into global thinking—including variations in consumer preferences, infrastructure, and employee expectations.

This case study reinforces our conclusion that the best definition of "global" is "integrated," not "international." Companies with international activities have greater need for multiple forms of integration, but they do not always build the linkages across countries or products or functions that allow them to think about all of their resources simultaneously and therefore to tap the power of the whole. The key to success in the global economy is for companies to behave in a more integrated fashion—to tap the collaborative advantage that comes from being able to use all their resources and being able to work across boundaries.[18] That means becoming knowledgeable about local needs, skillful at managing local changes, and expert at forging cross-boundary relationships—and doing this in many places at the same time with a global, or holistic, strategy in mind.

Endnotes

1. Kanter, R. M. 1995. *World Class: Thriving Locally in the Global Economy.* New York, NY: Simon and Schuster.

2. Kanter, R. M. 1997. *Rosabeth Moss Kanter on the Frontiers of Management.* Boston: HBS Press, Chapter 1.

3. Barnevik, P. and Kanter, R. M. 1994. *Global Strategies.* Boston, MA: HBS Press.

4. Kanter, R. M. 1995. *World Class: Thriving Locally in the Global Economy.* New York, NY: Simon and Schuster.

5. Pablo, A. 1994. Determinants of Acquisition Integration Level: A Decision-Making Perspective. *Academy of Management Journal,* August 803-836.

6. Olie, R. 1994. Shades of Culture and Institutions in International Mergers. *Organization Studies,* 381-405.

7. Smith, K. and Quella, J. 1995. Seizing the Moment to Capture Value in a Strategic Deal. *Mergers & Acquisitions,* January/February 25-30.

8. Very, P., et al. 1996. A Cross-National Assessment of Acculturative Stress in Recent European Mergers. *International Studies of Management and Organization,* Spring 59-86.

9. Begly, T., and Yount, B. 1994. Enlisting Personnel of the Target to Combat Resentment. *Mergers & Acquisitions*, September/October 27-32.

10. Reece, R. 1996. Easing the Transition During a Merger or Acquisition. *Bank Marketing*, August 38-42.

11. *The Wall Street Journal*. 1997, February 14. Merged Firms Often Face Culture Clash; Businesses Offer Advice on Ways to Avoid Minefields. Feb. 14, 9A.

12. Galpin, T. and Robinson, D. 1997. Merger Integration: The Ultimate Change Management Challenge. *Mergers & Acquisitions*, January/February 24-28.

13. *The Wall Street Journal*. 1997. Side Effects: Cross-Border Merger Results in Headaches for a Drug Company; Pharmacia and Upjohn Faces Culture Clash; Europeans Chafe Under U.S. Rules; Even Logo is Troublesome. Feb. 4, 1A.

14. Very, P., et al. 1996. A Cross-National Assessment of Acculturative Stress in Recent European Mergers. *International Studies of Management and Organization*, Spring, 59-86.

15. Hakanson, L. 1995. Learning through Acquisitions: Management and Integration of Foreign R&D Laboratories. *International Studies of Management and Organization*, Spring/Summer 121-157.

16. Harrington, L. 1997. Making the Most of a Merger. *Transportation and Distribution*, January 36-40.

17. Hakanson, L. 1995. Learning through Acquisitions: Management and Integration of Foreign R&D Laboratories. *International Studies of Management and Organization*, Spring/Summer 121-157.

18. Kanter, R. M. 1997. *Rosabeth Moss Kanter on the Friontiers of Management*. Boston: HBS Press, Chapter 20.

Managing the Global Workforce: Challenges and Strategies

Reading 1.2
Karen Roberts
Ellen Ernst Kossek
Cynthia Ozeki

The line went dead. Steve Prestwick slowly hung up the telephone, wondering what he could possibly say to the executive committee monitoring the Singapore R&D center project. Shortly after being assigned to help staff the facility, he had attended a committee meeting that left him excited about tapping into the potential of the company's large global work force. "Get the best people from everywhere," said one executive. "Don't just rely on information from headquarters. Try to find out what the people in Europe or Japan might know," chimed in another. And from the CEO, "Let's use this as an opportunity to develop a global mindset in some of our more promising people." The vision sounded great, and Steve's role seemed simple: put together a team with all the experts needed to get the new facility up and running smoothly in its first two years.

Right away Steve began having trouble finding out who had the right skills, and even where the choices seemed obvious, he wasn't getting anywhere. The engineer who refused the assignment over the telephone was the best the company had in her field. She told him that spending two years in Singapore wouldn't really help her career. Plus, it would be hard on her children and impossible for her husband, a veterinarian with a growing practice. Not only did he need a top engineering manager, but Steve also had to find a highly competent corps of technical researchers who knew about the company and its approach to R&D. He also needed technicians who could set up the facility. He thought he would bring in people from the U.S. to select and set up equipment, then lead a research team of local engineers that the U.S. engineers would train in company practices and technologies. To his chagrin, most of the U.S. technical people he had talked to weren't interested in such an assignment. A European perspective might

Source: K. Roberts, et al. Reprinted with permission of Academy of Management, PO Box 3020, Briar Cliff Manor, NY 10510-8020. "Managing The Global Workforce: Challenges and Strategies," K. Roberts, E. Ernst Kossek, & C. Ozeki, *Academy of Management Executive*, Vol. 12, No. 4 (1998). Reproduced by permission of the publisher via Copyright Clearance Center, Inc.

be useful, but he didn't even have records on possible candidates from the other overseas offices. Steve was on his own, and he had less than a week to come up with a plan.

What Can Steve Do?

Although Steve is fictional, he is facing a composite of real problems for global HR managers. The need to develop a global perspective on human resource management has been part of the managerial landscape for well over a decade, but there is no consensus about what tools to use. Adler and Bartholomew noted that organizational "strategy (the what)... is internationalizing faster than implementation (the how) and much faster than the managers and executives themselves (the who)."[1] Steve has been given an assignment that reflects his organization's commitment to manage globally but little guidance about how to meet his goals.

The challenges, strategic approaches, and diagnostic framework we present are based on interviews with senior managers in large corporations with reputations for excellence in international operations. We chose the firms in this study using three criteria. First, we wanted firms experienced in operating internationally that could comment on the evolution of transnational HR management. Second, we wanted variation across industries to assure that we were not uncovering information idiosyncratic to certain types of industries. Third, we selected firms whose recruitment policies indicated a commitment to the strategic use of HRM in global management.

We sent the most senior international HR professional in each firm a letter describing our study and requesting an interview. We asked that they identify any other HR professionals in their organization whom we might also interview. Based on this process, we interviewed 24 professionals at eight firms.[2] The letter listed four questions that we wanted to cover during the interview:

1. What are the key global pressures affecting human resource management practices in your firm currently and for the projected future?

2. What is the level and substance of knowledge about human resource issues that human resource professionals should possess?

3. What are examples of leading edge international human resource practices in your organization?

4. To what extent is international knowledge needed by entry level professionals in human resource management at your organization?

The questions were deliberately broad, reflecting our exploratory approach. Each interview lasted 1½ to 2 hours. During the interviews, we asked for any additional materials the HR managers thought would be valuable to our study. Once we had begun to analyze our interview information, we used follow-up phone calls both to those we interviewed as well as to other professional contacts to supplement or clarify the data from the interviews.

The information from these interviews was distilled into a two-dimensional framework. One dimension was the set of challenges these executives saw confronting global managers. The second was a set of four prototypical strategies to address these challenges.

The Challenges_____

In the course of each interview, we asked these executives to describe their vision of the ideal global international labor market. Three broad features emerged from their responses:

1. Deployment: easily getting the right skills to where they are needed in the organization regardless of geographical location;

2. Knowledge and innovation dissemination: spreading state of the art knowledge and practices throughout the organization regardless of where they originate; and,

3. Identifying and developing talent on a global basis: identifying who has the ability to function effectively in a global organization and developing those abilities.

Although skill deployment, information dissemination, and talent identification have long been basic HR challenges, in the global environment, these issues are overlaid with the complexities of distance, language, and cultural differences. Part of the challenge to global management is to reinterpret successful past practices in terms of these complexities.

Deployment

All the organizations had a history of operating internationally, but had relied on a headquarters-subsidiary structure and the traditional expatriate model of human resource staffing where U.S. nationals held most positions of authority. This arrangement was adequate in yesterday's international organization because leadership, decision-making authority, and organizational power flowed from the parent site to the foreign subsidiaries. Today, however, new technologies, new markets, innovation, and new talent no longer solely emanate from headquarters but are found cross-nationally, making the expatriate model obsolete.[3] Further, the cost of deploying an expatriate has become excessive. One Merck and Co., Inc., executive estimated that it was three times more expensive to have an expatriate than a local national in any given job.

All of the organizations were developing alternative ways to get the right people to where the work is on an as-needed basis. The key innovation is that organizations are making distinctions between when it is necessary to physically move a person to a particular location and when the person's skills can be delivered through other means. Permanent transfers are no longer seen as the only method for delivering certain services to parts of the organization, giving way to short-term assignments and virtual deployment. Getting managers to stop relying on physical transfers and to think globally about resources is not easy.

Managers will use company-wide job postings when there is a formal job opening, but will not think outside their units, let alone countries, when it comes to finding the expertise to solve a specific problem, such as poor market response to a new consumer product or dysfunctional work relationships that are due to cross-cultural ignorance.

Knowledge Dissemination/Innovation Transfer

The HR executives cited two global information flow blockages: disseminating knowledge from one location to another and spreading innovation. Under earlier expatriate structures, information flowed from the center out. Current global organizations need structures where all units concurrently receive and provide information. Valuable market and production technology information are being produced outside the parent location. One example of the perils of not using local expertise in collecting market information is Marks & Spencer, Britain's largest retailer. The company failed routinely overseas until it found its niche by selling M&S branded clothes in Hong Kong, a former British colony.[4]

The executives at both Dow Chemical Co. and Merck saw this challenge as being one of cross-functional communication, where the greatest opportunities for growth and innovation are at hand-off points between functions. These executives saw hand-off opportunities as easily lost in a global environment, primarily because of the difficulties of establishing cross-cultural trust. As one manager noted:

> As long as diversity is not valued, trust of people from different backgrounds is not developed. There is a tendency to duplicate functions so one does not have to rely on people one does not trust. As a result, rather than having a single global enterprise, many international companies are operating more like a collection of lots of smaller companies.

All of the executives we interviewed noted that language compounded the trust problem. Although English was the business language in all of these organizations, halting speech, misused words, strange grammar, and mispronounced words can subtly undermine the perception that the speaker is competent.

Talent Identification and Development

One executive at General Motors Corp. began his interview with us by noting that:

> ...the key global issue [for GM] is how to transform the organization internally to become globally competitive. Even for employees who may never go overseas, it is necessary to constantly sensitize everyone to the fact that they are in a global business.

All the executives reiterated this theme in one way or another. But, eventually, each interview came to the reality that not everyone in the organization is going to thrive and prevail in a global environment. Therefore, one of the larger challenges of managing the global labor force is identifying who is most likely to grasp the complexities of the transnational operations and function well in that sort of environment. As one Merck executive described it:

> In the 1940s, transactions were the basis for determining the types of skills managers needed. The [new] challenge to [global human resource management] is to learn to talk in terms of "stories." Organizations need people who understand the business and who are able to see where the business is going globally and the cultures that need to be bridged, people able to manage conflict and change.

One aspect of this challenge is that the scope of the transnational organization is so large that just collecting information about employees is difficult. Also, all of the executives we interviewed acknowledged that there were cultural biases in the selection process that probably caused talented people to be overlooked. One Amoco Corp. executive gave the example of their operations in Norway. Norwegian work-family values differ from those in the U.S., and it is common for men who are senior in their organizations to leave work at 3 p.m. to pick up their children after school. While U.S. norms are beginning to tilt somewhat more toward family in the work-family balance, leaving early still signals a lack of commitment to the job in most U.S. workplaces.[5] The Amoco executive noted that it was very difficult for U.S. managers to trust that their Norwegian employees would get the job done in a crisis and thus had trouble seeing them as potential global managers. Duplicative staffing was sometimes the result.

A final component of this challenge was motivating employees to want to spend time overseas. Most of the executives considered overseas experience a *sine qua non* for promotion to top jobs in their organizations. But, for a variety of reasons, many talented employees do not want to move overseas. One executive noted that, "talent marries other talent," and that spousal careers are increasingly an obstacle to overseas assignments.[6] Another point, made by both Merck and Amoco, was that the expected growth in their industries was in locations that were not viewed as desirable by employees from developed countries. An Amoco executive noted that in some West African countries where Amoco had operations, 30 to 35 percent of the population was thought to be HIV positive, dramatically undermining the appeal of those countries to potential expatriates.

Four Strategies for Managing the Global Workforce

The managers we interviewed described how their organizations had moved away from the traditional expatriate assignment and the new arrangements they were using to meet the three challenges above. Tables 1 through 4 summarize the key points of each of the strategies.

Table 1. Aspatial Careers

Who	What
Globally oriented, highly mobile people, with proven ability and company loyalty	Corps of experts with borderless careers on long-term overseas assignments

How		
Deployment	Knowledge Dissemination	Talent ID & Development
Geographically relocate employees with high level skills and rich cross-cultural perspective	Employees with in-depth global experiences & networks in leadership positions across sites	Rotation as development

Implementation Points

- Encourage company over country culture
- Assign within culturally homogenous regions
- Use pan-region selection meetings
- Evolve selection criteria that are shared across countries
- Provide cross-cultural training for families
- Recognize family life-cycle realities

Aspatial Careers

Aspatial careerists have borderless careers, typically working in multiple countries over the course of their lives. The chief difference between the aspatial career and the expatriate assignment is that these careers exist in an environment where authority and expertise are no longer thought to reside exclusively at the parent company. Aspatial careerists can come from any part of the globe.

Aspatial careers can take several forms. An employee may live and work overseas with frequent moves; others may have a geographically stationary home base but are required to travel and to have the ability to think about the organization in ways that are spatially neutral. If they relocate, their families go with them.

The aspatial careers model does not overcome the high costs associated with the traditional expatriate model. As a result, only a small percent of most organizations' employees follow aspatial career paths. GM estimates that only about 900 of its employees pursue aspatial careers. Merck has approximately 250 employees on this path out of a workforce of 37,000.[7]

Aspatial careerists are usually managers, not technicians. Over the course of their several moves, they accumulate rich contextual knowledge, also known as tacit or implicit knowledge. Successful aspatial careerists develop an in-depth understanding of global organizations because they have managed across cultures and know how culture affects work.

Table 2. Awareness-Building Assignments

Who	What
High potential employees early in their careers	3 to 12 month assignment

How		
Deployment	**Knowledge Dissemination**	**Talent ID & Development**
Technically competent, high potential employees	Cross-cultural immersion to produce global perspective	• Screening for ability to function out of own culture • Develop globally aware future performers

Implementation Points

- Use to bridge geofunctional disconnects
- Rotate employees with demonstrable competence
- Manage the adjustment cycle
- Use to develop local nationals

They have also developed extensive global networks that help them identify and draw on expertise throughout their organizations. These managers' global insights tend to filter through the organization rather than be distributed by means of explicit training or the introduction of new technology. One exception is when companies use aspatial careers to develop technical personnel below the top management level. A plant manager at Dow described cross-national rotation of engineers as part of a strategy for cross-training and to assure comparability of engineering skill level across Dow plants in all countries.

Through long rotations with in-depth experience, aspatial careerists acquire globally applicable skills. One company had a manager who had begun his career as a health care expert in France. He then spent four years in London, three in Tokyo, and three in Switzerland, at each point deepening his health care expertise and expanding his network. He had become a repository of cross-cultural health care information as well as a someone who knew the players across these different sites. His gradually accumulated information made him an insightful manager and valuable to the company.

The talent identification potential of aspatial careers is not yet fully realized. Several companies noted that they are beginning to explicitly view their aspatial careerists as a recruiting pool for the highest level of corporate management. The underlying logic is that those who have rotated across different countries have the global perspective needed at the top of the organization. However, none of the companies we interviewed had fully committed to reliance on aspatial career experience

Table 3. SWAT Teams

Who	What
Technical specialists	Short-term, project-length assignments

How		
Deployment	**Knowledge Dissemination**	**Talent ID & Development**
Specialized skills on an as-needed basis	Transfer of technical processes & systems	Specialized skills honed through varied & frequent applications

Implementation Points

- Best SWAT team member has single contributor mindset
- Use to spread acultural innovation
- Good at smaller locations or at start-up
- Recognize clear limitations

as an indicator of top management potential. Rather, several admitted that their companies still had difficulties with recognizing the value-added of overseas experience when reintegrating those who have been overseas into home country operations.

Awareness-Building Assignments

The primary purpose of awareness-building assignments is to develop cross-country sensitivity in high-potential employees in a short time. These assignments last anywhere from 3 months to one year. Families are not expected to relocate, so that depending on assignment length, regular home visits might be part of this strategy. Usually this assignment is made early in one's career and typically an employee will only have one such assignment.[8]

At the end of an awareness-building assignment, a high potential employee is expected to have a broadened cultural perspective and an appreciation of the diversity in the organization. One of the Dow executives summarized the purpose of these assignments:

> Overseas assignments are no longer used just to get the "overseas stamp"...We may transfer them to acquire knowledge available only overseas, or perhaps as way to export a leading-edge practice to an overseas location. Often, though, an overseas assignment is not specifically a technical transfer—we are going more for [developing an employee with an] 'open mind.'

GM also incorporates a training component in the form of short-term cross-function transfers and/or cross-plant training. This can be a

Table 4. Virtual Solutions

Who	What
Non-rotating employees who need overseas connections	Electronic communications

How

Deployment	Knowledge Dissemination	Talent ID & Development
Videoconferencing & e-mail allow virtual deployment	Web pages, bulletin boards, intranets, distance learning & interactive training disperse information across locations	GHRIS, electronic job posting, video & virtual interviews ID and screen for assignments

Implementation Points

- Encourage virtual friendships
- Couple with cross-culture awareness training
- GHRIS works best with standardized information
- GHRIS trade-off between standardized information & universal access
- Global job posting for clearly defined jobs
- Don't expect instant results

mechanism for innovation dissemination. GM has found that rotated employees must demonstrate technical competence to be accepted at the overseas site. As one GM executive described it:

> If the need is to cultivate openness and develop cross-cultural awareness, it has to be done early in one's career. However, the reality is that those who go overseas first have to demonstrate technical competence to be accepted in a different location, and this is more necessary than cultural awareness.

Several firms use these assignments to acculturate local nationals who after the rotation will spend most of their careers in their home countries. These assignments serve as screens for global awareness potential. Awareness-building assignments are not long enough to develop in-depth cultural knowledge. However, an employee who can shed provincialism and learn that value can be added from any location in the company is one who is likely to function effectively in the global organization.

SWAT Teams

SWAT teams are highly mobile teams of experts, deployed on a short-term basis, to troubleshoot, solve a very specific problem, or complete a clearly defined project. (The name derives from the special weapons and tactics units used by many police departments.) SWAT teams play a role like that of the technical troubleshooter, an individual sent to a foreign location to analyze and solve a particular operational problem.[9]

SWAT teams comprise nomadic experts who are identified internationally and deployed as internal consultants on an as-needed basis. As a Dow executive described the objective of this approach, the company does not "expect to move people across areas but does want to leverage resources across our different businesses." At GM, the SWAT team takes the form of an expert network, internal consultants deployed throughout the organization. The actual amount of time spent overseas varies with the purpose or project but in general is under three months.

The primary strength of this approach is that it permits the organization to cultivate highly specialized knowledge and expertise on a limited basis, and to apply that expertise wherever it is needed within the organization. One difference between SWAT teams and awareness-building assignments is that there is no explicit developmental component to the SWAT team model other than to complete whatever project is defined. Development of cross-cultural awareness on the part of the SWAT team members may be a by-product of the job but it is not its intention.

Once a SWAT team has been assembled, it can be redeployed each time a situation requiring its skillset emerges. Frequent opportunities to apply their skills in different settings can add significantly to the existing skill accumulation of team members, providing the developmental component to the SWAT team strategy.

Virtual Solutions

Virtual solutions are a collection of practices that exploit the rapidly evolving electronic communication technologies. These include use of all forms of the Internet and intranets, videoconferencing, electronic expert systems, and electronic databases coupled with user-friendly front-end systems. The chief advantages to this strategy are the low cost of communication and the uncoupling of real time from virtual time. Awareness-building and virtual solutions are the strategies with which most of the firms we interviewed had had the least experience, but also were the approaches they saw as having the most potential for managing and developing the global workforce.

Internet and intranets, including e-mail, are the most democratic form of overseas deployment, allowing communication among employees regardless of organizational level. Videoconferencing has a similar advantage; however, videoconferencing facilities are a scarce resource compared with e-mail in most organizations. Both Dow and Merck managers said that their videoconferencing rooms were in constant use.

Virtual international teams design software at IBM Corp. Communication through intranets allows for 24-hour product development. One team includes software developers from the U.S., several former Soviet Union states, and India. The work is usually initiated in the U.S. At the end of the day, the U.S. team transmits its files via the intranet to the Soviet team, which works on the project until the end of the work day. The Soviet team then sends its work on to the Indian team whose work day ends at the start of business for the U.S. team, which picks up the files and continues the production cycle.

A more sophisticated virtual deployment tool is the use of virtual reality. NASA uses virtual reality to train international teams of astronauts.[10] These teams need to perform complex tasks requiring lengthy training. Actually convening these teams of astronauts from different countries at a single geographical location for months at a time is prohibitively expensive and disrupts family life. A virtual simulation of a repair of the Hubble telescope was constructed for training purposes and allowed team members to simulate the repair as though in the same room. One Russian and one U.S. member virtually shook hands at the end of the repair exercise. However, this simulation took months to develop. While virtual reality is almost as good as being there, it is also almost as expensive.

All the companies have web pages on the Internet with company background and product information, as well as public information about new developments. E-mail is in common use and electronic bulletin boards to solve technical problems were becoming more common. At the time of our interviews, comparable intranet systems with proprietary information were in development. This sort of communication is one mechanism to break down some of the barriers to information flow erected by technical chauvinism. Reiterating the theme of cross-cultural distrust, one GM executive noted that "technically skilled people in one country feel their training and skills are superior [to those of employees from other countries] and they have little to learn from their international counterparts." He noted this was a substantial problem in motivating technical employees to rotate overseas and that use of e-mail and electronic bulletin boards is expected to ameliorate this problem as technical solutions are offered cross-nationally and recognized as valid.

One solution not yet widely implemented is distance learning. Ford Motor Co. uses this commonly to continuously update the skills of its engineers, videotaping classes that employees can play individually or as a group. The students can then hold discussion groups and interact with the instructor who holds electronic office hours at a predetermined time. Another version is a highly interactive broadcast class where students can interact with the instructor across networks that permit student questions and discussion, even pop quizzes. However, distance learning is still in its infancy and was not cited as a commonly used tool.

All the firms had Global Human Resource Information Systems (GHRIS), which allowed for global job posting. The companies stressed that talent identification below the highest level on a global basis was key to the success of the company. Amoco Corp., Dow, and Merck used their GHRIS to store career data about their employees useful for selection and, on a more limited basis, for job posting. Amoco has implemented a worldwide job posting system that allows all employees to use electronic systems to learn about and apply for jobs.[11]

Diagnosing the Challenges

We developed a diagnostic framework for evaluating each of the challenges and deciding among the four strategies.

Diagnosing the Deployment Challenge

The challenge of global deployment is getting the needed skills from one part of the organization to another inexpensively. Not all of the tools associated with each of the strategic solutions were equally effective in all situations. There are two components to deciding among the deployment strategies: contact time required and extent to which the skills can be applied out of cultural context.

If the need is for on-going on-site leadership, in-depth cultural understanding, and/or skills that can only be successfully applied if culturally embedded, use aspatial careers. To provide short-term training or skills application that requires cultural sensitivity, use awareness-building assignments. SWAT teams offer on-site technical skills, knowledge of production process, operations, and/or systems that need to be implemented, with little cultural content. Virtual solutions provide frequent, brief iterative interactions, with only a little cultural component to the interaction, or a wide sweep of the organization to search for or communicate technical details or information.

Diagnosing the Knowledge and Innovation Dissemination Challenge

The information organizations need to stay competitive ranges from highly technical to informally communicated background information. The effectiveness of each of the four strategies depends on the type of knowledge or innovation being disseminated. Choosing among the four strategies depends on the technical complexity of the information that is to be shared and the extent to which it must be culturally embedded. If the knowledge or innovations to be disseminated can be successfully shared only when communicated in a cultural context, use aspatial careers. Awareness-building assignments succeed when the knowledge is primarily cultural awareness and cross-cultural sensitivity training. If the knowledge is defined technology or practices with minimal cultural content, use SWAT teams. If the knowledge requires on-going and frequent information exchanges among dispersed employees, use virtual solutions.

Diagnosing Talent Identification and Development Challenges

Development of a global mindset is essential to operating globally. Executives are looking for a similar set of characteristics among their global managers.[12] Merck looks for people who have a broad perspective and can intelligently apply practical leadership skills to guide change in the organization. Baxter International looks for "patience, flexibility, communication skills, intellectual curiosity about the rest of the world." GM looks for a skillset that includes "communication skills, the ability to value diversity, and the ability to be objective."

Cultural training notwithstanding, a manager from Merck noted the difficulty of finding people with this skillset:

> Merck uses two-thirds selection and one-third development... [We rely more on selection than development in our selection criteria because] it is difficult to impart needed skills, and people don't get that much out of classroom training—they are more likely to remember what they had for dinner than what went on in the training session... We are looking for people with curiosity and a mix of skills.

This suggests that organizations should select well, then develop. Companies that need to identify and develop leaders with in-depth cultural knowledge and proven cross-cultural abilities and are willing to spend time and money to have those people, should use aspatial careers. To identify and develop high potential performers with an understanding that they are functioning in a global organization and an appreciation of cultural diversity, companies should use awareness-building assignments. SWAT teams provide mobile and technically competent specialists whose skills tend to be needed on a short-term basis. Virtual solutions identify employees using shared selection criteria to fill vacancies with well-understood job requirements.

Implementing the Strategies _____

Following are examples of how companies implemented each of the strategies, including some of the obstacles they have encountered.

Implementing the Aspatial Career Strategy

All the companies encourage the development of a culture of company over country. Baxter has deployed leadership throughout the organization regardless of national origin: the VP for the European region is of U.S. origin located in Germany; the VP for the Diagnostics division is an Italian located in Switzerland; the VP of Cardiovascular is Irish and located in France; the Hospital group is led by a French person in Belgium. This is not just a happy accident but the result of an explicit strategy on Baxter's part to develop a company-over-country identity, where the managers focus on the competitive strategies of the entire company, not only for the region in which they reside. Baxter has eliminated country-based organization and reorganized by product group or business function. Also, the position of country general manager has been eliminated to encourage a business-over-country orientation.

These geographically fluid careers are more successful if rotations occur within culturally homogenous regions. Both Baxter and GM have divided their global operations into regions, and Baxter is deliberate about rotating employees within rather than across regions as much as possible. This policy is consistent with results from a study of Singaporean managers showing that the cultural similarity between origin and destination locations positively affected employee and spouse willingness to relocate.[13] GM also uses a regional basis for determining benefit plans, distinguishing between intracontinental (policies reflecting continent-wide norms) and intercontinental policies (policies applied at GM sites worldwide). This distinction simplifies within-region rotations.

Schlumberger uses a "borderlands career track" version of aspatial careers in which rotating employees move often across adjoining borders. The cultural homogeneity of border areas allows the company to move people quickly with minimal adjustment.[14]

One identification mechanism used by several companies is the pan-regional meeting. This meeting takes place regularly, three to four times a year, where higher- (but not just the highest-) level managers and sometimes technical people within a geographical region meet to exchange information and network. The meetings last several days to a week and are used to showcase potential asaptial careerists. HR people are included and charged with identifying potential talent for global reassignment. Dow holds four annual meetings, one in each region, where managers are asked to recommend, review, and present the top 1.5 percent of the employees in terms of high management potential. Because it is important for managers to present very talented people, these annual meetings are high pressure events. These meetings are used also to identify candidates for awareness-building assignments.

An informal outcome from Dow's meetings is the evolution of a shared understanding of what is meant by global competencies. This evolves out of formal identification and presentation of high potential talent at the pan-regional meetings. Each meeting serves as an iteration in the development of global selection criteria. This evolving understanding of the managerial traits required by the global organization is used to identify candidates for both aspatial careers and awareness-building assignments.

A key component to motivating talented employees to go overseas, even for a short time, is their belief that the organization values overseas experience. This will be especially true for aspatial careerists, but also true to a lesser extent for awareness-building assignments and

SWAT team employees. Most organizations send a mixed message to employees about the value of overseas experience.[15]

There is often a sharp decline in authority, responsibility, and autonomy for the employee returning to the parent company. Most aspatial careerists are at or near the top of the overseas organization and in many cases behave like CEOs. Their jobs at the parent site are of necessity of lower status. The more hierarchical an organization, the more difficult this problem will be. Structuring jobs of returning aspatial employees to allow sufficient autonomy and identifying explicit ways to fully utilize their overseas expertise is important. GM does this by using returned overseas employees in the first round selection process for aspatial careers and awareness-building assignment candidates.

The firms varied in how they valued overseas experience. At one firm, it was impossible to receive more than 1000 Hay points (from the Hay Group's method of evaluating jobs based on technical skills, problem-solving, and accountability) without an international experience, so employees were willing to relocate to avoid that career ceiling. At another extreme, one executive candidly described his organization as having a top management that stressed overseas experience; below top management, however, was a headquarter-centered culture, where overseas experience was viewed as inferior.

GM sets up home-based mentor relationships between each overseas employee and what they call a repatriation facilitator. This provides a support system for the overseas employee but also helps home-based employees value what the overseas employee can contribute upon return. GM also uses home leave where rotated employees present their overseas projects and show how they will contribute to home operations. GM has found that repatriated employees are more successful when brought back into a unit where the manager has had some overseas experience.

Recognizing family needs is key to successful aspatial career deployment. According to numerous studies, family circumstances are the leading cause of overseas assignment failures.[16] Spousal careers and child care are important family considerations and cited in one survey as the top family reasons to refuse an overseas assignment.[17] Cultural awareness training for family members was just beginning at several of the companies we studied and held promise for smoothing family transitions. GM uses relocation facilitators and assigns mentor families to aspatial career families early in their assignments. Job seeking assistance and/or partial remuneration for loss of job income for spouses were provided by most of the companies we studied, but these were considered feasible only if the family was staying overseas at least two years.

It is also important to recognize that all asaptial careerists may not stay aspatial forever. Although some individuals will spend their entire careers outside of their native countries, most eventually return to the parent site. One driver of this decision is family life-cycle change, which pushes an employee to move the family back home. For example, executives wanting their children to go to U.S. high schools so they can get into U.S. colleges was a factor noted by GM.

Implementing the Awareness-Building Assignment Strategy

The missed opportunities at hand-off points described earlier by a Merck executive are often the result of geofunctional disconnects. These are points where functional and geographical boundaries are coterminous, compounding cross-functional cooperation problems. Awareness-building assignments can effectively bridge these gaps when they are used to collect consumer market information. Amoco uses awareness-building assignments to develop product preference sensitivity in employees who design products used or sold overseas. Two examples of the need to develop intimate knowledge of local markets are Procter & Gamble's faulty start selling all-temperature detergents to Japanese housewives who wash clothes only in cold water and GM's attempt to sell two-door trucks to Chinese with a strong preference for four-door vehicles.[18] Baxter learned this lesson after medical equipment intended for Japan was designed and sized using U.S. patients as the standard. The firm now has a cross-cultural training program, often in the form of awareness-building assignments, for engineers who design products for global markets.

Awareness-building assignments blur the traditional distinction between learning and contributing jobs. Most of the executives we interviewed noted that these assignments should be used judiciously. The awareness-building benefit will be lost if the rotated employee is perceived as having nothing to offer the overseas site. The challenge is to select people early enough in their careers that the assignments serve as screens for future potential but not so early that they have few skills to offer.

Merck gives awareness-building assignments to more mature employees, believing that generating a global mindset is more a selection than a developmental issue, and that mature workers can develop a global awareness if the predisposition is there. Both Merck and Baxter note, however, that language ability limits the candidate pool. At Merck, this has meant that more overseas employees are rotated for awareness-building assignments in the U.S. than the other way around.

Awareness-building assignments must avoid the negative effects of what is termed the "intercultural adjustment cycle."[19] A Dow executive described a cycle on long-term overseas assignments. During the first three months, employees are euphoric about the new country, soak up the culture, and enjoy the superficial differences between the overseas post and the home country. Because most rotated employees are top performers in their home country, however, by the third month they become discouraged by the drop in their productivity and by their lack of linguistic or cultural fluency. During the next three to six months, relocated employees and their families begin to miss their home countries and find fault with the overseas sites. At about nine months, the employees regain the confidence they had before being sent overseas and function as competent members of the overseas society.

Most aspatial careerists will pass through the cycle to regain their sense of competence, but an awareness-building assignment may not last through the entire adjustment cycle. An assignment that ends during the euphoric period will leave the employee with a superficial understanding of the overseas location. An assignment ended during the trough of the cycle may leave the employee soured about overseas experiences and negative about the global scope of the organization. Rather than trying to avoid the adjustment cycle, organizations should use training to prepare employees for it. The virtue of the adjustment cycle is that its low point prompts individuals to reconceptualize their mental frames and begin to develop in-depth understanding of the new cultures.

Since a solution to the problem of motivating aspatials to go to unattractive locations is to develop indigenous talent, Amoco, Baxter, and Merck give awareness-building assignments to local nationals. Rotations to headquarters familiarize them with the company mission and culture, while rotations to various worldwide production locations familiarize them with the operations. Local nationals must be given challenging assignments in the U.S. or the rotation may be demotivating.

Implementing the SWAT Team Strategy

Two factors seemed to help optimize the staffing of SWAT teams. First, despite the likelihood that work will be done on a team basis, individual contributor-type employees with a technical orientation are the best candidates. Second, because technical challenges are what motivate them, mechanisms such as outside training are needed to keep SWAT team members on the leading edge.

SWAT teams are best used to export clearly defined technologies or practices. While some training may have to take place at the overseas site to allow those employees to become users, knowledge or innovations conveyed by a SWAT team do not usually have a developmental or cross-cultural component. The SWAT team approach is most easily applied in a manufacturing setting where production processes are less dependent on cultural idiosyncracies. For example, GM uses what they refer to as internal consulting teams to collect information about best manufacturing processes and to disseminate them to other plants worldwide.

In some cases, SWAT assignments are used at sites that are too small to have a sustained need for certain skills, especially in developing countries. In Pakistan, for example, where the human resource/industrial relations function is a part-time job, a traveling unit of negotiators travels from site to site at contract negotiation time, completes the negotiations, secures a contract, and leaves. Both GM and Merck use teams of internal experts and external consultants to do global benefit planning. These teams immerse themselves in local government regulations and set up the benefit plan for each site.

SWAT team assignments can be useful in setting up new operations where start-up skills are needed for a brief period. Amoco uses SWAT teams when it is deciding whether or not to permanently locate in a country. Because location usually depends on finding oil and securing drilling rights, Amoco may be in a country for a relatively long time before withdrawing.[20] Using SWAT teams during start-ups also requires more cultural-awareness training than the conventional SWAT team assignment.

SWAT teams have their very clear limitations, tending to draw on the manufacturing model to conceptualize deployment and information dissemination challenges, and applying that model to nonproduction situations. The pure SWAT team approach will be effective only when interpersonal relationships and cultural understanding are of minimal importance to the transfer of knowledge or innovation. The development of interpersonal relationships and cultural awareness is time consuming and the benefits are often intangible, but in many cases these are necessary prerequisites for information exchange and effective working relationships. If these are needed, the SWAT team strategy will fail.

Implementing the Virtual Solutions Strategy

The virtual solutions model allows cross-national relationships to form below the level of top management. Virtual communications that are not necessarily task-oriented but that foster interpersonal exchanges enable task information to flow more smoothly. In addition, opportunities for innovation can occur at electronic hand-off points if information about production methods, problems, and solutions is shared informally.

In most cases, electronic communication is not yet a perfect substitute for direct contact. Small misunderstandings can become full-blown e-mail wars because of the absence of such communication cues as tone of voice and facial expression. Cultural differences and differing abilities in the language of the exchange increase the likelihood of misunderstanding. Thus, virtual deployment is best used in conjunction with some other form of cultural awareness building. Recognizing this, one Dow executive encourages modest expectations for e-mail initially—to develop in employees "a different mentality, to get them to agree that there are more than one way to skin a cat."[21]

Both Dow and Baxter use employee questionnaires designed by international teams to collect information about operations, practices, and values across the firm to build cross-cultural databases. These databases can be retrieved by employees throughout the organization and can supplement other cultural training for virtual solution users. The Baxter survey is customized to fit local conditions and uses local terminology appropriate to each culture. The Dow instrument measures climate as well as management practices.

All of the companies had a Human Resource Information System (HRIS) in place, but varied in the degree to which it could be characterized as a global system. Merck has developed templates that vary with the employee's level in the organization. Employees lower in the organization are less likely to be relocated globally and thus fewer data are required about them for the GHRIS. Approximately one hundred pieces of data are entered into the GHRIS for lower level employees, compared with approximately four hundred entries for higher level employees.

Storing benefit information continues to be a GHRIS challenge. Dow has developed regional benefit models and determined that approximately 80 percent of the data needed for any given employee is standard across nations. The remaining nonstandard 20 percent is country-specific. However, some of this nonstandard information can be collapsed into a smaller number of models, each with its own data template. One example, cited by Dow, is that while there is no worldwide set of educational certifications, most countries' educational systems can be classified into one of a few models. Decisions about which information can be standardized globally and which need to reflect local custom were made after a series of global stakeholder meetings.

One Dow executive commented that to be truly valuable, a GHRIS must be a dynamic tool, evolving over time. He also said that this is easy to say, but something of a headache to implement. One significant gap between the ideal and the reality of a GHRIS is the ability to combine universal access with standardized information. Amoco uses a kiosk system to allow employees to enter information about themselves but has found that not all employees have the ability to do this. Dow has faced the same challenge and has decided to sacrifice universal access for completeness of standardized information.

Global job posting works best for those jobs with relatively well-understood skill requirements. The more subtle or idiosyncratic the skill requirements, the more difficult the job description is to translate globally. As noted earlier, employees below a certain level are not likely to rotate internationally, so clarity about skill requirements also helps screen out certain types of postings for which the company reasonably wants to recruit only locally.

There are technological hurdles to implementing the virtual solutions model, and one should not expect instant results. Even when using established technologies like video broadcasting, learning will take on new forms and periods of adjustment will be required.

What Can Steve Do? _____

There is no instant solution to Steve's problem. The people he wants with the skills he needs are not going to convene in Singapore to work together for two years. But, by employing a combination of strategies, Steve can accomplish his goal. He can:

- Select a SWAT team to come in and set up the equipment, a clearly defined task that can be accomplished in a short time with minimal interpersonal contact. Technical people from Tokyo, just a few hours away by plane, could fly in three or four times to set up the equipment and conduct inspections once the facility is running.

- Virtually connect the talented engineer with the Singapore team using e-mail, the phone, and video conferencing, combining this with a short-term awareness-building assignment to foster personal relationships with the technical team and build cross-cultural understanding.

- Ask European, Asian, and South American regional heads to set up regular regional talent ID meetings to nominate potential people for both aspatial career and awareness-building assignments at their next regional conference. The list can be used to select people to conduct initial training sessions and handle early troubleshooting in Singapore as well as a few who may be suited for a longer-term assignment to the new facility.

- Post jobs on an internal bulletin board or intranet web site with full details about the skills required, so that interested and qualified people can also volunteer for Singapore assignments.

- Set up a web page for the site and e-mail technically capable people throughout the organization to stay tuned for brainstorming sessions during the R&D process. Good ideas will win prizes.

- Start scouting for a local national to head up the R&D center, then begin the development with an awareness assignment to headquarters to teach about company culture.

This version of using the four strategies to manage a cross-national workforce differs from the traditional staffing mindset with which Steve initially approached the problem. These strategies allow firms operating on a global basis to make the best use of their widely dispersed internal resources and find innovative solutions to their HR problems.

Endnotes _____

1. Adler, N. and Bartholomew, S. 1992. "Managing Globally Competent People," *Academy of Management Executive*, 6(3), 52.

2. The companies included: Amoco, Baxter, Dow (interviews at both U.S. and Canadian locations), General Motors, IBM, Merck, and Wyeth-Ayerst. Some information about distance learning as a knowledge dissemination/innovation transfer tool was also collected from Ford Motor Co.

3. See Taylor, S., Beechler, S., and Napier, N. 1996. "Toward an Integrative Model of Strategic International Human Resource Management," *Academy of Management Review*, 21(4), 959-985 for a description of the information flows in a globally integrated organization.

4. *Fortune*. 1995. "Retailers Go Global." February 20, 102-108.

5. *Fortune*. 1997. "Is Your Family Wrecking Your Career (And Vice Versa)?" March 3, 70-90.

6. This is consistent with the findings of a study by Brett, Stroh & Reilly of *Fortune* 500 company managers who were willing to relocate. They found that spouse willingness to move was the most significant factor in an employee's willingness to move. See Brett, J., Stroh, L., and Reilly, A. 1993. "Pulling Up Roots in the 1990s: Who's Willing to Relocate?" *Journal of Organizational Behavior*, 14(1), p. 49-60.

7. This total workforce number excludes employees of recent acquisitions by Merck.

8. Use of these assignments as a tool is still evolving and this aspect could easily change.

9. Schuler, R., Fulkerson, J., and Dowling, P. 1991. "Strategic Performance Measurement and Management in Multinational Corporations," *Human Resource Management*, 30(3), 365-392.

10. Loftin, R. B. 1996. "Hands Across the Atlantic," *Virtual Reality Special Report*, 3(2), 39-41.

11. See Kossek, E. E. 1993. "Globalization: What Every Human Resource Professional Should Know—Examples from Amoco Production Company," presented at the National Research Symposium of the Human Resource Planning Society, June.

12. Their list corresponds closely to that described in Tung, R. 1993. "Managing National and Intranational Diversity," *Human Resource Management*, 32(4), 461-477.

13. Ayree, S., Chay, Y. W., and Chew, J. 1996 "An Investigation of the Willingness of Managerial Employees to Accept an Expatriate Assignment," *Journal of Organizational Behavior*, 17(3), 267-283.

14. This strategy may not be for every organization, at least as it is implemented by Schlumberger. These paths require a move every three years. At the time of the move, employees are only permitted to move up to 2000 pounds of personal effects and are expected to take the next plane out once a new assignment has been made. As one employee commented, "they treat their people like cattle." See Kossek, E. E., cited above.

15. See Oddou, G. and Mendenhall, M. 1991. "Succession Planning for the 21st Century," *Business Horizons*, 34(1), 26-34 for a brief description of this problem.

16. See Arthur, W. and Bennett, W. 1995. "The International Assignee: The Relative Importance of Factors Perceived to Contribute to Success," *Personnel Psychology*, 48, 99-115, and Tung, R. 1981. "Selection and Training of Personnel for Overseas Assignments," *Columbia Journal of World Business*, Spring, 68-78.

17. Greenfield, C. 1996. *Work/Family Game*. Boston: Towers Perin.

18. An alternative way of expressing this is that companies producing overseas to sell overseas need to identify sources of customer value. See Bartness, A. and Cerny, K. 1991. "Building Competitive Advantage through a Global Network of Capabilities," *California Management Review*, 35(2), 78-103, for a full discussion of the identification process.

19. Grove, C. L. and Torbiorn, I. 1985. "A New Conceptualization of Intercultural Adjustment and the Goals of Training," *International Journal of Intercultural Relations*, 9(16), 205-233.

20. See Kossek, E. E. cited above.

21. After saying this, he noted that "more than one way to skin a cat" was precisely the type of phrase that needed to be eliminated from international communications.

Part 2

STRATEGY AND INTERNATIONAL HUMAN RESOURCE MANAGEMENT

Convergence or Divergence: Human Resource Practices and Policies for Competitive Advantage Worldwide

Reading 2.1
Paul Sparrow
Randall S. Schuler
Susan E. Jackson

Abstract

The world is becoming far more competitive and volatile than ever before, causing firms to seek to gain competitive advantage whenever and wherever possible. As traditional sources and means such as capital, technology or location become less significant as a basis for competitive advantage, firms are turning to more innovative sources. One of these is the management of human resources. Whilst traditionally regarded as a personnel department function, it is now being widely shared among managers and non-managers, personnel directors and line managers. As the management of human resources is seen increasingly in terms of competitive advantage, the question that arises is: What must we do to gain this advantage? Many of the most successful firms now have to operate globally, and this gives rise to a second question: Do firms in different parts of the globe practice human resource management (HRM) for competitive advantage differently? Because of their importance, these two questions form the primary focus of this investigation. Data from a worldwide respondent survey of chief executive officers and human resource managers from twelve countries are cluster analysed to identify country groupings across a range of human resource policies and practices that could be used for competitive advantage. Differences and similarities on fifteen dimensions of these

Source: Paul Sparrow, Randall S. Schuler, and Susan E. Jackson. "Convergence or Divergence: Human Resource Practices and Policies for Competitive Advantage Worldwide." *International Journal of Human Resource Management,* 1994, (5)2, pp. 267–299. Reprinted by permission.

policies and practices are statistically determined and the results interpreted in the light of relevant literature. This investigation concludes that there is indeed a convergence in the use of HRM for competitive advantage. However, in pursuing this convergence there are some clear divergences, nuances and specific themes in the areas of HRM that will take the fore and in the way in which specific aspects such as culture, work structuring, performance management and resourcing will be utilised. These patterns of HRM bear understanding and consideration in managing human resources in different parts of the world.

Introduction ———————————————————————————————

As firms pursue, aggressively, their short term and long term goals, they are realising that their success depends upon a successful global presence (Ghoshal and Bartlett, 1989). In turn, their success as global players is being seen increasingly as dependent upon international human resource management:

> . . . virtually any type of international problem, in the final analysis, is either created by people or must be solved by people. Hence, having the right people in the right place at the right time emerges as the key to a company's international growth. If we are successful in solving that problem, I am confident we can cope with all others (Duerr, 1986, p. 43).

In a comparative context, human resource management (HRM) is best considered as the range of policies which have strategic significance for the organisation (Brewster and Tyson, 1991) and are typically used to facilitate integration, employee commitment, flexibility and the quality of worklife as well as meeting broader business goals such as changing organisational values, structure, productivity and delivery mechanisms. Therefore, in order to explain the various "brands" of HRM on a worldwide basis in sufficient detail, any analysis must include ". . . subjects which have traditionally been the concern of personnel management and industrial relations . . . as well as . . . more innovative and strategic approaches to people management" (Brewster and Tyson, 1991, p. l).

This increasing reliance upon successful HRM as a key to gaining competitive advantage in the global arena is mirroring the same phenomenon that effective firms witnessed during the 1980s on the domestic scene. As technology and capital became commodities in domestic markets, the only thing left to really distinguish firms, and thereby allow them to gain competitive advantage, were skills in managing their human resources (Reich, 1990). Whilst attention has been devoted to international comparisons of production systems and management strategies for many years, the comparison of people management systems has until recently been overlooked (Brewster, Hegewisch and Lockart, 1991; Pieper, 1990). Yet in most business situations the technical solution to specific issues has been understood, whilst the associated implementation problems of how to change behaviour, improve performance, predict future performance and make the best use of available talents remain the most significant obstacles. Bournois and Metcalfe (1991) argue that in widening a firm's strategic focus beyond the confines of its national boundaries, the human element becomes paramount. Therefore in the global arena we find CEOs acknowledging the importance of the issue:

> . . . Limited human resources—not unreliable capital—are the biggest constraint when companies globalise. (Floris Maljers, CEO, Unilever, Bartlett and Ghoshal, 1992, p. 126).

Successful Global Human Resource Management

If long run as well as short run corporate goals are dependent upon successful global HRM, an interesting question is: What is successful global management of human resources? At the risk of oversimplifying, we argue that it is best defined as the possession of the skills and knowledge of formulating and implementing policies and practices that effectively integrate and cohere globally dispersed employees, while at the same time recognising and appreciating local differences that impact the effective utilisation of human resources.

This definition of the successful global management of human resources can be decomposed into two distinct components of international HRM. The first component represents the body of knowledge and action that multinational firms use in allocating, dispersing, developing and motivating their global workforce. The major HRM concerns tend to focus on expatriate assignment, payment schemes and repatriation (Black, Gregersen and Mendenhall, 1993; Dowling and Schuler, 1990). Concerns for third country and local nationals are reflected in issues relating to the management of global operations, such as who is going to run the various geographically dispersed operations? Thus relatively few individuals tend to be encompassed by this component of international HRM.

The second component represents the body of knowledge and action concerned with actually staffing and running the local operations. The topics and issues enacted at this level are essentially focused around an understanding of local differences relevant to attracting, utilising and motivating individuals (Adler, 1991; Poole, 1986; Punnett and Ricks, 1992).

As Ronen (1986) suggested, for global firms to be successful in managing their worldwide workforces, they need to have an understanding and sensitivity to several local environments. They must utilise local information and adapt it to a broader set of human resource policies that reflect the firm itself. Of the two components of successful global HRM, this appears to be the lesser developed. Consequently, the focus of this article is on providing a greater understanding of selected aspects of HRM on a worldwide, comparative, basis.

Human Resource Practices and Concepts for Gaining Competitive Advantage

Porter (1980) suggested the concept of gaining competitive advantage to firms wishing to engage in strategic activities that would be difficult for competitors to copy or imitate quickly. Schuler and MacMillan (1984) applied this concept to HRM. They, and others since (for example, Reich, 1990) have suggested that firms can use HRM to gain competitive advantage because it is difficult for competitors to duplicate. That is, while technology and capital can be acquired by almost anyone at any time, for a price, it is rather difficult to acquire a ready pool of highly qualified and highly motivated employees.

At the global level, firms can seize competitive advantage through the selection and use of human resource policies and practices. The most important questions to ask then are: What human resource policies and practices can firms consider using in their worldwide operations that might assist them in gaining competitive advantage? Are they likely to be the same across countries? Is there some uniformity that firms can pursue in their efforts to successfully manage their worldwide workforces? As Moss-Kanter (1991, p. 153) reported in her worldwide survey of 12,000 managers:

> . . . While the survey results indicate that the emergence of a global culture of management is more dream than reality, they also uncover the leaders of the dream. For the most part, traditional industrial enterprises—larger, older, publicly held manufacturing companies with long planning horizons—are leading the drive toward globalization.

Given the analysis by Moss-Kanter (1991) and Porter (1990), it seems reasonable to proceed on the basis that any understanding of comparative HRM would aid firms in seeking to develop and implement human resource policies and practices worldwide to gain competitive advantage.

Key Policies and Practices in Gaining Competitive Advantage

While there are several specific ways that firms can gain competitive advantage with HRM policies and practices, it is most useful to gather data on generalisable policies and practices that are consistently seen as central to the management of human resources. In order to provide a basis for international comparison, we elected to focus on five major groupings of HRM policies and practices identified in the literature (see Poole, 1990; Schuler, 1992; Walker, 1992). Broadly, these include: culture; organisation structure; performance management; resourcing; and communications and corporate responsibility.

Culture. The present study addresses two aspects of culture. The first is the problem of creating a culture of empowerment, of including all employees in the decision making and responsibility of the organisation. This aspect of HRM represents a significant trend in a number of U.S. and U.K. organisations (Lawler, 1991; Wickens, 1987). How important is it worldwide? The second aspect is the promotion of diversity management and the development of a culture of equality. These two practices are tied together by a policy of inclusion, of bringing everyone into the operation and treating them equally with respect.

Organisation Structure. Associated with the issue of culture is that of organisation structure. Organisation structure refers to the relationship among units and individuals in the organisation. It can be described as ranging from a hierarchical, mechanistic relationship to a flatter, horizontal and organic relationship (Burns & Stalker, 1961). Obviously, these represent rather contrasting approaches to structuring organisations. Although their impact on individuals has been explored, more investigation specifically related to comparative HR appears warranted. Are all countries pursuing strategies of reducing the number of vertical layers (delayering) with the same vigour?

Performance Management. Another important group of HRM policies and practices reflects those associated with performance management. This process links goal setting and rewards, coaching for performance, aspects of career development and performance evaluation and appraisal into an integrated process. As firms seek to "manage the most out of employees" they are turning their attention to issues associated with employee performance. Because of the nature of international competition, the specific concerns in performance management are with measuring and motivating customer service, quality, innovation and risk taking behaviour (Peters, 1992).

Resourcing. As important as motivating employees once they are employed are issues associated with obtaining the most appropriate individuals (external resourcing); training and developing them with regard to technology and business process change; and managing the size of the workforce through reductions, downsizing and skills reprofiling. Beer, et al. (1984) describe these issues as part of a human resource flow policy. Seen in aggregate, we also regard them as part of a total resourcing dimension to HRM, as discussed by a number of writers (Boam and Sparrow, 1992; Mitrani, Dalziel and Fitt, 1992; Torrington, Hall, Haylor and Myers, 1991).

Communication and Corporate Responsibility. The fifth and final group of HRM policies and practices to which we give consideration are those by which firms may seek to describe their philosophy of communication and corporate responsibility. These two aspects of HRM capture the flow and sharing of information, internal and external to the organisation (Daft, 1992). Both can be vital as firms seek to empower and include employees in the organisation; and, as they seek to recognise and incorporate aspects of the external environment such as the general quality of the labour force, legal regulations, or concerns about environmental quality and social responsibility.

In summary, while these five groupings of HRM policies and practices may not capture all the human resource policies and practices relevant to global firms seeking to gain competitive advantage, they represent some of the major contemporary policies and practices being considered by academics and organisations, and are, therefore, worthy of international comparison.

The current literature suggests that these five aspects of HRM policies and practices may have varying levels of effectiveness throughout the world (Moss-Kanter, 1991; Porter, 1990). Indeed, Whitley (1992a) notes that as organisations move towards greater integration there is increasing recognition of national differences in higher level business systems. Despite increasing internationalisation within many industries, national institutions remain quite distinct. The role of the state and financial sectors, national systems of education and training, and diverse national cultures, employment expectations and labour relations all create "national business recipes, "each effective in their particular context but not necessarily effective elsewhere. These different national business recipes carry with them a "dominant logic of action" that guides management practice. This logic of action is reflected in specific management structures, styles and decision-making processes, growth and diversification strategies, inter-company market relationships and market development (Hofstede, 1993).

The institutional argument against unconstrained globalisation and business integration runs broadly as follows. There are a number of different and equally successful ways of organising economic activities (and management) in a market economy (Whitley, 1992a). These different patterns of economic organisation tend to be a product of the particular institutional environments within the various nation states. The development and success of specific managerial structures and practices (such as HRM) can only be explained by giving due cognisance to the various institutional contexts worldwide. Not all management methods are transferable. The effectiveness therefore of any worldwide conceptualisation of HRM will very likely be constrained by the different institutional contexts for national practice.

Hypotheses and Expectations

Based on the work of Moss-Kanter (1991) and Hofstede (1993), two hypotheses are developed in direct relationship to the concept of convergence or divergence of human resource policies and practices. Moss-Kanter (1991) found in her worldwide survey of management practices and expectations that the results could be clustered, not necessarily according to geography but according to culture. Thus she coined the phrase "cultural allies" to signify results from several countries being identical (eg. U.S., U.K. and Australia) and "cultural islands" to signify results from individual countries being unique from other countries (e.g., Korea, Japan). Using her results and rationale, leads to these testable hypotheses:

Hypothesis 1:
In regards to using human resource policies and practices for competitive advantage, there will be cultural islands and cultural allies. The cultural islands will be Korea and Japan and the cultural allies will be Europe, North America, U.K. and Australia; and Latin America.

Our second hypothesis is more tentative, more exploratory than the first. Thus while we can propose cultural allies and islands to exist, given the existing literature we are unable to make specific predictions about how human resource policies and practices will differ across nations. While it might be argued that they will reflect national cultures (it might also be argued that they will reflect differences in local law, custom and union-management history), we have no guidance suggesting specific relationships between aspects of culture and specific human resource policies and practices. This research is intended to provide such information. Thus at this time, what we are able to offer is a second and somewhat exploratory hypothesis:

Hypothesis 2:
There will be differences in which human resource policies and practices are seen as important for gaining competitive advantage across nations.

Methodology _____

Questionnaire. To explore these hypotheses, we conducted secondary analyses on data obtained as part of a larger international survey conducted in 1991. This was a worldwide study of human resource policies and practices conducted by IBM and Towers Perrin. The survey data which forms the basis of the analysis in this paper has been published elsewhere (Towers Perrin, 1992). In developing the survey questionnaire, some of the authors of this paper were invited to incorporate policies and practices and then write survey items that represented the academic and practitioner research and literature through 1990. These items were reviewed for representation and agreement by a series of other academics and practitioners identified by the IBM Corporation.

A major topic addressed in one section of the questionnaire was "human resource concepts and practices for gaining competitive advantage." In this section, respondents were asked to indicate the degree of importance they attached to each item in their firm's attempt to gain competitive advantage through human resource policies and practices. They indicated this for the current year (1991) and for the year of 2000. For the purposes of this study, we have analysed the data for the year 2000. This allows us to consider the extent to which future plans and expectations within the firms surveyed are likely to converge.

The specific firms included were those identified jointly by IBM and Towers Perrin as being the most effective firms in highly competitive environments in each of several countries. Details of the sample are provided by Towers Perrin (1992). In summary, the following information is of relevance in order to raise attention to the nature of the sample and the limits to which the data may be generalised. Effective firms in highly competitive environments were identified for each country surveyed. Given the global nature of firms discussed in the introduction, major employers in one country were, in some cases, subsidiaries or divisions of firms headquartered in other countries. In all cases, Towers Perrin (1992) surveyed two executives from each firm. Invitation letters and questionnaires were mailed to respondents in Spring 1991. The respondents included the chief operating officers and the senior human resource officers (2,961 respondents or 81% of the sample). Of these respondents 22% were from firms that employed over 10,000 employees, 46% were from firms employing 1,000 to 10,000 employees and 32% were from firms employing less than 1,000 employees. The other 19% of the sample comprised leading academics, consultants and individuals from the business media. The total sample of respondents were located in twelve countries throughout the world (the figures in brackets denote the sample size for each country): Argentina (42), Brazil (159), Mexico (67), France (81), Germany (295), Italy (212), the United Kingdom (261), Canada (120), the United States (1,174), Australia (94), Japan (387) and Korea (69).

The strategy of gathering data from major employing organisations led to a natural bias in the sample towards those countries with significant numbers of large organisations (e.g., the United States, Japan, Germany and the United Kingdom). To overcome the potential bias this might introduce into the analysis, the statistical tests (as discussed later) used to establish significant differences between national samples are those that control for sample size. The analysis that follows then is primarily based upon responses from respondents in effective firms in highly competitive environments in twelve countries worldwide responding to surveys that were translated into the language of the representative country.

When survey responses are used for comparative analysis, there are a number of issues that have to be acknowledged. Different political, economic, social and cultural considerations lead to a reinterpretation of management agendas at a local level. For example, in carrying out the pilot studies for their surveys on European HRM, Brewster,

Hegewisch and Lockart (1991) noted that identical questions about specific HRM tools or issues were interpreted differently by respondents within their national cultural and legal context. For example, the issue of flexible working in Britain and Germany has been linked to demographic change and the need to reintegrate women into the labour market, whereas in France flexible working is seen as a response to general changes in life style and has little to do with female labour force participation. Another problem is that the actual level of rating is difficult to interpret. For example, a low rating to a particular item might reflect the fact that the firm does not think the issue critical because they do not have the competence or desire to pursue the issue, or it might reflect the fact that the firm is very good already in the area under question and so no longer thinks the issue critical (although it will still form part of their activity). Survey findings reflect a pot pourri of past cultural constraints and future expectations based on new practices. Surveys are also cross-sectional and only examine perceptions (current or future) at one point in time. The analysis in this paper is based on expectations and plans for the year 2000, and therefore should not be coloured by short term factors (such as economic problems) that might influence respondents. Nevertheless, ratings reflect current mindsets only and these may change over the next ten years as organisations implement the findings of the survey. The data are then not a guarantee of eventual action. Great care is needed in interpreting comparative survey results and where possible we support the survey findings by reference to other published work.

Having noted the methodological constraints of empirical survey work, we would point to the general dearth of large scale empirical data and the opportunities afforded by an analysis of the Towers Perrin worldwide data. The addition of new empirical data we believe outweighs possible limitations. The statistical analysis in this paper therefore uses the Towers Perrin (1992) survey data to shed light on hypotheses described above:

- is there any underlying pattern (i.e., statistical clusters of countries) in the national data on HRM policies and concepts?

- what is the nature of differences between countries or groups of countries across a range of HRM variables?

Statistical Analysis. We analysed the responses to 38 questions asked about various HRM practices and concepts. In the first analysis we used the cluster analysis to ascertain whether there was any pattern in the anticipated HRM policies and concepts across the twelve countries included in the sample.

Once the underlying clusters (or grouping of countries) were identified, the differences between the importance these clusters of countries attribute to various HRM policies and practices were analysed. In order to facilitate this analysis of difference, the 38 survey questions were reclassified (on a conceptual basis) into 15 underlying dimensions. These dimensions identify elements of culture change, structuring the organisation, performance management, resourcing, and communication and corporate responsibility. They, therefore, broadly correspond with current conceptualisations of strategic human resource management as discussed in the Introduction (see for example Schuler, 1992; Walker, 1992). Questions relating to each of the dimensions examined are listed in Figure 1. It is important to note here that we have grouped surveyed items on a logical basis rather than an empirical basis.

Figure 1: The Fifteen HRM Dependent Variables and the Questionnaire Items Combined to Create Them

---

CULTURE CHANGE VARIABLES:

(1) Promoting an Empowerment Culture
Facilitate full employee involvement
Require employees to self-monitor and improve
Promote employee empowerment through ownership

(2) Promoting Diversity and an Equality Culture
Promote corporate culture emphasising equality
Manage diversity through tailored programmes

ORGANISATION STRUCTURE AND CONTROL VARIABLES:

(1) Emphasis on Flexible Organization/Work Practices
Require employee flexibility (i.e., jobs and location)
Flexible cross-functional teams/work groups
Flexible work arrangements
Utilize non-permanent workforce

(2) Emphasis on Centralisation and Vertical Hierarchy
Maintain specialised and directed workforce

(3) Emphasis on Utilising I.T. to Structure the Organization
Promote advanced technology for communications
Provide more access to information systems

(4) Emphasis on Horizontal Management
Increase spans of control and eliminate layers
Establish multiple and parallel career paths

PERFORMANCE/ PROCESS MANAGEMENT VARIABLES:

(1) Emphasis on Measuring and Promoting Customer Service
Reward employees for customer service/quality
Peer subordinate customer ratings

(2) Emphasis on Rewarding Innovation/Creativity
Reward employees for innovation and creativity
Opportunity includes autonomy, creative skills
Reward employees for enhancing skills/knowledge

(3) Link Between Pay and Individual Performance
Reward employees for business/productivity gains
Focus on merit philosophy, individual performance

(4) Shared Benefits, Risks and Pay for Team Performance
Implement pay systems promoting sharing
Flexible benefits
Share benefit risks and costs with employees

RESOURCING VARIABLES:

(1) Emphasis on External Resourcing
Emphasize quality university hiring programmes
Recruit and hire from non-traditional labour pools

(2) Emphasis on Internal Resourcing—Training & Careers
Identify high potential employees early
Emphasize management development/skills training
Require continuous training/retraining
Provide basic education and skills training

(3) Emphasis on Internal Resourcing—Managing Outflows
Provide flexible retirement opportunities
Develop innovative and flexible outplacement

COMMUNICATION/CORPORATE RESPONSIBILITY VARIABLES:

(1) Emphasis on Communication
Communicate business directions, problems and plans

(2) Emphasis on Corporate Responsibility
Active corporate involvement in public education
Ensure employees pursue good health aggressively
Offer personal/family assistance
Encourage/reward external volunteer activities
Provide full employment (life-time security)

Results _____

Hypothesis 1. The dendogram in Figure 2 shows the result of the successive fusions of countries, starting from the most similar. There are five resultant clusters of countries. The first cluster initially comprises the Anglo-Saxon business culture countries of the United Kingdom,

Figure 2: Rescaled Dendogram Showing the Average of the Twelve Countries

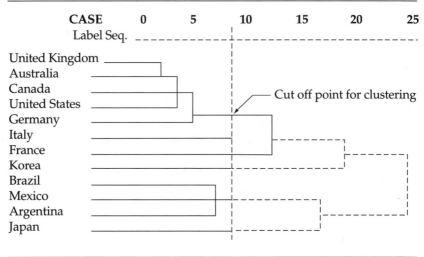

Australia, Canada, and the United States. These countries (the most similar) are subsequently joined by Germany and finally by Italy. The second cluster (a cultural island) consists solely of France. The third cluster is another cultural island consisting of Korea. The fourth cluster reveals another set of cultural allies comprising the South American or Latin countries of Brazil, Mexico, and Argentina, whilst the fifth cluster represents another cultural island consisting of Japan alone. These results, which are largely consistent with those we hypothesised, are discussed and interpreted later in this article primarily in relation to two other studies that have considered international patterns in business practice: the work of Hofstede (1980; 1993) on culture and the work of Moss-Kanter (1991) on attitudes toward change.

Three of the clusters only contained a single country. In order to complete the analysis of HRM differences between the other two clusters the United States was chosen to represent the Anglo-American cluster (as the largest sample contained within the cluster) and Brazil was chosen to represent the Latin American cluster on the same basis. The results are summarised in Table 1. Scores which are significantly[1] "higher" or "lower" (using the Standard Error of Difference in Proportions) than those of other countries on each variable are highlighted in the shaded boxes. In some cases, three grades of significant difference existed, i.e., higher, medium and lower.

---

[1]The term *significant differences, significant*, etc., refers to a statistical difference at the .05 level or lower.

Table 1: Summary of Differences in HRM between the Five Clusters of Countries

Survey Items	U.S. Anglo-Amer. Cluster	FRANCE	JAPAN	KOREA	BRAZIL S. American Cluster
Differences between the five clusters of countries on the Culture Change Variables					
Promoting Empowerment Culture	71.0% HIGHER	64.0%	52.7% LOWER	64.3%	78.7% HIGHER
Promoting Diversity and Equality Culture	53.0% HIGHER	36.5% LOWER	42.5% LOWER	49.5%	47.5%
Differences between the five clusters of countries on the Structuring Variables					
Emphasis on flexible work practices	59.8% HIGHER	39.8% LOWER	54.5%	53.3%	47.3% LOWER
Emphasis on centralisation and vertical hierarchy	6.0% LOWER	53.0% HIGHER	30.0% MEDIUM	51.0% HIGHER	10.0% LOWER
Emphasis on utilising IT to structure the organisation	50.0%	54.5%	46.0% LOWER	64.0% HIGHER	62.5% HIGHER
Emphasis on horizontal management	62.0%	55.5%	61.0%	58.5%	68.5%
Differences between the five clusters of countries on the Performance Management Variables					
Emphasis on measuring and promoting customer service	67.5% MEDIUM	82.0% HIGHER	50.0% LOWER	51.5% LOWER	66.5%
Emphasis on rewarding innovation/creativity	70.3%	62.7%	66.3%	67.3%	74.0%
Link between pay and individual performance	67.5%	64.5%	72.0%	70.0%	60.5%
Shared benefits, risks and pay for team performance	71.3% HIGHER	49.7%	40.1% LOWER	49.3%	60.7% MEDIUM
Differences between the five clusters of countries on the Resourcing Variables					
Emphasis on external resourcing	57.5%	50.0%	56.5%	42.0%	52.0%
Emphasis on training and careers	71.0%	60.7%	64.0% LOWER	81.5% HIGHER	73.3%
Emphasis on managing outflows	29.5% LOWER	40.5%	26.5% LOWER	34.0%	42.5% HIGHER
Differences between the five clusters of countries on the Communication and Corporate Responsibility Variables					
Emphasis on communication	85.0%	86.0%	83.0%	72.0%	81.0%
Emphasis on corporate responsibility	39.0%	28.6%	32.4%	37.4%	41.6%

Exploratory Differences on Hypothesis 2.   In this section we outline those comparisons that resulted in significant differences regarding HRM practices to be used to gain competitive advantage. Interpretation and discussion of these differences is left until later in the paper. On the Cultural items Japan scores significantly lower on Promoting an Empowerment Culture compared to the Anglo-American representative United States and the Latin American representative Brazil whilst the United States scores significantly higher on Promoting Diversity and an Equality Culture compared to France and Japan.

On the Structuring items the United States scores significantly higher on Emphasis on Flexible Work Practices compared to France and Brazil. Nearly all the comparisons on the Emphasis on Centralisation and Vertical Hierarchy variable are significant. France and Korea score higher than Japan and Japan scores higher than the United States and Brazil. Variations on the Emphasis on Utilising I.T. to structure the organisation are less marked, but Japan scores significantly lower than Korea and Brazil and the United States scores lower than Brazil. No significant differences were found between the clusters on the Emphasis on Horizontal Management variable.

Less variation was found between the clusters on the **Performance Management** items. There were no significant differences on the Emphasis on Rewarding Innovation/Creativity and Link between Pay and Individual Performance variables. The extent to which emphasis was put on Customer Service and its measurement varied significantly. France placed significantly higher emphasis on customer service than the United States, whilst the United States placed more emphasis on customer service than Korea and Japan. The emphasis placed on Shared Benefits, Risks and Pay for Team Performance also varied significantly. The United States placed greater emphasis on this than Brazil, France, Korea and Japan. The Japanese score was also significantly lower than that for Brazil.

The **Resourcing** items yielded virtually no significant differences. Korea placed a higher Emphasis on Training and Career Management than Japan whilst Brazil placed greater Emphasis on Managing Outflows of staff than the United States and Japan.

Finally, there were no significant differences between the cluster country representatives in their emphasis on **Communication and Corporate Responsibility.**

Discussion and Summary

There are several ways in which we could discuss the results of this analysis of possible differences among firms from different nations as they seek to gain competitive advantage through their HRM practices. We could look at differences between countries across each of the fifteen dimensions of HRM that have been examined, or focus on overall country strategies (as reflected by the different priorities given to each area of HRM), or consider the relationship between cultural stereotypes of nations and the results obtained in this study. Each of these approaches provides complementary insights; therefore, we discuss the findings from all three angles.

Relationship to Cultural Stereotypes

It is useful to compare and contrast the results regarding our hypothesis (particularly the national clusters of countries) to other identified clusters of countries associated with cultural stereotypes (Adler, 1991; Hofstede, 1980; 1993; Phatak, 1992; Johnson and Golembiewski, 1992; and Laurent, 1991); or with studies on the management of change (Moss-Kanter, 1991). The Anglo-American cluster identified in this study contains very similar members to those identified in Moss-Kanter's (1991) study of 12,000 survey respondents worldwide. The United States, Australia, the United Kingdom and Canada were also grouped into a common cluster by Moss-Kanter (1991). There is an Anglo-American or Anglo-Saxon business culture that unites these countries. It is stereotyped in terms of openness and equality. This is reflected in the results on both the culture change items (particularly the "promoting diversity and equality" variable) on which the Anglo-American cluster scores significantly higher than for example France and Japan. Firms in the Anglo-American cluster see this cultural openness as one of their most important ways of gaining competitive advantage, reflecting the academic literature that describes future problems of demography in terms of the need to cope with diversity (Johnston and Packer, 1987). This cultural stereotype of openness and equality is also reflected in the results on the structuring items, where the Anglo-American cluster places a significantly higher emphasis on the criticality of flexible work practices and the lowest emphasis on the need for centralisation and vertical hierarchy. It is interesting to note that in Moss-Kanter's (1991) study, Germany formed part of a North European cluster of countries, and Italy formed part of a Latin cluster of countries. In contrast, our study suggests that where people management issues are concerned, the relative emphasis these countries expect to give in the year 2000 to the fifteen dimensions of HRM places them in the Anglo-American camp.

Our study indicated that Japan stands alone with a unique cluster of HRM emphases. This was also the case in Moss-Kanter's (1991) study which is why she called Japan a cultural island. It is interesting to note that although Japan faces even more severe demographic problems than the Anglo-American countries it does not place as high an emphasis on the cultural variables of empowerment, diversity and equality but places greater emphasis on centralisation and vertical hierarchy. Japan gave lowest importance for gaining competitive advantage to promoting empowerment, diversity and equality, reflecting the cultural importance given in Japan to respect for authority and its more homogeneous ethnic culture.

In Moss-Kanter's (1991) study France formed part of a North European cluster of countries. The only difference noted in this study is that Germany does not share the same pattern of HRM emphases as France. The results obtained for the French cluster also strongly reflect Hofstede's (1980) findings on culture. In Hofstede's analysis French managers have a higher Power distance score (68) in comparison for example with British managers (35). There are greater differences in formal power across management hierarchies in France and managers are more tolerant of such inequalities of power. French managers also have a higher Uncertainty avoidance score (86) in comparison to British managers (35) and might be expected to seek to eliminate uncertainty and ambiguity in their tasks. The way in which the manager-subordinate relationship enables them to do this nevertheless remains a delicate point in France (Poirson, 1993). The fear of face to face conflict, the way in which authority is conceived, and the mode of selection of senior managers all act as powerful cultural forces that make it difficult for French organisations to readily adopt Anglo-American management concepts (such as performance management). Rojot (1990) paints French corporate culture as one that creates situations in which subordinate managers seek more responsibility, but in fact remain passive, fear to commit themselves to specific objectives and mostly look for protection from above. Senior managers rule autocratically and see the organisation as an elite school in which they are the most intelligent and subordinates therefore cannot conceivably have valid ideas. French managers are therefore more possessive of their individual autonomy. Their reaction is: "I know my job, if I am controlled, this means they have no confidence in me" (Poirson, 1993). Even where Anglo-American concepts of HRM are adopted, they become ". . . the stake of a different game" (Rojot, 1990, p. 98).

Both our study and that of Moss-Kanter (1991) revealed Korea as another cultural island. The Korean results in our study reflect Korea's higher emphasis on protectionism, strong sense of corporate paternalism, preference for centralisation and greater optimism for the future, as noted by Moss-Kanter (1991). The utilisation of information technology to help do so appears consistent with the image of Korea as a nation that is respectful of authority and very hierarchically organised.

Recently, attention has been directed to the unique features of Latin America in terms of HRM (Baker, Smith, Weiner, 1992; Baker, Smith, Weiner and Jacobson, 1993; Nash, 1993). Moss-Kanter (1991) identified a Latin cluster of countries consisting of South American nations, Italy and Spain. Similarly, we found that the South American countries of Mexico, Argentina and Brazil clustered together. The one difference was that Italy seems to adopt an Anglo-American perspective on future

HRM practices for competitive advantage. Recent analyses of HRM in Italy and the European Latin countries (Camuffo and Costa, 1992; Filella, 1991) support this finding. The Latin cluster has many features similar to the Anglo-American cluster such as promotion of an empowerment culture, high decentralisation, high emphasis on using IT to support structuring in organisations, and a high desire to seek a sharing of benefits and risks in reward systems which may reflect the high levels of privatisation occurring in those countries. The Latin cluster differs from the Anglo-American cluster in that it places more value on the need to manage outflows from organisations and less emphasis on the need for flexible work practices.

National HRM Strategies

In this section we discuss the survey findings in relation to national patterns of HRM and draw upon other research to provide the necessary context to interpret the survey findings. Naturally, this section focuses on differences between countries. These differences should not be overstated, however, for balanced against these are the underlying convergences that are reducing many of these differences. These convergences will be discussed in the following section.

> . . . European-style class consciousness, a serious socialist movement . . . penetration of Marxist ideology in "old Europe" . . . have variously served to structure both the perception and reality of superior-subordinate and management-worker relations in industry (Lawrence, 1992, p. 12).

Lawrence (1992) argues that HRM is essentially an Anglo-Saxon construct that has been "grafted on"—but has not "taken root"—in continental Europe. Classic HRM functions such as recruitment, socialisation, training and development are determined by different conceptions of management in Europe, and underpinned by a related set of values. Historically, HRM has not had the same élan and in part has been socially and culturally by-passed. When compared with American (or indeed British) concepts of HRM, a European model needs to take account of a number of factors. The distinctions drawn between concepts of HRM prevalent in continental Europe as opposed to the Anglo-American model (Brewster and Hegewisch, 1993; Pieper, 1990) include more restricted employer autonomy, difficult hiring and firing decisions, lower geographic and professional employee mobility and a stronger link between type of education and career progression. There is an increased role of "social partners" in the employment relationship, a stronger role of trade unions influence in the setting of HRM policy, collective bargaining at the state and regional level and direct co-determination at the firm level. Finally there are higher levels of government intervention or support in many areas of HRM, a state role in education through public school and university systems, formal certification systems influencing personnel selection and careers and more comprehensive welfare policies.

It is therefore all the more interesting that Germany and Italy, as two continental European countries, actually fell within the Anglo-American cluster. However, a preliminary analysis of this cluster suggests that whilst the constituent members are all more alike each other than they are alike the other countries (France, Korea, Japan and so forth), there are still likely to be some significant differences in HRM practices within the cluster. Germany and Italy only "joined" the Anglo-American cluster towards the end of the mathematical forcing process (see Figure 2), and could be considered as worth separate investigation. A useful area for further investigation would be to investigate national pathways and statistical differences within the regional clusters.

The characteristics of French HRM (recently discussed by several authors such as Barsoux and Lawrence, 1990; Besse, 1992; Poirson, 1993; and Rojot, 1990) as revealed by our analysis supports many of the cultural distinctions drawn above. For example, the strong French educational élite, distinct cadres of management, and extremely rigid hierarchical approach to both performance and career management is reflected in the significantly lower rating given to a culture based on diversity and equality as well as a significantly higher emphasis given to centralisation and vertical hierarchy. However, the context within which HRM in France is practiced has changed considerably over the last ten years (Poirson, 1993; Rojot, 1990). Increased and globalised competition, the growth of multinational organisations, the shortening of product life-cycles, and the growing importance of product quality have all provided a new justification of managerial authority in France, and a new language amongst the employers' associations and bodies has legitimised a number of management and HRM practices, including performance management (Rojot, 1990). A 1987 survey by Hay France of 220 French organisations employing more than 65,000 managers found that 91% had a policy of fixing individual objectives for managers, 81% evaluated performance in relation to these objectives and 87% had an annual performance appraisal review meeting. This renewed fervour for and emphasis on objectives-based performance management is reflected in the French sample high rating for the need to emphasise the promotion and measurement of customer service.

Many of our findings reflect the existing competence and perceived priorities in the Japanese HRM system (see Aoki, 1988; Dore, 1986; and Koike, 1987) and reveal the unique approach to HRM created by its internal labour market. Japanese HRM has been characterised by hierarchical pyramid-type organisations with bureaucratic control. The Japanese respondents rated an emphasis on centralisation and vertical hierarchy as significantly more critical than the Anglo-American cluster (30% compared to 6%). However, the Korean and French samples placed an even greater emphasis on these issues. Performance in Japan is evaluated in the long term and there is a model of life-time employment. Skills are firm-specific and there is a reliance on in-house specific on-the-job training. Not surprisingly our Japanese sample rated the need to manage outflows from the organisation significantly lower than Brazil or France and placed a lower emphasis on training and development (linked to careers as opposed to jobs) given the existing high levels of informal on-the-job training.

Communication in Japan is more informal and relies on managerial networks. Promotion systems (particularly to senior management level) are more geared to an educational elite (Koike, 1987; Whitley, 1992b), female participation rates are low and there is a marked labour market segmentation between core (65% to 90%) employees and lower status, higher mobility, temporary workers. This is reflected in the survey finding that the Japanese sample provide a significantly lower rating to the criticality of promoting a culture that promotes diversity and equality (42% compared to 53% in the Anglo-American cluster).

Japanese wage differentials are based on hierarchy and have remained fairly stable, despite the pressures for change discussed later. Bonuses in Japan are not regarded as a reward or dividend of profit as in the Anglo-Saxon countries, but are taken more for granted and assumed to be part of regular earnings despite the fact they account for around 33% of nominal salaries (Aoki, 1988). They do not decrease even in difficult times (Sano, 1993). Jobs are also highly segmented. The survey data reflected this paradox with the Japanese sample giving a significantly lower rating to pay systems that share risks and benefits or reward team performance (40% compared to 71% in the Anglo-American cluster).

More recently a number of reviews have pointed to growing pressure for change in the Japanese model of HRM (see for example Sano, 1993; Sasajima, 1993; and Takahashi, 1990). Japanese organisations are facing a crisis and their traditional patterns of HRM are under structural pressure to change. Increasing difficulties are being faced in maintaining employment security and automatic pay increase systems. Demographic pressures have resulted in an aging workforce with an increasingly long length of service (Sano, 1993), creating fears about skills shortages and upward pressure on labour costs. Education levels have increased markedly, as have female participation and part time work (these pressures are also apparent in the U.S. and Europe). It is interesting to note that the Japanese sample provided the lowest rating to the importance of promoting an empowerment culture. This could be interpreted in two contrasting ways: a reflection of the fact that the Japanese HRM system already achieves this and so it is a lower priority for the future, or a recognition by Japanese managers that external pressures may interfere with their ability to maintain this type of culture.

Some authors have argued that in Japan new technology is being used increasingly to deskill jobs and combine business processes because productivity of more senior and skilled employees is falling. However, our survey data does not appear to reflect this concern. The

Japanese sample viewed the use of IT to structure the organisation as significantly less important compared to, for example, the Korean and Brazilian samples.

Wilkinson (1988) has noted that some features of the Korean labour system resemble those of the Japanese, such as the segmentation of the labour market (our data supported this with both countries rating the need to promote an empowerment culture or culture based on diversity and equality as low) and overall philosophy behind their reward systems (similarly supported by our analysis showing no significant differences between Korea and Japan on any of the four dimensions used to examine performance management). However, a number of writers have noted a number of striking differences between Japanese and Korean labour systems (Biggart, 1989; Chung and Lee, 1988; Deyo, 1989; Michell, 1988; Park, 1992; Sharma, 1991; Shin and Chin, 1989; Whitley, 1992b; Yoo and Lee, 1987). In relation to Japan, labour turnover in the manufacturing sector is high (Amsden, 1989) and managerial mobility is high (Biggart, 1989). This is perhaps reflected in our finding that Japan places a low emphasis on the importance of managing outflows from the organisation (27%) in comparison to Korea (34%), although the difference is not significant. Similarly, Michell (1988) reported lower employer commitment to employee welfare in Korea than Japan, mainly because its labour intensive industries (such as textiles) are following cost leadership strategies. Even in capital-intensive industries, lifelong employment is not seen as an ideal. Our analysis revealed that the Korean sample placed a significantly higher emphasis on work structuring through the use of IT and on centralisation and the vertical hierarchy. These are two dimensions of structure that are often associated with newly industrialising countries and their attempts to drive cost savings and improvements to the business process and productivity.

Attention has also been drawn to the greater scope for manager and owner discretion in Korea, more authoritarian and directive supervisory style focused on task performance as opposed to the facilitation of group performance (Parl, 1992; Whitley, 1992b), limited scope for supervisors to organise groups' work and lower levels of autonomy for workers in comparison to Japan (Deyo, 1989). We found only a marginally lower emphasis on the importance of horizontal management in Korea than in Japan and a more marked (but still insignificant) difference in the importance given to communication (72% in Korea, the lowest of all five clusters, compared to 83% in Japan). Perhaps reflecting a national desire to reduce this differential, recent moves towards democratisation and the atypical Korean trend towards greater unionisation (Park, 1992), the Korean sample placed higher importance on promoting an empowerment culture than did Japan (which as discussed previously may feel it has already achieved much in this area).

Recruitment decisions, whilst based on a university elite as in Japan, also differ in Korea. Shin and Chin (1989) argue that Korean selection and promotion decisions are more influenced by personal and regional networks and relationships than in Japan. Therefore, despite the acute labour shortages experienced in Korea since 1986 (Park, 1992) the lower level of formality in selection is reflected in our results, which show that in Korea only 42% of the sample felt that an emphasis on external resourcing was critical, compared to 57% of the Japanese sample, although again the difference was not significant. Amsden (1989) has also drawn attention to the high wages and fringe benefits (such as company housing, bonus payments and schooling for children) that characterise the Korean reward system. This is essentially a paternalistic system (without the Japanese guarantee of lifelong employment) in which loyalty is less directly incorporated into rewards systems than in Japan. However, as already noted, there were no significant differences between Japan and Korea on the four dimensions of performance management, although the Korean sample placed a lower emphasis on reward systems that share both benefits and risk or pay for team performance, but a higher emphasis on linking pay and individual performance, which seems to reflect the description of reward systems given by Amsden (1989).

Predictions About HRM Practices for Competitive Advantage

The comparison of differences thus far have been made using the data for the year 2000. These data were used for two primary reasons: First, using HRM to gain a competitive advantage takes time, thus historical data would not be as much use as data which reflects expectations and plans for the year 2000. Second, data for the year 2000 would enable us to assess the extent to which there is a convergence or divergence occurring worldwide in the practice of HRM.

In making predictions about HRM practices and policies for competitive advantage, it is necessary to establish the baseline from where we started. In this study, the baseline is 1991. If we look at these results in conjunction with the results for the year 2000 we not only have a better basis for prediction but also for comparison across the clusters. Table 2 shows the differences in the importance ratings from respondents for the 15 dimensions of HRM.

One clear pattern revealed by Table 2 is that the respondents in all the clusters rated all HRM items higher in the year 2000 than they did in the year 1991. This appears to be consistent with the academic and professional literature that suggests that the management of people is becoming a more significant force in organisations, particularly now that capital, technology and the like are readily available to everyone. It also reflects the points we made in the section on national strategies which showed that in France and Japan there are increasing pressures to adapt their highly nationalistic models of HRM. Another observation and prediction is that while people management is becoming

Table 2: Differences in HRM between the Five Clusters: Change from 1991-2000

Survey Items	U.S. Anglo-Amer. Cluster	FRANCE	JAPAN	KOREA	BRAZIL S. American Cluster
	Differences between the five clusters of countries on the Culture Change Variables				
Promoting Empowerment Culture	41-71 +31%	38-64 +26%	40-53 +13%	34-64 +30%	41-79 +38%
Promoting Diversity and Equality Culture	31-53 +22%	20-37 +17%	28-43 +13%	18-50 +32%	23-40 +25%
	Differences between the five clusters of countries on the Structuring Variables				
Emphasis on flexible work practices	26-60 +34%	24-40 +16%	32-55 +23%	15-54 +39%	17-47 +30%
Emphasis on centralisation and vertical hierarchy	0-6 0%	15-53 +38%	13-30 +17%	25-51 +26%	11-10 -1%
Emphasis on utilising IT to structure the organisation	16-50 +34%	19-55 +36%	21-46 +25%	23-64 +41%	21-63 42%
Emphasis on horizontal management	36-62 +34%	30-56 +26%	37-61 +24%	30-59 +29%	37-69 +32%
	Differences between the five clusters of countries on the Performance Management Variables				
Emphasis on measuring and promoting customer service	40-68 +28%	47-82 +35%	31-50 +19%	34-52 +18%	36-67 +31%
Emphasis on rewarding innovation/creativity	35-70 +35%	32-63 +31%	41-66 +25%	40-67 +27%	40-74 +34%
Link between pay and individual performance	52-68 +16%	42-65 +23%	44-72 +28%	45-70 +25%	48-61 +13%
Shared benefits, risks and pay for team performance	40-71 +31%	23-50 +27%	18-40 +22%	23-49 +26%	24-61 +37%
	Differences between the five clusters of countries on the Resourcing Variables				
Emphasis on external resourcing	24-58 +34%	37-50 +13%	41-57 +16%	40-42 +2%	23-52 +29%
Emphasis on training and careers	38-71 +33%	43-61 +18%	52-64 +12%	60-82 +22%	59-73 +14%
Emphasis on managing outflows	13-30 +17%	13-41 +28%	7-27 +20%	7-34 +27%	14-43 +29%
	Differences between the five clusters of countries on the Communication and Corporate Responsibility Variables				
Emphasis on communication	57-85 +28%	57-86 +29%	74-83 +9%	62-72 +10%	48-81 +33%
Emphasis on corporate responsibility	18-39 +21%	14-29 +15%	16-32 +16%	18-38 +20%	27-42 +15%

important in all the countries surveyed, the countries will continue to exhibit differences, both in degree and in kind. For example, when it comes to promoting an empowerment culture, the Japanese are increasing as are the French, but the Anglo-American cluster is increasing much more, (40-71% vs 40-53%).

When examining Table 2 it is important to keep these percentage differences in mind. They often provide explanatory evidence as to why the differences are indeed different. For the item "emphasis on communication" both Japan and Korea have small differences compared to the Anglo American cluster. However, an examination of the original percentage shows that both Japan and Korea had originally rated this item substantially higher than the Anglo American cluster. Is this suggesting that the Anglo American cluster is "playing catch-up"? Are we to assume that an understanding of future events is to be found in the Asian nations? Probably not. These differences more likely still reflect cultural and economic differences. Note that while Japan and Korea are geographical neighbours to the United States, overall their results are rather different. In fact, Australia is regarded by some as being in the Asia Pacific region, yet it falls into the Anglo-American cluster in the original analysis.

These observations about Table 2 being so noted, what other predictions about convergence can we offer concerning HRM practices and policies for competitive advantage?

1. The Culture Change dimensions: Firms in all clusters are seeing that it is likely to be useful to empower their employees more than today, and to promote a more diverse and egalitarian culture. As the world's workforce becomes more educated it is demanding more involvement and participation in workplace decisions and events. Task and knowledge, as well as employee needs and abilities, appear to be driving this trend in human resource practices. A related prediction here is that there will be continued examination of the role of the manager, with continued pressure for change in that role.

2. The Structuring dimensions: Following from the first prediction is the second: as the task and knowledge determine the involvement of employees and the role of the manager, they also impact the structure of the operation. In particular, they make it necessary for work practices to be more flexible to change as the skills and abilities needed to do them change. This removes the sole responsibility for decision making from the hierarchy to those in the know and those generally nearest the action.

3. The Performance Management dimensions: There is likely to be enhanced emphasis on obtaining performance and making performance a centre of attention. In particular, performance related to serving the customer would appear to be of most importance. This will be closely followed by an emphasis on the performance related to innovation, new products and services (of

course, designed with the customer in mind). To reinforce these emphases, remuneration schemes at both the individual and team level are likely to be implemented in significant numbers during this decade. There will be a greater sharing of risks and rewards. With the emphasis on promoting a culture of equality, this might also mean that greater sharing will occur at all levels of management and non-management employees.

4. The Resourcing dimensions: Flexibility will be desired and sought regarding all areas of the business. Just as there is likely to be more flexibility with regards to job assignments and decisions, there is likely to be more flexibility regarding staffing decisions, both at the entry and exit stages. That is, firms might be likely to seek greater use of part time or temporary workers to fill positions, and not bring them into full time employee status. Perhaps for the full time employees, firms will dedicate more resources to training and retraining. This will make the current workforce (the one that is more empowered and is making more decisions) more important to the organisation. Nevertheless, even this workforce may need to be replaced. Knowledge is doubling every seven years. To capture this, firms may need to be constantly incorporating new members and new ideas. This will demand constant change and adaptation by all. For some this may mean a need to exit the organisation. Consequently, firms will be equally concerned about managing the egress of employees. They will want to ensure that this is predictable and that employees with key skills, today and in the future, do not suddenly leave the firm.

5. The Communication and Corporate Responsibility dimensions: While organisations are likely to get more involved in community activities, particularly training and education, they are likely to still want employees to focus on the firm. Consequently, they will devote more resources to communicating and sharing the goals and objectives of the organisation with all employees. This will facilitate the empowerment of employees and help ensure that the decisions made by employees are as consistent with the needs of the business as those made by top management.

Conclusions —————————————————————————————————————

The function of managing people in organisations is perceived as important today for firms to gain competitive advantage. This level of importance, however, pales in comparison to the importance it is expected to have in the year 2000. While this is likely due to greater access organisations have to capital and technology, it is also likely due to a growing recognition that people do make a difference. Thus this relatively under-utilised resource called "people" is likely to receive greater attention from organisations throughout this decade, at least for firms seeking to be effective in highly competitive environments.

While "to receive greater attention" is likely to vary across firms, it is not expected to vary widely concerning several key themes or foci. These include the following: a greater emphasis on empowerment, equality, diversity management, flexibility in job design and assignment, flatter organisational structures, customer-based measures of performance and related remuneration schemes, flexibility in staffing decisions, training decisions and exiting decisions, and greater communication of the objectives and goals of the firm to all employees.

Finally, although the country clusters reported in this study did illustrate differences to these key themes, they also reflected similarity. The differences are probably better described as being more "in degree" than "in kind." Thus while it might be tempting to conclude that there is clearly a convergence rather than divergence in the practices and policies used by organisations to manage their human resources, this might be overstating the reality (as well as the complexity) of managing human resources effectively. Employees do reflect the larger society and culture from which they come to the organisation. From this they bring education and skill, attitudes toward work and organisation and general expectations about their role and responsibility in the organisation. The impact and relevance of these should not be understated. Thus while it may be tempting to conclude by using the term "convergence," it may be more an attempt to simplify reality prematurely.

References

Adler, N.J. (l991) *International dimensions of organisational behaviour.* Boston: PWS-Kent.

Amsden, A.H. (1989) *Asia's next giant.* Oxford: Oxford University Press.

Aoi, M. (1988) *Information, incentives and bargaining in the Japanese economy.* Cambridge: Cambridge University Press.

Baker, S., Smith, G., Weiner, E. and Jacobson, K. (1992) "Latin America: The big move to Free Markets," *Business Week,* June 15, 50-62.

Baker, S., Smith, G., and Weiner, E. (1993) "The Mexican worker." *Business Week,* April 19, 84-92.

Barsoux, J.L. and Lawrence, P. (1990) *Management in France.* London: Cassell Education Limited.

Bartlett, C.A. and Ghoshal, S. (1992) "What is a global manager?" *Harvard Business Review,* 70 (5): 124-32.

Beer, M., Spector, B., Lawrence, P.R., Mills, D.Q., and Walton, RE. (1984) *Managing Human Assets.* New York: The Free Press.

Besse, D. (1992) "Finding a new raison d'etre: Personnel management in France,", *Personnel Management,* 24(8), 40-3.

Biggart, N.W. (1989) "Institutionalised patrimonialism in Korean business." Program in East Asian culture and development research, *Working Paper No. 23, Institute of Governmental Affairs.* University of California: Davies.

Black, J.S., Gregersen, H.B. and Mendenhall, P. (1992) *Global Assignments.* San Francisco: Jossey-Bass.

Boam, R. and Sparrow, P.R. (1992) (eds.) *Designing and Achieving Competency.* London: McGraw-Hill.

Bournois, F. and Metcalfe, P. (1991) "HR management of executives in Europe: structures, policies and techniques." In C. Brewster and S. Tyson (eds.) *International Comparisons in Human Resource Management.* London: Pitman.

Brewster, C. and Hegewisch, A. (1993) "Personnel management in Europe: a continent of diversity," *Personnel Management,* 25 (1), 36-40.

Brewster, C., Hegewisch, A. and Lockhart, J.T. (1991) "Researching human resource management: methodology of the Price Waterhouse Cranfield Project on European trends," *Personnel Review,* 20 (6), 36-40.

Brewster, C. and Tyson, S. (1991) (eds.) *International Comparisons in Human Resource Management.* London: Pittman.

Burns, T. and Stalker, G.R. (1961) *The Management of Innovation.* London: Tavistock.

Camuffo, A. and Costa, G. (1992) "Strategic human resource management — Italian style." *Sloan Management Review,* 34 (2), 59-67.

Chung, K.H. and Lee, H.C. (1988) (eds.) *Korean Managerial Dynamics.* London: Praeger.

Daft, R.L. (1992) *Organization Theory and Design.* St. Paul, Minneapolis: West Publishing.

Deyo, F.C. (1989) *Beneath the Miracle: Labour Subordination in the New Asian Industrialism.* Berkeley, CA: University of California Press.

Dore, R.P. (1986) *Flexible Rigidities.* Stanford: Stanford University Press.

Duerr, M.G. (1986) "International business management: its four tasks," *Conference Board Record,* Oct., 43-7.

Dowling, P.J. and Schuler, R.S. (1990) *International Dimensions of Human Resource Management.* Boston: PWS-Kent.

Filella, J. (1991) "Is there a Latin model in the management of human resources?" *Personnel Review,* 20 (6), 14-23.

Ghoshal, S. and Bartlett, C.A. (1989) "The multinational corporation as an interorganisational network," *Academy of Management Review,* 15(4), 603-625.

Hofstede, G. (1980) *Culture's Consequences: International Differences in Work-Related Values.* London: Sage.

Hofstede, G. (1993) "Cultural constraints in management theories." *Academy of Management Executive,* 7 (1), 81-93.

Johnson, K.R. and Golembiewski, R.T. (1992) "National culture in organization development: a conceptual and empirical analysis," *International Journal of Human Resource Management,* 3 (1), 71-84.

Johnston, W.B. and Packer, A.E. (1987) *Workforce 2000: Work and Workers for the 21st Century.* Washington, D.C.: U.S. Govt. Printing Office.

Koike, K. (1987) "Human resource development and labour management relations." In K. Yamamura and Y. Yashuba (eds.) *The Political Economy of Japan. 2. The Domestic Transformation.* Stanford: Stanford University Press.

Lawrence, P. (1992) "Management development in Germany." In S. Tyson, P. Lawrence, P. Poirson, L. Manzolini and C.S. Vincente (eds.) *Human Resource Management in Europe: Strategic Issues and Cases.* London: Kogan Page.

Laurent, A. (1991) "Managing across cultures and national borders." In S.G. Makridakis (ed.) *Single Market Europe: Opportunities and Challenges for Business.* London: Jossey Bass.

Lawler, E.E. (1991) "The new plant approach: A second generation approach," *Organizational Dynamics,* Summer, 5-15.

Michell, T. (1988) *From a Developing to a Newly Industrialised Country: the Republic of Korea, 1961-82.* Geneva: International Labour Organisation.

Mitrani, A., Dalziel, M. and Fin, D. (1992) (eds.) *Competency-Based Human Resource Management.* London: Kogan Page.

Moss-Kanter, R. (1991) "Transcending business boundaries: 12,000 world managers view change," *Harvard Business Review,* 69 (3), 151-164.

Nash, N. (1993) "A new rush into Latin America," *The New York Times,* April 11, Sec. 3, 1-6.

Park, D.J. (1992) "Industrial relations in Korea," *International Journal of Human Resource Management,* 3 (1), 105-124.

Peters, T. (1992) *Liberation Management: Necessary Disorganisation for the NanosecondNineties.* London: Macmillan.

Phatak, A.V. (1992) *International Dimensions of Management.* Boston: PSW Kent.

Pieper, R. (1990) (ed.) *Human Resource Management: an International Comparison.* Berlin: de Gruyter.

Poirson, P. (1993) "The characteristics and dynamics of human resource management in France." In S. Tyson, P. Lawrence, P. Poirson, L. Manzolini and C.S. Vincente (eds.) *Human Resource Management in Europe: Strategic Issues and Cases.* London: Kogan Page.

Poole, M.J.F. (1986) *Industrial Relations: Origins and Patterns of National Diversity.* London: Routledge.

Poole, M.J.F. (1990) Editorial: "Human Resource management in an international perspective," *International Journal of Human Resource Management,* 1, 1-16.

Porter, M.E. (1980) *Competitive Strategy: Techniques for Analysing Industries and Competitors.* New York: Free Press.

Porter, M.E. (1990) *Competitive Advantage of Nations.* New York: Free Press.

Punnett, B.J. and Ricks, D.A. (1992) *International Business.* Boston: PWD-Kent.

Reich, R.B. (1990) "Who is us?," *Harvard Business Review,* 68 (1), 53-64.

Ronen, S. (1986) *Comparative and Multinational Management.* New York: Wiley and Sons.

Rojot, J. (1990) "Human resource management in France." In Pieper, R. (ed.) *Human Resource Management: an International Comparison.* Berlin: de Gruyter.

Sano, Y. (1993) "Changes and continued stability in Japanese HRM systems: choice in the share economy," *International Journal of Human Resource Management,* 4 (1), 11-28.

Sasajima, Y. (1993) "Changes in labour supply and their impacts on human resource management: the case of Japan," *International Journal of Human Resource Management,* 4 (1), 29-44.

Schuler, R.S. (1992) "Strategic human resource management: linking the people with the strategic needs of the business," *Organizational Dynamics,* 21 (1), 18-31.

Schuler, R.S. and MacMillan, I. (1984) "Creating competitive advantage through human resource management practices," *Human Resource Management,* 23, 241-55.

Sharma, B. (1991) "Industrialisation and strategy shifts in industrial relations: a comparative study of South Korea and Singapore." In C. Brewster and S. Tyson (eds.) *International Comparisons in Human Resource Management.* London: Pitman.

Shin, E.H. and Chin, S.W. (1989) "Social affinity among top managerial executives of large corporations in Korea," *Sociological Forum,* 4, 3-26.

Takahashi, Y. (1990) "Human resource management in Japan." In R. Pieper (ed.) *Human Resource Management: an International Comparison.* Berlin: de Gruyter.

Torrington, D., Hall, L., Haylor, I. and Myers, J. (1991) *Employee Resourcing.* Wimbledon: Institute of Personnel Management.

Towers Perrin (1992) *Priorities for Competitive Advantage: a Worldwide Human Resource Study.* London: Towers Perrin.

Walker, J. (1992) *Human resource strategy.* New York: McGraw-Hill.

Whitley, R. (1992a) (ed.) *European business systems: firms and markets in their national contexts.* London: Sage.

Whitley, R. (1992b) (ed.) *Business Systems in East Asia: Firms, Markets and Societies.* London: Sage.

Wickens, D. (1987) *The road to Nissan.* London: MacMillan.

Wilkinson, B. (1988) "A comparative analysis." In *Technological Change, Work Organisation and Pay: Lessons from Asia.* Geneva: International Labour Organisation.

Yoo, S. and Lee, S.M. (1987) "Management style and practice of Korean Chaebols," *California Management Review,* 29(4), 95-110.

The Link Between Business Strategy and International Human Resource Management Practices

Reading 2.2
Allan Bird and
Schon Beechler

Introduction

Research on international HRM has blossomed in recent years yet much of this research has been in the area of staffing. Reasons for focusing almost exclusively on this area, especially among practitioners, appear to stem from the high costs of making poor staffing decisions. Two issues which have been extensively researched are these: (1) staffing of parent country nationals vs. host or third country nationals; and (2) appropriate criteria for selecting expatriates. Some limited attention has also been directed at related expatriate issues, including compensation and type of training for expatriates.

In addition to research on expatriates, a few writers have examined the role of HRM in formulating and implementing business strategy at an international level. The focus of this work is on HRM's role in the formal design of business strategy, as well as its role as an enhancer of strategy, concentrating specifically on HRM's role in implementation.

In the general literature most work linking strategy and HRM has been prescriptive and focused on domestic settings, yet clear associations between strategy and human resource activities have been found. We can classify studies of linkages between human resource management practices and business strategy into two categories. The first group conceptualizes strategy-HRM linkages in a broad, macro perspective. These authors use one of a variety of strategic typologies and then relate specific strategies to general categories of HRM policy.

Source: Allan Bird and Schon Beechler. "The link between business strategy and IHRM practices." Reprinted by permission of the authors.

Porter, for example, identifies two generic strategies: (1) overall cost leadership; and (2) differentiation. In his discussion of the skills, resources and organizational requirements needed for each strategy, Porter alludes to a strategy-manager match and considers some of the HRM policy implications that grow out of this match. A *cost leadership strategy* is based on the experience cost curve concept. This strategy places the company in a low-cost position where it can earn above-average returns despite strong competition. Under a cost leadership strategy, job requirements are those of establishing tight cost controls, making frequent reports, enforcing strict rules, and establishing incentives based on quantitative methods.

By contrast, a *differentiation strategy* is a strategy based on distinguishing the company's products or services from those of competitors. By providing unique and distinctive, non-price value, the company can insulate itself through customer loyalty. A differentiation strategy requires an emphasis on coordination, incentives based on qualitative methods, and the maintenance of quality and technological leadership.

Macro perspectives, such as Porter's, are useful in delineating possible strategy-human resources linkages, yet they lack specificity and fall short in their regard for the myriad details of HRM policy and practice. A remedy to this shortcoming is found in studies that have a micro perspective, attempting to trace relationships between strategy and individual HRM policies. Micro research, for example, proposes specific linkages between business strategies and selection practices or staffing and training practices that are likely to be found under different career systems. Mainstream HRM has adopted a micro perspective, attempting to trace relationships between strategy and individual HRM policies. Studies in this category often utilize one of the macro perspectives as a foundation for their more specific analyses.

However, while the existing research employing a macro perspective lacks specificity, studies in the second category of micro-focused approaches suffer a shortcoming of their own. They seek to identify linkages which extend from business strategy down to actual human resource policy applications; however, generally they focus only on a single function, failing to take into account how business strategy might influence other, related HRM functions.

Background _____

Both micro and macro approaches linking strategy and HRM fail to explicitly recognize the assumptions upon which they are predicated. There are two general assumptions which underlie all models connecting HRM practices and business strategy. First, it is assumed that the selection and mix of human resource practices are determined by the specific strategy a firm adopts, which is itself influenced by environmental constraints such as government regulations, competitor actions, etc. Second, it is assumed that firms achieving a tighter fit between alignment of environmental constraints, strategy requirements, and HRM practices will perform better than those that do not.

Failure to recognize these two assumptions has led researchers to ignore some of the complexities inherent in multinational firms. For example, consistency found between a parent company and its foreign subsidiaries with regard to business strategy and HRM policies has often been assumed. Differences between the environment of a parent organization and those of its foreign subsidiaries, however, may create strong pressures for the firm to modify its local operations in each country. This is particularly true with respect to HRM policies. Labor markets, union influence, worker skill level and skill variety, along with legal requirements relating to hiring, compensation, and dismissal practices are all likely to differ significantly from one country to the next.

The second contingency assumption specifies that effective performance is a result of the alignment of internal operations to the external environment. Given the potential cross-national variations cited above, multinational firms that achieve internal consistency (between parent and foreign subsidiary) would appear to run a high risk of misalignment with the external environment. Looking at these two assumptions together, the implication for multinational firms is one of competing pressures: internal pressures for consistency between strategy and HRM practices, and external pressures for consistency between HRM practices and the environment.

Recognition of competing pressures on HRM practices is a return to the well-documented dilemma of "standardization versus differentiation" that pervades debates of how to administer international operations. There is a dynamic tension between the need for the overseas affiliate to adapt to local conditions versus the need to integrate across the MNE as a whole. To date, most approaches have suggested that resolution of this dilemma is determined by the relative strength of the competing forces.

A Strategic Framework

We propose an alternative approach that focuses on the *extent to which a MNE firm requires consistency* between parent and subsidiary business strategy and between parent and subsidiary HRM practices. In doing so, we suggest that these twin needs for consistency are determined by (1) the strategies that firms adopt; and (2) the nature of the international competition in which they are involved. Internal and external pressures are filtered by two strategic choices that MNEs make. Firms decide on the strategy they will pursue and the domain within which they will pursue it.

The Environment-Business Strategy Match

One way of viewing the external environment of MNEs is to identify the nature of international competition in the industry in which a firm is involved. There are two types of industry competition. A *multidomestic* industry is one in which competition in a given country is essentially independent of competition in other countries. For example, the soft drink industry in Japan is not influenced by competition in the soft drink industry in China. Insurance and retailing are characteristic multidomestic industries. By contrast, an industry such as that of commercial aircraft manufacturing, involves competition where activities in one country have a significant influence on activities in another. For example, competition in the petroleum industry occurs across nations, with oil wells in one country, refineries and processing facilities in another, and various end-users located in those two countries as well as others. Industries of this type are labeled *global.*

Differences between the two types of competition are reflected in the varying demands for coordination that each imposes. Global industries exhibit greater coordination needs than do multidomestic industries. The need for coordination implies pressure for internal consistency.

While MNE environments can be classified into global versus multidomestic types, firms' strategic orientations can also be classified in terms of orientation with regard to two broad types: *cost leadership* and *product differentiation.* A cost leadership strategy, as alluded to earlier, seeks to achieve competitive advantage by being the least-cost producer of a product, while a product differentiation strategy seeks competitive advantage by providing unique value to a product.

Originally these two strategic archetypes were put forward as mutually exclusive. A firm could pursue a cost leadership strategy, for example, only at the exclusion of a product differentiation strategy. Indeed, "being stuck in the middle" was considered one the of the weakest positions a firm could occupy. However, recent research concludes that a single firm can successfully pursue both strategies.

Simultaneous efforts at cost leadership and product differentiation do not, however, suggest equal weighting between the two. Indeed, though changes in environmental pressures may encourage firms to adopt a combined strategy, organizational imprinting—locking into a particular view of the environment early in an organization's life—and the development of distinctive competencies within a firm may result in a persistent bias toward one or the other. For example, Sony and Matsushita both seek to compete on the basis of cost and product variety. Nevertheless, Sony's roots and corporate culture help maintain a preference for differentiation over cost. Similarly, when push comes to shove for Matsushita, the choice is in favor of cost.

Because the cost-differentiation distinction remains persistent in practice, it can be usefully employed in discussions if cost leadership and product differentiation are thought of as opposite ends of a continuum. Consequently, firms may locate themselves at any point along the continuum that reflects the mix of cost and differentiation strategies they are pursuing.

Since a strategy of cost leadership seeks to achieve competitive advantage by being the least-cost producer of a product, then this strategy requires a firm to focus on functional policies. Under a cost leadership strategy, internal operations of a firm command attention and the drive is for internal efficiency.

A product differentiation strategy, on the other hand, seeks competitive advantage through the ability of a firm to provide unique value to a product, one that will be more localized in terms of its appeal to a particular foreign market or segment. Using a strategy of differentiation, firms are less concerned with cost and more concerned with identifying what special value they are able to add. A differentiation strategy requires a firm to develop an external focus, to be intimately aware of what its customers desire.

When a MNE's strategic orientation is considered in combination with the type of international competition in which it is involved, we can map out the requirements for consistency. As shown in Figure 1, the four combinations of MNE strategic orientation and international competition exhibit their own unique requirements for consistency between the parent company and the overseas subsidiary.

Figure 1. The Pressures for Consistency Resulting from MNE Strategic Orientation and the Nature of International Competition

---

STRATEGIC ORIENTATION

	Cost	**Differentiation**
Multidomestic	• Strong pressure for consistency between parent & subsidiary strategy; • Strong pressure for consistency with local external environments	• Weak pressure for consistency between parent & subsidiary strategy; • Strong pressure for consistency with local external environments
International Competition		
Global	• Strong pressure for consistency between parent & subsidiary strategy; • Weak pressure for consistency with local external environments	• Weak pressure for consistency between parent & subsidiary strategy; • Weak pressure for consistency with local external environments

---

Pursuing a cost leadership strategy in an industry characterized by multidomestic competition generates the highest levels of stress on the parent-subsidiary relationship. The strategy of cost leadership, and its accompanying internal focus on efficiency, creates strong pressures for standardization in the business unit's strategy across countries. At the same time, the multidomestic nature of the industry provides strong encouragement for the firm to adapt to local conditions in order to compete with local and multinational competitors.

Firms pursuing a cost leadership strategy in an industry where competition is global, though experiencing strong pressures for internal consistency, will feel lower levels of pressure to conform to the myriad local external environments of its subsidiary operations. This is not to suggest that environmental constraints and pressures will be unimportant for MNEs in this quadrant. Rather, pressures will be lower relative to firms in the multidomestic-cost leadership quadrant which must respond to local competitor actions.

Pursuing a differentiation strategy in an industry characterized by multidomestic competition leads to low levels of stress on the parent-subsidiary relationship. The strategy of differentiation and its accompanying external focus aimed at providing unique value to its customers generate weaker pressures for standardization across countries. At the same time, the multidomestic nature of competition suggests that a firm should adapt to local conditions.

By contrast, a differentiation strategy in an industry where competition is global affords MNEs with the widest range of latitude in consistency requirements. Internal pressures for alignment of parent and subsidiary strategy are lower than for firms following a cost leadership strategy. Simultaneously, the global nature of the industry in which the MNE competes suggests that pressures to adapt to the local external environment will also be relatively weak.

Regardless of whether a firm competes in a multidomestic or global competitive environment, the efficiency orientation of a cost leadership strategy places greater emphasis on internal consistency than does a differentiation strategy. Second, localization pressures associated with a multidomestic competitive environment make it harder for MNEs to achieve consistency than in a global competitive environment. Therefore, consistency between parent and subsidiary business strategies will have a greater impact on firm performance in MNEs employing a cost leadership rather than a differentiation strategy. Moreover, firms competing in a multidomestic competitive environment will experience greater difficulty in achieving consistency between parent and subsidiary business strategies than firms competing in a global competitive environment.

The Business Strategy-HRM Strategy Match

If a MNE's performance is based on its capacity to internally align its operations in a way that allows it to match environmental constraints, then there must be a way to determine whether or not a firm is properly aligned with its environment. More than any other function within a MNE, the management of human resources is decentralized. With the exception of matters related to expatriates and international assignments, the vast majority of HRM affairs are handled at the level of the subsidiary. Consequently, a consideration of business strategy-HRM strategy linkages must necessarily shift attention away from a MNE's business strategy at the parent level and its position in international competition to a focus on how these two factors interact with subsidiary-level business strategy to influence the choice of HRM strategy.

At the subsidiary level, the requirement for internal consistency may be interpreted as the degree of integration with the parent company necessary for success. For example, due to strong pressures for internal consistency and relatively weak pressures for external consistency, we would expect subsidiaries of MNEs competing in global industries with a cost leadership strategy to be highly integrated with the parent. On the other hand, subsidiaries of MNEs pursuing a product differentiation strategy in multidomestic industries are more likely to be less integrated with the parent.

Human Resource Management Strategies

Business strategy determines how a firm competes in a given business. Firms select business strategies in accordance both with evaluations they make about the environment in which they wish to compete and the resources available within the firm. In order to develop and implement a business strategy, however, it is necessary to break it down into its various components or to develop functional strategies. These functional strategies are further decomposed into policies which, when implemented, become practice.

Policies can be thought of as decision rules. They are procedures that organization members are expected to follow. Practices, on the other hand, are less formal than policies and can be thought of as the actual decisions taken by organization members. Practices thus reflect those procedures that are actually carried out. In the international context, for example, a MNE may have a worldwide policy of equitable pay schemes for all of its employees, but how that policy is translated locally can vary from country to country. Thus, for a single firm, practices may differ across countries while the policy remains consistent.

Our framework predicts that if a firm's strategy is congruent with the external environment, firm performance will be higher than if its strategy does not match the environment. However, consistency between a plan (strategy) and the external environment is only a first step. It does not directly predict firm performance. Rather, firm performance is determined by the application of the plan, through the implementation of functional policies, including those contained in a HRM strategy.

A number of classification schemes have been suggested for categorizing HRM strategies. One widely used typology defines three types of HRM strategies. A *utilizer strategy* deploys the human resources of the firm as efficiently as possible through: (1) the acquisition and dismissal of personnel in accordance with the short-term needs of the firm; (2) the matching of employee skill to specific task requirements. An *accumulator strategy* builds up the human resources of the firm through: (1) the acquisition of personnel with large, latent potential; (2) the development of that latent potential over time in a manner consistent with the needs of the organization. A *facilitator strategy* is focused on new knowledge and new knowledge creation. It seeks to develop the human resources of the firm as effectively as possible through the acquisition of self-motivated personnel and the encouragement and support of personnel to develop, on their own, the skills and knowledge which they, the employees, believe are important.

Determination of the appropriate HRM strategy for a given subsidiary can be achieved by assessing the intersection of subsidiary's business strategy with its degree of integration with the parent. Appropriate combinations are shown in Figure 2.

Figure 2. The Implications for HRM Strategy of Subsidiary Strategic Orientation and Degree of Integration Between Subsidiary and MNE

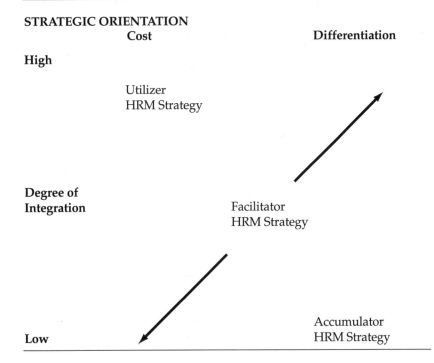

STRATEGIC ORIENTATION

Cost   **Differentiation**

High

Utilizer
HRM Strategy

**Degree of
Integration**   Facilitator
                               HRM Strategy

                                               Accumulator
Low   HRM Strategy

Because a utilizer HRM strategy helps to maintain a lean workforce by acquiring or dismissing employees as and when skills are required, this strategy is more appropriate to a cost leadership business strategy. The utilizer strategy is effective not only because of its efficiency orientation, but also because of its high level of flexibility, making it easier to fit subsidiary human resources with the demands of the parent (high integration). With decreasing integration, the utilizer strategy may still remain somewhat effective. However, as pressures for local adaptation increase, the subsidiary is less able to implement a utilizer strategy, particularly if it is not in line with local norms and customs.

A facilitator strategy is appropriate in a wide range of circumstances because it can handle HRM demands along both dimensions. The facilitator is qualitatively different from the utilizer and the accumulator in that it seeks to support new knowledge creation. Complex and evolving human resource demands, resulting from strong pressures in opposing directions for both strategic orientation and integration, call for an evolutionary, learning orientation.

An accumulator HRM strategy facilitates the flexibility required under a differentiation strategy by providing an excess pool of employees with latent potential which can be tapped as needed. An effective accumulator strategy would be easiest to pursue under conditions of low need for integration with the parent. As the demand for integration rises, the accumulator strategy breaks down because of the increasing influence of the parent company which stem from its desire to exercise tighter control as a result of the subsidiary's increased centrality to the MNE's overall operations.

We would expect that those subsidiaries which match their HRM strategy to their combination of business strategy and degree of integration with the parent will perform better than those that do not. The following briefly summarizes the main ideas developed so far:

1. Among subsidiaries employing cost leadership business strategies and having a high degree of integration with the parent, those which adopt a utilizer HRM strategy will perform better than those that employ an accumulator or facilitator HRM strategy.

2. In subsidiaries employing product differentiation business strategies and having a low degree of integration with the parent, those which adopt an accumulator HRM strategy will perform better than those that employ a utilizer or facilitator HRM strategy.

3. Finally, for subsidiaries pursuing both cost leadership and differentiation strategies, those which adopt a facilitator HRM strategy will perform better than those that employ a utilizer or accumulator HRM strategy.

Consistency in Parent-Subsidiary HRM Strategy Alignment

Although HRM constitutes the most decentralized of all MNE functions, it is also true that the increasing globalization of MNEs has brought about an increased desire and need for greater coordination and consistency between parent and subsidiary. Application of the above framework in assessing HRM practices in both the parent and subsidiary provides a means by which to determine the extent to which the two are in alignment. Moreover, the relationships in Figure 1 indicate that the need for parent-subsidiary alignment of HRM activities may vary depending on the strategic orientation of the MNE and the nature of international competition for the industry in which it competes.

Firms pursuing a cost leadership strategy in industries characterized by multidomestic competition will strive for consistency in HRM activities. However, they will do so in the face of strong pressures to modify their practices from one country to the next. In such a situation, consistency between parent and subsidiary in the application of a utilizer HRM strategy may not only be difficult to carry out, but lead to a loss of local competitiveness as well. For example, pressure to adapt locally is usually amplified for HRM practices because labor, blue- and white-collar combined, represents an area where cost reductions may make a significant contribution to implementing a cost leadership strategy. Adapting to local labor conditions in an attempt to obtain cost advantages, however, may introduce greater disparity between parent and subsidiary with accompanying increases in the cost of monitoring and managing the overseas operation.

By contrast, firms employing a cost leadership strategy in industries typified by global industries will seek consistency in a more amenable context. While experiencing internal demands similar to those of cost leadership firms in multidomestic industries, they pursue consistency in a setting more willing to forgive a measure of local insensitivity. Aligning a utilizer HRM strategy in both parent and subsidiary may be more easily achieved. Additionally, firms in this quadrant are likely to achieve a higher degree of parent-subsidiary alignment than are firms in the other three.

We can conclude that firms employing a cost leadership/utilizer combination competing in industries characterized by global competition will achieve a higher degree of integration between parent and subsidiary than firms with similar combinations competing in industries characterized by multidomestic competition. Furthermore, firms employing a cost leadership/utilizer combination competing in industries characterized by global competition will perform better than firms with similar combinations competing in industries characterized by multidomestic competition.

MNEs with a differentiation strategy in industries characterized by multidomestic competition will experience relatively weak internal demands for parent-subsidiary consistency. Simultaneously, pressures on subsidiaries to be sensitive to local conditions make it difficult to achieve alignment between parent and subsidiary HRM practices. Unlike a utilizer HRM strategy, however, an accumulator HRM strategy is more appropriate since it emphasizes the accumulation of resources and possesses more organizational slack and latent human resources potential. The result is greater flexibility in human resource activities and less stringent requirements for consistency. Firms in this quadrant exhibit a lower degree of consistency than firms in the other three quadrants but this also means that consistency requirements may be less important.

Firms employing a differentiation/accumulator combination competing in industries characterized by multidomestic competition achieve a lower degree of integration between parent and subsidiary than firms with similar combinations competing in industries characterized by global competition. By contrast, firms employing a differentiation/accumulator match competing in industries characterized by multidomestic competition will perform better than firms with similar combinations competing in industries challenged by global competition.

Finally, MNEs with a product differentiation strategy in an industry where competition is global confront internal pressures for alignment that are lower than for firms with a cost leadership strategy. Simultaneously, the global nature of the industry in which these firms compete indicates that local external environment pressures are also weak. Alignment of parent and subsidiary HRM activities for firms in this quadrant is less critical to firm performance than for firms employing a cost leadership strategy. This leads to the conclusion that firms employing a differentiation/accumulator combination competing in industries characterized by global competition achieve a higher degree of integration between parent and subsidiary than firms with similar combinations competing in industries with multidomestic competition. Additionally, firms employing a differentiation/accumulator combination competing in industries characterized by global competition will perform better than firms with similar combinations competing in industries where competition is multidomestic.

Conclusion

This framework constitutes a model bridging macro and micro perspectives on the linkages between business strategy and HRM practice in MNEs. It concludes that there must be consistency between parent-level business strategy and subsidiary-level HRM strategy.

The framework also provides direction to HRM managers by clarifying the extent to which there is a need for consistency between parent and subsidiary in multinational operations. In doing so, it provides both a rationale and a means for them to sort through the dilemmas involved in trying to integrate parent and subsidiary operations.

Novell: Transforming Culture[1]

Case 2.1
Marjorie McEntire

"Culture is everything—how can you study it?" Jesse Hassler[2] recalled her graduate school professor's words from twenty years ago. He said that organizational culture was not a legitimate research topic because it was difficult to isolate, measure, and analyze variables. "Give it up," he advised her. Yet, as the senior vice president of human resources at Novell, the world's largest networking software company, she was charged with transforming the organization's culture. Despite her professor's directive, the shelves in her office were filled with well-thumbed anthropology and organizational culture and change books. These books did not specifically address information technology (IT) companies, but contained sound principles that Jesse had used to influence change throughout her human resource management career.

Jesse, hired two years ago, had been a member of the search committee that recruited and trained Novell's new executive team, including Dr. Eric Schmidt,[3] the CEO and Chairman of the Board. He was the second new CEO in three years, following the departure of the entrepreneur who built Novell from a startup into a worldwide organization.

Several years before Jesse arrived, the director of human resources had been assigned to create a Novell culture amid the company's tumultuous mergers and acquisitions period. Today, Jesse faced a dramatically changed company—Novell was pared down to about half its mid-1990s size and surviving remnants of a worldwide organization were scattered throughout six continents.

Jesse's first step as the senior vice president of human resources was taking stock of Novell—she spent the first six months on the job talking to Novell people. She didn't have historical documents for review—one executive quipped that Novell couldn't make money writing history. Old timers (employees of more than eight years) provided insight into Novell's basic assumptions but most employees were reluctant to describe the human resource issues through which the company had wrestled—they feared alienating past and present colleagues who were still influential in the global software community.

Source: Marjorie McEntire. "Novell: Transforming Culture." Reprinted by permission of the author.

81

Novell's new executive team was depending on her vision, ingenuity, sensitivity, and skills to engineer Novell's cultural transformation. In order to direct changes, she needed both leadership support and employee cooperation worldwide.

She was ready to design a strategy. The *roadmap* that preceded the recent release of the company's newest software provided insight into Novell processes. Jesse's colleague, the vice president of product development, said that this software release required the efforts of hundreds of engineers, programmers, and testers throughout Novell:

> My job is to take the products that are on the roadmap and make sure they ship on time. It's making sure that we're listening to the customers. It's making sure that the products are actually doing what the customers say they want. Working with the sales force, working with the marketing team. All of that is what I do daily. We have a process we go through every other month, which we call a roadmap review. We take three days—12 hour days—and go through every product on the roadmap: look at its feature set, what customers are targeting, is this still valid, what are we missing, what does this need to be competitive, etc. And we will adjust the roadmap accordingly, making sure that the products actually are what the customers are asking for. It's a rigorous process. (Martinez, 1998)[4]

Transforming a culture was a more sophisticated and subtle task than aligning product development and finance with corporate objectives— her task encompassed all functional areas. As she faced the biggest challenge of her career—designing a roadmap to transform an international organizational culture to meet the 21st century—Jesse reviewed Novell's strategy, human resource context, leadership, international structure, cultural barriers, and the *constant look and feel* that the company hoped to create.

Networking—Product and Strategy

Novell, founded as a hardware company in Provo, Utah in 1983, launched the era of computer networking. Today, Novell identifies itself as a networking company that intends to become a world leader in Internet software. As the fifth largest software company in the world, Novell defines its niche in the *1997 Annual Report*:

> Everywhere we look networks matter. Customers around the world are deploying networks to transform every aspect of their business. As the world's largest network software company, Novell believes that the network is the centerpiece of every computing endeavor. More businesses run their networks with Novell's NetWare than all other alternatives combined. Novell now intends to become a leader in Internet software that makes possible increasingly intelligent interconnected networks. (1998)

Jesse noted that Novell's business strategy also reflects networking—establishing social connections throughout the world and building on these associations. Today, according to Dr. Eric Schmidt, the CEO and Chairman of the Board, "solid partnerships are critical to success in a networked world" (1998). Novell ties together the concepts of computer and human networking in its official statement of purpose: "Novell solutions give people and organizations the secure, manageable networks they need to compete, innovate, and build communities in an interconnected world (Novell, 1998a)."

Novell markets products and support throughout the world through a *partner and leverage* model that begins with one-person outposts in widely dispersed targeted geographical areas. One veteran Novell manager described the initial process: "In the early days, we would go into a country, hold a seminar, and say, 'Now, this is networking, this is the concept. Anybody want to sell this?' Anybody who raised their hand got to sell it." He continued, "Because software is developed and is shipped around the world, it's easy to set up representation indirectly, grow the market to the point where you can bring in your own people, and then continue to grow it."

One-person outposts do not have extensive contact with headquarters and the people who work in them typically are lower-level employees. As sales increase in an area, Novell establishes formal organizational structures to increase the company's visibility and credibility. When the local market (a country or a cluster of companies) reaches the $5 million revenue level, Novell establishes an office. One manager explained: "When Novell sets up a local office and hires local people, there is almost a straight-up jump in growth rate because local businesses say, 'Okay, Novell is serious about my country.'" Starting with small sites, Novell has established a worldwide organization amid external turbulence and internal tumult.

Removing Dissatisfiers ————————————————

Acquisitions, mergers, divestitures, multiple presidents, revised executive teams, and layoffs have characterized Novell for almost two decades. Each strategy has been designed to align the corporate vision and resources in order to expand the organization. Despite these efforts, Novell's financial performance has declined for several years—until recently. Analysts cite Novell's rapid expansion—Novell's strategy for competing with Microsoft—as a key factor in its poor financial performance.

Within the past four years, two CEOs have led Novell, and five new hires now sit on the thirteen-member executive team. Dr. Eric Schmidt, the newly hired 43-year-old CEO, came to Novell from Sun Microsystems, Inc., where he was chief technology officer. Schmidt has a B.S. in electrical engineering from the University of California at Berkeley and a Ph.D. in computer science from Princeton. He is known for possessing "a deadly combination of technological know-how and a penchant for demanding the near impossible" (Cooper, 1998). Schmidt's 1997 salary and bonus totaled $729,143 (Copeland, 1998).

Schmidt led a retrenchment that focused on three priorities: (1) realigning Novell's business model with the market in order to restore the company's financial performance, (2) accelerating the rate of new product releases, and (3) establishing new rigor within Novell's management team (Novell, 1998a).

Jesse recalled how employees throughout Novell immediately felt the impact of Schmidt's sudden and severe changes. In a year of declining revenues, he established direction, reduced the workforce, and consolidated facilities. Seven layers of management were replaced by four and 1,000 people were laid off, decreasing the workforce by 17%. The company sold major subsidiaries such as WordPerfect and UnixWare, reversing the merger and acquisition trend of the early 1990s.

New products, designed for a worldwide market, are integral to Novell's new direction that is now in its "infant growth phase" (Caron & Thomas, 1998). Schmidt described the importance of new products:

> . . . to me, NetWare 5.0 is incredibly important because it removes the dissatisfiers of the historical association with Novell . . . My feeling when I came to this company was that this was a multiyear process—to take Novell from where it was to where it needs to be—as the innovator in the networking space. So, the first year was to stabilize the business. The second step is to post NetWare 5.0, where you get all of these interesting new services that are just now enabled by this new architecture. (Caron & Thomas, 1998)

Schmidt continued, "Clarity of direction and strategy are essential for software companies to sustain growth. The Novell that I joined in April 1997, mid-way through the company's fiscal year, had lost touch with this simple truth. In seven months, we have corrected that" (Novell, 1998a).

Less than two years after Schmidt took office, he said, "Our strategy is clearly working" (Novell, 1998b). During the fourth fiscal quarter of 1998, Novell reported 11 percent increase in revenue over the fourth quarter of fiscal 1997, "shedding the red ink and layoffs of a year ago" (Fidel, 1998). At the end of 1998, Novell was listed as number five of Utah's top ten performing stocks, showing a 142% increase in closing price compared to the end of 1997 (Oberbeck, 1999). The financial upturn was the result of aligning physical and human resources.

The IT Human Resource Context _____

Jesse knows that people comprise the IT competitive advantage. In an industry in which a monthly salary of $10,000 is considered minimum wage, human assets such as computer skills, an unrelenting work ethic, and the ability to work across borders are premium. IT executives, developers, programmers, marketing, sales, and support people are characterized as highly educated, innovative, independent, and fiercely driven workers. Schmidt, who "doesn't vacation," sets the pace at Novell (Copeland, 1998). Books and articles advise Jesse how to motivate this breed with practices such as flexible hours, telecommuting, and the lure of working with cutting edge technology—sometimes as substitutes for high salaries and stock options (Alexander, 1998). Most of this advice is aimed at the U.S. employee.

Novell recruits employees from other IT companies—the executive team's pedigree includes IBM, Data General, Wang, Digital, Sun, Xerox, and Hewlett-Packard. A recent IT labor shortage in Silicon Valley, the location of Novell's San Jose offices, made it difficult to fill positions—Internet experts are in great demand.

Universities located near Novell's San Jose, California and Provo, Utah offices supply IT engineers, managers, and sales and marketing personnel. Major universities such as Stanford and the University of California at Berkeley provide IT labor for the surrounding Silicon Valley. In Utah, Brigham Young University, the University of Utah, and several smaller regional schools supply employees who have both technology and language skills.

Jesse had heard about Novell's "secret weapon" long before she was hired. Novell has an arsenal of employees who speak languages in addition to English. Novell's headquarters are located near universities in which a large percentage of the students have lived in foreign countries while serving missions for The Church of Jesus Christ of Latter-day Saints. More than half of the MBA students at the University of Utah and Brigham Young University speak a second language. Bilingual skills benefit initial communication with foreign markets and product translation.

Novell employs approximately 4,600, in contrast to its peak of 8,460 in 1994. Employees include veteran Novell staff, members who joined Novell through mergers and acquisitions, and new hires. Novell also has 27,000 channel partners or resellers—15,000 are in the U.S. (Novell, 1998c). Aligning the perspective of Novell's field associates with the company's vision is a continuing challenge, illustrated by one executive's description of "bullying" early European distributors:

> We called the shots, and they [distributors] learned, after a time, that we were usually right . . . And our dealer councils were war. They loved us because they were making money but

they hated us because we were telling them what to do...One day in Europe, the European distributors had formed this coalition to tell us [Novell leaders] what to do. And so I showed up at the Distributor Conference and I stood up to give them a speech and they all had this agenda of what to do that afternoon. And I just came head on and said, "Look guys, this is a world of change and here's what has to be done to compete. You've got all these competitors out there that are trying to kill us. This is what we're going to do and we need people who are willing to change and go forward. If you don't like change, then maybe you should start growing corn because that's the same year after year—and get out of this business."

Jesse realized Novell's current retrenchment directive was similar in approach to the above corn speech: change or die. From what she knew about cultural change, she doubted that such a strident mandate, even from Novell leaders, would be effective in transforming the culture.

Leadership

Twelve people comprise the Novell executive team—ten men and two women:

- Chief Executive Officer and Chairman of the Board
- Senior Vice President and Chief Information Officer
- Senior Vice President and General Counsel
- Senior Vice President, Worldwide Sales
- Senior Vice President, Human Resources
- Senior Vice President, Novell Products Group
- Senior Vice President, Customer Services
- Senior Vice President, Corporate Marketing
- Senior Vice President, Strategy and Corporate Development
- Chief Scientist and Vice President, Advanced Development
- Vice President, Operations
- Chief Technology Officer

All of these executives are Caucasians and are U.S. educated (most have at least a master's degree). Three of them—the CEO, senior vice president of marketing, and senior vice president of strategy and corporate development—joined Novell in 1997 to "strengthen the management team" (Novell, 1998a).

Jesse pays close attention to language because it is a primary cultural artifact and transmitter. "Focused Management," a recently adopted term, describes the new "clarity of focus" and "new rigor within Novell's executive management team," a "significant shift" for the company (Novell, 1998a). Schmidt said, "In the last quarter of fiscal 1997 we demonstrated how a shared, singular focus on product delivery and expense management—along with tight focus on a set of product initiatives—has the potential to return the company to profitability" (Novell, 1998a).

International Strategy ————————————————————

Unlike Coca Cola, a company that produces beverages in tens of flavors targeted at different markets throughout the world, Novell delivers uniform products worldwide—only the language differs. An international manager explained: "The products all operate the same, but as far as the interface, as far as the look on the screen, it could be in a different language—but behind the scenes, it all operates the same." During a tour in which Schmidt promoted Novell throughout Europe and Japan, he said, "An important challenge for Novell...is to expand our leadership in international markets" and described "great enthusiasm for new, localized versions of Novell products" (1998). He continued:

> As the old slogan says, "Think globally, act locally." Our progress in the Japanese marketplace reflects our status and commitment as a global leader in networking. It's critically important, as we move forward in 1998, that we consider all our responsibilities and activities in the context of a worldwide company. (1998)

Novell's international strategy began with Ray Noorda, who is recognized as Novell's founder. He came to Novell Data (later named Novell) as a consultant in 1983 with the mission to rescue the floundering computer company. He later took over as president. Noorda's vision led Novell's early success and today, the company retains his values of innovation, cost control, and international scope. His international perspective permeated the development of all Novell's products:

> Noorda made it clear that from a vision standpoint, [products] had to reach around the world. Whenever we did something that was highly successful, his next statement would be, "Okay, how are we going to get this out there?" He was very, very clear about his expectations. You didn't dare not have your worldwide plan in place when you went to talk to Ray. When you went in with a corporate advertising plan and you said, "We are going to be the *Wall Street Journal* and the *New York Times*," he would say, "And? And you would say, "The *Financial Times in London* and *Wall Street Journal-Asia*."

Noorda's initial push for internationalization and Schmidt's emphasis on developing these markets has established Novell's international presence. Currently, international markets provide approximately half of annual revenue: 47% in 1995; 50% in 1996; and 45% in 1997 (Novell, 1998a).

Novell's recent focus clearly has been on fixing the business. An international perspective is implicit throughout all of Novell's initiatives, but is explicitly stated in the company mission: "Novell's mission is to become the leader in Internet and intranet software by supplying the world with directory-enabled networks" (Novell, 1998c). Worldwide offices mirror the direction and practices of the U.S. offices—the global strategy of business alignment and product delivery is not altered at the local level except to reflect local language and legal requirements.

International Structure _____

Expanding international markets means that Novell must build sales and support in existing markets and enter new countries. Novell's early success came in the developing markets that had poorly developed infrastructures and used English as a business language—these are no longer criteria for entering markets. Novell's three geographic regions evolved from business volume and political considerations: (1) Americas, (2) Asia Pacific, and (3) Europe, Middle East, Africa. Each has several regional offices and additional sales offices. Teams, headed by country managers, lead the regional offices and Novell generally staffs these offices with local people rather than export U.S. headquarters employees to run them. For example, a Novell Benelux Team leads the Belgium regional office and a five-member Novell Osterreich Team leads the Austrian regional office (their photo appears on the Novell Austria website).

Japan Ltd., a joint venture, is one of Novell's largest regional offices and employs nearly 200 people and oversees more than 1,600 resellers and ten Original Equipment Manufacturers (OEMs) that sell Novell products. In Japan, Schmidt described the importance of Novell's international markets and cited the achievement of providing Novell products in Kanji, giving credit to the leadership of country manager, Shigechika Takeuchi. A key to growth is "getting to market faster with localized products that account for differences in language and alphabet" (Schmidt, 1998).

International economic events may benefit Novell's international expansion. For example, Asia's economic crisis created unexpected opportunities for Novell because firms needed to integrate their internal computer systems quickly (Reuters, 1998).

International Management _____

Novell began using local people in 1988, when the country offices were first set up—anyone who could speak a local language and was willing to sell Novell products was recruited to head an international operation. One manager recalled:

> [The local offices] were incredibly autonomous. Although someone who had been sent over from the U.S. managed them at the top management level, there was a real heritage from the very beginning at Novell of hiring local people to run the offices. That is a really important success factor—the three or four people who were actually running the country organizations were local folks. A lot of U.S. companies don't do that when they are small. They send little entourages over to set up offices. That is the first misstep a U.S. company can make.

Table 1. International Offices

Regional Offices (26)

Americas (3)	Asia, Pacific (5)	Europe, Middle East, Africa (18)	
Canada	Australasia (Mirror Site)	Austria	Middle East
United States	Australia	Belgium	Netherlands
Latin America	Hong Kong	Czech Republic	Norway
	Japan	Denmark	Poland
	New Zealand	Finland	Switzerland
		France	South Africa
		Germany	Spain
		Israel	Sweden
		Italy	UK & Ireland

Regional Sales Offices

Americas	Asia, Pacific	Europe, Middle East, Africa	
Argentina	Australia	Austria	Italy
Brazil	China	Belgium	Middle East
Canada (Calgary,	Hong Kong	CIS & Baltic	(Dubai, United
Hull, Montreal,	India (Bangalore,	Czech Republic	Arab Emirates)
Toronto, Vancouver)	New Delhi)	Slovak Republic	Netherlands
Chile	Japan	Denmark	Norway
Columbia	Korea	Finland	Poland
Mexico	Malaysia	France	Portugal
Venezuela	New Zealand	Germany	South Africa
United States	(Auckland, Wellington)	(Berlin,	(Johannesburg,
(each of 50 states &	Singapore	Frankfurt,	Cape Town)
Washington, D.C.)	Taiwan	Munich)	Spain (Madrid,
	Thailand	Hungary	Barcelona)
		Ireland	Sweden
		Israel	Switzerland
			United Kingdom

The growth of the German market illustrates Novell's international management development. A guitar player opened Novell's German distributorship—he spoke German, knew the company, and understood the vision of international growth. As the market grew, additional distributors were located. Novell eventually required more personnel and expanded its organizational structure to respond to increased headquarters requests. Initial distributors were replaced with more sophisticated personnel and a vice president replaced the director. Eventually, Novell's matured German connection became one of Novell's three worldwide technical support centers (the others are in the U.S. and Australia). According to a manager, "That's a natural transition for any company that wants to go international . . . they have to determine the threshold points, where there's enough revenue to justify moving in."

Novell's "worst case" is to appoint an American, living in another country, as a regional vice president or senior executive. The ideal scenario is to appoint a local senior executive who has worked in the U.S. corporate offices and has returned to the international arena.

Barriers

When developing Novell's worldwide organization, the company faces challenges typical of firms that expand into international markets. Several headquarter's managers told Jesse that Novell employees were parochial. One returned expatriate said, "I have been striving for eight years to get people in the U.S. to think internationally, to think globally—I don't think it will ever happen . . . people live in the U.S., speak English, and don't want to understand other countries." He continued:

> There are, however, key pockets of people who really want to get international and to learn and to become a global company. Novell has improved significantly over the past years, but I don't think we will ever reach a point to where everyone is thinking globally and everyone has the right hats on. We can continually try to educate people in thinking global in any decision that they ever make—that one decision that they make here affects the rest of the world.

Language differences hamper personal communication and product design. One executive described the struggles Novell had when developing international products:

> The disadvantage of an American company trying to go international versus a European company trying to go international, is that American engineers cannot get it through their heads that there's another language spoken anywhere. They always hardwire something into their code that makes it tough to expand it out. And you have to continually be in there saying, "Think of international. Make it so somebody else can change the language in it." And if you stop doing that for one week, they forget. You have to have a zealous person in the company who must make a jerk out of themselves all of the time. We begin to think that everyone can communicate if we all speak English—if we just speak slowly. It took eight years to finally get that into Development's head: "Look, we're an international company. Would you stop hard coding the messages?" I don't think it really started to change until we started sending the engineers to Europe to sit and deal with their customers that they'd been screwing up.

Nationalities within the same geographical area perpetuate cultural prejudices. One European Novell manager said, "If I have to have a foreign boss, it had better be an American, because I will not have an

English boss." He summarized the perceptions of Europeans by saying that the French will not work for German bosses and the Germans will not tolerate French bosses. They will, however, perform for a Canadian, American, or Australian boss.

In addition to status conflicts, communication patterns differ between nationalities. Profile sketches of German, French, European, and Japanese employees describe Novell managers' onsite experience:

- The Germans want everything in rules and they want everything to be very clear and specific. The more rules there are, the more respect they have for you and the more willing they are to participate.

- The French will never agree with you. The goal cannot be consensus with the French because there is no such thing there. The goal can never be to have them happy because they will never communicate satisfaction, so you just have to know that. You have to know that you do not keep working on them until they are happy—you just do what you have to do. They will never agree that what you have done is good, so the more room you can give them to maneuver, which is sort of the opposite of the Germans—the more they will draw their own conclusions and come to where you want them to come.

- Your European employees never work for you. They work for their country. So if you think they're working for you, you're really crazy. Now, their objective is to sell your product, but in their own way. They know more than you do, they think, and they probably do. But the fact is, they'll never work for you. They say they are—they'll nod their head and then they'll do what they think needs to be done, and that probably saves a lot of companies. But if you don't know what's going on, you could spend a lot of money that you don't need to because if you try to start a campaign—you might as well not spend the money. Give them the money and let them do something else with it.

- The Japanese use language that makes you think they are agreeing with you, but they never agree in meetings. The culture says that when they say their word for "yes," all it means is that they understand what you have said. And then they register everything in a meeting and then they leave and then they decide. Then they come back. If you want to renegotiate, they re-register the new information and then they leave and decide, then they come back. Everything is done behind closed doors in Japan and you are never invited into the inner sanctum.

Local country laws, customs, and political events sometimes require Novell to adapt its business model when entering new countries. Jesse learned that in Brazil, Japan, and India, Novell altered its standard practices to accommodate unique markets, with varying results. For years, Novell failed at attempts to enter the Brazilian market. When a businessman approached Novell with an offer to take the company's business inside Brazil, Novell accepted. The contract, designed by the opportunist, allowed him to have an exclusive Brazilian Novell distributorship—a violation of Novell policy. Several years later, untangling this legal fiasco cost the company a lot of money. Novell's successful Japanese entry underscored the importance of social networks and joint ventures. Novell's Indian distributor pirated software from the company in order to avoid paying tariffs. National restrictions prohibit Novell from entering certain countries—Pakistan and Afghanistan have restrictive import laws and the U.S. government prohibits Novell from selling products in Iran, Iraq, and Cuba. In restricted countries, privateers typically steal and pirate Novell software. In the face of national barriers, Novell works through alliances and diplomatic channels to conform to local requirements.

Novell attempts to counter employee tunnel vision through exchange programs and organization-wide communication. Several managers told Jesse that employees do not understand other countries unless they live abroad. In Novell's exchange program, key U.S. engineers exchange places with engineers from other countries for two or three week periods. One manager explained, "They have their eyes opened about what is going on in other parts of the world. When they return to their assignments, they are excited and can teach others and say, 'Hey, it really is different over there—and we need to do this and that.'"

International experience is valued when it is coupled with a firm grasp of Novell's business imperatives such as product delivery and expense management. National and cultural arenas are the settings in which Novell products are imposed. Other than translating products into local languages, Novell does not tailor its software to local markets. Acquiring an understanding of local perspectives, however, is crucial for effective marketing.

Marketing a Constant Look and Feel

Customers and employees should encounter a uniform Novell look and feel when they interact with Novell offices worldwide, including ad campaigns and telephone support. The balance between Novell headquarters control and local autonomy fluctuates. One manager described how local campaigns sometimes resist corporate direction: "I can remember seeing local European ad campaigns that were frightening things. One in particular had a picture of the Ayatollah on it and it had some political joke. We all in the U.S. went, 'No! I don't think we had better do that.'" Global advertising campaigns, however, do not always translate to local settings:

> After such [inappropriate] incidents in Europe, Novell headquarters people became hard-nosed about using the logo in marketing. They insisted that the same ads were used worldwide but cultural differences became apparent—certain things didn't translate. For example, an ad that was based on American football didn't apply to citizens in other countries and the Europeans and Asians pushed back hard saying, "Hey this ad doesn't mean anything over here."

A global approach may also have unexpected political repercussions. For example, when Novell sponsored an ad campaign called "Selling Red" (Novell's logo color), Europeans resisted:

> When that hit Europe, selling red was connected with the Soviet Union, so it was not a positive thing. People in the U.S. tried to implement the campaign but the European employees said, "Yeah, OK, OK, OK," and then didn't promote the campaign—they knew what the effects would be.

International rhetoric and artifacts pepper Novell headquarters. Jesse heard words such as *global* throughout the day. She watched clocks broadcast the time in several countries and looked at flags from Asia, South America, and Europe that hung on the walls. Novell's international offices are even posted on the company's home page, along with e-mail access. She reflected on one veteran Novell manager's summary of the company's diverse and competitive international environment: "Novell has always been changing . . . It is a changing environment. It is true today—but different tomorrow... It is trying to stay ahead of the game."

Case Problem: Transforming Culture ⸺⸺⸺⸺⸺⸺⸺

Jesse sat at her desk after almost everyone else had left for the day. She thought of a Novell executive who said his company's best resources were the ones that drove home every night. That resource, people, was the essence of her work—not software design, marketing plans, or financial statements. She faced transforming an organizational culture on an IT schedule—not within the timeframe of societal or even typical organizational change in which new behavior patterns may not be evident for five years. One year in an IT company is long-term.

To transform Novell's culture, Jesse had the support of the CEO and pockets of employees who envisioned a global organization. She had electronic access to everyone in the company—the Novell Global Network Operations Center used its own ManageWise network to manage its worldwide network (Weinberg, 1998). How was she to create a *roadmap* leading to Novell's cultural transformation? Was creating a global Novell culture as feasible as building a global Novell product in which everything was identical except the language? What will this new organizational culture look like?

References ⸺⸺⸺⸺⸺⸺⸺⸺⸺⸺⸺⸺⸺

Alexander, S. (1998). Ten tips for keeping workers happy. *CNN interactive.* <wysiwyg://16http://www.cnn.com/TECH/computing/9812/16happy worker.idg/> (Dec. 29, 1998).

Caron, J., & Thomas, S. (1998). Sitting Pretty. *LAN Times*. <wysiwyg://43/http://www.lantimes.com/98/98aug/808b009a.html> (December 8, 1998).

Copeland, L. (1998, November 9). Eric Schmidt: Novell—This button-down executive is managing a reversal of fortunes at the beleaguered networking giant. *Reseller News: 815*. <http://www.novell.com/lead-stories/inthenews.html> (January 6, 1999).

Fidel, S. (1998). Novell sheds the red, nets $102 million. *Deseret News*. <http://deseretnews.com/dn/view/0,1249,15000176,00.html?> (November 11, 1998).

Martinez, D. (1998). *Guiding Novell's products*. <http://www.novell.com.lead_stories/98/dec16> (December 19, 1998).

McEntire, M., Derr, C. B., & Meek, C. (1996). *Novell's global strategy: "Bytes are somewhat narcotic."* CIBER Case Collection, Indiana University CIBER distributed by *ECCE@Babson*.

Novell, (1998a). 1997 *Annual Report*. <http://corp.novell.com.au/text/corp/it/97annual/managdisc.html> (December 8, 1998).

Novell, (1998b). *Novell reports fourth fiscal quarter 1998 results*. <http://www.novell.com/press/archive/1998/11/pr98148.html> (December 20, 1998).

Novell, (1998c). Novell highlights. <http://www.novell.com> (January 6, 1999).

Oberbeck, S. (1999, January 1). Tech stocks set the pace in a turbulent year. *Deseret News*, p. E1.

Reuters. (1998). Novell sees Asia opportunities. *CNETNEWS.COM*. <http//www.news.com/News/Item/0,4,27582,00.html> (December 3, 1998).

Schmidt, E. (1998). *Dr. Eric Schmidt's Dispatch from Japan January 9, 1998*. <http://corp.novell.com.au/text/corp/ir/esjapn97.html> (December 8, 1998).

Weinberg, N. (1998, September 21). Tough marching orders. *Network World*.

Endnotes

1. This case is based on public documents including annual reports, news articles, and website postings.

2. Jesse Hassler is a fictitious person—a literary device used to frame the case.

3. Dr. Eric Schmidt is the actual CEO of Novell. References to him are cited from public documents.

4. All quotations, unless accompanied by citations such as this, are excerpts from the historical case, *Novell's Global Strategy: "Bytes are Somewhat Narcotic"* (McEntire, Derr, & Meek, 1996). Quotations are from Novell employees and former employees.

The Anstrichehof Infrared Coating Corporation—AICC

Case 2.2
Alberto Zanzi
Paul Lemieux

"Well, I'm really not surprised," Ron Wheeler thought to himself as he looked in disgust at SwissAir's monitor. The "Arrivals" display video terminal read as follows:

> 11 MAR 1988   FLIGHT 402 - ZURICH 1 HOUR DELAY

It had been that kind of a day. More than the usual amount of bull at work, the Friday night traffic jam in the Sumner Tunnel, and now that he was finally inside the terminal, the flight from Zurich was late. If there was one thing he hated more than a trip to Logan Airport, it was a trip to pick up Dr. Buerlanger at Logan.

"I guess it comes with the territory," he sputtered barely under his breath. As executive vice president of AICC, he felt responsible to personally pick up the directors from AICC's parent company, Masseverk AG. The visits were becoming more frequent and more tense; this time Dr. Vogtgartener was also coming.

Ron found a corner table in the Skyway Lounge, ordered a Lite (an American beer!), and set out his workpapers in front of him. He had a right to be in such a foul mood. AICC was in major trouble. That trouble was traveling toward him at 1,100 miles per hour at 30,000 feet.

He sat back and thought about his beloved AICC. Started in 1968, its growth had been steady but not earthshaking. They actually shipped over $18 million worth of infrared products in 1986. Their current employment of 225 people was their highest level ever. AICC manufactured infrared band-pass filters and antireflection coatings for use in a wide variety of biochemical, military, and aerospace applications. AICC filters were on the job in communications satellites, blood analyzers, burglar alarms, and literally hundreds of other places. The growing worldwide market for commercial applications currently exceeded $250 million. Since the largest competitor only had 25 percent of the market, AICC's potential for continued growth was quite good.

Scource: Alberto Zanzi and Paul Lemieux. "The Anstrichehof Infrared Coating Corporation" 1989. Suffolk University. Reprinted by permission.

Ron marveled at the contrast to Masseverk AG, the parent firm. With 1986 revenues of over four billion Swiss francs ($2.8 billion), Masseverk was a significant force in European industry. Although over 60 percent of their production was military, their optics division, which included AICC, accounted for 12 percent of their total sales. AICC's president, currently a Dr. Mueller, reported directly to Dr. Buerlanger at the optics division headquarters in Zurich.

For the first five years after Masseverk had bought the company, AICC had lost money. Although they had managed to make a small profit last year, this year they barely broke even, and the trend at year end was down, with a bullet. To make things worse, all the good technical people were leaving just when the competition was getting tougher.

There was the memo from Dr. Buerlanger in front of him. As he began to reread it for the sixth time, he felt his ulcer kick up.

MEMORANDUM
TO: Dr. W. Mueller, Pres. AICC
CC: Mr. R. Wheeler, Exec. V.P.
FROM: Dr. J. Buerlanger, Mgr. Masseverk AG., Dir. AICC
SUBJECT: 1987 Performance

Needless to say we are extremely disappointed in your recently reported year end figures, especially after our repeated exhortations that you make improvements. We continue to fail to understand why your technical efficiency remains weak in spite of continued capital equipment investments on our part.

We thought it was sufficiently clear in our memo of 22 FEB 1986 that the new capital of nearly 3.8 Million SFr (2 Million US$) that we invested at that time was supposed to cure whatever was needed, and your predecessor readily agreed. It seems unlikely that the . . .

"Ladies and gentlemen! Your attention please! SwissAir Flight 402 from Zurich has been delayed one additional half hour."

"Waitress, another Lite, please. There goes any hope of making it home in time for the Celtics game. Now, where was I," he mused, as his agitation increased.

. . . seems unlikely that the present management team will ever reach the minimum level of success which Masseverk AG demands from all its subsidiary companies.

As some immediate and direct action on our part seems desirable, in fact unavoidable, I ask you to prepare in advance of our meeting on 12 MARCH 1988 at your location any defenses you wish to raise. Dr. Vogtgartener and myself have some thoughts on structural changes at AICC which may prove effective, but may not be your preference.

As always and best regards,

Dr. J. Buerlanger

Ron bottomed-up his second beer and wandered over to the plate glass windows overlooking the runway. A light rain was starting to fall. He allowed his mind to wander back to his early days at AICC. In retrospect, they were beginning to look like the good old days. "I'm starting to sound like my father," he thought wryly to himself.

When Ron started in 1973, proudly toting his new Suffolk M.B.A. under his arm (a nice supplement to his B.S. in chemistry from Northeastern), AICC hadn't been invented yet. It was a nice, fresh, American company, with a pleasantly high tech name, Infra-Tech. The founder, George Mason, was the man for all seasons, the life of the party, the perennial entrepreneur who was fully involved in everything and made everything work. Infra-Tech was vibrant, growing, alive, and exciting. Direct communication between employees was unhampered by rigid rules and regulations. Each employee felt a sense of involvement and contribution. People worked hard and derived satisfaction from their jobs. Productivity and creativity were high. Under Mason's informal style of leadership, the company flourished.

In the late 1970s, though, Infra-Tech started to lose its edge. Infrared technology was developing at a lightning pace. State-of-the-art equipment was expensive, and margins were slim. Infra-Tech's growth became stifled by lack of investment capital. They had good ideas, but they did not have the resources to bring those ideas to the market. Gradually, as the competition got the edge with better equipment, Infra-Tech tried to buy back its market share by cutting prices. Shortly after the margins disappeared, so did the cash. When Masseverk AG began looking for an American base for its infrared coating business in 1980, the match looked like a natural. The Swiss firm was a world recognized name in infrared technology; they would add their financial and technical strength to Infra-Tech. It had to be a winning combination.

Back in the lounge, Ron thought to himself how the vanishing foam on his beer was like his evaporating hopes over the AICC years. He had been a strong and early supporter of the buyout. But almost immediately things started to go wrong.

Dr. Buerlanger arrived with the contracts, the capital, and a new organization chart. George Mason was replaced with a Swiss national, who proceeded to alienate most of the Infra-Tech managers. By the end of the second year, most of the creative people had quit or been fired. Mason had run his firm in a loose, freewheeling manner, but he had encouraged close, frequent, and direct communication. No organization chart. No memo. No bull. Now all that was changed.

Dr. Buerlanger came from a different world. At Masseverk AG, where he had worked his whole long and successful career, company structure was hierarchical and very rigid. Employees were loyal and hardworking, and they knew their place. The working environment was strict and formal.

Wheeler was reminded of a meeting two years ago in Zurich. He recalled how he was out of sorts because all he could get with his meal was dark Swiss beer, no Lite. To his right, he had overhead Dr. Buerlanger make a comment to Dr. Vogtgartener under his breath about how the American's bad taste in beer was only surpassed by his childish impatience, disloyalty, and lack of organization. Dr. Buerlanger must have sensed Wheeler's attention because he turned his back slightly and continued in his native Suisse-Deutsche[1]:

Dr. B: Seriously, Herr Doctor, I cannot understand these Americans. They are bright, but they don't have any regard for the way things should be done. Everyone wants to be in charge. The technicians want to tell the scientists about ion exchange. The salesmen want to tell the supervisors how to run the plant. No one has any respect for order and control.

Dr. V: Believe me, I understand your disappointment. We have given them the opportunity to come here and learn from our success, but it is no use. They are hopelessly uncivilized. They carry their democratic ideas into the workplace; it is no surprise that the structure collapses.[2]

Dr. B: I would be content to deal with the EC [European Economic Community—ed.] countries; these are people I can understand. But the American market is too lucrative to ignore. I suppose we will have to continue to try to educate them to the correct way of doing things.

"Organization! Organization! Organization!" Wheeler thought over and over. "Ever since they have tried to make us an organization, we have stopped being an enterprise." Just that afternoon an angry exchange had taken place between Dave Howard, Manufacturing Manager, and Michael Steiner, Director of R&D. The stark contrast between now and Infra-Tech was foremost in Ron's mind as he recalled the scene in the corridor.

Howard: Where were you when Jonesie started up the 1500 Hi-Vac! He blew away almost $80,000 worth of germanium in two runs before Larry from QC shut him down!

Steiner: What do you mean "Where was I?" Where were you? You're the manufacturing manager, not me. Look on the wall in Wheeler's office next to manufacturing. That's you there, not me.

Howard: Listen, Mike. You know as well as I do that chart is Dr. B's little fantasy. You're the only one here who knows the right way to start up the 1500 Hi-Vac. We can't afford to foul up like this,

---

[1]Translated by the editor.

[2]Dr. Vogtgartener used the word *gefallenundversagenvollig*, a colloquialism which I have translated as "collapse." The literal meaning has a sense of total failure — ed.

      or the Swiss will take their francs and go home. I got a kid in college and orthodontist bills to pay!

Steiner: Look Dave, it's nothing personal. But I've got to play it safe at least until I can get my résumé out on the street.

Howard: Well, do what you have to. But I'll tell you this much. This business is too complicated to run like the army. If we're gonna survive, we gotta learn to talk. And then we gotta learn to help each other out . . . not just hide behind the organization chart.

      "Ladies and gentlemen! Your attention please! SwissAir Flight 402 from Zurich is now arriving at gate 12. Disembarking passengers can be met at the U.S. Customs exit in the lower lobby in approximately 30 minutes."

      "Well, here they are. Buerlanger and Vogtgartener with another organization chart, and . . . ," thought Wheeler, "I don't even know if I'm on it!" The possibility of another president, the fourth in seven years, made Ron's ulcer kick up again. He pulled out the manilla folder which held tentative plans for a management leveraged buyout; he had been toying with the idea for six months, but it wasn't quite ready.

      "Half an hour for customs? Waitress! I'll have another Lite, please."

Exhibit 1. Anstrichehof Infrared Coating Corporation Comparative Balance Sheet

	1981	1982	1983	1984	1985	1986	1987
Assets							
Current assets							
Cash	822,042	83,893	34,794	60,453	33,526	42,534	55,979
Accounts receivable	544,860	862,158	1,620,623	1,224,444	1,798,451	2,414,426	2,138,830
Inventories	363,029	641,220	1,772,533	1,988,948	1,508,320	1,813,490	1,757,092
Prepaid expenses	36,764	10,840	43,399	36,804	26,384	61,403	43,195
Total current assets	1,766,695	1,598,111	3,471,349	3,310,649	3,366,681	4,331,853	3,995,096
Equipment and Leaseholds, Net	1,610,522	4,119,974	3,686,767	3,598,186	3,543,186	3,589,534	3,995,455
Intangible Assets	92,340	81,262	58,774	30,028			
Total Assets	3,469,557	5,799,347	7,216,890	6,938,863	6,909,867	7,921,387	7,990,551
Liabilities & Equity							
Current Liabilities							
Notes Payable	256,122	719,511	1,100,000	2,600,000	2,100,000	1,750,000	3,400,000
Accounts payable accruals			1,763,529	1,607,329	548,434	1,564,220	614,781
Salaries, wages, taxes	139,864	42,610	69,871	48,805	59,592	134,536	127,568
Income taxes payable						450,288	
Deferred tax, current							10,710
Due to affiliates	36,802			589,210	2,000,000		92,141
Current portion, LTD				315,625	315,625	315,625	315,625
Total Current Liabilities	432,788	762,121	2,933,400	5,160,969	5,023,651	4,214,669	4,560,825
Deferred Taxes							4,590
Long Term Debt		2,525,000	2,525,000	2,209,375	1,893,750	1,578,127	1,262,502
Equity							
Capital	3,300,000	3,300,000	3,300,000	3,300,000	4,300,000	2,015,601	2,015,601
Retained earnings (deficit)	(263,231)	(787,774)	(1,541,510)	(3,731,481)	(4,307,534)	112,990	147,033
Total Equity	3,036,769	2,512,226	1,758,490	(431,481)	(7,534)	2,128,591	2,162,634
Total Liabilities	3,469,557	5,799,347	7,216,890	6,938,863	6,909,867	7,921,387	7,990,551

Exhibit 2. Anstrichehof Infrared Coating Corporation
Comparative Statement of Income

	1981	1982	1983	1984	1985	1986	1987
Net Sales	2,305,046	6,101,116	8,456,087	8,888,253	14,795,246	18,275,256	17,916,961
Cost of Sales	1,601,356	4,822,067	6,817,782	8,749,517	12,583,515	13,747,058	13,906,623
	703,690	1,279,050	1,638,305	138,735	2,211,731	4,528,198	4,010,338
General, Administrative Expense	590,303	710,670	775,411	1,098,033	1,049,720	1,519,662	1,504,070
Selling Expense	161,408	547,316	646,117	742,743	634,106	873,087	961,367
Product Development	88,344	228,534	204,855	227,656	98,544	1,320,469	1,177,992
	840,055	1,486,520	1,626,383	2,068,432	1,782,370	3,713,218	3,643,429
Other Expense	126,865	317,072	765,658	260,274	1,005,414	250,756	306,566
Income Taxes						428,100	23,300
Earnings (Deficit)	(263,231)	(524,543)	(753,736)	(2,189,971)	(576,053)	136,125	37,043

Exhibit 3. Anstrichehof Infrared Coating Corporation Organization Chart

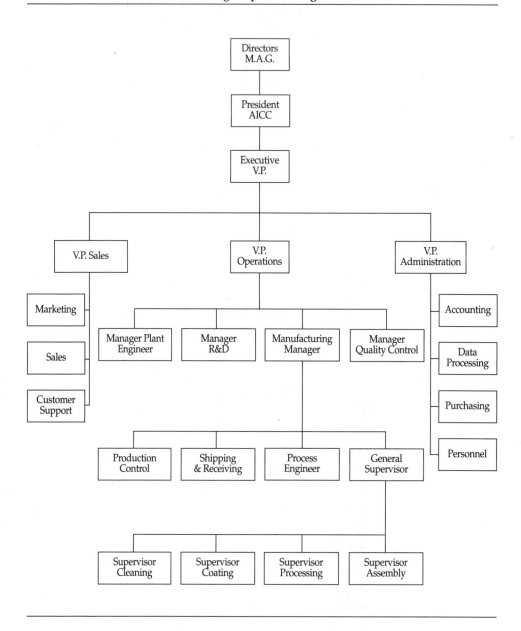

Part 3

STAFFING FOR INTERNATIONAL OPERATIONS

Flexible Working in Europe

Reading 3.1
Chris Brewster
Lesley Mayne
Olga Tregaskis

Around the world, the concept of flexible working practices,[1] the extent of such practices and the implications for practitioners and policy makers in the area, have been much discussed. These are critical issues for employers, trade unions and governments. In Europe, in particular, recent opinions from the European Court of Justice have raised the political profile of the subject and the Commission, the civil service of the European Union (EU), is committed to further action on this issue in 1997. This article uses evidence from Europe to explore the implications for the state, for individuals and for employers.[2]

The paper presents evidence on developments in flexible working from European countries. In this discussion, "flexible working" covers only working time and contractual variations (temporary contracts, outsourcing, etc). The paper summarises the debates on the topic; outlines the reasons for the massive growth in flexible working that has been seen in Europe; and draws conclusions about the implications for governments, individuals and for employers.

Theories of Labour Flexibility

The concept of "labour flexibility" remains, both in theoretical and practical terms, highly problematic. Despite the huge volume of literature devoted to the so-called "flexibility debate" relatively little progress has been made in resolving many of the problems associated with the concept.

In the literature, the term "flexibility" is applied to a series of quite distinct (if related) theories. There are those which have been labelled "post-Fordist": a category which covers a range of variants, but is characterized by the work of such writers as Piore and Sabel (1984),

Source: Chris Brewster, Lesley Mayne and Olga Tregaskis. "Flexible Working in Europe," Journal of World Business, 32(2), 1997. Reprinted by permission of JAI Press Inc.

Mathews (1989a, 1989b, 1990, 1992), Lash and Urry (1987), Katz (1985) Kern and Schumann (1987), Tolliday and Zeitlin (1986) and Streeck (1987). For these writers, who generally concentrate on the manufacturing industry, new technology is the key to a more flexible form of production, more responsive to increasingly rapid changes in the market: such developments may depend for their success upon a more skilled, motivated and flexible workforce. The focus of this stream of writing has been on production systems rather than employment. A more critical, "neo-Marxian" (Clegg, 1990, pp. 21 1) or "neo-Fordist" (Wood 1989b, p. 21) group of writers has also been concerned with flexible production, though taking a more negative view of its likely effect on individuals and including discussion of the impact on labour markets (Bramble, 1988; Bramble & Fieldes, 1989, 1992; Harvey, 1989, 1991). An alternative conception of flexibility is provided by researchers in the operational management area.

Finally, and most relevantly here, there has also been an important set of literature focussed on employment flexibility: labelled by some as "managerialist" (Bagguley, 1991: 164) or "neo-managerialist" (Clegg, 1990, p. 210) and typified by the work of Atkinson (1984, 1985a, 1985b, 1987; Atkinson & Gregory, 1986; Atkinson & Meager, 1986). His work has been subjected to critiques which have attempted to demonstrate the limited utility and lack of theoretical robustness of his work, rather than attempting to build upon the insights which it provides or to develop a more comprehensive theoretical framework based on it—some, indeed, attempted to deny the growth of flexibility (see for example: Pollert, 1988a, 1988b). Nonetheless, Atkinson's work has been extremely influential. His vision of flexibility has influenced policy debates internationally (OECD, 1986a, 1989).

Reasons for the Growth of Flexibility ———————————————————

Atkinson (1985a) argues that three main factors have contributed to moves to greater flexibility. The first two concern economic difficulties experienced by the advanced economies in recent times. The argument is that, since the late 1960s or early 1970s, the advanced capitalist economies have been in crisis (Boyer, 1987; Harvey , 1989; Piore & Sabel, 1984; Mathews, 1989a, 1989b) and that the drive for more flexibility is dictated by the need to overcome the crisis (Meulders and Wilkin, 1987, p. 16). More typically, perhaps, neo-managerialist theory essentially presents flexibility as a pragmatic managerial response (Bagguley, 1991, p. 153) to a given set of circumstances, the cause of which is not at issue.

Atkinson (1985a, 1987) provides a brief, largely descriptive, account of economic pressures for greater flexibility, in terms of generalised recession and an increasingly competitive and volatile market environment. Recession, he argues, has made increased competitiveness a management priority, and in an environment unconducive to investment, this has involved management reliance on increased labour productivity and reductions in unit labour cost (Atkinson, 1985a).

Pressure for greater flexibility is also said to derive from the "particularly unstable and (since 1945) unprecedented market conditions experienced in recent years" (Atkinson, 1987, p. 88). In addition to increased competition, and in the context of slow growth, markets have become more volatile, with a correspondingly greater immediacy between the recognition of market opportunities or pressures and the need to respond to them. Uncertainty about demand has led to uncertainty about labour requirements, and employers have sought ways to make labour both cheaper and more easily variable in quantity (Atkinson, 1985a).

The third factor said to necessitate greater flexibility is technological change. Technology is changing more quickly than ever before. This, it is said, necessitates the creation of a workforce which is able to adapt to the demands of new technologies as they emerge. Such adaptability allows enterprises to obtain maximum advantage from advances in technology. Furthermore, technology is characterised by computer controlled production systems. While not always the case, in some instances the new technologies have led to a blurring of the distinction between conception and execution of tasks. In such cases, workers need to be more highly skilled and sophisticated since they are required to perform a wider range of more complex tasks than has been typical (Atkinson, 1985a). Therefore, the general effect of technological change has been to increase the need for a workforce which can be redeployed to new and/or more complex jobs as necessary.

The net effect of this combination of economic and technological pressures is said to be a situation in which:

> Employers are increasingly looking for a workforce which can respond quickly, easily and cheaply to changes . . . ; such a workforce will be able to contract as readily as it expands to meet market requirements; such a workforce must not result in increased unit labour costs . . . ; finally it must be capable of deployment over time to meet the needs of the job exactly through recourse to a range of working time options (Atkinson, 1985a, p. 9).

Others have argued that some elements at least of the drive for greater flexibility come from labour market "pull"—the opportunity it provides for sections of the labour market that would not otherwise be available for work or to retain valued staff who would otherwise leave.

There are a significant number of flexible workers who prefer to work in that way (Social Europe, 1991; Wareing, 1992). Almost certainly, this will include some people who are justifying to themselves the employment pattern that they have, in reality, been forced to accept.

The majority are people who have deliberately, with more or less enthusiasm, chosen to adopt these flexible work patterns (Commission of the EC, 1990). These might be people who have made decisions about balancing work, income and other aspects of their lives in a less typical way; people who do not want to tie themselves to organizations for long periods of time (for reasons of temperament, or because their skills are so marketable that they can increase their salary with each career move); or people who are combining one job with other, perhaps unpaid, work.

There are additional advantages to employees of flexible working beyond those of career choice or just getting at least some kind of job. Flexible work patterns can be seen as "family friendly." There are many parents who would argue that part-time, shift or homeworking allows them to spend more time with their children; there are other careers, of children or elderly or disabled people, who are unable to work in a "typical" pattern and therefore can only work if nonstandard hours are available. While this has undoubtedly been a factor, the growth of flexible working at a time of mass unemployment cannot be explained to any great extent by pull factors.

These changes and the development of a more flexible labour market have been controversial. They are seen by some to have taken our societies back towards the early years of the industrial revolution, with the creation of a significant underclass of underprivileged and "vulnerable" workers. They are seen by others as evidence of an uncaring and irresponsible approach to employees by employers—sometimes associated with a desire to "de-unionize" the workforce.

Some will argue that the development of the flexible workforce is a long-overdue move away from an insistence on standard forms of employment towards forms which can be more responsive to the needs of employees and their families. Finally, there are many who will see the development of flexibility as a means of making the labour market more responsive to economic requirements, able to deliver a cheaper and/or more productive—and therefore more efficient and competitive—workforce.

This paper draws on currently available and new data to explore these issues in detail.

Methodology ————————————————————————————————

The evidence being used here is data collected by the Cranfield Network on European Human Resource Management (Cranet-E).[3] In 18 European countries identical questionnaires (subject to local "translation") were distributed to senior HR or personnel specialists in organizations of over 200 employees over four rounds of data collection, starting in 1989 with five countries; increasing in each round of collection since then. The data covers all sections of the economy and is in broad terms representative. Practically all major, "household name" companies in each country, and many smaller ones, were surveyed. The survey also included major public sector organizations; key employers in nearly every country and particularly important in Europe. Well over 20,000 questionnaires have been collected including nearly 6,000 collected in 1995. This paper draws mainly on the first 14 countries to report in the 1995 survey round, but will use the trend data where appropriate. (For full details of the methodology see Brewster, Hegewish & Mayne, 1994; Brewster, Tregaskis, Hegewish & Mayne, 1996b).

The survey covers various forms of flexibility in working time; contracts; place of work; task or job; and in the financial package. For reasons of space constraints, the data presented here is that for time and contractual flexibility.[4]

All research is compromise and the limitations of this research are clear. Among them, two are worth noting specifically in this context. First, our evidence is, almost inevitably, drawn from the legitimate economy; the shadow economies of the various European countries are excluded. Second, the Cranet-E data is drawn from companies with more than 200 employees; smaller organizations are excluded, at least from our comparative analyses. Interestingly, it is likely that the inclusion of those individuals and organizations excluded by this research would serve to strengthen the arguments addressed in this paper.

Findings _____

Flexibility

The first key finding is that flexibility is substantial and growing. It affects large numbers of organizations and individuals and is growing right across Europe. (An interesting sidelight on this is that many commentators, lawyers and practitioners with little experience of Europe have argued that employment in that continent is rigid and *inflexible*.)

For the purpose of this paper just a few examples of extent and trends will be presented: we focus on the most commonly used forms of working time flexibility (part-time and shiftworking) and contractual flexibility (short-term contracts and subcontracting). Considerable amounts of further evidence are available in Brewster et al. (1996). This will enable a lengthier discussion of the findings and their implications.

There are, of course, differences in levels and growth rates of the various forms of flexibility; and of course there are instances where in a particular country or for a particular type of flexibility the trend is actually downwards. Overall, however, the upward trend is very clear. This trend is found in nearly all countries and in nearly all sectors of the economy and is not dependent on economic cycles.

Part-time Working is the most widely used form of flexibility. The degree of flexibility in part-time work has been debated: the argument is that if someone is doing regular part-time work, and has other commitments which cannot be moved, then they are not themselves very flexible. However, from the viewpoint of the management, part-time employment—which can often in practice be easily shrunk or extended or, in some cases, moved to a different place in the day—is more flexible than standard full-time work.

Part-time employment is playing an increasingly important role in Europe. One in seven people in the European Union is working part-time, and part-time employment has been the major area of employment growth during the last decade. However, definitions of part-time work and, even taking that into account, the levels of part-time work, vary greatly between different European countries. There are also variations in the treatment of part-time workers in legal and social security systems (Brewster, Hegewisch & Mayne, 1993). Given that a substantial majority of part-time workers in the EU are female, it is no surprise to find that there is also a correlation with child care arrangements (Rees & Brewster, 1995).

Broadly, there is a North-South divide. Part-time employment is highest now in the Scandinavian countries and in the Netherlands where, after very rapid growth during the last decade, by the end of the 1980s over 30% of the labour force, and six out of ten women, worked part-time. Denmark, Norway, Sweden and the U.K. also have an overall part-time share of over 20%, with more than four out of ten women working part-time. In northern Europe there are very few organizations which do not use part-time work. Some organizations, such as the major banks and retail chains employ a considerable proportion of their workforce this way. At the other end of the spectrum are the southern and more agricultural countries such as Greece, Portugal, Spain and to some extent Italy, and Ireland, where part-time employment is well below 10% of all employment. And part-time working is increasing right across Europe (see Table 1).

Sweden, which has high levels of part-time working and where there was trade union pressure to convert part-time jobs into full-time ones, was the only country to have more organizations decreasing the use of part-time working than increasing it. In many countries more than half the organizations had increased the use of part-time work with hardly any reducing it.

Shiftworking is not a new form of working; it is essential in some industries where equipment, services and production processes must continue on a 24 hour cycle. Examples as diverse as newspaper production, public transport and utilities, food production and delivery and hospital and emergency services illustrate the need for continuous production and services. New technology, as well as debates over work sharing and working time reductions, have put shiftworking into the limelight during the 1980s. Ever more expensive technology has

Table 1. Changes in the Use of Part-Time across Europe (percentage employers)

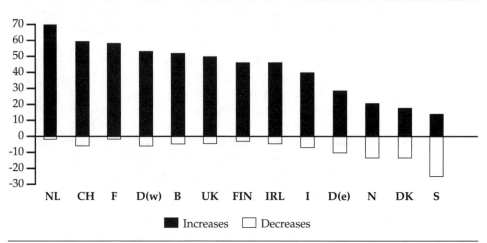

Increases ☐ Decreases

Source: Cranet-E, 1995

increased competitive pressures on employers to extend operating hours and increase productivity; at the same time working time reductions for the individual employee were facilitated by introducing new shift patterns which extended plant utilisation and gave management greater flexibility in working time arrangements (Blyton, 1992; Bielenski, Alaluf, Atkinson, Bellini, Castillo, Donati, Graverson, Huygen, & Wickham, 1993).

A key development in recent years has been the spread of shiftworking to industries, such as telephone sales and banking, where it has not been used previously.

Concern with the impact on employees' health and social welfare of changing working patterns, new shift arrangements and work during unsocial hours led the European Commission to introduce a new Directive on working time. Limits on night work and requirements for periods of rest once a week have obvious implications for many shiftworking patterns, particularly some of the newer and more varied patterns now operating. The implementation of the Directive will require some legislative adjustments in most Community member states, particularly in the U.K. which currently has very little working time legislation.

It is not easy to get comparable figures on the incidence of shiftworking among employees in Europe. Our research at the organizational level shows that across Europe shiftworking (paid and unpaid) is a widespread practice; only in Denmark, Norway and Sweden are there less than 80% of organizations using shiftworking (Brewster et al., 1994). Once again the picture of widespread increases is clear.

Table 2. Changes in the Use of Shiftwork across Europe (percentage employers)

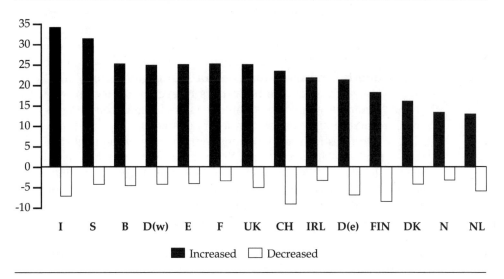

These increases in flexibility are not restricted to working time. They apply in the same way to contractual flexibility. There are a range of methods by which organizations can get work done. In some cases these involve contracts of employment which are quite distinct from "typical" contracts in more significant ways than just a change to the time at which the employee works—they may involve short-term or even casual employment, for example. Or they may involve getting the work done through a non-employment option: as an example this article takes the example of subcontracting.

"Non-Permanent" Employment is a phrase used to cover any form of employment other than permanent open ended contracts. To some extent "temporary" and "fixed term" contracts are substitutes, and which is used most heavily in a country depends largely on legal and quasi-legal regulations and national expectations; therefore the two forms are considered jointly.

Temporary work in Europe plays a lesser role in the overall labour market than part-time employment and its growth during the 1980s is less dramatic; however, as with part-time employment, levels and growth rates of non-permanent employment vary substantially across Europe.

In general it is the poorer countries of the European Community which have the highest levels of employees on such contracts. Non-permanent employment is highest in southern countries such as Greece, Portugal and Spain where the percentage of the workforce on such contracts is over 15% and lowest in Luxembourg, Belgium and Italy at around 5%.

At organizational level our research shows that the use of non-permanent employment is widespread: used by 8 or 9 out of every 10 employers in all countries. The "wealth divide" however is clearer when we look at the share of those organizations in each country which are high temporary/casual or fixed-term users (those where at least 10% of the workforce are on such contracts); in Spain, Portugal, Turkey and Ireland more than one fifth of organizations are "high users." However, there are high users in every country: in the U.K., Flymo (a company making lawnmowers and engine components) has one third of its employees on temporary contracts.

Growth rates for non-permanent employment varied substantially during the 1980s, increasing rapidly in some countries while remaining at a low level or declining in others (OECD, 1991). The largest increases occurred in France, where the proportion of non-permanent employment for both men and women more than doubled between 1983 and 1989 (to 9.4% of the female and 7.8% of the male workforce); Ireland, Greece and the Netherlands also show positive increases (Commission of the EC, 1992). In all the countries in our survey, except Norway, the growth in the number of organizations using short-term contracts far outweighed the numbers reducing their use (see Table 3).

For employees, the evidence is that, in contrast to part-time working, most employees with a temporary or fixed-term contract would prefer a permanent one. The drive to increase their use has come from managers. They see five main advantages from short-term contracts.

Table 3. Change in the Use of Temporary Contracts across Europe (percentage employers)

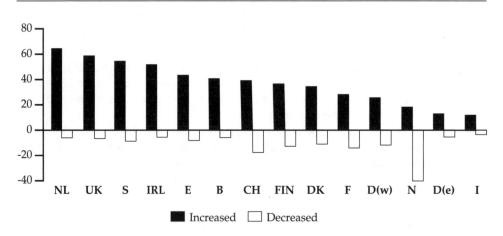

1. First, it is frequently the case that managers know that work needs to be done, but they do not know how long that demand will last or whether further work will accrue. When Rank Xerox transformed its U.K. copier and printer business in the face of competition from the Far East the management decided only to grow through the use of temporary employment until they had more certainty that the growth could be sustained.

2. Second, employers know that some jobs will only involve a short period of time (in addition to obvious examples such as seasonal work, or construction this would include, for example, the decision by American Express to use temporary workers whilst services were being moved to a centralised location).

3. Third, managers believe that in many cases the costs of short-term recruitment will be less since less care may be needed in selection, temporary employees will require less—sometimes zero—administration for sickness or pension schemes, etc. This was the reason given by the U.K.'s telephone giant BT—although it argues that it has now moved on to a more strategic use of temporary workers. (Of course, managers may be wrong about the real costs of temporary employment, see Nollen, 1992).

4. Fourth, short-term appointments may be an answer to an immediate problem where skills are otherwise unavailable. In these, and a number of less important ways, short-term employment is extremely flexible. In most cases, crucially, the complications involved in terminating long-term contracts are absent: it is easy to dispense with the services of these employees.

5. A final major advantage for many managers is that short-term employment is the ideal way to access whether a particular employee would "fit in" if taken on as a permanent staff member. Several of the airlines, from the giants like BA and Lufthansa to the new small "niche" airlines like Air Dolomiti, now take on nearly all new employees as temporary workers, only confirming in permanent employment the very best performers. It has clear advantages over even the best selection system.

Subcontracting is "the displacement of an employment contract by a commercial one as a means of getting a job done" (Atkinson & Meager, 1986). For some employees this will make little difference in terms of flexibility: they might well be a permanent full-time employee in the contractor firm. In many other cases, however, this system—which has always been common in industries like construction—will mean the displacement of more traditional contracts of employment with individuals by contracts for services with other organizations. The employment relationship will have been superceded by a commercial relationship and the organization which is giving out the contract will have no further concern with employment issues—these will have been passed on to the contractor. In many of the public sector organizations in our sample subcontracting is a response to tightening financial constraints, but in many of the large private sector employers such as Hewlett Packard, BT or the brewery businesses subcontracting is an attempt to concentrate on their core business. Of course, even in the private sector there are many organizations which use subcontracting as a way for line managers to overcome headcount restrictions.

In all major west European countries there is an increase in subcontracting (see Table 4). Only a minority of organizations in the public or private sectors in any country have decreased the use of subcontracting. In West Germany and the Netherlands, half of all organizations surveyed indicate that subcontracting has increased. In Spain, Switzerland, France, Finland, Ireland and the U.K. one third or more of all organizations have increased their use of subcontracting. Very small percentages of organizations in any country say that they have decreased their use of subcontracting (other than Norway, where slightly more organizations decreased their use of subcontracting than increased it, largely as a response to new legislation in the run-up to the vote on EU membership). There appears to be generally less uptake of subcontracting in the Nordic countries than in other parts of Europe with Denmark, Finland and Norway having a quarter or more of their organizations not using subcontracting. Subcontracting is used by fewest organizations in Ireland and East Germany, both having more than a third of organizations not using it.

Table 4. Change in the Use of Subcontracting across Europe (percentage employers)

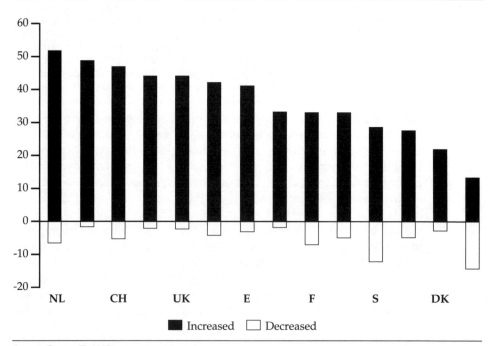

Source: Cranet-E, 1995

There are a wide variety of other flexible employment patterns available—some of them very new and very imaginative. A number of organizations have taken up particular forms of flexible working time in a major way, but in general they are less widespread. They include such approaches as annual hours contracts, weekend working and term-time working; networking; consultancy arrangements and tele-working. All are much smaller in extent; but all are growing.

Taken overall, the evidence is incontrovertible: there has been a substantial change in Europe's labour markets. Employers now have open to them, and are using more extensively, a wider range of means of getting work done. In every EU country in our research a clear majority of employers in our sample report that the range, extent and use of nearly all forms of flexible working hours and contractual arrangements is increasing. There is no obvious sign that these changes have "peaked" or are likely to reduce.

If the first finding is that flexibility is extensive and growing, the second is that **the convergence of trends does not equate to similarity: the various countries in Europe are still very different in their use of flexibility.**

The evidence shows a clear and widespread trend to increase flexibility across Europe. However, the trend is starting from markedly different bases. The form, extent and nature of flexible working that employers are most likely to use is different in the different countries. Issues such as the role of trade unions and collective bargaining; the influence of the church; family structures; whether Sunday is a working day (with shops open, etc.); and legislation in a wide range of areas outside employment (transport, shop opening, banking) as well as employment legislation itself, all vary from country to country, so this should not surprise us. Interestingly, despite this national variability, flexibility is not determined by employment legislation per se. The North/South divide on the use of part-time and non-permanent work, which emerges from much of the data, indicates that there is a complex of factors involved in the use of particular forms of flexibility. Both highly-regulated and low-regulated countries use considerable amounts of flexibility and in many cases show very similar levels of increase. The analysis of the labour market pull and employer demand factors at the beginning of this paper indicates that employers everywhere across Europe are facing the same pressures to use their human resources in the most cost-effective manner. The national context is a more powerful predictor of the use of flexibility by employers than size of organization or sector, although within the national boundaries these variables may also be important.

There is now an ever wider variety of ways of getting work done. This rather clumsy formulation is more accurate than talking of ways of employing people, because many of these forms of flexibility (subcontracting, agency work, consultancy work, etc.) are in fact alternatives to employment. Flexibility has significant advantages for employers: it acts to reduce risk, to reduce costs, to match work available more closely to the requirement for it, and it enables organizations to expand and reduce their labour capability more readily in line with demand. There are also problems; of commitment, of training; of communication and of managerial ability to control and motivate flexible workers. For most employers, however, the benefits outweigh the problems and, hence, there has been a substantial increase in flexible working. And the increase has taken place in nearly every European country, whatever the nature of their employment law. What is happening is that working patterns and contracts are established according to a complex of factors— employers' needs, competition, the sales market, the availability of particular skills, the bargaining power of employees, (the British Post Office, as one instance suffered a series of strikes in 1996 when it tried to introduce a form of flexibility they called "teamworking" and failed to get it in), managerial understanding, tradition and employment legislation. It is the combination of these factors which determines the extent of particular practices in any one country.

Finally, in terms of the findings reported here the research found **no evidence of a direct link between flexibility and increased unemployment.**

One of the major claims made for flexible working is that it will reduce unemployment: this should occur because the increased efficiency and competitiveness of organizations will lead to an upturn in the total economy and also because there is a clear substitution effect— replacing one eight hour contract with two four hour contracts, for example, means two people in the labour market, one less on the unemployment register, two people earning salaries and possibly two people paying taxes. A counter-argument is that flexible working may attract into the workforce people who would not otherwise have registered for work, thus having little effect on unemployment rates. In some cases the substitution is of, to stay with the example, one full-time job by one part-time job (or one standard employment by one temporary job, etc.) so that unemployment is not reduced whilst the benefits of employment to the individual and the economy are reduced. Some forms of flexible working—overtime for example (Spink & Brewster, 1989); or task flexibility—may in fact reduce employment opportunities (Minford, 1995).

This fails to survive the test of evidence. The most regulated societies in Europe such as Portugal and (outside the EU but in the European free trade area) Norway, have less flexibility, but the lowest levels of unemployment. Taking Europe as a whole there appears to be some correlation between increased employment and high use of part-time work. In some of the Nordic countries—Denmark, Sweden and Finland—there is a negative correlation: organizations with more than 10% of their workforce on part-time contracts are rather less likely to have increased their employment by more than 5% over the previous three years. Norway is different and, like Germany, France, Spain, Ireland, Italy, the Netherlands and the U.K., organizations there with more than 10% of the workforce part-timers are more likely to have increased their total employment than organizations with a smaller proportion of part-timers.

The trends show a wide variation and provide little comfort to any of the more didactic commentators. At organizational level, part-time work is sometimes linked to job creation and sometimes linked to the reduction in employment. The argument that flexibility can be a valuable step towards job creation is borne out on an overall basis for some kinds of flexibility in many countries, but even in those countries there is a substantial minority of cases where job loss is linked to increased flexibility.

The position would be more straightforward if there were convincing evidence that increased flexibility is statistically correlated with increased levels of employment. That is not the case. Whether organizations are increasing in size of employment or decreasing in size of employment they are likely to be increasing their use of flexible forms of working. Furthermore, if jobs are created, but in such a form that they involve low salaries, government subsidies, limited spending power and insecurity, then many of the advantages that would flow from job creation are lost.

Discussion ⎯⎯⎯⎯⎯⎯⎯⎯⎯⎯⎯⎯⎯⎯⎯⎯⎯⎯⎯⎯⎯⎯⎯⎯⎯⎯⎯⎯⎯

The evidence, therefore, shows that there has been a drive to develop different forms of working practice, including some that may not even involve employment, right across Europe. This drive is created by the requirement to use the most expensive item of operating costs—the labour that an organization uses—in the most cost-effective manner. It is not determined by legislation although the national circumstances (including such factors as history, culture, trade unions, markets and legislation) do have a profound effect and one that militates against convergence.

Going beyond the evidence adduced here, there are some important implications of these developments for European society, as indicated in Figure 1.

The Different Interests

The implications of flexible working for individuals, for the state and for employers are quite distinct. Figure 1 indicates the relationships involved.

For the individuals flexible working patterns can provide additional opportunities to work, can enable family incomes to be supplemented and can allow work to be fitted in with family responsibilities. However, the transfer of the costs means that flexible work is often low

Figure 1. Implications for European Society

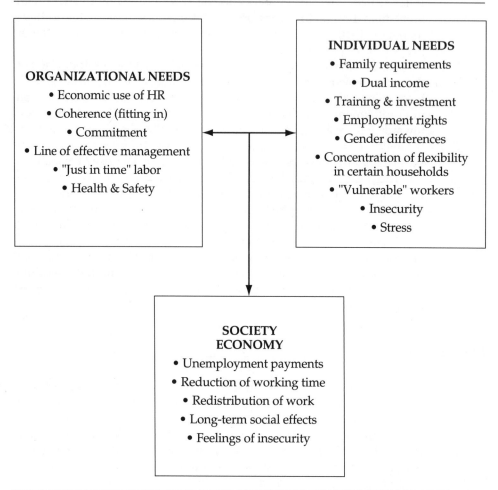

paid. It is the individual and the family who bear the cost of not working on standard hours and contractual arrangements. In addition, these
workers may well be expected to arrange for and to pay for their own
training and skill updating. The transfer of risks means that many individuals and the families that they support cannot be sure of employment much beyond the immediate future. This becomes more than just
an immediate financial problem for the families involved; it has a major
issue on the rest of their lives, because so much of our society is built on
the assumption that most people have standard employment. Thus the
ability to purchase goods on credit, to have bank loans, to arrange housing and to provide pension arrangements are all dependent, to some
degree in every European country, on having a full-time long-term job.

A further potential impact of the growth of such flexibility will be pressure on the provision of equal opportunities. There seems little doubt that in many cases organizations are failing to provide flexible workers with equal access to salaries, financial and nonfinancial benefits and to opportunities for training and development, promotion and the like.

Governments will also have to address these changes in the labour markets more directly. One important implication concerns the effect on government finances. The problem of "dependency ratios" has been exercising many analysts throughout Europe. As people stay on longer in full-time education and join the workforce later; and as people retire earlier and live longer; so the proportion of those contributing to government finances shrinks compared to those making demands on them. Some governments, notably the British in the 1980s and early 1990s, saw the greater efficiency of flexible working as one way of alleviating this problem. However, even if it reduces unemployment, flexible working tends to increase the number of those in employment who because they do not work enough hours per week, or enough weeks in the year, end up paying no taxes and indeed may still, in much of Europe, be drawing benefit from the State even though they are in work. The trade unions in Britain estimated that the difference between the creation of a quarter of a million full-time jobs at average male earnings and the creation that took place in 1996 of a quarter of a million part-time jobs for women was not far short of 1.5 million dollars of tax revenues (TUC, 1996).

For society in general the costs have been transferred directly, because the State will supplement low earnings and provide support for the unemployed. The costs have also been transferred indirectly in that the requirements for training, for health and safety and for the provision of other relevant benefits will have to be borne by the State. The transfer of risk means that during periods of unemployment, between short-term contracts, for example, the State will again be expected to provide support. And there are arguably many indirect aspects of this transfer in terms of the effects of insecurity and stress on health levels, in terms of pension arrangements and in terms of housing support. It appears, for example, that part-time jobs are likely to be replacing full-time jobs on a one for one basis, rather than that full-time jobs are being replaced by two part-time jobs to cover the same number of hours. Even if two people were getting work rather than one, though, the overall benefit may be extremely limited if one or both remain on income support, do not pay tax (or even in many cases National Insurance) and have little extra money to spend in the economy. The increased flexibility in Europe means that risks and costs have been transferred from employers to individuals and to the State. This may make the employing organizations more efficient, but not necessarily make the country more competitive.

There are also wider societal implications of these changes in working practices; there are the implications of flexible working on the social security system, on housing and on pensions, to take just some instances. Since the markets here currently depend on the assumption that most people have full-time permanent jobs the decline of that form of employment may have far-reaching effects.

One major set of implications relates to employers, organizations need flexible use of labour, and in particular time and contractual flexibility, in order to ensure the most economic use of what is, in most cases, the most expensive single element of their operating costs. But increased flexibility is not without its problems for organizations. There is evidence that employers are less ready to invest their resources in the training of employees who will not be in a position to provide a long-time, long-term payback of that investment. The implications of these developments for skill levels in the EU, widely acknowledged as being an important component of competitiveness, are negative. Other problems center around the problems of establishing rational policies, administering the system, and particularly around communication and commitment.

The problem that managers face is that if they make only a limited and instrumental commitment to the people working for them, it is hard to see why those people should give their employer their whole-hearted commitment. Much of at least the popular writing on management tells us that the future will belong to those organizations with the most motivated, enthusiastic and committed staff—the ones ready to "go the extra mile" for the customer, to come up with better ways of doing the job and respecting confidences. Yet the evidence is that employers are increasingly unready to make any substantial commitment to their workers. There is room for some serious debate here. The usual response to a lack of commitment on the part of the workforce would be increased communication, but flexibility makes that problematic too; the workers will rarely meet together, may not be at work when their boss is, may not see the person they report to as their employer and may have left soon after any communication.

Employers such as the U.K.'s BT or the Swedish Electrolux are working hard to go beyond the use of flexible working as a short-term measure to take a more strategic view, working out where and in what circumstances they can use flexibility most effectively and where long-term, full-time employment is more advantageous and what they can do about the problems that flexibility brings. But this is no easy task. The absolute necessity for employers to adopt more flexible employment means that the problems that flexibility brings need to be addressed much more coherently and systematically by employers and a much more strategic approach adopted. In Europe, arguably, there is already far more flexibility that most commentators have understood hitherto. This may be one area—unlike so many others—where management practice is outstripping management theory. A practice that is little discussed is widespread.

At least the debate has begun.

Endnotes

1. This is an area bedeviled with terminological problems. This paper adopts the terminology most commonly used in Europe, even though it has certain linguistic connotations which may be inaccurate. Even in Europe some commentators prefer the (equally inaccurate) term "atypical working" and some trade unionists talk about "vulnerable work." Certain aspects of this subject are referred to as "contingent working" in the United States of America.

2. This paper is based upon a detailed analysis of the data collected by the Cranfield Network on European HRM (Cranet-E) which was conducted for DGV (A) of the European Commission. The report "Working Time and Contract Flexibility in the European Union" (Brewster, C., Mayne, L., Tregaskis, O., Parsons, D. & Atterbury, S.) was published in September 1969. The support of DGV is gratefully acknowledged, but the views expressed in this article are those of the researchers only and should not be taken to represent those of the Commission.

3. Cranfield Network on European HRM (Cranet-E) is a research network of major business schools across Europe. Current members include: Prof. Dirk Buyens, De Vlerick School voor Management; Prof. Henrik Holt Larsen, Copenhagen Business School; Prof. Arja Ropo, University of Tampere; Prof. Sylvie Roussillon, Groupe ESC Lyon; Prof. Dr. Wolfgang Weber, University of Paderborn; Prof. Wolfgang Mayrhofer, Fakultät Wirtschaftswissenschaften; Dr. Nancy Papalexandris, Athens University of Economics and Business; Dr. Patrick Gunnigle, University of Limerick; Prof. Marco Biagi, Ordinario nell'Universita delgi, Studi di Modena; Drs. Jacob Hoogendoorn, Erasmus Universiteit; Prof. Odd Nordhaug, Norwegian School of Economics and Business Admin; Rita Cunha, Universidade Nova de Lisboa; Prof. Ricard Serlavos, ESADE; Dr. Monica Wåglund, the IPF Institute; Prof. Dr. Martin Hilb, University of St. Gallen.

4. Analysis of the data on task or functional flexibility and on pay flexibility is still to be completed.

References

Atkinson, J. (1984). Manpower strategies for flexible organizations. *Personnel Management*, (August): 32-35.

Atkinson, J. (1985a). *Flexibility, uncertainty and manpower management.* IMS Report No 89, Institute of Manpower Studies, Brighton.

Atkinson, J. (1985b). Flexibility: planning for the uncertain future. *Manpower Policy and Practice*, 1(Summer): 26-29.

Atkinson, J. (1987). Flexibility or fragmentation? The United Kingdom labor market in the eighties. *Labor and Society*, 12(1): 87-105.

Atkinson, J. & Gregory, D. (1986). A flexible future: Britain's dual labor market force. *Marxism Today*, (April): 12-17.

Atkinson, J. & Meager, N. (1986). *Changing working patterns: How companies achieve flexibility to meet new needs.* London: National Economic Development Office.

Bagguley, P. (1991). Post Fordism and enterprise culture: Flexibility, autonomy and changes in economic organization. Pp. 151-170 in R. Keat & N. Abercrombie (Eds.), *Enterprise culture.* London: Routledge.

Bielenski, H., Bielenski, H., Alaluf, M., Atkinson, J., Bellini, R., Castillo, J. J., Donati, P., Graverson, G., Huygen, F., & Wickham, J. (1993). *New forms of work and activity: A survey of experiences at establishment level in eight European countries.* Working paper, European Foundation for the Improvement of Working and Living Conditions, Dublin.

Blyton, P. (1992). The search for workforce flexibility. Pp. 295-318 in B. Towers (Ed.), *Human resource management.* Oxford: Blackwell.

Boyer, R. (1987). Labor flexibilities: Many forms, uncertain effects. *Labor and Society*, 12(1): 107-129.

Boyer, R. (1986): *La flexibilidad del trabajo en Europa: un estudio comparativo de las transformaciones del trabajo asalariado en siete países, entre 1973 y 1985.* Madrid: Ministerio de Trabajo y SS.

Bramble, T. (1988). The flexibility debate: Industrial relations and new management production practices. *Labor and Industry*, 1(2): 187-209.

Bramble, T. & Fieldes, D. (1989). *Post Fordism: Utopian fantasy or historical break?* Paper delivered to the 1989 TASA Conference, Melbourne, December.

Bramble, T. & Fieldes, D. (1992). Post Fordism: Historical break or Utopian fantasy. *Journal of Industrial Relations*, 34(3): 562-579.

Brewster, C. J., Mayne, L., Tregaskis, O., Parsons, D. & Atterbury, S. (1996a). *Working time and contract flexibility in Europe.* Report prepared for the European Commission, DGV.

Brewster, C. J., Tregaskis, O., Hegewisch, A. & Mayne, L. (1996). *Comparative Research in Human Resource Management: A Review and an Example*, 7(3): 585-604.

Brewster, C., Hegewisch, A. & Mayne, L. (1994). Flexible working practices: The controversy and the evidence. In C. Brewster & A. Hegewisch (eds.), *Policy and practice in European human resource management: The Price Waterhouse Canfield survey.* London: Routledge.

Brewster, C., Hegewisch, A. & Mayne, L. (1993). Trends in HRM in Western Europe. In P. Kirkbride (Ed.), *Human resource management in the new Europe of the 1990s.* London: Routledge.

Brewster, C. (1995). Towards a 'European' model of human resource management. *Journal of International Business Studies*, 26(1): 1-21.

Clegg, S. R. (1990). *Modern organizations: Organization studies in the postmodern world.* London: Sage.

Commission of the European Communities 1990 Employment in Europe (pp. 87-100). Directorate-General V, Brussels.

Commission of the EC (1992). The position of women on the labor market: Trends and developments in the 12 member states. *Women of Europe supplements No 36.* Brussels, EC.

Harvey, D. (1991). Flexibility: Threat or opportunity? *Socialist Review, 21*(1): 65-77.

Harvey, D. (1989). *The condition of postmodernity.* Oxford: Basil Blackwell.

Katz, H. (1985). *Changing gears.* Cambridge, MA: MIT Press.

Kern, H. & Schumann, M. (1987). Limits of the division of labour. *Economic and Industrial Democracy, 8*(2): 151-170.

Lash, S. & Urry, J. (1987). *The end of organised capitalism.* Cambridge: Polity Press.

Matthews, J. (1989a). *Tools of change: New technology and the democratisation of work organization.* Sydney: Pluto Press.

Matthews, J. (1989b). *Age of democracy: The politics of post Fordism.* Melbourne: Oxford University Press.

Matthews, J. (1990). The post Ford pill. *Australian Left Review, 118*: 26-30.

Matthews, J. (1992). New production systems: A response to critics and a re-evaluation. *Journal of Australian Political Economy, 30*: 91-128.

Meulders, D. & Wilkin, L. (1987). Labor market flexibility: Critical intro-duction to the analysis of a concept. *Labor and Society, 12*(1): 3-17.

Minford, P. (1995). *Submission to panel of independent forecasters: Her Majesty's treasury.* Her Majesty's Stationery Office, November.

Nollen, S. D. (1992). The cost effectiveness of contingent labor. In *Proceedings 9th World Congress,* Vol. 6 (communication abstracts) International Industrial Relations Association, Geneva.

OECD. (1986a). *Flexibility in the labor market: The current debate.* Paris: Author.

OECD. (1989). *Labor market flexibility: Trends in enterprises.* Paris: Author.

OECD. (1991). *Employment outlook.* Paris: Author.

Piore, M. J. & Sabel, C. (1985). *The second industrial divide: Possibilities for prosperity.* New York: Basic Books.

Pollert, A. (1988a). Dismantling flexibility. *Capital and Class, 34*: 42-75.

Pollert, A. (1988b). The 'flexible firm': Fixation or fact? *Work, Employment and Society, 2*(3): 281-316.

Rees, B. & Brewster, C. (1995). Supporting equality: Patriarchy at work in Europe. *Personnel Review, 24*(1): 19-40.

Social Europe, working time, employment and production + - capacity; reorgani-zation/reduction of working time. (1991). Supplement 4/91 DGV European Commission.

Spink, R. M. (1990). *Overtime working in the U.K.* PhD thesis, Cranfield University, Cranfield School of Management.

Streeck, W. (1987). The uncertainties of management in the management of uncertainty: Employers, labor relations and industrial adjustment. *Employment and Society*, 1(3): 281-308.

Tolliday, S. & Zeitlin, J. (1987). *The automobile industry and its workers: Between Fordism and flexibility*. New York: St. Martin's Press.

TUC. (1996). *Submission to the chancellor of the exchequer prior to the 1996 budget*. TUC, London.

Wareing, A. (1992). Working arrangements and patterns of working hours in Britain. *Employment Gazette*, (March): 88-100.

Woods, S. (Ed.). (1989). P. 21 in *The transformation of work*. London: Hutchinson.

The International Assignment Reconsidered

Reading 3.2
Nakiye A. Boyacigiller

Close to 41% of the major U.S. multinational corporations (MNCs) plan on reducing the number of U.S. nationals assigned overseas.[1] And yet, most MNCs see an increase in the international interaction most managers will be facing. Therein lies a paradox. Just when the need for international expertise is growing, U.S. MNCs are reducing the number of Americans sent overseas, thus depriving both the country and themselves of the opportunity to increase the international experience and knowledge base of our current and future managers.

The orientation most MNCs take toward international assignments needs to be reconsidered. U.S. MNCs must view expatriation as a strategic tool, a very different perspective from that traditionally used. Historically, firms sent managers and professionals overseas to fill positions on a seemingly ad hoc basis, paying little attention either to their selection and training or to the role they could play in the overall organization. Moreover, American firms frequently sent Americans overseas because of ethnocentric attitudes ("We have to assign Americans to key positions because foreigners can't be trusted to handle the job.") Both approaches created problems. Individuals sent overseas without adequate training often failed. Indiscriminate staffing with Americans created resentment among qualified local nationals.

Fortunately, a growing number of human resource professionals and researchers in this area are beginning to speak in terms of strategic international human resource management.[2] International assignments should be utilized to develop future managers with a global orientation and to manage key organizational and country linkages.

Consider two overseas branches of the same U.S.-owned international bank opened in 1975. Both grew to equal size as measured by loans, deposits, and employment. Yet the two branches use very different personnel staffing practices. In Branch A, only 7% of the professionals and managers are U.S. nationals, while in Branch B, U.S. nationals number close to 30%. Why the difference? Is it explained by location? Branch A is located in Copenhagen, Denmark, while Branch B is in Cairo, Egypt. Or

Source: Nakiye Boyacigiller. "The International Assignment Reconsidered." Reprinted by permission of the author.

can it be explained by internal organizational characteristics, such as the branches' complexity? The answer is both.

As suggested by the above example, there are a multitude of national and organizational characteristics that influence the relative utilization of U.S. and local nationals in overseas affiliates. Yet previous research in this area, while providing direction on the employee characteristics to emphasize in selection decisions, has not focused on organizational and national characteristics to consider when staffing overseas affiliates.

To fill this void in our knowledge of international staffing practices, a study was conducted of a major U.S. financial institution, here called ICB, to determine which organizational and environmental factors influence the use of U.S. nationals abroad.[3] ICB is structurally comprised of four regions: North America; Asia; Latin America and the Caribbean; and Europe, the Middle East and Africa. The present regional structure was established in 1974 to "decentralize [ICB's] approach to a coordinated global wholesale banking strategy."[4] The study includes all 84 foreign branches of ICB. Located in 43 different countries, the branches are wholly owned by ICB.

These ICB branches are involved in both wholesale (corporate) and retail (individual) banking to varying degrees. The Asian branches deal primarily in trade finance, while their European counterparts are mainly wholesale operations catering to large multinationals. In Latin America, much of the activity has been project lending and retail banking. The branches differ tremendously in size and scope of operations and the kind of businesses in which they engage. There are significant differences both across regions and within regions.

The study was designed to test the following hypotheses:

- *Political risk:* Greater levels of political risk will lead to a greater proportion of U.S. nationals in professional positions.

- *Cultural distance:* The greater the cultural distance between the host country and the U.S., the greater the proportion of U.S. nationals in professional positions.

- *Competition:* The greater the level of competition with other finance institutions, the greater the proportion of U.S. nationals in professional positions.

- *Interdependence:* The greater the interdependence between the branch and corporate headquarters, the greater the proportion of U. S. nationals in professional positions.

- *Complexity:* The more complex the branch operations, the greater the proportion of U.S. nationals in managerial and staff positions.

- *Cost:* The variance in the cost between a local national and an expatriate will not have an influence on the proportion of U.S. nationals in the branch.

Environmental (Country) Factors to Consider When Staffing Overseas Units _____

This research revealed three factors—political risk, cultural distance, and competition—to be particularly important in explaining the utilization of expatriates in a foreign unit.[5]

Political Risk

What is the level of political risk in the country and how can it be managed? Conventional wisdom suggests that in countries where political risk is high, it is important to have a local profile, that is, to appear to act and look like a local firm. This approach would require minimal use of U.S. personnel.

Politically risky countries are often the most difficult for managers in corporate headquarters to understand. In addition, studies have shown that inherently volatile situations (like one of high political risk) are often accompanied by decisions based on judgments rather than specific structural arrangements to deal with the uncertainty.[6]

Yet how are these judgments to be made? The knowledge and insight a well-placed U.S. national can provide to corporate executives is crucial in environments where garnering the necessary information is problematic. Understanding how to interpret economic, political, and financial signals in an alien environment is difficult even when one is located in the country in question. When one is sitting thousands of miles away in an entirely different milieu, reaching erroneous conclusions is all too possible. Parent nationals located in overseas operations can be important conduits of information. This study found that ICB utilizes more expatriate managers in countries with high political risk ratings, as was hypothesized.

Cultural Distance

Cultural distance refers to the extent that two cultures differ. Key dimensions of culture include such characteristics as how collectivistic or individualistic the culture is, how time is perceived, and how rigidly sex roles are defined. When two cultures differ significantly on these and other cultural dimensions, it is more difficult for individuals from these cultures to communicate and work well together. Strategically placed U.S. nationals play an important interpretative role between the host country culture and the U.S. headquarters offices. This bridging role is clearly evident in a Scandinavian manager's description of an MNC's operations in Japan:

> Nowadays there seems to be a tendency towards "over-Japanization" of the foreign company in Japan; i.e., the top management is, after initial stages of starting up business, staffed entirely with Japanese executives. It has been observed

that this can create serious problems particularly in the communication with the head office overseas. In one actual case, the Japanese president of a joint venture company got so frustrated with this communication problem that he actually resigned and returned to the large Japanese corporation he originally came from. The occasional visitor from the head office cannot possibly understand all the complexities of carrying out business in Japan, and what the Japanese executive in the related case actually wanted was to have an able person from the head office permanently stationed in Japan and with whom he could discuss the various problems on the spot.[7]

My research found that the greater the cultural distance between the host nation and the U.S., the greater the proportion of U.S. nationals in subsidiary management.

Competition

This research found the competition existing in the local environment of the host country to lead to fewer U.S. nationals in the foreign branches. There are two logical explanations as to why this would occur. First, greater competition indicates a greater number of firms (local and foreign) where local nationals are able to acquire banking experience. With ample situations for training in finance and banking, local nationals became more attractive to ICB.

Secondly, in a competitive market, local nationals are a critical resource in garnering more local business. Local nationals often provide critical links to local commerical communities, thus allowing the MNC to gain new business. This is especially true, given that some countries where competition was found to be the highest (e.g., Indonesia, Bahrain, and Malaysia) are also countries where good contacts with local government and business officials are very important.

Cost

Every CEO laments the high cost of sending Americans overseas on assignment. Total expatriate compensation comes to about 2.5 times the employee's U.S. base salary, when such expenses as cost-of-living adjustments, tax equalization, housing, and education are included.[8] Yet the cost of expatriation needs to be understood in a broader framework. First, thinking about cost in averages rather than focusing on individual countries creates a fallacy. The cost of living varies greatly across international borders, thus focusing on average costs can mask real differences. For example, in 1983, the cost of a $36,000-a-year American employee was $61,500 a year in Tokyo, $41,000 in Hong Kong, $71,000 in Bahrain, and $36,000 in Argentina.

Secondly, MNCs need to address the cost issue within a broader frame-work of what the company seeks to gain through overseas assignments. If they use international assignments to develop future upper-level managers with a global orientation and the ability to manage key organizational issues, then absolute cost must be viewed from a very different perspective. While costly in the short term, international assignments appear more useful when perceived as a long-term investment.

Still, one important caveat must be made regarding cost. It is always an important consideration when employees sent overseas fail. Previous research suggests that the reason many U.S. firms have not sent many Americans abroad is their high failure rates overseas.[9] Another study found that when compared to Japanese and European expatriates, American expatriates tend to have significantly larger failure rates (e.g., early returns due to lack of adaptation or ineffective job performance on the job).[10] The failures are not surprising given that assignments are often made hastily, with insufficient time and care paid to selection and training. Studies show that when choosing individuals for overseas sojourns, MNCs focus on technical and managerial competence, assuming that technically competent managers will automatically function effectively overseas. Unfortunately, this is often not the case. Characteristics such as adaptability, ethnocentrism, and the family's resistance to an international sojourn are often neglected and yet frequently lead to overseas failure.[11]

Characteristics of the Foreign Affiliate to Consider When Staffing —————————————————————

After considering the national factors, several characteristics of the overseas affiliate should be considered when deciding on an appropriate staffing policy. The most important are interdependence, complexity, and control mechanisms.

Interdependence

Subsidiaries of MNCs do not operate as closed systems. Typically, they have resource links to other subunits within the MNC as well as ties to firms and customers in host, home, and other countries. This interdependence with other organizations creates important implications for staffing. For example, if a foreign affiliate maintains a high level of interdependence with the U.S. headquarters, placing some U.S. expatriates in management positions facilitates intraorganizational communication and relations. Given significant interdependence with headquarters or other U.S. affiliates, U.S. nationals perform an important role in managing the uncertainty that derives from interdependence. This is clearly evident in the comments of the non-Swedish president of a Swedish joint venture on the appointment of a Swede to the position of production manager:

It was absolutely necessary that Mr. X was appointed. Before he came we were never able to receive any attention from the product divisions when we needed faster deliveries for some reasons or when we needed special blueprints for our own production. As a result, we sometimes had serious production delays. He [Mr. X] has improved the situation a lot in many instances just by knowing whom to contact in Sweden.[12]

Alternatively, if the foreign affiliate has its most important resource ties within the host country, then parent country managers do not provide an equivalent benefit. Intracountry, as opposed to intercountry, interdependencies are best managed by local nationals.

Complexity

Most multinational corporations are comprised of units that differ widely in their levels of complexity. The complexity of an assembly plant in Western Europe is undoubtedly much lower than the complexity of an R&D lab in the same location. Controlling units that have disparate levels of complexity is difficult for MNCs. Complex tasks imply "an increase in information load, information diversity, or rate of information change."[13] Consequently, the amount of information processing necessary to control complex operations is much greater than the information processing required to control less complex units. Given that communication and control is facilitated among managers of the same nationality, it is not surprising that more complex units had more U.S. nationals assigned to them.[14]

Control Mechanisms: Socialization

Given ICB's decentralized approach to global banking strategy, the firm requires several specific control mechanisms to ensure that employees in foreign affiliates act in concert with the parent organization. As an ICB executive stated:

If your major strength is a network of global operations, you must provide that network with a strong *esprit de corps*. As operations are decentralized, we cannot tell the branches what to do. Yet if a branch turns down the loan request of a person that is a key customer for our firm, just because that particular loan does not make sense for that particular branch . . . then the company will risk losing an important customer. Yet the more you decentralize the more you localize those decisions and risk that particular loan not be made. We must make sure that the customer is managed worldwide.

Three ways an organization can achieve control are bureaucratic rules, the use of hierarchy, and socialization. Of these, socialization is the most flexible and least obtrusive. Parent country nationals can provide an invaluable role in socializing local nationals into the MNC's ways of doing business. This is especially important in MNCs where increasing rules and standards may not be possible (because of high complexity and/or differentiation of operations) and increasing socialization may be the only mechanism for increasing control.

Conclusions: Consider Both ————————————————————

Both organizational and country characteristics need to be taken into account when determining how to staff an overseas affiliate. First, and most important, one must assess the interdependencies between the subunit, the host government, local businesses, and corporate head-quarters. Complexity, political risk, and cultural distance increase the inherent difficulty of doing business in the foreign country and gener-ally require greater expatriate presence. In contrast, extensive local competition in the host country in turn increases the importance of local nationals as conduits to the local market.

International staffing decisions need to be tied to other strategic decisions. The emphasis during staffing should be on long-term orga-nizational development and management development and above all on long-term commitment to learning about international markets. If high-potential individuals are carefully selected and trained for over-seas positions, they will not only facilitate the maintenance of an inter-national network of operations in the short term but should be allowed to continue providing informational support upon their return to the U.S. The international education that future executives could acquire in these types of assignments cannot be replicated in any classroom.

Endnotes ————————————————————————————————————

1. Kobrin, S.J. *International Expertise in American Business: How to Learn to Play with the Kids on the Street.* New York: Institute of International Education, 1984.

2. See for example, Adler, N.J. and Ghadar, F. "Globalization and Human Resource Management." To be published in Alan Rugman (ed.), *Research in Global Strategic Management: A Canadian Perspective,* Volume One. Greenwich, Conn.: JAI Press, 1989.

3. For more detail, see Boyacigiller, N.A. "The role of expatriates in the management of interdependence, complexity and risk." Working paper 8703. San Jose State University, Department of Organization and Management.

4. An ICB internal document.

5. An expatriate refers to a parent country national assigned overseas; (e.g., an American IBM employee stationed in Japan for three years). A host national refers to a local national working for the multinational in his or her own country (e.g., a Japanese national working for IBM in Japan).

6. Leblebici, H. and Salancik, G.R. "Effects of environmental uncertainty on information and decision processes in banks." *Administrative Science Quarterly,* 1981, 578-596.

7. Delaryd, B. *The Japan Economic Journal,* May 30, 1972, 20.

8. "High cost of overseas staff." *World Business Weekly,* April 27, 1981, 4, 48.

9. Kobrin, S.J. "Expatriate reduction and strategic control in American multinational corporations." *Human Resource Management,* 1988, 27 (1), 63-76.

10. Tung, R.L. "Expatriate assignments: Enhancing success and minimizing failure." *The Academy of Management Executive,* 1987, 1, 2, 117-125.

11. Tung, R. L. "Selection and training of U.S., European, and Japanese multinational corporations." *California Management Review,* Fall 1982, 57-71.

12. Leksell, L. *Headquarter-Subsidiary Relationships in Multinational Corporations.* Stockholm School of Economics, 1981.

13. Campbell, D.J. Task complexity: A review and analysis. *Academy of Management Review,* 1988, 13 (1), 40-52.

14. On the challenges of managing a multicultural work force, see Adler, N.J. *International Dimensions of Organizational Behavior.* Boston, Mass.: Kent Publishing, 1986. For an in-depth study of the role of the manager, see Mintzberg, *The Nature of Managerial Work.* New York: Harper & Row, 1973.

Computex Corporation

Case 3.1
Martin Hilb

Goteborg, May 30, 1985

Mr. Peter Jones
Vice President—Europe
Computex Corporation
San Francisco / USA

The writers of this letter are the headcount of the Sales Department of Computex Sweden, A.S., except for the Sales Manager.

We have decided to bring to your attention a problem which unsolved probably will lead to a situation where the majority among us will leave the company within a rather short period of time. None of us want to be in this situation, and we are approaching you purely as an attempt to save the team the benefit of ourselves as well as Computex Corporation.

We consider ourselves an experienced, professional, and sales-oriented group of people. Computex Corporation is a company which we are proud to work for. The majority among us have been employed for several years. Consequently, a great number of key customers in different areas of Sweden see us as representatives of Computex Corporation. It is correct to say that the many excellent contacts we have made have been established over years; many of them are friends of ours.

These traits give a very short background because we have never met you. What kind of problem forces us to such a serious step as to contact you?

Problems arise as a result of character traits and behavior of our General Manager, Mr. Miller.

Firstly, we are more and more convinced that we are tools that he is utilizing in order to "climb the ladder." In meetings with us individually, or as a group, he gives visions about the future, how he values us, how he wants to delegate and involve us in business, the importance of cooperation and communication, etc. When it comes to the point, these phrases turn out to be only words.

Mr. Miller loses his temper almost daily, and his outbursts and reactions are not equivalent to the possible error. His mood and views can change almost from hour to hour. This fact causes a

Source: Martin Hilb. "Computex Corporation." © 1985, University of Dallas. Reprinted by permission.

situation where we feel uncertain when facing him and consequently are reluctant to do so. Regarding human relationships,
his behavior is not acceptable, especially for a manager.

The extent of the experience of this varies within the group
due to our location. Some of us are seldom in the office.

Secondly, we have experienced clearly that he has various
means of suppressing and discouraging people within the
organization.

The new "victim" now is our Sales Manager, Mr. Johansson.
Because he is our boss, it is obvious that we regret such a situation, which to a considerable extent influences our working
conditions.

There are also other victims among us. It is indeed very difficult to carry through what is stated in our job descriptions.

We feel terribly sorry and wonder how it can be possible for
one person almost to ruin a whole organization.

If this group consisted of people less mature, many of us
would have left Computex Corporation already. So far only
one has left the company due to the above reasons.

From September 1, two new Sales Representatives are joining
the company. We regret very much that new employees get
their first contact with the company under the present circumstances. An immediate action is therefore required.

It is not our objective to get rid of Mr. Miller as General
Manager. Without going into details, we are thankful for what
he has done to the company from a business point of view. If
he could control his mood, show some respect for his colleagues, keep words, and stick to plans, we believe that we can
succeed under his leadership.

We are fully aware of the seriousness of contacting you, and
we have been in doubt whether or not to contact you directly
before talking to Mr. Miller.

After serious discussions and considerations, we have reached
the conclusion that a problem of this nature unfortunately cannot be solved without some sort of action from the superior. If
possible, direct confrontation must be avoided. It can only
make things worse.

We are hoping for a positive solution.

Six of your Sales Representatives in Sweden

Peter Jones let out a long sigh as he gazed over the letter from
Sweden. "What do I do now?" he thought, and began to reflect on the
problem. He wondered who was right and who was wrong in this
squabble, and he questioned whether he would ever get all the information necessary to make a wise decision. He didn't know much about
the Swedes, and was unsure whether this was strictly a work problem
or a "cross-cultural" problem. "How can I tease those two issues
apart?" he asked himself, as he locked his office and made his way
down the hallway to the elevator.

As Peter pulled out of the parking garage and onto the street, he began to devise a plan to deal with the problem. "This will be a test of my conflict management skills," he thought, "no doubt about it!" As he merged into the freeway traffic from the on-ramp and began his commute home, he began to wish that he had never sent Miller to Sweden in the first place. "But would Gonzalez or Harris have done any better? Would I have done any better?" Few answers seemed to come to him as he plodded along in the bumper-to-bumper traffic on Interstate 440.

Recruiting a Manager for BRB, Israel

Case 3.2
William Roof
Barbara Bakhtari

BRB Inc., a multinational electronics corporation, plans to establish a new subsidiary in Israel. The firm's base is in Los Angeles, California, with a second overseas headquarters in England. The U.S. office staffs and operates six North American divisions and three South American subsidiaries. The U.K. office is responsible for operations in Europe and Asia. The Israeli venture is the company's first business thrust in the turbulent Middle East.

During the past 10 years, BRB's phenomenal growth resulted largely from its ability to enter the market with new, technically advanced products ahead of the competition. The technology mainly responsible for BRB's recent growth is a special type of radar signal processing. With Fourier transforms, BRB's small, lightweight, and inexpensive radar systems outperform the competitions' larger systems in range, resolution, and price. It is this type of lightweight, portable radar technology that has enormous potential for Israel during conflicts with the Arab States.

BRB's human resource functions in the United States and Europe each boast a vice president. John Conners is the Vice President of Human Resources in the United States, and Francis O'Leary is the Vice President of Human Resources in the United Kingdom. Paul Lizfeld, the CEO of BRB, contacted the two vice presidents and told them to recruit a general manager for the Israeli operation. "I don't care who finds him, but he better be right for the job. I cannot afford to replace him in six months. Is that clear!" Lizfeld told them to look independently and then coordinate together to select the right person. They knew that their jobs could be in jeopardy with this task.

The two human resource operations were independent, and each was managed individually. Recruiting processes differed between U.S. and U.K. operations. Each had different organizational structures and corporate cultures. The only link between the two was Lizfeld's strong micromanagement style, which emphasized cost control.

Source: William Roof and Barbara Bakhtari. "Recruiting a Manager For An Israeli Subsidiary." Reprinted by permission.

U.S. Operations ————————————————————————————

John Conners has worked for BRB for the past 20 years. He started with a degree in engineering and worked in the engineering department. After earning his M.B.A. in human resource management from UCLA, he transferred to the human resource department. Management felt that someone with an engineering background could hire the best technical employees for BRB. With BRB's high turnover rate, they felt that someone who could relate to the technical side of the business could better attract and screen the right people for the organization. BRB promoted Conners to vice president three years ago, after he hired the staffs for the subsidiaries in Peru and Brazil. Except for the general managers, they were all correct fits. Conners felt that the problem with the general managers was an inability to work with Lizfeld.

John Conners looked at many different strategies to determine how to begin recruiting for the Israeli position. He wanted to be sure he found the right person for the job. The first step in choosing the ideal candidate was to determine the selection criteria.

Conners defined the task in Israel to include control and management of BRB's Israeli operations. The GM must work with the Israeli government both directly and indirectly. The political unrest in Israel also requires the GM to conduct sensitive transactions with the Israeli government. This person would also work directly with Lizfeld, taking direction from him and reporting regularly to him.

As with many countries in the Middle East, Israel was in turmoil. Conners actually knew very little about the Israeli culture, but decided to ask different associates who had past dealings with Israel. He knew that the threat of war constantly hung over Israel. The country was also suffering from high inflation rates and troubled economics. Lately, he also learned that the country had become divided over certain political and cultural issues. The person accepting this job needed nerves of steel and extraordinary patience.

Conners decided the selection criteria that would be important for the candidate included technical skill, cultural empathy, a strong sense of politics, language ability, organizational abilities, and an adaptive and supportive family. He also felt that the GM would have to have the following characteristics: persuasiveness, ability to make decisions, resourcefulness, flexibility, and adaptability to new challenges. Now all he needed to do was find a person who had all these attributes.

He decided to begin his search for candidates within the organization. He knew this route had both advantages and disadvantages. Since BRB was still in the beginning stages of internationalization in Israel, a "home country" presence might prove to be very helpful. Lizfeld would appreciate this. The disadvantages would be many. It might be very difficult to find someone willing to relocate in Israel. The increased cost of living and the political unrest make it a tough package to sell. Conners knew of the "Israeli mentality." He also knew he would have to take care in sending someone who might either overpower the Israelis or break under their aggressive business style. Conners knew that Lizfeld wanted to have the home country atmosphere in Israel and planned to be very active in the management of Israeli operations.

The second option Conners had was to recruit from outside the company. The ideal candidate would have both domestic and international experience. Conners could recruit either by contacting an employment agency or by placing an ad in the *Wall Street Journal*. He thought he could find a person with the right qualifications, but he also knew it would be difficult to find someone Lizfeld liked outside the company. Conners had hired two managers for the South American offices, and Lizfeld had driven them over the edge within six months. Conners knew that he had to be extra careful. One more "unqualified" candidate might put his own job on the line.

Conners found three potential candidates for the Israeli position. One candidate, Joel Goldberg, was a recommendation from the headhunter Conners had commissioned. Goldberg had thirty-five years of electronics and radar experience. He had been CEO of Radar Developments Incorporated, a major electronics corporation in New York. Goldberg had taken control of Radar Developments Incorporated in 1981. By 1986, the company had tripled sales and increased profits fivefold. Goldberg had the technical knowledge to perform the job. He also had the necessary individual characteristics Conners felt would be important for this position. Goldberg had studied in Israel on a kibbutz for two years after college, spoke fluent Hebrew, and was a practicing Jew. He wanted to retire in Israel in a few years. Conners worried that Goldberg would not stay with the company long enough to establish a solid organization. Goldberg also liked running his own show, and that created a potential problem with Lizfeld.

The next candidate was Robert Kyle, Vice President of BRB's radar electronics department. Kyle had been with BRB for more than twenty years and headed two other international divisions for BRB in Japan and Canada. Kyle was familiar with the international process and the BRB corporate culture. Lizfeld had given him excellent reviews in the other two international positions. He had strong management skills and was highly respected both within the organization and in the industry. Kyle received his Ph.D. from MIT in electrical engineering and his M.B.A. from Dartmouth. He had the technical expertise and was familiar with the company and its procedures. Conners was afraid of Kyle's cultural acceptance in Israel since he did not speak the language and was not familiar with Israeli attitudes. He could require Kyle to participate in extensive cultural training, but Conners still had some reservations about sending a gentile to head operations in Israel.

The last candidate was Rochelle Cohen, an Israeli who relocated to the United States in 1982. She originally relocated to assist the head of the electronics division of Yassar Aircraft, an Israeli company that opened its first international office in 1978. Cohen did very well and brought Israeli thoroughness and assertiveness to the U.S. operations. She now wanted to move back to Israel to be with her family. Additionally, her fiancé recently relocated in Israel, and she wanted to return to marry and raise a family. Cohen had experience in the international circuit, having worked in the United States, United Kingdom, and Israel, but Conners was still worried about hiring her. Although she had the political knowledge and the proper connections in the Israeli government, the problems were her young age, lack of technical expertise, and sex.

Conners contacted O'Leary to see what progress he had made. Knowing the consequences that would come from this decision, Conners realized it was going to be a difficult one to make.

U.K. Operations ————————————————————————

Francis O'Leary reflected on his past eight years with BRB. His rise from the strife-torn east side of Belfast to BRB's corporate vice president for human resources was extraordinary. While most Irish business careers in large English firms peak at middle management, O'Leary's actually began at that point. He proved his capabilities through hard work, constant study, and an astute ability to judge the character and substance of people on first sight. His task of finding a suitable general manager for the new division in Israel offered a challenge he readily accepted.

O'Leary excelled at recruiting and hiring innovative employees who brought technical ideas with them to BRB. The management structure at BRB in England did not support internal growth of technology and innovation, so new ideas and technological advances were not rewarded with commensurate fiscal incentives. As such, turnover of experienced innovators forced O'Leary to recruit and hire innovation on a "rotating stock" basis. It was this success in hiring innovators that broke him from the shackles of middle management and thrust him to the top of the corporation. Four years ago, through a well-planned and well-executed recruiting program, O'Leary hired Rani Gilboa, a young Israeli engineer and former Israeli army officer. For Gilboa, the need for lightweight, inexpensive battlefield systems drove a desire to approach the problem from a new aspect: signal processing. After graduate study in this field, Gilboa sought and found a company that would support his concepts. That company was BRB. Gilboa's subsequent contributions to BRB's profits secured his and O'Leary's positions atop their respective disciplines within the firm.

Since that time, O'Leary had other successes hiring innovators from Israel. This stemmed largely from his tireless self-study of Israeli culture. With a feel for the Israeli people rivaling that of an "insider," O'Leary enjoyed success in pirating established innovators from Israeli firms. Now, he faced the task of recruiting and hiring a general manager for the newly established electronics division near Haifa.

Selecting the right manager would be more difficult than expected. With his knowledge of the Israeli culture, O'Leary knew intuitively that an Israeli should head the new division. Acceptance by the division's employees, ability to speak Hebrew, spousal support, and knowledge of Israeli government regulations and tax structures were vital to the success of the new division. Unfortunately, BRB's CEO preferred home country presence in the new division and directed O'Leary to recruit with that as the top priority. After O'Leary presented a strong case, however, the CEO agreed to review all candidates. Another potential problem arose when Lizfeld, the CEO, announced a hands-on management style with plans to participate actively in the management of the Israeli division. To O'Leary, this meant that Western values, along with the current innovative recruiting strategy practiced in England, would extend to Israel as well.

Until recently, O'Leary's recruiting for management positions concentrated on internal promotions. A known performer from within was a better bet than an outsider. When current employees could not meet the job requirements, O'Leary typically turned to newspapers as his primary source of candidates. The recent emergence of reputable executive placement services in England gave him an additional sourcing tool. At times, O'Leary had turned to social contacts, job centers, and the internal labor market as candidate sources, but the percentages of good leads from these were comparatively low .

After months of reading résumés, introductory letters, and job applications, three candidates emerged for the position in Israel. It was now up to O'Leary to decide the candidate he would recommend to Lizfeld.

Michael Flack worked for BRB for more than nineteen years. After graduating from Cambridge College with a degree in general engineering, Flack joined the company as a mechanical engineer. Initially, he worked in the mechanical design group of the radar division. After five years, BRB promoted Flack to engineering section manager. While in this position, he enjoyed various successes in radar miniaturization design. During his eleventh year, BRB again promoted Flack to department head in the manufacturing engineering group. Emphasis in this position shifted from design to production. During his seventeenth year, he became director of engineering design, where he was responsible for managing forty-three engineers' efforts in new-product design.

Flack had no international experience, and he was a reputed "tinkerer." He liked to spend time in the labs designing mechanical components along with his engineers. This generated tremendous esprit within his department but often resulted in inattention to his administrative responsibilities.

Rani Gilboa thought his friend Yair Shafrir was perfect for the position. Shafrir was currently vice-president of engineering at Elta

Electronics in Israel. Elta is one of Israel's top radar firms, with several products proven in actual combat during the last Arab-lsraeli conflict. Shafrir received his degree in electrical engineering from the University of Jerusalem. He had spent his professional career in Israel, usually changing companies to accept promotions. He had been with four companies since graduating from the university nineteen years ago. Shafrir was a strong-willed, organized individual who took pride in his record of technical management accomplishments. He had been able to complete projects on schedule and within budget over 70 percent of the time, a rare feat for an Israeli company. This record resulted mainly from the force of his personal leadership and strength of will. With his entire career spent in Israeli companies, O'Leary had little doubt that Shafrir could manage BRB's new electronics division. Culturally, he was perfect for the job. O'Leary had concerns, however, about Paul Lizfeld's injection of Western culture through his active management plan. The obstinate Shafrir, with no international business experience, might resent the interference.

A well-placed advertisement in the *London Times'* employment section drew a number of responses. One of the three final candidates responded to the ad about four weeks after it appeared in the *Times*.

Harold Michaelson was an English citizen of Jewish faith. Michaelson's family fled Poland in 1938 when Harold's father insisted that the "Nazi madman" would never attack England, especially after Prime Minister Chamberlain's successful visit to Munich. Harold was born to the newly naturalized couple in 1940. Later, he attended college in the United States, where he earned both bachelor's and master's degrees in electrical engineering at Georgia Tech. After graduating, Harold spent two years with General Electric until his father's illness forced him to return to England. He accepted an engineering position with Marconi, and he has remained with that company. Shortly after his return, his father died. Michaelson continued to take care of his mother for the next year. Mrs. Michaelson had always dreamed of living in the Jewish homeland—a dream not shared by her husband. One year after his death, she joined her sister's family in Haifa. Harold had readily accepted a position with Marconi in Israel to work on the new Israeli defense fighter LAVI. Unfortunately, cancellation of the LAVI program also canceled his chances to work in Israel for Marconi. At the time of the interview, Harold was vice president of engineering for Marconi's air radio division. He was also the youngest vice president in the corporation. His background in engineering and administrative functions, coupled with his ability to speak Hebrew, made Harold a strong candidate for the position. During the interview, he mentioned his mother's failing health and her refusal to leave Israel. He intended, if selected, to take care of her there. O'Leary wondered if that was Harold's main reason for wanting to live in Israel. Would he still want to live and work there if he lost his mother? O'Leary was anxious to discuss his candidates with John Conners.

Part 4

MANAGEMENT DEVELOPMENT

Women Managers and International Assignments: Some Recommendations for Bridging the Gap

Reading 4.1
Efrat Elron
Ronit Kark

Though the number of women expatriates is on the rise, international assignments still remain a rarity for women. In 1996, women accounted for only 14% of the total expatriate managerial population (Solomon, 1998) and only 4% of the executives holding the highest managerial positions in international subsidiaries (Elron, 1997). As companies face growing global competitive pressures, it becomes increasingly important to realize the organizational advantages of having women expatriates. At the same time, it is necessary to understand the reasons for the low number of women expatriates and to begin to find ways to overcome the obstacles women face in procuring overseas assignments.

The number of women managers has grown dramatically over the past two decades, and they now account for more than 40% of the managers in the U.S. workforce (although only 3% have reached the level of senior manager). Studies comparing the leadership styles of men and women and their effectiveness as managers have reached several conclusions: (1) Women have a tendency to adopt a more democratic participative managerial style and a less autocratic or directive managerial style than men (Eagly & Johnson, 1990). (2) Contrary to the expectation that women will lead in an interpersonally oriented style and men in a task-oriented style, female and male leaders do not differ in their use of these two styles in organizational settings (although gender differences were found in laboratory experiments and assessment studies (Eagly & Johnson, 1990). (3) Transformational leadership (similar to the concept of charismatic leadership) motivates followers by transforming their needs, values, preferences, and aspirations, while changing the followers' focus from

Source: Efrat Elron and Ronit Kark. "Women Managers and International Assignments: Some Recommendations for Bridging the Gap." Reprinted by permission of the author.

self-interest to collective interest. Many studies (Yukl, 1998) point to a positive relationship between transformational leadership and effectiveness. Women leaders in a variety of contexts were found to be highly transformational (e.g., Druskat, 1994). (4) The research literature focusing on gender and the effectiveness of leaders shows that aggregated over organizational and laboratory studies, male and female leaders were equally effective (Eagly, Karau, & Makhijani, 1995).

Women as Expatriates: A Forgotten Resource

In the past decade, the status of formal hierarchy as a major source of organizational authority has declined, while cooperation, teamwork, and workers' participation have become more important. Due to these changes, there is a need for managers to adopt transformational leadership approaches that incorporate participation and the ability to nurture and develop subordinates. The need for such new patterns of modern management is highly evident in transnational environments, which are increasingly organized into networks of equals and can therefore enable organizations to perceive women, as well as men, as talented domestic and expatriate managers. Based on the findings of the research literature cited above, women would seem to be prime candidates to manage in transnational environments.

One of the key global issues facing companies today is how to transform the organization internally to become globally competitive. Therefore, one of the major challenges of managing the global workforce is to identify and utilize *all* top performers who will be effective in a global environment. The larger the pool of candidates for any job, the more likely that the best people will be selected. To increase the number of candidates for expatriate positions, which are critical to both the formulation and the implementation of a company's strategy, companies need to consider men and women equally.

An additional challenge of managing the global workforce involves harnessing the benefits of its diversity. Diversity and the multiple perspectives it brings can be a source of innovation, which is a key component of global competitiveness. Moreover, diversity at the upper levels of overseas subsidiaries has been shown to directly enhance subsidiary performance (Elron, 1997). By bringing a new form of diversity to international operations that have been primarily male dominated, expatriate women can have an impact on their company's bottom line.

Overseas Adjustment Issues

Success in overseas assignments depends on the personality, skills, and behaviors of the expatriate. It can be argued that women may have a certain advantage in overseas assignments due to their past experiences and socialization. For example, the Other-Oriented personality dimension has been found to relate to the expatriate's adjustment in the host country (Mendenhall & Oddou, 1985). This dimension consists of activities and attributes that enhance the expatriate's ability to interact effectively with host-nationals and includes relationship skills, being willing to communicate with host-nationals, and having respect and empathy for others.

Studies on women in leadership positions reveal that women lead with more relational and empathetic styles than do men (Helgesen, 1990). Patterns unique to women's socialization make them comfortable with encouraging participation and facilitating inclusion, sharing power and information, and enhancing others' self-worth (Rosener, 1990). All these specific skills are related to the Other-Oriented dimension.

Another dimension that relates to the success of expatriate managers is the Perceptual dimension (Mendenhall & Oddou, 1985), which involves the consciousness of social cues and behaviors, attentiveness to them, and the ability to interpret them. In organizations men tend to perceive women—and women tend to perceive themselves—as the "other"—even as "outsiders." Not being a part of the dominant majority in an organizational setting and experiencing the status of "other" most likely requires women to develop high levels of adaptation, as well as higher levels of sensitivity and understanding of social cues. This experience, then, may help women on overseas assignments to formulate accurate perceptions of their encounters with host-nationals, where they are once again in the role of the "other."

Barriers to Expatriate Assignments _____

Despite the potential advantages of utilizing women in global assignments, the number of women in these positions remains low. Discrimination against sending women overseas still exists. Women expatriates who were interviewed by Adler (1987) reported that they had difficulty convincing their companies to grant them their foreign assignments. Their reports reflect findings from interviews with human resource vice presidents and managers from North American companies (Adler, 1994). More than half the firms reported resisting assigning women overseas because they assumed that female managers generally were not willing to go abroad. The firms also reported that they believed that women managers would face cultural biases in a foreign location.

Women in organizations also face the "glass ceiling," a barrier that prevents them from reaching the upper-middle or senior-level positions from which many expatriate managers come. Moreover, the same mechanisms that cause the glass ceiling are also part of the reason why women who do reach these positions are overlooked as candidates for overseas assignments. Thus, understanding the barriers that women face is important not only to organizations, but also to women managers—as more companies expand their global presence, overseas assignments and international experience become critical to a manager's promotion and advancement.

A common perception is that women are less motivated than men to become international managers. Are women really less interested than men in going on overseas assignments? Nancy Adler (1984) surveyed more than a thousand graduating MBAs from the United States, Canada, and Europe and found that men and women were equally interested in pursuing international careers. More than 80% of the MBAs—with no differences between men and women—indicated that they wanted an international assignment at some point during their careers. In practice, however, family and other concerns may cause some of the women (and men) to change their responses when an actual offer for an overseas assignment materializes.

Many women who are potential candidates for overseas assignments face the challenge of dual-career marriages. The challenges associated with spousal adjustment seem to be magnified from the point of view of male partners. Western society tends to judge men by their careers more than it does women. Thus, men face a higher risk of being unable to adjust when accompanying a woman expatriate manager because it is less acceptable for men not to work or to become the secondary breadwinner, as may be necessary in the foreign location. Limited employment opportunities, visa restrictions on work permits, and company nepotism rules that prohibit the employment of both husband and wife are among the barriers to finding employment overseas and to career advancement for the expatriate's partner.

The role of the spouse has been identified as critical in successful expatriation (Black & Stephens, 1989). Companies, however, do not always consider the needs of the expatriate's partner. When asked to identify the best and worst aspects of the experience of living abroad, expatriate employees reported more unfavorable than favorable family-related experiences by a ratio of four to one (Guzzo, Noonan, & Elron, 1993).

Examples of unfavorable family-related experiences included difficulties related to the spouse's career and family stress. When asked about the assistance they received from their companies, expatriate managers reported that they rarely received help in locating spousal employment outside the firm and that very few spouses were employed in the firm itself (Guzzo, Noonan, & Elron, 1994).

What Should Firms Do?

International firms need to take a more proactive approach to dual-career couples. This approach should include corporate activities that expatriate spouses say are the most important to them (Punnett, 1997):

- Partner career counseling and job placement both before departure and in the foreign location. Coordination of employment networks with other international organizations would enhance the effectiveness of such services.

- A pre-move trip in order to make employment contacts.

- Office space and secretarial support in the foreign location if needed for job hunting.

- Compensation for the partner's lost wages and benefits.

- For expatriate couples who opt for commuter marriage, financial benefits packages aimed at meeting the special needs commuting entails, including telephone and airfare expenses.

Global assignments, by their very nature, affect the entire family and not just the employee on the assignment or the spouse. Currently, many career women still hold the major responsibility for managing the house and the family (Hochschild, 1989) and may therefore be more reluctant to relocate the whole family for the sake of their own careers. To help expatriate women and their families with the move, companies must offer comprehensive pre-departure training for the whole family. Part of the training should be aimed specifically at explaining the advantages of an international move for the family (e.g., experiencing new surroundings together, language and educational opportunities, etc.), as families that perceive the move positively adjust better to living in the host country (Caligiuri, Hyland, Joshi, & Bross, 1998). And when the expatriate and her family reach their foreign location, the company should continue its assistance by helping the family find schools for the children and reliable child-care providers.

Not only can these programs help solve the specific problems of the dual-career couple, but they can also improve the expatriate woman's perceptions of organizational support and with it her positive view of the organization. These positive attitudes, in turn, enhance the expatriate's organizational commitment and adjustment to the host country (Guzzo, Noonan, & Elron, 1994; Caligiuri, Hyland, Joshi, & Bross, 1998).

Women Managers and Cultural Biases _____

Almost all cultures have different expectations of how men and women should behave. Decision-makers are concerned about a woman's ability to function effectively in countries where strong biases against women in managerial roles exist (Adler, 1994). This concern at least partly explains the tendency of U.S.-based companies to send women to English-speaking countries (Moran, Stahl, & Boyer Inc., 1988), where the culture is more similar to the United States, although there is no evidence that women perform better in these countries than elsewhere.

Interviews with expatriate women regarding cultural biases reveal a somewhat different picture. Westwood and Leung (1994) report that overall the gender differentiations and sexist practices and attitudes found in Hong Kong are not invasive in the work environment. Business pragmatism takes precedence there; provided people can perform, gender in the workplace is something of a nonissue for many of the locals.

Women expatriates are seen first as foreigners and only secondly as women by most host-nationals (Adler, 1987). They are therefore less constrained than the local women by the limiting norms of the local culture. Consequently, even in cultures where local women do not normally become managers, being female is not necessarily a handicap for an expatriate female manager. Furthermore, the presence of women expatriates who serve as role models may expand managerial options for local women, thereby increasing the pool of local candidates for positions in the subsidiary.

In a survey of women managers on international assignments in countries around the world (Adler, 1987), more women described their gender as an advantage than as a disadvantage. They said they may find a warmer welcome because they are a novelty, and because they are more visible, clients are curious about them and want to meet them. Women managers often benefit from a halo effect—because they are rare, they are assumed to be outstanding by the host-nationals. Difficulties do exist, however, for women on international assignments. The women in the study had encountered some unequal treatment and sexist attitudes and behaviors and were well aware that they had to strive harder than men (Westwood & Leung, 1994).

What can companies do both to correct misconceptions and to solve the real problems that are still out there?

- Do not assume that foreigners will treat women expatriates the same way they treat local women.

- Provide pre-departure training for women that includes not only information on the culture, values, and traditions of the host country and its people but also an analysis of how these may affect the woman manager in particular. For example, what is considered sexist in the United States may not be in the host culture. It is important that the training not be perceived as a way to discourage women from international assignments. The sessions should include tactics for addressing potential difficulties, rather than merely listing potential problems (Feltes, 1993).

- At the foreign location use local consultants who are familiar with both the culture and the needs of local businesses to identify potential difficulties.

- Establish clear and consistent rules of conduct at the work site.

- Avoid appointing a single "token" woman to a location when possible. Filling multiple positions with women will be perceived as a commitment to promote the best regardless of gender and will also enable the women expatriates to find support among their colleagues. Moreover, women have been found to be more effective as leaders when their subordinates and colleagues include women as well as men.

- Provide a strong show of support from senior management, which will give expatriate women more credibility as competent managers.

Home Company Barriers: Glass Ceilings and Glass Walls_____

Corporate "glass ceilings" and "glass walls" help to explain why women find it harder than men to get expatriate assignments. The glass ceiling phenomenon includes all the subtle and obvious barriers resulting from personal and organizational biases that have prevented talented women from advancing to the influential leadership positions from which many expatriates are chosen. Glass walls (Lopez, 1992) refer to the barriers that have limited women's lateral mobility in organizations, blocking their entrance to various jobs and organizational domains that are defined as masculine, expatriation being one of them. It is important to note that in most situations the discrimination against women is not deliberate but is part of a system of unconscious behaviors and values that exist in the culture of many organizations.

One dynamic that limits women is the tendency to "think manager—think male," which is a global phenomenon (Schein, Mueller, Lituchy, & Liu, 1996). Traits that are assumed to belong to men (e.g., a tough-minded approach to problems, analytical abilities, a capacity to set aside personal, emotional considerations in the interest of task accomplishment) are perceived as contributing to managerial and organizational effectiveness. As these perceptions are more salient the higher up on the organizational ladder the position is, women find it harder to get promoted to top positions.

It is often difficult—if not impossible—to predict the outcomes of decisions and organizational processes. As a consequence, managers try to fulfill their need for some form of certainty in a world of uncertainty by surrounding themselves with people whom they trust. Oftentimes, we perceive those who are most similar to us as more trustworthy than others. Hence, senior male managers often tend to promote other male managers, causing a deselection of women. The role of the expatriate involves even more uncertainties than does the domestic manager's role, and experience and empirical knowledge about the characteristics and qualifications needed to succeed overseas are usually not widely manifested throughout most companies. Therefore, this "similar-to-me" effect very likely plays a central role in the recruitment of expatriate managers (Antal & Izraeli, 1993).

Also related to the notion of glass walls is the translation of the traditional division of labor between men and women into the current issue of the domestic versus the expatriate manager. Typically, the private sphere, or the household, was seen as the woman's place, whereas the man was more visible in the public sphere, or the workplace. It has been suggested that globalization is redefining the boundaries between the private and the public domains.

If this is true, then the national managerial "space" is becoming the domestic arena, whereas overseas managerial positions are viewed as a more valuable (Calas & Smircich, 1993) but also more dangerous and adventurous domain. Thus, an organization may tend to "keep" women in safer domestic management positions, while sending men to the more dangerous and heroic international positions.

The biases described above may also continue to operate once women expatriates are overseas. The women expatriates interviewed by Adler (1987) found the company often limited their opportunities and scope of activities. They revealed that most of their problems were a result of their relationships with peers and superiors in their own home companies, rather than with clients, local managers, and workers.

Better use of human potential, including women's potential, will make multinational corporations more competitive in the global environment. A firm can do many things to improve the selection and support of its women expatriates. A committed firm will first and foremost increase the awareness of its decision-makers to both the biases and the real problems that could be affecting their human resource selection practices for overseas assignments. Moreover, such firms will ask women whether they want to go abroad, rather than assuming that they are not interested. Company decision-makers might also keep the following points in mind.

- Ask both seasoned women expatriates and women candidates for future overseas positions what kind of support they believe is needed to help them succeed. Too often human resource managers assume they know what expatriates need, when, in reality, they do not have a clear understanding of the expatriate experience.

- Help women break through the glass ceiling and glass walls. Consider implementing an organization-wide diversity program, if necessary, to increase women's chances for being selected to expatriate positions.

- Implement career development programs. Actively encourage women managers to consider the advantages of a global assignment, and ask them to include the possibility in their career plans.

- Publicize the success of women expatriates and have them serve as role models. Bring in women repatriates or women expatriates who are on home leave to discuss their experiences with groups of employees. Also, have them support and give more detailed information to women managers who have been assigned as future expatriates.

- Grant women expatriates on assignment the full status that comes with their job to signal the company's commitment to them.

A woman who is interested in becoming an expatriate can do the following to enhance her chances of being selected:

- Actively manage your career. Be persistent in educating your company about the possibilities and advantages of sending women abroad and about your own personal value as an expatriate. Point out the assumptions that might wrongly influence decisions about your overseas assignments.

- If a global assignment is a high priority, initially condition your acceptance of employment on the availability of such opportunities.

- Contact other expatriate women for help before you leave and when you are on the assignment. An active network of women can be supportive and valuable.

- Discuss the implications of an international assignment and strategies to overcome possible difficulties with your partner before it becomes a reality.

Conclusion

Women expatriate managers are too important for multinational corporations to overlook in their international staffing processes. Human resources managers and senior managers, together with the women of their corporations, need to understand and fight against the biases that lead to the exclusion of women from global assignments. By creating an action plan that works toward increasing the number of women in the worldwide managerial workforce, they can increase the effectiveness of their organizations as well.

References

Acker, J. (1990). Hierarchies, jobs, bodies: A theory of gendered organizations. *Gender & Society*, 4, 139-158.

Adler, N. J. (1994). Women managers in a global economy. *Training and Development*, April, 731-736.

Adler, N. J. (1987). Pacific Basin managers: A gajin, not a woman. *Human Resource Management*, 26(2), 169-191.

Adler, N. J. (1984). Women do not want international careers: And other myths about international management. *Organizational Dynamics*, Autumn, 66-78.

Antal, A. B., and Izraeli, D. N. (1993). A global comparison of women in management: Women managers in their homeland and as expatriate. In E. A. Fagenson (Ed.), *Women in management: Trends, issues and challenges in managerial diversity*, 52-96. Newbury Park: Sage Publications.

Black, J. S., and Stephens, G. K. (1989). The influence of the spouse on American expatriate adjustment and intent to stay in Pacific Rim overseas assignment. *Journal of Management*, 15, 429-544.

Calas, M. B., and Smircich, L. (1993). Dangerous liaisons: The "feminine-in-management" meets the "Globalization." *Business Horizons*, March-April, 71-81.

Caligiuri, P. M., Hyland, M. M., Joshi, A., and Bross, A. (1998). Testing a theoretical model for examining the relationship between family adjustment and expatriates' work adjustment. *Journal of Applied Psychology*, 598-614.

Druskat, V. (1994). Gender and leadership style: Transformational and transactional leadership in the Roman Catholic Church. *Leadership Quarterly*, 5, 99-109.

Eagly, A., and Johnson, B. (1990). Gender and leadership style: A meta-analysis. *Psychological Bulletin*, 108, 233-256.

Eagly, A. H., Karau, S. J., and Makhijani, M. G. (1995). Gender and the effectiveness of leaders: A meta-analysis. *Psychological Bulletin*, 117, 125-145.

Elron, E. (1997). Top management teams within multinational corporations: Effects of cultural heterogeneity. *Leadership Quarterly*, 8, 393-412.

Feltes, P., and Robinson, R. (1993). American female expatriate and Civil Rights Act of 1991. *Business Horizons*, 36(2).

Guzzo, R. A., Noonan, K. A., and Elron, E. (1993). Employer influence on the expatriate experience: Limits and implications for retention in overseas assignments. In *Research in personnel and human resource management*, 323-338. Greenwich, CT: JAI Press.

Guzzo, R. A., Noonan, K. A., and Elron, E. (1994). Expatriate managers and the psychological contract. *Journal of Applied Psychology*, 79, 600-608.

Helgesen, S. (1990). *The female advantage: Women's ways of leadership*. New York: Doubleday Currency.

Hochschild, A. R. (1989). *The second shift*. New York: Avon Books.

House, R. J., and Howell, J. M. (1992). Personality and charismatic leadership. *Leadership Quarterly*, 3, 81-108.

Lopez, J. A. (1992). Study says women face glass walls as well as ceilings. *Wall Street Journal*, March 3, B1-B8.

Martin, P. Y. (1996). Gendering and evaluating dynamics: Men, masculinities, and management. In: D. Collins & J. Hearn (Eds.), *Men as managers, managers as men: Critical perspectives on man, masculinity and management*, 186-209. London: Saga.

Mendenhall, M., & Oddou, G. (1985). The dimensions of expatriate acculturation: A review. *Academy of Management Review*, 10(1), 39-47.

Moran, Stahl, and Boyer Inc. (1988). *Status of American female expatriate employees: Survey results.* Boulder, CO: Moran, Stahl, & Boyer Inc.

Punnett, B. J. (1997). Towards effective management of expatriate spouses. *Journal of World Business*, 32, 243-357.

Punnett, B. J, Crocker, O., and Stevens, M. A. (1992). The challenge for women expatriates and spouses: Some empirical evidence. *International Journal of Human Resource Management*, 3, 585-592.

Rosener, J. (1990). Ways women lead. *Harvard Business Review*, 68, 119-125.

Schein, V., Mueller, R., Lituchy, T., and Liu, J. (1996). Think manager-think male: A global phenomenon? *Journal of Organizational Behavior*, 17, 33-41.

Solomon, C. M. (1998). Women expats: Shattering the myths. *Workforce*, May 1998, 5-10.

Westwood, R. I., and Leung, S. M. (1994). The female expatriate experience: Coping with gender and culture. *International Studies of Management and Organization*, 24(3), 70-85.

Windham International and the National Foreign Trade Council. (1996). 1996 Global Relocation Trends Survey Report. New York.

Yukl, G. (1998). *Leadership in organizations.* Englewood Cliffs: Prentice Hall.

Management Development: An African Focus

Reading 4.2
Merrick L. Jones

Anyone interested in issues of Third World development is painfully aware of the complexities, contradictions, and cruel paradoxes involved. Recent events in Africa have thrown the issues into stark focus. Africa is a cockpit of turbulent change, where the transition from traditional societies to modern nation states confronts those involved with painful and complex puzzles. The myriad problems facing the continent are reflected daily in Western newspapers. Great human tragedies unfold as whole nations are devastated by droughts and other natural calamities. Famine, population growth, deforestation, the advancing deserts, civil wars, border disputes, military coups, political intrigues, one-party states, tribalism, guerrilla movements: the catalogue is reported with scant sympathy—indeed, it sometimes seems, with gleeful smugness. Meanwhile, the peoples of Africa struggle with the awful natural and man-made problems that confront them in building nation states within the arbitrary boundaries bequeathed to them by the departed colonial powers. No one can doubt that it will be a long and supremely difficult struggle. There have been, and will be, many failed experiments, many dead ends, many setbacks in the process. But one central reality seems inescapable: in coping with acute scarcity of resources and lack of developed infrastructure, great skills of management and organization will be imperative.

The question is: Will the importation of management concepts and practices from the industrialized West meet Africa's needs? Questions concerning the transferability across nations of management concepts and practices are complex and controversial. There is as yet no consensus about the nature of the arguments involved or about how empirical data can usefully be obtained and compared.

Onyemelukwe [1] considers the educational implications, asserting that "The belief is that whatever is not going well can always be rectified by training. The result is a staggering investment in foreign-orientated training schemes with little in the way of return in investment." And:

Source: Merrick L. Jones. "Management Development: An African Focus." This article first appeared in *Management Education and Development*, Volume 17, Part 3, Autumn 1986, pp. 202–216. We are grateful to the Editor for permission to reprint it here.

Looking through courses and lectures on management organised in various parts of Africa by universities and institutes of management, one is faced with a galaxy of do-it-yourself kits and shorthand prescriptions. . . . it is the refusal of many authors and researchers in the field of management to give a significant place to social and cultural factors that limits the usefulness of their work.

In this paper I consider some of the issues in relation to an investigation of managerial thinking in one African country, Malawi. In particular, I focus on the data concerning the way Malawian managers think about their work, and implications for management education and training. Very briefly, the study involved 105 Malawian senior and middle-level managers from both the private and public sectors in a questionnaire survey designed to elicit their thinking on aspects of their work, especially their satisfactions and their relationships with subordinates. The questionnaire was based on an instrument used originally by Haire, Ghiselli, and Porter [2] in 14 countries, and subsequently in similar studies in many other parts of the world (including 3 African countries). In addition, 47 managers were involved in a semi-structured interviewing survey, which was intended to focus on similar issues and to provide insights on the contextual fabric of the Malawian manager's world. The aims of the study were:

1. to investigate managerial thinking about a limited number of important issues in a national context (Malawi);

2. to compare data from this investigation in a practical way with those produced by similar studies in other countries;

3. to examine factors in the Malawian context that might account for similarities and differences between the thinking of the Malawian managers and that of other managers;

4. to relate these findings to the education and training of managers in Malawi, and to consider their appropriateness; and

5. to consider possible areas for further investigation.

In this paper my intention is to focus mainly on item 4 above. Before considering the data from the study and their implications for the education and training of Malawian managers, it might be useful to present *very briefly*, some relevant information about the country.

Malawi is located in southern central Africa, bordering Zambia to the west, Tanzania to the north east, and Mozambique. By African standards it is not a big country, its area totaling 118,500 square kilometers, of which about one-fifth comprises the great lake that dominates the country, Lake Malawi. However, Malawi's population density is about four times as high as the African average, at 47 persons per square kilometer overall. At the time of the last population census, in 1982, Malawi's population stood at a little over 6.5 million.

In common with other nations in this part of Africa, Malawi has a turbulent history, experiencing long periods of stability and at other times the eruptions of migratory peoples entering the region from other population centers. Although the details of these movements are still being elaborated, it is clear that the great lake, the third biggest in Africa, has been a focal point for centuries in this part of the continent. In more recent times, the territory that now constitutes Malawi was subjected to the depredations of slave traders operating from the Indian Ocean coast, and to the influx of Ngoni peoples from the south, driven to their northward odyssey by the turmoil, in what is now the Republic of South Africa, caused by the rise of the great Zulu empire. Another powerful influence was the coming of European missionaries and explorers in the latter half of the nineteenth century. As the scramble for Africa divided the continent into spheres of influence for the European powers at the turn of the century, the area of the lake eventually became the British colony of Nyasaland.

Unlike other British colonies in Africa, Nyasaland offered no exploitable natural resources and did not attract large numbers of European settlers. Evidence suggests that Britain's attitude toward its colony of the lake was at least ambivalent, and possibly at times downright unenthusiastic. An attempt in 1953 to form a federation in central Africa consisting of Northern Rhodesia (now Zambia), Southern Rhodesia (now Zimbabwe), and Nyasaland was doomed to failure. The independent nation of Malawi emerged after a long and complex struggle that had its roots early in the present century, but developed as a significant movement during the 1950s.

The "wind of change" was then gathering strength in southern Africa, and the British colonies there were experiencing a common, if individually manifested, movement toward self-government. For Malawi the crucial moment came when Dr. H. K. Banda returned to Nyasaland, in July 1958, after having lived and practiced medicine in the USA, Europe, and Ghana for many years. From that day, events were set in train that led, with historical inevitability, to independence from Britain in July 1964 and, in 1966, to the status of a republic within the Commonwealth. Dr. Banda became President (and in 1971 was made the Life President) of the new Republic of Malawi. The story of Dr. Banda's apparently historic destiny in liberating the country of his birth from its colonial masters is extraordinary, and his continued dominance as leader of Malawi is an overwhelming factor in the nation's development. Since this reality forms a part of the national context in which Malawian organizations function and Malawian managers work, it may be useful to explore briefly the nature of Malawi's political milieu.

Since the 1960s we have observed the achievement of independence by most of Africa's former colonial territories. The dominant picture we in the West receive of Africa through our media is one of a continent in a turbulent transition, with national regimes apparently changing, sometimes violently, with bewildering frequency. Some states seem to have tried almost every conceivable form of government, from multi-party democracy to military dictatorship, in search of a suitable system. Malawi has been notably absent in reports of such developments. The overwhelmingly powerful and pervasive influence of the Life President on all facets of Malawian life is important, because we could expect that the consequences of such a situation would inevitably include the ways in which organizations operate and managers behave.

Turning to Malawi's economic position, the country is, in terms of per capita income, one of the world's poorest nations. At independence the country had a small industrial sector and a rudimentary economic infra-structure. Few exploitable mineral resources have been located in any quantity. The policies of the government since independence therefore have emphasized the development of agricultural, transport, and commu-nications infrastructure. As a landlocked country, Malawi faces problems, sometimes acute, in routing its crucial agricultural exports and its imports. Problems of transporting goods great distances across difficult terrain are frequently aggravated by climatic conditions and guerrilla activity. Since Malawi's independence, the protracted war in Rhodesia (now Zimbabwe) and the continuing civil insurrection in Mozambique have presented intractable difficulties for Malawian administrators and businessmen.

Malawi, by African standards, enjoys a good climate for a variety of agricultural activities and is blessed with relatively productive soils. There has been impressive development in the production of a number of cash crops, including tobacco, tea, coffee, and sugar, which form the bulk of the country's exports. In addition, greater yields of subsistence crops, importantly maize, have been consistently achieved. Malawi is one of the few African countries that are largely self-sufficient in staple foodstuffs.

Although the industrial base remains modest in size, development in this sector also has been impressive. The following figures relating to paid employment in Malawi (1980) are relevant:

> Total in paid employment—294,707
> In professional, technical, and related posts—21,716 (7.4%)
> In managerial/administrative occupations—4,127 (1.5%).

These figures, supplied by the Manpower Planning Unit, Office of the President and Cabinet, relate to December 1980 and are the most recent available in this form. By 1983 (the latest figures available), the number of individuals in paid employment was approximately 387,000, over fifty percent of whom were engaged in agriculture.

Malawian Managers

It would be neither possible nor relevant to report in this paper the details of findings from the interviewing and questionnaire surveys. My intention is to put forward some fairly direct statements about Malawian managers and the organizations in which they work, and to consider their implications for management development. These statements appear to reflect as directly as possible the data produced by the investigation.

In general terms, management education and training have attracted some rather critical comments, and it may be useful to look very briefly at this wider context before we focus on the Malawian situation.

Safavi [3], reporting on a project involving the 57 countries and territories of Africa during a 4-year study of management education and development programs, paints a "gloomy picture" of "a number of areas of conflict between classroom and culture, between Western theory and African reality." A number of observers have similar concerns. Nyerere (cited by Onyemelukwe [1]) has observed that the training of African managers appears to have been designed to divorce them from the societies it is supposed to equip them to serve. Hofstede [4] claims that Western management theories, although widely taught, are not practiced by non-Western managers. Successful managers "perform a cultural transposition of ideas . . . there is no single formula for management development to be used in different cultures" (p. 380); there is a need to ascertain what constitutes "success" in a particular culture. Hyden [5] comments on the absurdity of what he calls "technique peddling" by Western management consultants in Africa, exemplified by bizarre attempts to undertake Organization Development (OD) consultancies (with their accompanying American individualistic, humanistic values) in African organizations: "The African personality is full and wholesome in a sense that does not tally with the demands of systematic rationality." Yet African managers "have been molded in a type of management thinking that makes them strangers in their own environment" (p. 159).

It is difficult to dispute the view that strategies and methods used to educate and train African managers have generally been based on Western theories and practices, with little, if any, consideration of the environments in which African organizations function. What can be done to change the situation? Simply asserting, as so many observers do, that management education and training must take cognizance of the environmental realities of Africa does not get us very far. Do the data from this study of Malawian senior and middle managers provide any pointers? It is perhaps appropriate to preface the discussion of the issues with two notes of caution.

First, it is important to avoid the common assumption that education and training can be relied upon to accomplish changes in human behavior and thinking. There is a line of reasoning (or rather, assumption) that:

TRAINING
(usually equated with classroom-based courses)
↓
INDIVIDUAL LEARNING
↓
IMPROVED INDIVIDUAL JOB PERFORMANCE
↓
IMPROVED ORGANIZATIONAL PERFORMANCE

At each level the assumption can be challenged, and experience indicates that, without positive managerial action, the training of individuals rarely leads to improved organizational performance. I am therefore conscious of the need to exercise caution in advancing ideas about the education and training of Malawian managers, especially since I believe that the causes of important aspects of their thinking are to be found in fundamental national sociocultural and political elements.

Second, there is at present no way of judging with any degree of accuracy the extent to which Malawian organizations and management have developed distinctive features. Malawi was a British colony, and is now a member of the Commonwealth. Its systems (for example, in education, communications, industry, commerce, technology, health care, public utility provision, and government organization) would be familiar to British expatriates and visitors. The major language of business and government is English. Most Malawian administrators and executives will have been trained on the Western model, many of them in Britain; and, as the data confirm, most have worked with expatriate (predominantly British) managers, often taking over from an expatriate boss. The study has shown that traditional modes of social and family organization still inhere in contemporary Malawi as fundamental aspects of the life of individuals, even those, such as managers, who have moved out of the rural subsistence economy to paid employment in the expanding urban sector. To ask the question "How Westernized are Malawian organizations and managers?" is not to anticipate a precise answer, but to realize that more research will be necessary before we can even begin to make useful judgments about this important issue.

Using the data from this study, supplemented by those from other relevant studies, I propose the following general statements about Malawian managers and the organizations in which they work, which may serve as a useful base for a discussion of relevant strategies for management education and training:

1. Malawian organizations function in an environment of acute resource scarcity, economic uncertainty, and highly centralized political power.

2. These organizations tend to retain the major characteristics of structures developed in the colonial era, namely, rather rigid bureaucratic, rulebound hierarchies.

3. Organizations tend to be viewed by society as a whole as having a wider mission than is generally understood in the West, being expected to provide socially desirable benefits such as employment, housing, transport, and assistance with important social rituals and ceremonies; considerations of profit maximization and efficiency may be viewed as secondary or incidental.

4. There is among Malawian workers a generally instrumental orientation toward work, involving high expectations of the benefits, to the worker and his extended family, that employment

brings, but less in the way of loyalty and commitment to the organization (or profession) that is said to typify the employer-employee relationship in the West.

5. There is in Malawian society an emphasis on prestige and status differences, creating relationships of dependency, which in organizations finds expression in wide differentials between organizational levels, particularly between managers and workers, extreme deference to and dependence upon one's boss, and a paternal, concerned, but strict style of management.

6. The collectivist values of Malawian society are reflected in organizations in the high regard managers have for their subordinates as people; in a view of workers as a network of people rather than as human resources; in an emphasis on maintaining relationships rather than on providing opportunities for individual development; in an emphasis on "highly ritualised interpersonal interactions which often place greater value on the observance of protocol than the accomplishment of work-related tasks" [6. p. 159]; in a desire by workers for a close relationship with the boss; and in a reluctance by managers either to accept individual blame for mistakes or to criticize individual subordinates in a direct manner.

7. Malawian managers tend to view their authority, professional competence, and information as personal possessions, rather than impersonal concomitants of their organizational role, and as a source of status and prestige.

8. This, coupled with the emphasis on the wide differential—in status, power, education, experience, and perceived ability—between managers and workers makes Malawian managers very reluctant to delegate authority, to share information, and to involve subordinates (who may be perceived as a potential source of threat) in decision-making processes.

9. Malawian managers regard security as an important factor in their work, to be reinforced by unchanging structures, detailed procedures, and close supervision of subordinates.

10. Malawian managers desire a good relationship with their boss, whom they perceive as a key figure, but frequently find this to be a problematic relationship because the boss manages them in a manner similar to that they employ with their own subordinates; this may find expression in dissatisfaction with their perceived opportunities for autonomy and self-actualization.

11. Individualistic (as opposed to universalistic) criteria tend to influence organizational behavior; hence, insecurity is increased because decisions cannot be consistently predicted, and blame for mistakes tends to be assigned on a personalized basis.

12. Malawian managers have constantly to be sensitive to political pressures and aware of developments that might affect them as power coalitions change.

13. Malawian managers tend to recognize their role in achieving organizational performance (this, on the basis of our limited data, does not seem to apply to civil servants to the same degree), and to emphasize their individual professional or technical expertise rather than their "managerial" functions.

14. Malawian managers have a keen awareness of the necessity to acknowledge and manage their wider social obligations to extended family and kinship systems, and of the possible conflicts that may thereby exist in relation to their formal organizational roles.

15. Malawian managers often find their relationships with expatriate bosses and colleagues problematic and tend to view expatriate executives as lacking in the sensitivity they view as essential, especially in their dealings with workers.

The data from the study appear to confirm that the demands of formal organizations create tensions and conflicts for Malawian managers. It is well understood that the processes of industrialization on the Western model demand the utilization of technical and scientific knowledge, but it is perhaps less clearly recognized that the use of such knowledge depends somewhat on the acceptance of the values and "world view" that are its sociocultural foundation.

The data from this study provide several examples of the tensions and problems that can occur when Western management ideas and practices are transplanted into a non-Western environment. There is, for instance, the apparent contradiction that Malawi is a newly independent nation in the process of rapid change, a characteristic shared by all African states to a greater or lesser degree and likely to continue. Yet the organizations that are to be instrumental in bringing about and managing change are, as a number of commentators have observed, generally bureaucratic, rigid, and rule-bound. On the level of managerial motivation, there is another apparent contradiction: Malawian managers reflect in many aspects of their thinking African traditional, communalistic values, yet they stress the importance of their needs for autonomy and self-actualization at work (the individualistic focus more characteristic of Western societies).

Jenkins[1] and Rutherford,[2] in studies of Malawian managers, remark on the strong, expressed need for structure, guidelines, and clear direction (reflecting a preoccupation with security). This apparent acceptance of "universalistic" criteria for behavior in organizations is contrasted with the evidence that managers regularly bypass organizational structures and make decisions on the basis of "particularistic" (i.e., what the managers in the study referred to as "personalized") criteria.

Education and Training of Malawian Managers _____

Organizational behavior is influenced by a complex set of interrelated factors. The Western notion of "rational" behavior is itself the product of such factors, but it is not automatically applicable in other contexts. What appears to a Western observer of African organizations to be "irrational," on closer examination can be seen to reflect a set of values that are different from, but no less valid than, those of the West. For this reason I take the view, in considering the education and training of Malawian managers, that it would be unrealistic and inappropriate to advance prescriptive proposals for changing the existing realities of Malawian organizational life.

The following propositions are intended rather to accept the socio-cultural, economic, and political realities and to suggest how Malawian managers might be assisted to be effective and, if they so desire, to change existing systems and practices:

1. Because the Malawian environment is less stable and predictable than is the case in the industrialized nations, "the probability of planned actions going wrong is high . . . margins of error are likely to be particularly large" [5. p. 157]. It is therefore important to recognize that the use of Western planning techniques cannot be assumed to guarantee any anticipated outcome. Malawian managers will need to reflect on experiences, since independence, of planning and its effectiveness, and to identify the particular factors that have influenced success or failure.

2. There is a need to acknowledge the collectivist values that inhere in contemporary Malawian society and to consider which Western management practices and techniques might tend to contradict them. For example, it is not difficult to understand why Western performance appraisal and Management by Objectives schemes may find intellectual acceptance by Malawian managers, yet fail in practice. Seddon [7] has observed that in many African societies it is a sign of weakness to admit incompetence or ignorance. Mistakes are believed to be beyond the control of individuals, and the maintenance of "face" is of crucial importance. There is a highly developed sensitivity to individual criticism, "the most powerful contingencies determining behavior (informally) are 'social evaluations'— pride and shame." In my study there was considerable evidence of a reluctance by managers to criticize individuals.

   In such circumstances, the use of Western practices for assessing individual performance appears to be inappropriate. For Malawian managers to have to learn such practices without a comprehensive analysis of their chances of success and their consequences in terms of Malawian values seems both impractical and wasteful.

3. Similar considerations apply to teaching Malawian managers about the benefits claimed, in the Western context, for delegation of authority, sharing of information, and a generally more participative management style. In the situation I have described, such practices can be seen to contradict many Malawian social values, and have little chance at present of successful adoption. It is important, however, that Malawian managers clearly understand the consequences of their current management style, which (1) tends to push decisions upward in the

organizational hierarchy; (2) involves managers in routine, trivial activities; (3) hinders the sharing of information within the organization, thus possibly reducing its capacity to anticipate and cope with change; (4) encourages highly dependent subordinate behavior; (5) reduces opportunities for subordinates to engage in more interesting work; and (6) on the evidence of my interview survey, appears to be a source of dissatisfaction for managers in terms of relationships with their bosses.

4. Malawian managers require highly developed political skills, both in monitoring developments that may affect them, as "particularistic" criteria influence decision makers inside and outside their employing organizations, and in their relationships with organizational superiors, colleagues, and subordinates. Such skills are not necessarily a major focus in Western management development strategies.

5. Malawian managers require well-developed diplomatic skills, particularly in two contexts. First, their bosses expect them to behave in a deferential manner, far more than is the case in Western views of such a relationship. It seems important that the implications of this type of relationship should be examined in relation to organizational performance. If managers are to be able to cope with change and to provide solutions to emerging problems, will their extreme deference to, and dependence on, more senior executives not inhibit them? Malawian managers expressed dissatisfaction with this relationship and wanted more opportunities (clearly delineated, nevertheless) for autonomy. They also wanted their bosses to behave in a more predictable (i.e., "universalistic") manner and to give them recognition for good performance. In such circumstances of dependency and unfulfilled expectations, Malawian managers need diplomatic and influencing abilities of a high order. Secondly, as we have seen, Malawian managers are often faced with demands from outside the organization, from extended family and kinship groups and (less frequently) from the Party. Such demands may well conflict with the manager's organizational role, and he will need to be skilled in explaining the demands and limitations under which he operates in the organization.

6. When Malawian managers are taught the paramount Western organizational values of effective and efficient use of scarce resources, it is important that they consciously consider and understand the implications of implementing these values in Malawian society, where there is a greater concern for social relationships than for performance, where there are social expectations about the role of organizations that are greater than is customary in the West, and where the notion of considering the individual as a "resource" is strange.

7. Malawian workers tend to have higher expectations about the organization's ability and willingness to accept a degree of responsibility for their welfare and development than is the case in the industrialized West. At the same time, there is a more instrumental attitude toward work, involving fewer considerations of loyalty to the organization. In these circumstances, managers could well consider the

implications in terms of employee motivation. Western assumptions about the desirability of self-expression and fulfillment appear to be inappropriate, and uncritical teaching of Western motivation theories to Malawian managers needs to be challenged.

8. The managers in this study indicated that they derived considerable satisfaction from the use of their professional or technical competence, and were generally concerned about performance (this was decidedly less so in the case of the Malawian civil servants in the study). These strengths might be used in developing managers' understanding of their more directly managerial functions if it can be shown that job satisfaction can be enhanced when management work is viewed as requiring equally prestigious, admirable skills, and that effective performance is more likely when professional and technical expertise is reinforced by managerial capabilities.

9. Although the presence of expatriate managers will lessen in significance, it is at present an area of concern for many Malawian managers. Since it is not realistic to expect that expatriate executives will be selected primarily on the basis of their cultural sensitivity, it might be useful if Malawian managers were helped to understand more about the backgrounds, perspectives, and values of the expatriates. This may go some way in enabling Malawian managers to handle their relationships with expatriates effectively.

Strategies and Methods ————————————————————————

Turning to considerations of appropriate methods for education and training of Malawian managers, I suggest that the foregoing discussion indicates that the following *outcomes* are priorities:

- In an environment of turbulent change, learning should become a conscious and continuous process for Malawian managers.

- Malawian managers should develop a profound awareness of, and sensitivity to, the sociocultural context in which they operate.

- They should also have a clear understanding of the implicit demands of Western management ideas and practices, and of the facets of Malawian society that might be congruent and incongruent with such demands (for example, deference and dependent relationships).

- There should be a deliberate and reasoned rejection of the uncritical adoption of Western (or other alien) organization and management theories.

- Managers and educators should acknowledge, analyze, and reflect upon the experience of Malawian organizations and develop from it indigenous explanatory concepts.

- Malawian managers should develop more confidence in the validity of their own experiences and their views on management (rather than deferring to outsiders).

When we consider how such outcomes might be achieved through education and training, several factors have to be borne in mind. First, just as Western management ideas must be critically examined in the light of Malawian sociocultural realities, Western notions concerning the education and training of managers have to be understood in terms of the assumptions they make about people and the values that influence them. Many current Western ideas about management development can be seen clearly to reflect values such as individual responsibility for self-actualization; learning as problem solving, involving puzzlement, perturbation, even discomfort for the learner; the value of self-discovered knowledge as opposed to prescribed knowledge; a view of the teacher-learner relationship as involving interdependence and assumed equality; development as involving risk and change for learners; a view of the professional as an individual of independent judgment, self-confident in his relationship with his employing organization; and an increasing degree of openness in relationships. Contrasted to this I have detailed Malawian values that might be expected to influence management education and training, including the collectivist (as opposed to Western individualist) nature of social relationships; greater awareness of hierarchical levels and deference to authority, which, according to Clarke[3], is expressed in the teacher-learner relationship by "a greater need (by the learner) for clear and unequivocal direction . . . and regular face-to-face contact"; education seen as a way to enhance status rather than for personal growth; learning viewed as a way of avoiding risk by acquiring additional information, to be hoarded and protected as a source of power; and training viewed as a threat rather than an opportunity for self-actualization if it involves an admission of ignorance or shortcomings.

In addition, managers indicated in the questionnaire survey that the most effective ways in which they had learned their managerial abilities were: by doing, by discussing real problems with colleagues, through training by the boss, by observing effective managers, and by analyzing their successes and failures.

This seems to suggest that approaches to management education and training in Malawi should include the following general criteria:

1. As Hyden [5] has noted: "For a manager to be effective he needs to be sensitive to and work in response to his proximate environment. Many African managers lack a grasp of how they can combine good management with effective response to their environment" (p. 59). People are intuitively and experientially aware of their environment, but it is suggested that managers need to be helped to develop a fuller understanding of and sensitivity to the sociocultural facets of their environment that affect their roles. This will involve teaching strategies that draw upon the experiences of managers and encourage them to reflect on the implications for future action.

2. It must be made clear in organizational policies that the organization accepts a substantial share of responsibility for the development of individuals, and that further education and training do not imply that a manager is incompetent or lacking in some area. It must be understood that management development does not involve a risk for the individual and that the learning environment will be supportive.

3. Learning strategies and methods should reflect the collectivist nature of Malawian society. This would imply that methods should be avoided that focus on individual performance (especially shortcomings). Small-group methods and other supportive techniques seem to be appropriate.

4. There needs to be an explicit focus on continuous learning from experience. Learning opportunities in the organization (such as deputizing for an absent boss, introduction of structural or technological change, launching of a new product, coping with unanticipated difficulties) should be identified and utilized. This will demand that attention be given to developing skills in analyzing successes and failures in a conscious, structured way.

5. Management education and training should help managers understand the processes of organizational change. As noted earlier, the structures of Malawian organizations tend predominantly to be rigidly bureaucratic (embodying security and stability in an environment of accelerating change). Managers need to understand the implications of such organizational patterns for the effective performance of the roles Malawian society expects organizations to undertake.

6. Managers should be trained in coaching skills, in order to be fully effective in developing subordinates. Organizations need to ensure that the job descriptions of managers include the coaching of subordinates as a priority function.

7. Management development strategies should include structured, on-the-job, developmental activities.

8. The group-oriented methods and problem-solving focus of Action Learning suggest that it might be worthwhile to experiment with this approach to management development. Revan's [8] notion of "comrades in adversity" may address the needs of Malawian managers for security and social interaction while enabling them to identify real problems and to use their shared experience to develop solutions.

Conclusion

In the literature about the transfer of Western management concepts and practices, one can detect a developing dichotomy. Some writers assert that the imperatives of organizational life are so powerful, so pervasive, that the "culture of production" will sweep aside local variations in culture, values, and behavior. Others would claim, on the contrary, that in some countries the culture is so distinctive and so enduring that imported notions about organizations and their management will be radically modified or even rejected. The findings from the study of Malawian managers upon which this paper is based provide evidence that both tendencies are present. The "convergence-divergence" debate will continue as cross-cultural research adds to the stock of data for comparison.

For management educators this is inconvenient. It demands that strategies for management development should recognize the complex and distinctive realities of the contexts in which managers perform. The search for relevance will, I suspect, be a crucial task.

Endnotes

1. Jenkins, C. "Management Problems and Management Education in Developing Economies: A Case Study of Malawi." Working paper. University of Aston, Management Centre, 1982.

2. Rutherford, P. "Attitudes of Malawian Managers: Some Recent Research." Unpublished paper. University of Malawi, 1981.

3. Clarke, R. "Independent Learning in an African Country, with Special Reference to the Certificate of Adult Studies in the University of Malawi." Ph.D. thesis. University of Manchester, Department of Adult and Higher Education, 1981, 240.

References

1. Onyemelukwe, C. *Man and Management in Contemporary Africa.* London: Longmans, 1973.

2. Haire, M., Ghiselli, E., and Porter, L. *Managerial Thinking: An International Study.* New York: Wiley, 1966.

3. Safavi, F. "A Model of Management Education in Africa." *Academy of Management Review,* 1981, 6(2), 319-331.

4. Hofstede, G. *Culture's Consequences: International Differences in Work-related Values.* London: Sage, 1980.

5. Hyden, G. *No Shortcuts to Progress: African Development Management in Perspective.* London: Heinemann, 1983.

6. Blunt, P., and Popoola, O. *Personnel Management in Africa.* London: Longmans, 1985.

7. Seddon, J. "The Development and Indigenisation of Third World Business: African Values in the Workplace." In Hammond, V. (ed.), *Current Research in Management.* London: Frances Pinter/ATM, 1985.

8. Revans, R. *The Origins and Growth of Action Learning.* Bromley: Chartwell-Bratt, 1982.

Management Development in Europe: A Study in Cultural Contrast

Reading 4.3
Peter Lawrence

Our starting point is that the management of human resources (HRM) is essentially an Anglo-Saxon construct. It has been "grafted on" rather than "taken root" in Continental Europe, where the classic HRM functions—recruitment, socialisation, training, development—are rather more determined by different conceptions of management, underpinned by related values. These same underlying beliefs and assumptions also colour the varied approaches which are taken to the making of managers in these countries. The purpose of this article is to throw the different European approaches to management development into sharp relief first by making the contrast with the American situation clear and then by drawing out the differences within Europe—most notably France and Germany.

Management's American Origins

Discussion of the origins of management is sometimes obscured by the fact that management is at the same time an activity, an idea, and a subject (Lawrence, 1986:2-5). As an activity, management has clearly existed for centuries. Past instances of the discriminant deployment of resources and the effective co-ordination of manpower abound, from the building of the pyramids to the organising of the army that Napoleon took to Moscow in 1812. But engaging *in* it is different from having an idea *of* it, and it is the latter which is the American *démarche*.

It was in the USA, that is, that the idea of management crystallised. Management was first identified and labelled in the USA, seen as a phenomenon that could be extrapolated, analysed, and made the subject of generalisation. The most potent cause of this development, no doubt,

Source: Peter Lawrence. "Management Development in Europe: A Study in Cultural Contrast." *Human Resource Management Journal,* 3 (1), Autumn 1992. Published by IRS/PPL, 18-20 Highbury Place, London, N5 1QP. Reprinted by permission.

was the unusual circumstance of America from the end of the War of Independence (1783) until the last unclaimed land was distributed at Fort Sill, Oklahoma (1890): namely, a vast, empty continent was "filled in"—too much space and too many resources crossed with too few people and too little time. And the shortage of people betokened an even more acute shortage—of drive, entrepreneurialism, versatility, adaptability, and the opportunistic exploitation of circumstance and resource; that is to say, a shortage of (some of) the ingredients of management. And the sense of shortage led to a corresponding valuing, indeed valorisation, of these qualities.

It is a short step from the conceptualisation and valuation of management to the conviction that it is teachable: the Americans took this step. The world's first business school, at Wharton, Pennsylvania, was established in 1881 (cf. the London Business School established in 1965). Wharton was the first of many. By the 1950s business education, as we know from William Whyte's *Organisation Man* (1956), was not only a mass phenomenon but a mature one, inviting satirical treatment (management education has yet to become an object of satire in Europe).

The transition from a concept of management to the *teachability* of management itself expresses a variety of American values, with proactivity, a drive to efficiency, and equality of opportunity all playing a part. The American world view is active not contemplative, oriented to the here and now not the life thereafter, and above all to the conviction that man can and must shape his destiny. All this inclines an efficiency-conscious people to:

- be aware;
- work out how;
- formulate if possible;
- pass it on (teach).

So far we have argued for management's American origins, but in general terms. It is possible to go further and see the emergence of HRM and "management development" as pre-eminently American phenomena. There are a number of issues here. First is the general consideration that Americans, having invented management, espouse all its specialisms, techniques, and the "supporting cast" of business school teachable subjects. Thus the Americans invented mass production, marketing, and corporate strategy, just to take three lead examples. But more than this, the USA is the land par excellence of social science. While Britain, and to a lesser extent Continental Europe, discovered sociology in the 1960s and scrambled to establish sociology departments at universities, these had routinely existed in the USA for half a century. This tends to be obscured by the fact that it was the Europeans who produced all the "founding fathers"—Weber, Marx, Durkheim, Simmel, and so on—with the Americans making a systematic contribution to social theory only in the mid-twentieth century. But if Europe had the "officers" the USA had "enlisted men" in abundance. Indeed the inter-war period is something of a golden age in American empirical social science with a plethora of community studies, research on stratification systems, ethnic minorities, race relations, poverty, crime, and juvenile gangs.

This empirical outpouring did not end with the 1930s. When the Japanese bombed Pearl Harbor in December 1941 they unleashed not only an American military response but also a sociological one! A distinctive feature of the American war effort was its reflexive nature; it studied itself in the making. Americans wanted to understand the human and organisational dimensions of belligerence, and to profit from the understanding. It is sometimes said that the Second World War in the United Kingdom gave birth to operations research: in the United States it gave rise to group dynamics and leadership studies. In the post-war period the American preoccupation with people and groups enjoyed a new flowering. Consider that all the theories of motivation are American, so are virtually all the leadership studies, so is group dynamics, studies of supervisory effectiveness, informal organisation, work group behaviour, and much organisation theory and analysis. All this is a powerful thrust to the development of HRM, and to management as a teachable activity.

There is also an important facilitating factor. This is the absence in the USA alike of European-style class consciousness, a serious socialist movement, and any penetration of Marxist ideology. In "old Europe" these have variously served to structure both the perception and reality of superior-subordinate and management-worker relations in industry. But the American comes to these with an open mind. In the absence of any prestructuring these phenomena must be seen in their own terms, their own irreducible human and social terms. So that group dynamics, supervisory styles, context-specific leadership, and formal and informal systems have a greater relevance and immediacy.

One obvious manifestation of these tendencies is the American fascination with the organisation itself. Precisely because it is a man-made construct, "the organisation" is endlessly fascinating to Americans. Whereas the Germans, for example, see the organisation as a secondary consequence of engaging in manufacturing activity, in the American view the organisation is both primary and perfectable. Because people have made it, people can improve it, endlessly "tinker" with it (= OD) to get improvements in efficiency, effectiveness or enhanced interpersonal cooperation. Managerial leaders can be taught how the system works and thus be equipped to modify it.

Finally, the American concern with people—as individuals, in groups, as organisational members—is also heightened by American rejection of European élitism. As the land without monarchy, aristocracy or papacy, the USA is the society where people are primary, equal and important. People cannot be judged secondary to an idea, are less easily relegated to the status of role incumbents. So if people are primary, and equal, there must be a greater concern with their motivation, leadership, satisfactions and concerns, and with the dynamics of their cooperation.

For such reasons the USA is the country par excellence of HRM and formal management development, both in terms of practice and of the academic, research-driven underpinning. A major contention of this article is that these conditions and values, and therefore their results, are not replicated in Continental Europe in the same plenitude. But what of the "intermediate state," Britain?

HRM, Management Development and the British View of the Human Condition _____

There can be little doubt the HRM is "alive and well" in Britain. It is included on every conceivable management course from DMS to MBA, there is a flourishing Institute of Personnel Management which acts as a qualifying body as well as an interest group, and while it would probably be unrealistic to expect any staff function/department to enjoy the highest prestige, low esteem has traditionally been reserved for engineering (Gerstl and Hutton, 1966), design and production (Gill and Lockyer, 1978) rather than personnel. It must be equally clear that this is not because Britain shares with the USA any of the features or values explored above. Indeed, the only thing that Britain in this connection would appear to share with the USA is not being Continental European. So how is this parallel development of HRM in Britain to be explained?

It seems to this writer that the answer must lie in a number of intersecting negatives, but let us at least begin on a more positive note. For most of this century Britain has recognised that industry and management are not national strengths and there has been a corresponding tendency to "look up" to other countries whose superior economic performance was attributed in part to quality of management. For most of the twentieth century the USA has been the business role model. If you wanted to know how to do it you went to the USA to observe the professionals, and came back and did it in Britain—if you had the nerve and the trade unions would let you. This sustained British admiration of American business lasts at least until the 1970s, and is manifest in a number of shared enthusiasms—short termism, equity financing, mergers and acquisitions, financial planning, budgetary control, strategy, and management education. For all of these the enthusiasm evinced in Britain is observable, but later on less so than in the USA. So this standing of HRM and management development in Britain is in part a reflection of extended mid-century admiration for that dominant transatlantic economy. But there are other considerations.

A number of writers have identified an anti-industrial strain in British culture and society (Barnett, 1972; Wiener, 1981) and this anti-industrialism is also a well-worked theme in the "industrial novels" of the mid-nineteenth century, for example Disraeli's *Sybil* and Dickens's *Hard Times*. The essence of this genre is that industry is variously rejected as soulless, depersonalising, calculating, and overly-materialistic. Not an enterprise for the gentleman, or the intellectual, or for anyone with finer feelings. But note that the critique implies a plea for HRM, where the mission of personnel is to re-personalise a dreary and mechanistic operation. It also implies a vital need to teach managers "interpersonal skills," communication, leadership, and so on.

A similar thesis-antithesis may be perceived in the British undervaluation of *Technik*. Engineers have traditionally enjoyed lower standing in Britain than in Continental Europe (Hutton and Lawrence, 1981), the technical functions, including production, have lower relative status in British industry (Lawrence, 1980; Lockyer and Jones, 1980). Furthermore, the tendency in Britain has been to stereotype the engineer pejoratively as interpersonally inadequate, at ease only when communing with his machines. Here again the playing up of the human side of enterprise as a crucial managerial role is a very British response.

There are further antithetical elements. The persistence in Britain of subjective class consciousness renders communication (across class lines, in industry across authority lines) more problematic. Hence people, managers and supervisors, need to be coached in it, need to be made aware of the barriers by means of case studies and role plays. Or again the traditionally poor industrial relations in British industry are a stimulus to professional HRM. Poor industrial relations "flag up" a need for training—in communication again, in supervisory skills, in negotiation, and in being familiar with "the British system of industrial relations," a common course component. It also shapes the consciousness about the priorities to be included in management education, training and development processes. Furthermore, a number of elements already canvassed—anti-industrialism and class consciousness, aristocratic disdain and employee intransigence—all render motivation relatively more problematic than in other industrial societies. Once again, it is a challenge for management development.

Finally, this negatively induced concern with communication, negotiation, supervision and motivation in British industrial society is paralleled and sustained by a positive conviction. If there is one thing that "our glorious history" teaches us, it is that great men matter—from Clive to Churchill, from Wolf to Dowding. The British tendency to reject technology as depersonalising and administrative systems as mundane is matched by a valorisation of the human and individual. Human qualities, individual talents, creativity, social ease and political grasp are what matter; the ability to move others is decisive, leadership is at a premium. Again, it is a national inclination that works in favour of HRM. Personnel is the function charged with the selection, recruitment, and development of human talent, with "the care and feeding" of leaders. This is not a disposition that one finds, for instance, in matter-of-fact Sweden, or in the anti-heroic Netherlands.

We have deliberately spent some time exploring the differential underpinning of HRM and the nature of managerial priorities in the two key Anglo-Saxon countries as a backdrop to understanding Continental Europe. It is in fact because so many of the considerations explored in the British and American connection do not apply in mainland Europe, that HRM does not have the same élan there, indeed is in part socially and culturally by-passed. Let us begin with France.

Personnel Management and the Making of Managers in France ___

It should be said at the outset that the distinctions made in this article between countries are not of a "black and white" kind. In these discussions of the origin, standing, and nature of both the personnel function and role of management development we are dealing of course in matters of relative importance and national emphasis. With this qualification let us begin to situate the personnel function and French conceptions of management with a brief historical reference.

In the previous discussion of Britain it was suggested that part of the *raison d'être* for the personnel function was a need to civilise industry, to give manufacturing a human face. These arguments are not inapplicable to France but they are less important for that country. In the British case the humanising mission of personnel derives long term from the black imprint of the industrial revolution on the folk memory. Say "industry" to a British school child and he/she thinks of slums, squalor, and child labour in the cotton mills. All this applies rather less to France. In that country the industrial revolution started later than in Britain, and was far less comprehensive. France remained persistently if not predominantly rural until after the Second World War. It is generally agreed that industrialisation was only completed in France in the 1950s, part of the development connoted by the phrase *les trentes glorieuses,* the thirty years of growing prosperity after the Liberation. There are occasional French novels decrying the ills of industrialisation, but "the industry novel" is not a genre as in nineteenth century Britain. Or again the civilising mission of personnel, very obvious in the British case, is inappropriate in the case of France. In that society industry has been civilised from within by the quality and educational élan of the management élite, an idea that will be developed in the next section.

Another part of the *raison d'être* for the personnel function in general, and the management development activity in particular, is the conviction that industry has "special needs" in terms of the skills and capabilities of those who staff it. At the blue-collar level this simply means the development of craft skills and operating capabilities, but at management level there is an implicit distinction. This is that the skills of the manager (private sector, profit making) will need to differ somewhat from those of the administrator (public sector, non-profit making) where the former is historically recent and the latter, like the poor, has always been with us. The present writer has argued elsewhere (Lawrence, 1986:17-19) that the distinction is valid, that both the ambiance and values of public and private sector organisations differ, and that different capabilities are required by those who run them. But interestingly, this distinction is less salient for France, which country is distinguished by projecting a valorisation of public service models into the later twentieth century.

The heroes of French history have been authoritarian centralisers; one looks in vain for a Disraeli extending the franchise to industrial workers or for an Andrew Jackson articulating populist aspirations. In the French case the centralisers range from Cardinal Richelieu, Cardinal Mazarin and Louis XIV in the seventeenth century, through Robespierre's 1792-93 Committee of Public Safety during the Revolution and Napoleon shortly after, to Clemenceau and of course General de Gaulle in the twentieth century. And what these centralisers have done is to centralise power and decisions in the hands of a state bureaucracy, whether royal, revolutionary, imperial or presidential. In other words, France has long standing as a bureaucratic state. It is more bureaucratic than its neighbours, and bureaucratic forms are given more credence. Indeed it has been argued by Crozier (1963) that the French actually like bureaucracy, their individualism making them prefer the impersonal dictates of bureaucratic regulation to the willful direction of a physically present superior.

Historically, there is an interesting twist to this story. The Fourth Republic in France (1946-1958), from its inception until its transformation into the Fifth Republic with enhanced presidential power to the benefit of Charles de Gaulle, was unstable. Marked by too many political parties, unstable and fluctuating coalition governments and short-lived ministries, the Fourth Republic is viewed by the French as something rather shameful (although it presided over effective post-war reconstruction and growing prosperity, and enacted some desirable reforms) and there is a sense of national relief when de Gaulle comes to power. The interesting thing is that throughout the period 1946-1958 ministerial instability is compensated by bureaucratic continuity; it is the state service rather than a succession of short-lived premiers who ran France; the triumphs of the period are the triumphs of a technocratic civil service rather than those of parliamentarians. And the role of the state service raises its standing and even its esteem with the public at large.

The thrust of these remarks is that whereas in other countries management, coming later, felt a need to differentiate itself from civil administration, coming sooner, this dysjunction is much less in France.

There the state service enjoys higher prestige than in the Anglo-Saxon countries, is regarded as a suitable or at least plausible model for industrial organisation, with the result that the public sector v private sector distinction is much less marked. The relative closeness is furthered by the fact that senior posts in both the state service and in private industry are staffed by people with the same educational background, of which more in the next section. In addition, there is also mobility between the sectors, from public to private, whereby civil servants in mid-career may move to posts at or near the top in private industry; this institution is known as *pantouflage*. The result of this greater public sector v private sector closeness is a diminished role for management development, in a milieu less inclined to view the demands of industrial management as distinctive.

Management Development and French Understanding _____

In the previous section we have explored "the outer edges" of management consciousness in France. It has been argued that industry in France did not in the twentieth century need to combat the negative image of early industrialisation, as was the case in Britain. That French industry was seen at an earlier stage than British as offering an appropriate career to intelligent and educated people, and therefore had less need to be "civilised" by a personnel function that would "respectably relate" it to the wider society. Furthermore, less discontinuity is perceived in France as between civil administration and industrial management, the standing of the former is high, and the two are linked by recruitment from a common educational source reinforced by some mobility from the state service into industry. What is more, profit-making companies in France differ less in terms of both organisational structure and *modus operandi* from the state bureaucracy. All these considerations imply a different and modified role for the personnel function in France and for the management development responsibility. But there is more.

Management development is less salient in France because in that country management is regarded more as a state of being than as the result of fashioned development processes within the company. It is or connotes an identity, more than an activity or set of capabilities. This is signalled in the term *cadres* by which managers are collectively known. This term was adopted in the 1930s, a period of troubled relations between organised labour and the *patronat* or class of business owners. With regard to these tensions the *cadres* were meant to be disinterested, impartial, distinct also from the owning class, devoted in technocratic style to the efficiency of the company. It is a solidaristic concept. It is an important label. Being a *cadre* cuts you off from other groupings, and automatically means you have things in common with all other people who are *cadres*. This solidarism is reinforced by the military ring (and origin) of the term, cf. *quadri* in Italian, though this is less widely used to designate managers in Italy than the ubiquitous *cadres* in France.

It is sometimes said that France has gone further towards making management a profession than have other industrial societies, and there is some truth in this. The reference here is not so much to professional excellence (though there is absolutely no suggestion that French managers are inferior) but again to self-identity. The entity *cadres* in France is not "fuzzy at the edges." One does not have debates in France as in Britain, about whether or not the foreman is part of junior management. In French companies people know who is, and who is not, a *cadre,* an understanding that is readily reflected in remarks such as *"en deux ans j'espere passer cadre"* (in a couple of years I hope to make it into the ranks of the *cadres*). This quasi professional unity is reinforced by other factors. The *cadres* have benefited much from the postwar economic development and rise in prosperity, the *trentes glorieuses* referred to earlier. The *cadres* are viewed if not exactly as the architects of this achievement then at least as those who presided over it and made it happen, and are thus further differentiated from the *patronat* (owners), many of whom were discredited by collaboration with the Nazis in the 1940-44 occupation period.

Or again *cadres* are treated separately by the state for the purposes of unemployment administration. They have for decades been the focus of attention by advertisers and especially advertisers of luxury and fashionable goods and services. This, of course, is not unknown in other countries, but there is a difference in France. This is that there the *cadres* have a stronger claim to be an educational and cultural élite as well as a disposable income élite. A further feature which is definitely French is that the *cadres* have been courted by the political parties in France. One speaks indeed of trying to capture the *cadres* vote (the nearest and much narrower equivalent in English, now discredited, would be going for the Yuppie vote).

But the most powerful factor acting upon the management development issue in France is that society's distinctive understanding of the management task. In France management is seen much more in ratiocinative terms, as being about analysis and rational decision. The qualities sought in *cadres* are correspondingly powers of analysis, synthesis, evaluation, and articulation. French management adverts are peppered with calls for such qualities as *la rigueur* and *l'esprit de synthèse* (Barsoux and Lawrence, 1990:47). There is a general "playing up" of these qualities at the expense of the Anglo-Saxon qualities of drive, pugnacity, self-starting, motivating communication.

In the French case, the demand is matched by the supply. France is unusual in having a two-tier system of higher education, where the "mere universities" are outclassed by the superior *grandes écoles*. From the standpoint of the able and ambitious, the system works like this. One attends a *lycée* (selective part of a secondary school), and works towards the *baccalaureat* exam, the equivalent of "A" levels in England or of *Abitur* in Germany, which is taken at the age of 18 and admits to university. But significant choices have already been made. There are different versions of the *baccalaureat* in the sense of different groupings of subjects and subject emphasis. Though there is an economics and business subjects *baccalaureat,* someone aiming at an eventual career in management would not take it! Instead the able and ambitious go for "bac C," the option that includes most maths and natural science, since these are thought to be the best test of intellectual and reasoning ability.

Having passed the bac one might go to university, but again the able and ambitious candidate, especially if male, will not do this (except for subjects such as medicine or computer science only offered at university). Instead our future manager will have his or her sight fixed on entry to one of the *grandes écoles.* To this end one enters an *école préparatoire* (known colloquially as a *prépa*) for an intensive two-year preparatory course. This is the most testing time in the aspirant's life, and (ex) *prépa* students speak routinely of working 70 and 80 hours a week. These labours culminate in taking the *concours,* nationally competitive exams that admit to the *grandes écoles.* This is the most important hurdle one ever has to scale; when it has been cleared, one is made for life. While the course at the typical *grande école* is not a rest cure and the final examination there is taken seriously, the system is "front end-loaded": it is getting in that is difficult and important, once there one is likely to succeed, educationally and occupationally.

The *grandes écoles* are élitist and exclusive. They admit not only on the basis of intense competition but also in small numbers—hundreds not thousands. There is no completely agreed list of the *grandes écoles,* but they are generally thought to number 140 to 160 or so establishments. Many are technical; engineering schools, both general technical and engineering subject specific. Others are commercial or business schools, known commonly as *Sup de Cos* (= *école supérieur de commerce*); and there are a few specialist schools such as the *Ecole Normale* which trains selective secondary school teachers. The *grandes écoles* are arranged in a prestige order that is clear to French people. The most prestigious of the engineering schools is the *Ecole Polytechnique;* the most prestigious of the *Sup de Cos* is HEC (*Haute Ecole de Commerce*), one of the three that are situated in Paris and known collectively as the *trois grandes parisiennes.*

The *grandes écoles* are the gateway to both management careeers and to higher posts in the state service. Not every *cadre* is *grande école* educated, but most are. They are massively overrepresented in the ranks of the chief executives: a 1990 *L'Expansion* survey of 100 chief executives found indeed that 28 of them came from the *Ecole Polytechnique* alone. Most name companies recruit exclusively from the *grandes écoles,* technical and commercial. To enter a company from the *grande école* means achieving *cadre* status early and being on what is known as the *voie royale* (royal road) to success. Non-*grande école* graduates who become *cadres* will variously do it at smaller, less renowned companies, it will take them longer; their career ceiling will be lower, and their *cadre* status will be tied to seniority and performance in the company that "ennobled" them. They will not possess "portable" credentials.

The thing to emphasise is that there is a high congruence between the French understanding of the essential nature of management on the one hand and the output of the education system on the other hand. From *lycée* to *grande école* the emphasis is on formal learning, the development of educated cleverness, numeracy, literacy and a stylish competence with the French language, together with a high level of formal reasoning ability and *culture générale*. All this fits very nicely in a milieu that conceives of management as being about ordering and deciding on the basis of analysis and synthesis, rather than about inter-personal manoeuvring, motivating, and implementing.

This is not to say that there is no "management development" of the graduates of the *grandes écoles* that companies recruit. But it tends to be more of a validating and grooming exercise. Young graduates are sent on assignments abroad, go out on fact-finding missions to the manufac-turing facilities in the provinces, or serve as an *attaché de direction* (PA to senior management). There is also a diagonal promotion route from research and development into general management; serving as the head of research units, or of planning, strategy, or development entities is all seen as an opportunity for the upwardly bound recruits to play their strengths and to cultivate the generalist label so important for progress into the higher ranks. Thus there is management development, but its role is modified by an assumtion that the important act of selec-tion has already taken place at the *concours* (entry to the *grandes écoles*) and been reaffirmed by *grande école* graduation. The task of management development is further simplified by the conviction that all the most important qualities the successful manager should possess are *already* in place and have been publicly certified by the education system.

So far in this article emphasis has been given to the deep-seated contrasts between the understanding of the nature of management in France and that existing in the Anglo-Saxon countries. These differ-ences, it has been suggested, have a profound impact upon the ways in which managers are made and upon the content of the knowledge transmitted to them. The thrust of the argument can be further elabo-rated if we now also bring into the picture an account of management development in another European country. At this point therefore it is worth looking briefly at the situation in Germany.

Management and Management Development in Germany ————

As with the previous analyses of Britain, America and France, it is worth beginning with a view of the general HRM scene before looking more closely at the conception of "management" and hence the way management might be learned. Germany offers a very interesting contrast with the USA and indeed is virtually a mirror image of the American norm. (Our discussion here refers to the personnel function in West Germany as it existed from 1949 to 1990; what are now called the New Federal States [East Germany] required separate treatment.) It should be said straight away that this does not imply any criticism of German personnel managers, they are not lacking in some way compared with their American and British counterparts. It is rather that a range of institutional factors have turned German personnel officers into a body of reactors, implementers, and law-enforcers. The first of these constraining factors is the force of law.

In Germany tradition, diffuse expectations, and custom and practice count for less, and the law counts for more. This reflects not only the relative newness of the (West) German state with its written constitution and Basic Law (1949) but also the much vaunted low tolerance for ambiguity (Hofstede, 1980). It is difficult to express such notions as "grey area" in German, and the German language in general does not lend itself to "fudging." More soberly a wider range of employment issues are legally regulated in Germany than in Britain, wage agreements have the force of law, and there is a system of labour courts. German personnel officers are much more concerned to do what the law commands, are more disposed to ask themselves in any exercise of discretion what it would look like in the labour court. It is not for nothing that the traditional qualification set of the German personnel manager is the equivalent of an LL.B plus a PhD in Law, although a small survey revealed the *de facto* range of qualifications to be somewhat wider (Lawrence, 1982: 31-3).

Second, there is the weighty matter of wage negotiations. In Germany wages are typically negotiated at a level above that of the individual company/employer between employers' associations and trade unions on a *Land* (state) by *Land* basis. This system does not in fact cover *all* German companies: smaller ones may not be members of the relevant employers' federation, and some very large ones, such as Siemens, may go it alone. With these exceptions German personnel managers seldom do what their British colleagues often do and their American colleagues invariably do—negotiate wages. But if they do not have authority, they do have responsibility. The wage agreements that emerge from the negotiations referred to above are in the form of endless pay scales, to which individual employees have to be fitted. This in turn necessitates complicated systems of job-grading, valid independently of particular job incumbents. All this is hard work, and it falls on personnel. So although the authority of initiative may be absent, the burden of implementation is very much present.

Third, there is the codetermination system, established in (West) Germany by law in the early 1950s, and in particular the institution of the elected *Betriebsrat* (works council). While there are clearly benefits to management from the German industrial democracy system of which the *Betriebsrat* is a central part, it does not serve to enhance the proactivity of the personnel function. Indeed the *Betriebsrat* decides some things in its own right, and is a watch-dog for all things that interest it. The personnel department in a sense services it, anticipates its concerns, provides up-front information, offers clarifications as demanded, and takes away critical issues raised in the *Betriebsrat* to "work on them" and provide "a management response." The other half of the equation is that this loss of proactivity by personnel in Germany tends to "free up" line management and particularly production managers.

The general drift of the arguments advanced in this section is to suggest that these several factors cast personnel management in Germany into a reactive mode, which, in turn, militates against an Anglo-Saxon style valorisation of the management development activity. But there is more. One of the earliest accounts of German management has as its major theme the idea that the German tradition venerated the entrepreneur and not the manager (Hartmann, 1959). Indeed the term manager came into use late, and was originally used to designate people running prize fights and road shows rather than industrial enterprises. It is also worth noting that the Germans never developed their own general-purpose term for manager, but simply say "manager" (with a capital M)—clearly indicative. Again tracing out these language peculiarities, the Germans cannot quite bring themselves to say "managerial" which should be *managerhaft* in German. Instead they say *unternchmerisch* (entrepreneurial) which has very positive connotations.

Management education of a general kind also came late to Germany. There is an undergraduate course that approximates to our first degree in management or business administration, the subject being called *Betriebswirtschaftslehre* or business economics. The interesting thing is that throughout most of the post-war era it was regarded as a bit inferior, something for second rate students. First rate people, on the other hand, did *Volkswirtschaft* or political economy, although it had less relevance for a career in management; industry followed the public estimation by hiring graduates in *Volkswirtschaft* on the grounds that they would be brighter. This state of affairs has now changed, but only in the 1980s, with *Betriebswirtschaftslehre* rising in esteem and increasing its enrolments substantially.

At the next level up, that of the MBA, Germany until very recently had nothing at all. The problem is compounded by the fact there are no Master's degrees in Germany anyway in the sense of a degree between the bachelor's and the doctor's (although some German universities call the first degree an MA to confuse foreigners!). In the last few years some MBA courses have sprung up in Germany, and revealingly some of them are franchised by universities in other countries (it is one of our invisible exports).

To round out this picture of management rejection it might be added that there is no equivalent in Germany of the BIM (British Institute of Management) nor any general management course/qualification akin to the DMS (Diploma in Management Studies). Germany does have an approximate equivalent of the IPM (Institute of Personnel Management) but it is a rather low profile affair compared with the British organisation: the present writer has interviewed personnel managers at patently respectable German companies who have not even heard of it.

This relatively weak concept of management, together with the belated emergence of general management education, does not, of course, bode well for management development. But there is another, and important element in this set of problems. The Germans typically have difficulty with the idea of management as something general, as something that can be viewed in the round, taken apart, and generalised about. When Germans look at a company they do not see a need for management: they see a variety of departments and functions requiring specialised knowledge and experience.

This specialist view of management also informs the German view of manager mobility. Germany is not a country where inter-company mobility is viewed as bad, as it is, for instance, in the Netherlands. But Germans expect that the mobility will take place within the same industry. In their view you cannot go from being, say, a purchasing officer in a machine tool company to an equivalent job in textiles: you would forfeit your expertise and have wasted the last ten years. The same sort of thinking informs mobility between functions. It simply does not make much sense, except for mobility between contiguous technical functions (design, production, maintenance, engineering, quality control). This specialist understanding of the management task is also perceptible in the organisation structure of German companies. These tend to be structured in big functional slabs with only a thin layer of general management at the top. Nor do German companies share the British predilection for breaking companies down into smaller units (profit centres) with generalist managers in charge of them.

All of the issues canvassed here militate against a flourishing management development activity in Germany. This does not, of course, mean that it is non-existent. It is often there in German companies but it is less widespread, less salient, more restrained by the reactive mode of the personnel function, and above all it gets away to a slow start because of the traditional German conviction that it is specialist knowledge (especially technical) and experience that are crucial.

Conclusions ————————————————————————————

We have looked at Britain and the USA as a springboard for focussing on personnel and management development in France and Germany.

In neither of these countries is the Anglo-Saxon model to be found, albeit for different reasons in each case. There is no suggestion that this makes either the French or the Germans "worse managers" or "less professional." The non-universality of the Anglo-Saxon norm is attributable rather to two other considerations. First, these nation states have different configurations of institutions—educational, political, and economic—that impinge on management. Second, they exhibit different understandings of what management "is all about" and of the necessary qualities that managers should bring to it.

It is worth noting how much difference has surfaced from this simple line of inquiry: management development in two European countries. This result should be seen as salutory at a time when there is an increasing tendency towards rather facile "internationalism."

References

Barnett, Corelli. 1972. *The Collapse of British Power.* New York: William Morrow.

Barsoux, Jean-Louis and Peter Lawrence, 1990. *Management in France.* London: Cassell.

Crozier, Michel. 1963. *The Bureaucratic Phenomenon.* London: Tavistock Publications.

Gerstl, J.E. and S.P. Hutton. 1966. *Engineers: The Anatomy of a Profession.* London: Tavistock Press.

Gill, R.W.T. and K.G. Lockyer. 1978. *The Career Development of Production Managers in British Industry.* London: Report to the Joint CBI/BIM Advisory Panel on Management Education.

Hartmann, H. 1959. *Authority and Organization in German Management.* Princeton, NJ: Princeton University Press.

Hofstede, G. 1980. *Culture's Consequences.* Beverley Hills: Sage Publications.

Hutton, S.P. and P.A. Lawrence, 1981. *German Engineers: The Anatomy of a Profession.* London: Oxford University Press.

Lawrence, P.A. 1980. *Managers and Management in West Germany.* London: Croom Helm.

Lawrence, P.A. 1982. *Personnel Management in West Germany: Portrait of a Function.* Berlin: Report to Internationales Institut für Management und Verwaltung.

Lawrence, P.A. 1986. *Invitation to Management.* Oxford: Blackwell.

Lockyer, K.G. and S. Jones, 1980. "The Function Factor." *Management Today.* September, 5: 64.

Whyte, William H. 1956. *The Organisation Man.* New York: Simon & Schuster.

Wiener, Martin. 1981. *English Culture and the Decline of the Industrial Spirit. 1950-1980.* Cambridge: Cambridge University Press.

Career Management of Highfliers at Alcatel

Case 4.1
Christophe Falcoz
Sylvie Roussillon
C. Brooklyn Derr

Alcatel-Alsthom

Alcatel is a quintessentially French company. Its corporate offices have always been in Paris, and for years all of its main subsidiaries were French. Until October 1995, most of its top managers were also French. In many ways, Alcatel provides a perfect case study of the French methods of managing highfliers.

Recently, however, Alcatel has diversified and established subsidiaries in several different countries. A large number of non-French executives now work for the corporation, and these executives come from widely differing cultural, organizational, and national backgrounds. At the same time, following a decade of steady growth during the 1980s, major technological and market shifts have forced the Group and its subsidiaries to undergo radical restructuring and rationalization. Current business conditions require new areas of specialization and competency in managers—skills that are sometimes lacking in the top managers who led the firm so successfully until 1992, when it achieved a record profit of 7 billion francs (about $1.4 billion). These recent challenges have raised crucial questions about how best to identify high-potential employees and prepare them to assume top management positions.

Alcatel-Alsthom is France's third largest employer, after the Postal Service and the national water company (La Générale des Eaux). There are about 45,000 managers in Alcatel, 23% of the approximately 104,000 employees. It's the second largest French exporter, with more than 110 billion francs in profits earned abroad in 1994. The Group's profits rank 44th internationally, 21st in Europe, and 4th in France, after Elf-Aquitaine, EDB and Renault. Alcatel's main activity is telecommunica-

Source: Sylvie Roussillon, Christophe Falcoz, and C. Brooklyn Derr. "Career Management of Highfliers at Alcatel." Adapted by permission.

Table 1. Alcatel's Profit and Employees

Total 1994	France	Rest of Europe	Rest of World
Total Profit: 336 million	27.6%	39.4%	33%
Employees: 197,000	41.2%	45.5%	13.3%

tions. In 1994, 67.3% of Alcatel's business was in telecommunications, while only 17.2% of its business was for GEC-Alsthom (energy and transportation), 9.2% for CEGELEC (electrical engineering, 2.4% for SAFT (accumulators) and 3.9% for services and miscellaneous.

As the above table shows, the Group maintains a strong Franco-European character. But it's important to note that Alcatel ranks as one of the top three international telecommunications equipment groups, next to AT&T and Motorola. Alcatel is unquestionably a leader in this industry, with dominant market shares in most European countries and a significant reputation in technology.

Challenges Facing Alcatel

Technological Transformations in the Industry

Ever since the telecommunications environment began to destabilize in the 1980s, the international telecommunications equipment market has been mushrooming. Technological innovations, American and European deregulation, and a growing split between the private and public sectors have all affected the industry, which grew at a rate of about 3.6% per year between 1989 and 1995. In 1995, the industry achieved about $545.5 billion in international profits related to goods and services.

The technological revolutions in the telecommunications industry require that competitors cope with new market patterns and new competitive challenges. One major industry change is the merging of the formerly separate fields of data processing, telecommunications and electronics. In fact, with the development of digital networks, the distinction that used to exist between vocal communication and data transmission is rapidly disappearing.[1] The number of computer engineers hired by Alcatel—several hundred per year over the last five years—and the growing importance of such subsidiaries as Alcatel TITN Answare are a clear indication of the new alliance between data processing and telecommunications.

New technology and services for information transmission—including cables, satellites, optical fibers, telephone lines, digital networks, and Hertz transmission equipment—have also been important elements of change in the industry. So has the field of micro-electronics. Telephone networks can now be used as virtual computer networks, interconnected with powerful mainframes using software that greatly enhances the performance of telephone exchanges. Miniaturization of electronic components has reduced production costs. At the same time, the ever-increasing demand for efficient data exchange between international firms and their markets has greatly increased global demand for information processing within the telecommunications industry. The growing, relatively new market for cellular telephones—which were originally only convenience products—is a perfect example of this development. The cellular telephone industry has grown beyond its traditional markets and has become extremely competitive. Alcatel has not done well in this area, however; its international market share was only 10% in 1995, which represented only 4.5% of its profits.

The push for standardization, combined with the increasingly rapid spread of basic technologies, creates new concerns for firms like Alcatel. Alcatel, which has never been strictly regulated—nor shielded against competition by protectionist legislation—now faces new competitors. Computer firms like IBM, integrated circuit and semi-conductor manufacturers, and even software firms like Intel and Microsoft have all entered the market with competitive low-cost products. Alcatel, with its higher labor and overhead costs, is suddenly at a disadvantage.

Given these new market conditions, investment in research and development has become critical to survival. Yet innovation is complex and expensive. Nor can it be done in isolation from other research efforts within the industry. Alcatel has signed a number of technology transfer and standardization agreements to avoid this isolation, and also to help it stay abreast of unexpected changes in international standards.

The most important consequence of all these developments is that an industry that once relied on technological superiority alone must now become an industry able to supply "custom-built" solutions for increasingly demanding customers. The integration of data-processing and telecommunications, the growing importance of customer services and marketing, the need for flexibility and rapid reaction to increasingly specific demands, and the push for new innovations done in cooperation with competitors, have all become real challenges. Engineering logic once reigned supreme in this industry, but new challenges now require a revolution in corporate mentality.

Foreign Subsidiaries

Because of a virtually uninterrupted series of takeovers and mergers, the Group has become a kind of shifting jigsaw puzzle that includes about 200 companies and holdings in France and about 700 abroad. As a result, Alcatel faces several difficult challenges. It must integrate the different centers of the Group and establish a common corporate culture, while at the same time accommodating the unique national cultures of foreign customers, where most of the growth is now occurring. In the process, the company must help its managers to develop the skills required for these new market conditions—as well as the skills needed to cope with the changing environment within the more mature markets.

The management style of the head office is not management by formal authority, but rather by informal influence. Teamwork is important, and is used to arrive at compromises acceptable to the subsidiary managers. However, that management style hasn't been very effective in achieving integration between foreign subsidiaries, which are closely tied to their own national cultures and to the markets within those cultures.

A couple of examples illustrate the difficulties and risks of isolating the subsidiaries within the Group. In one case, Alcatel SEL, the German subsidiary that Alcatel acquired from ITT, changed its domestic strategies and performed badly for two years. Even though Alcatel normally allows its subsidiaries a large degree of autonomy, in this case general management requested that SEL change its strategy. SEL managers resisted. In response, Alcatel dramatically changed its approach, and fired most of the managers at SEL.

Isolation also hurts research and development. For instance, at one time five subsidiaries were conducting very similar research on ATM terminals; all five, in fact, were developing new state-of-the-art technologies. When this type of duplication has occurred, subsidiaries have often resisted abandoning their research projects in favor of another subsidiary in another country. This leaves the final decision to the head office—a decision that is made more difficult when each subsidiary points out the national specificity of its market.

A similar situation arose during lengthy negotiations to make subsidiary names uniform. CIT, for example, was changed to CIT-Alcatel and finally to ALCATEL CIT. A similar process occurred with ALCATEL SEL. In each case, a difficult process proved how strongly each company was attached to its own history and background.

The unification of brands and names took place after the Group was renamed Alcatel-Alsthom from CGE on January 1, 1991. The purpose of this name unification was to make the structure of the Group more clear to its customers and to help the subsidiaries understand that, though they were often in competition with each other in the global market, they had to speak with the same voice. But "home-town thinking"—a national subsidiary + a national market + a national culture + a unique history—is dying a hard death. In 1995, the head office resorted to shuffling groups of products around the subsidiaries in an attempt to make their product-activity matrix less dependent on local fiefdoms. But the strategy wasn't particularly effective.

The autonomy so dear to the subsidiaries plainly poses a couple of questions related to issues of coordination and subsidiary independence: how far can the parent company intervene in the choice of local managers? And how much horizontal cooperation can exist between managers in different subsidiaries?

Alcatel's HIPO Selection Methods _____

All of these challenges mean that the selection and training of top managers has become more critical to the company's success than ever before. New methods of HIPO selection are gaining ground within the Group, especially among the foreign subsidiaries. As Alcatel has consciously allowed each business unit to maintain its autonomy and national characteristics, a diversity of models has emerged. This decentralization of power has been a key element in the history of Alcatel's high-potential management policy.

At the same time, traditional models are still very much in use. For the last 25 years, Alcatel groomed its high-potential employees in traditionally French ways. During that time, neither the selection criteria nor the profiles of the managers themselves changed much. This is most clearly seen in the criteria used to select the CEO and other top-echelon officers.

The Competitive Examination Model

The succession of men who have led the Group shows clearly the importance that the French place on a limited number of professional schools. These highly competitive French schools aren't business schools but are schools of engineering and public administration. In the case of Alcatel, a degree from a single university—Polytechnique[2]—has become a crucial qualification for reaching the highest echelon.

Besides having the correct degree, top managers at Alcatel, which is a private corporation, have usually spent a lengthy period working for the national government. This period of service seems to be an important springboard to high management positions in large French corporations—which is not surprising, given the close connection between government and business in France. The careers of top Alcatel managers from 1965 to 1995 as illustrated in Table 2 demonstrate this phenomenon. We call this process for selecting future leaders the "Competitive Examination Model."

For example, in 1982 G. Pebereau became CEO of Alcatel. At the time, Pebereau's career was one of the most impressive among top French business leaders. He entered Polytechnique University at the age of 19; upon graduating five years later as an engineer, he worked for the Ministry of Public Works (*Ponts et Chaussees*), then went on to become head of several government departments. Pebereau left government service at the age of 37 to join the former Alcatel (CGE) as Deputy Director General of CIT.

Here, he worked to reposition the group around its most profitable activities. He sold a subsidiary to Saint Gobain and purchased 44% of Framathome. In 1983 he helped acquire a share worth 10 billion francs in Alsthom, held at that time by Thomson CSF. This first real step in the process of takeover was facilitated by the personal relationship

Table 2. Education and Public Service of Alcatel CEOs

CEO From/To	Diploma	Public Service
1965-70	Polytechnique, Ecole Superieur D'Electricité	Mayor, Senator, Minister
1970-82	Polytechnique	Head of Public Works Ministry
1982-86	Polytechnique	Head of Public Works Ministry, Ministry for Equipment
1986-95	Polytechnique	Finance Ministry, Paris Airports Administration
1995-present	Polytechnique	

between the CEOs of the two firms. And, true to French tradition, the takeover was helped along by government participation. At the time, the CEO of Thomson was himself a Polytechnique graduate and a member of the Ponts et Chaussees. The resulting cooperation between CIT and Thomson, which came to an end in 1990, resulted in differentiated activities within the French electronics industry: CGE focused on telecommunications equipment and Thomson on hi-fi, household appliances, electronics for national defense, and data processing.

The takeover by Alcatel of ITT's telecommunications business in Europe helped it achieve its present size, doubled its profits, and made it an international force. The credit for this ITT merger doesn't go to Pebereau, however, but to P. Suard, his successor. Suard spent two years at the Finance Ministry, from 1966 to 1968, then five years at the Paris Airports Administration. He joined CGE in 1973 and three years later took over Câbles de Lyon, a subsidiary that was struggling at the time. There Suard gained a reputation of being a shrewd financier, capable of carrying the company through the most difficult of economic recoveries.

From 1984 onward, Pebereau, impressed by this young man from Savoy, took him on to help complete the merger agreement with ITT. In 1986, at about the time Alcatel was becoming privatized, Suard was appointed CEO of CGE—by the French Minister for the Economy, Finance and Privatizations. The appointment of a CEO by a government minister is just one more unusual aspect of French capitalism, demonstrating the fact that in France there is a strong link between top government officials, politicians in office, and the heads of both public and private companies. These political/business connections mean that changes in capital ownership, either public or private, have little effect on the criteria used in the selection of CEOs, or in the scrutiny given them during the selection process.

The current CEO of Alcatel replaced Suard when he encountered legal problems. S. Tchuruk came directly from the oil industry, after a long career there. Tchuruk had joined Mobil Corportion in 1964, where he remained for 15 years, becoming Director of Strategic Planning, Director of Human Resources and then finally CEO of MOBIL Benelux. He then spent six years with the group Rhône-Poulenc, becoming CEO in 1983. Three years later, the government appointed him chairman of the board of Orkem (formerly CDF-Chimie). And in 1990, Tchuruk became President and CEO of TOTAL, the government-sponsored French oil company.

The only common strand in the careers of Tchuruk and his predecessors is the fact that they all graduated from Polytechnique. In fact, Tchuruk spent his whole career in the business world, outside the realm of the political/administrative elite. Still, Tchuruk is a member of the same old-boy network. The way this network functions is typical of the Competitive Examinations Model, in which success in an informal "test" leads to membership in an influential group. And the group works to help its members succeed.

In this case, the test is simple, even if recruiters don't acknowledge it, you must have the "correct" alma mater. Besides Polytechnique, two other universities are strongly represented among Alcatel's top echelon. About 140 Polytechnique graduates hold highly responsible positions at Alcatel, 60 top executives are graduates of HEC (France's leading business school), and 14 went to ENA (France's elite public administration school). Alcatel isn't alone in its preferences. Some 56% of the CEOs of the 200 leading French corporations are graduates of one of these three schools.[3]

At Alcatel, the presence of so many engineers among top management has had a strong influence on the corporate culture and market approach. Alcatel is a company that emphasizes production and research and development, probably because Polytechnique graduates have steered the company in that direction. However, the need to develop other areas, such as marketing, has become a major challenge for Alcatel. As we shall see, Alcatel's new models for managing highfliers should significantly help the Group meet these challenges.

The Feudal Model

Besides the technical and engineering culture and the importance of certain elite schools in the French parent company, a third dynamic shapes Alcatel's traditional management development strategies: the "Feudal Model." In this model, informal co-opting mechanisms structure the organization at the highest levels, and networking within subsidiaries is an important step in attaining high management positions.

When legal action was brought against P. Suard,[4] the crisis resulted in a redefinition of management teams within Alcatel and several of its subsidiaries. The new teams were homogenous and very loyal to one another. Around the beginning of 1995, a select executive committee of nine was set up under the chairmanship of Suard; five of these had already sat on the management committee in 1991. To these were added the President-CEOs of Cegelec, SAFT and GEC-Alsthom and the financial director of Alcatel-Alsthom.

At the time, only two members of the 19-member general management team at Alcatel were not French. Among that group were eight graduates of Polytechnique, two from ENA, and one from HEC. Most of these managers had responsibilities both at the Alcatel-Alsthom corporate office and at the Alcatel subsidiary office. Seven of the 19 managers had been members of the Cables de Lyon, where P. Suard was president from 1976 to 1986. Five of these former Cables de Lyon cronies were also on the board of directors. Suard had built up a virtual fiefdom.

It's important to note that the human resources manager of Alcatel is not a member of these two committees, nor is the director of communications. None of the top 19 managers has any specific background in marketing, commercial development or production. Where there is an obvious need to serve and satisfy the customer, no one within the inner circles has a working knowledge of how to accomplish this.[5]

Titles and job descriptions often have little to do with true influence and power within the company. There seems to be little connection between the formal hierarchical structure and the relationships that exist within the informal decision-making bodies. Anyone seeking to climb to the top must decipher, by interpreting situational and personal cues, the true power structure. In most cases, of course, they must also learn to work within this informal power network.

The Professional Model

A different model for identifying highfliers exists within the Group's subsidiaries and can be illustrated by a look at Alcatel Bell (Alcatel Belgium). Alcatel Bell is one of the companies acquired from ITT in 1987.

In Belgium, an "executive" is defined differently than in France. Within Alcatel Bell, an executive is anyone who manages people below the level of engineer and/or who is responsible for several important projects. Executives are mostly university graduates in the humanities or various specializations, and usually have five years of experience.

The pay scale is an important tool used in identifying who among these executives are highfliers. First, each new recruit is formally assessed by his/her immediate superior. The written assessment is used to plan salary increases. If the immediate supervisor predicts four salary increases over the next five years, and that the person will reach a level of grade twelve or higher (on a scale of 1-20) before age 50, the person is identified as a highflier.

In each department, a certain number of these individuals are selected by the Human Resources Department and given a career counseling session. After further interviews with HR and immediate superiors, each department develops a short list of ten or so candidates for further development. These candidates are then sent to an external development and assessment center. Some of them may then be referred to the central Human Resources Management Department and to the central Management Committee for training at the parent company, for example in the PACE program. Those who have not been shortlisted may be offered other support positions.

In this "Professional Model," a diploma from a certain elite school isn't the main criterion for success. Instead, the company carefully defines the characteristics of a good executive, and gives the candidate several years of experience. A person makes his or her career within a single division, developing necessary areas of expertise as he/she climbs the ladder rung by rung.

In contrast to the French subsidiaries, Alcatel Bell identifies and develops highfliers with the help of external specialists. Alcatel Bell is also careful to avoid creating perceptual imbalance between the treatment given to highfliers and non-highfliers. The management techniques used for HIPO employees are the same—although modified—as those used for all employees.

Within the entire Alcatel Group, several similar models are in use. Other foreign subsidiaries, particularly in Germany and the United States, use different forms of the Professional Model. But since Alcatel is a French firm managed by the French, it's inevitable that the Competitive Examination Model described earlier is dominant throughout the firm in selecting top managers. In addition, the mosaic-like, expansionist structure of the firm makes it a theater of hidden power struggles.

Endnotes

1. Commutation and transmission are now carried out digitally by using a computer coding system that has replaced the old analogue technique.

2. Polytechnique, called "X," is the most prestigious of the French engineering schools and is under the Ministry of Defense. The top graduates go to public ministries: Bureau of Mines (15 per year), Public Works (12 per year), Telecommunications (2 per year), Armament (1 per year).

3. Other engineering schools are strongly represented in Alcatel-Alsthom, but the graduates tend mostly to be employed in a specialization close to that taught at their school. For example, a hundred or so come from ESTP and are essentially in Cegelec and Alsthom, about 50 from the Ecole Nationale Superieure de l'Aéronautique et de l'Espace are with Alcatel Espace, 80 are from les Ecoles des Mines, and involved in specialized engineering, and so on.

4. P. Suard was taken to court on a charge of political and financial corruption.

5. A marketing department was created at Alcatel's head office in January of 1995.

References

Alpha, the Alcatel-Alsthom company magazine

Bauer, M. and Bertin-Mourot, B. (1987). "Les 200: comment devient-on grand patron?" in *L'Epreuve des Faits*, (Paris: Seuil), 123-145

Bourdieu, P. (1987). "Variations et invariants: elements pour une histoire structurale du champ des grands écoles," *Actes de la Reserche en Science Sociale*, 3-30

CANAL TEL, the Alcatel Business Systems Division Magazine

Cohen, E. and Bauer, M. (1985). *Les Grandes Maneuvres Industrielles* (Paris: P. Belfond Publisher), 181-203

EUROSTAF (1991), "l'industrie mondiale des telecommunications: enjeux economiques, stratégies industrielles, performance financière," (for further information on telecommunications industry)

Gallard, P. and Constanty, H. (October 7, 1994). "Alcatel: le chamion est nu," *Le Nouvel Economiste*, no. 966

Jolinet, J. P. (1990). "Le retour de Thomson dans les télécoms civilies," *L'Usine Nouvelle*, no. 2251, vol. 18.1

Lettre de l'IDATE (October 1995), no. 5, "Reseaux et Télécoms" (for information on the telecommunications industry)

Nexon, M. (September 26-October 9, 1995). "Radiotéléphone" trois hommes pour un réseau," *L'Expansion*, no. 483

Nexon, M. and Fortin, D. (November, 1995). "Reconstruive Alcatel," *L'Expansion*, no. 512, 10-22

Andreas Weber's Assignment to New York: A Case Study in Expatriate Repatriation and Career Planning

Case 4.2
Günter K. Stahl
Mark E. Mendenhall

Andreas Weber's mind would not stop racing. Normally, an intense run in the evening had the effect of dissipating his worries, but tonight it was not working. The further he jogged along his standard route, the more he could not get out of his mind the letter he knew he must write tomorrow. "How had it all come to this?" he wondered. The thought triggered his mind back seven years to the initial event that had set in motion the process that led to his current trouble.

Andreas remembered the occasion clearly; Herr Goerner, the Managing Director, had walked into his office unannounced and asked him to participate in a company-wide international management development program. The Managing Director had gone on to explain that the program involved an international assignment with the intention of fostering the professional development of young, aspiring managers. After their overseas assignments, the trainees would constitute a pool of internationally experienced young managers with the potential for senior management positions at corporate headquarters. Andreas had accepted the offer on the spot, with pride. He had worked hard and had felt that his efforts had finally paid off.

His next memory was a jumble of classes that all had to do with issues related to globalization and overseas adaptation. Right after the program started, an unexpected vacancy had occurred in the New York branch of the bank, and Andreas was asked if he was interested in the position. He remembered calling his wife, Lina, to talk it over

---

Source: Günter K. Stahl and Mark E. Mendenhall. "Andreas Weber's Assignment to New York: A Case Study in Expatriate Repatriation and Career Planning." Reprinted by permission.

and they had both quickly agreed to accept the position. Two months later he was transferred to New York.

> Andreas remembered the day of his arrival in the U.S. as if it were yesterday. He had arrived at JFK Airport early in the afternoon. No one had come to pick him up, so he took a taxi and went directly to the New York branch of the bank. Once at the bank he was uncertain where to go. No one had told him who he should contact after his arrival, so he went straight to the head of the corporate finance department where he was supposed to work. When he entered his office and told the secretary that he was the new manager from Germany, she looked at her notebook, shook her head and told him that they were not expecting anybody. Confused, Andreas rushed to the HR department and soon found out that several misunderstandings had occurred. First, it was not the corporate finance department but the credit department that had requested his transfer. Second, contrary to what he was told in Frankfurt, there was only a non-management position vacant. They were looking for a credit analyst, basically the same job that he had done in Germany.

> Andreas shook his head in reaction to the memory: "There I stood, in what was supposed to be my new office, three pieces of luggage on the desk, and wondering whether I should stay or take the next plane home!"

Why he decided to stay in New York he never quite could figure out; it had been simply a split second decision to make the best of the situation. The whirl of the next two months took over his memory: images of rushed days and nights trying to learn the ropes of a new office with new procedures, looking for a place to live, meeting new people, and of exploring new places raced through his consciousness. Then a clear memory intervened the collage of memories of those first two months—Lina's arrival.

Lina and their three-year-old daughter, Anne-Marie, followed Andreas to New York two months after his arrival. They moved into a small house in the outskirts of New York. Lina knew New York pretty well, since she had lived there for 6 months as an intern in a New York-based reinsurance company; she arrived excited to re-discover her favorite cafés, art galleries, and museums.

Except for occasional attacks of homesickness, Lina was satisfied with her new life. The week after they had moved into their new house they received a dinner invitation from a young married couple that lived next door. To their surprise, their American neighbors quickly embraced the Webers. After two or three months they had gained several more new friends. Since there was no chance for Lina to get a working permit, she joined one of her new acquaintances in doing voluntary work at an art museum. Anne-Marie spent every second afternoon at a local kindergarten, so Lina had plenty of time to pursue her own interests. Then, at the end of their first year in the U.S., a second daughter, Elena, was born. When the Webers stepped off the plane at JFK after their first home leave to Germany, it felt more like they were coming home than returning to a temporary assignment.

Professionally, things had also developed nicely. The New York branch of the bank had been right at the beginning of a boom-phase that lasted for several years. Throughout the boom, the bank's staff increased significantly. After eight months of working in the back office, Andreas was promoted to supervisor of a group of credit analysts. Then, one year after his first promotion, an unexpected vacancy occurred at the senior management level. The deputy head of the rapidly expanding corporate finance department had quit, and the bank had to fill his position with a manager who spoke fluent German, who was familiar with the finance departments of a number of German and other European companies, and who was instantly available. Andreas was asked if he was willing to extend his foreign service contract for another three years and accept the position as deputy head of the corporate finance department. After discussing it with Lina, Andreas accepted the offer.

Then, in the fifth year of his assignment, Andreas made another step upward in his career. His boss retired, and Andreas was promoted to head of the corporate finance department. He was now one out of five managing directors in the branch. When Andreas signed his new contract, it was agreed that he would stay with the New York branch of the bank for another three years and would then return to the bank's German headquarters in Frankfurt.

These were warm memories, memories that somewhat buffered the intensity of Andreas' emotions of frustration and anger at his current situation. But as he continued on his run, the warmness of the past dissipated into the turmoil of the present. He felt tense again, and the beauty of the park's foliage, resplendent in full autumn color, did nothing to ease the burden he felt. His current troubles came to the forefront of his mind and would not leave.

"It all started with that promotion," he muttered to himself. As head of the corporate finance department, Andreas' professional as well as his private life had unexpectedly changed. He was now responsible for a huge area—his business activities no longer concentrated on North American subsidiaries of foreign-based companies, but on their headquarters in Europe and East Asia. In the first six months of his new job Andreas had traveled more than 100,000 miles, mainly business flights to Europe. Due to Andreas' extensive travelling, Lina began to complain. She felt alone, and she began to be concerned about the children's education. Anne-Marie was now nine years old and had spent most of her life outside of Germany. Lina was also concerned about their oldest daughter missing out on a German high school education. Anne-Marie's German language skills had gradually deteriorated over the last two years, and that troubled Lina as well. Their second daughter, Elena, was attending kindergarten, and except for the yearly home leave, she had no contact with other German children. Elena's German was quite poor. In fact, both Anne-Marie and Elena considered themselves Americans.

Lina had also become more and more discontent with her life as a housewife. Obtaining a working permit in the U.S. remained impossible, and it was more difficult for her to find new volunteer activities to quench her interests. To make things worse, Lina's father fell ill and died in that same year, before she could return to be by his side, leaving her mother alone. Andreas remembered the long conversations he had had with Lina during this time, many of which were by telephone from hotel rooms in far away places; and when he was home, in the quiet of their living room. Many times they had talked as they walked through the same park he was now running through.

"It was an extremely difficult situation," Andreas remembered, "not so much for the children, but for Lina and me... From a professional standpoint, my assignment to New York was the best thing that could ever happen to me: I worked in the financial center of the world; I liked my job, the freedom of being away from the corporate bureaucracy, the opportunities to travel; I became a member of the senior management team at a very young age—impossible if I stayed in Germany... Personally, we were also happy: the children felt at home in New York; we had quickly been embraced by our neighbors and the expatriate community; we had many friends here... the question we continually wrestled with was: "does it make sense to give this up for the uncertainty of a return to Germany?" In principle, the answer would clearly have been: "no. But on a long-term basis, moving back to Germany appeared to be the best solution for our children and for Lina's mother. After all, we felt responsible for their future."

After several weeks of consideration and discussion, Lina and Andreas had decided to move back to Germany. This was about a year ago. Immediately after the decision had been made, Andreas had contacted the bank's corporate headquarters in Frankfurt and informed the human resource executive in charge of international assignments about his decision. Three weeks later Andreas received a short letter from him, stating that there was currently no position available in Germany at his level, but that chances were good to find a suitable return assignment within the next six months. Since then Andreas had had several meetings with managers at corporate headquarters, as well as with managers of domestic branches of the bank, but he had not been offered any reentry position.

Lina had become discouraged. She had told her mother immediately after their decision of their intention to return, but 8 months had passed, and her mother kept asking when they were coming back home. Andreas' parents were persistent in their queries as well. Finally, last week, Andreas had received a telephone call from the corporate

HR department in Frankfurt, in which he was informed that they had found a challenging return assignment as deputy head of a medium-sized branch of the bank in the Eastern part of Germany.

The memory of opening that letter and reading it, and the resultant emotions of anger, betrayal, shock, disbelief, and frustration all came back to him. He stopped running, and sat down on a park bench alongside the jogging trail.

"Not only will I earn little more than half the salary that I currently make in New York, I will not be able to use my skills and experiences that I have gained in this new position; I will be out of touch with all the important decisions being made at headquarters; and on top of that, I will be posted to one of the least attractive regions of Germany!" he thought, bitterly.

Andreas continued his thoughts: "The bank's HR policy—if there ever was any rational policy—punishes those who are really committed to the organization...If you are an outstanding performer, they send you abroad. There is no career planning whatsoever. You are posted abroad, and if there just happens to be a job vacant when you return, you are lucky. If not, they let you wait and wait and wait, until you finally accept the most ridiculous job offer...Our senior executives never cease to emphasize how important internationally experienced managers are to the company, but this is only lip service!" He began to wonder if he should accept the offer after all. He wondered if they should just stay in New York and make their home here. But then images of Lina, Lina's mother, Anne-Marie, Elena, and his parents, and all of their combined needs enveloped him.

Leaning back on the park bench, he blankly stared down the path that would lead out of the park and into the street, that in turn would lead him to his sub-division and then home.

Part 5

PERFORMANCE APPRAISAL AND COMPENSATION

Rethinking International Compensation

Reading 5.1
George T. Milkovich
Matt Bloom

We are on the verge of a worldwide restructuring of compensation and reward systems. Even long-established, seemingly carved-in-granite cultural norms, such as lifetime employment in Japan and industry-wide bargaining in Germany, are weakening in response to the pressures of a global economy. So also are our previously hard-and-fast assumptions about international compensation—the idea that pay systems should keep expatriates "economically whole" and the notion that local compensation should be tailored to fit national cultures.

True, from a global perspective, there are still substantial differences in the ways people get paid. Consider, for example, that the pay packages offered by the same multinational operating in both Shanghai and Bratislava are very different. In Shanghai, the package may emphasize housing allowances and bonuses intended to retain scarce critical skills, while in Bratislava the package will place greater emphasis on productivity-based gainsharing and base pay.

Yet the logic of market-based economics suggests that these differences will narrow as players worldwide cope with similar pressures. All are affected by intense competition for customers and critical skills; all are influenced by global financial markets; and all seek to understand and leverage the enormous (and increasingly less restricted) flow of information and technology across national boundaries. All strive to harmonize their regional and global manufacturing and distribution systems. Exhibit 1 depicts some of the global forces at work.

While all companies playing in the international market face similar pressures, responses differ. In Europe, the French are changing their compensation systems only gradually. French voters continue to place a high value on their country's wide-ranging social safety net. Consequently, French managers are using share-the-work schemes to cope with the country's high unemployment. Other Europeans, notably the British, permit the

Source: George T. Milkovich and Matt Bloom. "Rethinking International Compensation." Reprinted from Compensation & Benefits Review, Jan/Feb 1998. Copyright © 1998 American Management Association International. Reprinted by permission of American Management Association International, New York, NY. All rights reserved. http://www.amenet.org.

Exhibit 1. Global Forces

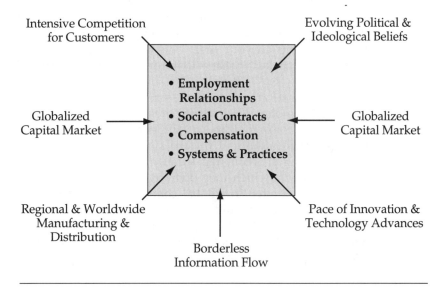

parties to adopt more variable systems, including stock options and performance-based schemes. So even though the pressures created under market-based economies are similar, the players who determine how people get paid have considerable freedom when choosing how to respond.

Different responses to globalization highlight the fact that compensation and reward systems are part of the overall relationships between people and employers around the world. These relationships are entwined with social, political, and economic contexts. We are witnessing different approaches to balancing these pressures within those relationships. The changes occurring bring to mind the old children's game of rock-scissors-paper: rock crushes scissors, scissors cuts paper, and paper covers rock. Rock, scissors, and paper interact with each other in the same way the pressures depicted in Exhibit 1 interact and, in turn, cause compensation and reward systems to adapt.

Creating Global Mind-sets _____

The pressures generated by globalization and market-based economies create unprecedented opportunities for multinational employers. Increasingly, company leaders are recognizing that global mind-sets are required to meet these challenges—and create opportunities.

A global mind-set means adopting values or attitudes to create a common mental programming for balancing corporate, business unit, and functional priorities on a worldwide scale. Such a mind-set has enormous intellectual and thus competitive advantages. According to Jack Welch, CEO at General Electric, "The aim in a global business is to get the best ideas from everyone, everywhere...I think [employees] see that if you are going to grow in GE, you are not going to have a domestic background all your life." This perspective goes beyond "think globally, act locally." It seems to imply the converse: "Think locally but act globally."

Compensation and reward systems can become crucial tools to support this global mind-set—or they can form major obstacles blocking the way. For organizations competing in worldwide markets, managing compensation and reward systems has always depended on understanding the economic, social, and political changes occurring in the countries in which they operate. What is emerging is that some companies are adopting global compensation and reward strategies that are aligned with and signal their global mind-sets. Rather than only reacting to and matching local conditions, companies with a global perspective shift to finding how they can best use compensation and rewards to compete on a worldwide basis.

Expatriate and National Systems Thinking _____

Ask compensation directors to describe how international compensation and rewards are managed in their firms, and they typically offer one of two responses. Some describe their recent efforts to modify the balance sheet approach for paying expatriates. Most of these efforts attempt to better align compensation costs with the purposes of different global assignments by distinguishing between developmental and longer-term technology transfers and leadership roles.

Other compensation directors think in terms of different national cultures. They point out the importance of localizing compensation decisions within broad corporate principles. Their purpose is to better align compensation decisions with differences in national cultures. Usually the broad corporate principles seem to be relevant only at 10,000 meters, as in "support the corporate values and global business strategy."

The reality is that local conditions dominate the compensation strategy. Justifications of this practice inevitably include statements like, "You must understand that the United States has a highly individualistic national culture. In other places in the world, particularly Asia, people are comfortable with more collective values. Security is more important than risk taking. You need to be sensitive to 'saving face,'" and so on. These executives seem to believe that something called "national culture" is a critical (perhaps the most critical) factor when managing international compensation.

Now ask those same executives the question posed above, but delete the word *international*, i.e., "Describe how your organization manages compensation." Executives now talk about initiatives to create a common culture of ownership and performance. They say they want to build flexible, agile cultures through practices such as broad banding, broad-based stock option eligibility, 360-degree assessment, and competency-based projects.

So, on the domestic front, they place emphasis on strategic choice and on crafting compensation strategies to help create an organization culture sensitive to markets and performance. Yet internationally, concern with aligning compensation with different national cultures dominates. Most managers subscribe to this approach as consistent with the belief that competitive advantage is achieved via transforming multinationals into local companies.

This view conforms to the often-heard conventional wisdom that the best, indeed, the *only* way to manage international compensation is to tailor it to local conditions and the national culture—to think globally but act locally. Too often the reality is a matter of *reacting*, not acting, locally.

Traditionally, "International" Means "National" ——————————

Generally, the traditional perspective is based on the premise that different national systems of compensation and reward are strategic. Discussions, for example, focus on contrasting the German, Japanese, and U.S. approaches. To a large measure, this view reflects the critical importance of government, laws, and regulations, especially tax policies, in determining pay practices. Consequently, understanding these regulations and perhaps undertaking initiatives to change them remain important responsibilities in international compensation.

But this national-system approach goes beyond focusing on regulatory differences among nations; it rests largely on three tenuous assumptions:

1. that national borders largely define the important attributes of people and must be considered when designing compensation and reward systems,

2. that differences between nations are greater and more relevant to managing international compensation than differences within nations, and

3. that something called "national culture" exists and is a significant factor in global approaches to compensation and reward.

Nations and Regions versus Strategies and Markets ——————————

Does it still make sense to view international compensation in terms of national systems when there appears to be considerable variation in compensation and rewards *within* nations as well as between them?

Recent studies in China, for example, report substantial differences in pay and reward systems associated with differences in the governance and ownership. In general, pay packages provided in state-owned enterprises emphasize services, benefit allowances (housing, food, healthcare, childcare, etc.) and relatively lower cash. Joint ventures and wholly foreign owned subsidiaries use widely divergent approaches, some emphasizing highly risky variable pay, others emphasizing careers, training opportunities, and moderate cash.

Studies of Japanese companies' HR strategies report differences in compensation approaches associated with organization profitability, size, degree of unionization, capital-labor ratio, and exposure to global competitive forces. For example, Japanese companies operating in protected domestic markets are more likely to use the more performance- and ability-based schemes. Among Korean chaebols, factors such as labor market conditions, customer and supplier relations, economic conditions, and technology account for differences in compensation strategies.

Studies of person-based rewards in samples from Hungarian and U.S. companies suggest that political, economic, and institutional forces, rather than national cultures, explain differences in Hungarian and U.S. reward practices. Recent surveys in the Central European countries of Slovenia and Slovakia also report differences among companies in their use of variable performance-based pay schemes, allowances and services, and even in the ratios of top managing directors' salaries to the average worker.

While the recent evidence does not suggest that national boundaries (national wage systems) should be ignored or overlooked, it does suggest that sufficient discretion for individual organizations exists within these national systems to allow organizations to customize compensation and reward systems. Hence, business strategy and markets are more appropriate than countries as the unit of analysis for globalizing compensation.

The Strategic (In)Significance of National Cultures

Are compensation and reward systems in a global context better understood by examining differences in *national* cultures—or by examining more *local* cultures, particularly those within organizations?

The assumption that compensation systems must fit national cultures is based on the belief that "most of a country's inhabitants share a national character ... that ... represents mental programming for processing ideas and information that these people have in common."[1] This belief, put forth by Geert Hofstede, leads to a search for distinct national characteristics whose influence is then assumed to be critical in managing international compensation systems.

Typical of this mode of thinking is the widely used list of cultural attributes proposed by Hofstede (power distance, individualism-collectivism, uncertainty avoidance, and masculinity/femininity) or by H. K. Trompenaar (individualism versus collectivism, achievement versus ascription, universalism versus particularism, neutral versus affective, specific versus diffuse).

Following this view, some argue that compensation systems in countries where the culture emphasizes respect for status and hierarchy and thus produces higher power distance scores (Malaysia and Mexico) should exhibit more hierarchical pay structures, while those manifesting low power distance (Australia and the Netherlands) would choose more egalitarian systems. In nations identified as individualistic (U.S., U.K, Canada), compensation and rewards would support employability and individual and performance-based pay. Those in more collectivist nations (Singapore, Japan) would choose more group-based approaches, and so on.

This national culture approach prescribes that compensation and reward policies must be aligned with and reinforce attributes of national culture. Proponents of this approach might argue, for example, that "Giving the kind of direct performance feedback required under most merit and bonus plans fails to account for saving face, which is so crucial in Asian cultures." Or they might say, "In Germany, MBO was favorably received, because Germans prefer decentralization and formal rules."

One might well react to such thinking by pointing out that it engenders blatant stereotyping. It parallels such biased notions as "all women desire time off because of their caring and nurturing values, while all men desire more time at work to pursue their more aggressive values."

It has long been recognized that compensation and reward systems, because of their social as well as economic significance, exemplify and reinforce cultural norms. However, this does not mean that social and cultural norms necessarily coincide with national boundaries. Indeed 100 years ago, writers recognized that mining and textile companies developed their own unique social norms—and that the compensation systems of these companies reflected those norms.

The idea of a "national culture" requires a leap of logic in assuming that social norms and cultural values are solely national in character. Clearly, geopolitical boundaries alone do not determine cultural values and social norms. Nations comprise a variety of subgroups and subcultures, and anecdotal and empirical evidence suggest that local cultural values as well as values within organizations differ significantly.

Consider, for example, that the former Czechoslovakia included the Czechs and Slovaks; now each of these two republics includes groups that exhibit Hungarian and Roman cultural characteristics. Historically, China has always been a composite of several groups; even today, Chinese make culturally laden distinctions between Shanghai, Beijing, and Hong Kong.

Listening to U.S. politicians during election time, one quickly realizes that the United States is made up of many different subcultures that do not conform to geographic boundaries. As pluralism and other influences of globalization increase around the world, some cultural researchers believe that the cultures of small subgroups will become much more important for shaping human behavior than norms at larger societal or national levels. Even when viewed at the national level, revisions may already have occurred. Recent studies suggest that work-related values are changing in China and the U.S. and that these changes are related to differences in reward allocation preferences.

Indeed, it seems increasingly inappropriate to begin analysis for compensation systems at the national level. We recently completed a study of values placed on individualism-collectivism and risk taking at four companies, two in the U.S. and two in Slovenia. The averages of these intra-country distributions were slightly different: Slovenian employees tended to be more individualistic and more inclined to take risks than U.S. employees. Yet Hofstede's work suggests that Yugoslavs, of which Slovenia is a former republic, should be risk averse and collectivistic. The striking feature, however, was that the variances of the distributions were virtually the same. Thus, one can find risk averse collectivists and risk-taking individuals in the U.S., Slovenia, and most likely in many other nations as well.

Our research suggests that paying attention to average levels across national cultures may be misleading. It fails to account for the significant variation within countries that creates sufficient overlap with the distributions in other countries. Closer analysis reveals that political, economic, institutional, and other forces (rather than national culture) explain a significant amount of variation in the expressed desires of employees from different countries. For example, U.S. workers may desire two weeks of vacation, not because of culture, but because that is the norm in the U.S. In Germany, the norm is one month or more. Transfer a U.S. worker to Germany, and the employee will likely want the month; two weeks will no longer be sufficient.

Does It Pay to Be Different? _____

Are compensation and reward systems in a global context better understood by examining competitive strategies of specific enterprises, or by focusing on differences in national culture and institutions (e.g., public policy)?

Obviously, national public policy, which reflects social contracts among unions, employers, financial institutions and people, is an important influence on compensation and reward systems. For example, differences in the use of stock options in Germany and Japan compared with the United States and the United Kingdom are directly related to national tax and regulation policies. Differences in marginal tax rates are directly associated with the use of variable pay schemes. In Korea or Japan, for example, employees prefer increases in bonuses and allowances (not based on performance) rather than base pay increments. Social security and national health insurance rates paid by employers are calculated on base pay, not bonuses or allowances. In the U.S., many benefit forms are not subject to income tax and are therefore a relatively tax effective way to increase the value of employment for people.

The degree of discretion available to managers when they respond to governmental initiatives is often not a simple matter of compliance. Except in rare cases, firms usually have alternatives in terms of the strength and pervasiveness of their response to governmental actions.

For example, structuring compensation practices around U.S. tax laws has led to some very creative and innovative new compensation schemes (e.g., deferred compensation plans, ESOPs, phantom stock options). These are used by some firms, but certainly not all. Thus, even the "how" of complying with public policies is a strategic choice.

In the same way, firms operating within so-called national cultures exhibit a variety of responses. Each organization's human resource policies and practices create a distinctive and unique culture that influences people's attitudes and work behaviors. Those people who do not fit the organization culture because they possess different values will either not join or will soon leave the organization.

Signaling Organization Cultures, Not National Cultures _____

Compensation and reward systems can become an important signal of an organization's culture and values. As such, the systems help create cultures or mind-sets that are different and distinct from the cultures and values of competing firms. Hewlett-Packard and Microsoft both compete vigorously for software engineers, yet each company exhibits a different corporate culture, signaled by and reinforced in their respective compensation systems. The same logic applies to Toyota and Toshiba—different cultures and different compensation and reward systems.

Given sufficient variation in values among the people in the labor pools of a nation, firms can structure compensation policies that are consistent with the firm's culture and simultaneously attract individuals from the applicant pool who have similar values. When considered from a strategic perspective, organizations can customize compensation systems to help create a culture and attract a workforce that possesses the values, knowledge, skills, and abilities that support the organizations' strategic goals and objectives.

Strategic Flexibility: Managing Multiple Deals _____

Strategic flexibility in global compensation and reward systems starts with understanding how the company plans to win. What is its strategic intent? What is its global mind-set?

As depicted in Exhibit 2, strategic flexibility is based on the premise that understanding and managing total compensation in a global business shifts thinking away from using a balance sheet to keep expatriates economically whole or relying on stereotypical notions of differences among nations. The focus, rather, is on understanding and leveraging differences within and between nations.

To be sure, national laws, particularly tax and welfare regulations, are important forces. Yet logic argues that understanding differences and variability within as well as between nations reinforces strategic concerns. In the U.S., no manager presumes all the people are equal to the U.S. average; differences matter. It's the same around the world. In addition, the focus on differences helps managers think in terms of shaping a common mind-set and creating and energizing a workforce with shared values and the capabilities necessary to achieve success.

If the global business strategy involves paying less attention to boundaries, sharing ideas and intelligence, harmonizing manufacturing and the distribution process to take advantage of economies of scale, and presenting one face to the customer, then a global compensation system should be crafted to signal this—and reward behaviors to achieve it.

At the same time, we need to recognize that creative tension occurs when a global business strives to achieve a common mind-set and the

---

Exhibit 2. Rethinking International Compensation
Traditional to Strategic Flexibility

TRADITIONAL	STRATEGIC FLEXIBILITY
Ensure Expatriates' Balance Sheet	⟶ Create Global Mind-set; Achieve Strategic Priorities
Focus on Differences Among Nations	⟶ Leverage Differences Within Nations
Act Like National Culture	⟶ Grow Corporate Culture
Focus Total Compensation Package	⟶ Manage Total Value of Employment and Relational Forms
Manage Multiple Compensation Systems	⟶ Manage Multiple Deals

common strategic objectives while simultaneously operating in numerous, complex, rapidly changing markets and locations.

Strategic flexibility means that companies achieve advantage by customizing multiple compensation and reward systems. This is already the state of practice in companies operating in multiple markets or employing contingent and core workforces. The art is to avoid the chaos created when multiple systems go off in multiple directions. This results in numerous compensation systems, one for each country in which the company operates. To overcome the chaos, the company must ensure that the multiple deals signal the organization's global mind-set and support its strategic priorities.

The strategic flexibility model presumes that all these complexities cannot be predetermined and indeed are constantly changing. So an adaptive, more flexible approach is required—one that creates a total value of employment consistent with local conditions, while at the same time forging the common mind-set required by business priorities. It supports business priorities not through a set of chameleon-like systems tailored to varying conditions, but from systems that focus attention on what matters to business success and influences employees' actions consistent with an organization's priorities.

Creating and managing multiple deals to support a global business is consistent with the current practice of broadening the definition of total compensation to include the total value of employment. As shown in Exhibit 3, total compensation includes cash, benefits, and long-term incentives as well as employment security conditions, flexible work schedules, learning opportunities, and so on. There is a growing realization that focusing only on the financial forms of total compensation creates transactional relationships that can be easily copied or purchased by competitors. Financial returns alone cannot extract the unique, value-adding ideas and behaviors possessed by empoloyees. Financial returns alone are ineffective in creating the common mind-set that creates peoples' willingness to share the insights and tacit knowledge required to achieve and sustain advantage.

Relational Returns _____

Broader thinking that includes both financial and relational returns is required. Relational returns may bind individuals more strongly to the organization because they can answer those special individual needs that cannot be met as effectively with economic returns (e.g., providing for childcare via the noneconomic return of flexible work schedules, versus the financial return of salary to pay for childcare; the flexible schedule puts a parent, not a caregiver, at home). The total value of employment, comprising both relational and financial returns, creates broad, flexible exchanges or deals with employees. Multiple deals

Exhibit 3. Total Value of Employment

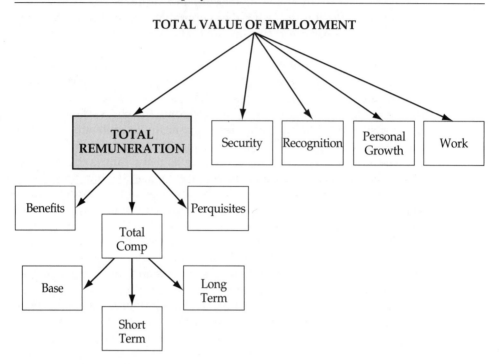

encompass a broad range of exchanges and can help create commitment to common values, goals, and the pursuit of mutually beneficial long-term objectives.

Thus, an adaptive, more flexible approach is required. It must permit multiple employment relationships that allow organizations to recognize local conditions when necessary, while at the same time creating the common mind-set among employees required to direct their efforts toward strategic priorities. This approach recognizes that variations in beliefs, opinions, and values within countries provide opportunities for organizations to attract people who thrive in the organization's unique culture, rather than trying to make the organization conform to national cultures.

Flexibility, choice, and managing risk form the essence of this thinking. It begins by viewing the employment relationship as an exchange. Under this view, both the employer and employee make contributions and extract returns from the relationship. A critical principle is that the returns offered by the employer are the primary determinants of the contributions provided by employees. That is, what employees are willing to give to the organization is determined in large part by what the employer is willing to give to the employee.

There is no chicken-and-egg search here; the employer's choices come first and determine the employees' response. However, once this relationship is underway, it becomes dynamic and recurring.

Total Compensation

The objective, then, is to structure the total value of employment so that employee contributions support organizational goals.

The model in Exhibit 4 groups different forms of total compensation into three sets: core, crafted, and choice. It includes any return an organization can offer that employees see as a reward or a return for the contributions they make on the organization's behalf.

The *core* section of the model includes compensation and reward forms that signal the corporate global mind-set (e.g., creating a performance/customer service culture or a culture of ownership, ensuring a basic level of services and benefits). Specific practices may vary according to market and local conditions but must be consistent with the core policies.

The *crafted* set of compensation elements in Exhibit 4 assumes that business unit or regional leaders have discretion to choose among a menu of total compensation forms that may be important to gain and sustain advantage in the markets in which they operate. For example, some form of housing assistance (loans, allowances, dormitories) may make sense in Shanghai, whereas in London or Tokyo, transportation assistance may make more sense. A single company with operating units in San Jose and Kuala Lumpur may find that specific elements (e.g., risk sharing, bonuses, language training, and flexible schedules) may be more important in California than in Kuala Lumpur.

Exhibit 4. Strategic Flexibility: Core, Customize, and Choice

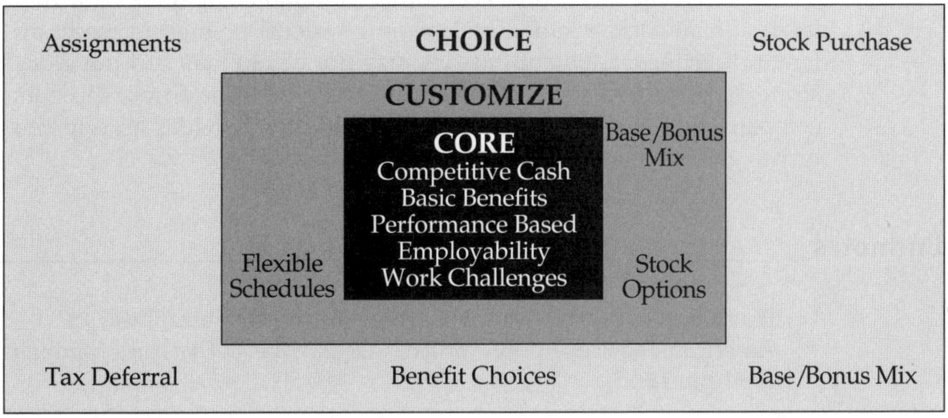

The critical focus of the crafted alternatives is to offer operating units the ability to further customize their total compensation package to achieve their business objectives. This crafted portion is created within the framework of core returns so that it supports and reinforces corporate priorities and culture as well. Thus, managers of R&D units can craft returns to support their goals and satisfy the preferences of scientists, while the sales units can craft a different set of returns consistent with sales goals and preferences of sales personnel.

Finally, the alternatives in the *choice* set offer flexibility for employees to select among various forms of total compensation. Analogous to flexible benefits, the choice set shifts the focus of customizing compensation from managers to employees. Examples here might include opportunities to take educational leaves to become eligible for regional or global assignments, 401(k)-like wealth creating arrangements, or differing employment security arrangements (e.g., contract terms for managers and professionals).

The choice set recognizes the difficulties in identifying national cultures by taking the notion of customizing to the individual level. Within a total cost framework, employees would be given the opportunity to select from a set of returns those that are of most value to their particular situations.

So the strategic flexibility model offers managers the opportunity to tailor the total compensation system to fit the context in which they compete within a framework of corporate principles. Additionally, the approach offers some opportunity for employees to select forms of returns that meet their individual needs as well.

Many companies are already using some of this strategic flexibility model. In global organizations, the business units or regions often have discretion to customize their compensation system within corporate guidelines. For some companies, the strategic flexibility model simply draws existing practices under one umbrella. For example, it treats expatriates as simply another group, much like sales disciplines.

At the same time, however, other companies operate with their international compensation and reward systems pointed in many different directions. Global mind-sets may not be obvious and the global strategic priorities may not be supported. For these firms, directing compensation and reward systems strategically provides an opportunity to gain a competitive advantage.

Endnotes

1. Hofstede, Geert. "Motivation, Leadership and Organizations: Do American Theories Apply Abroad?" *Organizational Dynamics*, Summer 1980, pp. 42-55.

Expatriate Performance Appraisal: Problems and Solutions

Reading 5.2
Gary Oddou
Mark Mendenhall

For more and more companies, gaining a competitive edge increasingly means making decisions that reflect an acute understanding of the global marketplace—how other countries utilize and view marketing strategies, accounting and financial systems, labor laws, leadership, communication, negotiation and decision-making styles. Gaining a knowledge of these components is most directly accomplished by sending managers to work in an overseas subsidiary and utilizing them on reentry.

Our research shows clearly that expatriates develop valuable managerial skills abroad that can be extremely useful to their development as effective senior managers. Based on current research on expatriates, including our own surveying and interviewing of more than 150 of them, probably the most significant skills expatriates develop as a result of their overseas assignments include the following:

- Being able to manage a workforce with cultural and subcultural differences

- Being able to plan for, and conceptualize, the dynamics of a complex, multinational environment

- Being more open-minded about alternative methods for solving problems

- Being more flexible in dealing with people and systems

- Understanding the interdependencies among the firm's domestic and foreign operations

These skills are the natural outgrowth of the increased autonomy and potential impact expatriates experience in their international assignment. In fact, in our study, 67 percent reported having more independence, and they also indicated they had more potential impact on the operation's performance than in their domestic position. With

---

Source: This article was written especially for this book.

increased decision-making responsibilities in a foreign environment, expatriates are subjected to a fairly intense working environment in which they must learn the ropes quickly.

The skills expatriate managers gain are obviously crucial to effectively managing any business operation, particularly at the international and multinational level. Nightmares abound in the business press of the inept decisions sometimes made by top management due to ignorance of cross-cultural differences in business practices. The ability to plan and conceptualize based on the complex interdependencies of a global market environment with significant cultural differences is required of top management in MNCs.

In short, expatriates can become a very valuable human resource for firms with international or multinational operations. However, one of the most serious stumbling blocks to expatriates' career paths is the lack of recognition of the value of expatriation and the informality with which firms accurately evaluate their expatriates' overseas performance. Although the attributes expatriates gain overseas can and do translate into concrete advantages for their firms, a quick glance at the skills previously listed indicates intangibles that are often difficult to measure and usually are not measured—or are measured inaccurately—by present performance evaluation methods. Hence, it is critical to more closely examine this potential stumbling block to expatriates' careers and to make specific recommendations to improve the process and accuracy of such reviews.

Appraising the Expatriate's Performance _____

Several problems are inherent to appraising an expatriate's performance. First, an examination of those who evaluate an expatriate's job performance is relevant. Those evaluators include the host national management and often the home office management.

Host National Management's Perceptions of Actual Job Performance

That local management evaluates the expatriate is probably necessary; however, such a process sometimes is problematic. Local management typically evaluates the expatriate's performance from its own cultural frame of reference and set of expectations. For example, one American expatriate manager we talked to used participative decision making in India but was thought of by local workers as rather incompetent because of the Indian notion that managers, partly owing to their social class level, are seen as the experts. Therefore, a manager should not have to ask subordinates for ideas. Being seen as incompetent negatively affected local management's review of this expatriate's performance, and he was denied a promotion on return to the United States. Local management's appraisal is not the only potential problem, however. In fact, based on our research with expatriates, local management's evaluation is usually perceived as being more accurate than that of the home office.

Home Office Management's Perceptions of Actual Job Performance

Because the home office management is geographically distanced from the expatriate, it is often not fully aware of what is happening overseas. As a result, for middle and upper management, home office management will often use a different set of variables than those used by local management. Typically, more visible performance criteria are used to measure the expatriate's success (for example, profits, market share, productivity levels). Such measures ignore other, less visible variables that in reality drastically affect the company's performance. Local events such as strikes, devaluation of the currency, political instability, and runaway inflation are examples of phenomena that are beyond the control of the expatriate and are sometimes "invisible" to the home office.

One expatriate executive told us that in Chile he had almost single-handedly stopped a strike that would have shut down their factory completely for months and worsened relations between the Chileans and the parent company in the United States. In a land where strikes are commonplace, such an accomplishment was quite a coup, especially for an American. The numerous meetings and talks with labor representatives, government officials, and local management required an acute understanding of their culture and a sensitivity beyond the ability of most people. However, because of exchange rate fluctuations with its primary trading partners in South America, the demand for their ore temporarily decreased by 30 percent during the expatriate's tenure. Rather than applauding the efforts this expatriate executive made to avert a strike and recognizing the superb negotiation skills he demonstrated, the home office saw the expatriate as being only somewhat better than a mediocre performer. In other words, because for home office management the most visible criterion of the expatriate's performance was somewhat negative (sales figures), it was assumed that he had not performed adequately. And though the expatriate's boss knew a strike had been averted, the bottom-line concern for sales dollars overshadowed any other significant accomplishments.

The expatriate manager must walk a tightrope. He must deal with a new cultural work group, learn the ins and outs of the new business environment, possibly determine how to work with a foreign boss, find out what foreign management expects of him, and so on. He must also understand the rules of the game on the home front. It is difficult, and sometimes impossible, to please both. Attempting to please both can result in a temporarily, or permanently, railroaded career. So it was with an individual who was considered a "high potential" in a semiconductor firm. He was sent to an overseas operation without the proper product knowledge preparation and barely kept his head above water because of the difficulties of cracking a nearly impossible market. On returning to the United States, he was physically and mentally exhausted from the battle. He sought a much less challenging position and got it because top management then believed they had overestimated his potential. In fact, top management never did understand what the expatriate was up against in the foreign market.

In fact, expatriates frequently indicate that headquarters does not really understand their experience—neither the difficulty of it nor the value of it. One study found that one-third of the expatriates felt that corporate headquarters did not understand the expatriate's experience at all. In a 1981 Korn/Ferry survey, 69 percent of the managers reported they felt isolated from domestic operations and their U.S. managers. It is clear from others' and our own research that most U.S. senior management does not understand the value of an international assignment or try to utilize the expatriate's skills gained abroad when they return to the home office. The underlying problem seems to be top management's ethnocentricity.

Management Ethnocentricity

Two of the most significant aspects of management's inability to understand the expatriate's experience, value it, and thereby more accurately measure his or her performance are (1) the communication gap between the expatriate and the home office and (2) the lack of domestic management's international experience.

The Communication Gap. Being physically separated by thousands of miles and in different time zones poses distinct problems of communication. Not only does the expatriate have difficulty talking directly with his manager, but usually both the U.S. manager and the expatriate executive have plenty of other responsibilities to attend to. Fixing the day-to-day problems tends to take precedence over other concerns, such as maintaining contact with one's boss (or subordinate) in order to be kept up to date on organizational changes or simply to inform him or her of what one is doing. Most of the expatriates in our research indicated they had very irregular contact with their home office and that often it was not with their immediate superior. Rarely did the boss initiate direct contact with the expatriate more than once or twice a year.

The Lack of International Experience. The old Indian expression "To walk a mile in another man's moccassins" has direct meaning here. How can one understand what another person's overseas managerial experience is like—its difficulties, challenges, stresses, and the like—without having lived and worked overseas oneself? According to one study, more than two-thirds of upper management in corporations today have never had an international assignment. If they have not lived or worked overseas, and if the expatriate and U.S. manager are not communicating regularly about the assignment, the U.S. manager cannot evaluate the expatriate's performance appropriately.

Of course, how the U.S. manager and foreign manager perceive the expatriate's performance will depend partly on the expatriate's actual performance and partly on the managers' *perceptions* of the expatriate's performance. Up to now, we have discussed the managers' perceptions of the expatriate's performance. Let's now turn our attention to what usually composes the expatriate's *actual* performance to better understand why evaluating it is problematic.

Actual Job Performance

As repeatedly mentioned by the expatriates in our study and in other research, the primary factors relating to the expatriate's actual job performance include his or her technical job know-how, personal adjustment to the culture, and various environmental factors.

Technical Job Know-How. As with all jobs, one's success overseas partly depends on one's expertise in the technical area of the job. Our research indicates that approximately 95 percent of the expatriates believe that technical competency is crucial to successful job performance. Although common sense supports this notion, research shows that technical competence is not sufficient in itself for successful job perfomance. For example, an engineer who is an expert in his or her field and who tends to ignore cultural variables that are important to job performance will likely be ineffective. He or she might be less flexible with local personnel, policies, and practices because of his or her reliance on technical know-how or because of differences in cultural views. As a result, the host nationals might become alienated by the expatriate's style and become quite resistant to his or her objectives and strategies. A less experienced engineer, with less technical competence, might be more willing to defer to the host country's employees and their procedures and customs. A shade of humility is always more likely to breed flexibility, and in the long run, the less experienced engineer might develop the trust of the foreign employees and might well be more effective than the experienced engineer.

We have been given numerous examples by expatriates, in fact, where this has been the case. One expatriate who represented a large construction firm was sent to a worksite in India. The expatriate was an expert in his field and operated in the same fashion as he did in the United States. He unintentionally ignored local work customs and became an object of hatred and distrust. The project was delayed for more than six months because of his behavior.

Adjustment to a New Culture. Just as important as the expatriate's technical expertise is his or her ability to adapt to the foreign environment, enabling him or her to deal with the indigenous people. Nearly every expatriate in our survey felt understanding the foreign culture, having an ability to communicate with the foreign nationals, and being able to reduce stress were as—if not more—important to successful job performance than was technical competence. Regardless of how much an expatriate knows, if he or she is unable to communicate with and understand the host nationals, the work will not get done.

An expatriate's adjustment overseas is also related to at least two personal variables: (1) one's marital and family status (that is, whether accompanied by a spouse and children) and (2) the executive's own personal and the family's predisposition to acculturation. Research clearly indicates that expatriates who have their family abroad are often less successful because of the stress on the family of being in a foreign environment. The stress on the spouse negatively affects the employee's concentration and job performance. With an increasing number of dual-career couples being affected by expatriation, the problems are even keener. A number of expatriates reported that their formerly career-positioned spouse suffered from depression most of the time they were overseas. Moving from experiencing the dynamics of a challenging career to having no business-world activity and being unable to communicate the most basic needs is a grueling transition for many career-oriented spouses.

Company variables affecting cultural and work adjustment also come into play. The thoroughness of the company's expatriate selection method and the type and degree of cross-cultural training will affect expatriate adjustment and performance. In other words, if the firm is not selective about the personality of the expatriate or does not appropriately prepare the employee and dependents, the firm may be building in failure before the manager ever leaves the United States.

All these factors influence the expatriate's learning curve in a foreign business environment. More time is thus required to learn the ins and outs of the job than for the expatriate's domestic counterpart who might have just taken a comparable position stateside. In fact, most expatriates say it takes three to six months to even begin to perform at the same level as in the domestic operation. Hence, *performance evaluations at the company's normal time interval may be too early to accurately and fairly reflect the expatriate's performance.*

A Summary of Factors Affecting Expatriation Performance_____

In summary, an expatriate's performance is based on overseas adjustment, his or her technical know-how, and various relevant environmental factors. Actual performance, however, is evaluated in terms of perceived performance, which is based on a set of fairly complex variables usually below the evaluator's level of awareness. Much of the perceived performance concerns perceptions of the expatriate and his or her situation. Depending on whether the manager assessing the expatriate's performance has had personal overseas experience or is otherwise sensitive to problems associated with overseas work, the performance appraisal will be more or less valid. *The bottom line for the expatriate is that the performance appraisal will influence the promotion potential and type of position the expatriate receives on returning to the United States.* Because expatriates generally return from their experience with valuable managerial skills, especially for firms pursuing an international or global market path, it behooves organizations to carefully review their process of appraising expatriates and the evaluation criteria themselves.

Guidelines on How to Appraise an Expatriate's Performance ——————

Human Resource Personnel: Giving
Guidelines for Performance Evaluation

Human resources departments can do a couple of things to help guide the evaluator's perspective on the evaluation.

A basic breakdown of the difficulty level of the assignment should be done to properly evaluate the expatriate's performance. For example, working in Japan is generally considered more difficult than working in England or English-speaking Canada. The learning curve in Japan will take longer because of the very different ways business is conducted, the language barrier that exists, and the isolation that most Americans feel within the Japanese culture. Major variables such as the following should be considered when determining the difficulty level of the assignment:

- Operational language used in the firm

- Cultural "distance," based often on the region of the world (for example, Western Europe, Middle East, Asia)

- Stability of the factors affecting the expatriate's performance (for example, labor force, exchange rate)

Many foreigners speak English, but their proficiency does not always allow them to speak effectively or comfortably, so they rely on their native language when possible. In addition, they usually do not speak English among themselves because it is not natural. In Germany, for example, one expatriate said that while relying on English allowed a minimum level of work to be performed, the fact that he did not speak German limited his effectiveness. Secretaries, for example, had very limited English-speaking skills. German workers rarely spoke English together and therefore unknowingly excluded the expatriate from casual and often work-related conversations. And outside work, he had to spend three to four times the amount of time to accomplish the same things that he did easily in the United States. Most of the problem was because he could not speak good enough German, and many of the Germans could not speak good enough English.

Although sharing the same language facilitates effective communication, it is only the surface level of communication. More deep-rooted, cultural-based phenomena can more seriously affect an expatriate's performance.

Countries or regions where the company sends expatriates can be fairly easily divided into categories such as these: (1) somewhat more difficult than the United States, (2) more difficult than the United States, and (3) much more difficult than the United States. Plenty of information is available to help evaluate the difficulty level of assignments. The U.S. State Department and military branches have these types of ratings. In addition, feedback from a firm's own expatriates can help build the picture of the varying level of assignment difficulty.

Rather than having the manager try to subjectively build the difficulty level of the assignment into his or her performance appraisal, human resources could have a built-in, numerical difficulty factor that is multiplied times the quantity obtained by the normal evaluation process (for example, somewhat more difficult = x 1.2; more difficult = x 1.4; much more difficult = x 1.6).

Evaluator: Trying to Objectify the Evaluation

Several things can be done to try to make the evaluator's estimation more objective.

1. Most expatriates agree that it makes more sense to weight the evaluation based more on the on-site manager's appraisal than the home-site manager's notions of the employee's performance. This is the individual who has been actually working with the expatriate and who has more information to use in the evaluation. Having the on-site manager evaluate the expatriate is especially valid when the on-site manager is of the same nationality as the expatriate. This helps avoid culturally biased interpretations of the expatriate's performance.

2. In reality, however, currently the home-site manager usually performs the actual written performance evaluation after the on-site manager has given some input. When this is the case, a former expatriate from the same location should be involved in the appraisal process. This should occur particularly with evaluation dimensions where the manager is trying to evaluate the individual against criteria with which he or she is unfamiliar relative to the overseas site. For example, in South America the dynamics of the workplace can be considerably different from those of the United States. Where stability characterizes the United States, instability often characterizes much of Latin America. Labor unrest, political upheavals, different labor laws, and other elements all serve to modify the actual effects a supervisor can have on the productivity of the labor force in a company in Latin America. A manager who has not personally experienced these frustrations will not be able to evaluate an expatriate's productivity accurately. In short, if production is down while the expatriate is the supervisor, the American boss tends to believe it is because the supervisor was not effective.

3. On the other hand, when it is a foreign, on-site manager who is making the written, formal evaluation, expatriates agree that the home-site manager should be consulted before the on-site manager

completes a formal terminal evaluation. This makes sense because consulting the home-site manager can balance an otherwise hostile evaluation caused by an intercultural misunderstanding.

One expatriate we interviewed related this experience. In France, women are legally allowed to take six months off for having a baby. They are paid during that time but are not supposed to do any work related to their job. This expatriate had two of the three secretaries take maternity leave. Because they were going to be coming back, they were not replaced with temporary help. The same amount of work, however, still existed. The American expatriate asked them to do some work at home, not really understanding the legalities of such a request. The French women could be fired from their jobs for doing work at home. One of the women agreed to do it because she felt sorry for him. When the American's French boss found out one of these two secretaries was helping, he became very angry and intolerant of the American's actions. As a result, the American felt he was given a lower performance evaluation than he deserved. When the American asked his former boss to intercede and help the French boss understand his reasoning, the French boss modified the performance evaluation to something more reasonable to the American expatriate. The French manager had assumed the American should have been aware of French laws governing maternity leave.

Performance Criteria

Here again, special consideration needs to be given to the expatriate's experience. Expatriates are not only performing a specific function, as they would in their domestic operation, they are also broadening their understanding of their firm's total operations and the inherent interdependencies thereof. As a result, two recommendations are suggested.

1. Modify the normal performance criteria of the evaluation sheet for that particular position to fit the overseas position and site characteristics.

Using the Latin American example referred to before might serve to illustrate this point. In most U.S. firms, maintaining positive management-labor relations is not a primary performance evaluation criterion. Stabilizing the workforce is not highly valued because the workforce is already usually a stable entity. Instead, productivity in terms of number of units produced is a highly valued outcome. As such, motivating the workforce to work faster and harder is important. In Chile, however, the workforce is not so stable as it is in the United States. Stability is related to constant production—not necessarily to increasing production—and a stable production amount can be crucial to maintaining marketshare. In this case, if an expatriate is able to maintain positive management-labor relations such that the workforce goes on strike only two times instead of twenty-five times, the expatriate should be rewarded commensurately. In other words, while the expatriate's U.S. counterpart might be rated primarily on increases in production, the expatriate in Chile should be rated on stability of production.

How can such modifications in the normal performance criteria be determined? Ideally, returned expatriates who worked at the same site or in the same country should be involved in developing the appropriate criteria or ranking of the performance criteria or both. Only they have first-hand experience of what the possibilities and constraints are like at that site. This developmental cycle should occur approximately every five years, depending on the stability of the site—its culture, personnel, and business cycles. Reevaluating the criteria and their prioritization periodically will make sure the performance evaluation criteria remain current with the reality of the overseas situation. If expatriate availability is a problem, outside consultants who specialize in international human resource management issues can be hired to help create country-specific performance evaluation forms and criteria.

2. Include an expatriate's insights as part of the evaluation.

"Soft" criteria are difficult to measure and therefore legally difficult to support. Nevertheless, every attempt should be made to give the expatriate credit for relevant insights into the interdependencies of the domestic and foreign operations. For example, if an expatriate learns that the reason the firm's plant in India needs supplies by certain dates is to accommodate cultural norms—or even local laws—such information can be invaluable. Previously, no one at the domestic site understood why the plant in India always seemed to have such odd or erratic demands about delivery dates. And no one in India bothered to think that their U.S. supplier didn't operate the same way. If delivering supplies by specific dates asked for by their India colleagues ensures smoother production or increased sales and profits for the Indian operation, and if the expatriate is a critical link in the communication gap between the United States and India, the expatriate should be given credit for such insights. This should be reflected in his or her performance review.

To obtain this kind of information, either human resource or operational personnel should formally have a debriefing session with the expatriate on his or her return. It should be in an informal interview format so that specific and open-ended questions can be asked. Questions specific to the technical nature of the expatriate's work that relate to the firm's interdependencies should be asked. General questions concerning observations about the relationship between the two operations should also be included.

There is another, even more effective way this aspect of performance review can be handled. At regular intervals, say, every three to six months, the expatriate could be questioned by human resource or operational personnel in the domestic site about how the two operations might better work together. Doing it this way helps maximize the possibility of noting all relevant insights.

Conclusion ———————————————————————

With the marketplace becoming increasingly global, the firms that carefully select and manage their internationally assigned personnel will reap the benefits. Today, there is about a 20 percent turnover rate for expatriates when they return. Such a turnover rate is mostly due to firms not managing their expatriate's careers well. Firms are not prepared to appropriately reassign expatriates on their reentry. This obviously indicates that firms do not value the expatriate's experience. This further carries over into the lack of emphasis on appropriately evaluating an expatriate's performance. Appropriately evaluating an expatriate's performance is an issue of both fairness to the expatriate and competitive advantage to the firm. With the valuable experience and insights that expatriates gain, retaining them and effectively positioning them in a firm will mean the firm's business strategy will be increasingly guided by those who understand the companies' worldwide operations and markets.

The Road to Hell

Case 5.1
Gareth Evans

John Baker, Chief Engineer of the Caribbean Bauxite Company of Barracania in the West Indies, was making his final preparations to leave the island. His promotion to production manager of Keso Mining Corporation near Winnipeg—one of Continental Ore's fast-expanding Canadian enterprises—had been announced a month before and now everything had been tidied up except the last vital interview with his successor, the able young Barracanian, Matthew Rennalls. It was vital that this interview be a success and that Rennalls should leave his office uplifted and encouraged to face the challenge of his new job. A touch on the bell would have brought Rennalls walking into the room but Baker delayed the moment and gazed thoughtfully through the window considering just exactly what he was going to say and, more particularly, how he was going to say it.

John Baker, an English expatriate, was forty-five years old and had served his twenty-three years with Continental Ore in many different places: in the Far East; several countries of Africa; Europe; and, for the last two years, in the West Indies. He hadn't cared much for his previous assignment in Hamburg and was delighted when the West Indian appointment came through. Climate was not the only attraction. Baker had always preferred working overseas (in what were termed the developing countries) because he felt he had an innate knack—better than most other expatriates working for Continental Ore—of knowing just how to get on with regional staff. Twenty-four hours in Barracania, however, soon made him realize that he would need all of this "innate knack" if he was to deal effectively with the problems in this field that now awaited him.

At his first interview with Hutchins, the production manager, the whole problem of Rennalls and his future was discussed. There and then it was made quite clear to Baker that one of his most important tasks would be the "grooming" of Rennalls as his successor. Hutchins had pointed out that, not only was Rennalls one of the brightest Barracanian prospects on the staff of Caribbean Bauxite—at London University he had taken first-class honors in the B.Sc. Engineering Degree—but, being the son of the Minister of Finance and Economic Planning, he also had no small political pull.

Source: Gareth Evans, "Road to Hell." Intercollegiate Case Clearing House. Boston. Reprinted by permission.

The company had been particularly pleased when Rennalls decided to work for them rather than for the government in which his father had such a prominent post. They ascribed his action to the effect of their vigorous and liberal regionalization program which, since the Second World War, had produced eighteen Barracanians at mid-management level and given Caribbean Bauxite a good lead in this respect over all other international concerns operating in Barracania. The success of this timely regionalization policy has led to excellent relations with the government—a relationship that had been given an added importance when Barracania, three years later, became independent, an occasion which encouraged a critical and challenging attitude toward the role foreign interests would have to play in the new Barracania. Hutchins had therefore little difficulty in convincing Baker that the successful career development of Rennalls was of the first importance.

The interview with Hutchins was now two years old and Baker, leaning back in his office chair, reviewed just how successful he had been in the "grooming" of Rennalls. What aspects of the latter's character had helped and what had hindered? What about his own personality? How had that helped or hindered? The first item to go on the credit side would, without question, be the ability of Rennalls to master the technical aspects of his job. From the start he had shown keenness and enthusiasm and had often impressed Baker with his ability in tackling new assignments and the constructive comments he invariably made in departmental discussions. He was popular with all ranks of Barracanian staff and had an ease of manner which stood him in good stead when dealing with his expatriate seniors. These were all assets, but what about the debit side?

First and foremost, there was his racial consciousness. His four years at London University had accentuated this feeling and made him sensitive to any sign of condescension on the part of expatriates. It may have been to give expression to this sentiment that, as soon as he returned home from London, he threw himself into politics on behalf of the United Action Party who were later to win the preindependence elections and provide the country with its first Prime Minister.

The ambitions of Rennalls—and he certainly was ambitious—did not, however, lie in politics for, staunch nationalist as he was, he saw that he could serve himself and his country best (for was not bauxite responsible for nearly half the value of Barracania's export trade?) by putting his engineering talent to the best use possible. On this account, Hutchins found that he had an unexpectedly easy task in persuading Rennalls to give up his political work before entering the production department as an assistant engineer.

It was, Baker knew, Rennalls's well-repressed sense of race consciousness which had prevented their relationship from being as close as it should have been. On the surface, nothing could have seemed more agreeable. Formality between the two men was at a minimum; Baker was delighted to find that his assistant shared his own peculiar "shaggy dog" sense of humor so that jokes were continually being exchanged; they entertained each other at their houses and often played tennis together—and yet the barrier remained invisible, indefinable, but ever present. The existence of this "screen" between them was a constant source of frustration to Baker since it indicated a weakness which he was loath to accept. If successful with all other nationalities, why not with Rennalls?

But at least he had managed to "break through" to Rennalls more successfully than any other expatriate. In fact, it was the young Barracanian's attitude—sometimes overbearing, sometimes cynical—toward other company expatriates that had been one of the subjects Baker had raised last year when he discussed Rennalls's staff report with him. He knew, too, that he would have to raise the same subject again in the forthcoming interview because Jackson, the senior draftsman, had complained only yesterday about the rudeness of Rennalls. With this thought in mind, Baker leaned forward and spoke into the intercom. "Would you come in Matt, please? I'd like a word with you," and later, "Do sit down," proffering the box, "have a cigarette." He paused while he held out his lighter and then went on.

"As you know, Matt, I'll be off to Canada in a few days' time, and before I go, I thought it would be useful if we could have a final chat together. It is indeed with some deference that I suggest I can be of help. You will shortly be sitting in this chair doing the job I am now doing, but I, on the other hand, am ten years older, so perhaps you can accept the idea that I may be able to give you the benefit of my longer experience."

Baker saw Rennalls stiffen slightly in his chair as he made this point so added in explanation, "You and I have attended enough company courses to remember those repeated requests by the personnel manager to tell people how they are getting on as often as the convenient moment arises and not just the automatic 'once a year' when, by regulation, staff reports have to be discussed."

Rennalls nodded his agreement, so Baker went on. "I shall always remember the last job performance discussion I had with my previous boss back in Germany. He used what he called the 'plus and minus' technique. His firm belief was that when a senior, by discussion, seeks to improve the work performance of his staff, his prime objective should be to make sure that the latter leaves the interview encouraged and inspired to improve. Any criticism must, therefore, be constructive and helpful. He said that one very good way to encourage a person—and I fully agree with him—is to tell him about his good points—the plus factors—as well as his weak ones—the minus factors—so I thought, Matt, it would be a good idea to run our discussion along these lines."

Rennalls offered no comment, so Baker continued: "Let me say, therefore, right away, that, as far as your own work performance is concerned, the plus far outweighs the minus. I have, for instance, been most impressed with the way you have adapted your considerable theoretical knowledge to master the practical techniques of your job—that ingenious method you used to get air down to the fifth-shaft level is a sufficient case in point—and at departmental meetings I have invariably found your comments well taken and helpful. In fact, you will be interested to know that only last week I reported to Mr. Hutchins that, from the technical point of view, he could not wish for a more able man to succeed to the position of chief engineer."

"That's very good indeed of you, John," cut in Rennalls with a smile of thanks. "My only worry now is how to live up to such a high recommendation."

"Of that I am quite sure," returned Baker, "especially if you can overcome the minus factor which I would like now to discuss with you. It is one which I have talked about before so I'll come straight to the point. I have noticed that you are more friendly and get on better with your fellow Barracanians than you do with Europeans. In point of fact, I had a complaint only yesterday from Mr. Jackson, who said you had been rude to him—and not for the first time either.

"There is, Matt, I am sure, no need for me to tell you how necessary it will be for you to get on well with expatriates because until the company has trained up sufficient people of your caliber, Europeans are bound to occupy senior positions here in Barracania. All this is vital to your future interests, so can I help you in any way?"

While Baker was speaking on this theme, Rennalls had sat tensed in his chair and it was some seconds before he replied. "It is quite extraordinary, isn't it, how one can convey an impression to others so at variance with what one intends? I can only assure you once again that my disputes with Jackson—and you may remember also Godson—have had nothing at all to do with the color of their skins. I promise you that if a Barracanian had behaved in an equally peremptory manner I would have reacted in precisely the same way. And again, if I may say it within these four walls, I am sure I am not the only one who has found Jackson and Godson difficult. I could mention the names of several expatriates who have felt the same. However, I am really sorry to have created this impression of not being able to get on with Europeans—it is an entirely false one—and I quite realize that I must do all I can to correct it as quickly as possible. On your last point, regarding Europeans holding senior positions in the Company for some time to come, I quite accept the situation. I know that Caribbean Bauxite—as they have been doing for many years now—will promote Barracanians as soon as their experience warrants it. And, finally, I would like to assure you, John—and my father thinks the same too—that I am very happy in my work here and hope to stay with the company for many years to come."

Rennalls had spoken earnestly and, although not convinced by what he had heard, Baker did not think he could pursue the matter further except to say, "All right, Matt, my impression *may* be wrong, but I would like to remind you about the truth of that old saying, 'What is important is not what is true but what is believed.' Let it rest at that."

But suddenly Baker knew that he didn't want to "let it rest at that." He was disappointed once again at not being able to "break through" to Rennalls and having yet again to listen to his bland denial that there was any racial prejudice in his makeup. Baker, who had intended ending the interview at this point, decided to try another tack.

"To return for a moment to the 'plus and minus technique' I was telling you about just now, there is another plus factor I forgot to mention. I would like to congratulate you not only on the caliber of your work but also on the ability you have shown in overcoming a challenge which I, as a European, have never had to meet.

"Continental Ore is, as you know, a typical commercial enterprise— admittedly a big one—which is a product of the economic and social environment of the United States and Western Europe. My ancestors have all been brought up in this environment for the past two or three hundred years and I have, therefore, been able to live in a world in which commerce (as we know it today) has been part and parcel of my being. It has not been something revolutionary and new which has suddenly entered my life. In your case," went on Baker, "the situation is different because you and your forebears have only had some fifty or sixty years' experience of this commercial environment. You have had to face the challenge of bridging the gap between fifty and two or three hundred years. Again, Matt, let me congratulate you—and people like you—once again on having so successfully overcome this particular hurdle. It is for this very reason that I think the outlook for Barracania— and particularly Caribbean Bauxite—is so bright."

Rennalls had listened intently and when Baker finished, replied, "Well, once again, John, I have to thank you for what you have said, and, for my part, I can only say that it is gratifying to know that my own personal effort has been so much appreciated. I hope that more people will soon come to think as you do."

There was a pause and, for a moment, Baker thought hopefully that he was about to achieve his long awaited "breakthrough," but Rennalls merely smiled back. The barrier remained unbreached. There remained some five minutes' cheerful conversation about the contrast between the Caribbean and Canadian climate and whether the West Indies had any hope of beating England in the Fifth Test before Baker drew the interview to a close. Although he was as far as ever from knowing the real Rennalls, he was nevertheless glad that the interview had run along in this friendly manner and, particularly, that it had ended on such a cheerful note.

This feeling, however, lasted only until the following morning. Baker had some farewells to make, so he arrived at the office considerably later than usual. He had no sooner sat down at his desk than his secretary walked into the room with a worried frown on her face. Her words came fast. "When I arrived this morning I found Mr. Rennalls already waiting at my door. He seemed very angry and told me in quite a peremptory manner that he had a vital letter to dictate which must be sent off without any delay. He was so worked up that he couldn't keep still and kept pacing about the room, which is most unlike him. He wouldn't even wait to read what he had dictated. Just signed the page where he thought the letter would end. It has been distributed and your copy is in your 'in tray.' "

High Technology, Incorporated: The International Benefits Problem

Case 5.2
Rae Andre

Part A

At High Technology Incorporated (HTI), the benefits policy for international assignments states that:

> Wherever legally possible, HTI will attempt to provide the employee with Home Country benefits under the Life Insurance, Disability Pension and Social Security Plans during temporary international assignments.

HTI employees typically spend one to three, and sometimes as long as four years overseas. Historically, during this time, many employees have received benefits equaling or surpassing those of the home country. Recently, company policy has shifted toward equalizing benefits across countries. The system has been less than perfect, however, with some employees finding that their stay overseas has reduced their benefits. At a 1984 conference for the corporate personnel managers of local companies, Jack Cooke, HTI Corporate International Benefits Manager, commented on HTI's difficulties in fairly compensating its U.S. employees abroad. During his discussion, he made the following points.

Home Country Coverage

In 1984 HTI carried out an audit of employees and inventoried people for the purposes of determining offsets—the benefits given to overseas employees to offset loss of home country coverages for pensions, insurance, and similar benefits. The issue was to examine offsetting benefits

---

Source: Rae Andre. "High Technology, Incorporated: The International Benefits Problem." Reprinted by permission of the author.

to determine (1) if there was enough funding and (2) if the funding was allocated to the appropriate areas.

HTI gathered pension and benefits data for each employee on overseas assignment. A benefits book was published for each individual. The audit revealed that there was a considerable amount of overfunding (in the plans of four countries) and some underfunding—people with no plans at all. Cooke believed that HTI was not fulfilling its promise to provide equitable contracts to employees sent overseas. The audit pointed up the fact that whereas HTI was providing adequate funding, the money was being put in the wrong buckets—it was not being well distributed among the countries and individuals who needed it.

Cooke noted that the employees' main fear concerns the security of their coverage. He vividly recalls the old saying "Don't worry . . . but don't die or get sick on assignment!" and how it applied to a Canadian employee in Scotland. The employee died on the last night of his assignment. When his wife was questioned by Scottish authorities shortly after the death, it was discovered that the man had been covered by Canadian Social Insurance (federal social security), and so was ineligible for death benefits in Scotland. The Scottish social security agency refused to pay a death benefit and returned all HTI contributions to the wife, saying the employee should not have been covered in the first place.

The Scottish case highlights the need to review the current local policy to determine when coverage should apply and what steps should be taken to ensure continuity of coverage. Currently the company does not cover the employee under foreign programs when an employee cannot be maintained in a home country plan. A lack of coverage results in one of two major ways.

First, the home country legal requirements or plan documents may not permit participation by nonresidents. For example, a citizen and resident of Country A is transferred to Country B. Country A does not provide certain coverages, retirement income coverage, for example, to its citizens if they live outside Country A. HTI does not provide this coverage either.

Second, nonnationals in the home country are not allowed to stay in home country programs. For example, a citizen of Country B is working in Country A. In Country A, he is only covered for health insurance for a specified period, after which, unless he becomes a citizen, he will not be covered. Again, HTI has no policy to cover him.

To give a real-life example: "What about my pensions in the U.K.?" is a question often asked by "permanent" British employees living in the U.S. From the company's viewpoint, it may be difficult to decide what "permanent" means. Cooke pointed out that any American citizen on a United States payroll is covered by U.S. Social Security anywhere in the world. This type of problem only arises with HTI employees from nations other than the United States.

Additional Issues ——————————————————————————————————

Cooke identified several other problems that he felt needed to be addressed. One was that the permanent relocation policy did not address past service: What happens if a person relocates permanently out of their home country? How should their benefits, especially their pension benefits, be calculated? Another problem was that the company and employee sometimes differed about how to define home country. If an employee had been in a country other than his or her country of origin for ten years or more, which was the employee's home country? Also, there were some employees with *no* evident home country.

Cooke sent questionnaires to the personnel heads in the various countries concerned, asking them to tell him what problems they would face in attempting to make the international benefits program more equitable. Three major issues were identified.

1. *Legal.* The first issue was complying with legal requirements in the various host countries. Of the three issues, this was considered to be the most serious. For example, sometimes employees found themselves involuntarily vested in host country plans by law, when HTI would have preferred them to be covered in the United States. Cooke pointed out that to date corrective action on this particular problem has involved alerting line management of the situation and developing recommendations.

   The home country law sometimes excludes nonresidents from coverage in their home country. As an example, if a U.K. (English) resident is outside the U.K. for more than three years, he or she has to leave the retirement plan. Extensions are possible, but only for the fourth year. The nonresidents can buy back into the U.K. plan later on. But in the meantime, the company has chosen to provide coverage for subsequent years.

2. *Financial.* Two issues arise here. The first is liability for past service. For example, with the case just mentioned, who pays for the uncovered years? The host country? The individual? HTI? Also, individuals may lose coverage due to local fiscal requirements. For example, a country might not have a sliding scale for social security benefits, thus putting the well-paid individual at a disadvantage relative to his home country peers.

3. *Administrative.* Not all HTI facilities even *have* pension plans. And among those that do, there are different requirements. Some have a minimum age of twenty-five, some do not. Some have a one-year waiting period for eligibility, some do not. Some have voluntary participation, some do not. And some are benefit plans, whereas some are contribution plans.

At the time of Jack Cooke's talk, these issues at HTI were far from solved. The policy was that when HTI moved someone permanently, the employee would get the sum of the benefits from the country left and the new country. However, because of high inflation in many countries, this often meant that the employee was losing money.

PART B

HTI: Cooke's Recommendations _____

HTI's Corporate International Benefits Manager, Jack Cooke, feels that the company's benefit policy should be revised. The problem is summarized by him as follows: "If HTI moves someone permanently, they get the sum of the parts, and the money left in the other country is often losing money for them due to inflation. This is all they get and it's not adequate." Cooke recommends that the HTI policy be revised to read:

> Assignments shall not result in loss of retirement and retirement-related benefits to the employee, whether compulsory or voluntary, calculated in accordance with the program in effect in the Home Country.

Cooke believes that for temporaries—people on international assignments of up to four years—the problem should be fixed locally. "Whatever the component—risk insurance, annuity, or pension plan—we should sit down with local counsel to provide substitute coverage that equals what they had at home." This may not lead to double coverage since HTI tries to get temporary people excluded from local plans wherever possible. Sometimes HTI chooses to live with the double coverage.

Cooke weighed the pros and cons of providing the employee with the sum of the parts earned in their different countries of employment plus vesting them and updating them in their home country. The advantages are that this policy:

- Reflects the employee's HTI career in each country
- Updates vested benefits so that total benefits are current
- Provides equitable treatment with employees in the home country
- Allows the company to retain control
- Is understood by employees
- Is simple to administer and provides more company flexibility than the alternative (i.e., moving people from country to country and changing their benefits each time, which employees resist)

The disadvantages of this policy are that it

- Is administratively complex
- May not recognize continuous service for survivorship and disability benefits
- Will be affected by exchange rates (i.e., severe inflation)
- May not achieve retirement income objectives

Cooke noted that through their research HTI found that other companies had not solved the problem either.

P A R T C

The Bandits _____

HTI faces an additional problem, one faced by most international companies. The problem is reclassifying people from temporary to permanent. Cooke noted, "We have thirteen to fourteen American 'bandits' living in Geneva, Switzerland. Their kids can't even speak English, and they own ski chalets. They have home leave benefits that are more generous than others. But they are 'temporary,' and they are so powerful we can't get them to change to permanent status." The same problem is found among some employees who live in the United States. Exhibit 1 indicates how many bandits of various nationalities are employed by HTI.

On the other hand, if HTI does change the bandits' designated home country, the new home country must give them benefits as if they spent their entire career there. This can be costly to the company in some instances, but it can also be an inducement: "Come over to Switzerland at age sixty-three and we'll fix you up. If the company does not do this, it reduces its flexibility to move people."

Exhibit 1. Employees on Extended Assignments

	Assignment Years				
	4-5	5-7	7-10	10 +	Total
To Switzerland	13	18	11	7	49*
To U.S.	9	18	6	1	34

*From Germany n = 11, Netherlands n = 8, U.K. n = 17, U.S. n = 13.
Source: Sample of 550 expatriates.

Part 6

LABOR AND
EMPLOYEE RELATIONS

Strategic Management of Worker Health and Safety Issues in Mexico's Maquiladora Industry[1,2]

Reading 6.1
Mark C. Butler
Mary B. Teagarden

Mexico is a country ripe for worker health and safety abuse. Economically, the country is striving aggressively to attract investment and create jobs. Geographically, it shares a 2000 mile border with the United States, whose more stringent pollution regulations make Mexico a tempting destination for factories running away from environmental restrictions; and for manufacturers looking for a cheap, albeit illegal, toxic waste dump. In addition, stringent worker health and safety regulations in the United States "encourage" firms to flee to nearby Mexico to exploit less rigorous enforcement. Against these forces are, for example, barely 100 industrial pollution inspectors and a six-year-old law covering emissions of 12,000 substances—versus the 75,000 regulated in the United States. To compound the issue, there is the classic enforcement problem that comes with underpaid civil servants and wealthy violators: bribery. Approval of the North American Free Trade Agreement (NAFTA) between Canada, Mexico, and the U.S. intensifies the importance of these issues because it is expected to increase trade between these countries.

Differences in business practices, business standards, values and norms guiding behavior are inherent in international business. These differences are particularly evident when comparing business activities in developed and developing countries, and perhaps stand in sharpest contrast when examining issues such as worker health and safety. Internationally, multinationals (MNEs) commonly face settings where the "rules of the game" are far more ambiguous, contradictory, and dynamic than in domestic contexts. The strategies MNEs use to manage these cultural and contextual differences have a significant impact

Source: Mark C. Butler and Mary B. Teagarden. "Strategic Management of Worker Health and Safety Issues in Mexico's Maquiladora Industry." Reprinted by permission of the authors.

on their overall organizational effectiveness. Human resource management (HRM) practices can be used to align MNE and host country affiliate norms, values, standards, goals, and objectives. The strategic use of HRM, a view based on a long-range future, extends this alignment into the future in an effort to insure a major long-term positive impact on the host country affiliate's productivity and effectiveness.

This article begins with a discussion of strategic HRM and the benefits of reconciliation of MNE-affiliate differences in Mexico's maquiladora industry, which primarily consists of manufacturing facilities located along the Mexico-U.S. border. We provide an overview of the maquiladora industry and the North American Free Trade Agreement (NAFTA), then discuss the strategic importance of worker health and safety issues in this context. Finally, we present HRM design alternatives, and use the strategic HRM perspective to identify recommendations for managing differences and, more generally, to discuss global competitiveness.

Strategic Human Resource Management and the Maquiladora Context _____

Strategic human resource management is the design and implementation of human resource systems to support the firm's short- *and* long-term strategic objectives. The predominant theme in strategic HRM literature concerns the need to fit HRM strategy to the larger organizational context, specifically, to the firm's business and functional strategies. Strategic HRM is believed to promote productivity *and* overall organizational effectiveness (Devanna, Fombrun, and Tichy, 1984). This is accomplished in part by increasing worker satisfaction and investing in worker development. In contrast to the traditional view of HRM which is typically reactive, control oriented, and productivity focused, the strategic orientation is decidedly proactive in nature. Specifically, the importance of viewing traditional aspects of HRM—recruitment and selection, training, appraisal, compensation, and employee relations—from both short- and long-term perspectives affords an organization the opportunity to gain or maintain competitive advantage.

Global Competition

In the increasingly competitive global marketplace there appears to be a convergence of many manufacturing techniques, those traditional areas where competitiveness has been enhanced by increasing efficiencies. The "hard" techniques (and advantages) of Total Quality Management, Integrated Manufacturing and Design, Just-in-Time Inventory Control, Process Mapping, Benchmarking, and Best Practices are rapidly diffused internationally as compared to the "soft" techniques associated

with HRM (Von Glinow and Teagarden, 1988). This diffusion has resulted in increased expectations of high quality and productivity as the
new bases of competitiveness: the level of the playing field has risen for
all competitors. The advent of these "hard" techniques suggest, at a
minimum, the need for a more strategic focus on recruitment, selection,
and training issues. However, those MNEs able to incorporate *and*
move beyond the more rapidly diffused "hard" techniques to develop
effective approaches for managing human resources will win future
competitiveness challenges.

Strategic HRM provides a compelling rationale for reconciling MNE-
affiliate differences in business practices, business standards, values and
norms: from a long-term perspective strategic HRM contributes to development of a capable, effective, world-class workforce. HRM serves additional, important purposes for MNEs operating internationally.
International strategic HRM practices are used to enhance MNE control
in foreign affiliates, and as a mechanism for bridging cross-cultural issues
that are often at the heart of MNE-affiliate differences (Milliman, Von
Glinow and Nathan, 1991; Dowling and Schuler, 1990; Adler and Ghadar,
1990). Consequently, in an international setting, strategic HRM emphasizes strategic fit issues, control issues, and cross-cultural issues.

Traditionally, two generic competitive strategies have been identified: competition based on overall cost leadership, where the firm is a
low cost producer; and competition based on differentiation, where the
firm competes using, for example, quality, customer responsiveness, or
service (Porter, 1980). Increasingly, MNEs find that remaining competitive in the global marketplace requires them to integrate these perspectives and produce high quality, low cost products with sufficient speed
to meet consumer demands. As MNEs encounter these more sophisticated challenges, they find that they must shift from traditional to
more strategic HRM system designs.

Maquiladoras and Global Competition

From the short term perspective, maquiladoras represent a source of
"cheap labor." The "cheap labor" concept, however, deserves closer
inspection. If "cheap labor" were the only criterion, then less industrialized countries like People's Republic of China (PRC), India, Thailand, or
Viet Nam would offer more attractive manufacturing sites than Mexico
because their wage rates are lower. Mexico offers additional benefits
such as proximity to the U.S. and higher levels of productivity—in terms
of output *and* quality—than these alternatives. MNEs that compete on
cost, but are not sensitive to issues such as worker health and safety, run
the risk of increased costs. In the short-term these costs come in the form
of turnover, absenteeism, and time lost due to illness; in the long-term
they risk increased regulation (cf. Barrera Bassols, 1990).

Over twenty percent of maquiladora production is done in plants using world class state-of-the-art technology that affords high quality and manufacturing flexibility. Ford, General Motors, Hewlett Packard, AT&T, and other MNEs identify Mexican plants as their highest quality producers in the world. This sentiment is echoed by Japanese MNEs such as Sony, Hitachi, and Sanyo. German MNEs like Mercedes Benz are opening Mexican operations to take advantage of high quality at a relatively low price. Even maquiladoras that use lower levels of production technology are challenged by the need to produce low cost, high quality products. The strategic challenge for MNEs is to produce relatively low cost, high quality products with sufficient speed to meet consumer demands.

Patterns of HRM in the Maquiladora Industry

To meet this global challenge well trained, loyal, committed workers are critical maquiladora resources. MNEs do not develop such workers by implementing short-term HRM thinking. This requires HRM programs that enhance individual performance through selection, training, development, and attention to culturally appropriate reward systems—all dimensions associated with strategic HRM thinking. This strategic approach can be contrasted with a more traditional approach that is encountered in maquiladoras that have a short-term, "low-cost" orientation.

Devanna, Fombrun and Tichy (1984) identify four types of assumptions about people that underlie HRM system design: (1) the nature of the employment contract; (2) the degree of participation in decision-making; (3) internal versus external labor markets; and (4) group versus individual performance. We have contrasted and extended traditional and strategic maquiladora HRM characteristics using these categories in Table 1.

As seen in Table 1, maquiladoras which embrace the strategic perspective invest in development of their human assets, workers who contribute to attainment of the firm's strategic objectives. For example, these firms implement training *and* development programs, make higher use of culturally appropriate reward systems, and develop internal labor markets. Additionally, issues regarding management of worker health and safety move to the foreground and are proactively managed when viewed through this strategic HRM lens. The next section will introduce the maquiladora industry, and identify MNE-affiliate differences relating to worker health and safety.

An Overview of the Maquiladora Industry ————————————

The Mexico-United States border is longer than any other between a developed and a developing country in the world. In 1965, Washington, D.C. and Mexico City established the Border Industrialization Program

Table 1. Dimensions of Traditional and Strategic Maquiladora HRM Systems

Characteristic	Traditional Maquiladora HRM System	Strategic Maquiladora HRM System
Time Horizon	Short-term	Long-term
Employment Contract	Work for Pay	Meaningful Work for Loyal, Committed Service
Training Objectives	Necessary Task Specific	Task Specific *and* Developmental
Decision-Making & Power	Top Down	Shared (Regarding Tasks)
Labor Market	External	Internal
Group vs. Individual Performance	Individual	Combination
Basis for Control	External, Mechanistic	Internal, Behaviorally Driven
Culturally Appropriate Rewards	Low Use	High Use
Basis for Competition	Cost	Cost *and* Differentiation

which created a free trade zone for work processing along the border. While the zone has been extended to allow location in most of Mexico, more than 80% of the maquiladoras are still located within 50 miles of the U.S. border. Maquiladoras—which are factories, assembly, or processing plants—are used to take advantage of the Border Industrialization Program. Maquiladoras are most commonly called maquilas or, less frequently, twin plants or in-bond facilities.[3] The agglomeration of maquilas are also referred to as the maquiladora industry, although they represent myriad industrial sectors.

Maquiladoras have proven attractive to foreign and Mexican investors alike, and there are now over 2,300 maquiladora facilities employing nearly 500,000 workers. They provide jobs for one tenth of Mexico's workforce, and are its most dynamic economic sector accounting for four-fifths of Mexico's manufactured exports and two-fifths of its total exports to the United States. Mexico is the U.S.'s third largest trading partner after Canada and Japan, numbers one and two respectively. With the passage of NAFTA, many economists believe that Mexico will become the U.S.'s second largest trading partner in the very near future.

The maquiladora industry is comprised of firms seeking (1) cheap, abundant labor and low costs of the other factors of production, such as manufacturing space, utilities, and so forth; (2) quick access to the U.S.

market; and (3) relaxed worker health and safety standards. These maquiladoras produce an array of goods including consumer electronics, electronic parts and assemblies, apparel, automotive equipment and accessories, furniture, toys, health care products and food. Many of the manufacturing processes use "vast quantities" of toxic materials including solvents, heavy metals, acids, resins, paints, plastics, oils, varnishes, and pesticides. The largest single maquiladora product category, electronics, often involves the use of solder flux and organic solvents that are flammable and can cause skin irritation and eye damage (Jenner, 1991).[4]

Maquiladora Worker Health and Safety

There is virtually no margin for disputes over basic rights or minimum working conditions in any organization operating in Mexico—these are prescribed and defined by Mexican Labor Law. Article 3 of the 1970 Labor Law states that employment is a right and duty of each individual, and demands liberty and dignity to those that toil. The law requires that work must be effected in a way that assures life, health, and an economic improvement for the worker and his or her family. In exchange, the worker's principle obligation is to personally execute the task contracted for under the direction and dependency of those in charge (Urbina, 1972).

Mexican Labor Law further stipulates that all employers provide employees with minimum levels of training and the formation of training committees to include management and workers. According to the law, training should allow the worker to improve skills, prepare for higher positions that may become available, improve worker productivity and general welfare, and minimize work accidents (Price, Waterhouse, 1990). Although training dictated by the law is not subsidized by the government, a tax deduction for the program costs and expenses is allowed. All training programs must be submitted to the Labor Ministry Board for approval.

Finally, labor law also requires the formation of health and security committees to insure that all companies meet the minimum requirements for health and safety on their premises. These committees are comprised of management *and* worker representatives, and work in conjunction with labor authorities to analyze and investigate causes of work-related accidents and illnesses; to develop safety practices and procedures; to communicate these to the workforce; and to oversee compliance. Both the Social Security and Labor authorities are empowered to issue safety regulations and to inspect sites to evaluate compliance with minimum work standards; to develop special standards in accordance with the type of industry or activity; and to impose sanctions for noncompliance.

In summary, existing laws, which are designed to protect Mexican workers, seem to be adequate to that purpose. In fact, such laws could be described from a generally proactive, or strategic HRM framework. Nevertheless, an interesting, but separate issue revolves around compliance with these laws. As in the U.S., organizations vary in their level of commitment to compliance with such laws, which sets the stage for creation of performance gaps such as those discussed in more detail below.

Maquiladora Workplace Conditions

Conditions relating to worker health and safety vary greatly in maquiladoras. Sklair (1989:173) cautions, "It is important to distinguish between Fortune 500-type firms—those with a corporate image they wish to protect, at least on the surface—and the mass of reasonably well run small and medium sized maquilas on one hand, and the limited group of atrocious factories that would be a scandal anywhere in the world, on the other."

Even among the best run maquilas it is possible to identify very great performance gaps between what is legally required and what actually occurs. Nevertheless, hard data on working conditions in maquilas is extremely scarce.[5] According to a report in *Technology Review,* "not only do U.S. and Mexican maquiladora managers attempt to deny access to their plants and their workers, but the Mexican government discourages inquiries and health studies" (LaDou, 1991).

What investigators have been able to piece together is that while working conditions in maquiladoras vary greatly, they are often inferior to those in the U.S. and other developed countries.[6] Many plants are inadequately ventilated, poorly lighted, and accidents resulting from inattention to safety procedures and the absence of safety equipment are frequent. According to one report, "Nogales maquiladoras reported more than 2,000 accidents in 1989—three times the accident rate of factories on the U.S. side of the border" (Satchell, 1991).

Workers in many maquilas report that sanitation is poor, production quotas are high, noise is excessive, and machinery is often unsafe. They receive few rest periods and in the electronics industry must perform long hours of microscopic assembly work. Many regularly handle hazardous materials, however the protective gloves, clothing, and other safeguards routinely required in U.S. plants are rare. To make matters worse, workers often lack safety instruction on the hazardous materials they are handling, either because they are not available or they are not written in Spanish. Many workers complain of grueling production schedules and factory fumes.

One report of interviews with dozens of employees in border communities identified complaints of headaches, vision and respiratory problems, and skin diseases caused by soldering fumes, solvents and other chemicals, particularly in the electronics assembly industry. While some plants supply protective gloves, few women wear them because they hamper dexterity and prevent workers from maintaining fast-paced production schedules (Satchell, 1991). Additionally, few men use protective gear because of "machismo"—use of such protection is not considered sufficiently masculine.

The following passage describes a worst-case example of the extent of the performance gap between what is legally required and what may occur. It is based on a study of long term effects of exposure to hazardous chemicals by Dr. Isabel de la Alonso of the Matamoros School of Special Education. The maquiladora in question is the former U.S. company, Mallory Capacitors:

> The Matamoros exposures occurred for full workdays over many months. The women often had to reach into deep vats of PCBs with no protection other than rubber gloves. Many of the workers developed the chloracne rash these chemicals normally cause. The children of these workers, however, were born with unusual characteristics that fell outside well-documented conditions such as Down's syndrome. With degrees of retardation ranging from mild to profound, these children had broad noses, bushy eyebrows, webbed and deformed hands and feet, and other distinctive birth defects. The mothers all reported that their jobs involved washing capacitors (small devices that hold electrical charges) in a chemical mixture they knew only as "electrolito." As they worked with the liquid it would cover their hands and arms and splash on their faces (Satchell, 1991).

Some of the affected mothers have filed a lawsuit against Mallory Capacitors claiming negligence. However, Mallory has changed ownership twice since the women were exposed, and the case is currently "under review" until the liable parties can be determined. Again, we reiterate that this is a worst-case example. Nevertheless, worst-case examples reflect negatively on all maquiladoras and foreign investors in general.

North American Free Trade Agreement Implications

In June 1991 the governments of the three North American nations— Canada, Mexico, and the United States—began negotiating a free trade agreement, referred to as the North American Free Trade Agreement, or NAFTA, and all three governments signed initial approval in October 1992. NAFTA is designed to reduce or eliminate barriers to trade and investment flows and went into effect on January 1, 1994. NAFTA's goal is ". . . to progressively eliminate obstacles to the flow of goods and services and to investment, provide for the protection of intellectual property rights, and establish a fair and expeditious dispute settlement mechanism" (U.S. Department of State, 1991).

Currently, both Canada and Mexico are extremely dependent on the U.S. as a trading partner—over two thirds of their trade is with the U.S.—and as a primary source of foreign investment. Some refer to the relationship as "the elephant and two ants." NAFTA will intensify the economic interaction between the U.S., Canada, and Mexico and criticism of NAFTA has come from myriad sources.[7] According to Clement and Gerber (1992) there are four basic themes in this criticism:

1. Labor and community groups in (mainly) Canada and the U.S. strongly attack the potential decline of the manufacturing

sector, loss of jobs, and deterioration of living standards that could result from freer trade and from MNCs moving to lower cost locations and the resulting disruptions to communities that would follow. In this view the NAFTA is frequently likened to a gigantic *maquiladora*.

2. Environmentalists in all countries, viewing the poor environmental enforcement record in Mexico, foresee a significant exodus of Canadian and U.S. firms to escape the stricter enforcement in their countries, aggravating both regional and global pollution.

3. Human rights groups in the three countries point to the absence of truly democratic processes and human rights violations in Mexico and advise that increasing trade links would implicitly condone such behavior.

4. In both Mexico and Canada NAFTA opponents are concerned with the potential loss of cultural identity, sovereignty and political autonomy that could result from a closer, more open relationship with their much larger and more powerful trading partner.

In light of this NAFTA-related criticism, MNE activities will be under heightened scrutiny, and MNEs will face increased pressure to respond to MNE-affiliate differences. From a reactive perspective, it is in the MNE's best interest to at least minimally comply with Mexico's worker health and safety regulations. They expose themselves to risk otherwise. From a strategic perspective, proactive management of worker health and safety issues sends an important message to employees that they are valued, and being cared for by management. Such paternalism is valued and expected by Mexican workers. A spillover benefit that accrues to MNEs through proactive management of worker health and safety issues is enhancement of their reputation in the local community and in the global marketplace.

Implications for Human Resource Executives _____

Mexico is currently an off-shore manufacturing "hot spot," and is expected to remain so, and grow in importance under NAFTA. Attractiveness of off-shore sites, however, shifts with changes in labor cost and availability, and other related costs. Maquiladoras, or any other off-shore manufacturing option, only remain an attractive alternative so long as they are able to help MNEs achieve or sustain global competitiveness. The recommendations offered in the following section apply as well to Thailand, Viet Nam, or Kenya as they do to Mexico.

Control-Based HRM Design

As mentioned earlier, MNEs can have a short-term productivity objective. For these MNEs, a control-based HRM design is sufficient, but not without cost. Control-based HRM strategies rely on power-coercive techniques, which are primarily based on negative reinforcement approaches such as docking pay, public chastisement, and employee termination as a solution to a variety of problems (e.g., tardiness, errors). These control-based designs are typically implemented in a relatively short time frame. They are, however, also associated with high levels of conflict, much of it rooted in cross-cultural issues. In maquiladoras this conflict results in increases in turnover and absenteeism, and higher costs associated with selection and training. It is not uncommon for MNEs to abandon their maquiladora operation due to the costs associated with an over reliance on this conflict-laden approach. For MNEs that use this HRM design and continue maquiladora operations, reports of quality and productivity deficiencies abound.

Human Relations-Based HRM Design

The longer-term human relations-based HRM design is a middle stance in which MNEs meet both increased productivity and improved worker satisfaction objectives. Human relations-based strategies rely on rational-empirical techniques, such as training or cross-training for specific tasks, and use of culturally appropriate rewards such as subsidized lunches, make-up kits, and records. These necessarily require more time to implement than do control-based HRM designs. An advantage to human relations-based designs is that they typically produce lower levels of conflict than control-based designs. Since implementation of this design typically results in productivity gains and satisfaction improvements, they are also associated with lower levels of turnover and absenteeism, and reduced selection and training costs. Given these benefits, maquiladoras that pursue this less conflict-laden design would likely emphasize both task-related and quality-focused worker training programs.

Human Resource-Based HRM Design

Finally, MNEs can simultaneously pursue productivity, satisfaction, and development objectives. In this case, a long-term human resource-based design is necessary. Such long-term HRM designs rely on normative-reeducative techniques, are process oriented, and aimed at generating improvements in worker satisfaction and development. These techniques include, for example, task specific training and cross-training *and* developmental training that could range from work-related quality or supervisory training to completion of high school education. While this design must be implemented over a longer period of time, attainment of its objectives is associated with the lowest level of conflict, and with maximum gains in productivity, levels of satisfaction, and overall employee development. Consequently, turnover and absenteeism are lower in maquiladoras using this design. However, training and selection costs, at least in the short-term, are likely to be higher than those encountered in maquiladoras pursing shorter-term HRM designs. However, an emphasis on training and selection results in a workforce capable of producing world-class quality products that meet demanding customer schedules. Figure 1 illustrates the costs and results of these three HRM strategies.

We feel there is a compelling reason for MNEs to consider the strategic human resource-based HRM design outlined above: customer preferences change over time. Those who are satisfied with low cost at this point in time may well expect low cost, high quality, and rapid delivery in the future—especially if global competitors up the ante. Development of a workforce that can deliver on these more sophisticated demands takes investment in training and development, and time. MNEs that opt for strategies that yield only short term benefits place themselves at risk in the long term competitive arena where ability to compete on cost, quality-based differentiation, and speed are likely to be critical.

Figure 1. HRM Strategy Costs and Benefits

Strategies Model
Based on the following management objectives:
- Worker Productivity
- Worker Satisfaction
- Worker Development

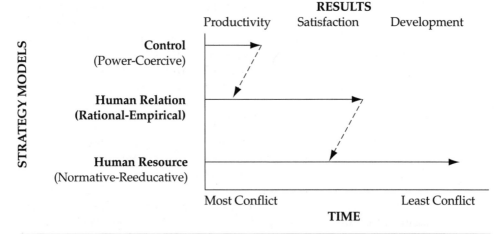

Note: From M.C. Butler and M.B. Teagarden (1993) Strategic Management of worker health, safety and envlronmental issues in Mexico's maquiladora industry. *Human Resource Management,* 32(4). Based on R. Chin & K.D. Benne (1976) General strategies for effecting change in human systems. In W.G. Bennis, K.D. Benne, R. Chin & K.E. Corey (eds.), *The Planning of Change* (3rd ed.). New York: Holt, Rinehart & Winston.

Conclusions and Future Directions _____

The foregoing discussion identifies a serious question that must be asked: How do we go about the task of solving the variety of problems identified in this article? We suggest that the strategic HRM perspective provides powerful rationale for problem solution. What we advocate is a systematic study conducted through the human resource function of organizations that currently work in the international context. In particular, those organizations that operate facilities both in the U.S. and in Mexico should be examined. While an extensive amount of anecdotal evidence exists which suggests a path that *should* be followed, such data are also somewhat insufficient for a broader range of organizational purposes.

To clarify and specifically identify the path, which would eliminate any insufficiencies in data which currently exist, a more scientifically rigorous and systematic approach is warranted. This approach must combine both quantitative and qualitative data collection methods in order to build on work that has accumulated to date. Further, the study should document (a) the extent to which the worker safety and health and environmental problems discussed earlier actually exist, (b) whether or not such occurrences vary by industry, and (c) what specific HRM strategies are currently being employed (if any) to resolve the identified problems. In short, the goal of future activity is to identify the human resource management "best practices" that can be most effectively matched to resolving the complex problems noted above. Without such a systematic approach, worker safety and health issues in the maquiladora setting will continue to go unresolved, jeopardizing countless numbers of workers as well as prospects for improved economic health between Canada or the U.S. and Mexico.

Endnotes _____

1. Adapted from M.C. Butler and M.B. Teagarden (1993) Strategic management of worker health, safety and environmental issues in Mexico's maquiladora industry. *Human Resource Management,* 32(4). An earlier version of this manuscript received the Minerva Education Institute Irwin/Proctor & Gamble Award for Research Contributions to Worker Health, Safety and Environment at the 1992 National Academy of Management Meeting, Las Vegas, Nevada.

2. We would like to acknowledge the valuable contribution of two anonymous reviewers, Professor Miguel Angel Valverde of CETYS in Tijuana, Baja California, and many of our MBA graduate students and International Business and Management undergraduate students to this project. (John Hendon, Chris Feno, Marianne Sozio, Mike Adams, Jonas Almstrup, Pom Assoratgoon, Chris Barber, Al Stark, Konrad

Larson, Jeff Parkinson, John Patton, Lin Farmer, Linlee Austell, and Tehseen Lazzouni).

3. Twin plant stems from the belief that there would be similar plants on each side of the border; the U.S. side completing capital intensive functions and the Mexican side labor intensive function. In fact, less than 10% of the maquilas have a twin plant in the U.S. The in-bond term stems from the requirement that raw materials and supplies shipped to Mexico be processed and then reexported to the U.S. To guarantee reexport these inputs are bonded.

4. For a more detailed discussion of the maquiladora industry see M.B. Teagarden, M.C. Butler, and M.A. Von Glinow (1992) *Organizational Dynamics,* Winter, 20(3), 34-47.

5. Studies that address working conditions in maquilas are predominantly in Spanish. Two notable studies include *Condiciones de Trabajo en las Maquiladoras de Ciudad Juarez* [Maquiladora Work Conditions in Ciudad Juarez] by Dalia Barrera Bassols, Mexico, D.F.: Instituto Nacional de Antropologia e Historia, 1990; "La salud y la mujer obrera en las plantas maquiladoras: El caso de Tijuana," [Health and female maquiladora workers: The case of Tijuana] by Jorge Carrillo and Monica Jasis, *Enfermeria Hoy,* (June 1983), 4, 20-33. English translations of Spanish language citations are bracketed throughout the manuscript. Translations were done by M.B. Teagarden.

6. This description of working conditions is based on a synthesis of the work of Barrera Bassols (1990); Gross (1991); Jenner (1990); Kammer and Tolan (1989); LaDou (1991); "Minimal Safety Rules . . . " (1989); Moyers (1990); Pasternak (1991); Sanchez (1989); Satchell (1991); Sklair (1989); and the authors' observations.

7. There are myriad views of the costs and benefits of NAFTA. For example, see *Columbia Journal of World Business,* Summer 1991, 26(2); the *American Review of Canadian Studies,* Fall 1991, 21(2/3); NACLA (1991) The new gospel: North American Free Trade. *Report on the Americas,* 24(6); AFL-CIO (1991) Exploiting both sides: U.S.-Mexico 'Free Trade.' Washington, D.C.; and USITC (1991) *The likely impact on the United States of a Free Trade Agreement with Mexico.* Washington, D.C.: United States International Trade Commission, Publication 2353.

References _____

Adler, N.J. and F. Ghadar (1990) Strategic human resource management: a global perspective (pp. 235-260). In R. Piper (ed.), *Human Resource Management in International Comparison.* Berlin: de Gruyter.

Barrera Bassols, D. (1990) *Condiciones de Trabajo en las Mauiladoras de Ciudad Juarez: El Punto de Vista Obrero.* [*Work Conditions in Ciudad Juarez Maquiladoras: the Worker's Point of View.*] Mexico, D.F.: Instituto Nacional de Anthropologia e Historia.

Clement, N.C. and J. Gerber (1992) The North American Free Trade Agreement: its implications for California. Paper presented at the US/Canada/Mexico Free Trade Agreement Conference, Jesse M. Unruh Institute of Politics, University of Southern California, January 23.

Devanna, M.A., C.J. Fombrun and N.M. Tichy (1984) A framework for strategic human resource management (pp. 33-51). In C.J. Fombrun, N.M. Tichy and M.A. Devanna (eds.) *Strategic Human Resource Management,* New York: John Wiley & Sons.

Dowling, P.J. and R.S. Schuler (1990) *International Dimensions of Human Resource Management.* Boston: PWS-Kent.

Gross, G. (1991) Presto! Maquiladora toxic waste disappears. *San Diego Union,* Sunday, June 16, Al, Bl, B4-5.

Jenner, S.R. (1990) Conference offers ways to handle hazardous waste at maquiladoras. *San Diego Business Journal: Special Report Maquiladoras,* August 6, 23.

Kammer, J. and S. Tolan (1989) Toxic drums hold water for workers. *Arizona Republic,* April 19.

LaDou, J. (1991) Deadly migration: Hazardous industries' flight to the third world. *Technology Review,* July, 47-53.

Milliman, J., M.A. Von Glinow and M. Nathan (1991) Organizational life cycles and strategic international human resource management in multinational companies: implications for congruence theory. *Academy of Management Review,* 16(2), 318-339.

——— (1989) Minimal safety rules lure firms to border. *Arizona Republic,* April 17, Al.

Moyers, B. (1990) *Global Dumping Ground.* Washington: Seven Locks Press.

Pasternak, J. (1991) Firms find a haven from U.S. environmental rules. *Los Angeles Times,* Tuesday, November 19, pp. Al, A24.

Porter, M. (1980) *Competitive Strategy.* Free Press: New York.

Price-Waterhouse (1990) *Doing Business in Mexico.* New York: Price Waterhouse & Company.

Sanchez, R. (1989) Contaminacion de la industria fronteriza: riesgos para la salud y el medio ambiente [Contamination in the border industry: health and environmental risks] (pp. 155-184). In Gonzalex-Arechiga, B. and R. Barajas Escamilla (eds.), *Las Maquiladoras: Ajuste Estructural y Desarrollo Reaional. [The Mauiladoras: Structural Adjustment and Regional Development.]* Tijuana, B.C., Mexico: El Colegio de la Frontera Norte (COLEF).

Satchell, M. (1991) Poisoning the border: many American-owned factories in Mexico are fouling the environment and their workers aren't prospering. *U.S. News & World Report,* May 6, 32.

Sklair, L. (1989) *Assembling for Development: the Mauila Industry in Mexico and the United States.* Boston: Unwin Hyman.

Teagarden, M.B., M.C. Butler and M.A. Von Glinow (1992) Mexico's maquiladora industry: Where strategic human resource management makes a difference. *Organizational Dynamics*, Winter, 20(3), 34-47.

Urbina, A.T. (1972) *Nuevo Derecho del Trabajo—Teoria Integral [New Labor Law—Integral Theory].* Mexico, D.F.

Von Glinow, M.A. and M.B. Teagarden (1988) The transfer of human resource management technology in Sino-US cooperative ventures. *Human Resource Management*, 27(2), 201-229.

U.S. Expatriates and the Civil Rights Act of 1991: Dissolving Boundaries

Reading 6.2
Sully Taylor
Robert W. Eder

This paper explores the impact of the extraterritoriality provision in Title VII of the 1991 Civil Rights Act on U.S. corporate international staffing policies, identifies key research questions that arise as a consequence to this U.S. law, and reveals how U.S. employment laws contribute to dissolving corporate global boundaries.

> You are the director of human resources at a large southwestern teaching hospital. This hospital has a cooperative program with a major teaching hospital in Saudi Arabia. Each year several doctors from your hospital spend the year in Saudi Arabia teaching and doing research. The stay in Saudi Arabia is generally considered both lucrative as well as professionally rewarding.
>
> This morning you had a visit from two of the doctors in the hospital who had been rejected for assignment to Saudi Arabia. They were very upset, as they are both very well qualified and ambitious. You had carefully explained to them that while the selection committee was impressed with their abilities, the fact that they are Jewish had decided the members that it would be best if they were disqualified from consideration. In spite of vigorous protest from the two doctors, you had held your ground and supported the committee's decision. However, as you sit at home reading that evening, the situation replays itself in your mind, and you think about the decision and feel a little uncertain.

Is the director of human resources correct in supporting the committee's decision? What should be the criteria used by the committee, and the director of human resources, to make a selection decision such as this? Do the doctors have any legal recourse?

Source: Sully Taylor and Robert W. Eder. "U.S. Expatriates and the Civil Rights Act of 1991: Dissolving Boundaries" from *Advances in International Comparative Management* (1994). Reprinted by permission of JAI Press Inc.

Questions like these are growing in U.S. MNCs, and gaining increasing urgency due to two trends. On the one hand, all multinational corporations (MNCs) face both the need for more top managers with an international perspective, and the need to place their best people overseas. MNCs are becoming increasingly dominant in both global and U.S. economies. The U.S. alone has more than 3,500 MNCs, 25,000 companies with overseas branches or affiliates, and around 40,000 companies doing business abroad on a sporadic basis (Prentice, 1990: 633). This has led to an increasing emphasis on international experience for senior managers (Adler and Bartholomew, 1992; Kobin, 1992; Porter, 1990). At the same time, overseas operations of MNCs represent a growing portion of the profitability of these firms (Bartlett and Ghoshal, 1991). As a consequence, there is pressure on multinationals to select their best people to manage their overseas operations.

Recent changes in the United States Civil Rights Act have important implications for the selection of U.S. expatriates. The main purpose of this article is to explore these implications. The article first places expatriate selection within the context of changing U.S. workforce demographics. Then, the legal status of the extraterritorality of U.S. employment laws is reviewed, including the Civil Rights Act of 1991. The final section of the paper explores unresolved legal issues, the likely impact of the 1991 Civil Rights Act on the international staffing policies of multinational firms, and areas in need of additional international management research.

International Selection and the Changing U.S. Workforce_____

The U.S. workforce is changing. It is becoming more demographically diverse (*Workforce 2000*). What are the consequences of these changes for international staffing?

1. Women and minorities will comprise a larger proportion of the labor pool from which to draw candidates for overseas positions. By the year 2000, only 15% of the new entrants to the U.S. labor force will be white males.

2. Women and minorities, who have been kept from top level corporate positions as well as from overseas positions ("Why Women . . .", 1990; Adler, 1984) will increasingly demand access to overseas postings as these become more and more critical to senior level executive career advancement (Adler and Batholomew, 1992).

New legal pressures from the 1991 Civil Rights Act encourage and support these two trends. U.S. EEO laws represent a formidable but as yet unrealized pressure on U.S. MNCs to increase the number of expatriates drawn from non-traditional groups. Before explaining the effect these changes in the law will have on U.S. MNCs' international staffing policies, let us first review the history of U.S. EEO laws with regard to this issue.

Brief History of Legal Decisions Regarding International Selection

Perhaps reflective of the ethnocentric mindset of the U.S. Congress when it crafted Title VII of the Civil Rights Act of 1964, the language of Title VII did not clearly indicate whether the law applied to U.S. citizens who are working abroad. Section 702 of Title VII exempts from Title VII coverage the "employment of aliens outside any State." At first, lower courts reasoned that legislative intent was to apply Title VII protections to the employment of citizens outside the U.S., though no specific language to that effect was stated in the legislation. As the following brief review illustrates, the courts later reversed themselves and withdrew that protection, leading to the necessity of an amendment to Title VII to clarify the coverage of U.S. citizens working abroad for U.S. firms.

Building the Case for Extending Civil Rights Protections to U.S. Expatriates. As summarized in the attached legal chronology exhibit (Exhibit 1), a series of court cases created the argument for the extraterritoriality of civil rights protections. In *Love v. Pullman* (1976) the court ruled that Black Pullman porters who were American citizens employed in Canada by an Illinois corporation were entitled to the full protection of Title VII, and that aliens (i.e., Canadian citizens) employed by the same U.S. firm were protected under Title VII during that portion of the workweek when the alien was working in the U.S. In *Bryant v. International Schools Services, Inc.* (1980), American citizens residing in Iran and hired by an American corporation were accorded full protection under Title VII against alleged discriminatory practices, as were American citizens hired in Frankfurt, West Germany to work for a Martin Marietta plant (*Seville v. Martin Marietta Corp.*, 1986). Also, in 1986 the Fifth Circuit Court of Appeals ruled that Jewish doctors who were refused a position in the Baylor College of Medicine's program in Saudi Arabia, allegedly because of their religion, were covered under Title VII. (*Abrams v. Baylor College of Medicine*).

In related court cases, the courts ruled in *Kern v. Dynalectron* (1984) that a BFOQ (bona fide occupational qualification) argument could be supported by a U.S. firm operating helicopter service to Mecca, Saudi Arabia to require pilots who were U.S. nationals to be Muslim, when local law punishes non-Muslims entering Mecca with death. Though U.S. non-Muslim pilots were adversely treated by the company's practice, the court used the Title VII statute with regard to BFOQ defense to rule in favor of the employer. Not all cases have been built solely around Title VII. In *EEOC v. Radio Free Europe* (1989), the court upheld

Exhibit 1. Chronology and Impact of Major Legal Decisions Affecting Overseas U.S. Employees of U.S. Corporations

Year	Case/Law	Impact
1976	*Love v. Pullman*	Upheld the extraterritoriality of Title VII, i.e., American citizens working for American firms overseas *are* protected by Title VII.
1980	*Bryant v. International Schools Services*	Upheld the extraterritoriality of Title VII, i.e., American citizens working for American firms overseas *are* protected by Title VII.
1980	*Mas Marques v. Digital Equipment Corp.*	Established that the foreign subsidiary of an American firm has to have sufficient contacts with parent firm in order for Title VII to apply. To determine whether involvement is "sufficient," a 4-part test should be applied: (1) degree of interrelated operations. (2) degree of common management. (3) centralized control of labor relations. (4) common ownership of labor relations.
1984	*Kern v. Dynalectron*	Upheld that it is a legitimate BFOQ to be a Muslim for a job in Mecca as local law punishes non-muslims entering Mecca with death.
1986	*Seville v. Martin Marietta*	Upheld the extraterritoriality of Title VII, i.e., American citizens working for American firms overseas *are* protected by Title VII.
1986	*Boureslan v. ARAMCO*	Held that Title VII does *not* apply to U.S. citizens abroad. Stated that there was no clear congressional intent for extraterritoriality.
1986	*Abrams v. Baylor College of Medicine*	Held that it is *not* a legitimate BFOQ to be a non-Jew to work in Saudi Arabia as there is no explicit local law prohibiting Jews from working in the country.
1989	*EEOC v. Radio Free Europe*	Upheld the application of the Age Discrimination Act of 1964 to American workers in U.S. firms overseas, as long as local law is not violated.
1991		Supreme Court upheld *Boureslan v. ARAMCO* decision.
1991	Amendment to Title VII	Specifically states that Title VII is applicable to U.S. firms overseas. Negates *Boureslan v. ARAMCO*.

the application of the Age Discrimination Act of 1964 to U.S. workers employed by U.S. firms overseas, provided local law was not violated.

Reversing Course: Boureslan v. ARAMCO (1986). In *Boureslan v. ARAMCO* (1986), the Fifth Circuit Court ruled that Title VII does not afford extraterritorial protection to U.S. citizens and dismissed the suit. The Supreme Court upheld the ruling of the Fifth Circuit Court on March 26, 1991 by a 6-3 vote. The majority on the Supreme Court reasoned that the U.S. Congress had been silent on the geographical or transnational scope of Title VII protections and therefore, argued against extraterritorial application of Title VII statutes in the absence of "a clear congressional expression of intent to the contrary." This argument was bolstered by subsequent Supreme Court decisions (e.g., *Espinosa v. Farah Mfg. Co.*, 414 US 86 (SCt, 1973), 6 EPD 64,014.) that ruled Section 702 of Title VII covers aliens employed within the U.S., further reaffirming the "within U.S. border" interpretation of Congressional intent. Furthermore, the Supreme Court contended that requiring American employers to comply with Title VII in countries where religious and social customs are wholly at odds with U.S. civil rights protection, places American firms in the difficult position of either refusing to employ U.S. citizens abroad or discontinuing business in that country.

Ironically, it was Judge King's strong dissent in the Fifth Circuit Court of Appeals case, *Boureslan v. ARAMCO* (1986), that eventually became incorporated in Section 109 of the Civil Rights Act of 1991. Judge King argued that the rule of reasonableness should be applied to a state's attempt to apply its law in a transnational context. In accordance with international law, employers overseas could not be expected to take action that directly conflicted with the existing laws of the foreign country. Furthermore, Judge King argued that to the extent that foreign assignments were important considerations in employment advancement, the failure to extend Title VII protections to U.S. citizens abroad would constitute adverse career advancement effects for women and minorities.

Civil Rights Act of 1991. It would be left to the current U.S. Congress to clarify the extraterritoriality of Title VII, as it had with its amendment of the Age Discrimination in Employment Act (26 USC 630(f)). The Civil Rights Act of 1991 had been several years in the making, and a point of considerable partisan politics. The law was initially written to overturn a series of recent Supreme Court Cases, of which *Boureslan v. ARAMCO* was but one, that undermined the effective enforcement of Title VII statutes.

The Civil Rights Act of 1991, Section 109 (P.L. 102-199, Section 109105 STAT. 1077-1078), amended the Civil Rights Act of 1964 and the Americans with Disabilities Act of 1990 to include coverage of U.S. citizens employed in a foreign country, provided that compliance with this provision would not cause the employer to violate the law of the foreign country in which the workplace is located. To be covered under this provision the U.S. citizen must be employed overseas by a firm controlled by an American employer. Control can be determined in several ways: interrelation of operations, common management, centralized control of labor relations, or common ownership or financial control of the corporation and the employer.

Impact of the Extension of Extraterritoriality of Title VII _____

Mitsuko Hanada was frustrated and upset. She walked determinedly down the sidewalks of the fashionable Roppongi district of Tokyo, unmindful of the cold wind and rain, trying to decide what to do. If she were in the States she would know immediately!

Up until this morning Mitsuko had been pretty content in her job at Uptown KK, a large U.S. firm in the communications business. She had been hired straight out of her MBA program in the U.S., like the other five Americans in her section, because of her Japanese language ability, and given responsibilities and duties far above what a fresh MBA could expect in a first job. Moving to Tokyo one year ago, she had settled in happily, possibly because of the network of family she had from her issei parents. But today she had learned that three of the Americans who had been hired with her, all men, were receiving one-third more salary than she, and moreover getting help with apartment rent subsidies and other amenities. When she inquired about this, she was informed that their personnel affairs were being managed by the personnel manager in charge of expatriates, while she was the responsibility of the regular personnel manager, and that the differences stemmed from this administrative decision. When she had asked why males and females were being differentiated, the personnel manager had alluded vaguely to some differences in qualifications between the two groups.

Differences in qualifications!! Huh!! If there were any greater qualifications, they lay with the women, not the men!! Mitsuko gave a very American snort of disgust, startling the other pedestrians, and considered what she should do. Boy, if only she had been hired in the U.S.!!!

The impact of the extraterritoriality extension of Title VII falls into three categories: (1) the unresolved legal issues that must be clarified; (2) the effect on the policies of MNCs and their host countries; and (3) research questions that will need to be addressed. Mitsuko's situation illustrates one of the several unresolved legal issues that has not yet been resolved, as will be discussed below.

Unresolved Legal Issues

There are at least four legal questions that remain to be clarified as a result of the amendment to Title VII to cover U.S. citizens working abroad:

1. What are foreign "laws"? What is a "law"?

2. What constitutes "sufficient control" by a U.S. MNC of its overseas subsidiary?

3. Can the entire family be legally considered when an MNC makes a selection decision regarding international staffing?

4. How can Title VII be enforced overseas? Who is going to do it?

Let's consider each of these unresolved questions in turn.

1. What are foreign "laws"?

A key issue is what constitutes a foreign law. What the U.S. defines as "civil law" may have a very different definition in a foreign country. Civil law may give deference to a particular religious doctrine, or permit localities to promulgate regulations or local conditions that have the effect of discriminating unfairly but in a manner that is consistent with the "laws" of that country. U.S. courts will have to consider what constitutes the "law" of a foreign locale and the extent to which social customs or traditions are considered inviolate. If, for example, a foreign country had such strong social taboos against women working in business that it was not uncommon for violators to be stoned, could this be regarded as a "law"? U.S. courts in employment discrimination suits have typically examined the reasonable risk of injury to the employee and whether critical tasks in the job description simply could not be performed in a specific foreign context as a basis for rejecting the employee's unfair discrimination suit. The uncertainty regarding where the courts are likely to fall within the broad continuum of options in interpreting what constitutes foreign law will likely stimulate the growth of international employment law firms in the U.S. for years to come.

Other countries show much greater deference to local custom than the U.S. when applying their equal opportunity laws. For example, Japan's Ministry of Labor in 1986 offered the following official guideline to Japanese employers as an exception to Japan's own equal opportunity requirements when employing women overseas:

> . . . where the working environment or social situation such as custom and practices of a country would make it difficult for women to realize their abilities. Here, the major reference is to working in foreign countries. This exception can severely limit the recruitment of women to jobs which would require periods of working overseas. . . . it includes not only present jobs but also jobs which, in the future, as a result of job rotation, will require overseas assignments. (MOL 1986: 49-52) (*Source:* Lam, 1992)

Clearly, Japanese MNCs are permitted to broadly include "customs and practices of a country" in disqualifying a Japanese woman not only from overseas assignment, but also from promotion considerations domestically if there is a reasonable expectation that the promotion would require future job rotation overseas to the country in question. It is difficult to envision U.S. courts interpreting foreign law as broadly as the Japanese. However, it is possible that U.S. multinational firms may claim that they suffer a global economic disadvantage given the way in which other countries apply their own EEO laws to the international situation.

2. What is "sufficient control"?

The determination of when a foreign firm is sufficiently controlled by an American firm received its initial guidelines from the 1980 court case *Mas Marques v. Digital Equipment Corp.* A key consideration is whether the U.S. firm has sufficient involvement in the foreign subsidiary's personnel policies to conclude that the U.S. parent firm is jointly responsible for the allegedly discriminatory behavior. As firms take on a more multinational structure with complex joint venture arrangements and other strategic alliances, the determination of "sufficient control" in employment policies by the U.S. firm will likely become more problematic. Is a U.S. citizen working in a joint venture abroad in which its employer controls 49% of the assets covered by Title VII? What coverage does an employee have if the joint venture is evenly split into thirds among the parent country and two foreign firms? As illustrated in the case of Mitsuko above, is a U.S. citizen recruited in the U.S. to work in Japan by the Japanese subsidiary of an American MNC covered under U.S. EEO laws? Mitsuko herself (for this is a real case) decided that she did not have any legal recourse, and reluctantly accepted the situation. Yet the area of "sufficient control" remains murky, and answers to the kinds of questions posed above are elusive and subject to court interpretation.

3. Can the family be considered in the assignment of a candidate to an overseas position?

A third issue relates to the role of the family in overseas assignments. Typically, it is the family and not the individual that is sent overseas for a two to five year assignment. Inquiries regarding one's spouse and family members have clearly been regarded as inappropriate in the U.S. in considering a person's qualifications for a position (e.g., inquiry of marital status, spouse's occupation, family plans). However, in overseas selection, it has been argued that interviews with the other members of the family unit to determine their likelihood of successful acculturation is critical to a successful overseas placement (Dowling and Schuler, 1993; Tung, 1988; Adler, 1991; Black, Gregersen and Mendenhall, 1992). Adjustment problems of spouse or children are often a key reason for overseas assignments to be prematurely ended, at considerable cost and inconvenience to the firm. However, it would seem that under the Civil Rights Act of 1991, it is now inappropriate to base an overseas selection decision on information gathered regarding the candidate's family unit.

A key legal question that arises is whether firms will be able to prove that the transfer overseas represents a clear and significantly different situation from a domestic transfer, and thus can consider the family of the candidate in their decisions. With the exception of laws in the host country that may be violated by the presence of a family member, it is difficult at this time to see whether a firm can treat the international transfer as different from the domestic transfer with regard to this issue. In fact, if U.S. MNCs are successful in making a business necessity argument based on documented costs associated with failed job placement due to family unit incompatibility with the new culture, there is no reason why such an argument couldn't be made with regard to a *domestic* transfer. As the United States becomes more regionally and ethnically diverse, concerns over the acculturation of the family unit may become more of a factor in domestic transfer success. This would be a logical development as national boundaries continue to dissolve in the global economy of the twenty-first century, as regions of one's own country become more foreign than a move overseas. For example, a Boston-based firm may have the need to transfer key executives to both domestic and international sites. For a family that has lived in the Boston metropolitan area their entire life, a potential transfer to El Paso, Texas may easily offer more of an acculturation challenge than a transfer to Toronto, Canada. Why should the issue of cross-cultural adjustment skills only be relevant for the transfer to Toronto? Are there not domestic transfers with comparable transition costs that also strain an employee's and the employee's family's ability to culturally adapt?

4. How can Title VII laws be enforced overseas?

A final legal issue involves the enforcement of U.S. EEO laws overseas. The issue of enforcement gives rise to a number of questions. Will the U.S. government be required to set up EEO offices in all the countries where U.S. MNCs are conducting business? If not, will it be a function assumed by the U.S. embassy, and if so, will embassy staff be trained in how to handle EEO complaints? Given the close relationships between the embassy and the business expatriate community in most foreign countries, will it be possible to maintain the privacy of individuals bringing a complaint overseas? Where will cases be heard and decided? If in the U.S., will this place an undue financial burden on the employee, who will have to return to the U.S. for court proceedings?

Policy Implications for International Human Resource Staffing

The extension of Title VII to overseas staffing can be expected to impact MNC policy in at least four ways. The most critical impact may be on the choice of international human resource management strategy. Other issues involve the effect of adherence to Title VII guidelines on host countries, the impact on the recruitment and selection process, and the influence on the approach to training for overseas postings. Each of these policy implications will be examined in turn.

> The meeting to select a replacement for Hal, the General Manager of the Mexican subsidiary of Tayer Manufacturing had gone much longer than anyone expected. A rather glum silence had descended on the small group appointed to select the best candidate. Finally, Sam White, the vice-president in

charge of personnel, leaned back in his chair and spoke to the group, holding Susan Troy's file in his hand as he talked.

"Look, no matter how you cut it, Susan is the best candidate. She speaks Spanish, has the technical and managerial background we need, did real well up in Canada. And she wants the job! There is really no way around it. Bill is the next best candidate, and he doesn't even come close. Heck, he doesn't even speak Spanish, and he doesn't even have a passport. I think we really have to accept the fact that Susan is the one we need to pick, no matter how difficult you think it might be for her down there. Remember, the 1991 amendment to the EEO laws simply won't let us consider the machismo aspect of all this. Besides, I think Susan can do the job."

Silence decended again. Kirk Latham, the CEO, sighed and got up and served himself another cup of coffee. Suddenly, on the way back to the table, he stopped.

"Wait a second. We've been thinking too narrowly! We have a perfect replacement for Hal, who's been sitting under our noses all this time. Gaspar Zavala could do Hal's job in a minute. He's been vice-president for operations for three years, and he runs the show every time Hal is gone, whether it's to visit up here or on annual leave. Gaspar was up here himself for three months last year, so he really knows how things are done both here and there. Gosh, why didn't I think of him before!"

As Kirk spoke the rest of the group looked up, and gradually began nodding at the saneness of the suggestion. Boy, if only they had thought of that earlier, it would have saved them several hours sitting in this windowless meeting room!

1. Impact on international human resource management strategy.

The most serious policy implication of Title VII may be on the choice of international human resource management strategy. For firms that are aware of the extraterritoriality of the Civil Rights Act, the change in law may pressure them to take a polycentric approach to overseas staffing. The higher perceived legal liability from the enactment of this law can be minimized by switching from an ethnocentric (i.e., preferring to send U.S. citizens from American corporate headquarters to manage overseas enterprises) or geocentric (i.e., choosing the best qualified candidate for the position overseas regardless of home country, host country, or third country nationality) to a polycentric approach that searches for the best qualified host country national to fill the overseas position (Dowling and Schuler, 1993; Perlmutter, 1969). Firms may emphasize the selection of key host country hires who are temporarily transferred to the United States to receive corporate training and socialization in the firm's business philosophy. A recent example is the intensive training Disney provided hundreds of key French personnel who were to open Euro-Disney outside of Paris, which included indoctrination to the unique Disney corporate and management culture. Such a shift in overseas staffing strategy reduces the number of U.S. citizens assigned to overseas operations. Therefore, the Civil Rights Act of 1991 may actually reduce the number of opportunities U.S. citizens will have for acquiring international experience, which, as stated above, has become a necessary part of the preparation for effectively managing MNCs.

In addition to decreasing the amount of international experience among top managers in U.S. firms, a push towards polycentrism may have serious implications for both the corporate strategy and competitiveness of U.S. multinational firms. It could result in corporate reluctance to enter a relatively unfamiliar overseas market and limit the ability of the U.S. firm to react to shifting labor, resource, and customer markets worldwide (Bartlett and Ghoshal, 1989). Instead, preference may be given to entering into joint venture agreements with host country firms, or to other forms of strategic alliances that permit the U.S. firm to avoid sending U.S. expatriates abroad. In short, foreign investment decisions may become sub-optimized and result in lower firm performance and a decrease in competitiveness.

2. Effect on host countries.

A second policy implication of the extraterritoriality of Title VII deals with its effect on host countries. For firms that choose to retain a geocentric or ethnocentric approach to international staffing, there will be the need to actively recruit women and minorities for overseas positions. But, as these firms begin to send members of these groups to their overseas subsidiaries, women and minority employees within those overseas affiliates will be exposed to managers from groups that are usually underrepresented in business in other countries. One consequence could be a change of expectations of these local employees, regarding promotions to both managerial positions and postings overseas. In order to maintain a sense of internal equity, the U.S. firm may include women and minorities employed in its overseas affiliates in the pool from which it draws its international managers. These employees may in turn be noticed by women and minorities in local firms, whose own career aspirations may be altered as a result. In short, the extraterritoriality of Title VII may lead to diffusion of U.S. social policy. This diffusion of the social effect of Title VII may, as a consequence, have policy implications for non-U.S. firms, and eventually, for employment policies in the host countries in which they operate. Whether this diffusion of U.S. social policy is beneficial or detrimental to the host country is a separate, but fascinating, issue.

3. Impact on the recruitment and selection process.

Assuming U.S. firms continue to employ U.S. citizens abroad, even if to a lesser extent than under the Civil Rights Act of 1991, the recruitment and selection process has been made considerably more complex. First, firms will have to post available overseas positions in a more open manner, as is already required for domestic positions. The practice of a few key executives meeting behind closed doors to discuss an overseas selection, meeting with the pre-ordained choice, and quickly preparing the individual to go abroad would appear to be inconsistent with legal expectations for equal opportunity to all those able and willing to be considered. Likewise, individuals could no longer make special deals that involve explicit commitments to a particular overseas assignment as part of a career move or compensation enhancement. Furthermore, advertisements by U.S. firms for overseas assignments, regardless of where the advertisement is placed, would have to be in compliance with U.S. civil rights laws with regard to the statement of qualifications. Except where compliance with U.S. civil rights laws would cause the employer to violate the law of a foreign country in which the workplace is located, specific references to race, gender, age, or religion would be prohibited.

On the positive side, a move to a more open job posting system would require firms to integrate overseas assignments with managerial career planning, which would require a more long-term perspective to be taken in the overseas staffing decision. As employees see the postings for overseas positions, they will seek information on how to acquire experience and training that makes such assignments attainable, leading to greater career planning. Moreover, this long-term perspective could potentially reduce part of the repatriation problem, when managers return to the United States, only to find there is little thought to how their recent international experience will be valued or utilized by the firm (Adler, 1991).

4. Effect on the design of training programs.

A final policy implication of the application of Title VII to overseas assignments is the effect it will have on the design of training programs to prepare candidates for their sojourns abroad. First, there is an effect on the training process. As Black and Mendenhall (1990) observe, social learning theory states that it is desirable to have the person who models new behaviors be as similar to the trainee as possible. This implies a need for more women and minorities with overseas business experience to act as cross-cultural trainers. Regarding the content of the training, the "cultural toughness" dimension regarding women and minorities of the host culture will need to be calculated (Mendenhall and Oddou, 1985). This will influence both the behaviors and skills the candidates will have to learn, which may be different from those needed by white males. Some caution is necessary here, however. Some women and minorities may actually find discrimination against them in the foreign culture easier to deal with than their white male counterparts since they have dealt with discrimination in their own country. Interviews with black U.S. women expatriates in

Japan indicate that they perceive little or no difficulty in dealing with the slights against them as foreigners and as women because such incidents have always been part of their existence (Taylor and Napier, 1993). Finally, there may be an effect on the length and timing of the cross-cultural training, with women and minorities requiring greater training once in country as there are fewer local country nationals with whom they can identify and from whom they can learn how to manage effectively in that country.

Implications for Research in International Management

There are also implications of the extraterritoriality of Title VII for research in the field of international management. Two of the most urgent research questions are, first, the validation of selection criteria and methods for overseas assignments, and, second, determining what factors will mediate the impact of the extraterritoriality of Title VII on the international staffing behavior of U.S. MNCs.

    1. Validation of selection criteria.

Previous research and practice provide guidelines regarding the selection criteria and measures that should be used. Tung (1981) identified four main groups of variables that are related to expatriate success, and hence should be used in selecting expatriates for overseas assignments: (1) technical competence; (2) personality traits or relational abilities; (3) environmental variables; and (4) family situation. With regard to the third category, environmental variables, researchers (Jones and Popper, 1972; Pinfield, 1973; Torbiorn, 1982) have found that some cultures are more difficult to adapt to than others, depending on the culture of origin for the expatriate, a dimension termed cultural toughness (Mendenhall and Oddou, 1985). Black, Gregersen and Mendenhall (1992) outline a slightly different set of factors from Tung.

In short, researchers have made some progress in identifying what makes an expatriate able to function effectively overseas, and therefore what criteria should be utilized in the selection decision. However, validation of the suggested criteria has not been undertaken in separate studies, creating a gap in our research knowledge that must be addressed given the increased political risk facing U.S. MNCs. Both construct and criterion related research is required to establish the predictive and incremental validities of each of the selection criteria currently in use. Black et al. (1992) recommend which selection methods are most relevant for each selection criterion. However, these recommendations must be tested before they can provide the sort of validity that can withstand the legal scrutiny of the courts. As Black et al. point out, there is little academic or practitioner consensus with regard to which selection criteria should be used to identify highly qualified expatriates. Criteria receiving widely variant opinions with regard to importance include foreign language proficiency, family support, and prior overseas experience.

There has also been little research with regard to the relative weight that should be given each category of selection criteria. In one study, Tung found that the fourth category, family situation, was the primary reason for failure among expatriates (Tung, 1982), and recommended that firms include the spouse and family in making selection decisions. As noted above, this is a recommendation which if followed may create some legal risk. The weights may also be partially determined by the national origin of the firm. Recent research indicates that the national origin of a firm influences which variables will be emphasized in the selection decision (Stone, 1991), which could indicate either a cultural belief in the importance of some variables over others, or that cultures vary in the way they define the roles of an expatriate. Finally, Black et al. (1992) recommended that the firm determine which factors are most important for a particular assignment. In sum, a key part of validating the selection criteria will be determining how much weight to give each selection criterion within the decision model the firm chooses to use. The utility of this selection model for the firm will be a function of, not only the validity coefficient (i.e., multiple R) for the battery of tests, but also the adequacy of an applicant pool from which an overseas assignment is made, the historical pattern of success or failure in past similar selections, and the overall cost of the selection procedures that are used.

A second major area that will need to be addressed is the validation of different methods of selection. Black et al. (1992) noted that the variety of methods available to firms is much greater than what is actually utilized, and includes such approaches as assessment centers, work samples, biographical and background data, standardized tests, interviews and references. At present firms tend to underutilize the range of both criteria and selection methods available to them: ". . . the short-term approach of most multinational firms leads them to rely on . . . the least reliable and valid selection methods (interviews and references)" (Black et al., 1992: 73-74).

Before leaving this section, it should be noted that even if researchers are successful in validating expatriate selection criteria, past research indicates that firms ignore the recommendations of researchers concerning international selection. The actual overseas selection practice of MNCs does not utilize accumulated selection validation research. Some research has indicated that technical expertise is used as the primary selection criterion by U.S. MNCs (Baker and Ivancevich, 1971; Miller, 1973; Tung, 1981), ignoring the other categories of criteria because technical expertise is so much easier to determine than other factors. However, as Black et al. (1992:56) note, ". . . (the) people with the best technical skills are not necessarily those with the best cross-cultural adjustment skills. In fact, a global assignment failure (poor performance or premature return) is generally the result of ineffective cross-cultural adjustment by expatriates and their families, rather than the outcome of inadequate technical or professional skills." Firms also apparently avoid even attempting to measure non-technical, human relations skills. In her study, Tung (1981) found that only five percent of firms formally assess a candidate's relational ability, even though the relationship abilities of expatriates have been identified as important to overseas success. Finally, only between 40% and 50% of all firms interview both candidate and spouse for an overseas position, even though the family has been shown to be an important determinant of overseas success (Tung, 1981). While the extension of Title VII to the overseas assignment makes it legally risky to consider the family as part of the selection decision, it is still noteworthy that most U.S. MNCs have been ignoring the considerable research evidence that suggests this as an important selection criterion. In sum, researchers will also have to determine, as part of their validation of selection criteria and methods, the factors that inhibit firms from utilizing the findings concerning how to successfully select candidates for overseas.

2. Factors that will mediate the impact of the extraterritoriality of Title VII.

A second major research question that arises from the extension of Title VII to the international arena is what factors will influence its impact on firm behavior. Two obvious factors that will be important are the risk averseness of the firm, and its stance regarding multiculturalism. Risk averseness is the probability that the firm could face discrimination lawsuits from the extraterritoriality of Title VII, and the potential magnitude of the settlements. It is probably a function of the firm's history of past lawsuits, as well as its risk minimization stance due to its industry. Banks, for example, will tend to be more risk averse because of the large role government plays in overseeing the industry, and the consequent necessity of justifying actions to regulating authorities.

Multiculturalism is the degree to which the firm is proactive in encouraging diversity in its workforce, both domestic and international. This may be a function of top management philosophy and the percentage of the workforce overseas. These two dimensions have been mapped against each other in Figure 1, resulting in four quadrants that give some indication of the potential effects on the behavior of the firm.

Figure 1. Differential Impact on Expatriate Selection of Women and Minorities in Response to 1991 Civil Rights Act

		Commitment to Multiculturalism	
		Low	High
Risk	Low	Minimal Effect On Firm (1)	Proactive Assignment of Women/Minorities Overseas (3)
Averseness	High	Minimize Expatriates/ Polycentric Strategy (2)	Calculative Response/ Validate Process First (4)

Firms in quadrant 1 are not proactive with regard to multiculturalism in their workforce, and hence do not have in place many mechanisms for increasing the number of women and minorities at different levels of the organization. With regard to risk averseness, these firms do not perceive that there is much legal risk from lawsuits, perhaps because they have not been the target of them in the past, either for size or geographic location reasons. For these firms, it is proposed that the effect of the extraterritoriality of Title VII will be relatively minimal. Firm behavior will not likely change; there will be little interest in promoting expatriate selection.

Firms in quadrant 2 are risk averse, and will avoid putting themselves in a position that might increase the probability of lawsuits. At the same time, these firms have traditionally not been at the forefront of nurturing cultural diversity in their workforces. These firms will be discouraged from utilizing expatriates due to the extraterritoriality of Title VII. For these firms, a polycentric approach may replace an ethnocentric approach, or the firm may emphasize the use of third country nationals if there is an insufficient supply of capable host country nationals. Another possibility is that firms in this quadrant may attempt to distance themselves legally as much as possible by changing their overseas investments to joint ventures or through subcontracting operations. Obviously the industry of the firm also influences the degree to which it can move in such a direction. This approach is most likely to be effective when the firm's production can be undertaken outside of the firm, or when there are sufficient legal protections of its distinctive technology or trademark to make alliances safe alternatives.

The third quadrant consists of firms who perceive low legal risk and have a proactive approach to multiculturalism in the firm. Many of these firms have a history of avoiding discrimination lawsuits by actively promoting women and minorities. These firms will be proactive in inducing members of these two groups to work overseas as a consequence of Title VII. Moreover, the 1991 Title VII law can help them persuade such candidates to undertake an overseas assignment because now the law clearly states that they will be protected even while working overseas.

Finally, in quadrant four are those firms who see a high legal risk from lawsuits, probably from having experienced a number of such suits in the past. These firms tend to be perceived as having deep pockets and thus are often targets of discrimination suits. At the same time, these firms cannot avoid going overseas. Compared to firms in quadrant three, companies in this group are as publicly committed to multiculturism, but must be more careful in proceeding in a manner that does not unreasonably increase legal risks. Firms in the steel and transportation industries would fit this profile, as would law firms. For these companies, overseas investments are usually direct and wholly owned. It is predicted that these firms will, as a consequence of the extraterritoriality of Title VII, take a more calculative response with regard to assigning women and minorities overseas, complying with the legal requirement to change recruitment and selection approaches, validating selection criteria and processes, but not taking an unrestrained proactive approach to inducing women and minorities to go overseas.

Conclusions ────────────────────────

By establishing the extraterritoriality of Title VII, the 1991 Congress clearly signaled that U.S. MNCs have an obligation to follow the strictures laid out by U.S. society wherever they are operating, abroad or at home. The law has removed the ambiguity that existed concerning whether U.S. citizens can rightfully claim civil rights protection while serving their companies abroad, although as was discussed above, some legal issues remain to be resolved, and are subject to further court interpretation.

Possibly the most interesting aspect of the establishment of the extraterritoriality of Title VII is that it is yet another signal of the degree to which nation states are becoming superseded by the economic interdependence of the world. By requiring U.S. MNCs, which together hold the largest investment overseas, to adhere to the same legal and social standards as they do at home, there is in effect a diffusion of American social mores and cultural values to other countries. Again, our point is not to debate whether the U.S. stance on promoting women and minority rights in the workplace is socially or morally superior to that in other countries. The fact is that countries which have put less emphasis on equal employment opportunity for all their citizens, and that have not enacted laws to support it as a consequence, will find within their borders firms with a proactive stance with regard to the hiring and promotion of women and minorities. While this staffing policy may initially impact only foreign workers, the necessity of maintaining internal equity in an overseas subsidiary may lead the firm to extend equal employment opportunity practices to host country nationals. Thus while certain countries may not wish to promote equal opportunity for either social or religious reasons, they may find within their midst a modern Trojan horse from which spills out agents of change created by the extraterritoriality of Title VII.

As a side issue, it is ironic that at a time when U.S. MNCs are required to extend civil rights protection to U.S. citizens working abroad, foreign firms operating in the U.S. are often permitted to prefer home country nationals over host country U.S. citizens for key managerial positions, in accordance with a mosaic of Friendship, Commerce, and Navigation treaties. For example, the Seventh Circuit Court of Appeals ruled that Japanese subsidiaries operating in the U.S. may legally prefer Japanese citizens over U.S. citizens and that Title VII prohibitions against discrimination on the basis of national origin do not apply (*Fortino v.*

Quasar Co., 1992). In effect, a "glass ceiling" for all U.S. employees working in Japanese-owned firms is in effect. In some industries (e.g., microelectronics) a U.S. manager may have more career opportunity and more U.S. Civil Rights protections working for a U.S. MNC overseas than for a foreign-owned MNC operating in the manager's own home country.

U.S. MNCs face a number of challenges in making the transition to a world in which their overseas staffing is covered by Title VII. The greatest challenge is to re-examine their recruitment and selection of candidates for overseas positions, and bring these procedures up to a standard of validation commensurate with procedures used for domestic hires. As mentioned previously, there is also the necessity of changing the training and career planning procedures to facilitate utilization of women and minorities in overseas positions. While some firms will be more proactive than others in trying to achieve these goals, and some will try to avoid the question entirely through alternative foreign investments, there is no doubt that on the whole the extraterritoriality of Title VII represents a significant challenge for U.S. MNCs with regard to international human resource management.

References _____

Adler, N. J., and Bartholomew, S. (1992). Managing globally competent people. *Academy of Management Executive*, 6(3):52-65.

Adler, N. J. (1991). *International Dimensions of Organizational Behavior.* Boston: PWS-Kent.

Adler, N. J. (1984). Expecting international success: Female managers overseas. *Columbia Journal of World Business*, 19 (3), Fall, 79-85.

Adler, N. J. (1984). Women in international management: Where are they? *California Management Review*, 26(4), Summer, 78-89.

Baker, J. C. and Ivancevich, J. M. (1971). The assignment of American executives abroad: Systematic, haphazard, or chaotic? *California Management Review*, 13(3): 39-41.

Bartlett, C. and Ghoshal, S. (1989). *Managing Across Borders.* Boston: Harvard University Press.

Black, J.S., Gregersen, H., & Mendenhall, M. (1992) Global Assignments: Successfully Expatriating and Repatriating Global Managers. San Francisco: Jossey-Bass Publishers.

Black, S. and Mendenhall, M. (1990). Cross-cultural training effectiveness: A review and a theoretical framework for future research. *Academy of Management Review*, 15(1): 113-136.

Benson, P. G. (1978). Measuring cross-cultural adjustment: The problem of criteria. *International Journal of Intercultural Relations*. Spring, 21-37.

Business Week, (1991). Were Civil Rights Laws Meant to Travel? January 21, page 36.

Coulter, T.A. (1990). Testing the United States' commitment to international law: The conflict between Title VII and treaties of friendship, commerce, and navigation. *Wake Forest Law Review,* 25: 287-313.

Dowling, P. J. and Schuler, R. S. (1993). *International Dimensions of Human Resource Management* (2nd ed.). Boston, MA: PWS-Kent.

Dowling, P. J. and Welch, D. (1988). International human resource management: An Australian perspective, *Asia-Pacific Journal of Management* 6(1): 39-45.

Doz, Y. (1991). Ciba-geigy-management development, in M. Mendenhall and G. Oddou (eds.), *International Human Resource Management.* Boston: PWS-Kent.

Jones, R.R. and Popper, R. (1972). Characteristics of peace corps host countries and the behavior of volunteers. *Journal of Cross-cultural Psychology,* 3: 233-245.

Kobrin, (1992). Multinational strategy and international human resource management policy. *Wharton WP,* 92-14.

Lam, A. C. L., (1992). *Women and Japanese Management,* London, Routledge, Chapman and Hall, Inc.

Mendenhall, M. and G. Oddou. (1985). The dimensions of expatriate acculturation: A review, *Academy of Management Review,* 10(1): 39-47.

Miller, E. L. (1973). The international selection decision: A study of some dimensions of managerial behavior in the selection decision process. *Academy of Management Journal,* 16: 239-252.

Perlmutter, H. V. (1969). The tortuous evolution of the multinational corporation. *Columbia Journal of World Business,* 4, Jan.-Feb., 9-18.

Pinfield, L. T. (1973). Sociocultural factors and inter-organizational relations. *Academy of Management Proceedings,* 33rd Annual Meeting, Boston.

Porter, M. E. (1990). *The Competitive Advantage of Nations.* New York: The Free Press.

Prentice, R. (1990). The muddled state of Title VII's application abroad. *Labor Law Journal,* Sept., 633-640.

Ronen, S. (1989). Training the international assignee, in I. Goldstein (ed.), *Training and Career Development.* San Francisco: Jossey-Bass.

Silver, G. D. (1989). Friendship, commerce and navigation treaties and United States discrimination law: The right of branches of foreign companies to hire executives "of their choice." *Fordham Law Review,* 57: 765-784.

Simon, H.A., and Brown, F. (1991). International enforcement of Title VII: A small world after all? *Employee Relations Law Journal,* 281-300.

Stone, R. J. (1991). Expatriate selection and failure. *Human Resource Planning,* 14(1): 9-18.

Taylor, S., and Napier, N. (1993). Successful women expatriates: The case of Japan. Paper presented at the Academy of International Business, Hawaii, October 22.

Torbiorn, I. (1982). *Living Abroad: Personal Adjustment and Personnel Policy in the Overseas Setting*. New York: Wiley.

Tung, R. (1988). *The New Expatriates: Managing Human Resources Abroad*. Cambridge, MA: Ballinger.

Tung, R. L. (1981). Selection and training of personnel for overseas assignments. *Columbia Journal of World Business*, 6(1): 66-78.

Tung, R. L. (1982). Selection and training procedures of U.S., European, and Japanese multinationals. *California Management Review*, 25(1):57-71.

Workforce 2000. (1987). Indianapolis: Hudson Institute.

"Why Women Still Aren't Getting to the Top." (1990). *Fortune*, July 30, pp. 40-62.

Effective Rightsizing Strategies in Japan and America: Is There a Convergence of Employment Practices?

Reading 6.3
Tomasz Mroczkowski
Masao Hanaoka

Managing Workforce Reductions

The American Quick Fix Approach

The downsizing programs of many American companies are poorly planned, badly managed, and do not bring about expected improvements in company performance. Downsizing is no longer driven by immediate market conditions. Only 19.5 percent of firms included in the 1995 American Management Association surveys on *Downsizing in the United States* reported operating losses in the year preceding the cuts.[1] Driven by long-term strategic factors, downsizing has become an employment strategy, and 65 percent of firms that downsize in a given year do so again the following year. Although downsizing is expected to continue into the foreseeable future, policies intended to lessen job losses by reduced pay or hours or spreading the work (job sharing) are actually in decline. Rather than share the work to save jobs, many companies expand the work day for those still employed.

For those laid off, outplacement activity continues to rise, and is by far the most important form of assistance offered. Remarkably, whereas 40 to 45 percent of employers are willing to offer extended severance pay or health benefits, only 10 to 18 percent offer retraining. Right Associates, in a poll of 1,204 companies that had reduced employment levels, found that

Source: T. Mroczkowski and M. Hanaoka. Reprinted with permission of Academy of Management, PO Box 3020, Briar Cliff Manor, NY 10510-8020. "Effective Rightsizing Strategies in Japan and America: Is there a Convergence of Employment Practices?" by T. Mroczkowski and M. Hanaoka, Academy of Management Executive, Vol. 11, No. 2 (1997). Reproduced by permission of the publisher via Copyright Clearance Center, Inc.

only 6 percent had tried cutting pay, 9 percent had shortened work weeks, 9 percent used vacation without pay and 14 percent had developed job sharing plans.[2] This result contrasts sharply with a TIME/CNN poll of adult Americans that found that 80 percent of the respondents would prefer a 10 percent pay cut to a 10 percent reduction in the workforce.[3]

A 1991 survey by the Wyatt Company of 1,005 firms demonstrated that a majority of restructuring efforts fall far short of the objectives originally established for them: Only 46 percent of companies said their employment cuts sufficiently reduced costs over time, since in four cases out of five they had to replace some of the people they dismissed. Fewer than one in three said that profits increased as much as expected and only 21 percent reported satisfactory improvements in shareholders return on investment.[4] The AMA survey found that 47 percent of the companies reporting workforce reductions since 1990 increased operating profits in the year following the reduction and a smaller percentage reported number increased operating profits overall.

Collapsed employee morale is one recurrent effect of downsizing. Seventy to 80 percent of companies that administered cuts reported a negative impact on employee attitudes. Making matters worse, downsizing is often inadequately managed. A 1990 AMA poll of 1,142 companies that had downsized found that nearly half were badly or not well prepared for the cuts and had not anticipated the problems that developed. More than half had begun downsizing with no policies or programs to minimize the negative effects of cutting back. An author commenting on the results of the survey noted the fixation of corporate management on short term results while ignoring the disruptions in organizational relationships: "In the process, they misused and alienated many middle managers and lower level employees, sold off solid businesses, short changed research and development and muddled the development of their manufacturing floors."[5] According to some observers, sudden disruption of key relationships within a downsized organization leads to a loss of "corporate memory" that can be damaging to creativity and growth.[6]

The most recent 1995 AMA survey of downsizing sees a continuation if not an acceleration of many of these trends. Twenty-nine percent of companies surveyed expect to trim their workforces further in the coming years—the highest rate since the association began the surveys eight years ago. At the same time, company efforts to help workers stave off layoffs have declined. Five years ago, nearly 70 percent of firms offered demotions or transfers as a way to avoid layoffs. Last year the figure was down to 43 percent.

The Art of Japanese Restructuring: The 12 Stages of *Koyochosei*

Japanese companies are undertaking restructuring efforts on a scale much greater than at any previous downturn of the nation's economy. Nippon Steel alone has announced a program to cut $3 billion in operating costs within three years, chiefly by eliminating 10,000 administrative workers and 15 percent of its factory workers. Yoshiro Sasaki, the company's executive vice president, calls this process "Americanizing." Yet when pressed to say what will happen to the displaced employees, his reply suggests a misunderstanding of Americanization: "The workers will either retire or move to one of our subsidiaries or suppliers."[7]

The restructuring done in Japan during the post-bubble recession has been remarkable for its limited layoffs and for producing only a moderate rise in unemployment, which, in spite of overcapacity and poor profits, continues below U.S. levels. The Japanese term for "adjustment of employment levels" is *koyochosei*, a concept that has existed alongside that of "lifetime employment," and that was used widely during discussions of restructuring brought about by the rise in the value of the yen in 1986. Since 1990, with the pressures for restructuring more serious than ever, the term is heard much more often in discussions of Japanese policy, as, for the first time, is the viability of lifetime employment. *Koyochosei* describes the various methods of matching the number of staff actually employed to what is economically required.

A Ministry of Labor survey in August 1993 revealed that Japanese companies in many sectors believed they had too many employees and needed to reduce staffing levels.[8] The measures companies had already taken and those they planned to take in the future ranged from restrictions on overtime to making permanent staff redundant. These methods are categorized in Table 1.

The first stage methods, which have often been used in Japan, are the mildest of the measures available and do not give the employees any strong feeling of anxiety about their jobs. The intermediate stage cluster involves reducing recruitment, or not renewing contracts. This is generally achieved by not filling vacancies that arise, and by internal transfers. These measures give the employees a fairly strong feeling of anxiety

---

Table 1. The Three Stages of Japanese Employment Adjustment

First Stage	• reduction of hours worked by restricting overtime • reduction in number of hours/days worked • internal transfers
Intermediate Stage	• reducing intake of permanent staff • reducing/eliminating extra/part-time work • not renewing contracts/dismissing extra/part-time employees • not renewing contracts of employees dispatched by outside employment • temporary leave
Final Stage	• transferring staff to other companies • early retirement with preferential conditions • voluntary redundancies • compulsory redundancies

about their jobs. The final stage involves actually discharging employees from the company. Transferring staff to other companies and early retirement procedures have been resorted to by many companies in Japan. Voluntary and compulsory redundancies constitute the last resort, and these create an atmosphere of crisis in terms of fears about jobs.

First State Adjustments

The Ministry of Labor Survey shows that companies that have already restricted overtime (44.9 percent) and increased leave do not intend to take these measures any further in the future. Eleven percent plan to make more use of other methods, such as increasing somewhat the number of internal transfers. The usual type of transfer is job rotation, carried out in order to develop the skills of the staff, or transferring an appropriate member of staff to a vacancy that has arisen. In Japan, rotation is carried out about once to twice a year, or more often if necessary. In contrast, most *koyochosei* transfers consist of moving staff from indirect divisions to direct production divisions, with the objective of reducing indirect labor costs. The way overtime is managed in Japan is very different than in the U.S. where downsizing increases overtime for survivors.

Intermediate Stage Adjustments

According to the survey, there will be an increase in the proportion of companies dismissing or not renewing contracts of extra/seasonal, part-time workers from 9.6 percent to 12.1 percent. The proportion reducing or stopping recruitment of mid-career staff will remain around its already high level (37.0 percent), while the proportion carrying out temporary shutdowns is set to increase from 7.6 percent to 8.3 percent.[9]

The objective of temporary leave in Japan is to reduce the level of operations and hence labor costs. It often includes (and in the case of NKK was limited to) managerial and supervisory staff, and is accompanied by wage cuts of various sizes. At Minolta, for instance, the pay was cut 20 percent.[10]

Final Stage Adjustments

Shukko is the Japanese term for transferring staff to other companies (subsidiaries and suppliers). This option has two forms, *zaiseki shukko*, where staff are temporarily transferred but retain their employee status in the company, and *iseki shukko*, where staff are released to be employed by the other company. About 95 percent of the companies surveyed were carrying out *zaiseki shukko*, but also a very high 50 percent were carrying out *iseki shukko*. A measure that makes the older staff in larger companies extremely anxious, *iseki shukko* is in reality a combination of discharging staff and passing the buck to other companies, and is tantamount to early retirement from the original company.

Voluntary and compulsory redundancies are closely equivalent to western layoffs. In the former, volunteers for redundancy are sought among a particular group. Because the method does not involve coercion, it is used widely in Japan, where a softer approach is much more acceptable. Nevertheless, compulsory redundancies are not entirely uncommon. With the increased use of *koyochosei*, it appears that rigid lifetime employment systems have little future in Japan, although stable employment will continue to be used within a wide, flexible framework appropriate to the circumstances of individual companies. The overriding priority seems to be the survival of the company, with desirable employment practices based on secure employment.

In another recent survey, the Japan Productivity Center found that preservation of employment is still the declared basic policy of most managers and union leaders in Japan.[11] Nevertheless, most managers feel that the best qualified people should be allocated to appropriate jobs and that performance is a condition of employment.

The Ministry of Labor survey makes it clear that only a relatively small percentage of companies are actually using direct layoffs, whereas the majority are laboriously implementing employment adjustment using gradual and partial measures. These partial measures do not always have the same character as in Western companies. This reliance on patient gradualism in employment adjustment distinguishes the Japanese approach from typical western practice, especially American practice.

Japanese human resource management systems will continue to face pressures for constant change in the coming years. The rich and varied ways of calibrated employment level and wage adjustment designed to minimize adversary situations provide interesting lessons for Western companies struggling with the permanent restructuring of the 1990s.

Convergence and Divergence in American and Japanese Downsizing Practice

American Downsizing Practices

Employment maintenance is not part of the social contract between the management and workers of American corporations. For American companies, best practice in managing downsizing means making an honest effort to avoid layoffs, and, if they are deemed necessary, managing them competently and responsibly, offering assistance to those who will leave as well as to those who remain. U.S. companies differ widely in how they implement socially responsible rightsizing strategies.

General Electric, for example, has one of the most comprehensive approaches to managing layoffs. At its Pittsfield, Massachusetts, plant, GE worked closely with the International Union of Electrical Workers to set up a training and development center that assisted workers during and after layoffs, included teams of employees in the implementation of layoff procedures, and provided family counseling, location of job leads, and retraining programs. GE implemented a preferential hiring policy to help laid off workers find jobs in other GE facilities, and applied for funds from federal, state and local governments for training resources. About half of GE's laid-off workers entered some type of educational program, and 70 percent found other jobs, earning on average 80 percent of their previous wages.[12]

Duracell's program focuses on managing survivors of layoffs by increasing information exchange, rebuilding commitment to the corporation, and providing support to each employee individually. At its Waterbury, Connecticut, plant, Duracell lost only two survivors to other corporations and maintained productivity levels among remaining employees.

IBM's management of downsizing strongly resembles Japanese *koyochosei*. The company's first stage adjustments eliminated temporary work and overtime, encouraged voluntary transfer to other IBM plants, and permitted only minimum replacement of personnel. More drastic steps included early retirement incentives for older personnel, cancellation of contract services, voluntary and involuntary transfers to other company plants, and downgrading of jobs. At first, IBM was able to rely on first stage adjustments only and was able to keep sufficient numbers of employees at its plant in Burlington, Vermont, to build on when business improved. The worsening recession of the 1990s and increasing international competition forced the company to downsize more actively, cutting its workforce by more than 25,000 in 1992.

The 1994 AMA survey concluded that operating profits improved at companies that adopted a gradualist downsizing approach, starting with strategic analysis, followed by structural redesign before actual redeployment took place, spacing out the cuts over an extended period of time, concluding with morale building. The worst cases were those firms that avoided reductions in the past and had begun the process since 1992.

Lessons for American and Japanese Managers

The similarities between the Japanese way of restructuring employment and the American better practices of rightsizing are summarized in Table 2.

After painful restructuring, American companies in the mid-1990s are counted among the most competitive in the world. But the evidence of how often downsizing and restructuring have been mismanaged by U.S. companies suggest that complacency is uncalled for. The Japanese Federation of Economic Organizations (Keidanren), in a 1994 report devoted to corporate structural reform, warned: "While introducing new management techniques, Japanese firms must be mindful

Table 2. Japanese *Koyochosei* Compared with American Better Practices in Managing Rightsizing

Japanese Employment Adjustment: *Koyochosei*	Common Characteristics	American Rightsizing Better Practices
• Rightsizing is planned as a series of incremental steps aimed at lowering cost but with maximum possible preservation of jobs. A process divided into distinctive "stages" of employment adjustment is used.	• Careful planning of rightsizing follows a gradualistic approach with incremental steps. • Employees are consulted. • Enhanced communication. • Immediate reductions are avoided if possible and emphasis is on redeployment of manpower to higher value added tasks.	• Long Term Strategic analysis focuses on business goals, not staff reduction targets. Early warning systems used to identify potential layoffs. • Structural Redesign focuses on elimination of low value added tasks and redeployment of manpower.
• First, hours worked are reduced and internal company transfers are used. • Next, reductions of recruitment, non-renewals of contracts, pay cuts, and temporary leave occurs.	• Policies and programs put in place to minimize effects of negative downsizing. • Increased training and retraining.	• Participative process used in restaffing and redeployment with full and honest disclosure and a system of reviews and appeals.
• Actual discharging of employees from company does not start until previous measures are exhausted and then a process begins with external transfer to other companies, early retirement, and voluntary redundancies used before layoffs.	• Organizational recovery program used.	• Limited use of "sharing the pain" measures—if workforce demands it (transfers, job sharing, hiring freeze, shorter work hours, etc.) • Broad Outplacement Assistance. • Increased training and retraining. • Organizational Renewal, Morale Building and Performance Improvement.[17]

of retaining such positive elements of traditional Japanese practice that have proven their worth. It should also be remembered that the recent resurgence of U.S. industry is due in part to the adoption by U.S. firms of employee oriented Japanese management practices such as small group activities and the establishment of a productive dialogue between management and employees."[13]

American companies like Ford have rebuilt their competitiveness by adopting Japanese lean manufacturing systems and by reinventing teamwork and worker-management collaboration. Poorly planned and managed downsizing actions can be very destructive not only of workers' morale and commitment but also of teamwork and cooperation with management. Continuation of some of the present trends in American downsizing practice could lead to the reemergence of bitterly divisive adversary relations between labor and management. As a leading commentator wrote recently in the *Financial Times*: "Downsizing has gone too far and it is time to invest in factories and skilled workers."[14] American managers must be aware of these pitfalls:

- Improved profitability does not automatically follow downsizing; in certain cases, operating profits may decline.

- Productivity and cost reduction outcomes after downsizing are mixed.

- A recurrent effect of downsizing is collapsing employee morale and commitment.

- Downsizing often disrupts a firm's network of relationships between employees and teams of employees, destroying corporate memory vital for future growth and creativity.

- For service companies, customer satisfaction often plummets following downsizing.

Negative outcomes of downsizing are associated with sudden, poorly planned and executed programs that use employment reductions as a quick fix for company problems. In contrast, the Japanese approach to employment adjustment presented in this paper is characterized by gradualism and meticulous planning—characteristics also shared by American companies known for soundly planned and executed downsizing activities.

While there are useful lessons for many American companies to learn from the patient and systematic way in which the Japanese implement employment adjustment, American best practice cannot and need not go to the extremes of employment preservation used by the Japanese. U.S. managers should develop a strategy of rightsizing tailored to American conditions and to the circumstances of their companies. They should:

- Consider cost-cutting options other than employment reductions (e.g., pay cuts, unpaid holidays, reduced workweeks, and job sharing). If workforce reductions are necessary, managers should provide assistance and outplacement programs.

- Build support by full disclosure of information and dialogue with employees and demonstrate the company's good will and concern by explaining the measures the company is taking to minimize layoffs, and describing the assistance to be provided those who may lose jobs.

- Redesign work based on positions rather than people. New opportunities for the remaining workforce should emphasize the sharing of higher value added tasks, not higher work loads.

- Make the redeployment process seem fair and equitable. A system of reviews and appeals should be used.

- Preserve key elements of organizational memory, for example, through video interviews with departing employees. Employees with key organizational knowledge should be retained or hired as consultants.

- Provide generous outplacement assistance and benefits to those who have been laid off to minimize the downward mobility effects of downsizing. Managers should use available government resources.

- Plan for and provide leadership for organizational recovery, morale, and performance improvement.

The lessons for Japanese managers are quite different. However much they try to postpone change in employment practices, pressure to cut employment costs and overmanning are going to continue. More and more Japanese firms will have to make hard choices about employment adjustment, realizing that what they have done so far has not been enough. While the Japanese are likely to reject the practices of those American firms that have downsized drastically and indiscriminately, they may be well advised to study the best practices of those U.S. firms that have implemented well-prepared, successful programs of employment restructuring with accompanying programs of assistance and training for the laid-off. In this sense, they will be converging with the best American practice—a habit the Japanese have pursued for decades.

Corporate Japan has become acutely aware of the need for restructuring. Overmanning is publicly acknowledged by such business leaders as Ken Nagano, chairman of the Japan Federation of Employers Association (Kikkeiren). In urging restraint by Japanese workers in wage and bonus demands during the 1993 shunto annual wage negotiations, he stated that Japanese companies employ 1.2 million excess workers.[15] Even Japan's conservative Ministry of Labor reversed its long-held view that Japan has a structural labor shortage. In a report based on a 1993 industry survey, the ministry found that several industries were overstaffed. About three quarters of the seven million Japanese employees hired between 1987 and 1991 were white collar workers. More than half of manufacturing employees are white collar staff. A Nikkeiren report published in late 1991 contrasts the improved productivity of blue collar workers with the declining productivity of their white collar colleagues.[16] Thus, just as in the United States, a decision to seriously downsize by the Japanese would have to affect white collar as well as blue collar employees.

Japan continues to be stuck in a predicament of low economic growth, flat stock prices, sinking land values, and a banking crisis. In addition, the political and economic elite lack the vision and willpower to undertake the major restructuring necessary for recovery. These elites are aware that the developmental state model that served them so well after World War II has to be discarded, but there is no consensus about what should replace it. Lacking a vision of a new paradigm around which to organize change, Japan continues to tinker with and modify old structures.

In the past, the Japanese have shown a genius for selective adoption of the outside world's best practices. Since World War II, as shown in Figure 1, Japan's management system imitated and absorbed many American management techniques and subsequently evolved its own version of the enterprise system. The golden age of Japanese management, much studied and admired around the world, ended in 1990, ushering in a new set of challenges. Unprecedented international competition and accelerating global economic integration is pushing Japanese management into the new era of universalization.

Figure 1. Historical Evolution of Japanese Management after World War II.[16]

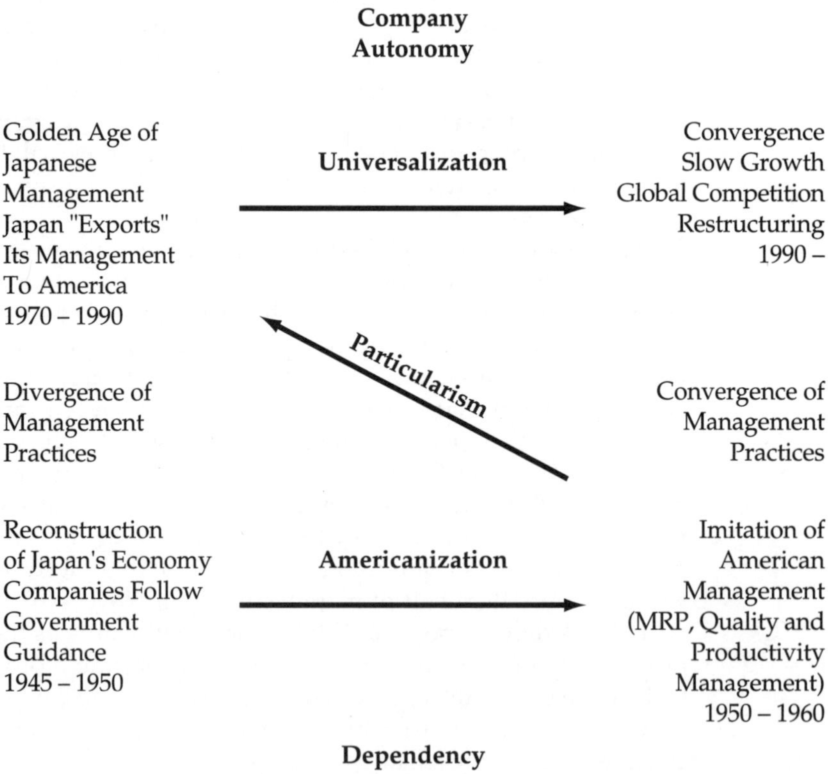

Company Autonomy

Golden Age of Japanese Management Japan "Exports" Its Management To America 1970 – 1990	**Universalization** →	Convergence Slow Growth Global Competition Restructuring 1990 –
Divergence of Management Practices	*Particularism* ↖	Convergence of Management Practices
Reconstruction of Japan's Economy Companies Follow Government Guidance 1945 – 1950	**Americanization** →	Imitation of American Management (MRP, Quality and Productivity Management) 1950 – 1960

Dependency

In this new era, Japanese companies will face increasing pressures to phase out practices that undermine their competitiveness. As they have historically, they are likely to blend continuity with change. The change most likely to occur will be the gradual emergence of a horizontal labor market.

The age of accelerating globalization of business implies a constant readiness to learn international best practices in every field. In the field of employment and human resources, convergence of best practices is likely to be much more complex and incomplete than, for example, in quality management. Japanese and American companies may move at different speeds, but long-term employment practices in the two countries may converge. Japanese social expectations are likely to become reconciled with layoffs and with the emergence of a large horizontal labor market. American corporate management, facing the challenge of permanent restructuring, may need to relearn the value of collaborative labor-management relationships, and implement restructuring and rightsizing with those relationships in mind.

Endnotes

1. *Academy of Management Survey*. 1995. Corporate downsizing, job elimination, and job creation. New York.

2. *Wall Street Journal*. 1992. Lack of communication burdens restructuring. November 2.

3. Greenberg, E. R. 1990. The latest AMA survey on downsizing. *Compensation and Benefits Review*. Vol 22.

4. Cascio, W. T. 1993. Downsizing: What do we know? What have we learned? *Academy of Management Executive*. 7(1).

5. *Wall Street Journal*, Ibid.

6. *The Economist*. 1996. Fire and forget? April 20.

7. *Industry Week*, 1994. Reengineering Vs. Tradition. September 5.

8. Ministry of Labor Survey. 1993 Manuscript. Tokyo.

9. *Ibid.*

10. *Industry Week*. Ibid.

11. *Nihonteku Keiei Saikochiku O Saguru* Japan Productivity Center, August 1992.

12. Feldman, D. C., Leano, C. R. 1994. Better practices in managing layoffs. *Human Resource Management*, Summer, 33(2).

13. *Keidaneren Review*. 1994. Special issue on the Japanese Economy.

14. *Financial Times*. 1996. America's recipe for industrial extinction. May 14.

15. For a critical assessment of post-bubble Japan, see: Wood, C. 1994. *The End of Japan Inc.*, New York: Simon and Schuster.

16. *Ibid.*

17. Marshall, Robert & Yakes, Lyle. Planning for a Restructured Revitalized Organization. *Sloan Management Review*. Summer 1994.

Anatomy of a Paraguayan Strike[1]

Case 6.1
Joyce S. Osland
Pedro Ferreira

Two labor union leaders were sitting in a café in Asunción, the capital city of Paraguay, looking back on the tumultuous events of recent months and wondering if it had all been worthwhile. Oscar Martinez and Roberto Ugarte were president and vice president (respectively) of the Engineers Labor Union (UIA) of ANDE, the parastatal electric power utility for the entire country. ANDE has four different labor unions for its 4500 employees. Oscar is an idealistic, engaging man in his early thirties. He is extremely bright and recently graduated at the head of his Executive MBA class. He teaches engineering classes on the side and is involved in numerous community projects to help the poor. Roberto is an intense man in his forties, who is known for his dedication to his work and family.

Both men hold prestigious jobs on two counts. First, engineers in Latin America are so highly regarded that, like doctors, they are addressed using the name of their profession—"Engineer Gonzalez" rather than "Mr." (Señor) Gonzalez. Second, the electricity utility in most Latin American countries is often the most respected and well-run government agency, perhaps due to its well-educated work force and its importance to the citizenry.

Labor Day, *el Dia del Obrero*, is a holiday celebrated on May first throughout Latin America. Work places are closed, employers host parties for workers, and labor unions organize parades and sometimes more serious forms of protest to improve worker conditions. Sometimes, there are "general strikes," which attempt to shut down an entire country or city by persuading sympathizers to stay home and show their solidarity with union demands. Even if citizens do not support a general strike, it is usually too difficult or dangerous to transport themselves to work. In Paraguay, May 1, 1996 was a special occasion since four labor union federations had convoked a two-day general strike for May 2 and 3. They were protesting government economic policies that they deemed harmful to the poor and government inaction in areas where they felt reform was needed.

Source: Joyce S. Osland and Pedro Ferreira. "Anatomy of a Paraguayan Strike." Reprinted by permission of the author.

The anatomy of this strike can only be understood within the broader context of the Paraguayan political situation and the events that led up to it within the UIA.

National Situation

Paraguay lived through a dictatorship headed by Alfredo Stroessner from 1954-1989. During much of this time Stroessner enjoyed the popular support of the people. He accomplished this via pronounced economic growth, social mobility (the lower classes could improve their lot by obtaining government jobs), control and manipulation of information, and convincing the public that other needs were more import than liberty.

In 1989, a coup d'etat was engineered by General Rodriguez, the father-in-law of Stroessner's son. Rodriguez had been Stroessner's right hand man. When he assumed power, Rodriguez initiated a period of democratic progress, with broad guarantees of freedom of expression and functioning opposition parties. As often occurs when totalitarian regimes fall, raised expectations and a particular set of hopes and beliefs flourished. Many Paraguayans began to attribute all the country's problems to Stroessner's dictatorship and believed that democracy would soon resolve these problems. They also believed that the corruption that was part and parcel of the dictatorship would be eliminated or at least reduced once freedom gave people the courage to denounce unethical practices. With corruption eliminated, people believed there would be a more equal distribution of wealth. If they just had patience and hope, the general welfare of the people would improve. These expectations were not realized, in part because corrupt practices continued in the democratic governments that followed the dictatorship. The only difference is that Paraguayan newspapers now have the freedom to publish numerous articles about corruption.

In 1993, the Engineer J.C. Wasmosy was elected president in an election that was considered to be fraudulent by the majority of the population. A businessman who became wealthy during the dictatorship, Wasmosy was the first civilian Paraguayan president in almost half a century. He enacted a series of economic measures, which were applauded by liberal sectors and by business. However, his actions were also criticized by those who believed that he was simply looking out for the interests of his fellow capitalists.

In contrast to the business sector, the economic expectations of people at the lower end of the social strata were not fulfilled. Paraguay has a set minimum wage that applies to most workers. The buying power of the minimum wage had decreased by 20% compared to the levels that existed prior to the coup d'etat in 1989. The *campesinos* (people who live in the country, usually small farmers or ranchers) are forced to sell products at lower prices, which caused problems of land ownership, unemployment, health and education. Although inflation has decreased from 30-40% annually to approximately 10%, interest rates are still very high (50%).

Since 1992, there have been a series of protests, strikes, road closures, and demands for political justice, mostly aimed against government policies, which were perceived as conflicting with the interests of the common people. A few people died in these protests, usually *campesinos*, but these actions had little impact on the government. In late 1995, the *campesinos* organized a march that was widely considered to be an admirable example of a peaceful protest. Nevertheless, the government did not know how to respond to their concerns in a timely fashion. When the government finally invited the *campesino* leaders to a dialogue, the latter said they were not interested. The purpose of their march was not to solicit solutions from a government that made promises it did not fulfill. Their purpose was to convict the government of a lack of interest in social problems and the diversion of resources to other priorities.

One of the most influential figures in Wasmosy's government, until April 1996, was General Lino Oviedo. The army general was very popular after the military coup of 1989 due to the bravery he demonstrated at that time and to the subsequent leadership he exerted over the military rank and file when he eventually succeeded General Rodriguez. In 1992, however, General Oviedo's image was beginning to deteriorate among some groups in light of his increasingly evident political aspirations. According to one Paraguayan, much of the populace was "fed up with having two presidents—one who held the reins of power and the other who had the tanks." This further increased the dissatisfaction of the populace.

On Monday, April 22, 1996, relations were ruptured completely between the President and General Oveido. There are differing versions about what actually occurred. Wasmosy claims he asked Oveido for his resignation, and the General refused. According to Oveido, Wasmosy asked him to take measures that would disempower the Congress, but the General refused. Everyone agrees that Oveido threatened to take over the government, and there was widespread concern that armed force and violence would result. Shortly thereafter, the U.S. embassy and Brazilian officials announced their support for Wasmosy. The university students staged a peaceful demonstration against a military takeover, and the danger of a military coup was defused. The middle and upper class, the media, the intellectuals, and a large part of the population hoped that this would be a positive turning point for Wasmosy's government. The unions, however, did not think Oveido's removal would produce deep-seated changes; in their eyes, the displacement of the military leaders simply meant greater power for the business leaders controlling the government. Right upon the heels of the heady drama of the attempted coup came Labor Day and the general strike.

Meetings of the UIA Union Leaders Prior to the Strike _____

The UIA leaders had a series of meetings and decisions prior to the strike when they were trying to decide whether or not they should go along with the other unions and strike. Snippets of these meetings follow.

UIA Executive Meeting—April 10, 1996

The leaders of UIA met, as they did every Wednesday. Among other agenda items, they needed to discuss an invitation from the federation of unions to participate in a congress to be held the following Saturday. At that meeting, the union representatives would decide whether or not to hold the threatened general strike. Five members were seated around a table in the union headquarters.

> **Oscar:** It sounds like we're all in agreement that the officers should attend the congress this Saturday. Then our next decision is—do you think we should strike?
>
> **Roberto:** Several of our members weren't happy with the position we took during the last strike. They didn't think it was enough to simply write a manifesto agreeing with the workers and then go to work as if it were "business as usual." It's the easy way out.
>
> **Miguel:** Well, at least we published a manifesto proposing structural changes and things the government should do to avoid a civilian outburst. (Please see Appendix 1) You'll never get all the engineers to go on strike when so many of them are managers.
>
> **Roberto:** If we want to wake up the government, manifestos aren't enough. The social situation is deteriorating, and the moment will arrive when there won't be anything left to do.
>
> **Victor:** I agree with Roberto. Besides, if we are in agreement that the government is neglecting the lower classes, why don't we pledge ourselves to the strike?
>
> **Miguel:** Don't forget though that in the six years of the UIA's existence, we have only participated in two strikes—one against the unethical privatizations and the other against corruption. In both cases, the participation of our members was pretty lukewarm, because there is always a lot to lose in these situations.

To Strike or Not to Strike?

After more debate, the group decided to call a general assembly meeting for all their members to decide what stance the UIA should take at the congress. At the assembly, the union members agreed to join the strike. Their reasons can be divided into two categories. The first category were ethical reasons. The members believe it is wrong to ignore the needs of the majority of the population. What use is it for some people to have a great deal of money when others are suffering for lack of resources? Furthermore, it is not fair for the government to focus only upon the interests of the politicians and their friends.

The second set of reasons were practical ones that touched upon the general welfare of the citizenry and self interest. The union did not perceive that it was benefiting from government policies, and the government was not living up to its side of their agreement on a previous labor contract with the union. The country's economic difficulties caused an increase in crime, particularly robberies and assaults, which affected everyone. If the poor eventually were to lose patience and rebel, everyone would suffer with the exception of the wealthy capitalists who would simply leave the country and live on money they have stashed overseas. Members of the UIA did not have this option.

UIA Executive Meeting—April 17, 1996

Oscar began the meeting by reporting on the congress held by the union federation.

> **Oscar:** As you know from reading the newspaper, the federation has decided to go forward with the strike on May 2nd and 3rd. If there is not a favorable response from the government, there will be another week-long strike before the end of the year.
>
> **Miguel:** The business owners will not like that!
>
> **Oscar:** I have a copy here of the main points the federation is asking for in connection with the strike. (See Appendix 2) There are more than twenty on the list, some of which are rather strange. The most important ones are a salary increase, improving the Instituto de Prevision Social (the social security institute) which, as we all know, is currently a disaster, and avoiding privatizations that benefit politicians or government officials who buy public resources at lower than market value. I don't agree with all these demands, but I think we have to show solidarity with the other unions so the government takes notice.
>
> **Victor:** I wanted to report that we've received a note from the Ministry of Justice and Work inviting us to a meeting the day after tomorrow. We made inquiries and none of the unions, other than the *amarillos*,[2] are planning to go. The invitations only went to unions like us that are not associated with any federation. This looks like a ploy to give the impression that the government wants to dialogue, but the unions don't. If they had wanted to discuss things, they should have done so before the deadline set by the Federation, which ran out on April 8. Now that the strike is irreversible, they are trying to discredit this pressure tactic and divide the unions.

UIA Meeting—April 30, 1996 (last meeting prior to the strike)

Miguel: Some people called to complain about the decision taken in the assembly to go on strike. I told them that if they wanted to discuss it, they should meet and explain their point of view.

Roberto: Some of them believe that public opinion is in favor of the government after last week's failed coup and Oveido's ouster.

Carlos: In my area the people from SITRANDE (a union for workers and technicians at ANDE) are commenting that we aren't going to have the necessary mass that we're hoping for. The danger of all this is that if the government thinks its position is stronger because of the failed coup and believes that the worker movement is losing steam, they might take advantage of the situation to get even with groups that have been protesting against them.

Roberto: In my department they are saying that we all have to agree on the strike, because there is a certain threat that this strike will be bloody, unlike the last one. Business can't allow this strike to be successful, because it will result in the week-long strike planned for the end of the year. Victor, what happened at the meeting between the ANDE executives and the Strike Committee?

Victor: I thought the attitude of the ANDE executives seemed irresponsible. They refused to talk about how we'd keep the system going with fewer people on the job. They just wanted to make sure all the engineers would be at work. They kept insisting that *all* positions were vital for the operation of the power system, even the administrative ones.

Miguel: How did the meeting end up?

Victor: No agreements were reached. Management said they would continue operating the system with the people who come to work—but without "subordinating" themselves to a strike committee.

Carlos: The situation is dangerous because the SITRANDE members only take orders from their own strike committee. We need to help organize this and figure out what workers are needed to keep the system operating during the strike. We should elect Victor as president of the strike committee of UIA, because he works in operations and will be informed about everything that occurs. All in favor, say aye.

A chorus of ayes followed Carlos' suggestion.

Oscar: SITRANDE has invited us to join them at the crossroads of Route 1 and the highway, which will be the principal point of friction between the strikers and the police. Any strike that is successful in blocking all traffic at this point is guaranteed at least a 50% success rate, because no one can get into downtown Asunción otherwise.

Roberto: I heard a police announcement on the radio warning that if the strikers tried to take this intersection, they were going to prevent it with violence if necessary.

Victor: The quantity of strikers at that point is usually so large, added to the throngs of people who are waiting at the various bus stops there, that it is impossible to clear the road. When the police clear out one side of the street, the other is already blocked again. The best the cops can hope for is an intermittent flow of traffic, and the resulting traffic jam will be so large that there will be no way into the city.

Carlos: The union delegate in my department, Samuel, will carry a cellular phone and keep us posted on what is going on. He'll be at the intersection early in the morning. I will have another cellular phone just in case the telephone service is cut off in our meeting place.

Discussion Between Oscar and Roberto—May 2, 1:10 a.m.

Shortly after midnight in the early hours of May 2nd, Oscar Martinez and Roberto Ugarte visited one of the sites in Asunción where union members gathered to make strike plans. Oscar and Roberto were concerned that only a handful of strikers were present. Those in attendance assured them, however, that the others would show up at five in the morning. On their way home they discussed their concerns about the coming strike.

Oscar: Roberto, what kind of turnout do you think we'll have?

Roberto: Well, the fact that last year's strike was peaceful has given the union members more confidence. There should be more protesters on the street as a result. What do you predict?

Oscar: I think people here in Asunción will not go to work, but I don't expect many of them to join the protest. Since the two days of general strike follow a holiday, some people may just treat this as a long weekend.

Roberto: SITRANDE can probably count on having between 300-500 strikers of their 2500 members at the main meeting point.

Oscar: I was calculating the numbers for our own union last night. Of our 140 members, thirty are senior managers, thirty are in jobs that are crucial to providing power service, and twenty are out of town or on vacation. I'll be happy if 25 of the remaining fifty show up at the union hall.

Roberto: APROANDE (the non-engineering professionals union) is the only union that is not going out on strike. Maybe they think they'll gain something later on by not participating.

Oscar: It would have been better if all the ANDE unions had formed a united front.

Roberto: True, but you know how hard it is to get that many people to agree. At least SITRANDE is committed to the strike, and there's no way management can replace their technicians since ANDE is the only electricity company in Paraguay.

Oscar: Let's get some rest; tomorrow may be a long hard day.

UIA Assembly Meeting—May 2, 7:00 a.m.

Some of the UIA members and the leaders gathered to monitor the strike's progress at the union hall. Because of their status, they did not protest in the streets. In horror, they watched and listened to live TV and radio coverage of a strike that had quickly turned violent. The police began harassing and attacking protesters at 4:00 a.m. in an effort to prevent the strikers from blocking the intersection of Route 1 and the highway. According to reporters, the police were beating members of the press as well as observers. People were calling the radio stations to complain about police brutality. Some of the SITRANDE protesters were beaten without provocation before they even reached the intersection. The police fired shots at them, and the protesters had to take refuge in a private home. The principle leaders of the union federation were arrested, beaten, and loaded into a truck heading to an unknown destination. Since union leaders have sometimes figured among the *desaparecidos* (people who simply disappear, apparently murdered by enemies, paramilitary groups, or the military, etc.) in Latin America, this caused a great deal of alarm. The general secretary of SITRANDE appeared on TV warning that if the leaders were not freed within an hour, ANDE technicians and workers on duty would leave their posts, essentially cutting off the electricity supply.

Oscar: Is there any word on the federation leaders?

Carlos: The mobil unit of the radio station is following the truck they were loaded into, since their lives might be in danger.

Victor: I just heard that the power line from San Lorenzo to Itaugua is out of service. They can't find any technical reason for the blackout. The instruments in the stations outside Asunción are not giving us the correct readings, so we're working blind. I think it's best that I go to the office in case the problem gets any more complicated.

Carlos: I have a cell phone call from SITRANDE members who are right in the middle of the protest. They are requesting some type of help from us. I can hear shots in the background. They say the shots are not being fired into the air but right over their heads. The police are beating people with clubs, and they are stampeding.

Oscar: Tell them to be careful and to give us a little time to see what we can do.

Carlos: Now the police are corralling them. They want a communication or something from us right away.

Oscar: Give me a moment to think.

A ringing telephone broke the tense silence in the room. It was Oscar's mother-in-law, saying, "The entire family is supporting you!" Oscar thanked her for calling and returned to weighing his options. "What's the right thing to do?" he muttered.

Oscar and his fellow officers decided to write a communique. Carlos suggested calling the president or senior management of ANDE. Oscar responded, "See if you can get them on the phone, but I don't think we have enough time. We have to do something that freezes the situation and avoids a power shutdown." Roberto and Oscar began to work over a legal pad at one end of the table. The other officers continued with their conversation.

> **Carlos:** I think that supporting SITRANDE at this moment when they are threatening to cut off the power would be an unpopular move. We'll lose public support if we go along with them. Worse yet, we're going to look like SITRANDE's caboose—they get involved in a fight and then drag us in after them.
>
> **Danilo:** If the SITRANDE workers walk off the job and cause a blackout, the consequences will be enormous.
>
> **Victor:** I just heard that the technicians in the distribution department handed a note to their boss and immediately left their positions. They are going to the intersection to help their fellow union members. The only people left on duty are two workers and the supervisor.
>
> **Miguel:** A friend of mine called from headquarters saying that everyone believes the breakdown in the San Lorenzo line was intentional. The maintenance workers were told to repair it, but they have refused until SITRANDE's strike committee approves the request.
>
> **Carlos:** This is getting worse and worse. Why don't we just let SITRANDE continue with their own fight? Why get involved in a conflict like this?
>
> **Miguel:** Don't you realize that people could be killed or wounded? If there is a blackout, things will be that much worse. There are hospitals in the country that don't have backup generators.
>
> **Carlos:** If you get involved in a strike, you have to be willing to pay the consequences.
>
> **Oscar:** We're wasting valuable time, and everything indicates that the situation is getting out of hand. Why don't we send out a forceful communique. A half-hearted gesture on our part at this point won't have any impact. We have to be aware of the danger we're courting, but this should give everyone more time—the police, the unionists, and the administrators of ANDE. Here's the draft we wrote just now. What do you think of it?

The officers all read and agreed to the communique. After several tries, they were successful in getting a telephone line to one of the largest local radio stations. Oscar read the following communique over the telephone in a solemn tone of voice, and his statement was broadcast over the air. (The first communique appears in Appendix 3)

Reactions to UIA's Communique

Reactions to UIA's announcement came fast and furious. The radio station that aired the broadcast interpreted the statement as irresponsibility on the part of the UIA for failing to guarantee electrical service to hospitals without backup generators.

Meeting with SITRANDE—May 2, 1996, 8:20-10:00 a.m.

SITRANDE immediately called the officers of UIA and asked for a meeting where they would plan out the next steps. The UIA officers jumped into a car and went to the meeting location, devising their strategy and position en route. Upon entering the meeting room, they found the SITRANDE members in a highly emotional state. Some men had been harassed by the police, beaten, and threatened with death. A policeman had aimed his gun and discharged the bullet right over the head of one of the leaders. These well-respected civil servants had never experienced this type of treatment before; they were in shock and appeared to be much more nervous than the UIA members.

As a result, the initial positions of the two unions were very different. The engineers did not want to endanger the country electricity system in any way, whereas SITRANDE wanted to fight back and demonstrate the force and cohesion of the electricity sector.

The meeting was a cauldron of conflicting ideas. Some wanted vengeance, others worried about the imprisoned leaders and the people who'd been injured. Still others vowed to take a firm stance with the government and yield nothing in what was now a full-fledged fight. Those who wanted to escalate the conflict made the following statements.

"We should contact the union at Itaipú, (the enormous dam that is the main source of electricity for both Paraguay and the neighboring region of Brazil), and get them to go on strike too."

"In this instance, cutting off the electricity is a matter of self defense until the federation leaders are released."

"Why should we be concerned about the life-threatening consequences of a blackout? The police were not worrying about human life when they were shooting guns at us this morning!"

"How many times has Paraguay had blackouts due to technical problems and no negative consequences resulted? Why would an intentional blackout be any different?"

"The San Lorenzo line should not be repaired or tested."

"We should knock out the large power cables, because this would force an immediate solution."

"Let's cut off power in the areas where the army is quartered!"

Others argued more calmly for considering the negative consequences to escalating the conflict:

"We can't put innocent lives at risk."

"Public opinion will be against us."

"Cutting off the power will give ammunition to those who want to privatize ANDE."

"Pulling the power plug should be the last and not the first weapon in the fight."

"We can't make a decision like this without the full vote of the general assembly."

After an hour and a half of discussion, the combined unions made the following decisions:

1. There will be no unilateral actions.

2. The two unions would send out a joint communique.

The purpose of the first resolution was to ensure that decisions would be made in a rational manner, taking all factors into consideration. No union or a subgroup would unilaterally cause a blackout. The purpose behind the second resolution was to present the two unions' side of the situation to the public, thereby pressuring the police to release the federation leaders and showing a united front to encourage the strikers in the streets.

The leaders of the two unions hammered out a joint communique which was released to the radio stations. (See Appendix 4)

After leaving the meeting, the UIA officers turned on the radio to hear that a rumor was circulating that two of the arrested federation leaders would be released shortly. The rest of the news, however, was disheartening.

- The president of ANDE, Ricardo Alvarez, had called the UIA irresponsible, citing Oscar and Roberto by name. He also announced that even if the technicians went out on strike, ANDE had an emergency plan that would guarantee service. Alvarez is an electrical engineer with an MBA from the same alma mater as Oscar. He has a relaxed, pleasant personality and good political skills. Union members griped that while they were worrying about trying to prevent more violence and blackouts from happening, Alvarez was concentrating on protecting his own image.

- A doctor complained that there was no electricity in the Sanatorio Cristian clinic, and ANDE had failed to restore service, thereby threatening innocent lives.

- Rumor had it that two of the arrested federation leaders would be released shortly.

- Some radio announcers began a slander campaign against the unions in the electricity sector.

As soon as they returned to their headquarters, the UIA officers checked on the clinic and discovered that it had not suffered a power outage and the doctor's claims were false. Their next call went to the ANDE engineers who specialized in operations to ask about the Alvarez's claim that ANDE had an emergency plan. A plan did exist, which relied primarily upon army personnel, to run a station that was refusing to operate. The success of the plan would depend upon whether or not the workers on duty would leave peacefully and whether the problem with the inaccurate instrument readings could be resolved. It was never determined whether the instrument system was sabotaged (and if so, by whom) or whether it was simply another technical problem that looked suspicious. The engineers were doubtful that the emergency plan would be successful; some worried that if the entire system went down it could be extremely difficult to get it up and running again.

The UIA officers figured that the negative publicity campaign was being orchestrated by ANDE itself. The radio station that led the campaign was the major recipient of ads and program support from ANDE. Therefore, the officers decided to go directly to this station and try to inform the public about the true facts of the situation and reassure them that there were no health clinics without electricity. When they arrived at the station, however, the announcer/owner would not let them speak. Instead, he proudly told his listeners that he would not give air time to "traitors like these." The union leaders regrouped and sent faxes to all the radio stations.

General UIA Assembly Meeting—May 2, 11:00-14:00

The UIA members met at their headquarters and heard a recount of the events of the day. Many of the members were unhappy about the efforts to discredit them by some of the radio stations. There was some good news however: the violence in the streets was virtually over by 8:00 a.m.; there were no major locations without electricity; and two of the federation leaders had been released, but refused their freedom until all the other leaders were released. For a moment, it looked as if things were returning to normal. Oscar breathed a sigh of relief—but this was just the calm in the eye of the storm.

- A radio news flash announced that the workers at Itaipú were threatening to shut down the largest hydroelectric plant in the world if the federation leaders were not immediately released. Since the workers did not specify whether only Paraguay would be affected, there was the possibility that Brazil would also be dragged into the conflict. It appeared as if SITRANDE had asked the Itaipú workers to take this measure without consulting UIA.

- Once again, Alvarez went on the air, complaining that the union leaders were irresponsible. He also went to court and obtained a restraining order that was served upon both unions.

- In response, another player entered the game. The Electricians' Association, with 3000 members, issued a manifesto supporting the ANDE unions and attacking its president, Alvarez.

- At noon, Oscar received a phone call from his wife, who said, "Oscar, don't you realize that you are endangering everyone?"

- The unions extended the deadline they had given the government to release the federation leaders by 1:00 p.m.

Meanwhile, the UIA assembly agreed upon the following conclusions. They had achieved their goals in the conflict. SITRANDE, however, was escalating the conflict unnecessarily. After a few phone calls to the dam, they concluded that the Itaipú workers would probably not shut down the turbines, and it was unwise to keep the populace on edge worrying about a blackout. Furthermore, it looked as if the federation leaders would be released very soon. Therefore, they decided to release a third communique clarifying their position and trying to calm the public. (See Appendix 5) This was read on radio stations around noon.

The conflict continued to escalate during the afternoon.

- Disaster struck again at 12:50 when the lights went out in an area that contained two large hospitals. The cause was a common technical problem concerning overheated cables, which was unrelated to the strike. Nevertheless, this produced a deluge of criticism against the UIA and SITRANDE. Alvarez went back on the air accusing the unions of slowdown tactics, a purposeful delay in restoring service to the hospitals. He said their leaders were criminally responsible for any loss of human life. Oscar called the same radio station to clarify that this was simply a technical problem that was repaired in forty minutes.

- The newscaster at Radiomundo, a friend of Alvarez, read a phony curriculum vita that portrayed Oscar as a "*Stronista*," a term applied to Stroessner supporters, collaborators, and/or profiteers.

- A representative of SITRANDE called Radiomundo to back up the veracity of Oscar's radio announcement and denounce Alvarez's actions. He also accused Alvarez of supporting General Oveido, claiming Alvarez had ordered two generators to be delivered to the general's headquarters during the failed coup attempt.

- Alvarez called back the radio station, denying this charge and lashing out again at the unions. Some of Oscar's friends said he should clear his own name and attack Alvarez. He refused, explaining that the UIA's objectives had been met and the radio fight was distracting attention from more important issues. Instead, Oscar called the person on Alvarez's staff who was friends with both of them. This person got Alvarez to agree to Oscar's suggestion that neither of them would speak on the radio again to keep ANDE from losing further prestige.

The Aftermath

- According to Oscar, just about everyone lost as a result of the strike. Two workdays were lost and in the following two days not much was accomplished. The unions were weakened, because it became obvious that a strike lasting longer than a day would require more public support than they could muster. The government did not change anything, but they became even less popular. They also lost whatever momentum they might have gained after removing Oveido from the scene. Social instability has increased, prompting the popularity of more authoritarian leaders, which may threaten the evolution of democracy in Paraguay. Wasmosy was not reelected by his party.

- Alvarez never did meet with Oscar. A week after the strike, the president initiated a criminal lawsuit against Oscar and the leaders of SITRANDE, but, as frequently occurs in Paraguay, nothing came of it.

- Just prior to the strike, Oscar had been selected for a faculty job at an industrial engineering school (professors in Paraguay have "day jobs" and moonlight as professors). A week after the strike, the job search was reopened. Oscar was tied with another candidate. A member of the faculty committee who was a friend of Wasmosy suggested that the other candidate be named, given Oscar's actions in the strike.

- Six moths after the strike, Oscar lost out on yet another professorship. This happened in spite of the fact that he was more qualified than the person who was appointed and had been teaching this course for four years, waiting for a vacancy to open.

- For a while after the strike, Oscar felt uncomfortable with some of his friends. In particular, he felt that his MBA classmates, who are business people who don't think much of the working class, did not approve of his actions.

- There have been no apparent negative repercussions for Alvarez. Oscar believes that people generally believed Alvarez's version of what occurred rather than his own. Oscar regrets channeling their communique through Radiomundo, which took attention away from the union demands to engineer a conflict between Alvarez and the union and its leaders. Alvarez enjoyed an advantage in this arena because he is friends with several radio announcers and the newspaper is anti-union. The unions believe this is because the newspaper owner wants to buy state businesses and the unions are against privatization.

- Oscar does not think his career has suffered within ANDE. He was promoted to a management job in Human Resources shortly after the strike by placing first on the selection exam. A month later a huge storm knocked out several towers in an isolated part of the country. Since Oscar had been responsible for maintaining high tension lines in the past, he went to the trouble spot without being asked. The president was also there; for 48 hours they worked together almost nonstop to repair the line. Both were grateful for the other's help. In Oscar's opinion, there is no rancor between them.

- Oscar's actions in the strike have helped him in his relations with the workers and technicians within ANDE. They trust him and are more willing to share information and problems with him.

In Oscar's opinion, the one positive outcome of the strike is that the engineers stood behind the workers and technicians when the strike became dangerous and helped prevent a country-wide blackout.

APPENDIX 1

MANIFESTO OF THE ENGINEERS LABOR UNION OF ANDE DECEMBER 1995

(This manifesto was released on the occasion of the first general strike, in which UIA did not participate.)

For the time being we manifest our deep concern for the lack of attention given by the National Government to the serious problems facing this country:

1. Lack of buying power of salaries given the cost of the *canasta familiar* (family basket of necessities)

2. The worker, rural farmer, and middle classes are indebted due to interest rates higher than the level of inflation and the decrease in their income

3. Lack of work, land and resources oriented to production

4. Deficient infrastructure and human resources

5. Lack of internal and external credibility of our legal justice system

6. Deficient handling of citizen complaints and state powers

7. Personal interests placed before the interests of the nation

8. A permissive climate towards corruption

The general strike and the *campesinos'* march are eloquent symptoms of the critical social situation of the country. The National Government should accept these legitimate complaints with wisdom and self-criticism.

Therefore, the Engineers Labor Union of ANDE proposes the following:

1. Reorient national politics towards the solution of social problems

2. Execute bipartisan policies

3. Implement plans for cultural revolutions of short, medium and long term, that will permit us to compete more effectively, a current requirement of market economies

4. Firmly brake the efforts of those, including the government, who try to destabilize reform

5. Dialogue and commitment to the public will, as evidenced in the last elections

6. Respect for public institutions and their officials for their role as servants of the people and not for political interests or sectarian economies

Finally, we express our confidence that people in power in the government will be reminded of their patriotic and moral values, so they can orient their minds and actions for the common good. The Paraguayan people will acknowledge and be grateful for these acts.

STEERING COMMITTEE

APPENDIX 2

DEMANDS* OF THE LABOR UNION FEDERATIONS
APRIL 13, 1996

1. Increase the minimum salary by 31%

2. Salary readjustment (increases) for public employees

3. Protection and reform of the Social Security Institute (IPS)

4. Benefit coverage for self-employed workers

5. Fulfillment of contracts signed with public and private workers

6. Fulfillment of specific contracts signed with transportation workers

7. Convocation of a referendum on privatization

8. Adoption of a policy of full employment

9. Support for the demands of the rural farmer organizations

10. Full participation of all social classes in the process of regional integration of the Mercosur (trading bloc of the southern Latin American countries)

11. Distribution of the National Labor Code

12. Repeal of Decree No. 6.478/94 regarding positions of trust

   * Some of these demands concerned previous contractual agreements that the government had not honored.

APPENDIX 3

FIRST COMMUNIQUE
ENGINEERS LABOR UNION OF ANDE (UIA)
MAY 2, 1996
7:50 A.M.

In light of the serious repercussions reported this morning and the arrests and beatings of union leaders, and protesters, we declare the following:

1. We send an urgent plea to the police to release the union leaders and protesters so they can freely exercise their constitutional rights.

2. SITRANDE (syndicate of workers of ANDE) has notified us of their decision to not guarantee the provision of electrical energy service, including the abandonment of key posts.

3. The UIA appeals to the common sense and wisdom of the police, because this could result in serious consequences—not only the possible loss of electrical power but extensive damage to the electrical system itself.

4. Since the members of UIA find themselves in a strike of solidarity with the working class, we will not guarantee the provision of electrical power as of 8:15 a.m. If SITRANDE pulls workers off the job, it will be physically impossible to guarantee service.

APPENDIX 4

SECOND COMMUNIQUE
SPECIAL GENERAL ASSEMBLY OF UIA AND SITRANDE
MAY 2, 1996
10:00 A.M.

Given the serious acts of violent repression and detention of union leaders, protesters, journalists, and workers in general, the strike committee of SITRANDE and UIA inform the general public of the following:

ANDE workers who respond to customer complaints throughout the country are no longer on the job.

Service complaints from hospitals and other essential services will be handled rapidly by the strike committees of both unions.

Neither union will be responsible for power cutoffs that are the result of acts of sabotage and/or the operation of the national electricity system by people who do not work for ANDE.

The operators of the stations, substations, and Acaray Central Hydroelectric plant will remain at their jobs until the strike committees deem otherwise.

If the national government does not release our unfairly detained colleagues, the strike committees of both unions reserve the right to take whatever measures they consider necessary.

Other decisions to be decided will be communicated solely to the media and the ANDE authorities.

STRIKE COMMITTEES OF SITRANDE AND UIA

APPENDIX 5

THIRD COMMUNIQUE
ENGINEERS LABOR UNION OF ANDE (UIA)
MAY 2, 1996

In light of the misinformation with respect to the electrical power service, the Engineers Labor Union of ANDE informs the general public of the following:

1. At no time has our union caused or will cause a cutoff in the provision of electrical energy.

2. This union promises to take care of energy outages that affect hospitals, clinic or other essential services where there is direct or indirect danger to human life. We will respond immediately and diligently repair the problems.

We have the technical means to accurately and immediately identify when outages affect the essential services mentioned above.

Endnotes _____

1. All names have been changed to protect the identity of the protagonists.

2. The *amarillos* or "yellow ones" support management in return for certain advantages like promotions, paid trips, etc., rather than fight for the workers' conditions.

Labor Relations at EuroDisneyland

Case 6.2
J. Stewart Black
Hal B. Gregersen

Only one year after the grand opening of EuroDisneyland, Robert Fitzpatrick left his position as EuroDisney's chairperson, citing a desire to start his own consulting firm. In April, 1993, Philippe Bourguignon took over the helm of EuroDisney, thought by some to be a sinking ship. EuroDisney faced a net loss of FFr188mm for the fiscal year ending September, 1992.[1] The European park also fell 1mm visitors short of its goal for the first year of operation, with the French comprising only 29% of the park's total visitors between April and September, 1992—a far cry from the predicted 50%.[2]

In addition to the financial woes weighing down on Bourguignon, he was also expected to stem the flow of bad publicity which EuroDisney had experienced from its inception. Phase Two development at EuroDisneyland was slated to start in September, 1993, but in light of their drained cash reserves (FFr1.1bn in May, 1993)[3], and monstrous debts (estimated at FFr21bn)[4], it was unclear as to how the estimated FFr8-10bn Phase Two project would be financed.

Despite this bleak picture, Michael Eisner, CEO of Walt Disney Co., remained optimistic about the venture: "Instant hits are things that go away quickly, and things that grow slowly and are part of the culture are what we look for. What we created in France is the biggest private investment in a foreign country by an American company ever. And it's gonna pay off."[5]

Source: J. Stewart Black and Hal Gregersen. "Training and Socialization at EuroDisneyland." This case was written by Research Assistant Tanya M. Spyridakis under the direction of Associate Professor J. Stewart Black, with the assistance of Associate Professor Hal Gregersen and Research Assistant Sonali Krishna as the basis for class discussion; it is not meant to illustrate the effective or ineffective handling of an administrative situation. Adapted by permission of the authors.

History_____

On March 24, 1987, Michael Eisner and Jacques Chirac, then the French Prime Minister, signed a contract for the building of a Disney theme park at Marne-la-Vallee. At the signing, Robert Fitzpatrick, fluent in French, recipient of two awards from the French government, and married to French national Sylvie Blondet, was introduced as the president of EuroDisneyland. Fitzpatrick was expected to be a key player in wooing support for the theme park from the French establishment.

Explanations for location choice included Marne-la-Vallee's close proximity to one of the world's tourism capitals (it is 20 miles from Paris), and approximately 300 mm people throughout France, Belgium, England, and Germany are within a day's drive or highspeed train ride. Good transportation was another advantage mentioned; one of the train/RER lines of the Paris Metro subway runs to Torcy, located in the center of Marne-la-Vallee. In addition, the French government promised to extend this line to the actual site of the park. The park is also served by A-4, a modern highway that runs from Paris to the German border, as well as a freeway that runs to Charles de Gaulle airport. Finally, the "chunnel" between France and England was expected to be completed near the time of EuroDisney's opening.

With a signed letter of intent in hand, Disney knew that the French government had too much at stake to let the project fail. This knowledge was enough to allow the company to hold out for concession after concession: the normal 18.6% VAT (Value Added Tax) on ticket sales was reduced to only 7%;[6] subsidized loans were secured to fund one-fourth of the building costs; contractual disputes would be settled by a special international panel of arbitrators, rather than by the French courts. Disney, however, did have to make a concession: it would respect and utilize French culture in its themes.

The park's development was to consist of two major phases. Phase One of the park would be a theme park as well as a complex of hotels, golf courses, and an aquatic park. Phase Two, slated to begin construction after the gates opened in 1992, entailed a community to be built around the park, including a sports complex, a technology park, a conference center, a theatre, a shopping mall, a university campus, villas, and condominiums.

In total, EuroDisney had 5,000 acres to play with. The theme park itself would initially occupy about 200 acres; totaling 730 acres by 1995.[7] Opening was set for early 1992, with a predicted attendance level of 11 mm visitors annually, and an estimated break-even point somewhere between 7 and 8 mm. Phase One's preliminary estimations on cost were $1 bn. This venture represented the largest single foreign investment ever in France. A French "pivot" company was formed to build the park with starting capital of FFr3bn, split 60% French, and 40% foreign.

Disney invested $160 mm directly into the project; a total of $600 mm in foreign investment was expected to flow into France each year.

At this point no definite plans for Phase Two had been laid out, making it difficult to do more than guess about the final size of the park. Costs, however, were expected to surpass the price tag of the first phase. In addition, in November, 1989, Fitzpatrick announced plans for a European version of the Disney-MGM studios, based on the original located at Disney World in Orlando, Florida. The studios would increase Disney's production of live action and animated filmed entertainment in Europe for both the European and world markets. Opening was projected for sometime in 1996.

Optimism was at an all time high; individuals and businesses alike raced to become part of the "Mickey Mouse money machine." "The phone's been ringing here ever since the announcement," said Marc Berthod of EpaMarne, the government body that oversees the Marne-la-Vallee region. "We've gotten calls from hotel chains to language interpreters—all asking for details on EuroDisneyland. And the individual mayors of the villages around here have been swamped with calls from people looking for jobs," he added.[8]

It was hoped that EuroDisney would provide the region some relief to their unemployment rate, which had hovered at 10% plus for the past several years. EuroDisney expected to generate as many as 28,000 plus jobs, from permanent park employees, to construction workers; a new laundry facility alone would employ 400 outside workers, just to wash the fifty tons of laundry expected to be generated per day by EuroDisneyland's 14,000 employees.

Cultural Chernobyl? ————————————————————————

The "deal of the century" as many called EuroDisney, came under protests from all sides. Communists and intellectuals protested heavily. Ariane Mnouchkine, a theatre director, described it as a "cultural Chernobyl." "I wish with all my heart that the rebels would set fire to Disneyland," thundered one intellectual in the French newspaper *Le Figaro.* "Mickey Mouse," sniffed another, "is stifling individualism and transforming children into consumers." Other criticisms of the park cited the project as another attack on France's cultural landscape, already under siege from American movies and music. The theme park was damned as an example of American "neoprovincialism."[9]

Never ones to suppress their emotions, the farmers of the Marne-la-Vallee region manned protests of their own. Incited over terms of the government's contract with Disney, in which the French government would expropriate the necessary land and sell it without profit to EuroDisneyland development company, farmers lined the roadside with signs such as "Disney go home," "Stop the massacre," and "Don't gnaw away our national wealth." Local officials, though sympathetic to the plight of the farmers, were unwilling to let their predicament interfere with the Disney deal. "For many years these farmers have had the fortune to cultivate what is considered some of the richest land in France," said Berthod. "Now they'll have to find another occupation."[10]

One other front to be contended with by Disney was the communist dominated labor federation—the Confederation Generale du Travail (CGT). The CGT was skeptical of Disney's job creation claims. The CGT fought against the passage of a bill which would give managers the right to establish flexible work hours. This was believed to be essential for the profitable operation of EuroDisney, especially with its seasonal attendance variations.

Working to allay fears of traffic congestion, noise, pollution, etc.—all stemming from the project—Disney launched an aggressive community relations program. Efforts included: inviting local children to a birthday party for Mickey Mouse, sending Mickey to area hospitals, and hosting free trips to Disney World in Florida for dozens of local children and officials. This type of public relations is a rarity in France; businesses make little effort to establish good relations with local residents.

Dress and Indoctrination at Disney ————————————————

Creating a fantasy worthy of the Magic Kingdom required more than just buildings and technology; it required people—a lot of people. Disney needed 12,000 plus employees for the theme park alone. Unlike either of the two U.S. theme parks, which have many seasonal and temporary, part-time college workers, these employees would be permanent cast members on the EuroDisney stage. "Casting centers" were set up in Paris, London, Amsterdam, and Frankfurt, in a drive to mirror the multi-country make-up/aspect of EuroDisney's visitors with the composition of the employees. It was nonetheless understood between the French government and Disney that a concentrated effort would be made to tap into the local French labor market. Overall, Disney was looking for workers with communications skills, spoke two European languages (French and one other), were outgoing, and liked to be around people.

As with all the parks, EuroDisney has its own "Disney University." Not being known for having the same definition of service, speculation abounded as to whether or not Disney would find enough Europeans with the right attitude for the job. However, with 24,000 applicants by November, 1991, this proved not to be a problem. "A lot of people made assumptions about France and Europe that have not turned out to be true. We find that we are attracting the same kind of people we did in the U.S.," said Thor Degelmann, a native Californian who has been with Disney for more than 25 years, and is EuroDisney's personnel director.[11]

Controversy did arise over Disney's strict appearance code, enforced in all of its parks. The rules are spelled out in a video presentation and in a guide book, given to all new cast members. The guide book details the requirements for just about everything one could imagine. Mens' hair must be cut above the collar and ears; no beards or mustaches allowed; all tatoos must be covered. Women must keep their hair in one "natural color," no frosting or streaking. Use of make-up is limited. False eyelashes, eyeliner, and eye pencil are completely off limits. Fingernails are not allowed to pass one's fingertips. Jewelry is allowed at an absolute minimum: Women can wear only one earring in each ear, but the earring must not go beyond the specified three-quarters of an inch diameter limit. Men and women alike are restricted to one ring per hand. In addition, women must wear the appropriate undergarments, and only transparent panty-hose are permitted. Cast members were also informed that they were expected to show up "fresh and clean" each day. A related training video contained a shower scene, indirectly saying that a daily bath was required.

French labor unions mounted protests against the appearance code, which they saw as "an attack on individual liberty." Others criticized Disney as being insensitive to French culture, individualism, and privacy, because restrictions on individual and collective liberties are illegal under French law, unless it can be demonstrated that the restrictions are requisite to the job and do not exceed what is necessary. Disney countered by saying that a ruling that barred them from imposing a squeaky-clean employment standard could threaten the image and long-term success of the park. "For us, the appearance code has a great effect from a product identification standpoint," said Degelmann. "Without it we wouldn't be presenting the Disney product that people would be expecting."[12] Degelmann also pointed out that many other companies, particularly airlines, had appearance codes just as strict, Disney's just happened to be written down. Aware of cultural differences, the company, according to Degelmann, had toned down the wording from the original American version. According to Degelmann no more than 5% of all applicants interviewed and provided the initial orientation, decided against working at EuroDisneyland.

EuroDisney also faced the challenge of getting the new cast members used to smiling and being polite to park guests on a consistent basis. Responding to a criticism of Disney's indoctrinating people, Degelmann stated, "You can't *make* someone be sincere all day. We select people who want to work here and are predisposed to do well in this environment. We don't try to change people, we arm them with the tools and motivation to perform."[13]

EuroDisneyland's Grand Opening _____

April 12, 1992. *France-Soir* enthusiastically predicted Disney dementia. "Mickey! It's madness," read its front page headline. Would-be visitors were warned of chaos on the roads. A government survey indicated half a million people carried by 90,000 cars might try to get in. Would people be turned away? French radio warned traffic to avoid the area.

By lunchtime the parking lot was less than half-full, suggesting an attendance level below 25,000. Speculative explanations ranged from people heeding the advice to stay away, to the more likely one-day strike that cut the direct rail link to EuroDisney from the center of Paris.

Queues for the main rides such as Pirates of the Caribbean and Big Thunder Mountain, were averaging around 15 minutes less than for an ordinary day at Disney World in Florida. Despite this fact, English visitors found the French reluctant to stand in line and wait. "The French seem to think that if God had meant them to queue, He wouldn't have given them elbows," commented one.[14] Different cultures have varying definitions of personal space. EuroDisney guests' problems ranged from people who either got too close or who left too much space between themselves and the person in front of them.

Other Problems Along the Way

Disney's first ads for work bids were all placed in English, which left small and medium-sized French firms feeling like foreigners in their own land. A data bank was eventually set up with information on over 20,000 French and European firms looking for work. The Chamber of Commerce, with the aid of Disney, developed a video text information bank that the smaller companies would be able to tap into. Local companies were told they would get work, but had to compete for it.

The building of EuroDisneyland was plagued by construction delays and modifications. All facades were given six coats of paint versus the standard one coat in the two U.S. parks. *Le Visionarium*, a 360-degree Circle-Vision screen movie, finished construction with $8-10 mm in extras. At one point Eisner ordered a $200,000 staircase be removed because it blocked a view of the Star Tours ride. This further hiked-up the EuroDisney bill, which already had to deal with construction costs being, on average, 20% higher than for similar jobs in the U.S. Another set back occurred when a fire, sparked by a short circuit, caused minor damage to the Sequoia Lodge while it was under construction.

Subcontractors also created headaches for Disney. Though already paid by Disney, the Gabot-Eremco construction contracting group had been unable to meet all of its obligations to the subcontractors it used on the EuroDisney project. Many of these subcontractors feared bankruptcy if not paid for their work in the park. Disney agreed to pay some of the money owed. Demands totaled $157 mm, stemming from work added to the project after the initial contracts had been signed; Disney conceded to about $20.3 mm.

Exhibit 1: Mickey Goes to France: The EuroDisney Deal

1984-1985	Disney negotiates with Spain and France for site of European Disneyland; France is chosen; protocol letter is signed by Eisner and Laurent Fabius, French Prime Minister.
1986	Farmers protest against government plan to expropriate necessary land.
1987	Disney and Jaques Chirac, French Prime Minister, sign letter of intent.
1988	Selects lead commercial bank lenders for the senior portion of the project. Forms the Societe en Nom Collectif (SNC). Begins planning for the equity offering of 51% of EuroDisneyland as required in the letter of intent. Disney and Michel Rocard, French Prime Minister, sign a rider to give Disney rights to the land immediately instead of 1989, as originally planned; construction begins.
1989	European press and stock analysts visit Walt Disney World in Orlando. Begin extensive news and television campaign. Stock starts trading at 20% to 25% premium from the issue price. Disney announces plans for a European version of the Disney-MGM Studios with a projected opening in 1996.
1991	Disney sets up "casting centers" in Paris, London, Amsterdam, and Frankfurt. Controversy erupts over dress codes.
1992	Disney bails out subcontractors. Pre-Opening party held at Buffalo Bill's Wild West Show; Threat of strike hangs over EuroDisneyland's Grand Opening. Grand Opening—April 12, 1992.
1993	Phillipe Bourguignon replaces Robert Fitzpatrick.

Source: *L'Expansion,* January, 1994.

It was thought that competition from French theme parks, which had significantly lower admission costs, might be a concern. However, Fitzpatrick did not appear to be daunted: "We are spending 22 billion French francs before we open the door, while the other places spent 700 million," he said. "This means we can pay infinitely more attention to details—to costumes, hotels, shops, trash baskets—to create a fantastic place. There's just too great a response to Disney for us to fail."[15]

With these bold predictions of his predecessor echoing in his ears, Bourguignon stared at his desk. Surrounding him were piles of financial statements drowning in red ink (to the tune of $500 mm), stock market reports chronicling EuroDisney's falling price from FFr166 on opening day to approximately FFr65, and newspapers full of stories of EuroDisneyland's cultural blunders. He wondered where he would find the magic to turn this kingdom around.

Endnotes

1. David Jefferson. "American Quits Chairman Post at EuroDisney." *The Wall Street Journal* (January 18, 1993): pp B1.

2. Ibid.

3. "Euro Disney: Waiting For Dumbo." *The Economist* (May 1, 1993): pp 74.

4. Peter Gumbel and Richard Turner. "Blundering Mouse: Fans Like EuroDisney But Its Parents' Goofs Weigh the Park Down." *The Wall Street Journal* (March 10, 1994): pp A12.

5. David Jefferson. "American Quits Chairman Post at Euro Disney." *The Wall Street Journal* (January 18, 1993): pp B1.

6. "Euro Disneyland: Mickey Hops the Pond." *The Economist* (March 28, 1987): pp 85.

7. "France, Disney Ink $2-Bil Contract to Construct Euroland." *Variety* (March 25, 1987).

8. Jaques Neher. "Mickey and Money for France." *The Journal of Commerce* (February 26, 1986): pp 1.

9. Richard Turner and Peter Gumbel. "Major Attraction: As Euro Disney Braces for its Grand Opening, the French Go Goofy." *The Wall Street Journal* (April 10, 1992): pp A1.

10. Jaques Neher. "Mickey and Money for France." *The Journal of Commerce* (February 26, 1986): pp 1.

11. Rone Tempest. "Challenging Casting Call For Disney; Help Wanted: Native American Indian, French-Speaking Preferred, To Play Sitting Bull in Wild West Show . . ." *Los Angeles Times* (November 8, 1991): pp A5.

12. "A Disney Dress Code Chafes in the Land of Haute Couture." *New York Times* (December 25, 1991): pp 1.

13. Anne Ferguson. "Maximising the Mouse." *Management Today* (September, 1989): pp 60.

14. Frank Barrett. "French Play Cat and Mouse with Mickey." *The Independent* (April 13, 1992): pp 10.

15. Steven Greenhouse. "Playing Disney in the Parisian Fields." *The New York Times* (February 17, 1991): pp C1.

Bibliography

Richard Turner and Peter Gumbel. "Major Attraction: As Euro Disney Braces for its Grand Opening, the French Go Goofy." *The Wall Street Journal* (April 10, 1992): pp A1.

David Jefferson. "An American Quits Chairman Post at Disney." *The Wall Street Journal* (January 18, 1993): pp B1.

Frank Barrett. "French Play Cat and Mouse with Mickey." *The Independent* (April 13, 1992): pp 10.

Joan Bakos. "Allons Enfants au Euro Disneyland!" *Restaurant Business* (April 10, 1991): pp 96-101.

"A Disney Dress Code Chafes in the Land of Haute Couture." *New York Times* (December 25, 1991): pp 1.

Robert Neff. "An American in Paris." *Business Week.* (March 12, 1990): pp 60-64.

Linda Bernier, Susan Roberts, and Elizabeth Ames. "Monsieur Mickey or Senor Miqui? Disney Seeks a European Site." *Business Week* (July 15, 1985): pp 48.

Mary Ann Galante. "Disney's Ambassador Guides Foreign Policy for a Magic Kingdom." *The Los Angeles Times* (May 27, 1987): pp 1.

Christopher Knowlton. "How Disney Keeps the Magic Going." *Fortune* (December 4, 1989): pp 111-132.

Jaques Neher. "Mickey and Money for France." *The Journal of Commerce* (February 26, 1986): pp 1.

"Can Disney Do it Again?" *Dun's Review* (June 1981): pp 80-82.

Irwin Ross. "Disney Gambles on Tomorrow." *Fortune* (October 4, 1982): 63-68.

Nigel Andrews. "Euro Disney and the Mouse that Soared." *The Financial Times* (April 11, 1991).

Myron Magnet. "The Mouse at Disney." *Fortune* (December 10, 1984): pp 57-64.

Stephen Koepp. "Do You Believe in Magic?" *Time* (April 25, 1988): 66-73.

Charles Leerhsen and Diona Gleizes. "And Now, Goofy Goes Gallic: A Little Bit of Orlando in Central France." *Newsweek* (April 13, 1992): pp 67.

Judson Green. "Brought to Account: Not a Mickey Mouse Organization." *Accountancy* (November, 1989): pp 16.

"Euro Disney: Waiting for Dumbo." *The Economist* (May 1, 1993): pp 74.

Roger Cohen. "Threat of Strike in Euro Disney Debut." *The New York Times* (April 10, 1992): pp 20.

Stanley Meisler. "Mickey, Minnie, and Cohorts Have a New Home in France." *The Los Angeles Times* (March 25, 1987): pp 1.

"Euro Disneyland: Mickey Hops the Pond." *The Economist* (March 28, 1987): pp 85.

Awata Fusaho. "Disneyland's Dreamlike Success." *Japan Quarterly* (January-March, 1988): pp 58-62.

Ellen Paris. "A Yen for Fun." *Forbes* (July 11, 1988): pp 38-39.

Hiroko Katayama. "Mouse Madness." *Forbes* (February 8, 1988): pp 152.

Tracy Dahlby. "Magic Kingdom East: Tokyo Disneyland Bets on Mikki Mausu." *The Washington Post* (April 10, 1983): pp F1.

Gale Eisenstodt and Hiroko Katayama. "Mickey Does Tokyo." *Forbes* (September 16, 1991): pp 16.

Hokaji Mino. "Tokyo Disneyland Inspires New Leisure Parks." *Business Japan* (July, 1988) pp 47-49.

Robert Wrubel. "Le Defi Mickey Mouse." *Financial World* (October 17, 1989): pp 18-21.

Rone Tempest. "Challenging Casting Call For Disney; Help Wanted: Native American Indian, French-Speaking Preferred, To Play Sitting Bull in Wild West Show . . ." *Los Angeles Times* (November 8, 1991): pp A5.

Jaques Neher. "Putting On a Show For the French; Disney Woos Europeans For Latest Theme Park." *The Washington Post* (April 2, 1989): pp H2.

"Euro Disney to Bail Out 40 Subcontractors;" *Los Angeles Times* (February 12, 1992): pp D5.

"New Disney Deal." *The New York Times* (March 12, 1992): pp D4.

Anne Ferguson. "Maximising the Mouse." *Management Today* (September, 1989): pp 57-62.

Cindy Gurlay. "Disney keeps O&M on tight rein in Europe; Ogilvy & Mather Intl.'s advertising contract with EuroDisneyland." *Information Access Company; Haymarket Publications Ltd. 1991* (March 28, 1991): pp 8.

Steven Greenhouse. "Playing Disney in the Parisian Fields." *The New York Times* (February 17, 1991): pp C1.

Peter Gumbel and Richard Turner. "Blundering Mouse: Fans Like Euro Disney But Its Parents' Goofs Weigh the Park Down." *The Wall Street Journal* (March 10, 1994): pp A1 & A12.

"Magic of the Magic Kingdom." *Los Angeles Times* (July 31, 1978): pp 1.

"Disney Magic Spreads Across the Atlantic; Popular U.S. Theme Park Prepares For Opening of Euro Disneyland Resort Near Paris in April, 1992." *Nation's Restaurant News* (October 28, 1991): pp 3.

Jane Sassen. "MICKEYMANIA" *International Management* (November, 1989): pp 32-34.

"France, Disney Ink $2-Bil Contract to Construct Euroland." *Variety* (March 25, 1987).

Suzanne Stephens. "That's Entertainment." *Architectural Record* (August, 1990): pp 72-79.

Judson Gooding. "Of Mice and Men." *Across the Board* (March, 1992): pp 40-44.

Chris Baum. "Euro Disney Awaits Mickey's Fans." *HOTELS* (October, 1991): pp 29-30.

Alan Riding. "Near Paris, Disney's Next Park." *The New York Times* (October 20, 1991): pp E6.

Robert Neff. "In Japan They're Goofy about Disney." *Business Week* (March 12, 1990).

Specialized Human Resource Topics in International Business

Part 7

CROSS-CULTURAL ISSUES IN PRODUCTIVITY AND QUALITY

Evolution of Mondragon: Changes in a Model of Worker Ownership

Reading 7.1
Warner P. Woodworth

Managing a business has traditionally been conceived of as a top-down process of making decisions. The owner or appointed administrators do the planning (Steiner, 1969), lead organizational events, and strive to achieve pragmatic results (Drucker, 1964).

Research on the process of managing emphasizes concepts such as control, strategy, and implementation of decisions. Perhaps too many traditional analyses cling to the assumption that organizational results come from the top, that excellence and/or effective cultures are derived from the upper echelon. This view suffers from a bias toward those in formal positions of power, attributing favorable characteristics to those who happen to occupy the top deck of the organizational chart. Such attitudes often tend to ignore the power and the contributions of those at lower levels.

However, another stream of early management thought has heavily emphasized the importance of shared power and worker participation. McGregor (1960), Likert (1967), and other early researchers laid the foundation for a bottom-up managing of organizations. Popular works of Ouchi (1981), Peters (1987), and Peters and Waterman (1982) have emphasized the importance of humane work structures, the use of groups, and democratic organizational values.

This article provides a brief overview of the trend toward a bottom-up approach and then focuses in depth on the Mondragon system of managerial democracy in Spain. It is suggested that new forces of global competition have led to unanticipated changes in Mondragon's operations. Finally, the implications of such an approach for researchers and American managers are evaluated by discussing the problems and prospects of contemporary worker-managed enterprises.

Source: Warner P Woodworth. "Evolution of Mondragon: Changes in a Model of Worker Ownership." Reprinted by permission of Warner P. Woodworth, Professor of Organizational Behavior, Brigham Young University.

Toward a System of Worker Participation in Management _____

The traditional form of labor-management relations in the United States has been the collective bargaining approach. Essentially an adversarial system growing out of earlier decades in this century, it has primarily consisted of fighting for bread-and-butter issues. More recently, new concerns have arisen which have broadened the agenda from wages to health and safety, job security, and so on. The latest thrust has been to institute a bargaining process which also emphasizes joint decision making and the social rights of workers.

Many firms have moved in the direction of work-place democracy, regardless of collective bargaining arrangements or unionization. Socio-technical strategies (Davis & Taylor, 1979; Hackman & Oldham, 1980) have attempted to give workers a voice in the redesign of their jobs. Autonomous work teams at various firms (Gylenhammar, 1977; Guest, 1979; Katzenbach & Smith, 1993) have functioned to alter the traditionally exclusive domain of management to make production decisions. Especially since the early 1990s, mainstream U.S. industry has begun to experiment with a variety of innovations to involve workers, at least partially, in the managing of conventional firms (Cummings & Worley, 1993; Dumaine, 1993).

A more dramatic shift toward worker participation is currently occurring in some 11,000 American firms with a degree of employee ownership. In the past decade, a number of major airlines, steel and trucking companies have given workers formal representation at the board-of-directors level in exchange for wage concessions. Although not state-mandated, as are the extensive systems of codetermination in Europe, the seeds of a broader, more fundamental change in power are being sown (Cutcher-Gershenfeld, 1991; Woodworth, 1984; Woodworth & Meek, 1995).

In the minds of most managers, and organizational researchers, efforts to involve employee-owners are probably viewed as still somewhat experimental (Bernstein, 1980; Whyte & McCall, 1980). The bulk of worker participation efforts are clearly controlled and usually initiated by management (Conte & Tannenbaum, 1978; Hammer & Stern, 1980; Mohrman & Cummings, 1989). The question of whether or not workers can actually run industry is debatable.

Internationally, some evidence is beginning to emerge that answers such a question affirmatively, or at least addresses its possibilities. The Mondragon system of worker-owned cooperatives sheds light on the possibility of a worker-managed economics. Drawing upon reports by other researchers and limited data of my own, a case is made for the potential of a bottom-up strategy for managing organizations.

The Original Mondragon Model_____

The Mondragon system consists of 103 small- to medium-sized industrial cooperatives in the Basque region of northern Spain. After several decades of severe unemployment in the town of Mondragon, including the ravages of civil war, the first small worker cooperative was established in 1956. Subsequently, other co-ops were created, all based on the practical need for jobs and on the democratic ideals of a labor-managed economy.

The cooperatives worked together in forming a support organization. Caja Laboral Popular (CLP) (The People's Savings Bank). It began to operate as a source of funding and expertise services in 1960. The CLP and the associations of cooperative continued to grow and expand. By the 1990s, the CLP had over 300,000 individual depositors and assets in excess of $3 billion. During the 1980s, Mondragon produced about 5% of the entire national output in certain consumer goods and comprises 14% of the total industrial output of the province of Guipuzcoa, where the Basque community is located (Bradley & Gelb, 1981; Woodworth, 1996). Annual sales in recent years have grown to over $5 billion (MCC, 1998).

General Structure

For nearly 40 years, the cooperatives of Mondragon were all internally organized in basically the same way. The members of each cooperative became the ultimate authority. The general assembly of all members met at least annually and was empowered to examine and approve the balance sheet and vote on organizational procedures. The assembly also elected those workers who were to serve on the supervisory board, which is a type of board of directors (Aranzadi, 1976).

The supervisory board appointed the managers who, in turn, were responsible to the board, and through it to the general assembly. This indirect accountability of management has proved to be one of the strengths of the Mondragon cooperatives. It is important to note that managers could never be on the supervisory board. Management was directly responsible for administrative tasks.

The management council functioned as an advisory and consultive body. The members of the council were usually managers, top executives, and outsiders with special expertise and skills.

The members of the cooperative also elected the social council, a body having wide prescriptive and advisory powers regarding all aspects of personnel management—work safety, social security, and wage levels. The watchdog council was the ultimate safeguard in ensuring the democratic running of the cooperatives' affairs. The general assembly elected three members to watch over the supervisory board and the two advisory councils and to inform cooperative members of any irregularities.

Figure 1 illustrates the organizational structure of the cooperative as it evolved over the past four decades.

Figure 1. Organizational Structure of the Mondragon Cooperatives

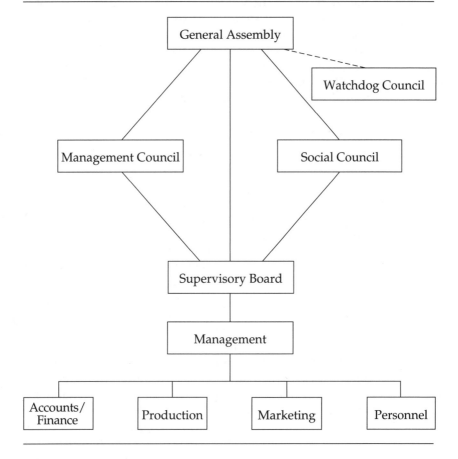

Membership

Mondragon's Contract of Association stated that "membership in the Associated Cooperative shall be voluntary and open to all persons who can render the services for which it was established, provided they agree to assume the responsibilities membership entails." This open-door policy has ensured that all those who desire and qualify for membership can apply for it. Members who decided to join and who had the needed skills or training paid an initial contribution in cash of approximately $3,000. This initial investment and the allocation of funds to the individuals' capital accounts made the workers 100% owners of the cooperative.

Decision Making

The major decisions of each cooperative were determined in annual meetings of the general assembly. Simple majority vote was sufficient in determining any policy, approval of a budget, admission of new members, or for disciplining violators. Decisions were not determined by the number of shares a person had in the company, but rather on the basis of one person/one vote. This bottom-up structure of workers' control provided a network of participation channels and ensured the democratic sharing of organizational power. Power was not concentrated in an elite group of decision makers at the top, but remained with the membership as a whole.

Distribution of Wealth

The Mondragon system is unique in that money does not stay strictly within the cooperative. Under the Cooperative Law of Spain, it is permissible to form "second degree cooperatives," organizations that are not entirely worker-owned and controlled but which have associated cooperatives as institutional members. The Caja Laboral Popular has been the primary second degree cooperative of the Mondragon system. It was designed to attract the savings of the local community and to invest the money in the associated cooperatives. The bank provided computer services, conducted feasibility studies for new cooperatives, and loaned up to 50% of the capital needed to launch a new business. Other bank support efforts included securing land for construction, designing new plants, and training workers as they launched their own new business ventures.

The initial capital contribution made by all new cooperators represented their capital share in the new enterprise. Thus, each new cooperative was financed in part by the capital contribution of its members and augmented by loans from the CLP. The employees' earning structure, being governed by solid principles and ideals of solidarity and equality, was different from that of a traditional firm. The maximum range of earnings was set at a 3:1 ratio. In other words, the gross earnings of the highest paid managers could not be more than three times that of the lowest paid worker-members.

Work Structures

Because the emphasis of Mondragon was on job creation and democratic control, work structures centered on training and job security. For example, in the past the cooperatives' policy has been to send workers back to school to develop further expertise rather than lay them off during slow or bad times. Sometimes workers were temporarily sent to other cooperatives.

Nevertheless, cooperative factories that compete in markets have to organize their work efficiently. This has led to the division and diversification of work and the implementation of new technologies. Jobs centered on teamwork rather than on assembly-line labor. The goal was to build a participatory organization by objectives, rather than the traditional management by objectives. For instance, in a new furniture factory, all the work is planned by worker teams. A performance index is allocated to the entire team, which then decides how these gains should be distributed among members.

In 1997, several industrial cooperatives jointly established a research and development (R&D) center called Ikerlan in order to compete more efficiently with new technologies and products made elsewhere. Much time and money are devoted to the design of new components for existing products, to the study of competitors' products, and to keeping abreast of international developments.

Social Organization

Because Mondragon was not a communal system, work and social life were somewhat segregated. However, Mondragon was a complex of organizations, and its cooperative structure and ideals have had an important spillover effect on social and community structures such as education.

Education has been an important part of the Mondragon model from the beginning. The first cooperative firm was preceded by 13 years of education. Jose Maria Arizmendi, the visionary priest whose ideals significantly shaped the Mondragon system, continually repeated the words, "Knowledge is power; socializing knowledge implies the democratization of power."

The League for Education and Culture was organized years ago as a full-fledged cooperative with a general assembly and supervisory board designed to support the socioeconomic system of Mondragon through education. There is great coordination between the educational system and the cooperatives. Students are trained in the skills needed by the cooperatives, and the students' training and research help shape the future. Students are not only trained technically but are also socialized regarding the ideals and functions of Mondragon.

The Results of Bottom-Up Management _____

In response to the query, "Can workers run industry?" the Mondragon experience by the early 1990s suggested an affirmative answer. Out of the rubble of war and economic stagnation, over 26,000 jobs have been created. Starting with one co-op in 1956, there were eight by 1960, 60 by 1970, and today a total of 103 cooperative firms. Some of the worker-owned firms grew fairly large, such as Ulgor, which had 3,400 members and six factories. It became the leading manufacturer of appliances in Spain, producing 300,000 refrigerators and 250,000 stoves a year. Some 25% of its products were marketed internationally. Other firms were smaller, ranging from agricultural equipment to steel construction, graphic arts, plastics, and robotics.

The worker cooperatives have been supported by second-degree institutions such as the peoples' bank, a localized system of social security called Lagun Aro which provides welfare benefits and cooperative medical care, an R & D center, a technical school, and a college of engineering. An elementary cooperative educational system of 44 schools, day-care centers, 14 housing co-ops, some fifty cooperative supermarkets, and 7 agricultural co-ops round out the community structure for building an egalitarian society.

The track record of these cooperative businesses is impressive. Of 103 business start-ups thus far, there have only been three failures, in contrast to the typical U.S. experience which suffers from a 50% failure rate in the first several years (Greene, 1985). Nor has the Mondragon system generally suffered massive layoffs during economic downturns. For instance, when the OPEC oil crisis hit in the 1970s, instead of losing their jobs as did their counterparts in traditional firms worldwide, Mondragon workers in hard-hit firms were simply transferred to the technical school for a few months to obtain new skills. Then they moved into other firms in the cooperative system which were experiencing growth, without losing a single day's pay in the process. In sharp contrast to most industries during that period, Mondragon increased employment by 7.5% while profits grew 26% and exports shot up 56% (Johnson & Whyte, 1977). More recently, total cooperative sales have increased each year, while industrial investment has grown 10-15% annually. Mondragon has a philosophy premised on Schumacher's *Small is Beautiful* (1973) logic, keeping the size of most firms well under 500 members. Such a scale seems to foster healthy interpersonal relationships and strong identification with the enterprise. An important result of this is that there has been only a one-day strike these decades of cooperative existence, and that was over job classifications in a large co-op. A labor relations climate such as this seems rather enviable when compared with the problems of distrust, alienation, and conflict which characterize all too many conventional firms.

1990s Evolution of Mondragon

During the pioneering decades of Mondragon's existence, the unique path that was pursued was heralded by many outside observers as a viable alternative to mainstream capitalism of the West, and state-controlled socialism of the East.

But in 1991 European market integration was begun and by 1992 unification began to challenge many of Mondragon's founding premises. In reaction to the European Community (EC) and growing economic globalization, Spain began to eliminate protective tariffs and state subsidies. Mondragon began to make internal adjustments in order to compete more effectively on this new, more level playing field.

Rancorous internal debates occurred between the old cooperative founders and new, young workers, managers and financial experts.

The attempt to create relative equality gave way first. From a 3:1 ration of top-paid to lowest paid workers, the ratio changed to 5:1 and then 6:1. Otherwise, the Basque co-op system could not attract the best engineers and executives. Even with these changes, however, Mondragon is still a model of rough equality, especially when compared to the 250:1 pay ratio in U.S. Fortune 500 firms.

The network of semi-autonomous cooperatives next became restructured as subunits of the new Mondragon Cooperative Corporation (MCC). As a single company, MCC now ranks as the Number Ten firm among all Spanish companies. It has been reorganized, not according to community location throughout the Basque region, but according to product lines. Today, three corporate divisions have been established: finance, manufacturing and distribution. Strategic planning has become centralized, costs have been cut, and tighter controls have been established (Tilly, 1996).

Other changes are equally far-reaching. Rather than hire new, permanent worker-owners, the manufacturing and distribution divisions began to hire short-term, temporary employees, further widening Mondragon's wage gap. MCC has even started to establish non-worker-owned factories outside of the Basque region, as well as in other countries (Woodworth, 1996).

The bank, Caja Laboral Popular, is now investing in a number of traditional capitalist enterprises, not only worker co-ops. In 1995 Mondragon broke with the past and put itself on the Spanish stock market. The effort was an attempt to raise cash for some of its struggling co-ops, thereby allowing non-owners, and even foreign investors, to obtain shares of MCC (Parry, 1995; White, 1995). The Corporation's Chairman, Javier Mongelos, was replaced by Antonio Cancelo, president of MCC's giant retail business, Eroski, in late 1995. He had led the expansion of MCC's retail efforts throughout Spain and parts of France, and was widely believed to be the best candidate for propelling MCC globally.

There have also been MCC manufacturing ventures outside of Spain, including a refrigerator plant in Morocco, washing machines in Iran, and a luxury bus joint venture in China. Other ventures include computers in France, three appliance plants in Argentina, and a components factory in the Czech Republic. Additional subsidiaries now operate in Mexico and Thailand, as well as a new joint venture in Egypt. Thus, MCC seems to be on the road to becoming a multinational corporation, expanding around the globe.

Essentially, the structural changes required for expansion have evolved through the creation of a parallel economic organization that operates alongside Mondragon's traditional system of worker ownership. The newly existing foreign firms and joint ventures operate outside the culture of cooperation. Says Jose Ignacio Garate, an MCC board of directors member: "We are learning to live with two different cultures" (White, 1995).

What this means, in effect, is that the new international expansion side of Mondragon uses a different organizational formula. Foreign enterprises do not operate, according to worker-ownership values. Management pay is based on market rates rather than a rough equality. Even modest downsizing occurred during Spain's economic recession between 1992 and 1994, leading to 1,400 co-op jobs lost. However, some 2,000 new jobs have been generated since that time, showing an overall net gain in employment.

Many of these recent changes started during the 2nd World Basque Congress held in Bilbao, Spain in October 1987. As one of only a few outsiders to participate in those meetings, I was struck by the growing conflict between those who fought to preserve the original elements of the Mondragon cooperative and new, loud voices pushing for radical changes, those more aligned to conventional business approaches. The Basque values emphasized using enterprises to create jobs, working in collaboration, sharing resources and expertise, humane work methods, power equalization, and a focus on utilizing the fruits of labor for community development and a better quality of life for all.

The alternative perspective argued for a scenario of "business as usual" in which the Mondragon complex would abandon its unique history and enter the hegemonic world of large, rich, transnational corporations. Since the 1987 Congress, the argument for transforming the cooperatives from democratically-run systems to a top-down, managerially-controlled hierarchical firm seems to be evolving toward victory.

At least up to a point. In essence, what seems to have occurred is a piecemeal evolution toward certain elements of traditional capitalistic firms, and that system now functions in tandem with the original Basque co-op system. Don Jose Maria's core values may not have been completely abandoned, but real questions arise as to whether or not the two systems can both be maintained. Can one serve both God and Mammon?

Supporters of MCC's change report that today there is a total of 32,400 employees of MCC, although many are now merely contract workers, not owners. With diversified holdings the company can now better withstand economic turmoil such as the unfavorable U.S. dollar—Spanish peseta exchange rate that first caused painful damage to the co-ops in 1989 (White, 1997). Furthermore, by opening itself to outside Spanish and foreign investors, MCC now can tap external sources of capital heretofore unavailable. In the past, cash shortages severely constrained the growth of the worker-owned firms. The only option was to borrow from commercial banks, clearly a competitive handicap. As it is presently structured, outside investors in the traditional business side of MCC have no voting rights, while dividends are paid from pre-tax profits.

My most recent visit to Mondragon was in the summer of 1996. Interviews with various managers and workers in the cooperative side of MCC suggested a good deal of anxiety about new steps being taken. On the one hand, pre-tax surpluses rose 33% in 1996, thereby buoying up cooperative reserves, as well as channeling billions of pesetas into the co-op promotion fund, Basque education, and worker-owned retirement accounts. But, as one manager suggested, "Most co-op members are rather confused by the pace and extent of so many recent changes" (Woodworth, 1996).

Future Research

In a comprehensive review of the literature, Strauss (1982) concluded that workers' participation in management

> has had only limited success. It has involved top leadership more than the rank and file, and it has almost ignored middle and lower levels of management. It has not brought substantial power or influence to the ordinary worker; nor has it unleashed workers' creativity or even actively involved them in making production decisions. (pp. 254-255)

Mondragon may be an exception to such assumptions. Yet, so far, economists have expressed the greatest interest in Mondragon, and the research to date emphasizes overall economic performance. What is less clear is why this success has occurred. These small- to medium-sized cooperatives suggest a rich data base for management and organizational researchers.

There is a need for academics to study important features of the Mondragon system. As yet, there is no systematic investigation of unique aspects of the Spanish cooperative which are most relevant for conventional businesses elsewhere. In the current quest for quality and productivity in American industry, it seems that all the hoopla about Japanese management may be a bit overdone. We ought to also consider lessons from across the Atlantic in northern Spain.

For instance, there has been much discussion in the United States about business life cycles—birth, growth, maturity, and decline (Hirschhorn & Associates, 1983; Kimberly & Miles, 1980). Some theorists argue that over time there is an inevitale bureaucratic stodginess and loss of entrepreneurial spirit. The evidence from Mondragon suggests that fossilization is not inherent in all corporate systems, and that renewal and revitalization processes may nurture an ongoing climate of entrepreneurship. One could postulate that by keeping the size of each co-op small, linking all firms with the R &D center, and creating a blue-collar entrepreneurial climate through worker ownership, a firm could be virtually guaranteed ongoing innovation. Will this "Small is Beautiful" climate of the old Mondragon endure in today's global

MCC? Certainly, this area is a fruitful and relevant issue for management researchers.

A long-standing debate between capitalist and socialist theorists is about which system is superior. The cooperatives of Mondragon suggest a potential third way which includes the strengths of grassroots capitalism and self-reliance combined with concern for the collective good and structures of workers' control.

To what extent are the two views compatible? Can the Mondragon system be evaluated along the lines of Likert's (1967) survey of organizations? Would such methodology reveal Mondragon to fit a System 4 ideal? Or would it move completely off the scale, perhaps to a new System 5?

Perhaps other conceptual models would be more appropriate. For example, Bernstein (1980) has delineated six components necessary for a truly democratic enterprise: participation in decisions, full sharing of company information, economic feedback, guaranteed individual rights, due process, and a democratic consciousness. What is needed is the application of such a model to the Mondragon experience, a testing process which might further refine the Bernstein or Likert models, as well as assess the effectiveness of workers' self-management as an organizational phenomenon.

The research implications of Mondragon suggest numerous other fruitful possibilities for investigation. For instance, Long's (1978) study of Employee Stock Ownership Plans (ESOPs) reported that worker-owners scored higher than non-owners on measures of company integration, satisfaction, and involvement. Further data on Mondragon could amplify the potential for employee ownership in facilitating the emergence of an economically and psychologically healthier work environment in the United States. Policy-related research along lines which would predict the conditions under which worker ownership leads to an improved quality of working life would be not only of theoretical interest, but also of practical use to employers, unions, and state and national legislators, as Brown and Reich (1993) suggest.

Future studies could also add important insights to the broader literature on management. Additional research may consider a largely neglected variable in evaluating participation, the degree of worker ownership of a firm. Figure 2 represents a two-dimensional approach for researchers.

What is needed is an empirical study which utilizes cases from each of the four cells, comparing them in terms of key issues such as economic performance, worker attitudes, degree of participation, mechanisms of participation, extent of stock ownership, and so on. A systematic collection of data from a sample of each cell would be useful in understanding the interplay between ownership and participation. Monitoring a project like this for a 3-5 year period would provide important longitudinal data currently unavailable.

Figure 2. Extent of Worker Participation

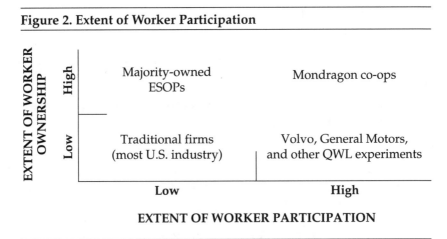

In such a study, firms with high ownership and high participation would seem to fit Dahl's (1979) criteria for a truly democratic process: equal votes, effective participation, enlightened understanding (access to information), final control of the agenda, and inclusiveness. It could be predicted that the Mondragon system would fully fit such criteria, but how would conventional U.S. firms stack up? Or even most employee-owned enterprises? Such research could raise further conceptual inquiry about what it really means to have a free and democratic society.

A study of this nature would also have implications for the action research of organizational development (Argyris, 1970; Beckard, 1969; Cummings & Worley, 1993). It would suggest, among other things, that organizational intervention could lead to a genuine redistribution of organizational power rather than simply tinkering with structure so that employees "feel good." Some theorists (e.g., Argyris & Schon, 1978; Mohrman & Cummings, 1989; Watzlawick, Weakland, & Fisch, 1974) have conceptualized different types of change, distinguishing between first order change, which grows out of an established framework, and second-order change. Mondragon may serve as a classic illustration of second-order change, in which the framework itself is significantly altered as workers themselves begin to design and manage the process of organizational evolution.

The issue of power raises another important line of research which might profitably flow from the Basque model. A predominant view of the literature is that management derives its power from its expertise, its ability to reward or punish, and/or the very legitimacy of its position in the organizational hierarchy (French & Raven, 1959; Mintzberg, 1983). Although such an interpretation seems warranted in the context of the conventional organization, other studies have questioned the validity of such a perspective. Tannenbaum, Kavcic, Rosner, Vianeilo, and Weiser's

(1977) work on authority across five different cultures is particularly important in delineating different sources of power. In the Mondragon system, decision-making power indeed flows from the general assembly to top management. Further research may provide more conclusive support for the notion that power can also be derived from below.

Another spinoff for future studies centers on the question of management/labor relations. Mondragon illustrates the essential trust needed between managers and workers, a condition which appears related to a flattened hierarchy, minimal class differences, including a 3:1 wage ratio, and so on. The more conventional corporate culture emphasizes social division, executive perks, and little information sharing (Jackson, 1983; Locke & Schweiger, 1979). Perhaps more research will reveal that what produces worker commitment is not an open-door policy but an opening of the books. Consistent with other data (Bernstein, 1980), Mondragon suggests that interpersonal feedback may not be as valued as economic feedback.

Finally, longitudinal research comparing Mondragon with other systems of participation and ownership may forge a new theory of business organization. The roots of such thinking are evident in the work of Braverman (1974) and others (Edwards, 1979), who argue that the structural reasons for conventional business derive from the historical push to make workers merely the executioners of managerial decision making. Taylor's *Scientific Management* (1911/1967) is the clearest evidence of early attempts to bifurcate thinking and work itself.

Mounting research in recent years, amplified now with the Mondragon evidence, may soon enable scholars to formulate a new paradigm which reintegrates workers and the organization. Whyte and McCall (1980), Lawler (1978), Cotton (1993), and others have begun to see these approaches to corporate democracy as forerunners of a new conceptual model. What should follow is the outlining of such a theory, one which links micro and macro analyses of worker participation to form a more comprehensive model of organizational effectiveness.

So far, the most extensive inside analysis of Mondragon is that of Cornell anthropologist, Davydd J. Greenwood and six team members of the Fagor Cooperative (Greenwood & Santos, 1991). Using participatory action research methods, the group collected data through a pilot questionnaire, followed by interviews, roundtables and a survey over four years. An anthropological "map" of Mondragon was developed by using such concepts as "hierarchy and equality," "cooperation and conflict," "unity of values and internal diversity," "ethnicity and social class," "charismatic leadership and member activism," and "the perfect system and historical development." This study, which might best be described as industrial anthropology, analyzed through processual methods the gap between the Mondragon ideal and its actuality, pointing to inherent contractions between the early vision of the Basque cooperative network and its ever-changing adjustments to new economic and political realities.

Implications for American Managers

The Mondragon experiment suggests some important issues for U.S. managers to consider. Of course, it could not be replicated in an across-the-board fashion in an American setting. One must acknowledge unique aspects of the Spanish experiments, such as economic deprivation, the Basque culture, and the communal network of Mondragon's cooperative economy. Although dominant values in America emphasize individualism (Harris & Moran, 1979), there are also regions with a strong collective orientation, as exemplified by the farm co-ops of Minnesota and the plywood co-ops of the Northwest (Schaaf, 1977). The transferability of the Spanish cooperative experience to America would necessitate an integration of co-op principles with solid operational strategies.

Moreover, Mondragon should not be dismissed as a mere case study because it consists of over 100 organizations intricately linked in mutually reciprocal ways with a dynamic that has lasted over four decades. A recent book by Canadian Greg MacLeod (1997) suggests a fascinating view of Mondragon's relevance to us today. A founder of Canada's extensive modern co-op movement in the 1970s, MacLeod's volume, *From Mondragon to America*, articulates a number of possible applications that the Basque system offers North Americans in today's economic conditions.

What are the lessons of Mondragon? A major conclusion is that managing from below can be as productive as top-down. Indeed, the central thesis of my research is that management is not a noun, but a verb demonstrating action. Managing is a process that can, in some circumstances, be effectively carried out by workers rather than solely by executives. Mondragon is an example of a worker-management partnership, an approach that challenges contemporary theories which hold that executives only should plan, control, and execute decisions.

Mondragon suggests that the full potential of workers has yet to be tapped. The cooperative system has transformed a mere job into a more meaningful, high-quality life which integrates the career, the family, and the larger political community. Instead of merely putting in their eight hours, co-op members are responsible decision makers and entrepreneurs. With full access to financial information, they help create and support sound business strategies. Equality and efficiency are not antagonistic, but mutually reinforcing.

A third lesson from the Basque experience is that important benefits accrue by creating mechanisms for sharing not only psychological ownership, but actual stock ownership. As Gurdon (1982) and Woodworth & Meek (1995) observe, a number of U.S. firms are recognizing this factor and extending ownership to their employees. However, other research is appearing which suggests that legal ownership on paper is not sufficient unless there is a concomitant system for participation and influence by worker-owners (Castro, 1989; Cohen-Rosenthal & Burton, 1987; Meek & Woodworth, 1982; Olson, 1982). Mondragon illustrates the need for a vibrant organizational climate that facilitates innovative experimentation to see what is possible. It also emphasizes the importance of institutionalizing bottom-up power structures to prevent regression to traditional managerial approaches in conventional firms.

Finally, Mondragon counters the myth that democratic decision making is by nature ineffective. Perhaps the most common response about worker participation from American managers is that cumbersome communication wastes time and blocks the ability to achieve quick results (Macy, Ledford, & Lawler, 1981). With Basque cooperatives, the evidence is in the other direction, implying that groups skilled in consensus methodology can out-perform conventional, hierarchical decision making. A handful of studies by the London School of Economics (Bradley & Gelb, 1981) and other researchers (Gorrono, 1975; Thomas, 1982; Thomas & Logan, 1982) reveal that in some industrial sectors, Mondragon profits are twice those of traditional capitalist firms. Overall, productivity has been higher in the Mondragon group than in conventional firms throughout Spain.

With its past clear articulation of core values and congruent business practices, the Mondragon model has shown that day-to-day decisions in worker-owned environments may be arrived at very effectively. For one Mondragon worker, a young woman who was also on her firm's board of directors in the 1980s, efficiency alone is not sufficient: "What we're really trying to prove here is that business and human needs are not necessarily contradictory. Our experience shows that a people's economics is possible." Whether such a view can survive the recent MCC shift toward that of conventional multinational corporations yet remains to be seen.

References _____

Aranzadi, D. (1976). *Cooperativismo industrial como sistema*. Bilbao, Spain: Editorial Elexpuru Hnos., S.A.

Argyris. C. (1970). *Intervention theory and method: A behavioral science view*. Reading, MA: Addison-Wesley.

Argyris, C., & Schon, D. (1978). *Organizational learning*. Reading, MA: Addison-Wesley.

Beckard, R. (1969). *Organization development: Strategies and models*. Reading, MA: Addison-Wesley.

Bernstein, P. (1980). *Workplace democratization: Its internal dynamics*. New Brunswick, NJ: Transaction Books.

Bradley, K., & Geib, A. (1981). *Obstacles to a cooperative economy: Lessons from Mondragon*. London: London School of Economics and Political Science.

Braverman, H. (1974). *Labor and monopoly capitalism*. New York: Monthly Review Press.

Brown, R. H., & Reich, R. B. (1993). Workplace of the future. *A report on the conference on the future of the American workplace*. Washington, D.C.: U.S. Department of Commerce and U.S. Department of Labor.

Castro, J. (1989). Eastern goes bust. *Time*, March 20, pp. 52-53.

Cohen-Rosenthal, E., & Burton, C. E. (1987). *Mutual gains: A guide to union-management cooperation*. Westport, Conn.: Praeger.

Conte, M. & Tannenbaum, A. S. (1978). Employee-owned companies: Is the difference measurable? *Monthly Labor Review, 101*, 23-28.

Cotton, J. L. (1993). *Employee involvement*. Newbury Park, CA: Sage.

Cummings, T. G., & Worley, C. G. (1993). *Organization development & change*. (5th ed.) St. Paul, Minn.: West.

Cutcher-Gershenfeld, J. (1991). The impact on economic performance of a transformation in workplace relations. *Industrial & Labor Relations Review*, vol. 44, pp. 241-260.

Dahl, R. A. (1979). Procedural democracy. In P. Laslett & J. Fishkin (Eds.), *Philosophy, politics and society* (5th series, pp. 97-133). New Haven, CT: Yale University Press.

Davis, L. E., & Taylor, J. C. (1979). *Design of jobs*. Santa Monica, CA: Goodyear.

Drucker, P. (1964). *Managing for results*. London: Pan Books, Ltd.

Dumaine, B. (1993). The new non-manager managers. *Fortune*, Feb. 22, pp. 80-84.

Edwards, R. (1979). *Contested terrain*. New York: Basic Books.

French, J. R. P., Jr., and Raven, B. H. (1959). The bases of social power. In D. Cartwright (Ed.), *Studies in social power* (pp. 150-167). Ann Arbor: The University of Michigan.

Gorrono, I. (1975). *Experiencia co-operativa en el pais vasco*. Bilbao, Spain.

Greene, R. (1985, October 21). Do you really want to be your own boss? *Forbes*, pp. 86-96.

Greenwood, D. J., & Santos, J. L. G. (1991). *Industrial democracy as process: Participatory action research in the Fagor cooperative group of Mondragon*. Stockholm, Sweden: Arbetslivscentrum.

Guest, R. H. (1979). Quality of work life—Learning from Tarrytown. *Harvard Business Review, 57*, 76-87.

Gurdon, M. A. (1982). Is employee ownership the answer to our economic woes? *Management Review, 71*, 8-14.

Gyllenhammar, P. G. (1977). *People at work*. Reading, MA: Addison-Wesley.

Hackman, J. R., & Oldham, G. R. (1980). *Work redesign*. Reading, MA: Addison-Wesley.

Hammer, T., & Stern, R. (1980). Employee ownership: Implications for the organizational distribution of power. *Academy of Management Journal, 23*, 78-100.

Harris, P. R., & Moran, R. T. (1979). *Managing cultural differences*. Houston, TX: Gulf.

Hirschhorn, C., & Associates. (1983). *Cutting back: Retrenchment and redevelopment in human and community services*. San Francisco: Jossey-Bass.

Huet, T. (1997). Can co-ops go global? Mandragon is trying. *Dollars & Sense*, November-December, pp. 16-19, 41-42.

Jackson, S. E. (1983). Participation in decision-making as a strategy for reducing job related strain. *Journal of Applied Psychology, 68*, 3-19.

Johnson, A. G., & Whyte. W. F. (1997). The Mondragon system of worker production cooperatives. *Industrial and Labor Relations Review, 31*(1), 18-30.

Katzenbach, J. R., & Smith, D. K. (1993). *The wisdom of teams: Creating the high performance organization*. Boston: Harvard Business School Press.

Kimberly, J. R., & Miles, R. H. (1980). (Eds.). *The organizational life cycle*. San Francisco: Jossey-Bass.

Lawler, E. E., III. (1978). The new plant revolution. *Organizational Dynamics, 6*(3) 3-12.

Likert, R. (1967). *The human organization*. New York: McGraw-Hill.

Locke, E., & Schweiger, D. M. (1979). Participation in decision-making: One more look. In B. Staw & L. L. Cummings (Eds.), *Research in organizational behavior* (Vol. 1, pp. 265-340). Greewich, CT: JAI Press.

Long, R. J. (1978). The effects of employee ownership in organizational identification, employee job attitudes, and organizational performance: A tentative frame work and empirical findings. *Human Relations, 31*(1), 29-48.

MacLeod, G. (1997). *From Mondragon to America: Experiments in community economic development*. Sydney, Nova Scotia: University College of Cape Breton Press.

Macy, B. A., Ledford, G. E., & Lawler, E. E., III. (1981). *The Bolvar quality of work experiment: 1972-1979*. New York: Wiley-Interscience.

MCC (Mondragon Corporacion Cooperativa). (1998). *Corporate profile*, Elkar, S. Coop.

McGregor, D. (1960). *The human side of enterprise*. New York: McGraw-Hill.

Meek, C., & Woodworth, W. (1982). Employee ownership and industrial relations: The Rath case. *National Productivity Review, 1*(2), 151-163.

Mintzberg, H. (1983). *Power in and around organizations*. Englewood Cliffs, NJ: Prentice Hall.

Mohrman, S. A., & Cummings, T. G (1989). *Self-designing organizations: Learning how to create high performance*. Reading, MA: Addison-Wesley.

Olson, D. G. (1982). Union experiences with worker ownership. *Wisconsin Law Review, 5*, 729-823.

Ouchi, W. G. (1981). *Theory Z*. New York: Avon.

Parry, J. N. (1995). Foreign players eye Mondragon. *The European*, May 19, p. 16.

Peters, T. J. (1987). *Thriving on chaos*. New York: Alfred A. Knopf.

Peters, T. J., & Waterman, R. H., Jr. (1982). *In search of excellence*. New York: Harper & Row.

Schaaf, M. (1977). *Cooperatives at the crossroads*. Washington, DC: Exploratory Project for Economic Alternatives.

Schumacher, E. F. (1973). *Small is beautiful: Economics as if people mattered*. New York: Harper & Row.

Steiner, G. (1969). *Top management planning*. New York: MacMillan.

Strauss, G. (1982). Workers' participation in management: An international perspective. In B. Staw & L. L. Cummings (Eds.), *Reasearch in organizational behavior* (vol. 4, pp. 173-265). Greewich, CT: JAI Press.

Tannenbaum, A. S., Kavcic, B., Rosner, M., Vianeilo, M., & Wieser, G. (1977). *Hierarchy in organizations*. San Francisco: Jossey-Bass.

Taylor, F. W. (1967). *The principles of scientific management*. New York: Norton. (Original work published 1941).

Thomas, H. (1982, August). *The dynamics of social ownership*. Paper presented at the Third International Conference of the International Association for the Economics of Self-Management, Mexico City.

Thomas, H., & Logan, C. (1982). *Mondragon: An economic analysis*. London: George Allen and Unwin.

Tilly, C. (1996). Mondragon: Still a model? *Dollars & Sense*, May-June, p. 38.

Watziawick, P., Weakland, J., & Fisch, R. (1974). *Change: Principles of problem formation and problem resolution*. New York: Norton.

White, D. (1995). Change of culture for the Basque co-operatives. *The Financial Times*, June 7, p. 30

——(1997). Mondragon helps itself to success: The Spanish co-operative is expanding along orthodox commercial lines. *The Financial Times*, June 10, p. 29.

Whyte, W. F., & McCall, D. (1980). Self-help economics. *Society, 17*(4), 22-28.

Woodworth, W. (1984). Hard hats in the boardroom: New trends in workers' participation. In J. B. Ritchie & P. Thompson (Eds.), *Organization and people* (pp. 403-413). St. Paul, MN: West.

Woodworth, W. (1996). Personal interviews with co-op managers. Mondragon, Spain.

Woodworth, W. P., & Meek, C. (1995). *Creating labor-management partnerships*. Reading, MA: Addison-Wesley.

Cultural Implications of Implementing TQM in Poland

Reading 7.2
Jennifer Roney

The globalization of organizations, partially brought on by rapid improvements in information flow capabilities, increased competition from emerging economies, and newly opened markets, has transformed organizational life (Thomas, 1996). Managers are now faced with a growing set of issues of how to manage and motivate individuals from diverse cultures who hold very different assumptions about work, time, and the world. The ways in which people from different cultures interact has become varied and complex. Multinational corporations, cross-cultural joint ventures, transnational teams, international consulting and marketing have all provided vehicles for this interaction. While we may recognize the need to address management of individuals who view the world differently, we often fail to see how the implicit cultural assumptions embedded in well-known managerial programs may be implemented in a way that is inconsistent with dominant cultural values. Total Quality Management (TQM) is one of these well-known programs and Valvex, a Polish company, illustrates the problem.

TQM is an integrated approach to management that represents a holistic management philosophy rather than a series of techniques. As such, TQM is embedded with cultural values and assumptions which are consistent with its culture of origin (predominantly Japanese). When TQM was implemented in a valve manufacturer in a farming village in southern Poland the impact of the cultural differences between the management approach and the cultural context became clear.

For Valvex, as with most Polish companies, the ripple effect of the dramatic changes of 1989 have turned the company virtually upside-down. In an attempt to make massive change quickly, the management has introduced Total Quality Management (TQM). Valvex employs approximately 600 employees and has supplied valves to the construction industry in Poland, the former Soviet Union, other east European

Source: Jennifer Roney. "Cultural Implications of Implementing TQM in Poland." *Journal of World Business*, 32(2), 1997, pp. 152-168. Reprinted by permission of JAI Press Inc.

countries and Cuba for 25 years. The company was privatized in early 1994 through a lease/buy plan. Valvex has remained a profit-making enterprise throughout the pre and post-communist periods. Increasing competition from other European suppliers and difficulties generating new customers for the product have threatened their previously secure financial picture. The Polish-American owner's recent efforts to introduce TQM to Valvex represent his attempt to address these challenges.

Total Quality Management

TQM asserts that exceptional quality is essential to maintaining competitive advantage and organizational survival. The management philosophy (Spencer, 1994) of TQM directs all strategic and operational policies in which the company engages (Deming, 1986). This "philosophy" is enacted within an organizational setting like a "prepackaged culture" (Beyer, Ashmos & Osborn, 1996). TQM is therefore embedded with its own set of cultural beliefs, norms, values and assumptions. Culture in organizations has been described as patterns of shared assumptions (Schein, 1992), socially acquired and shared knowledge that is embodied in organizational frames of reference (Martin, 1992) or as common and clear understandings (Meyerson, 1991). Implementation of TQM requires changes to the shared assumptions, frames of reference, and understandings that most organizations have developed through interaction with their environment. These changes will impact basic beliefs and values that employees hold about work (Beyer et al., 1996).

How these changes are made and what they come to mean to the organizational members impacts the receptivity of TQM and depends on the dominant values and assumptions that are evoked in the organization when the change is made. These dominant values and assumptions are influenced by the preferences and tendencies of the organizational members (the societal culture), and the product/service characteristics and norms (the industry culture), in addition to historical factors that are specific to the organization. The most powerful of these influences is the societal (or national culture). Deep-seated cultural values and assumptions appear to be quite insensitive to the transient culture of the specific organizations (Laurent, 1992) or the industry. Therefore, TQM must work within the context of the greater society in addition to the organization into which it is implemented.

TQM has been applied successfully in culturally diverse settings and the history of these applications suggests that over time, TQM takes on some of the host country's cultural values. The TQM that is predominantly introduced to eastern Europe, for example, embodies the influences of both the Japanese and the American cultures. At Valvex, the new owner has introduced an interpretation of TQM that emphasizes empowerment with individual rewards, cross-functional teamwork for problem solving and design, and measurement of quality processes with an eye toward the reduction of variance. The general TQM framework which is employed in Valvex is represented in Figure 1.

The Nature of Culture

Differences exist between national cultures in the way the members view the world (Stewart & Bennett, 1991), how they deal with uncertainty, the degree to which individuals are integrated into groups, the extent to which the less powerful members of organizations accept and expect that power is distributed unequally (Hofstede, 1984), how information is processed, conceptions of time (Hall & Hall, 1990), how individuals establish relationships with others, the modality of human activity, what a human being's relationship to nature is, and the character of innate human nature (Trompennars, 1994). Many of these differences have been characterized as paired value orientations which represent opposing tendencies. High incidence of each of the paired orientations exist in each society and even within a given individual, but cultural norms and expectations are generally based on a dominant shared value (one of the paired values). Though cultural patterns may and usually do reflect a capability to evoke either of the paired values, contextual cues stimulate perceptions that cultural members share and help them to select "appropriate" behavior, or suffer social consequences. Thus laws, means of social organization, codes of appropriate behavior, and preferred leadership styles, for example, are based on the dominant values within a given society. These influence policies and procedures, reward systems, and norms of accepted behavior within the organization. In addition, organizational members share expectations that policies will be consistent with these dominant values. Divergence causes conflict.

Figure 1. Total Quality Management Dimensions

Process Focus
Continuous Process Improvement
Measurement of Processes
Active Involvement of Suppliers and Customers

Long-term Customer Focus
Expanded Definition of Customer
Long Range Planning
Emphasis on Quality

Decentralized Control Structure
Teamwork
Empowerment
Visionary Leadership

To understand and address this conflict a four-step process of assessment can be applied.

1. First, you must isolate the values underlying the management approach to be implemented. In the example employed here, three values of the TQM philosophy that were significant to its introduction to the Polish factory are seen in Figure 2.

2. Second, you must isolate the dominant national cultural values and characterize them in comparison to the techniques (see Figure 2).

3. Third, you must chart the degrees of consistency or inconsistency on each of the key values.

4. The final step is to address the conflict in value orientations with management plans that promote values that are consistent with the management approach, or that adjust this approach to be consistent with the cultural context.

These four steps are applicable across cultural contexts (Taiwan, Nigeria, Argentina or Russia) and across management approaches. A brief look at the Polish context will help frame the Valvex example and present evidence of how an in-depth understanding of historical factors provides valuable insight into current cultural characteristics.

Poland _____

The Context for Managing in Poland

Modern Polish society can be viewed as the product of three significant influences: a history of foreign power (or foreign system) domination, a long history of agrarian traditions, and the Catholic church (Roney, 1996). The physical and political fortunes of Poland have undergone significant changes in the last 200 years and its borders have changed numerous times (Walters, 1988; Davies, 1982a, 1982b). In the late 18th century, Poland underwent a series of partitions, orchestrated by Prussia,

---

Figure 2. Comparison of Values and Assumptions

Polish Culture	TQM Philosophy
Power is assigned through **Ascription** "Who you are"	Power is assigned through **Achievement** "What you do"
Fatalistic Belief in a "powerful" other and a lack of personal control over destiny	**Deterministic** Belief in personal power over destiny
Simultaneously **Individualistic** and **Collectivistic**	Simultaneously **Individualistic** and **Collectivistic**

Russia, and Austria, which eventually eliminated Poland entirely as a sovereign state. The aftermath of World War I resurrected the Polish state for fifteen years, with new borders, including a large portion of Ukrainian and Lithuanian territory, producing the only period of self-rule in two centuries. World War II brought invasion by the Nazi army and another redistribution of property. One of the victors of the war, Russia, claimed a large portion of Poland's eastern region, but Poland was given as compensation a large section of land to their west from vanquished Germany. The end of World War II also brought to Poland a communist system orchestrated by the Soviet political powerhouse.

Polish traditions, the second influence, have remained strong, in part, because of the need to resist foreign power domination. Traditional land inheritance practices, for example, that require all living children receive a portion of the family farm land (Lewis, 1973; Polonsky & Drukier, 1980) have significantly influenced the way Poles organize their relationships. Plots of land were divided into very small pieces, but they represented a personal connection with Polish identity and thus remain extremely important. Collectivization of farming was strongly rejected and private ownership of farms was reluctantly tolerated by the communist government (Lane, 1973; Polonsky & Drukier, 1980). The Polish peasant farmers viewed communism as another period of foreign power domination and relied on church, family and community networks for facilitating daily life. Despite the distaste for political systems, Poles operate their daily businesses in a very political manner (Kennedy, 1992; Kostera, 1995). They view most contacts as political. Nonfamilial relationships are structured around an informal network of "connected" individuals for facilitating the acquisition of a wide range of basic needs, including farming products and home repairs (Hann, 1985).

The Catholic church, the final influence on modern culture addressed here, has played a significant role in defining the values of the Polish people (Wnuk-Lipinski, 1987). Basic beliefs in sacrifice and suffering, espoused by the Catholic doctrine, have given the Polish people a justification for their history of oppression by foreign powers. It has also given them a sense of common purpose and a safe haven for expressing nationalism. This same theme is seen in their literary figures of the 19th century, most notably Mickiewicz (Davies, 1982a), who wrote that the sacrifice and suffering of the Polish people represented a preordained destiny which would be rewarded in heaven.

These factors, blended over time, have shaped the Polish belief in what is right versus wrong and how things "ought to be" (their values). In addition, it has carved out the set of assumptions that explain for them the way the world works. These basic values and assumptions influence how the Poles react to various work situations and how they behave in organizations. The employees at Valvex enter their work place with this set of influences and ways of viewing the world.

After comparing the values of the cultural context, in this case the employees at Valvex, with the values of the management approach, in this case TQM, three possible consistency conditions might emerge. The first possible condition is that the cultural value may be consistent with the management approach and implementation may proceed. The second possible condition is that the national culture and management may rely upon different and contradictory dominant values in the pair. In this situation a solution must be found to facilitate successful implementation of the new management approach. In the final condition, the management approach and/or the culture may rely simultaneously on both of the paired values. This presents a different type of conflict and requires an innovative set of solutions. Each of these conditions is described below utilizing Valvex for illustration, and management solutions are suggested.

Valvex

Consistent Values

When consistency between values exists conflict is unlikely to ensue. This was the case, for example, with the implementation of TQM in U.S. companies as it relates to the focus on achievement based rewards. TQM espoused rewarding individuals for the accomplishment of defined behaviors that are consistent with organizational goals. This was consistent with American values and thus little conflict occurred related to this facet of TQM. Further, empowerment, which is frequently included in TQM implementation in the U.S., can be seen as a cultural adaptation of achievement orientation combined with individualism (detailed descriptions of both will follow), which are commonly held American values. Effective utilization of empowerment in organizations becomes an issue of consistency in management practice with policy more than a conflict with basic employee tendencies. Consistency in values should be expected with TQM's implementation in American companies because it represents a "coming home" of management ideas that were originated by Americans. This connection did not exist with the implementation of TQM in the Polish factory, Valvex, and thus the consistency with the most critical TQM values was not initially observed.

Inconsistent Values

Two sets of value orientations are in particular conflict as a result of the introduction of TQM at the Valvex factory and they present clear examples of inconsistent values. The first is the ascriptive assignment of power versus achievement. The ascription-achievement orientation addresses the means by which a given culture assigns status within the society. Achievement status refers to "doing," whereas ascriptive status refers to "being" (Trompennars, 1994). Ascription, as opposed to achievement, assigns status and power based on some type of characteristic of the individual, for example age, gender, social connections, education or profession. In ascriptive societies, like Austria, Argentina, and Arab states, status requires no justification, and simply implies "power." In addition, these societies associate status and power with position, and they attribute obligation to one's standing in society (Hofstede, 1984; Stewart & Bennett, 1991). Achievement oriented societies, like American, Canadian and Scandinavian cultures, place a high emphasis on skill and knowledge, and authority is assigned on this basis. Power comes with position only if the job is performed effectively.

The highly political nature of Polish society and the utilization of political networks of affiliation instituted during the communist era fostered the ascriptive nature of status assignment. Networks that linked individuals to the ruling class were the only means by which real power and status was attainable. Thus, managers in the communist period sought to protect their organizations from excess interference and their own status by maintaining critical relationship with key individuals, usually within the communist party structure (Kostera, 1995). This reliance on ascription and management connections with "power" centers continues in post-communist Poland. The reaction to one attempt by management to change the focus of awards demonstrates the conflict at Valvex.

Awards are an essential element of TQM implementation because they emphasize the behaviors which are valued by management and they celebrate employees' accomplishments. The new owner at Valvex was very concerned about the high absentee rate in this newly acquired company. This is a typical problem in state owned Polish companies because there is little incentive to come to work. Doctors are easily bribed to give excuses for extended time off for illnesses. The owner viewed this practice as a costly lack of commitment to the company which was inconsistent with TQM and vowed to correct the problem. A new point system was instituted that evaluated employee performance based on a series of quantitative measures which were used for pay increases and lay-off decisions. One of the most highly weighted criteria was attendance. After several months, however, he decided to emphasize the point with a new policy.

When I entered the factory one day to talk to the production workers, Alicja, a female production worker, told me that several of the employees were awarded television sets the previous day; those that had not taken sick days for the entire previous year. She said that there was a problem, however, because there were 40 people that had met the criteria but there were only 10 television sets awarded. Alicja told me that there were rumors, and lots of jealousy. People were saying, "why you and not me?"

Employees stated that it was either the supervisors and the technicians who fix and set the machines or those "close to the heart of the manager" (meaning the owner) that got the awards. When asked on what "basis" the awards were given, a trend emerged. They expressed their belief that a form of favoritism was used and they generally resented it. I began to understand how this was manifest by the employees when I was told the same story by several of the workers about Joanna. Joanna's temper apparently exploded in reaction to the awarding of the television sets. The televisions were awarded at a ceremony in the company cafeteria. All employees were encouraged but not required to attend. Those 40 employees that had met the criteria, as well as those that would actually receive the awards, were informed the morning of the ceremony. After telling all the employees who were assembled about the importance of perfect attendance, the owner of the factory called the ten recipients up to the front of the room and awarded the television sets. At this point he took questions for a short while and then he asked them to return to work. Joanna, knowing in advance what would happen at the meeting, was furious about what she had determined was a terrible injustice and had decided not to attend the ceremony. As the workers returned from the ceremony one of the recipients, a technician that repairs the machines, walked by Joanna's work table. She turned to him and yelled "get out of here you spy! You are what is wrong with this company!" Her reaction was described to me with little admonition for Joanna. Her fellow employees seemed to think that it was a perfectly justified thing to say. They spoke about Joanna simply reaching the end of her patience. When I asked Joanna about it several days later, she clearly did not want to talk about it with me.

I later discovered that the owner's decision to reward employees for perfect attendance was implemented by the management staff. When given the responsibility to decide to whom among the group to give the "limited" number of television sets, they relied on the only method they knew. The sets were given based on who was connected in the political network. This decision perpetuated the workers' belief that "nothing had changed." The old system of preference based on affiliation and not achievement was still at work. The result was an organization of employees split into two groups. The first were the people that did not get the television sets and resented those that did. The second group was the recipients of the television sets, who wished that they hadn't received them, because they were now accused of spying for management.

It is important to note that the process of favoritism based on criteria other than pure achievement is found in all societies. What is interesting to observe is the role that this process plays on the psyche of the Polish workers that are not part of the power structure. It serves to send a signal that achievement is actually devalued in the system and thus counterproductive to attaining personal objectives. Employees have learned to expect ascription to dominate in their public lives. This is true only, however, in the public sphere of life. The Polish people still highly value accomplishments when it comes to objectives that are not influenced by the "public" sphere. For example, farming that produces for the farmer's (employee's) personal needs is prized. They have learned to evoke a different value in public life than in their private lives.

This conflict in the Valvex factory is expected to continue as TQM is further introduced into the environment. In the TQM philosophy, personal achievement through creativity and innovation are highly valued. TQM focuses on personal or group achievement, particularly as a means of improving the organization as a whole. The belief is that individuals can each prosper when the organization as a whole prospers. All rewards, whether they be intrinsic or extrinsic, are based on personal or group achievement, hard work, and the acquisition of skills that will make an individual more beneficial to the organization.

The devaluation of achievement that is generated by ascription stifles opportunities to channel and reward individual efforts toward organizational objectives. This conflicts with the owners' objectives for implementing TQM. Attempts to live up to values embedded in Poland's culture necessitates that individuals spend energy on developing political alliances rather than on "hard work." Channeling personal efforts toward anything "public," as the organization is viewed, will be difficult in this environment. In addition, empowerment of the workforce would be seen as generally irrelevant if true "power" distribution is assigned through ascriptive means.

Though the television sets incident was not a direct product of the implementation of TQM in this factory, it does represent the sensitivity and volatility with which changes in the factory are currently met and points to the potential difficulties that TQM will produce. Rewarding the television sets was interpreted by employees based on their expectations, in this case of an ascription based system of favoritism. Although it was executed in a manner that was consistent with dominant expectations, it was espoused to be a change. The violent reaction arose from the perception that the change was superficial and spying became the explanation.

A second example of value incongruence occurs at the merging of the fatalism of the Polish culture and the determinism assumed in the TQM approach. Fatalism is viewed in opposition to determinism. They each describe an individual's relationship with nature and the perception of free will within the world context. As with all value orientations, both fatalism and determinism exist in all societies and in all individuals. Some cultures favor, however, the view that man is the master over his environment and they value harnessing and exploiting issues such as time, space, and change (Schneider, 1992). These cultures, for example America, Germany and the Scandinavian countries, that are classified as deterministic, have a belief that people are responsible as individuals or as a group for their actions and can affect the future. In addition, individuals in these societies find themselves unconstrained by environmental factors and capable of self-improvement.

In societies that tend to be more fatalistic than others, individuals share a perception of a lack of personal control over events. In these cultures, for example Arab, Chinese, and Indonesian peoples, dominion over events is believed to lie ultimately with a greater power such as God, fate, luck, government, one's social class, or history. They believe that the individual is subservient to, or in harmony with, nature, and that action taken by man will be overcome by the powers that control their destiny. Thus, responsibility for events lies not with the individual but with nature or fate.

A fatalistic view was expressed at all levels within the Valvex organization. The perceived external force that controls their fate, however, was different for men versus women and for various levels of authority within the organization (there are no women in positions of authority at Valvex). The women in the organization tend to look to some ambiguous "other" that is controlling their destinies. They use phrases like "we have to take it like it is" or "it is all planned, we have no control over it." They also focus on their changing economic predicament as being inevitable and uncontrollable. One female production worker responded to a question about whether they saw a greater disparity of wealth now as opposed to during communist times by saying: "people who have it are going to have it."

The men, including those in higher positions of authority, also assume very fatalistic attitudes. They, however, tend to focus on more specific targets for their subjugation. Due to the specific nature of these targets, they are changing with time. The men in lower levels of authority blame management and politicians for their state of affairs. They claim that they have little control in a world where powerful men rule their lives. The men in management, however, have changed their focus from the communist party, or the government, to the "market." They claim that market conditions now dictate their destiny, and thus they have little, if any, control over this situation. Regarding the centralized system that existed under communism, a product manager noted that they were directed by this government on all issues of capital investment, product line, and the quantity of products to manufacture. "Now," he says:

> the market dictates the machines and the number of people that we have in the factory...times are better and we are making investments. We are making lots of changes and it is very stressful. C'est la vie. It is getting better and better day by day. The salaries and wages...well, it is not like we can do everything, it is up to the market.

During communism this dominance of fatalism in employees in Polish organizations was an acknowledged and managed fact of state owned enterprises. The managers at Valvex, having the same tendencies themselves, accepted that in employees' attitudes because the managers were not rewarded for promoting self-motivated employees. TQM motivated training sessions and owner directives are now focusing on promoting self-determination. Change implementations, however, as described in the television set incident, have conflicted with the expectations that were developed in the training. The employees have drawn on their dominant tendency toward fatalism to explain the inconsistencies of expectations with actions by resignation to their "fate." Therefore, the actions of management have heightened and strengthened this fatalism rather than promoting the determinism that is subordinate in this culture.

This reliance on fatalism was incongruent with TQM which assumes a very different view of control. Issues of empowerment, decentralized decision making, and holistic process responsibility assume that individuals perceive control over events that impact them, and can act to change the circumstances and outcomes of those events. Finally, it assumes that the individuals who work within a TQM organization will hold the belief that they are responsible for their actions, can affect the future, and are capable of self-improvement. A major area of conflict between the deterministic TQM philosophy and the fatalistic Polish culture is in empowerment of employees. Empowerment requires the cognitive perception of an individual's ability to influence his/her environment and an acceptance of responsibility at the individual level (Thomas & Velthouse, 1990). Process diagnosis and improvement require that an individual believe that the risks associated with performing problem solving analysis and correction will have an impact. In addition, the drive to improve individual quality must be seen as having a tangible purpose. Attempts to establish reward systems to encourage individual decision making will be limited in a context where individuals feel that they have no control. For example, if the Valvex employees feel that the "market" is directing their futures, then it may be difficult to convince them that their hard work, attention to quality and restructuring of work processes will help them to influence the market in their favor.

Managers facing conflict between dominant cultural values and those embedded in a particular management approach must first recognize that the conflict exists. In the Valvex example, the conflict between orientations is evident in counterproductive attempts by the management to implement TQM, as interpreted by the new owner, and the seriously destructive behavior that it has generated. The television set incident, for example, was not expected to generate conflict. The managers, immersed in this culture, did not perceive difficulties with applying traditional means for selecting recipients of honors. It was only after several managers were approached by recipients of the awards with a request that they not be considered for awards in the future that the managers recognized the conflict.

The TQM approach can be implemented to evoke consistent values by analyzing the employees' view of the world. I do not suggest that management attempt to "change" the culture, but simply, or not so simply, to focus on ways that are within management's control to mitigate the most negative organizational impediments that are produced by a specific cultural characteristic. This can be accomplished by promoting the subordinate cultural value in a way that does not conflict with the dominant value. For example, at Valvex the conflict between achievement and ascription is evident only within the "public" sphere of Polish life. The Polish people do not fundamentally reject achievement as a means for privilege and power but they have learned to promote it only in their private lives. This knowledge can prompt the manager to work to blur the lines further between public and private lives promoting achievement in each. Those members of society, and within the organization with the most at stake in the ascriptive system, should be presented with new opportunities to maintain "power" but in a way that is consistent with promoting achievement orientation.

Several of the values held by Polish employees may conflict with any approach employed by management to modernize. Fatalism, for example, stifles the proactive behavior that is required to adapt to the growing complexity of Polish society. All modern, developed countries have experienced periods of transition; culture can and does change in response to external forces. In each case, however, the change is different in rate, and in kind, due to the unique qualities of the people. The early signs of cultural change are surfacing at Valvex and employees do appear to be tapping into secondary value orientations. The achievement orientation, for example, may be on the rise. The Valvex employees, at all levels, claim that achievement "should" be the means for status assignment in their society. However, fatalism or potentially self-serving interests, in the case of the managers, gets in the way of expecting this to actually happen. Management needs to find ways to foster this naturally occurring change.

Reliance on Both of the Paired Values

A third condition exists in evaluating the congruence of dominant values. In some societies and/or management approaches, both of the pairs of a particular value orientation are salient. This is the case in evaluating individualism versus collectivism in both the Polish culture and the TQM approach. Both individualistic and the collectivistic orientations of the Polish people, for example, influence behavior at Valvex. The individualism-collectivism dimension (Hofstede, 1983a; 1983b; Kluckhohn & Strodtbeck, 1961; Parsons & Shils, 1951) identifies the importance of the individuals in a society as compared to the group

(Schneider, 1992). It represents the level at which the culture tends to prefer to organize, make decisions, structure government, and structure reward and punishment systems. Individualistic cultures reward individual effort at the expense of the group, tend to make decisions at the highest levels of the authority structure, and encourage a highly competitive environment. In addition, individualism represents the pursuit of self-serving goals and a primary focus on their own interests and the interests of their immediate family (Morris, Davis, & Allen, 1994). Employees in individualistic societies, for example American, British, and Australian cultures, tend to view their relationship with the organization in a calculated manner, such as in relation to the particular compensation scheme or the status associated with employment (Boyacigiller & Adler, 1991).

At the other extreme is "collectivism" where individual accomplishments that place one person above another are discouraged or severely punished, group decision making is preferred, and authority is decentralized. Through birth right, or other forms of differentiation, individuals assume membership in particular "groups" from which it is difficult to detach themselves (Hofstede, 1984). They subordinate their individual needs and interests to the goals of the larger group for which they are a member. Often intergroup conflict results from a heavy emphasis on intragroup cooperation, sharing, and group harmony. Employees in collectivist societies, for example in Mexico, Korea and Japan, commit to their organization based on their relationship with other employees, such as managers, owners, or co-workers (Boyacigiller & Adler, 1991).

In Valvex, strong expectations existed for both individualism and collectivism. A significant struggle was often waged between the paired values. One example of individualistic and collectivistic tendencies co-existing at Valvex is the case of Janusz. Janusz is a male production worker around 30 years of age. He was slightly more educated than most of the workers in his work group and was savvy in his dealing with both management and his co-workers. When a new production machine was introduced to the assembly area, Janusz was one of two men selected to run the machine. The machine's introduction was met with serious difficulties and Janusz spent a great deal of his time correcting the problems by hand. This situation was compounded by the fact that his pay had actually decreased as a result of this move since he was now working on a salary.

Janusz was clearly frustrated with the difficulties of his new job, and one day he became nostalgic for the "old" way. He told me that it used to be that he could make a pretty good wage here. When he worked on his own, he could produce a high volume of parts. Since he was paid by the part he was able to bring home pretty good money. I asked him about the norms set by the engineers for the production. The norm was set as a production rate that a person should make for a given part in an eight hour shift. When the parts are assembled in groups, the norm for the group is the sum of the norms for the individuals. This is the method employed for performance evaluation, as well. Janusz had, in fact, told me in the past that they did not work over the norm that was set for the part because it caused the norm to go up. I witnessed many times groups that slowed down their work as they approached the norm. Some groups even stopped work, as much as an hour before quitting time, when the norm was reached. Janusz told me that when he works in a group he never exceeds the norm. It was a sort of agreement that they had amongst themselves. He confirmed that the reason they did this was to keep the norm from going up. If the norm goes up they have to work harder "every" day. All of the assembly groups that I spoke to at Valvex had this same agreement. Janusz told me, however, when he works by himself he does not have this agreement, so he can work as hard as he can to make some more money. I asked him why the group did not work together to make more money as a whole. He looked puzzled at this question, and then he said "it just isn't done that way. No one wants to work harder than they have to."

Janusz's behavior when he worked with the group was typical. Group sanctions are strong in Poland for attempting to step outside your group, by obtaining wealth, education or by fraternizing with higher status individuals. The penalty is severe social ostracism and in many cases exclusion from the existing set of networks. Group norms are established to protect the small group or societal interests not the organization's interests. Working hard in the interests of any "public" institution is irrational to most Poles. But, Janusz's individualistic behavior is also typical and it reflects what is most advantageous to the individual as long as it does not conflict with the group, or cause the person to elevate his/her standing in the society. This dual tendency is reflected in all of Polish society and is at the core of the Poles' image of themselves, which is of a nation capable of the most heroic collective efforts in times of emergency and incapable of living prosperously in quieter times due to extreme individualism and a fatal tendency to anarchy (Czarniawska, 1986).

Though the TQM philosophy is strongly rooted in the foundations of U.S. culture, which is very individualistic, the collectivism that is the cornerstone of Japanese society may have left its greatest impact here. Both individualism and collectivism values are seen in the TQM philosophy as it is interpreted by management in the Valvex factory. A focus on team decision making, engineering, and problem solving reflect the collectivistic nature of TQM. Yet, the focus on empowerment of individual workers, to the extent that they have ultimate power to shut down production lines, represents TQM's more individualistic American roots. TQM promotes a balance between solid individual behaviors and rewards, with a utilization of teamwork in key areas.

The dual orientations, of individualism and collectivism, of the Polish people would appear to be consistent with the dual orientations of the TQM philosophy. Difficulties arise, however, in channeling these competing orientations to capitalize on the power of each in the appropriate situation at Valvex. The balance between the two, particularly in Poland, where it is coupled with distrust and reluctance to assume responsibility, is a daunting task and to date has been unsuccessful at Valvex. For example, many individuals that had worked in cohesive groups were reassigned at Valvex to other work areas potentially reducing the negative impacts of strong sub-group cohesion. This action, however, has generated insecurity and tremendous suspicion which has been counterproductive. The power of collectivism does not lie solely in the small work groups, but also in the general sense of egalitarianism that was espoused by both the theoretical socialism and the Catholic church. Promoting one orientation, by rewarding for individual behavior, for example, may evoke the opposite orientation, strong collectivism.

In managing a culture or using a management approach with dual dominance value orientations channeling each appropriately becomes the primary objective. One possible approach to addressing this issue at Valvex would be to implement simple reward targets that are easily attainable and clearly defined and communicated in advance. They should be quickly acknowledged with rewards that are valued by the Polish people (money for example) and with no interpretation by the immediate power network (supervisors). The results should be documented with clear justification. This process would channel individualistic behavior toward specific objectives, prompted by the extreme need many of them have for cash, without threatening the group. In addition, the clear documentation of procedures and results signals to the Polish workers that management is not relying on the established ascriptive system utilized during communism, thus avoiding renewed conflict with other value orientations. It also provides evidence that the organization values individual responsibility. Analysis of the results should continue from the perspective of the cultural values that are impacted and adjustments should be made accordingly.

Conclusion _____

The major changes that have engulfed our world have highlighted our differences while they have brought us closer together. Major difficulties with transferring management practices, such as TQM, are partially a result of these differences. I have presented the inconsistencies that exist between the values embedded in the TQM management philosophy and those held by the employees of a Polish factory. This case highlights conflict that could occur in any context where management approaches, which are developed and implemented successfully in one culture, are introduced into vastly different cultures with different histories, political and social systems and thus different values. Three conditions of value consistency were presented and approaches to address each were discussed. The solutions presented here do not imply that management can, or even should, "change" the host culture to pave the way for successful implementation of unfamiliar management approaches. Instead, I propose a method for evaluating the differences in a systematic way that will facilitate for a flexible and observant management staff successful planning and implementation.

At Valvex, the Polish culture presents a resistance to TQM that is uniquely its own. Lessons learned from examining the issues that face management in Poland as a conflict of basic values and assumptions can be transferred to other cultural settings. Change will occur at Valvex, and it may resemble the values of TQM, but it will likely be in Poland's own image.

References

Beyer, J. M., Ashmos, D. P. & Osborn, R. N. (1996). *Contrasts in enacting TQM: Mechanistic vs. organic ideology and implementation.* Unpublished manuscript.

Boyacigiller, N. A. & Adler, N. J. (1991). The parochial dinosaur: Organizational science in a global context. *Academy of Management Review, 16:* 262-290.

Czarniawska, B. (1986). The management of meaning in the Polish crisis. *Journal of Management Studies, 23*(3): 313-331.

Davies, N. (1982a). *God's playground: A history of Poland,* Vol. 1: *The origins to 1795.* New York: Columbia University Press.

Davies, N. (1982b). *God's playground: A history of Poland,* Vol. 2: *1795 to the present.* New York: Columbia University Press.

Deming, W. E. (1986). *Out of the crisis.* Cambridge, MA: MIT Center for Advanced Engineering Study.

Hall, E. T. & Hall, M. R. (1990). *Understanding cultural differences.* Yarmouth, ME: Intercultural Press.

Hann, C. M. (1985). *A village without solidarity: Polish peasants in years of crisis.* New Haven, CT: Yale University Press.

Hofstede, G. (1983a). Dimensions of national cultures in fifty countries and three regions. Pp. 335-355 in J. B. Deregowski, S. Dziurawiec & R. C. Annies (Eds.), *Expiscations in cross-cultural psychology.* Lisse, Netherlands: Swets and Zeitlinger.

Hofstede, G. (1983b). National cultures in four dimensions. *International Studies of Management and Organization, 13:* 46-74.

Hofstede, G. (1984). The cultural relativity of the quality of life concept. *Academy of Management Review, 9:* 389-398.

Kennedy, M. D. (1992). Transformations of normative foundations and empirical sociologies: Class, stratification, and democracy in Poland. Pp. 83-95 in W. D. Connor, P. Ploszajski, A. Inkeles & W. Wesolowski (Eds.), *The Polish road from socialism: The economics, sociology, and politics of transition*. Armonk, NY: M. E. Sharpe.

Kluckhohn, R. & Strodtbeck, F. L. (1961). *Variations in value orientations*. Westport, CT: Greenwood Press.

Kostera, M. (1995). Differing managerial responses to change in Poland. *Organization Studies, 16*(4): 673-697.

Lane, D. (1973). Structural and social change in Poland. Pp. 1-28 in D. Lane & G. Kolankiewicz (Eds.), *Social Groups in Polish Society*. New York: Columbia University Press.

Laurent, A. (1992). The cross-cultural puzzle of global human resource management. Pp. 174-184 in V. Pucik, N. M. Tichy, & C. K. Barnett (Eds.), *Globalizing management, Creating and leading the competitive organization*. New York: John Wiley & Sons.

Lewis, P. (1973). The peasantry. Pp. 29-87 in D. Lane & G. Kolankiewicz (Eds.), *Social groups in Polish society*. New York: Columbia University Press.

Martin, J. (1992). *Cultures in organization: Three perspectives*. New York: Oxford University Press.

Meyerson, D. E. (1991). "Normal" ambiguity? A glimpse of an occupational culture. Pp. 131-144 in P. J. Frost, L. F. Moore, M. R. Louis, C. C. Lundberg, & J. Martin (Eds.), *Reframing organizational culture*. Newbury Park, CA: Sage.

Morris, M. H., Davis, D. L. & Allen, J. W. (1994). Fostering corporate entrepreneurship: Cross-cultural comparisons of the importance of individualism versus collectivism. *Journal of International Business Studies, 25*(1): 65-89.

Parsons, T. & Shils, E. A. (1951). *Toward a general theory of action*. Cambridge, MA: Harvard University Press.

Polonsky, A. & Drukier, B. (1980). *The beginnings of communist rule in Poland*. London: Routledge & Kegan Paul.

Roney, J. (1996). *Webs of resistance: A tale of Polish workers at the cultural crossroads of organizational transformation*. Unpublished doctoral dissertation, University of Utah.

Schein, E. H. (1991). What is culture? Pp. 243-254 in P. Frost, L. Moore, M. Louis, C. Lundgerg & J. Martin (Eds.), *Reframing organizational culture*. Newbury Park, CA: Sage.

Schneider, S. (1992). National vs. corporate culture: Implications for human resource management. Pp. 159-173 in V. Pucik, N. Tichy & C. Barnett (Eds.), *Globalizing management: Creating and leading the competitive organization*. New York: John Wiley & Sons.

Spencer, B. A. (1994). Models of organization and Total Quality Management: A comparison and critical evaluation. *The Academy of Management Review, 19*: 446-471.

Stewart, E. C. & Bennett, M. J. (1991). *American cultural patterns: A cross-cultural perspective*. Yarmouth, ME: Intercultural Press.

Thomas, A. S. (1996). A call for research in forgotten locations. Pp. 485-506 in B. J. Punnett & O. Shenkar (Eds.), *Handbook of international management research*. Cambridge, MA: Blackwell.

Thomas, K. W. & Velthouse, B. A. (1990). Cognitive elements of empowerment: An "interpretive" model of intrinsic task motivation. *Academy of Management Review, 15*(4): 666-681.

Trompennars, A. (1994). *Riding the waves of culture: Understanding diversity in global business*. Burr Ridge, IL: Irwin.

Walters, E. G. (1988). *The other Europe: Eastern Europe to 1945*. Syracuse, NY: Syracuse University Press.

Wnuk-Lipinski, E. (1987). Social dimorphism and its implications. Pp. 159-176 in J. Koralewicz, I. Bialecki & M. Watson (Eds.), *Crisis and transition: Polish society in the 1980s*. Oxford: Berg.

Designing and Supporting Transnational Teams: The Human Resource Agenda___

Reading 7.3
Scott A. Snell
Charles C. Snow
Sue Canney Davison
Donald C. Hambrick

Introduction ___

As multinational corporations expand to compete globally, many are benefiting from the use of *transnational teams*—individuals from different cultures working together on activities that span national boarders. When managed effectively, transnational teams help firms achieve the autonomy and flexibility needed to serve a variety of customers in different regions while obtaining the efficiencies afforded by an integrated organization (Bartlett & Ghoshal, 1989; Ohmae, 1985; Pascale, 1990). Working either within the firm's formal structure or as a complement to it, a transnational team can connect the best ideas and innovations from each part of the company and use them in ways that add value throughout the organization. They may form a nucleus from which a broader network of talent and relationships can be developed.

Some firms are making concerted efforts to realign their human resource (HR) strategies, policies, and programs to support and develop transnational teams. Our impression is that most HR professionals are aware of the emerging issues and challenges associated with managing across borders and cultures. In many companies, however, the efforts of these professionals to support and develop transnational teams are being hampered by institutionalized HR policies that reflect and perpetuate more traditional organizational arrangements (Adler &

Bartholomew, 1992). To facilitate change, both line and HR executives in leading companies are working with team leaders and members to establish more flexible approaches to team development.

The overall purpose of our article is to articulate a comprehensive agenda for aligning HR strategies, policies, and programs to produce effective transnational teams. Over the past few years, we have studied a wide variety of such teams in companies across the United States, Europe, and Asia. Their experiences provide guidance to firms regarding such matters as: (1) where and how transnational teams can be used best to achieve competitive advantage, (2) what fundamental design parameters underlie a team's composition and structure, and (3) how HR practices can enhance the performance of transnational teams. Drawing on our research findings, we present some exemplary practices used by successful teams and provide recommendations for how the HR function might view its role in developing transnational teams.

The Research Project

We conducted a worldwide research project sponsored by the International Consortium for Executive Development Research (ICEDR), a group of 31 large multinational corporations and 20 prominent business schools. ICEDR was established to address the organizational and managerial challenges posed by the global corporation.

The two-year study consisted of three phases: (1) in-depth interviews, (2) a questionnaire survey, and (3) a demonstration project. In the first phase, we worked with senior HR executives in ICEDR companies to identify teams with multinational membership that transacted business across national borders and represented a mix of firms in the United States, Europe, and Asia. Thirteen teams met these criteria. We interviewed more than 100 team members and their leaders about issues related to strategic purpose, team composition, training, job design, appraisal, rewards, and performance.

During the second phase of the study we expanded our sample of teams by contacting leaders of additional teams to invite their participation in completing a questionnaire. Each participant (team leaders and team members) was guaranteed confidentiality and was given a summary of our findings as well as a profile of the team benchmarked against the rest of the sample. The questionnaires were designed to assess the strategic contribution of the team, the HR practices used, and team performance. A total of 34 team leaders and 163 team members returned questionnaires (4.8 per team). Table 1 is a list of participating companies and teams.

The third phase of the research was a demonstration project designed to help firms translate the research findings into practice. HR specialists from The Wellcome Foundation (now Glaxo-Wellcome PLC) worked closely with two members of the research team to develop a multistage

Table 1. Sample of Companies and Transnational Teams

Company	Transnational Team
Alcatel/Alsthom	Corporate Purchasing
AT&T	Business Services Planning
BellSouth	Mobile Data
British Airways	Eastern Mediterranean Management Team
British Airways	Latin American/Caribbean Management Team
British Airways	Scandinavia Management Team
British Airways	Japan Management Team
British Gas	Full Field
British Petroleum	European Gas Business Development
Daimler-Benz	Trigat
Eastman Kodak	Photo CD Consumer Launch Team
Exxon Chemical	Viscosity Modifiers Worldwide
FIAT Group	CEAC Executive Team
FIAT Group	CEAC Purchasing Team
Fidelity	Continental Team
Ford-New Holland	NHGeotech
Glaxo-Wellcome	International Quality Assurance Coordination Team
Glaxo-Wellcome	International Quality Assurance Coordination Team II
Glaxo-Wellcome	Welferon
Glaxo-Wellcome	Retrovir
Glaxo-Wellcome	935 Team
Heineken	European Production Task Force
IBM-Latin America	Personal Systems Group
IBM-UK	International Airline Solutions Centre
KONE	MacGregor Navire Executive Team
Seagrams	South Region
Seagrams	SGBD
Siemens	General Management
Sparkomatic	Far East Operations
Toyota	Production Engineering
Unilever	Personal Care Marketing
Xerox-Fuji Xerox	Century Team
Xerox-Fuji Xerox	Century II Team
Zeneca	ZD 7288 Strategy Team

approach for improving team effectiveness. The company assembled a high-caliber HR team that used the results from phases 1 and 2 to identify "best practices" and then assessed the HR function's competencies in delivering the programs and services needed by transnational teams. HR practices derived from the demonstration project are currently being used to develop Glaxo-Wellcome's transnational research and development (R&D) and marketing teams. (See Snow et al., 1996 for a complete description of the demonstration project and its team-development model.)

Strategic Human Resource Management of Transnational Teams

Our starting point for understanding transnational teams is the identification of the teams' mission and strategic orientation. Most of the teams in our study face the challenge of balancing three concerns related to global competition: (1) *local responsiveness*, (2) *global efficiency*, and (3) *organizational learning* (Bartlett & Ghoshal, 1989). Kodak's Photo CD Consumer Launch Team, for example, is charged with customizing Kodak's marketing strategy for each country in western Europe. Such attention to local responsiveness requires that the team not only make allowances for unique demands and preferences across various cultures, but also develop facility in adjusting to changing market conditions and political/legal differences. The Kodak team example highlights the strategic importance of local responsiveness.

Other teams are charged with integrating widely dispersed activities to achieve global efficiency. Unilever, for example, uses transnational teams to combine 16 different operating companies into one global organization. Heineken, Alcatel, and Fuji-Xerox have transnational teams to achieve scale economies, rationalize production, and standardize products and processes to improve efficiency and lower costs. Whereas local responsiveness requires recognizing and instilling variety within the team, global efficiency requires coordination and integration. Those very different strategic orientations imply different priorities for managing team activities.

Finally, more than half of the teams in our study are expected to contribute to the process of organizational learning. To achieve technical as well as intellectual parity with their competitors, many teams develop innovative ways to leverage knowledge continuously around the world (Bartlett & Ghoshal, 1989; Kanter, 1983; Nonaka, 1991; Nonaka & Takeuchi, 1995). IBM's International Airlines Solutions Centre (IASC), for example, is the center of a complex network of technical and marketing experts who troubleshoot for IBM's customers in the airline industry. Because IASC is structured as a transnational team that develops synergies among individuals on five different continents, it has become a center of expertise that links knowledge located in one part of the world to problems that arise in another—in effect, institutionalizing learning within the organization as a whole.

Local responsiveness, global efficiency, and organizational learning are three major strategic drivers of transnational teams; in leading companies, HR strategies, policies, and programs must support each of

Table 2. Human Resource Practices for Transnational Teams

	Strategic Orientation		
HR Support Role	Local Responsiveness	Global Efficiency	Organizational Learning
Staffing	Value-adding Polycentric Dispersed	N minus 1 staffing Functional membership	Suprastaffing Geocentric Temporary members
Training & Development	Expand skill base Programs on strategy Temporary assignments	Professional culture New work methods Conflict & negotiations Technical & project management	Promote continuous learning Negotiating skills Interpersonal skills Project management
Team Design & Member Roles	Dispersed Specialized Local responsibility Delegated decisions	Global responsibility Interdependence Decentralized centralization Consensus decisions	Mutual exchange Shared information Rotational assignments
Rewards & Appraisal	Local appraisal Individual goals Individual appraisal Paid by home country	Team-based goal setting Appraisal based on others' input Central budget for pay Intrinsic rewards	Error embracing Evaluation based on learning Frequent feedback

those objectives. A comprehensive description of HR practices for transnational teams is shown in Table 2. We discuss each of the practices by giving examples from teams in our study.

Staffing a Transnational Team

The fundamental task in forming a transnational team is assembling the right combination of individuals who can work together to accomplish the team's goals. There is no universal formula for staffing a transnational team, but some guidelines can be followed to link staffing to business strategy:

Increase Variety on the Team to Improve Local Responsiveness. To achieve local responsiveness, a transnational team such as Kodak's Photo CD Consumer Launch Team must incorporate considerable variety within its membership. Variety can take several forms, but often transnational teams consist of *dispersed and specialized human assets* that enable the team to attend to local issues across countries, markets, products, and so on, and ensure that many different perspectives are brought to bear on the problems facing the team.

Several HR policies build variety and differentiation into a team. Transnational teams are not only multinational but often multifunctional. In addition, they are often staffed through a *polycentric* selection process whereby members are appointed from each of the functions, business units, and countries affected by the actions/outcomes of the team. Kodak's Photo CD Launch Team, for example, was composed of representatives from each of the major countries in which the product would be launched initially. Similarly, Heineken's European Production Task Force included representatives from each of the countries where Heineken breweries were located. Although a polycentric approach to staffing stems from an overriding concern about market and political sensitivities (e.g., dealing with local governments and unions), the effect is to expand the functional complexity and cultural heterogeneity of the team. However, carefully crafted variety and balance are essential to avoid the potential problem of one or two individuals (typically from the company's headquarters) dominating the dynamics of the team. To increase variety even further, new members tend to be added to the team only if they bring some *value-adding talent* to the team. Skill redundancy generally is not viewed as functional slack but as needless duplication. Variety in the team's composition is seen as essential to its ability to detect and respond to local issues.

Integrate the Team to Achieve Global Efficiency. The most significant challenge of transnational teams whose expected contribution is global efficiency is to combine the efforts of individuals into an integrated whole. Such transnational teams therefore establish HR practices that ensure members do not emphasize local interests over global concerns. Integration is the key, and teams such as Unilever's Personal Care team, Alcatel's Corporate Purchasing team, and IBM-Latin America's Personal Systems Group all use some variation on an approach we call "N minus 1" staffing to bring members together. With N minus 1 staffing, the transnational team is composed of fewer members than ordinarily would be necessary to complete the task. Some team members (and some leaders) complain about being overworked and understaffed, but N minus 1 staffing demands that team members cooperate to find the means whereby their collective effort makes up for the missing member(s). The approach has the effect of improving team integration as well as orienting the individuals to global issues rather than to more parochial concerns of a given country.

Use Network Staffing to Facilitate Organizational Learning. IBM's International Airlines Solutions Centre is an example of a transnational team that has mastered the development of an intelligence network. To create, transfer, and institutionalize knowledge, firms frequently staff their transnational teams with the best talent they can find—wherever it exists around the world. As a prototype for tomorrow's organization, IASC has been able to transcend the present organization structure to connect individuals and units that do not normally work together. Because the very best talent may be hidden within the organization's hierarchy, IBM and other firms such as AT&T, Unilever, and Alcatel have developed sophisticated information systems to tap these networks for specialized talent (Snell, Pedigo, & Krawiec, 1995).

Network staffing addresses two issues related to organizational learning: breadth of talent and rapid response. First, network staffing provides a broad base of skills and experiences from which teams can draw to address complex problems and business opportunities. By maintaining a pool of assets "on call" and accessible, teams can staff beyond their current needs to prepare for future strategic initiatives. Second, network staffing allows the team to reconfigure its membership as needs change. Given the dynamics of international business, transnational teams rarely have the luxury of keeping extra members (recall N minus 1 staffing). When the strategic focus is on learning, membership is frequently temporary, with new team members being brought in as experts on a particular problem and then released back into the network where they return to their home bases. In such cases, an active network augments what may be a very small core team (Snow & Snell, 1993).

Training and Developing the Team

Although training and development logically follow staffing, in reality much of the training the team members receive occurs before the team is put together. We have seen comparatively little training of intact teams, and consequently the group-skill levels of individuals—and of the team as a whole—are often inconsistent. Team training represents an important opportunity for the HR function in most multinational corporations. Glaxo-Wellcome's experience with the transnational team demonstration project (phase 3 of our study) showed that companies can do much more to develop effective transnational teams.

Expand the Range of Skills to Achieve Local Responsiveness. When transnational teams are oriented toward responding to local concerns, the developmental objective should be to *expand* the range of skills and experience on the team, though not to the exclusion of team unity. *Temporary assignment* (e.g., 2 to 4 weeks) is one technique that has proved effective for enhancing local responsiveness. Of course, if such assignments go on for too long or are too frequent, teams run the risk of losing input from individuals who cannot contribute because of their extended absences.

Interestingly, although most teams in our study were composed of members with international experience, we see no clear trend toward training the team *as a whole* to be locally responsive. As one manager told us, "Team training has the potential to homogenize the team and wipe away the very differences we want to accentuate." We have found, however, that training programs emphasizing the company's *strategies, structure, and processes* can have a substantial impact on the team's level of responsiveness to local issues. Such training is helpful for all teams but seems to be emphasized most for startup and emerging teams. Understanding strategy from the very beginning helps the team attend to various parts of the bigger picture and see how differences across countries, business units, and so on are important to the overall performance of the firm. Unfortunately, despite its potential effectiveness, this type of program is used infrequently.

Team Training Improves Global Efficiency. If the focus of the team's strategic orientation is global efficiency, the developmental agenda typically emphasizes team integration. For startup teams especially, companies such as Glaxo-Wellcome and Ford conduct *cross-cultural team-building* programs that are the next generation of what until now has been called "cultural awareness" training. The distinction between these two types of programs is important. Awareness programs (e.g., books and videotapes that describe various cultures) are most useful for legitimizing differences across cultures and sensitizing individuals to different customs and social norms. Such programs, however, are typically designed for knowledge acquisition and attitude change and may not provide the skills necessary for working through differences on the team. Cross-cultural team-building goes one step further, developing coherent work processes that take advantage of differences on the team by establishing ground rules and protocols that integrate members. When coupled with training in conflict resolution and negotiation skills, cross-cultural team-building can substantially improve integration and efficiency.

One of the most powerful forces for integration among team members is *professional culture*. Companies such as Alcatel, IBM, and MacGregor Navire, for example, believe that shared values among individuals in the same profession (e.g., engineers and scientists) frequently outweigh even wide country culture differences. In some cases, a team's professional culture is also stronger than the corporate culture. To take advantage of that fact, Alcatel has a comprehensive training program (called "The Alcatel Way") that blends professional, national, and corporate culture in a way that transcends individuals and teams to instill a global/local perspective within the entire organization.

Move from Individual to Organizational Learning. Training and development are an organization's formalized effort to institutionalize learning. Our interviews with team leaders, members, and HR executives made clear that most learning occurs at the individual level through training and other developmental experiences. Even in the best companies, less learning occurs at the team level, and disappointingly little learning takes place at the level of the organization as a whole. Ultimately, transnational teams can be a conduit through which learning at the individual level is synthesized and assimilated throughout the team and the entire organization (Nonaka & Takeuchi, 1995).

For IBM's IASC team, Glaxo-Wellcome's International Quality Assurance Coordination Team, and AT&T's Business Services Planning team, learning is at the top of the HR agenda. Team members focus on linking and leveraging knowledge through *continuous learning* rather than focusing on short-term performance issues. Across all the teams in our study, we found that programs emphasizing negotiation skills, project management, and interpersonal relations generally were associated with a team's ability to acquire, transfer, and utilize knowledge from other parts of the organization in addressing new problems and dilemmas.

Structuring Teamwork and Designing Roles

Some of the principal ways in which transnational teams differ from other work teams can be seen by examining their work structures and the responsibilities of individual members. Like those for staffing and training, guidelines for structuring teamwork can be linked to the strategic imperatives of local responsiveness, global efficiency, and organizational learning.

Assign Local Roles to Facilitate Responsiveness. Members of transnational teams who are geographically dispersed do not have the luxury of working side-by-side with their colleagues. When individuals are positioned in different countries to attend closely to local concerns, they must coordinate their activities across significant distances and cope with a host of logistical and communication problems. If it is essential to learn about and represent the specific concerns of different countries, member responsibilities tend to be *specialized* (though rarely completely autonomous), and decisions about those countries may be *delegated* very early in the team's development. For example, Kodak's Photo CD Launch Team had country representatives bid on parts of the implementation project (e.g., designing promotional displays) because of their areas of expertise and resource base. Those individuals then headed the activities with individuals (frequently non-team members) back in their home countries. To some extent such specialization aids efficiency, but mainly the decentralized decision making enables individuals to react quickly and responsively to local concerns. Kodak's approach is illustrative of those of other transnational teams that push action out to where response time is the fastest and expertise is the greatest.

Global Roles Improve Efficiency and Integration. One of the best ways to instill a *global perspective* among team members and keep them working toward the interests of the whole company is to assign global responsibility for a given task, project, or product to a particular individual. Alcatel's Corporate Purchasing team, for example, has individual Council Chairs in several countries. Each Council Chair has global responsibility for a family of products and puts together a subteam of individuals from appropriate locations to develop the best possible contract for the designated products. Unilever's Personal Care

Marketing team is organized similarly, with "decentralized centralization" helping to forge a global perspective while balancing the need for specialization and efficiency.

To orient members further toward global efficiency and integration, team leaders often try to base decisions on consensus, particularly at the early stages of team development or when addressing issues that concern the team's overall task. Such an approach to decision making must be balanced against the need for decentralization to ensure local responsiveness.

Mutual Exchange Engenders Organizational Learning. Because mutual exchange and *shared information* are vitally important for team learning, transnational teams must find ways to foster an ongoing dialogue among their members. One way is to formalize communication that is "upside-down" or "outside-in." AT&T's Business Services Planning team, for example, uses a planning process whereby members are periodically instructed by the team leader to learn as much as they can about the needs and interests of external constituents (e.g., business units, countries, customers) and then represent those concerns to the entire team. The planning process essentially involves a consolidation of ideas to find the best approach for reconciling a diversity of demands.

Rotational assignments (e.g., every 2 to 5 years) is another method teams use to foster organizational learning. Whereas short, temporary assignments can increase local sensitivity, individuals probably need to become truly immersed in a new context to learn enough to bring the value-adding knowledge back to the team. For example, the Century Team, a large group of engineers representing an international joint venture between Xerox Corporation and Fuji Xerox to develop the "world" copier, included 15 experienced Japanese engineers who spent up to five years in Webster, New York, learning and trading ideas about team processes. As a result, team members on each side of the ocean had an opportunity to analyze thoroughly and internalize the other's work styles and techniques.

Rewarding Transnational Teams

During the course of our study, we observed several reward and appraisal practices that ran counter to conventional wisdom about teams. At first we thought they might be isolated exceptions but soon observed a pattern across teams and began to understand the practices as team leaders revealed their logic to us. Ultimately, we concluded that reward and appraisal systems, perhaps more than any other area of HR, need to be managed carefully with a clear understanding of how they can be used to balance efficiency, responsiveness, and learning.

Use Individual and Local Rewards to Increase Local Responsiveness. To enhance local responsiveness, reward systems for transnational teams should reinforce the variety created through staffing, training, and work structures. Several teams use individual goal-setting and appraisal, which may seem inconsistent with traditional views of "teamwork." Even though organization members work in teams, however, they have individual responsibilities (Shaw & Schneier, 1995).

Despite the use of individual goal-setting, individual incentives are uncommon for a variety of reasons, some culturally based. A senior executive at Sumitomo Bank, for example, explained that individual incentives are anathema in Japan because their use implies that people are not already working as hard as they can (one would never assume such a thing of a loyal employee in Japan, let alone design a pay plan that makes the assumption explicit). Surprisingly, across our entire sample, where individual incentives (and goal setting) are used, they have a positive influence on local responsiveness. That broad generality *cannot* be applied to every team.

Teams typically try to highlight local differences by tying member compensation and appraisal policies to *home country units* rather than trying to establish uniform policies across the entire team. Where local concerns prevail, pay systems tend to vary dramatically from member to member within the same team. That practice seems to run counter to the objective of team development, but it can help ensure that team members retain some of their local affiliations; however, some important tradeoffs must be acknowledged with home-country rewards and appraisal. In addition to creating administrative difficulties, they can have a negative effect on team integration and efficiency. Team leaders and members at Alcatel and Glaxo-Wellcome, for example, indicate that the lack of team-based rewards prevents their working together as well as they might.

Team Rewards Improve Integration and Efficiency. In conjunction with home country reward systems, team member evaluations tend to be carried out by their home country managers. Nevertheless, the amount of input from team leaders and members to the home country manager appears to be increasing. At Alcatel, for example, home country managers retain responsibility for evaluating individual representatives to a given transnational team, but starting several years ago they began to get formal input from the corporate team leader.

One of the most surprising findings related to rewards is the infrequent use of formal team-based incentives. Combining individual, team, and home country rewards may be a move in the right direction for most transnational teams. For FIAT's CEAC Purchasing and Ford-New Holland's NHGeotech teams, rewards have individual, team, and corporate components. As with other HR matters, balancing global and local concerns appears to be critical in designing reward systems.

Reward Organizational Learning. Despite the importance of learning as a strategic objective for many transnational teams, we found little evidence that it is operationalized through appraisal and reward systems. Indeed, though rewarding individuals for new ideas can strongly enhance transnational team learning and innovation, that practice is not used frequently. Other practices that are generally acknowledged as fostering learning also tend to be uncommon, such as basing member evaluations on amount of learning (as in AT&T's Business Services Planning team), tolerating or acknowledging mistakes, and giving team members frequent performance feedback (Gross, 1995, 1997).

We attribute most of these inconsistencies to the fact that transnational teams are frequently used to initiate activities that are of strategic importance to the firm, and therefore need to show definitive results. Our conversations with team leaders and company executives, however, revealed that most companies rank organizational learning among the most important reasons for establishing and supporting transnational teams (Nonaka & Takeuchi, 1995). If this is true, we would argue that appraisal and reward systems must support learning that leads to innovation rather than focusing on short-term operational targets. Indeed, the payoffs from doing so appear to be substantial.

Recommendations for Human Resource Professionals —————————

The HR group can play an important role in helping transnational teams balance global, local, and learning issues. The following is an agenda for HR professionals, in the form of a set of practical recommendations describing how to develop and support transnational teams.

Recommendation 1: View the HR Group as a Transnational Team

In most multinational firms, the HR Department has both corporate and local offices—subunits that must work together to establish an integrated whole despite their competing demands and responsibilities. The dual orientation within the HR function requires it to be an effective transnational team. We urge companies to recognize and act on that fact. At Glaxo-Wellcome, for example, the corporate human resource group found that it had to undergo a team development process before it could effectively assist other transnational teams in the company. First, it had to formulate an HR strategy for facilitating team development in critical areas such as R&D and marketing. Second, it had to assemble a multinational team of process consultants to work with the teams. This step included the hiring of approximately 50 new HR staff and the formation of several new relationships with outside consulting firms. Third, the newly constituted HR group had to undergo its own team development process with assistance from a core group of outside researchers and consultants. After solidifying itself as a transnational team, the HR group was in position to launch a large training and consulting program aimed at developing the company's transnational R&D and marketing teams.

Recommendation 2: Develop a Worldwide Staffing Network

To help staff transnational teams, the HR group must adapt its human resource information systems to provide the foundation for a worldwide staffing network. The core of such a network is a computerized database containing information about potential transnational team candidates, including their work experience, previous performance, availability for team assignment, and skills. Most large companies have well-developed HR information systems for domestic planning purposes. Few companies, however, have systems that work effectively at the international level. Unilever and IBM are exceptions, as those companies have created sophisticated databases that enable HR personnel to identify potential team leaders and members. Ultimately, human resource information systems should be able to store not only historical data, but also individual preferences about the types of transnational teams on which individuals would like to work and their desired country locations.

Recommendation 3: Provide Team Training as Well as Individual Training

To develop transnational teams, the HR group should be prepared to offer training programs in at least three areas: (1) technical skills such as those required in project management and decision-making technologies; (2) team skills in areas such as interpersonal relations, conflict resolution, negotiations, and cultural sensitivity; and (3) company strategies, policies, and structures. Some are prerequisite programs that can be delivered before an individual is placed on a transnational team. Providing individual training in technical skills, as well as in company strategies and processes, is typical. Given the velocity of change in most multinational firms, coupled with the short expected response time of many transnational teams, few companies have the luxury of waiting until after the team is formed to do all the necessary training.

Other training experiences should be delivered to intact teams as soon as possible after they are formed. Developmental experiences focused on intercultural dynamics, group decision making and so on should be provided early so that effective interaction patterns become part of the team's daily operations, not just a set of skills acquired by its individual members. Too often teams postpone such training, assuming that administrative processes will develop along with task processes. That can be a grave mistake. Without appropriate group training, teams may develop dysfunctional processes that are difficult to correct later on.

In the most sophisticated companies, transnational teams that have been together for a long time meet periodically to review their team processes. The philosophy underlying these review meetings is that a team must constantly practice becoming a better team—improvement will not occur naturally.

Recommendation 4: Recognize That Many Transnational Teams Are Virtual Teams

Many transnational team leaders and members express a preference to be co-located so that it is quicker and easier to communicate and make decisions. For an increasing number of teams, however, this is an impracticality. The resources and responsibilities associated with a transnational team often are too geographically far-flung to make co-location feasible. Even when a team is co-located, as is true of British Petroleum's European Gas Business Development tea, the team leader and members may travel so frequently in their jobs that they are unable to hold meetings where everyone is present.

The HR group, therefore, should position itself to help transnational teams become virtual teams—stretched across space, time, and organizational boundaries and held together by an ever-increasing array of interactive technologies (Lipnack & Stamps, 1997). Virtual teams are already commonplace, and more will appear in the years ahead. These teams need all of the training and support required by co-located teams. In addition, however, they will look to the HR group for particular help in using multi-site management methods such as computer-based decision-support systems, management information systems, and planning and collaboration techniques. In large multinational firms where the HR group is itself a transnational team, it can serve as a model for virtual teams by being an adept user of appropriate management approaches.

Recommendation 5: Reevaluate the Career Development System

A company can operate many transnational teams successfully if it has a large pool of individuals whose work backgrounds include international experience. Because of cost reasons, however, most multinational companies in recent years have cut back substantially in their use of expatriates, the primary vehicle for obtaining international experience. As companies search for other means of leveraging international business knowledge and experience, the career aspirations and paths for many individuals who are interested in working on transnational teams will be affected.

Given the conditions in today's international business environment, it seems likely that multinational firms will emphasize three main alternatives to expatriation: (1) more frequent short-term international assignments that do not involve high relocation costs, (2) more emphasis on the selection of new employees who already have some international experience, and (3) larger amounts of outsourcing and heavier use of contingent workers. All of these potential moves have implications for the HR function. For example, if more managers and technical specialists are involved in short-term assignments, this creates a clear need for a worldwide staffing network and database as well as training that helps new team members to integrate and contribute quickly. More emphasis on the selection system also will require the HR group to determine the key international experience criteria associated with transnational team effectiveness. Lastly, outsourcing can only be cost effective if HR performs solid evaluations of the companies and workforces in the areas where the work is to be done.

Conclusion

Creating high-performing transnational teams is a complex and difficult endeavor. It requires much more than mere team training and education. Team development involves staffing, team composition and roles, performance appraisal and rewards, and career planning—the full complement of HR services. To achieve its potential, a transnational team also must integrate its activities with the company's business strategies.

The HR function within some multinational firms is already in a good position to support transnational team development. It has both the expertise and influence to help teams make a larger contribution to company success. In other multinational companies, the HR function has much work to do before it can fully support the efforts of transnational teams. Drawing from our study findings, we offer these latter companies a framework for thinking about the key HR issues of transnational teams and some broad recommendations for expanding the HR function's role in their development. With a clear agenda in hand, HR professionals can have a significant impact on the accomplishment of their company's international business objectives.

References

Adler, N. J., & Bartholomew, S. (1992). Managing globally competent people. *Academy of Management Executive, 6*(3), 52-65.

Bartlett, C. A., & Ghoshal, S. (1989). *Managing across borders: The transnational solution.* Cambridge, MA: Harvard Business School Press.

Gross, Steven E. (1995). Unleash the power of teams with tailored pay. *Journal of Compensation and Benefits, 11*(1), July/Aug., 27-31.

Gross, Steven E. (1997). When jobs become team roles, what do you pay for? *Compensation and Benefits Review, 29*(1), Jan./Feb., 48-51.

Kanter, R. M. (1983). *Change masters.* New York: Simon & Schuster.

Lipnack, J., & Stamps, J. (1997). *Virtual teams.* New York: John Wiley & Sons.

Nonaka, I. (1991). The knowledge-creating company. *Harvard Business Review, 69*(6), Nov.-Dec., 96-104.

Nonaka, I., & Takeuchi, H. (1995). *The knowledge-creating company: How Japanese companies create the dynamics of innovation.* New York: Oxford University Press.

Ohmae, K. (1985). *Triad power.* New York: Free Press.

Pascale, R. T. (1990). *Managing on the edge.* New York: Simon & Schuster.

Shaw, D. G., & Schneier, C. E. (1995). Team measurement and rewards: How some companies are getting it right. *Human Resource Planning, 18*(3), 34-49.

Snell, S. A., Pedigo, P., & Krawiec, G. M. (1995). Managing the impact of information technology on human resource management. In G. R. Ferris (Ed.), *Handbook of Human Resources* (pp. 159-174). Oxford, England: Blackwell Publishers.

Snow, C. C., & Snell, S. A. (1993). Staffing as strategy. In N. Schmitt & W. C. Borman (Eds.), *Personnel Selection in Organizations* (pp. 448-478). San Francisco, Jossey-Bass.

Snow, C. C., Snell, S. A., Canney Davison, S., & Hambrick, D. C. (1996). Use transnational teams to globalize your company. *Organizational Dynamics*, Spring, 50-67.

Endnote

1. This paper is based on research funded by the International Consortium for Executive Development Research. The authors gratefully acknowledge ICEDR's support.

How to Implement Total Quality Management in Strong Cultures: Alignment or Saturation?

Case 7.1
Asbjorn Osland

General Description

LITEP, Inc. is a family controlled U.S. based multinational corporation with very extensive production operations in Latin America that produce LITEP for industrialized markets, mainly North America and Europe. The company is one of the four major players in the industry. Several production divisions are located in the Central American country of Morazan. Each employs approximately 5,500 employees of whom around 500 are salaried; the rest are union members. LITEP, Inc. is the largest private employer in the country. During the 1980s the only areas of the country that developed economically, in real terms, were those located around the production divisions. LITEP, Inc. pays close to twenty million dollars each year in export and payroll taxes to the government of Morazan, a large contribution to the economy. LITEP is a labor intensive tropical export product.

The divisions are economies of scale operations. They are focused on exported volume of high quality LITEP. Quality is vital to the customer and volume is the key to lowering costs and increasing efficiency and productivity. This tension between a strategic emphasis on low-cost, commodity-like production versus maintaining market share through the sale of high quality LITEP is resolved through high volume production to dilute costs.

Historically the company provided hospitals, schools, public utilities, recreational facilities, airports, roads, and other such components of a community's infrastructure. However, the move to withdraw from the provision of infrastructure began more than 20 years ago and has continued. LITEP, Inc. has been attempting to confine itself to the production

Source: Asbjorn Osland. "How To Implement Total Quality Management in Strong Cultures: Alignment or Saturation?" Reprinted by permission of the author.

of high quality LITEP and interact with the surrounding community as a production partner rather than a paternalistic total institution. However, the village-like social environments around the divisions continue to be relatively closed, comparable to those found in old logging or mining communities throughout the world. The distinction between one's work and social roles are blurred in such company towns; one's status in the community reflects one's position in the company. The company is very figural in the gestalt of workers' lives.

Adoption of Total Quality Management within LITEP, Inc. ————

Throughout the 80s and 90s a number of different measures had been taken by LITEP, Inc. to improve quality, including the following: (1) a quality coordinator was named for the region to provide consultation to troubled areas and diffuse innovations to production operations, (2) quality bonuses were awarded to reward production, engineering, and shipping personnel for desirable quality outcomes in the market, (3) quality control and production personnel were periodically rotated from the Tropics to the North American and European markets, and (4) management had been incrementally improving the processing, packaging, and shipping processes.

Still, a more comprehensive approach to quality was sought. The director of organizational development and the vice president for engineering and quality had both come to LITEP, Inc. from a major food and beverage producer that had implemented a total quality management (TQM) program. They proposed this program to the CEO of LITEP, Inc. who supported it at the corporate level.

Playa Negra, a 65 year old production division, was one of the first sites. The TQM kick-off began there in late 1991. Bocagrande, a division with a full century of history, followed in March 1992. The objectives of the training programs administered in both sites were similar, in that they were developed by the organizational development section at headquarters. The objectives were as follows: (1) become familiar with the basic elements of total quality and understand what total quality can do for the company, (2) understand the key roles in implementing the transformation to total quality and how to work within a TQM culture, and (3) learn the basic steps in beginning a total quality program. The training seminars were to build enthusiasm for the TQM process.

The transition from traditional quality inspection of the final product to continuous improvement of work processes, a critical aspect of TQM, involved the following changes: (1) include the customers, mainly internal as these were production operations, in the analysis and revision of work processes; (2) focus on the prevention of quality problems rather than inspection; (3) manage the process rather than results—managers were to work with subordinates in problem solving rather than simply revising results for variances from targets; (4) encourage employees to participate rather than waiting to be told what to do; and (5) provide tools to teams of subordinates who would analyze problem related data using simple statistical tools such as Pareto charts, "fishbone" or cause-effect diagrams, control charts, histograms, and flow charts. The culmination of the process was their presentations to managers committed to listening rather than deciding based upon some data and too much intuition, as had previously been the case. This organizational learning was to foster greater customer satisfaction in the market.

In Playa Negra, in addition to the introductory seminars given by the TQM coordinator, dozens of employees attended workshops conducted by external consultants. Topics covered included facilitation skills, leadership in participative workplaces, and statistical process control.

In Bocagrande, seminars were conducted for 140 lower level salaried employees but with the departure of the human resources manager, the seminars stopped. The regional TQM consultant and the organization development consultant from the U.S. headquarters continued to support the quality council in Bocagrande. The Bocagrande council wanted internal facilitators to be trained to lead the training effort.

The TQM program is just beginning in San Juan, another old established production division of LITEP, Inc., to which Bernal Flores has just been assigned to the position of general manager (GM). We will now become eavesdropping flies on the wall of the San Juan LITEP employee club bar.

San Juan _____

Bernal Flore's wife was gone for a few days—visiting her mother in the capital—and since Bernal hated eating alone, he sat munching his sandwich in the bar. He had just been transferred back to the Tropics after a six month consultation assignment as assistant to the quality manager in Northern Europe. He had been assigned back to his native country of Morazan in Central America. Bernal was familiar with San Juan; he spent his first 14 years there. His father had been the production manager. At age 14 Bernal went off to school in the U.S. and continued through college. He even did a stint in the U.S. Marine Corps. His father had retired at the time he went to boarding school but maintained contact with his former colleagues and in 1978 helped steer Bernal into the company after he finished his military service. In the company Bernal rose through the ranks in production in various countries and after 10 years became the production manager of the largest division in the company. He served in that slot from 1988 to 1992. He also had done a two-year rotation as the regional quality manager immediately before that from 1985-87.

Bernal felt qualified to handle the GM's job in spite of the ever-present problems. Like his old boss said, "Stop bitching about problems. If there weren't any, you wouldn't have a job." He knew he would face many dilemmas; for example he had to cut costs at a time when his workers were feeling the pinch of inflation. He knew that the people in headquarters were skilled professionals and astute business people but he felt they sometimes lacked understanding of the strong cultural bonds that held the production divisions together and kept commitment so high—much higher than in the U.S. People here spoke of the company as though it were one's fatherland.

He also knew he would face a great deal of upheaval as Morazan was enduring the growing pains of the political transition from a military dictatorship to a democracy. Another source of uncertainty was the devaluation. The international financial community had forced the country to float the peso. It was now officially valued at six to the dollar whereas months before it had been artificially pegged at two to one. The financial people at headquarters were ecstatic as the dollar costs had dropped dramatically; salaries to his 5,500 workers were all paid in local currency. However, Bernal knew the union would be knocking on his door very soon, given the dramatic erosion in local buying power. The company also wanted to purchase some land from the new government. The old government had adopted a very nationalistic line and refused to sell to foreign multinationals. These issues made his job exciting and he looked forward to each day. His current problem was trying to figure out what strategy to follow in implementing TQM.

The regional TQM consultant, a fellow Latino, accompanied by the American organization development consultant from headquarters, left yesterday after spending several days introducing TQM to his senior staff. These two consultants were advocating that he proceed with an alignment strategy in introducing TQM. In their report the consultants described the alignment strategy in the following terms: "Alignment refers to getting the key stakeholders to buy in before it is diffused to the lower level employees. The fundamental assumption is that department heads need to be convinced of the merits of TQM before pushing it down the hierarchy. Otherwise they will thwart the efforts of their subordinates. If we frustrate the initial efforts of the subordinates, TQM will develop a bad name and fail."

Bernal continued reading the consultants' comments. "Therefore, we want to spend 12 months preparing the foundation for TQM at the senior levels before we begin a massive training effort to diffuse the TQM message to the lower levels. The time will give the senior managers an opportunity to assimilate the new way of thinking. They need time to adjust as they are the most turf conscious of anyone within the hierarchy; they have the most to lose in yielding position power to participation. What we propose is the following: (1) participative leadership training courses for senior managers lasting four days; (2) facilitator training of one week for those middle managers and technicians chosen to eventually deliver the courses to lower level employees; (3) monthly seminars and workshops for the quality council, mainly made up of department heads; (4) name a department head as the part-time TQM coordinator; and (5) implement several quality action teams to work on priority items identified by the quality council. Only after the above is completed should training by facilitators be pushed down to lower levels.

"The regional TQM consultant will consult to the department head you name as TQM coordinator and will visit San Juan monthly. Headquarters will develop training materials for his review to make them culturally appropriate. The above approach has been used successfully in Bocagrande and we recommend it."

Bernal felt that this plan sounded reasonable. Until last night, he would have gone ahead with it. Yesterday afternoon he played a quick round of golf with Francisco, the newly assigned materials manager who, coincidentally, had been the TQM coordinator at Playa Negra, before coming to Bocagrande. Bernal beat him by three strokes but then as GM one is never sure if one wins or is allowed to win. Their subsequent conversation made Bernal wonder how to proceed with TQM implementation in San Juan.

Bernal accompanied Francisco to the club bar for a few beers as payment for the loss. On the sidewalk leading to the bar, Bernal glanced around him at the very large trees, planted close to a century ago. The huge trees, draped with Spanish moss, provided a comfortable canopy that protected them from the tropical sun—like their traditions had protected them from some of the more trendy innovations headquarters had foisted on them in the past. They entered the bar. Francisco saw his wife and excused himself saying he would be back shortly.

Bernal looked around the bar and thought of how things don't change. He felt more like a businessman now than the historical archetype of the tough man conquering the wilderness—the legendary strongman of LITEP lore. Yet on the wall of the bar, a black and white photo of a former American GM, who later became the regional VP, continued to be displayed. It was turning yellow and curling at the edges. The photo showed a man wearing two six-shooters sitting on a mule. "Such memorabilia keeps the men proud," thought Bernal. He also recalled the incident where this same GM had been rather high handed with a merchant friend of his father. The merchant had bought the first car owned by a "civilian" (i.e., non-company) in San Juan. When it was delivered on the company train, the GM in the photo had initially refused to allow it to be unloaded saying he hadn't given his authorization. Bernal flashed back to the image of the GM mentioned above. He remembered him as a portly warm man who liked his whiskey, got on well with the politicians, and who threw great Christmas parties for the children of the employees and workers. Bernal also knew that he could be tough as well.

While absorbed in his thoughts, a few subcontractors, made wealthy through their exclusive contracts with the company, entered. They had both been long term company employees who had resigned to be established in business by the company, a safe way for the company to appease the government and increase the politically required local ownership of production. One of them, a large gregarious fellow named Churrasco, was carrying a large fish by the tail. He was affectionately called "Churrasco" because he had been burned as a child and a scar covered one cheek. The name (Spanish for "broiled steak") acknowledged the scar by naming it, thereby ignoring it physically and ironically eliminating the stigma. Churrasco raised the fish with a forward motion of his arm and flopped it down on the bar. A crowd gathered around to admire his catch. "Where did you catch it?" someone asked.

"Just a few hundred yards off the coast, past the point by the mouth of the river," responded Churrasco. Several men in the group gathered around the fish, mumbled a few complimentary comments and returned to playing dominoes.

Bernal turned to Churrasco and asked, "What's the real story?"

Churrasco smiled and admitted, "I bought it from a fisherman after I returned empty handed again from a whole day of fishing. Next weekend let's watch how many boats congregate in the spot where I said I caught the fish!" Bernal smiled and shook his head.

Then the two, Churrasco and his companion, began to chide Bernal about his boat breaking down—again. Bernal's recreational boating was seemingly cursed with maintenance problems. Like everything the GM did, his mechanical difficulties were also publicly discussed. "How could you let that happen to you. That wouldn't have happened to a gringo," Churrasco teased. Pointing to the former GM in the photograph, Churrasco continued, "The old man had a boat called 'Solo Mio' (only mine). Nobody touched this boat except to keep it ready for his personal and exclusive use. That was how real GMs should behave."

Now a millionaire due to his subcontracting with the company, Churrasco was a timekeeper, one of the lowest non-union positions, when Bernal was a child. Bernal had many fond memories of Churrasco's antics. Churrasco's attention was then diverted by some former colleagues who walked in. Bernal turned and watched the show he put on for his friends. He was regaling them about how he had joined a political party composed only of rich people. He was planning on befriending the next president and felt that this party was his "ticket." The former leader of the party he previously supported was now behind bars so he had to choose another.

Churrasco changed direction like a billiard ball in his conversations. He next launched into a loud diatribe against the owners of the company and the new TQM program that he swore never to use on his production unit, the most productive in the area. He turned to Bernal and began, "They want us to fire ten hourly workers right after they give themselves huge bonuses in a year when they lost money. And now they speak of TQM." Then with a soft tone laced with false lament, he continued, "I guess it's understandable that the company wants to modernize. However, while there are a large number of administrators of the old school, the change should be slow and we should part with a smile and leave the worst of times to the best prepared."

By "best prepared" he meant professionally educated; he had risen through the ranks. The "worst of times" referred to the then looming financial crisis; the stock price had fallen to one fifth its highest value in a two year-period.

Churrasco continued, "I've seen it four times. Every time they take over they make some money for a time and then run the company into the ground. What we need is someone who is from the divisions." He meant the only people one could trust were those who had been socialized within the company. Churrasco felt that one could not simply respond to short-term financial indicators. One needed to be committed to the way of life of the divisions.

Churrasco represented the type of employee who had built the company. In LITEP, Inc. there are professional engineers, accountants, and some college educated production specialists at various levels of the hierarchy, including those of the department heads and GM. However, most supervisors and some department heads, Churrasco's last position with the company, are not college graduates but rather hard working people who had been socialized within the company during their lengthy tenures—20 years was not uncommon—with the company. Metaphorically, one could say the production, transportation, exportation, and other employees directly involved with LITEP comprised an "army of enlisted men." They were committed, loyal, and obedient members of a highly structured hierarchy and were generally not professionals. Based on their skill, hard work, and political ability (in the organizational sense), some made it to the upper levels of the hierarchy but remained relatively insular in their views due to a lack of professional association outside the company.

Bernal was aware of the importance of this socialization and his understanding of traditional factors such as this sometimes caused him to balk at projects introduced from the outside, but TQM made sense to Bernal. His dilemma was how to sell it to the staff of San Juan. Bernal hoped the insularity of his direct reports would work to his advantage since those who achieved the rank of department head were usually very skillful at organizational politics. Their processing of information would give ample consideration to what they perceived the desires of Bernal to be, given their political sensitivity and socialization.

Bernal turned to Francisco, his golf partner, who had returned to the bar after conversing with his wife. Bernal asked Francisco about his former job as the TQM coordinator in Playa Negra. Francisco related, "The idea sounded great in the beginning and I was delighted that Armando [the GM of Playa Negra] entrusted me with the job. We had consultants come in from the outside who trained us in TQM and participative leadership. A quality council was named and we got rolling. Armando sat back and allowed the council to muddle along for almost two years. Some members of the quality council did little to support me and seemed to be more concerned about their turf than anything else. However, several of them 'bought in' and were supportive. The quality manager was probably the most cooperative even though he continued to be as autocratic as a manager from the early part of the century. Several area managers in production were also very supportive but they were kicked off the council one day when they didn't go to a meeting—the council felt it had become too large.

"Subordinates were trained, named to cross-functional teams, and we got rolling. But they couldn't get much done aside from one project where they used a PC to solve a shipping box distribution problem that had plagued us for years. Aside from that initial successful effort, things did not go well in the beginning. Department heads seemed to resist giving up any autonomy. Thus Armando decided, unilaterally, as the department heads on the quality council seemed to be incapable of supporting cross-functional teams, that we would move to departmental quality action teams. I thought this was tantamount to heresy—a regression to the old idea of quality circles. TQM was based on cross-functional teams. I thought he should have pushed harder.

"Armando said, 'I could jam this down the throats of my direct reports and force them to go along. They're good soldiers and they'll do as they're told. However, I could be transferred. The new GM will come in and could throw TQM out if there is no support from the department heads. The department heads will feel no sense of ownership of TQM if I push it too hard.'

"So we went with the departmental teams. Armando wanted everybody trained in the introduction to TQM—just like he made the whole division take effective communication seminars. It took us six months of training four days per week to get through all 500 plus salaried employees with the communication seminars. It took me nearly as long to train all the salaried personnel in the introduction to TQM. We also had several very good teams working on TQM in materials and production. Only at the very end of my stint as TQM coordinator did the council come around. They named a new president, the assistant manager, who ironically initially thought that TQM was a passing fad. He finally 'bought in' and they limited council membership to supporters."

Bernal asked Francisco, "How would you assess your contribution?"

In looking back on his two years of training and working with quality action teams, Francisco related, "I made some progress although serving in a staff coordinator role was frustrating, given the strong line orientation of Playa Negra. In the end, after the initial frustration of the cross-functional quality action teams, I grew to appreciate the disciplined commitment of Armando. He 'walked the talk' and did not allow himself to get seduced into the traditional authoritarian role of the GM vis-à-vis the quality council. Armando believed he had to refrain from imposing his will on the council. He also believed that we had to simultaneously work hard at various levels of the organization to overcome the inertia. He insisted we train, train, and train some more. He also pushed me to get the quality action teams up to speed. Eventually, we found that the best way to work with the teams was to assign a quality problem to a key operations manager. He or she was then empowered to choose the members of his or her team. These people met and analyzed specific problems. Significant improvements in quality outcomes resulted. The feedback from the market has been very positive."

However, Bernal knew from attending regional meetings that concurrently with the TQM implementation, a very significant change in shipping had also occurred. Nevertheless, he understood that the participants in Playa Negra felt positive about the process and that desirable outcomes had been achieved, regardless of the causation. Bernal knew that the GM of Playa Negra, Armando, was sold on TQM. In the Fall of 1993, after several years experience with TQM, Armando enthusiastically endorsed TQM at a regional meeting. Bernal knew that Armando was political and astute. He wouldn't stand up in front of his superiors and support a "lemon." Bernal could also see how Armando had restrained himself from intervening too quickly when the council and the cross-functional teams did not generate the desired results. Instead he focused on massive training and prodding quality action teams, through Francisco, to generate results.

Francisco continued with his monologue, "In retrospect, I called this the 'saturation strategy'—we saturated the lower levels of the organization with TQM thinking and methodology, the fuel of participation! At some point, the saturated underbelly of the organization spontaneously ignited and burned the derrieres of our turf conscious department heads. Only then did we begin the transition from management by results to participative management where teams, led by supervisors, worked together to solve problems."

Bernal listened intently. This was very much at odds with what the regional TQM and the American organization development consultants were recommending. Both told him that Francisco had done a good job but had been reluctant to receive their support. Apparently Francisco wanted to do it alone. Francisco continued, "I'm glad to be in a line position again. Staff jobs—like my TQM coordinator job—are terrible in production divisions. All the power is with the line managers. I guess I'd appreciate focusing on inventories rather than TQM."

Bernal walked with Francisco to his pick-up. Francisco told Bernal to look at the results of the employee opinion survey that an external researcher doing a dissertation, with the assistance of Francisco, had completed. They had contrasted TQM participants with non-participants in Bocagrande where the alignment strategy had been pursued and TQM participants and non-participants in Playa Negra where Francisco had retroactively named their ad hoc heretical approach the "saturation strategy." Bernal took the results with him to bed and promptly dozed off.

As the steam whistle blew the next morning, Bernal was reminded of his childhood. He found it amusing that the company still woke people up but he found it absolutely hysterical that the whistle went off two more times; the next blast was to remind people that it was time to head for work and the last indicated it was time to be at work. Such throwbacks to the paternalistic era of his father were reminders that the company had been a total institution. He was surprised to hear that they still made caskets for anyone who died. This he would have to cut out as it was embarrassingly paternalistic. But he thought it quaint that the company still had a key to a gate on one of the international crossings so that the LITEP trains could pass at night. What were not so quaint were the 1,200 illegal hook-ups to the company's electrical power distribution grid—and one of these powered five of Churrasco's freezers! The company would have to continue generating electrical power for the community in addition to its operations but he'd have to talk to Churrasco soon and also get his staff to educate the others over the next few years. The company could no longer afford to present itself as a cornucopia.

Bernal left home and went to the airport to await the seven seater company plane. He was flying out that day to the capital where the three GMs would make their budget presentations to the regional VP and his finance director.

Hotel Bar in Capital City

Bernal landed at the airport and was whisked off to the budget meeting. After 12 hours of managerial "interrogation" by the regional VP, with additional clarifications sought from his finance director, the three GMs were pleased to retire to the hotel bar. Morazan produced one of those great tropical beers that was light but satisfying on a hot day. Bernal always enjoyed seeing his colleagues, Armando, the GM of Playa Negra, and Karl, the GM of Bocagrande. He had worked with them for years and had spent many hours laughing at their stories in hotel bars just like this one. They were all well into their forties now and felt foolish hanging out at discos at night. Thus, talking about TQM seemed like the appropriate alternative for middle-aged, either slightly balding or portly executives.

Bernal had once worked for Armando and knew him well. Armando was from Playa Negra. His father had been associated with the company as a professional service provider but had died in a small plane he piloted when Armando was a boy. The legend, still told by the company pilots, was that his body had been ravaged by sharks close to the wharf where LITEP was still loaded. Armando was educated in the U.S. and completed a degree in the sciences. He began working for the company in a research capacity but quickly moved to production where he has spent his entire career of more than 25 years. Bernal admired him for his highly developed political skills and charismatic leadership qualities. Bernal thought to himself, "He may be balding but he's still huge and very fit." Armando struck an imposing image as he spoke with a thundering voice and walked about with large arms waving while addressing meeting participants. He combined an engaging manner with total authority; Bernal knew one could speak frankly with him and challenge him with well founded arguments yet one remained totally cognizant of his authority.

Armando's former controller once told Bernal, "He does half the work of a controller in that he makes people follow the rules and is very cost conscious."

Like most LITEP GM's, Armando's talents were in production, including labor relations, and general leadership. He more or less left the support functions (e.g., the controller's office and materials) alone as long as policy was followed, budgets respected, and targets met. He handled the career development and succession planning for key employees himself and tended to plan and then offer options to subordinates, rather than conversing with them to ask how they saw their careers developing.

Bernal recalled how he once overheard the American HR manager suggest to Armando that he alleviate his housing shortage by moving a clerk, the wife of a transferred professional, who was still living in a large house, previously suitable for her family but too large for one person, to an apartment. Bernal remembered Armando's response, "You don't understand anything. She couldn't show her face and I have to get along with her." Later Bernal tried to explain to the American HR manager how touchy such matters were to the tight, village-like cultures created in the company towns, like San Juan, Playa Negra, and Bocagrande.

Karl, the GM of Bocagrande, held similar convictions about the importance of the strong culture within LITEP divisions. For example, an assistant controller candidate proposed by the American HR manager was rejected by Karl because the candidate's wife would not join him. This concern for the individual's family situation struck the HR manager as unusual. Bernal explained to him that what Karl seemed to have been trying to emphasize was the requisite familial commitment to the LITEP culture. It was not just a job but a lifestyle.

Bernal had trained with Karl. Karl carried a European Community passport, held a green card from the U.S., was born in the Caribbean, grew up in Central America, and was educated in Europe as a military officer and served several years in a police action in an area beset with ethnic violence. His father worked for the company and he arranged for Karl to be employed by LITEP, Inc. Karl worked his way up through the ranks of production within LITEP, Inc. and after 15 years or so with the company became a GM.

Bernal enjoyed listening to Karl's tales of crises. Karl said the only remaining disaster that had not affected Bocagrande during his tenure was a volcanic eruption. During a crisis Karl led the charge and worked day and night to get production back on track. Bernal recalled that Karl was described fondly by his subordinates with the English word "pusher," meaning one who gets things done.

Karl was also much involved in the social life of the division. His avid support of a soccer tournament left him with a severed Achilles tendon. This slowed him down for a time but he managed to hobble around the production areas on his crutches. Karl spent most of his free time with company associates.

Karl got himself into trouble from time to time with headquarters as he was more assertive than political. He was very concerned about the impact of cost cutting on the quality of life for workers. However, given the economic crisis facing the Central American LITEP industry as a whole, due to trade barriers in Europe, Karl understood the need to continue reducing costs.

Bernal began the conversation with a question, "Now that you both have gone through this TQM process, what advice would you have for me as I'm just beginning?"

Karl spoke of how difficult it was to be neutral within the quality council. "Even if I ask a question, the others are trying to guess what's on my mind." He continued by saying that he felt they had made a mistake by not working more with the department heads from the start: "We had a quality council that included several people from lower levels of the organization. Some of them objected to some of the ideas I proposed so I loaded the council with people from my office or department or section heads I could count on. The quality council became a manager's council."

Bernal knew of Karl's approach with the council. A former colleague was still in Bocagrande and told him that the council was filled with people interested in doing what the GM wanted because they were from his office and dependent on him or others who were perceived as ingra-tiating (the Spanish term literally translates as "sock sucker"). The council was not even relatively autonomous, as the TQM dogma prescribed.

Karl had openly stated that he didn't like it when the council objected to the projects he proposed. To keep the quality process mov-ing in the direction he wanted, he chose to force the above change. To Karl, the TQM process was not a philosophy but rather a cafeteria of interventions from which he could select the appetizing portions (e.g., project teams, involvement of lower level employees, etc.) and pass over the less appealing items (e.g. an autonomous council).

Armando listened and indirectly countered, always sensitive to the personal dignity of those with whom he was conversing: "One has little to fear from participation. If you know the business, you can help people problem solve in a manner that enables them to develop. By giving people authority they will come to you and seek your input. This gives me more power than I would have if I simply told a passive work group what to do. I want proactive people seeking answers. However, if I already know the answer I don't ask them—I tell them what I want done."

Armando paused, took a sip from his glass, and continued. "I guess what I like most is getting a large organization to do what I want it to do. I see TQM as a chance to try something new."

Bernal thought to himself as Armando and Karl chatted with a visitor from corporate who also attended the meeting earlier that day. Bernal understood that at the conceptual level, leadership was the driving force behind the company's quality system but he didn't know whether to push for alignment, like Karl had done, to get the quality council to fall in line with how Karl perceived TQM methodology or saturate the lower levels like Armando had done in Playa Negra while waiting for the department heads in the quality council to gradually change and adopt the TQM approach.

Bernal knew that he had to be careful in pushing to overcome resistance to change with an innovation like TQM. He realized that organizational inertia was a concern but he also saw this as the continuity of a strong culture. It allowed the organization to keep on doing what it had been doing. His dilemma was to strike the appropriate balance that permitted innovation while preserving enough continuity to maintain an organizational foundation that members found motivating and meaningful. The intervention was not an isolated event; TQM was embedded in the context of a strong culture.

Armando and Karl returned to the table with Bernal and continued their discussion of TQM. Armando said, "I adopted a low key approach with the council rather than pushing it, in contrast to my standard aggressive approach to project implementation. The risk of dictating policy for the quality council was that the TQM effort could fizzle should my eventual successor not support the process. I sat and watched the council accomplish little for nearly two years. The council members eventually became frustrated with their lack of accomplishment. They changed the leadership and reduced the membership. However, when they appeared to end yet another inconclusive meeting in late July 1993, I finally intervened and ordered them to continue their meeting until they developed some direction. I didn't give them a specific direction but ordered them to find one."

As Armando and Karl excused themselves, Bernal was left with his question, "Should I pursue the alignment strategy and get the council on board first or the saturation strategy where I would work simultaneously at various levels—slowly with the council, massive training, and quality action teams?" Bernal opened his brief case and turned to the data that Francisco had given him from the surveys.

Organizational Transformation at Skoda in the Czech Republic: An HRM Perspective

Case 7.2
Dianne J. Cyr

Company Background

The story of Skoda is one of struggle and success. Skoda enjoys a century-long history of motor vehicle manufacturing in a small town in the Czech Republic, about sixty kilometers outside the thriving cultural and tourist center of Prague. Skoda has been a nucleus of manufacturing since the Austro-Hungarian empire. Despite early achievements, times became much harder during the former socialist era. The physical plant fell into disrepair and quality declined. However, this tale is one of transformation, and Skoda has once again become very successful in a joint venture partnership with the large German manufacturer Volkswagen. At the outset Volkswagen owned 31% of the venture, although this has since changed and the Germans now have 70% equity ownership of Skoda. At the most senior level the venture is run by a five person Board of Directors, comprised of two Czechs, (the Chairman and VP of Human Resources) and three Germans. This ratio remains stable since the joint venture start-up.

The joint venture was formalized in 1991 and immediately Volkswagen contributed financially to upgrade the facility, and began to infuse modern technology into the operation. The change envisioned for the plant was expansive, and international competition in the automotive industry meant Skoda had no choice other than to very quickly become altered from its earlier state. As outlined in the 1996

Source: Dianne J. Cyr. "Organizational Transformation at Skoda in the Czech Republic: An HRM Perspective, Executive Summary." This case was investigated and written by Dr. Dianne J. Cyr, Adjunct Professor, Simon Fraser University, Canada. It is intended to be used as a basis for class discussion rather than to illustrate effective or ineffective handling of an administrative situation. The author would like to gratefully acknowledge support from INSEAD, the Social Sciences and Humanities Research Council of Canada, the Czech Management Center, Canadian Consortium of Management School Members, and CIDA for this project. © Czech Management Center, 1997.

company annual report "characteristics of the Transformation process, from 1991 to the present" include:

- **Quality**—Quality has been enhanced to meet international standards.

- **Research and Development**—Research and development is emphasized to create new models for the changing market. To this end original models were replaced by a new family sedan in 1994 and a more luxurious model in 1996.

- **Supplier Industry**—Assistance is given to local suppliers to upgrade to international standards in order that quality parts and components can be purchased by Skoda while maintaining advantageous local cost levels.

- **Organization**—Modernization of production processes has been central to the transformation, and building a new state of the art integrated production plant was recently completed. A cornerstone of these new initiatives is close communication between customers, the workforce, management and suppliers. Qualification (ISO 9000) and involvement of Skoda employees is a deliberate part of the change process.

- **Production and Sales**—Production and sales have surged. After the model change in 1994 volume has steadily increased from 174,000 cars in 1994 to 208,000 cars (1995), 263,000 (1996), to a planned volume of at least 340,000 cars in 1997.

- **Workforce**—the workforce has been streamlined, and remuneration is above the average for the Czech industry. In return the expectation by management is for above-average efficiency. Training provided to employees is in alignment with international standards.

- **Profit/Loss**—After initial losses in the start-up period of the venture Skoda achieved break-even in 1996. In acknowledgment of the visible results of the restructuring process Skoda was elected Best Company of the Year in the Czech Republic in 1996. With a 1996 turnover of CZK 59 billion, Skoda is the second largest enterprise in the Czech Republic producing 5.5% of total Czech exports. Sales to customers increased by 24% in 1996 compared to the previous year.

Sharing Responsibility in the Joint Venture _____

From the outset, a goal of the venture was to transfer knowledge and expertise to locals from German expatriates on temporary assignment. Germans and Czechs managers were paired as part of a "tandem system" for the purpose of exchanging "know-how." In alignment with the philosophy of the VP of Human Resources at Skoda, who happened to be German, "integration not domination" of locals was important. After six years of operations, the question is how effective was this system?

The reviews are generally positive. The locals have learned much, and overall Czechs now have greater operational responsibility in the venture as the number of German expatriates continues to decrease.

According to a Czech manager:

> The phase of the know-how transfer is finished so the number of expatriates is decreasing, and before 1999 there should be a small group of foreign managers here who are focused on strategic issues. As Volkswagen has the majority of shares in Skoda the Volkswagen group will maintain decision power. So now we are defining the strategic positions which in the individual branches will always be occupied by foreign employees. Up to now we had a tandem system of pairing German and Czech managers, and now the Czech managers have been taking the responsibility of double functions.

A German manager remarks that in the early stages of the JV the tandem concept was both necessary and useful, and knowledge has transferred to locals. He mentions the senior HR manager as a case in point. In 1993 it was the German expatriate who had primary control in the human resources area, but that has currently shifted to the Czech manager holding the position. In turn there remains a German expatriate in the HR area who assists Czech managers in more of a support capacity, and who "works on special projects and makes the link back to the mother company."

Although a stated goal for the venture is sharing responsibility effectively between Germans and Czechs, this same German manager mentions how difficult the achievement of this aim is in reality. Instead, one person tends to take the lead. He recounts:

> We have Czech, German and international managers. The responsibility isn't shared. Some positions are either Czech or German. Nowadays there are more European managers with knowledge in Czech language... and the number of young Czechs with experience is Europe is also growing. That means today you have a mixture of Czechs and foreign managers. In the first years we had more tandem pairing. From my point of view, I think the tandem concept normally always needs one leader. You can't share the leadership. That's a problem with the tandem concept. But you can have a leader, and you can have a deputy. For example, you can say the foreign service manager is the boss for two years, and maybe during the last year that would change and the national manager would take over the responsibility, so that in the last year the foreign manager is like a consultant.

Further, both Czechs and Germans agree the effectiveness of the tandem system is related to the personalities of individual managers, and to the level of knowledge possessed by the German expatriate. A German manager remarks: "This [system] depends on the personal characteristics of the two managers. If this human chemistry works, then everything is O.K. There are cases where cooperation has not been the best. But generally we are abandoning this system, so Czech managers have responsibility of individual posts." Alternately, a Czech manager describes: "Not all experts coming from Volkswagen were the best. Sometimes Volkswagen interests prevailed to the interests of Skoda." A different Czech manager notes: "For some of the foreign managers they are at a mid-point here and they don't have the motivation to do their best."

As Volkswagen has the management contract for the venture, German expatriates tend to retain control of strategic positions, although Czech managers now have more responsibility than in the early stages of the venture. Based on results from a questionnaire survey[1] foreign managers are seen as having a similar level of involvement in the venture (3.5) as 4 years ago, although Czech managers appear to have gained in their level of responsibility (2.8 now compared to 2.4 in 1993).

As in early stages of the venture, Czech managers feel they have much to offer, especially considering the long history of automobile manufacturing in the original plant. However, some Czech managers mentioned their opinions were rarely solicited by their German colleagues. This sentiment is expressed by a Czech manager in the following way:

> They [Germans] come and they go, and change everything. They don't ask what was here before. How did you do things? What did you do well? What can we improve? And if they come and change everything, it's like saying it was done bad or wrong, and I am here to do it right. And after awhile people say it was already here. You should have asked.

Cultural/Sensitivity Issues _____

Many employees mentioned that cooperation between Germans and Czechs was more dependent on individual personalities than to differences in national culture. In part this has been due to a transition of the German managers who now are present at Skoda. As described by one Czech manager, in the early days of the joint venture the German expatriates did not try to understand the systems and culture of the Czech Republic (e.g. legal systems, historical issues, cultural differences). But over time, this has changed and the second "wave" of German expatriates are more sensitive to the Czech cultural condition. This appears to have led to cultural changes which have been generally perceived by both locals and foreigners as successful. It is interesting to note that on the questionnaire survey cultural differences are perceived as moderately respected, and this level of respect is slightly higher than four years ago (3.0 in 1997 vs. 2.8 in 1993).

A Czech manager describes the most difficult part of the change process is for Germans and Czechs to gain an understanding of each other. He adds:

> It's not just the languages, but also what the other party expected. Initially, there have been problems. For example, the Czech

party wanted to do something but the Germans didn't understand what it was. In the national character, the Czechs are more action-oriented and less theoretical, whereas the Germans are more concept-oriented and prepare things systematically. The initial problems were to make sure there are different ways to reach the same target.

Tied to national culture, but more in the realm of corporate values, workers indicated they still need to better understand the concept of competitiveness. However many of the concerns expressed by workers in 1993 (e.g. fear to take responsibility) appear to have moderated. A Czech manager summed the current situation in this way:

As you know we had a different system here for 40 years and it wasn't very good. And Czech people know how to work— they are smart, creative, and flexible. But we have forgotten what is the 'hard' work in work. So the point is to motivate people at work. And Czech people are a bit skeptical, as many things were presented in the last 30 years—and they [the Czech people] think they are right. So the point is how to motivate the people.

On the German side, the corporate culture emphasizes efficiency and organization. Under German guidance various changes have unfolded in this realm. A German expatriate outlines:

I think Skoda is maybe one of the best organized companies in the Czech Republic. We have the best trained people, and the best training department and working clothes for people ... New clothes, and they [the workers] should work with white hand gloves, and you can see many clean people and clean floors. And what you can hear from the people is we pay more money than in other companies, but you have to do much more.

And from the Czech perspective:

In terms of the Czech and German cultures, we both belong to European countries. Of course a lot of changes occurred when the Germans came. You can observe the tidy surroundings and also the culture of the labour relations and talks [with union representatives]. We [Czechs] had to learn how important it was to behave the Western way in commercial negotiations. And of course the bilingual environment brought some initial problems because not always could the interpreter be present. But continuously we reached some mutual understanding. The coming of the foreign colleagues changed the behavior of the Czech colleagues.

In addition, the Volkswagen culture focuses on discipline in order to achieve maximum productivity and quality. Although there is a requirement for changes in the former work ethic in the Czech plant, some managers question the intensity of the work required. A Czech manager notes: "Nowadays they [the workers] must work with great effort all eight hours. In the summer it is hot and very exhausting for the workers."

In another way, change has created a culture more focused on materialism. A senior Czech manager laments that some workers have lost an innate sense of loyalty to Skoda, and instead "adore money." He states "The pride of being a Skoda member has been lost. Only the old Skoda employees keep this patriotism, and the sons and daughters of older workers." This same manager notes that in order to get ahead, some employees have become "workaholics" who have become "Skoda persons and sacrifice everything for the company."

Communication

Over and over, employees mention communication has improved over the years, but is not without problems. Some managers state expats are in the company on temporary assignment and then leave, creating gaps in the information flow with no system in place to alleviate this situation. Alternately, communication in the company and between the company and the parent firm is enhanced through email, Intranet and the company newsletter. As such, information was described by several people as "cascading" from one level to the other. There are also two or three special events per year for management in order for everyone to better get to know one another. The improvements in communication are supported by the questionnaire results. Employees indicated they have enough information to do their jobs, and enough information about company policies.

One area which still requires improvement is how information is shared between mid-level managers and workers. A German manager mentioned that for some managers "to know something is power." He adds: "Especially for older managers they must learn a well informed worker is a better worker." This is a change in mind set from the older system.

Problems in communication due to language differences have significantly declined (3.9 in 1997 vs. 3.4 in 1993). Regardless, some employees feel communication issues still exist due to lack of a common language. A German manager mentions: "If you would like a career in this group, then you should learn German." Another Czech manager suggested both Germans and Czechs should use English as a common language, as the Czechs would not be at disadvantage as much linguistically. Czech managers found the language barrier prevented them from always expressing themselves, which was falsely perceived by German colleagues as a lack of opinion or participation on a topic.

Further, Czechs were concerned that a differing opinion might signal a lack of loyalty to the company. One Czech manager notes he was more open about communicating in the earlier stages of the venture, but found it important to be careful about what he said in order that information would not be used against him.

Staffing

The ranks of Skoda's employees are swelling and there are currently about 18,000 employees in the company. This is 1,000 more people than in 1993. Of the current total, 11,500 workers are on the production lines, and 6,500 are white collar workers. In addition to local workers, there are 75 expatriates at Skoda, down slightly from the number of expatriates in 1993.

The unemployment rate in the local region remains very low (4.5% in the Czech Republic) and 1% near Skoda. In real numbers this represents only 849 unemployed people locally. This poses a serious recruitment problem at the plant as the intention is to increase the overall number of staff by 5,000 over the next two years (recruiting about 250-300 new employees each month). In fact, the few number of eligible workers in the local area has necessitated hiring a large number of immigrant workers, many from Poland, to work on contract in the plant.

New managers are generally selected from young (usually under 35) top Czech graduates. They enter a selection center, undergo a battery of selection tests, and the successful candidates enter the selection pool. For older candidates who may fit the criteria for senior management, there is a more intensive selection process. The potential candidate requires appropriate professional and technical qualifications, and must have excellent recommendations from superiors. Senior managers are also recruited through headhunters and personnel agencies. All employees have contracts as required by the Labor Code, including part-time workers. Contracts specify the type of work, place of work, the day work begins, salary, and benefits. German workers likewise have contracts to specify benefits, rewards, etcetera.

The current system of selection and retention of managers is different from that in the past. In the early days of the venture managers who had a position in the plant before the joint venture started were allowed to remain, but with a requirement that they adapt to new procedures and circumstances. This group of managers were given the opportunity to prove themselves, otherwise they were slowly replaced. Much of the assessment of original managers took place in the period from 1994-95, and only those who were successful are still at Skoda. One Czech manager described this process: "Perhaps there were some similar characteristics among the managers who were replaced—they were not able to reach the targets. But they were not always the guilty ones...In a lot of cases the conditions for how to meet the target were not clear. So a lot of managers left by their own request or were replaced."

Absenteeism is problematic, and overall is averaged at 5.7% per month although this figure is much higher in certain areas of the plant (e.g. 13% in production). Despite these levels, absenteeism is reported to be low compared to other firms in the Czech Republic. The majority of illness occurs in the younger employee group (18 to 25 year olds), and amongst those 46 to 55 years of age. Absenteeism is also high in the lower paying jobs. The problem of absenteeism is exacerbated by a government policy which pays workers a maximum of 250 CZK in insurance benefits per day for illness, and which is sufficiently attractive to keep some workers off the job in order to get that rate—especially when it coincides with the weekend.

Training

The number of trainers is about 40, down from 60 in 1993. Much of the initial training identified for the transformation of Skoda has already been accomplished in the areas on technical, professional and management education. The current emphasis is on preparing employees to work effectively in the new production system, and training young Czech managers to eventually take the lead in the venture. According to the questionnaire survey, respondents were satisfied with training (more than in 1993), and most felt they had enough training for their jobs (3.7) and were learning new skills on the job (4.1).

With the introduction of the new production system, training is currently focused on informing employees how to best operate the system. The training emphasis is initially targeted to foremen and production coordinators. Two day programs emphasize key elements of the new system, teamwork, and total defect prevention management. As part of a "cascading system" foremen and coordinators are then responsible for providing on-the-job training to production workers. More senior supervisors also participate in more intense training averaging six days per year. According to some managers, there is currently a lack of training at the supervisory level, especially for future qualified leaders who must better understand that modern management means being more a coach, and less a disciplinarian.

A new training program for "high potential" future managers was started in 1995. Young Czechs are groomed for management positions in a program which combines formal training with job rotation to various posts to gain practical experience. This system parallels one in place at Volkswagen. Candidates for the program are selected in an assessment center, and approximately 30 are selected annually. As part of the assessment, potential managers must prove proficiency in either German or English. In addition, they undergo psychological testing, and a test of managerial knowledge (including language, mathematics, and intelligence). Group simulations are conducted, there is an individual presentation, and each candidate is interviewed as to why he or she wants to work at Skoda. Once selected as a high performer, the trainee is able to choose from a variety of departments where he or she would like to work. Training lasts approximately one year during which the trainee rotates to at least three job positions. During this time these "high potentials" attend specialized seminars on topics such as the theory of management, team building, or language training. In addition, each trainee completes a project on a top of interest.

Language training continues to be available in both English and German. As one Czech manager observes "An obligatory part of training for Germans should be to learn the Czech language." She adds: "When proving he or she is able to learn Czech, this is appreciated a lot and this [German] person is immediately accepted by this community. Basically this refers to line workers who appreciate a lot when a top manager is able to speak in the mother tongue."

Much of the training for managers and "high potentials" is outsourced to universities or institutions such as the Czech Management Center near Prague. Many Czechs have already received training in Germany, and have access to Volkswagen's global training program. Although training is available, one German manager suggests that to a degree training suffers due to financial restraint. He adds: "We need to invest more in the people in the next years."

Performance Review and Rewards

In December 1993 a new performance review system was implemented. By 1995, the review system was no longer used with production workers and was modified for managers. For the managerial group the process was simplified from a lengthy MBO type of system to a single page, and is completed once per year. The focus of the review is on performance of goals, innovation, entrepreneurship, ability to lead, personal skills, and job skills. Employees are asked to outline their future career goals. Review forms are signed by both the individual assessed and the supervisor. Different from earlier times, greater emphasis is placed on a coaching role between a supervisor and subordinate. German managers are reviewed by the headquarters staff.

Also in 1993, a new salary system was created using job descriptions based on models adapted from Volkswagen. There existed 12 salary groups. The system was modified in 1996 to include a bonus for production workers and other "normal workers" which was calculated based on (1) attendance, (2) an across the board amount based on quality and amount of production in the company, (3) a special bonus given from the managers on an annual basis and tied to performance (which can be up to 12% of total gross salary), and (4) overtime. Bonuses for managers are based on performance and are 2.5 times the base salary on average. Previously there was little difference between senior, mid-level and junior managers, but this is currently being addressed. In the case of both production workers and managers, the introduction of a performance bonus appears to have a positive effect in motivating workers. Certainly, the addition of rewards for performance responds to an earlier survey (1993) in which all workers strongly indicated their desire for a bonus system.

Although the basic reward system has been structured in a similar way throughout the life of the joint venture, there is currently greater emphasis by managers on rewards aimed to increase productivity and reduce absenteeism. As a result, managers have more discretion as to how they can reward employees based on performance criteria. In the last six months as part of a pilot project, the company has been experimenting with team rewards in keeping with the team philosophy encouraged at the plant.

Salaries have increased in order to attract new applicants to Skoda and to retain current employees. Overall, rewards are approximately twice the amount of 1993, and average a fixed rate of about 14,000 CZK per month over all employees. A Czech manager described the escalation in salaries is due to (1) an increase in sales and profitability at Skoda, (2) proximity to Prague and generally higher wage scales as a result, and (3) competition with other international companies to attract the best people. In addition, the fixed rate is supplemented by overtime pay. On the questionnaire survey, respondents indicated greater levels of satisfaction with salaries than in 1993 (3.0 in 1997 vs. 2.7 in 1993), although overall satisfaction with rewards remains moderate. Of interest, respondents indicate they feel salaries are now more based on ability and performance than previously (2.8 in 1997, 2.3 in 1993).

Beginning May 1997 a new and interesting development is evolving for Skoda managers on foreign assignment to other Volkswagen operations. If, for example, a Czech manager were to go on extended assignment to Spain, his or her salary would be adapted to the local conditions related to wages and cost of living indices. As such, Czech workers will receive the same compensation, benefits, and foreign service leave entitlements as other Volkswagen managers at a given location. In the past, Czech managers felt the system was inequitable, as German managers came to Skoda and continued to receive much higher salaries than local managers. Under the present system, German managers on assignment to the plant will experience decreased salaries, although the standard of living is guaranteed to remain the same while on foreign assignment.

In addition to monetary rewards, some degree of recognition is provided to workers. Apart from praise, managers can get company "souvenirs" from the warehouse and distribute to workers. For managers and other specialists, cars are provided from the company as a form of "perk." Opportunities are offered to young and aspiring Czech managers to train and work in the Volkswagen group worldwide, and this is viewed as a form of recognition for high performance.

Transforming for the Future

To date there has been much progress. Based on the thoughts of a German expatriate at Skoda, he states: "From the Volkswagen side it (the joint venture) was the correct decision. And for the Czech side, Skoda is the most important company in this country and 50% of the product is for export and this is very important for this country. Further, the brand name is much better than a few years ago."

Important in the change process has been the ability to change the minds of the people in order that they think more strategically and competitively to keep pace with global requirements. Much has been accomplished in this area. A German expatriate comments:

> Today there is a mixture between the two worlds [e.g. Communist and post-Communist]. So there are some parts of the old system that are still alive. The people need to be given the chance to grow in their own way. In five years, the average young Czech in management will be between 35 or 40, and they will be able to run the company. The most important question is will we give these young people the responsibility.

Alternately, a foreign expatriate outlines the ability for the locals to take greater responsibility is part of a spiraling process based on support and increased confidence. In his words: "People are afraid to take responsibility and it's not the people, but the system that was here before. It was dangerous because if one person had responsibility it was his fault if mistakes were made. On the other side, there is a great ability to accomplish things. What is missing is self-confidence." When further queried as to how confidence can be built, this same manager replied: "My proposal is that we must work together as a team. So everyone needs the opportunity to make suggestions, and everyone must be an equal in discussions. It took a long time for people to believe this. But it is necessary if we are to build confidence between managers and their people" Patience and tolerance for making some mistakes is imperative to this endeavor.

Also important is respect for the culture and achievements of the locals. A young Czech manager recounts:

> There is a tradition in the people here. And the manager needs to work of creativity. From the German side there is good organization. It is their mentality. And if we give each other room to work then we can compete with the world.

Endnote

1. The same 37-item questionnaire survey was distributed to a random sample of respondents at multiple levels of the company in 1993 and again in 1997. In the most recent sample 251 questionnaires were completed. Questionnaire items addressed issues related to strategy, culture, and HRM. Participants responded to each item on a 5-point Likert scale from 1 (low agreement) to 5 (high agreement). Refer to Appendix 1 for a complete reporting of the results for the 1993 and 1997 samples. In addition, the table displays results from the questionnaire for company samples in Poland and Hungary which can be compared to the Czech sample.

Appendix 1. Cross-Country Comparisons

Item	Poland		Czech Republic		Hungary	
	1993	1997	1993	1997	1993	1997
1. Local/foreign managers have similar goals	3.6	3.6	3.4	3.4	4.0	3.5
2. Foreign mgrs have primary responsibilities	3.9	3.8	3.6	3.5	3.0	2.6
3. Local mgrs have primary responsibilities	2.5	2.7	2.4	2.8	2.8	3.3
4. Better understanding of competitiveness	4.4	4.3	3.2	3.3	3.6	3.6
5. Company has long-term benefits	4.1	4.1	4.6	4.5	4.5	4.4
6. More concern for production than people	4.0	4.1	3.6	3.5	2.8	3.1
7. More emphasis on individuals than groups	3.6	3.2	3.2	3.0	2.8	2.6
8. Change is positive	3.6	3.8	3.8	3.6	4.1	3.4
9. Important to avoid mistakes	4.8	4.6	4.4	4.3	4.5	4.1
10. Control on the job	3.1	3.2	3.5	3.7	3.6	3.6
11. More concern for present than future	2.9	2.9	3.0	3.1	2.5	3.0
12. Need to go through supervisor	3.6	3.7	3.3	3.6	3.2	2.8
13. Good personal connections are important	4.1	4.2	4.2	4.1	4.0	4.0
14. Cultural differences are respected	3.6	3.5	2.8	3.0	4.4	4.3
15. Employees selected for technical skills	3.5	3.2	3.2	3.4	3.5	3.5
16. Fair chance for promotion	2.3	2.3	2.6	2.8	3.2	3.0
17. Concern about layoffs	4.2	3.8	2.8	2.9	1.9	2.0
18. Employees feel loyal	3.9	3.8	3.4	3.4	3.9	3.8
19. Have information to do the job	3.8	4.2	2.7	3.2	3.9	3.8
20. Have information about company policies	2.1	2.5	2.4	2.9	2.8	3.1
21. Managers listen to employees' ideas	2.7	2.8	2.6	2.8	3.7	3.3
22. Managers don't always share information	3.3	3.3	3.4	3.2	2.6	2.9
23. Communication problems due to language	3.4	2.8	3.9	3.4	2.9	2.3
24. Enough training for the job	4.2	4.2	3.4	3.7	4.0	3.8
25. Learning new skills on the job	4.1	3.8	4.0	4.1	4.1	4.0
26. Learning new skills in class	2.9	3.3	3.0	3.3	3.0	3.1
27. Sufficient training	3.0	3.3	2.9	3.2	3.7	3.0
28. Satisfied with salary	2.5	2.9	2.7	3.0	3.2	2.9
29. Salary based on ability/performance	2.8	3.1	2.3	2.8	3.4	3.0
30. Salaries depend on who you know	2.8	2.6	2.6	2.7	1.8	1.8
31. Should be bonuses	4.5	4.5	4.5	4.5	3.8	4.2
32. Enough company benefits	2.9	3.1	3.1	3.6	3.7	3.9
33. Rewards are fairly distributed	2.4	2.7	2.4	2.7	3.3	2.7
34. Understand job goals	4.3	4.3	4.3	4.3	4.5	4.2
35. Know what to do to get rewards	3.3	3.4	3.8	3.9	3.4	2.9
36. Receive feedback for performance	2.8	3.1	3.3	3.5	3.5	3.5
37. Future of company is positive	3.9	4.0	4.3	4.3	4.7	4.5

Sample

	FR/PL		GR/CZ		SW/HR	
	1993	**1997**	**1993**	**1997**	**1993**	**1997**
Number	284	237	189	251	120	88
Male	71%	86%	84%	65.7%	72%	62.4%
Average age	35.8	36.0	42.6	39.8	35.2	32.5
Years in company	8.4	9.8	19.3	16.8	2.3	3.4

HUMAN RESOURCE ISSUES IN INTERNATIONAL JOINT VENTURES

The Formation of an International Joint Venture: Marley Automotive Components

Reading 8.1
Randall Schuler
Peter Dowling
Helen De Cieri

In Maidstone and Lenham in Kent, and Bitton near Bristol, England, is the operation of Marley Automotive Components Ltd. In the late 1980s it entered into an international joint venture (IJV) with the US company, Davidson Instrument Panel-Textron of Portland, New Hampshire. An earlier article by the authors examined Davidson's perception of the IJV, including their reasons for the joint venture, the critical human resource issues they were facing and how they were planning to deal with several unfolding human resource issues. This article now portrays Marley's perceptions of the same issues. The purpose in using this case study to describe IJV issues is to offer information on human resource issues to readers considering an IJV as the route to globalization. Hopefully, this information will help companies to increase the chances of a successful IJV experience.

Because of increasing globalization and its attendant costs and risks, many firms are entering into international joint ventures (IJV). Although joint venture formation is proving to be an integral part of business strategy for multinational firms such as Glaxo, Grandmet, IDV, and Thorn-EMI, entering and operating them successfully is by no means a sure thing (Main, 1990). Research indicates that the failure rate of IJVs is between 50 and 70 per cent (Harrigan, 1986; Levine and Byrne, 1986). Some of the most significant barriers to success involve people issues—issues relating to international human resource (HR) management. Consequently, these issues are the focus of this article.

Source: Randall Schuler, et al. "The Formation of an International Joint Venture: Marley Automotive Components" by Randall Schuler, Peter Dowling and Helen De Cieri. *European Management Journal,* Vol 10, No 3, September 1992, pp. 304-309. Used by permission of the authors.

Specifically, this article describes many of the international human resource issues associated with forming and managing IJVs. It does this through an intensive case study of an IJV in its early stages of formation and development. It addresses critical start-up issues from the view of the British partner, Marley Automotive Components Ltd. These are the same issues addressed from the view of the US partner, Davidson Instrument Panel reported in an earlier article (Schuler et al., 1991). Given that the IJV has developed since our first article, this article also addressed several other unfolding HR issues identified in that first article.

The Parents: Marley PLC and Davidson-Textron_____

Marley PLC

Marley is one of the leading manufacturers of building materials in the United Kingdom and has similar operations in many countries throughout the world. Marley's products extend from roof tiles, roofing felt, bricks, aerated concrete blocks and concrete paving to pvc flooring, plastic plumbing and drainage goods. Marley also derives part of its profit stream from property transactions by exploiting the value of sites surplus to operational requirements. In addition, Marley is recognized and well-established as a major supplier of quality components to the European motor industry. The particular division that deals with the motor industry is called Marley Automotive Components Ltd. This division employs approximately 1,400 workers out of a total Marley workforce of 11,000.

The nature of the automobile industry has changed drastically during the past 20 years, and the effects have been felt by all auto makers. As the automobile industry has become globalized, success has turned on quality products that fit right and perform smoothly and reliably. But while quality has become a major concern to the auto industry so have cost and innovation. New products and new technology are vital to success, but without cost reduction new products cannot be offered at competitive prices.

The characteristics of the auto industry are, of course, reflected in all companies supplying it. Marley Automotive Components Ltd. is no exception. To succeed, they must adapt to the demands of the new environment. Doing so will bring rewards such as market share and even more important perhaps, an extensive, cooperative relationship with major automobile manufacturers.

Essentially gone are the days of the multiple bidding system, where winning meant delivering at the lowest cost, with no assurance that the next year will be the same. Today, the automobile companies use sole sourcing for many of their supply needs. Accompanying this is a greater sense of shared destiny and mutual cooperation:

> The component suppliers are having to change with the times. The multinational car manufacturers increasingly want to deal

with multinational suppliers, giving them responsibility for the design and development of sub-assemblies in return for single supplier status (*Financial Times*, 1 March, 1990, p. 8).

Thus, it is not unusual to have design engineers from suppliers doing full engineering design of the components they will supply to their customers.

An important aspect of the new cooperative, sole sourcing arrangement adopted by automotive markers is the willingness to conceptualize and form longer-term relationships. For Marley Automotive this meant the opportunity to establish an international joint venture. In the summer of 1989, Marley agreed to establish an IJV to supply instrumentation panels to a Ford Motor Company plant in Belgium starting in 1993. They chose as their partner for this venture the US firm, Davidson Instrument Panel.

Davidson Instrument Panel

Davidson Instrument Panel is one of 33 divisions of Textron, an $8 billion conglomerate headquartered in Providence, Rhode Island. Davidson Instrument Panel and its two sister divisions, Interior Trim and Exterior Trim, make up Davidson-Textron. All three divisions are component suppliers to the automotive OEMs (original equipment manufacturers). Davidson-Textron is the largest independent supplier of instrument panels for the US automobile industry.

Originally begun as a maker of rubber products for drug sundries in Boston in the early 1850s, Davidson moved its operations to Dover, New Hampshire, in the 1950s. Its headquarters now are located in Portsmouth. A staff in Portsmouth of fewer than 50 oversees the operations of two manufacturing plants, one in Port Hope, Ontario, and the second in Farmington, New Hampshire. The 1000-person operation in Port Hope is unionized, and the 900-person operation in Farmington is not.

The IJV: Davidson-Marley BV _____

By way of review and update, Davidson Marley BV, the name of the IJV, is a 50-50 partnership between a US firm and a British firm. It is located in Born, The Netherlands. Situated near Maastricht Airport, the location was selected because it is near its primary customer, Ford. Proximity to Ford was important, because the company required its sole source suppliers to meet its just-in-time inventory requirements. The location was also selected because of favorable accommodation by the local authorities and the fact that it is close to the Netherlands Car BV production plant (a potential customer). The facility is being constructed so that expansion can be easily incorporated and approved by the local council. The plot of land is sufficient for expanding by a factor of at least four.

There were several reasons for the IJV between Marley and Davidson. First, Ford Europe asked Marley (who had been supplying its needs for the Sierra line in the UK) to supply its needs for its world car to be produced at the Genk plant. Consistent with the world car concept, however, Ford Europe wanted worldwide sourcing. A joint arrangement with Davidson Instrument Panel made a great deal of sense. It filled the worldwide sourcing requirement and it was a company Marley knew and trusted. Marley had been a licensee of the Davidson technology for instrument panel skins and the foam injected to give it shape and substance.

This long-term arrangement had given each other time to get acquainted and learn about the other's management style and philosophy. The compatibility in their styles provided confidence that an IJV might be successful. They were also compatible in what they could contribute to an IJV. Marley had marketing skills, knowledge of the European market and the ability to oversee construction of the new facility and provide administrative support. Davidson had the technological expertise and complementary administrative skills.

Another reason for the IJV was to share the risk of a new venture. While Davidson wanted to get into Europe and Marley wanted to expand its automotive business, there was no guarantee that Ford would be successful in Genk. Marley's primary businesses are construction-related. To reduce its dependence on the construction cycle, it had decided to expand its automotive business. However, Marley did not want to do this without minimizing the risks. The sharing of rewards was worth the sharing of the risks with a long-term business associate.

A joint venture with Davidson at a greenfield site in Born also offered Marley the opportunity to introduce a new management style and structure. During the 1980s more than 100 Japanese firms have established operations in the UK. In doing so they have implemented their human resource practices of workforce flexibility, minimal job classifications and use of teams with a total quality strategy. Though practically unknown in British industry, including Marley's other operations, these practices seemed to be working well. These practices are described in extensive detail by Peter Wickens, the Personnel Director of Nissan Motor Manufacturing UK (1988). The opening of the greenfield site in Holland, and also the creation of another joint venture in the UK with a Japanese company, offered Marley the opportunity to learn more about the Japanese policies and practices and possibly extend them to other operations. This desire was certainly consistent with Davidson's methods of operations, since it has implemented many similar practices in its plants in New Hampshire and Ontario, Canada.

In deciding upon the IJV arrangement, Marley and Davidson had a choice here: they could either build a greenfield site or take over a brownfield site. While the brownfield option is faster and avoids all the aspects of construction, the two partners thought it was more important to build to their own specifications. It was critical to both that everything be designed to be compatible with a teamwork, flexible job assignment-orientation.

A final reason for the IJV location was the potential it offered for competitive flexibility. Locating the plant in Born places it near Audi, Volkswagen, Mercedes and Volvo operations. While these companies often supply their own instrument panel needs, Davidson-Marley BV could potentially offer a better product at a lower price. To help develop this potential, Marley established a small marketing company.

While not meant to be exhaustive, these were the major reasons for the IJV from Marley's perspective. They are certainly consistent with Davidson's motives and with those suggested in the literature (Datta, 1989; O'Reilly, 1988; Gomes-Casseres, 1989; Harrigan, 1987a; 1987b; Shenkar & Zeira, 1987; and Main, 1990). Nonetheless, this does not ensure success nor diminish the risk of failure.

Reducing the Risk of IJV Failure _____

Managing IVJs can be very difficult. The difficulties, and thus the reasons for failure, include:

- Partners cannot get along;

- Managers from disparate partners with the venture cannot later work together;

- Managers within the venture cannot work with the owners' managers;

- Partners simply renege on their promises;

- The markets disappear; and

- The technology involved does not prove to be as good as expected.

Both Marley and Davidson think that they can overcome the odds of failure in their IJV. Much of their confidence rests on the fact that they know what it takes for a good partnership to survive and flourish (as illustrated in Exhibit 1).

Despite the many positive features of the Davidson Marley BV IJV, there is a consensus that the very nature of joint ventures contributes to their failure—they are a difficult and complex form of enterprise (see Shenkar & Zeira, 1987b; Main, 1990; Brown, 1990). As described in our earlier article (Schuler *et al.*, 1991), the critical issues which IJVs face revolve around *control, conflict, goals, management styles* and *degrees of commitment.*

Who controls the IJV—from its inception through to the early critical staffing appointments—can lead to failure. The Davidson Marley BV IJV has a board of directors with two members from each parent. All major decisions are to be decided by this board. Whenever local

---

Exhibit 1. What is a good partnership?

---

1. Shared objectives (a joint mission)

2. Co-operation as equals (based on parity, no domination or paternalism)

3. Openness, mutual trust and respect of others as persons and their values, capabilities and objective understanding of their intentions

4. Building on each other's strengths

5. Reducing each other's limitations

6. Each has something the other needs (resources, access, etc.)

7. Pooled capabilities and resources permit taking on tasks neither could do alone

8. Two-way flow of communication (breakthrough of communication blocks)

9. Mutually perceived benefits

10. Commitment of leadership and middle management to find some shared values, without ignoring the fact that they are not identical

11. Co-learning flexibility

12. A win-win orientation

Dutch management or their staff encounter key issues, the board decides. To ensure that IJV development and production deadlines are not compromised, Ford requested that Marley retains one less share in voting on major issues until production starts in January 1993. This arrangement would help address any critical issues of control and conflict if such were to arise during the start-up period.

Other positive factors included joint selection of the general manager and human resource manager, and an arrangement whereby Marley supplies the local marketing knowledge and makes the arrangements with the local suppliers, while Davidson supplies the technology and the financial systems (including the financial controller for the operation). These arrangements thus remove many potential disagreements and conflict and form part of the IJV agreement. Thus, errors of omission are avoided by extensive discussion of issues and formal recording of all agreements.

In terms of goals, management styles, and the degrees of commitment, Marley believes that is has compatibility with Davidson on these three issues. It is important that firms interested in IJVs give serious consideration to the degree of cultural homogeneity. This is particularly the case with regard to North American and Western European countries which share a similar Western cultural heritage. These cultural similarities tend to obscure difficulties. Such obfuscation is all the more likely when the differences are subtle and not obvious during initial negotiations. For example, when dealing with Asian firms, because Western managers *expect* differences, they will be more sensitive to cultural diversity. When dealing with firms which are perceived to be culturally similar, managers will be less sensitive to differences which while being subtle are still important (Brown, 1990).

As a case in point, there are important differences in language usage between English-speaking countries: Americans tend to use the term 'plant' to refer to the building in which operations take place and machinery is located, while the British use the term 'plant' to include machinery. 'Natural wastage' means voluntary resignations and retirements in the UK but something rather different in the USA! It is important that both parties to a joint venture clearly define key terms early on in discussions to minimize the problems attendant with miscommunication. This suggests that firms entering into a joint venture establish a glossary of terms regardless of whether they think they have a common language. Where differences in definition exist or in broader matters such as what selection methods to use, it seems advisable to go with local custom.

Thus while it appears as if Marley and Davidson are on top of the critical issues that can give rise to IJV failure, they still face many human resource issues that are beginning to unfold in the evolution of their partnership. These issues include the assignment of managers, transferability of human resource, managers' time-spending patterns, human resource competency, management loyalty issues, and career benefits and planning (Shenkar and Zeira, 1990). The following sections show Marley's views on these issues.

The Assignment of Managers _____

The general manager for the IJV has been selected. He was selected by both parent firms from three Dutch finalists identified by the search firm Spencer Stuart. The process was done in a way consistent with European practices. Marley recognized the importance of adjusting to the employment practices of the host country rather than just imposing parent country practices on the otherwise local (i.e. European) operations. While there is considerable divergence with regard to the development of relatively high minimum standards of employment conditions as a consequence of European integration, there is divergence in terms of both specific human resource practices and implementation of HR policies. For example in comparing the UK and France on the use of reference checking:

> ...UK firms are still using references as proof of someone's fitness to do the job. More than 70 per cent of UK firms use them compared with just over 11 per cent in France (*Personnel Today*, February 5, 1991, p. 5).

In selecting the general manager for the IJV, Marley gave significant weight to experience in manufacturing. Interviews were used to evaluate the degree of fit with the operating style and management philosophy of the parents. Employment tests such as aptitude and personality were not used.

Once appointed, the general manager participated in selection of the IJV's human resource manager in February 1991, using a similar process. These managerial appointments coincided with the final property purchase and ground breaking for the new plant.

While both of these individuals could have been brought in even earlier to achieve greater feelings of ownership and involvement, this was not done due to cost considerations and the need to carry out these initial recruitment assignments jointly. However, this group has now been given the freedom to select, appraise, train and compensate the 250—300 employees who will be hired by August 1992. The current, relatively high unemployment rate in this region (around 8–9%) should ensure a sufficiently large applicant pool. Although Marley had nominal lead responsibility for initial recruitment, the strategy for recruitment, training and compensation was developed jointly by senior human resource executives at Davidson and Marley agreed upon by the Davidson Marley board.

Transferability of Human Resources

Both parent firms are committed to the success of the IJV and are transferring experienced employees to the IJV. Even with the most systematic planning process, unforeseen events will occur. For example, the engineers assigned to design the plant were supplied by Davidson. While highly qualified, they calculated measurements in feet, inches and US gallons. The local Dutch engineers had to convert these non-metric measures when letting contracts to Dutch firms and gaining approval from local authorities. Since Davidson will supply the financial controller, US accounting procedures will be used and a corresponding set of accounts will need to be established to meet Dutch auditing requirements.

Allocation of Start-Up Responsibilities

Initially, IJV staff will need to focus on immediate, short-term issues in establishing the joint venture. The IJV staff are not under pressure to produce an immediate profit since the business plan allows for a reasonable time horizon to achieve profitability. Marley has established a sales and marketing group in The Netherlands for the IJV to look for new contracts. Both parent firms will offer training programs and support, including technical training for key employees who will in turn train the other employees. Start-up costs will be shared by both parent companies.

Conflicts of Loyalty

For both parent companies, the work of the planning teams is essentially completed. The financial controller (a US expatriate) is scheduled for a three-year term after which a local will take over. The staff will then be entirely Davidson-Marley BV, and conflicts of loyalty to either parent company should be minimal—particularly as the venture grows and achieves success, according to Mr. Chris Ellis, Business Development Director of Marley.

The general manager and his key staff members are employed by Davidson-Marley BV and as such have career paths anchored within the joint venture rather than the parent companies.

Progress to Date

To date, the two parent companies of Davidson-Marley BV appear to be benefitting from a careful planning process and a longer-term perspective with regard to profitability. Although trial production runs are just beginning at the time of writing, there have been no obvious signs of partnership dissolution or disaster. Nonetheless both parents are monitoring their relationship, checking for danger signals of a deteriorating relationship including the existence of statements such as those listed in Exhibit 2.

Conclusion

For an increasing number of firms in many countries, 'going international' is no longer a choice—regardless of firm size or product. The world has become far too interconnected for many products and services to be offered within a domestic market context only. Faced with this reality, many firms in the advanced western economies are seeking to establish their presence in the world market. For example, many large British firms such as BP, ICI and Marks and Spencer have already developed a global presence. These firms entered the global arena relatively early via the direct establishment of their own subsidiaries. This mode of internationalization is less of an option for many firms today because the establishment of subsidiaries requires substantial commitment of time and resources.

Thus, many firms are considering entry into global markets via various forms of cooperative venture and strategic partnerships. One form of partnership currently receiving considerable attention is the international joint venture (IJV). The IJV is popular because both parties are able to share risk exposure (i.e. political and financial risk) and to optimize

---

Exhibit 2. Danger signs in partnerships

---

1. 'They have long term objectives, we don't.'

2. 'They get more than they give.'

3. 'Their strengths (market access) were overestimated.'

4. 'We don't communicate any more; we just let them do their thing.'

5. 'They compete with us more than they co-operate.'

6. 'They (or we) haven't assigned the best people.'

7. 'Our combined decision making is too slow, compared to competition.'

8. 'We are not organized to learn from them, (or our people don't feel they can learn much from them) but they absorb everything we give them.'

9. 'We have agreed that the best way to work is not to work together.'

10. 'They are developing organizational capabilities which will make us unnecessary in the future.'

11. 'Whoever cooked up this deal was pretty naive.'

12. 'Our commitment to the success to this partnership is declining rapidly: mutual trust and respect are minimal.'

---

the strengths of each partner (e.g. cash, experience, or technology). There are, however, many potential problems involved with the establishment of an IJV. These problems are often related to the quality of the relationship between the two partners, and the human resource decisions which flow from the relationship. We believe the Davidson-Marley BV case is a good example of an IJV where both partners have worked hard to develop the initial relationship and have taken human resource issues into consideration throughout the planning process. While this does not guarantee that Davidson-Marley BV will be successful, we believe the behaviors of the parent firms to date are good predictors for the future success of the IJV.

References

Bere, J. F. Global Partnering: Making A Good Match, *Directors and Boards*, 1987, 11 (2), 16.

Berlew, F. K. The Joint Venture—A Way into Foreign Markets, *Harvard Business Review* (July-August 1984), 48-54.

Brown, R. J. Mixed Marriages, *International Management* (December 1990), 84.

Brown, R. J. Testing Times, *Personnel Today* (February 5, 1991), 5.

Datta, D. K. International Joint Ventures: A Framework for Analysis, *Journal of General Management*, 1989, 14 (2), 78-91.

Drucker, P. F. *The New Realities* (New York: Harper & Row, 1989).

Gomes-Casseres, B. Joint Venture Instability: Is it a Problem? *Columbia Journal of World Business*, 1987, 22 (2), 97-102.

——Joint Ventures in the Face of Global Competition, *Sloan Management Review*, Spring 1989, 17-25.

Harrigan, K. R. *Managing For Joint Venture Success* (Boston, MA: Lexington Books, 1986).

——Managing Joint Ventures, *Management Review*, 1987a, 76 (2), 24-42.

——Strategic Alliances: Their New Role in Global Competition, *Columbia Journal of World Business*, 1987b, 22 (2), 67-69.

Hyatt, J. The Partnership Route, *INC.* (December 1988), 145-148.

Lasserre, P. Strategic Assessment of International Partnership in Asian Countries, *Asia Pacific Journal of Management*, September 1983, 72-78.

Levine, J. B. and Byrne, J. A. Corporate Odd Couples, *Business Week* (July 21, 1986), 100-105.

Lorange, P. Human Resource Management in Multinational Co-operative Ventures, *Human Resource Management*, 1986, 25, 133-148.

Lyles, M. A. Common Mistakes of Joint Venture Experienced Firms, *Columbia Journal of World Business*, 1987, 22 (2), 79-85.

Main, J. Making Global Alliance Work, *Fortune* (December 17, 1990), 121-126.

Morris, D. and Hergert, M. Trends in International Collaborative Agreements, *Columbia Journal of World Business*, 1987, 22 (2), 15-21.

Ohmae, K. The Global Logic of Strategic Alliance, *Harvard Business Review*, March-April 1989a, 143-154.

——Managing in a Borderless World, *Harvard Business Review*, May-June 1989b, 152-161.

——Planting for a Global Harvest, *Harvard Business Review*, July-August 1989c, 136-145.

O'Reilly, A. J. F. Establishing Successful Joint Ventures in Developing Nations: A CEO's Perspective, *Columbia Journal of World Business*, 1988, 23 (1), 65-71.

Roehl, T. W. and Truitt, J. F. Stormy Open Marriages Are Better: Evidence from U.S., Japanese and French Co-operative Ventures in Commercial Aircraft, *Columbia Journal of World Business*, 1987, 22 (2), 87-95.

Schaan, J. L. How to Control a Joint Venture Even as a Minority Partner, *Journal of General Management*, 1988, 14(1), 4-16.

Schuler, R. S., Jackson, S. E., Dowling, P. J. and Welch, D. E. The Formation of an International Joint Venture: Davidson Instrument Panel, *Human Resource Planning*, Vol. 15, No. 1, 1991.

Shenkar, O. and Zeira, Y. Human Resources Management in International Joint Ventures: Direction for Research, *Academy of Management Review*, 1987a, 12 (3), 546-557.

____International Joint Ventures: Implications for Organization Development, *Personnel Review*, 1987b, 16 (1), 30-37.

____International Joint Ventures: A Tough Test for HR, *Personnel* (January 1990), 26-31.

Stewart, T. A. How to Manage in the New Era, *Fortune* (January 15, 1990), 58-72.

Thomas, T. Keeping the Friction Out of Joint Ventures, *Business Review Weekly* (January 23, 1987), 57-59.

Tichy, N. M. Setting the Global Human Resource Management Agenda for the 1990s, *Human Resource Management*, 1988, 27 (1), 1-18.

Webster, D. R. International Joint Ventures with Pacific Rim Partners, *Business Horizon*, 1989, 32 (2), 65-71.

Challenges Facing General Managers of International Joint Ventures

Reading 8.2
Colette A. Frayne
J. Michael Geringer

Introduction

Driven by the fundamental changes which have occurred during the past decade, including trends toward internationalization of markets and competition as well as the increasing cost and complexity of technological developments, joint ventures have become an important element of many firms' international strategies (Harrigan, 1988; Moxon & Geringer, 1985; Perlmutter & Heenan, 1986). These ventures involve two or more legally distinct organizations (the parents), each of which actively participates in the decision making activities of the jointly-owned entity. It is considered to be an international joint venture (IJV) when at least one parent organization is headquartered outside the venture's country of operation, or if the venture has a significant level of operations in more than one country (Geringer & Hebert, 1989).

Although the frequency and strategic importance of IJVs have increased dramatically during the late 1980s and early 1990s (Geringer & Woodcock, 1989; Harrigan, 1988; Hergert & Morris, 1988), many IJVs have failed to achieve their performance objectives due to the unique challenges associated with managing these interfirm ventures (Geringer & Hebert, 1991; Holton, 1981; Harrigan, 1986; Pucik, 1988; Shenkar & Zeira, 1987). The challenge results from the presence of two or more parent organizations, which are often competitors as well as collaborators (Geringer, 1991; Hamel, 1990). This means that the IJV general manager (IJVGM) is placed in the unenviable position of balancing the frequently divergent or even opposing motivations, operating policies and cultures of the parents, as well as addressing the competitive requirements confronting the venture itself (Buckley & Casson, 1988; Frayne & Geringer,

Source: Colette A. Frayne and J. Michael Geringer. "Challenges Facing General Managers of International Joint Ventures." Reprinted by permission of the authors.

1990a; Ganitsky & Watzke, 1990; Lynch, 1989; Sullivan & Peterson, 1982). The challenge of this task is compounded by the tendency to use these ventures in risky, uncertain settings (Anderson, 1990; Bleeke & Ernst, 1991), and by the fact that the IJVGM must operate across unfamiliar national and corporate cultures. As a result, it is understandable that a large proportion of IJV failures are attributable not to financial or technical problems, but rather to "cultural factors," such as conflicts in management styles, cultures, operational practices and degrees of control (Devlin & Bleackley, 1989; Dobkin, 1988; Ganitsky & Watzke, 1990; Geringer, 1988; Shenkar & Zeira, 1987). Indeed, these factors help explain why many IJVs begin to experience operational problems even after years of relatively stable performance.

The critical role of the IJVGM and its relationship to the venture's operations have been acknowledged in several prior studies (Bleeke & Ernst, 1991; Deloitte, Haskins & Sells, International, 1989; Geringer & Frayne, 1990; Lynch, 1989). Yet, despite the unique managerial challenges associated with this job, the academic and practitioner literatures have not focused on the role and required skills of the IJVGM. In particular, there has been essentially no discussion of variables associated with successful or unsuccessful IJVGM performance, or training programs which might enable IJVGMs to prepare for—and function better within—the complex environment of the IJV. The absence of such training programs may inhibit efforts to form IJVs which can successfully achieve the strategic objectives for which they were established.

The objective of this paper is two-fold: (1) to identify the role of the IJVGM and the key contextual issues associated with this role, and (2) to propose a comprehensive training program for developing the skills which IJVGMs require in order to function effectively within the IJV context. The next section of the paper, which discusses the IJVGM's role and contextual issues, is based on data collected in interviews with parent company executives and IJVGMs involved in forming and managing 42 developed country and 62 developing country IJVs. (Appendix A contains a summary of the methodology employed in collecting these data.) On the basis of these contextual issues, we then propose a four-part training program to prepare IJVGMs for functioning effectively within the IJV environment. This program consists of training in: (1) general contextual skills, (2) specific contextual skills, (3) interpersonal skills, and (4) self-management skills. The paper concludes with a discussion of implementation issues associated with the proposed training program.

The Role and Context of the IJVGM

Frequently, the job of the general manager (GM) has been equated with that of an organization's chief executive. Yet, the IJVGM position by its very nature is subordinate to the chief executive and represents more of a middle management type of position. As defined by Uyterhoeven (1972: p. 75), a middle-level GM is a "general manager who is responsible for a particular business unit at the intermediate level of the corporate hierarchy." The job of a middle-level GM differs significantly from top-level GM positions, and in many respects it is more difficult (Aguilar, 1988; Kotter, 1982).

The problems confronting the IJVGM have been well documented in several prior studies of joint ventures (Anderson, 1990; Geringer & Frayne, 1990; Harrigan, 1986; Janger, 1980; Lynch, 1989). The IJVGM's role typically differs from that of a GM in a subsidiary which is wholly-owned. Further, a strong argument can be made that the role of the IJVGM tends to be much more difficult than that of similar intracorporate positions, particularly due to the contextual challenges associated with the position, as will be discussed below. In fact, 88 percent of the IJVGMs and 86 percent of parent company executives participating in this study indicated that IJVGM skills were different from the general management skills required for similar positions in the parent firms' wholly-owned subsidiaries. Further, 78 percent of IJVGMs and 62 percent of parent company executives indicated that the requirements of the IJVGM position were *more* challenging than those of similar GM positions in the firms' non-joint venture businesses. None of the IJVGMs and only 4 percent of parent executives indicated that the IJVGM position was less challenging than similar non-joint venture positions.

IJVGMs are usually expatriates, especially for ventures in developing country contexts and when the venture is in an early stage of its life cycle. Although they tend to confront many of the same problems as any expatriate (Tung, 1981), there are substantive differences associated with the IJVGM position. As several of the participating executives remarked, the additional challenges of the IJVGM position are often not readily apparent, particularly for managers who have not previously been directly involved with one of these ventures. Respondents identified differences in terms of both the *degree* as well as the underlying *nature* of the challenges confronting the IJVGM. For example, role conflict, ambiguity and overload are inherent to the practice of management. However, for general managers of IJVs, the degree to which these factors are present is typically magnified (Geringer & Frayne, 1990; Lynch, 1989). Fundamental differences were also evident in terms of the nature of the challenges, including issues arising from the presence of two or more different parent organizations. Overall, the contextual challenges associated with the IJVGM's role include the following five issues: (1) the presence of multiple parent companies, (2) the existence of divided loyalties, (3) the need for operational independence despite limited preparation and support, (4) responsibility which exceeds authority, and (5) pressure for rapid action. This section addresses each of these issues individually.

1. The Presence of Multiple Parent Companies

Perhaps the most fundamentally different aspect of the IJVGM's context is the presence of two or more parent organizations which share both ownership and decision making in the IJV. The difficulties arising from multiple parents are sometimes ameliorated when one of the parents assumes a very dominant role over the venture (Deloitte, Haskins & Sells, International, 1989; Killing, 1983; Lynch, 1989). This may occur, for example, when there are highly asymmetric divisions of equity (e.g., 80/20) or when a parent assumes the role of a "sleeping" partner and therefore has essentially no active involvement in the IJV's operations. Yet, even situations such as these may eventually result in challenges for the IJVGM (Olk & Bussard, 1988). The root of the problem is that the different strategies, power bases, time perspectives, cultures and operating practices of the individual parent organizations typically result in substantive differences regarding their respective goals for the IJV as well as the means for achieving these goals (Blodgett, 1991; Ganitsky & Watzke, 1990; Geringer, 1988). Given the existence of small numbers of partner organizations and information asymmetry among these partners, there is potential for opportunistic behavior by one or more of the partners (or by the venture employees themselves) in an attempt to promote attainment of their own objectives, to the possible detriment of their partner(s). Indeed, parent company executives often disagree with the IJVGM regarding whether—or how—to clarify directions with their partner, and frequently attempt to manage the IJV as an extension of their other, wholly-owned operations. Therefore, in order for the IJV to function properly, IJVGMs must often devote substantial amounts of their time and energy toward ensuring effective coordination of and communication between these divergent partner organizations (Brown, Rugman & Verbeke, 1989; Geringer & Hebert, 1989).

The challenges of being an effective manager in such an environment may be exacerbated by the manner in which IJVGM performance is evaluated. Only 9 percent of the IJVGMs in our sample reported that their performance was evaluated by parent firms exclusively using specific performance criteria. In contrast, for 42 percent of the IJVs, the parents reportedly did not employ *any* specific performance criteria for such evaluations. These results were consistent with Janger's (1980) finding that only 22 percent of his sample ventures used formal performance reviews to evaluate joint venture staff. Based on our interview data, the IJVGMs often did not know how well they were performing, nor did they receive clear indication regarding how to effectively run the IJV. Often, they were left with inconsistent expectations regarding what behaviors were required and had to rely on their own perceptions of what performance was expected. For some, it was not until they were replaced or the venture was dissolved that they realized they were not performing up to one or both of the parent companies' standards.

2. The Existence of Divided Loyalties

Due to the complexity resulting from multiple parents, IJVGMs must usually rely on the support, cooperation, or approval of a large number of people in order to achieve their goals. Yet, this task is exacerbated by the existence of divided loyalties, both of the IJVGM and of the other parent company and IJV personnel. For example, in attempting to respond to the conflicting demands of superiors within the parent firms, the IJVGM must simultaneously manage relationships with peers within one or another of the parent firms and who control critical resources. These peers often have more direct relationships—and more clearly defined career considerations—with the parent firm's senior managers, and less incentive to cooperate with the IJVGM on issues of pooled sales forces, corporate staff assistance, R&D or manufacturing assistance, and the like. Obtaining their support for the IJV is therefore a difficult proposition.

IJVGMs may also confront divided loyalties among their subordinates in the IJV itself, including the venture's managers, technical people, and other staff and line personnel. Because of their past experience and future prospects, these employees frequently exhibit strong allegiance to one or another of the parent firms—or to the host nation itself—rather than to the IJV. This situation may be exacerbated by the tendency for expatriate personnel to be paid according to home versus host country standards, which are often significantly higher than the compensation for local personnel performing similar roles. The IJVGM must not only recognize the possible existence of these divergent loyalties, but also find a means of focusing them effectively toward attainment of the venture's objectives. Success often requires balancing and tradeoffs. Yet, in the process of attempting to satisfy the demands of one set of relationships, the IJVGM may reduce his or her effectiveness in managing another. A common response of IJVGMs is to be reactive rather than proactive, and to address issues of a short term rather than a long term nature (Schaan & Beamish, 1988), which further limits their ability to achieve a consistent behavior pattern.

This tendency toward reactive management is exemplified by the case of a recently formed joint venture involving Japanese and American partners, and in which the IJVGM was appointed by the U.S. firm (Geringer & Miller, 1992). The Japanese partner's objective was to use the IJV to establish a base for learning about the North American market, while the U.S. firm wanted to learn about their partner's production techniques, particularly the "just-in-time" kanban system. Despite these objectives, the IJVGM vetoed repeated efforts by his subordinate managers (assigned from the Japanese partner) who wanted to ensure the effective execution of the kanban system in the IJV. The Japanese managers argued that the long term benefits would justify the additional costs. Yet, the IJVGM justified his short term, cost-focused decision as being a response to continued pressure by a U.S.

appointee to the IJV's board to "get results," particularly in terms of keeping operating costs in line with the budgeted levels.

To further exacerbate such situations, the IJVGMs themselves often experience divided loyalties. In virtually every case, they are directly responsible for the performance of the IJV, and they have a fiduciary responsibility to ensure that the interests of each of the partners are protected. Yet, most IJVGMs, particularly those which are involved in the actual start-up of a venture, are appointed by and have been employed within one of the parent organizations. Their experience within that parent firm has often acculturated them to a particular way of thinking and acting, one which is peculiar to that parent organization. These values may be reinforced by the IJVGMs' personal and professional relationships within the parent as well as by their perceptions that, once the IJV posting is completed, their career path will involve a return to the parent firm. Since their position often involves postings far from parent firm headquarters, IJVGMs are more prone to being ignored and forgotten, which can be detrimental to future career development. Although extensive efforts at networking with headquarters personnel can help overcome such isolation, it is difficult to maintain and improve such critical interpersonal relationships while effectively and impartially managing the complexity of the IJV itself. Thus, the role of the IJVGM is fundamentally influenced by the potential for divided loyalties, both their own and those of individuals upon whom they are dependent.

3. Need for Operational Independence Despite Limited Preparation and Support

Despite the challenges described above, newly appointed IJVGMs typically have little in the way of guidelines or support systems to help them into their new jobs and they consequently encounter greater difficulty in being effective. For example, Kotter (1982: p. 172) found that effective GMs, "relied on more continuous, more informal, and more subtle methods to cope with their large and complex job demands." As a result, Kotter maintained that outsiders were often a risky choice for GM, regardless of their talent and track record. He argued that an outsider rarely has detailed knowledge of the business and organization, or good, solid relationships with the large number of people upon whom the GM is dependent.

Yet, by the job's very nature, the IJVGM is an outsider to at least one of the parent firms. In addition to being an outsider, factors such as geographic distance, time zone differences, staffing limitations, language differences and communication problems often make it more difficult for the IJVGM to obtain assistance. For an intracorporate position, the new GM may receive training to prepare him or her for the specific job, including lines of communication, plans for the business unit, policies, and the competitive and politico-legal environment.

However, such training is seldom available for IJVGMs, particularly in the start-up phase of a venture involving two or more parent firms which embody disparate objectives, resources and policies. Since the parent firms themselves are often unsure of the exact form the IJV will assume (Deloitte, Haskins & Sells, International, 1989; Harrigan, 1986), providing appropriate training and other support to the new GM is often not possible. The barriers to providing such support are further increased by the existence of geographic and cultural differences associated with the IJV. These differences often require adaptation of policies and procedures for the requirements of the local context, yet these changes may thereby limit the usefulness of the organization's existing support infrastructure.

Given the constraints described above, the IJVGM often must be exceedingly entrepreneurial in order for the venture—and the IJVGM—to perform effectively. Especially at the start-up phase, and given the high costs associated with using expatriate personnel, there will generally be few specialists and supporting staff in the venture for the IJVGM to rely on for assistance on difficult issues. This situation may be perpetuated, since IJVs are often much smaller scale ventures than the parent company operations in which the IJVGM worked previously. Language and cultural differences, as well as infrastructure inadequacies in many developing country contexts which limit the number of qualified indigenous middle managers, serve to further inhibit access to and the effectiveness of relying on locally available support. The absence of adequate numbers of qualified middle managers may also inhibit the IJVGM's efforts to effectively utilize standard control and feedback systems. As a result, the IJVGM is forced to either obtain the requisite skills or information through other channels, despite the barriers of geography or time zone, or to operate on the basis of incomplete information or an inadequate resource base.

4. Responsibility Which Exceeds Authority

As noted above, the nature of the IJVGM role means that this manager assumes responsibility for the functioning and performance of the venture within an exceedingly complex operational context. However, the burden of this responsibility may be further increased due to the reality of limited authority which these managers are often able to wield. Although textbooks may state unconditionally that such an imbalance is wrong, having responsibility without a commensurate level of authority is another basic facet of most IJVGM positions. Indeed, particularly given the presence of divided loyalties among venture personnel, the existence of multiple partner firms, and the limited level of contextual training provided to most IJVGMs, these managers confront pressure to relinquish authority both up and down in the hierarchy. For example, while formal controls may sometimes be relaxed and IJVGMs permitted to exercise more authority as the venture establishes a track record, it is not uncommon for each parent to attempt to exert a substantial amount of control over the IJVGM during the venture's initial stages (Schaan & Beamish, 1988). It is also common for parent firms to more closely monitor IJVs and further constrain IJVGMs' authority when the venture's objectives are not being fully attained. This phenomenon has been termed the "failure cycle" (Killing, 1983), since it can serve to further undermine the IJVGM's authority and may eventually destroy the manager's ability and perceived ability to manage the IJV operations effectively (Anderson, 1990). Nevertheless, IJVGMs are expected to function effectively—and relatively autonomously—despite limited levels of authority over the venture's often inadequate and divergent human and other resources.

5. Pressure for Rapid Action

New IJVGMs are also frequently hindered in their efforts to acclimatize to their positions. For instance, Kotter (1982: p. 139) recommends that, initially, a new GM usually needs to spend considerable time collecting information, establishing relationships, selecting a basic direction for his or her area of responsibilities, and developing an organization under him or her. During the first three to six months, demands from superiors to accomplish specific tasks, or to work on pet projects, can often be counterproductive. Indeed, Kotter maintains that anything that significantly directs attention away from agenda setting and network building may prove to be detrimental.

Yet, despite the desirability of the above acclimatization process, IJVGMs can seldom afford that luxury. For example, several studies have noted that a major impetus for IJV formation is rapid market entry and exploitation of products or technologies during the early stages of their life cycles (Contractor & Lorange, 1988; Geringer, 1988; Janger, 1980). These demands to undertake substantive action are further exacerbated by the limited time frame characterizing most IJVGM postings. In this study's sample, for example, the average length of an IJVGM's assignment ranged from 3 to 5 years. In confronting such a situation, the new IJVGM is thus under pressure to take quick and decisive action, within an environment characterized by complexity, inadequate information and nonexisting relationships.

Conclusions and Implications Regarding the IJVGM's Context

Given the challenging context described above, the IJVGM represents a critical variable to the effective control and performance of the IJV (Deloitte, Haskins & Sells, International, 1989; Frayne & Geringer, 1990a; Lynch, 1989). Their posting to the IJV was viewed by the vast majority of the IJVGMs as being of major importance to their personal and career development, as well as to implementation of the parents' strategy—particularly in terms of effective coordination and control of the parents' international operations. The importance of this position was further echoed in comments of the parent company executives, as well as by these firms' willingness to absorb the very high costs associated with the IJVGM position. For example, particularly for ventures in less developed countries and at the early stages of the venture's life cycle, the IJVGM is almost always an expatriate and the full cost of sending a senior expatriate and their family abroad was estimated by several of the participants at being over $1 million (U.S.) for an average four year assignment.

Despite the challenges of the position, the IJVGMs reported that they received essentially no advance preparation for their assignment, although the ability to balance conflicting goals and practices across different corporate and national cultures was identified as essential to successful IJV implementation and performance. In fact, less than 25 percent of the IJVGMs interviewed in this study received any specialized training or other preparation for their IJV assignment, despite the fact that less than 10 percent had any prior IJV experience. When queried as to why this situation occurred, several of the IJVGMs attributed it to the failure of their parent organizations to engage in planning for the assignment (or succession) of the IJVGM, as well as to the limited time frame which commonly resulted from this lack of planning. Even when specialized training *was* provided to IJVGMs, however, the programs were generally limited to a cursory overview of the local language and culture and they were usually administered over a relatively short period of time (i.e., one or two days' duration). Mechanisms for ensuring transfer of training, which is essential to maintain the benefits of training over time, were not emphasized nor incorporated into any of the training modules that the IJVGMs reported that they received. Several of the parent company executives rationalized that, because of the relatively limited number of IJVs which their firms were involved in, they had been unable to develop institutionalized support mechanisms for systematically acquiring and disseminating the requisite information and skills.

Although training programs were generally not administered to IJVGMs, the potential usefulness of such training programs was recognized by both the IJVGMs and the parent executives. In fact, over 85 percent of the IJVGMs and 80 percent of the parent company executives believed that development and delivery of specialized training programs would substantially improve IJVGM performance. Many of these respondents commented that, in the absence of training programs, it would typically be 12 to 18 months before the IJVGM could make substantive contributions to the management of the venture and attainment of the IJV's strategic objectives. In addition, both IJVGMs and parent executives noted that substantive undertakings were generally not forthcoming during the final 6 to 9 months of an IJVGM's assignment, as he or she began physically and mentally preparing for repatriation. Thus, in the absence of specialized training programs, IJVGMs on an average 4 year assignment would often have only 1½ to 2 years in which they could perform effectively, and their effectiveness even during this time could be further hindered by the absence of adequate contextual or behavioral skills.

References

Aguilar, F.J. (1988). *General managers in action.* New York: Oxford University Press.

Anderson, E. (1990). Two firms, one frontier: On assessing joint venture performance. *Sloan Management Review,* Winter: 19-30.

Black, S., & Mendenhall, M. (1990). Cross-cultural training effectiveness: A review and theoretical framework for future research. *Academy of Management Review,* 15:113-136.

Bleeke, J. & Ernst, D. (1991). The way to win in cross-border alliances. *Harvard Business Review,* 69 (6): 127-135.

Blodgett, L.L. (1991). Toward a resource-based theory of bargaining power in international joint ventures. *Journal of Global Marketing,* 5 (1/2): 35-54.

Brown, L.T., Rugman, A.M. & Verbeke, A. (1989). Japanese joint ventures with Western multinationals: Synthesizing the economic and cultural explanations of failure. *Asia-Pacific Journal of Management,* 6 (2): 225-242.

Buckley, P. & Casson, M. (1988). The theory of cooperation in international business. In F. Contractor & P. Lorange (eds.), *Cooperative strategies in international business,* 31-54. Lexington, Mass.: Lexington Books.

Contractor, F. & Lorange, P. (1988). Why should firms cooperate? The strategy and economics basis for cooperative ventures. In F. Contractor & P. Lorange (eds.), *Cooperative strategies in international business,* 3-30. Lexington, MA: Lexington Books.

Deloitte, Haskins & Sells International (1989). *Teaming up for the Nineties — Can you survive without a partner?* New York: Deloitte, Haskins & Sells.

Devlin, G., & Bleackley, M. (1988). Strategic alliances—guidelines for success. Long Range Planning, 20 (3), 12-18.

Dobkin, J. (1988). *International technology joint ventures.* Stoneham, MA: Butterworth Legal Publishers.

Frayne, C.A. (1991). *Reducing Employee Absenteeism Through Self-Management Training.* Westport, Conn.: Quorum Books.

Frayne, C.A. & Geringer, J.M. (1990a). The strategic use of human resource management techniques as control mechanisms in international joint ventures. In G.R. Ferris & K.M. Rowland (eds.), *Research in Personnel and Human Resources Management,* Supplement Volume 2, 53-69, Greenwich, CN: JAI Press.

Frayne, C.A. & Geringer, J.M. (1990b). The relationship between self-management practices and performance of international joint venture general managers. *Proceedings of the Administrative Sciences Association of Canada,* 11 (9): 70-79.

Frayne, C.A. & Geringer, J.M. (1992). *A Self-Management Training Program for International Joint Venture General Managers.* Working paper, University of Western Ontario.

Frayne, C.A. & Latham, G.P. (1987). The application of social learning theory to employee self-management of attendance. *Journal of Applied Psychology,* 72: 387-392.

Ganitsky, J. & Watzke, G. (1990). Implications of different time perspectives for human resource management in international joint ventures. *Management International Review,* 30 (special issue): 37- 51.

Geringer, J.M. (1988). *Joint venture partner selection: Strategies for developed countries.* Westport, Conn.: Quorum Books.

Geringer, J.M. (1991). Strategic Determinants of Partner Selection Criteria in International Joint Ventures. *Journal of International Business Studies,* 22(1): 41-62.

Geringer, J.M. & Frayne, C.A. (1990). Human resource management and international joint venture control: A parent company perspective. *Management International Review,* 30 (Special issue): 103-120.

Geringer, J.M. & Hebert, L. (1989). Control and performance of international joint ventures. *Journal of International Business Studies,* 20(2): 235-254.

Geringer, J.M. & Hebert, L. (1991). Measuring Performance of International Joint Ventures. *Journal of International Business Studies,* 22(2): 249-263.

Geringer, J.M. & Miller, J. (1992). *Japanese-American Seating Inc.* (A). Case 9-92-G004, University of Western Ontario.

Geringer, J.M. & Woodcock, C.P. (1989). Ownership and control of Canadian joint ventures. *Business Quarterly,* Summer, 97-101.

Hamel, G.P. (1990). *Competitive collaboration: Learning, power and dependence in international strategic alliances.* Unpublished doctoral dissertation, University of Michigan.

Harrigan, K.R. (1986). *Managing for joint venture success.* Lexington, Mass.: Lexington Books.

Harrigan, K.R. (1988). Joint ventures and competitive strategy. *Strategic Management Journal,* 9 (2): 141-158.

Hergert, M. & Morris, D. (1988). Trends in international collaborative agreements. In F. Contractor & P. Lorange (eds.), *Cooperative strategies in international business,* 99-109, Lexington, Mass.: Lexington Books.

Holton, R.H. (1981). Making international joint ventures work. In L. Otterbeck (ed.), *The management of headquarters-subsidiary relations in multinational corporations:* 255-267. London: Gower.

Janger, A.R. (1980). *Organization of international joint ventures.* New York: Conference Board.

Killing, J.P. (1983). *Strategies for joint venture success.* New York: Praeger.

Kirkpatrick, D.L. (1967). Evaluation of training. In R.L. Craig (ed.), *Training and development handbook: A guide to human resource development:* 230-233. New York: McGraw-Hill.

Kotter, J.P. (1982). *The general managers.* New York: Free Press.

Lane, H.W. & DiStefano, J.J. (1988). *International Management Behavior.* Scarborough, Ontario: Nelson Canada.

Latham, G.P. & Frayne, C.A. (1989). Self-management training for increasing employee attendance: A follow-up and replication. *Journal of Applied Psychology,* 74: 411-416.

Latham, G.P., Saari, L.M., Pursell, E.D. & Campion, M.A. (1980). The situational interview. *Journal of Applied Psychology* 65: 422-427.

Lynch, R.P. (1989). *The practical guide to joint ventures and alliances.* New York: Wiley.

Mills, P. (1983). Self-management: Its control and relationship to other organizational properties. *Academy of Management Review,* 8: 445-453.

Moxon, R.W. & Geringer, J.M. (1985). Multinational ventures in the commercial aircraft industry. *Columbia Journal of World Business,* 20 (2): 55-62.

Olk, P. & Bussard, D. (1988). General manager succession in international joint ventures: Strategic management implications. Working paper 88-105. The Wharton School, University of Pennsylvania.

Perlmutter, H.V. & Heenan, D.A. (1986). Cooperate to compete globally. *Harvard Business Review,* 64 (2):136+.

Pucik, V. (1988). Strategic alliances with the Japanese: Implications for human resource management. In F.J. Contractor & P. Lorange (eds.), *Cooperative strategies in international business:* 487-498. Lexington, Mass.: Lexington.

Schaan, J.L. & Beamish, P.W. (1988). Joint venture general managers in LDCs. In F. Contractor & P. Lorange, (eds.), *Cooperative strategies in international business,* 279-299. Lexington, Mass.: Lexington Books.

Shenkar, O. & Zeira, Y. (1987). Human resources management in international joint ventures: Directions for research. *Academy of Management Review,* 12: 546-557.

Slocum, J. & Sims, H. Jr. (1980). A typology for integrating technology, organization and job design. *Human Relations,* 33:193-212.

Sullivan, J. & Peterson, R.B. (1982). Factors associated with trust in Japanese-American joint ventures. *Management International Review,* 30-40.

Thoreson, C.E. & Mahoney, M.J. (1974). *Behavioral self-control.* New York: Holt, Rinehart & Winston.

Tung, R.L. (1981). Selection and training of personnel for overseas assignments. *Columbia Journal of World Business,* 16 (1): 68-78.

Uyterhoeven, H.E.R. (1972). General managers in the middle. *Harvard Business Review,* 50 (2): 75-85.

Wexley, K. & Latham, G.P. (1981). *Developing and training human resources in organizations.* Glenview, Ill.: Scott Foresman.

Whetten, D. & Cameron, R. (1991). *Developing Management Skills.* New York: Harper Collins Publishers.

Young; G.R. & Bradford, S., Jr. (1977). *Joint ventures: Planning and action.* New York: Financial Executives Research Foundation.

Appendix _____

Details of Pilot Study Examining IJVGMs and Their Roles

To identify and develop appropriate training programs for IJVGMs, despite the limited existing literature on these topics, a pilot study was undertaken to examine IJVGMs and their roles. From a Statistics Canada database listing the population of two and three parent IJVs in manufacturing industries which were formed in Canada since 1981 and still in existence at the end of 1988, a sample of 48 ventures was randomly selected. The Canadian headquarters of each parent company, both domestic and foreign in origin, as well as the IJVGM were contacted. Participation was obtained from 101 managers involved with 42 JVs, including 41 current or prior IJVGMs and 60 parent company executives. Each parent company respondent had direct line responsibility for the IJV's operations, and virtually all had been intimately involved with the venture since its formation. Data on the IJVGM and his or her role were collected via a brief questionnaire, followed by in-person interviews to confirm and further probe responses. Questions addressed IJVGMs' managerial backgrounds, IJV responsibilities and performance. Respondents were also queried regarding the skills required for effective performance in IJVs, as well as potential IJVGM training needs.

A similar methodology was employed to examine these same issues, but in a developing country context. From public data sources on joint ventures in Indonesia, a sample of 100 IJVs in manufacturing industries and involving a developed country and a local firm were identified. Both the local and the foreign parent, as well as the IJVGM, were contacted for each of these ventures. Data were collected in semi-structured interviews from 107 executives involved in 62 IJVs, including 45 IJVGMs and 62 parent company executives. Each parent company respondent had direct line responsibility for the IJV's operations, and virtually all had been intimately involved with the venture since its formation.

Suji-INS K.K.

Case 8.1
William H. Davidson

Mike Flynn, president of the International Division of Information Network Services Corporation, was undecided as to how he could best approach several delicate issues with his Japanese joint venture partner. He needed to develop an agenda for his trip to Japan, scheduled for the following day. In many ways, he considered this trip of vital importance. For one thing, the problems to be discussed were likely to affect the long-term relationship between his company and the Japanese partner in the management of their joint venture. Moreover, this was his first trip to Japan in the capacity of president of the International Division, and he was anxious to make a good impression and to begin to build a personal relationship with senior executives of the Japanese firm.

Flynn had assumed the position of president several months previously in May of 1988. He was 40 years old and was considered to be one of the most promising executives in the company. After 2 years of military service followed by business school, he had joined a consulting company for several years prior to accepting a position with Information Network Services Corporation (INS). Prior to his promotion to the presidency of the International Division, he had served as managing director of INS's wholly owned subsidiary in Canada.

INS was a major provider of value added network (VAN) services in the United States. Its principal products included high-speed data communications (packet switching), data base management, transaction processing services, and a variety of industry-specific information services. The company's total sales for 1988 were roughly $250 million, and it had recently established successful presences in the United Kingdom and other European countries. International operations accounted for roughly 25 percent of the company's total sales, and the company's top management felt that international markets represented a major field for future growth.

The company's management recognized that in order to capitalize on the rapidly growing Japanese market, a direct presence was needed. By the mid-1980s, the company began to receive a number of inquiries

Source: William H. Davidson, "Suji-INS KK." © 1988. William Davidson School of Business, University of Southern California, Los Angeles, CA 90089. Reprinted by permission.

from major Japanese corporations concerning licensing possibilities. INS was particularly interested in the possibility of establishing a joint venture to provide VAN services.

The company, after 2 years of demanding negotiations, was successful in establishing a joint venture in Japan with Suji Company, a leading Japanese telecommunications equipment manufacturer. The arrangement was formalized in the summer of 1987.

Suji was one of the companies that approached INS initially to arrange a licensing agreement involving VAN technology and expertise. It appeared to be an attractive potential partner. Suji was a medium-sized telecommunication equipment vendor that was directly tied to one of the major Japanese industrial groups. The company had only limited sales to Nippon Telegraph and Telephone (NTT), the national telephone company. About half of its sales were exported, and the remainder went largely to other Japanese firms within the same industrial group. Suji had established a reputation for high quality, and its brands were well established.

In the mid-1980s, as the Japanese telecommunications market was deregulated, Suji began to explore opportunities in the telecommunication services market, particularly in paging and mobile phone services. Prior to deregulation, telephone and related services were monopoly markets served only by NTT. Under the terms of the 1984 New Telecommunications Law, other Japanese firms were permitted to offer these services to the general public. VAN services in particular could be initiated simply by notifying the Ministry of Posts and Telecommunications. The Ministry of International Trade and Industry had established several programs to provide incentives for new VAN services, including tax breaks and low-cost loans. Suji's management felt that VAN services would be a major growth area. Suji's management, after some investigation, concluded that the quickest and most efficient way to achieve entry into these markets was through either licensing or a joint venture with a leading U.S. company. Suji's management felt that timing was of particular importance, since its major competitors were also considering expansion into these markets. Suji's expression of interest to INS was timely, as INS had become increasingly interested in Japan. Suji was at first interested in a licensing arrangement, but INS, anxious to establish a permanent presence in Japan, wished to establish a joint venture.

The negotiations concerning this joint venture were difficult in part because it was the first experience of the kind for both companies. INS had virtually no prior experience in Japan, and for Suji this was the first joint venture with a foreign company, although it had engaged in licensing agreements with several U.S. and European firms.

The ownership of the joint venture was divided between the two companies, such that Suji owned two-thirds and INS one-third of its equity. Japanese law limited foreign ownership in telecom services vendors to one-third equity participation. In addition to a predetermined cash contribution, the agreement stipulated that INS was to provide network technology and the Japanese partner was to contribute facilities and network equipment. The joint venture was first to market data communication services and later was to introduce transaction processing services. The services were to be marketed under the joint brands of INS and Suji. The agreement also stipulated that both companies would have equal representation on the board of directors, with four people each, and that Suji would provide the entire personnel for the joint venture from top management down to production workers. Such a practice was quite common among foreign joint ventures in Japan, since given limited mobility among personnel in large corporations, recruiting would represent a major problem for foreign companies. The companies also agreed that the Japanese partner would nominate the president of the joint venture, subject to approval of the board, and the U.S. company would nominate a person for the position of executive vice president. INS also agreed to supply, for the time being, a technical director on a full-time basis.

INS had four members on the board: Flynn, Jack Rose (INS's nominee for executive vice president of the joint venture), and the chair and the president of INS. Representing the Japanese company were the president and executive vice president of Suji, and two senior executives of the joint venture, the president and vice president for finance.

By the fall of 1988, the venture had initiated tests of its data communication services, and a small sales organization had been built. Although the venture was progressing reasonably well, Flynn had become quite concerned over several issues that had come to his attention during the previous 2 months. The first and perhaps the most urgent of these was the selection of a new president for the joint venture.

The first president had died suddenly about 3 months before at the age of 68. He had been a managing director of the parent company and had been the chief representative in Suji's negotiations with INS. When the joint venture was established, it appeared only natural for him to assume the presidency; INS management had no objection.

About a month after his death, Suji, in accordance with the agreement, nominated Kenzo Satoh as the new president. Flynn, when he heard Satoh's qualifications, concluded that he was not suitable for the presidency of the joint venture. He became even more disturbed when he received further information about how he was selected from Jack Rose, the executive vice president of the joint venture.

Satoh had joined Suji 40 years previously upon graduating from Tokyo University. He had held a variety of positions in the Suji company, but during the previous 15 years, he had served almost exclusively in staff functions. He had been manager of Administrative Services at the company's major plant, manager of the General Affairs Department at the corporate headquarters, and personnel director. When he was promoted to that position, he was admitted to the company's board of directors. His responsibility was then expanded to include overseeing several service-oriented staff departments, including personnel, industrial relations, administrative services, and the legal department.

Flynn was concerned that Satoh had virtually no line experience and could not understand why Suji would propose such a person for the presidency of the joint venture, particularly when it was at a critical stage of development.

Even more disturbing to Mr. Flynn was the manner in which Satoh was selected. This first came to Mr. Flynn's attention when he received a letter from Rose, which included the following description:

> By now you have undoubtedly examined the background information forwarded to you regarding Mr. Satoh, nominated by our Japanese partner for the presidency of the joint venture.

> I have subsequently learned the manner in which Mr. Satoh was chosen for the position, which I am sure would be of great interest to you. I must point out at the outset that what I am going to describe, though shocking by our standards, is quite commonplace among Japanese corporations: in fact, it is well-accepted.

> Before describing the specific practice, I must give you a brief background of the Japanese personnel system. As you know, the major companies follow the so-called lifetime employment where all managerial personnel are recruited directly from universities, and they remain with the company until they reach their compulsory retirement age, which is typically around 57. Career advancement in the Japanese system comes slowly, primarily by seniority. Advancement to middle management is well-paced, highly predictable, and virtually assured for every college graduate. Competence and performance become important as they reach upper middle management and top management. Obviously, not everyone will be promoted automatically beyond middle management, but whatever the degree to which competence and qualifications are considered in career advancement, chronological age is the single most important factor.

> A select few within the ranks of upper-middle management will be promoted to top management positions, that is, they will be given memberships in the board of directors. In large Japanese companies, the board typically consists exclusively of full-time operating executives. Suji's board is no exception. Moreover, there is a clear-cut hierarchy among the members. The Suji board consists of the chair of the board, president, executive vice president, three managing directors, five ordinary directors, and two statutory auditors.

> Typically, ordinary directors have specific operating responsibilities such as head of a staff department, a plant, or a division. Managing directors are comparable to our group vice presidents. Each will have two or three functional or staff

groups or product divisions reporting to them. Japanese commercial law stipulates that the members are to be elected by stockholders for a 2-year term. Obviously, under the system described, the members are designated by the chair of the board or the president and serve at their pleasure. Stockholders have very little voice in the actual selection of the board members. Thus, in some cases, it is quite conceivable that board membership is considered as a reward for many years of faithful and loyal service.

As you are well aware, a Japanese corporation is well known for its paternalistic practices in return for lifetime service, and they do assume obligations, particularly for those in middle management or above, even after they reach their compulsory retirement age, not just during their working careers. Appropriate positions are generally found for them in the company's subsidiaries, related firms, or major suppliers where they can occupy positions commensurate to their last position in the parent corporation for several more years.

A similar practice applies to the board members. Though there is no compulsory retirement age for board members, the average tenure for board membership is usually around 6 years. This is particularly true for those who are ordinary or managing directors. Directorships being highly coveted positions, there must be regular turnover to allow others to be promoted to board membership. As a result, all but a fortunate few who are earmarked as heir apparent to the chair, presidency, or executive vice presidency must be "retired." Since most of these executives are in their late fifties or early sixties, they do not yet wish to retire. Moreover, even among major Japanese corporations, the compensation for top management positions is quite low compared with the U.S. standard, and pension plans being still quite inadequate, they will need respectable positions with a reasonable income upon leaving the company. Thus, it is common practice among Japanese corporations to transfer senior executives of the parent company to the chair or presidency of the company's subsidiaries or affiliated companies. Typically, these people will serve in these positions for several years before they retire. Suji had a dozen subsidiaries, and you might be interested in knowing that every top management position is held by those who have retired from the parent corporation. Such a system is well routinized.

Our friend, Mr. Satoh is clearly not the caliber that would qualify for further advancement in the parent company, and his position must be vacated for another person. Suji's top management must have decided that the presidency of the joint venture was the appropriate position for him to "retire" into. These are the circumstances under which Mr. Satoh has been nominated for our consideration.

When he read this letter, Flynn instructed Rose to indicate to the Suji management that Satoh was not acceptable. Not only did Flynn feel that Satoh lacked the qualifications and experience for the presidency, but he resented the fact that Suji was using the joint venture as a home to accommodate a retired executive. It would be justifiable for Suji to use one of its wholly owned subsidiaries for that purpose, but there was no reason why the joint venture should take him on. On the contrary, the joint venture needed dynamic leadership to establish a viable market position.

In his response to Rose, Flynn suggested as president another person, Takao Toray, marketing manager of the joint venture. Toray was 50 years old and had been transferred to the joint venture from Suji, where he had held a number of key marketing positions, including regional sales manager and assistant marketing director. Shortly after he was appointed to the latter position, Toray was sent to INS headquarters to become acquainted with the company's marketing operations. He spent roughly 3 months in the United States, during which time Flynn met him. Though he had not gone beyond a casual acquaintance, Flynn was much impressed by Toray. He appeared to be dynamic, highly motivated, and pragmatic. Moreover, Toray had a reasonable command of English. While communication was not easy, at least it was possible to have conversations on substantive matters. From what Flynn was able to gather, Toray impressed everyone he saw favorably and gained the confidence of not only the International Division staff but those in the corporate marketing group as well as sales executives in the field.

Flynn was aware that Toray was a little too young to be acceptable to Suji, but he felt that it was critical to press for his appointment for two reasons. First, he was far from convinced of the wisdom of adopting Japanese managerial practices blindly in the joint venture. Some of the Japanese executives he met in New York had told him of the pitfalls and weaknesses of Japanese management practices. He was disturbed over the fact that, as he was becoming familiar with the joint venture, he was finding that in every critical aspect such as organization structure, personnel practices, and decision making, the company was managed as though it were a Japanese company. Rose had had little success in introducing U.S. practices. Flynn had noticed in the past that the joint venture had been consistently slow in making decisions because it engaged in a typical Japanese group-oriented and consensus-based process. He also learned that control and reporting systems were virtually nonexistent. Flynn felt that INS's sophisticated planning and control system should be introduced. It had proved successful in the company's wholly owned European subsidiaries, and there seemed to be no reason why such a system could not improve the operating efficiency of the joint venture. He recalled from his Canadian experience that U.S. management practices, if judiciously applied, could give U.S. subsidiaries abroad a significant competitive advantage over local firms.

Second, Flynn felt that the rejection of Satoh and appointment of Toray might be important as a demonstration to the Japanese partner that Suji-INS was indeed a joint venture and not a subsidiary of the Japanese parent company. He was also concerned that INS had lost the initiative in the management of the joint venture. This move would help INS gain stronger influence over the management of the joint venture.

Rose conveyed an informal proposal along these lines to Suji management. Suji's reaction to Flynn's proposal was swift; they rejected it totally. Suji management was polite, but made it clear that they considered Flynn unfair in judging Mr. Satoh's suitability for the presidency without even having met him. They requested Rose to assure Flynn that their company, as majority owner, indeed had an important stake in the joint venture and certainly would not have recommended Satoh unless it had been convinced of his qualifications. Suji management also told Flynn, through Rose, that the selection of Toray was totally unacceptable because in the Japanese corporate system such a promotion was unheard of and would be detrimental not only to the joint venture but to Toray himself, who was believed to have a promising future in the company.

Flynn was surprised at the tone of Suji's response. He wondered whether it would be possible to establish an effective relationship with the Japanese company. Suji seemed determined to run the venture on their own terms.

Another related issue which concerned Flynn was the effectiveness of Rose as executive vice president. Flynn appreciated the difficulties he faced but began to question Rose's qualifications for his position and his ability to work with Japanese top management. During the last visit, for example, Rose had complained of his inability to integrate himself with the Japanese top management team. He indicated that he felt he was still very much an outsider to the company, not only because he was a foreigner but also because the Japanese executives, having come from the parent company, had known each other and in many cases had worked together for at least 20 years. He also indicated that none of the executives spoke English well enough to achieve effective communication beyond the most rudimentary level and that his Japanese was too limited to be of practical use. In fact, his secretary, hired specifically for him, was the only one with whom he could communicate easily. He also expressed frustration over the fact that his functions were very ill-defined and his experience and competence were not really being well utilized by the Japanese.

Flynn discovered after he assumed the presidency that Mr. Rose had been chosen for this assignment for his knowledge of Japan. Rose graduated from a midwestern university in 1973, and after enlisting in the Army was posted to Japan for 4 years. Upon returning home, he joined INS as a management trainee. In 1984, he became assistant district sales manager in California, Oregon, and Washington. When the company began to search for a candidate for executive vice president for the new joint venture, Rose's name came up as someone who was qualified and available for posting to Japan. Rose, although somewhat ambivalent about the new opportunity at first, soon became persuaded that this would represent a major challenge and opportunity.

Flynn was determined to get a first-hand view of the joint venture during his visit. He had many questions, and he wondered whether he had inherited a problem. He was scheduled to meet with Mr. Ohtomo, executive vice president of Suji Corporation, on the day following his arrival. Ohtomo, who had been with Suji for over 40 years, was the senior executive responsible for overseeing the joint venture. Flynn had not met Ohtomo, but he knew that Ohtomo had visited the United States and spoke English reasonably well. He wondered how best to approach and organize his meetings and discussions with Mr. Ohtomo. He also wondered if his planned stay of one week would be adequate to achieve his objectives. While practicing with chopsticks, he returned to reading *Theory Z,* a popular book on Japanese management, in the hope of gaining insight for the days ahead.

A Strategy-Driven Joint Venture in Hungary

Case 8.2
Dianne J. Cyr

Case Summary[1]

This case presents the unique operation of a team management system in a joint venture located in Hungary. The joint venture between the Austrian partner (Tiling International) and a collective of Hungarian companies operates under the watchful eye of the Austrian partner, but is basically without foreign management involvement on-site in Hungary. From the start, the Hungarian General Manager has had a strategic agenda for the venture that specializes in the production of quality roof tiles. His vision for the accomplishment of a customer-oriented focus involves the reduction of organizational hierarchy, and an emphasis on training (the latter was also strongly supported by the Austrians). How various human resource management policies and practices sustain or detract from the company strategic objectives is elaborated.

Establishing the Joint Venture

Mr. Csabai hurried to his office one cold morning in December. He was careful not to slip on the newly fallen snow as he considered the past and pondered the future of the pioneering joint venture that he led. He had a major role in the strategic evolution of the company, and to some degree he considered himself an "orchestrator" of events and an enabler of people. Mr. Csabai described the operation of the company as a "smooth hierarchy" in which staff is empowered to do things themselves. He illustrated his role using the following example:

> In an orchestra there are musicians and head musicians and they can play alone without the conductor. I am the conductor. It is enough for the conductor to sometimes say there is something missing, but the orchestra can only play well when they are allowed.

Source: Dianne J. Cyr. "A Strategy-Driven Joint Venture in Hungary." Reprinted by permission of the author.

Mr. Csabai also reflected on the unique history of the pioneering joint venture (JV) of approximately 170 employees in Hungary known as Roofex. Formed in 1984 and operational in 1985, it was one of the first five large joint ventures to be established in the country—a landmark event preceding the topple of the Communist regime in 1989. The joint venture has a complicated ownership structure. The venture was formed between the Austrian partner Tiling International that initially had 49 percent equity, and a collective of fourteen Hungarian partners who held 51 percent equity. In 1993 the ownership between the partners changed, and the Austrian partner expanded their equity in the joint venture to 57 percent. Initially, the JV consisted of one plant, but eventually two more were added. Annual production is 30 million tiles that are sold mostly to the Hungarian market. In addition, Tiling International buys 1.5 million tiles per year to sell in its own markets. Besides the Hungarian operation, the Austrians also have roof tile production facilities in the Czech Republic and Slovenia. Due to cheaper production costs in these regions, Roofex finds itself unable to competitively market its products to some other locations in Central/Eastern Europe.

When the JV was established both partners contributed substantial capital investments. Total capital for the venture was 299 Million Forints[2] of which the Austrians contributed 146 Million Forints and the Hungarians 153 Million Forints. The Austrian portion was kept in a local bank for the purpose of buying new equipment, and was to be paid back to the Austrian group. In addition, the Austrian partner was to supply new technology and other equipment. Tiling International had licensed technology to the joint venture and was responsible for the selection of raw materials and models for production purposes. Modern technology is part of the operation. In fact a computer plan is used to determine how many roof tiles are required for a building.

Both partners are interested in the profitability of the venture and have a long-term commitment to Roofex. Some Hungarian managers noted, however, that profits returned to Austria might be better reinvested in the factory. On a questionnaire survey completed by 89 employees in the JV (refer to the Appendix 1) the majority felt that overall, the local and foreign managers have similar goals for the company. More specifically, the Austrian partner wanted to expand to Central Europe, and provided technology and training in the Hungarian plant. The Hungarian managers were interested in obtaining new technology, management skills, and to learn more about market-oriented systems.

Sharing Responsibility Between the Partners

Formally, the joint venture operates under a Board of Directors which is comprised of two Austrians and three Hungarians. At the operations level, a seven person management team is responsible for Roofex. It is this team that determines the strategy for the venture, pending final approval from the Austrians and Board of Directors. Unlike many joint ventures between Western European partners and Central European partners, there is minimal involvement of Austrian expatriates on site in Hungary. Only one Austrian, the Technical Director, had been on assignment at Roofex and he left to return to the parent branch. Based on questionnaire results, respondents perceived the local managers to have primary responsibility for the day to day operation of the venture.

However, there is another side. In some ways and despite their physical absence, local employees saw the Austrians as imparting many of their ways on the JV. In a book compiled in Hungary about Roofex titled "The Customer is the King," a short segment describes that the Austrians wish to make the Hungarian factory a replica of the facility in Austria. Further, this tendency has an outcome of stifling innovation in the Hungarian plant. A quotation from this book elaborates this theme:

> In the case of innovation there is a big difference between the Austrian owners and the Hungarian managers. For the [Austrian] owners the investment in [the joint venture] is rather capital placement than innovation because they have brought a well-tried technology and organization system to Hungary. They strictly determined that the factory in Hungary had to be the exact copy of the Austrian one. They wanted to nip the suggestions for innovation and technical improvement of the Hungarian technical managers in the bud.

> Judging innovation from the Hungarian point of view is just the opposite. Comparing to Hungarian circumstances [Roofex] is a real technological, oganizational and market innovation. Apart from these, the product, the tile itself, is new and hasn't been used previously. In my opinion, the innovative ability of the two Hungarian managers is just as important a factor of the company's success as the things which [Tiling International] could give. They [the Hungarian managers] fulfilled the task of purchasing, production, and organization of selling [marketing] very well. They obtained success for the company by solving all the problems, changing norms which had been traditionally accepted, overcoming all the political influences and the administration difficulties.

A senior manager at Roofex further offered that Hungarians have the opportunity to excel if given the opportunity. He said,

> Hungarians are creative, proud, difficult to accept the ideas of others, but if we understand what they [Austrians] are thinking, then we are able to do better. But Austrians don't believe we can do as well as they. Austrians come and say they know better. They don't believe.

A quality manager substantiates that in some areas he feels the "Westerners don't have confidence in local operations." He cited the example that if there are problems related to quality, the Austrian partner turns to a branch operation in Germany for advice. The quality manager mentioned that testing could be done locally through contacts he has at the university—and for a better price. However, this had not been followed up and no explanation was given.

In addition, a manager noted the importance that the Western partner supports the local people, especially related to fair wages and minimizing layoffs. In 1989, when the quota systems changed and privatization began in Hungary, many companies closed and in general unemployment soared. The Austrian philosophy that originally emphasized that people should be satisfied, well paid and well trained became less important to maintain because of the glut of willing employees. This manager mentioned not only did worker morale decline, but so did quality. There was fewer staff, and people worked more. To make matters worse, workers took second jobs to make additional income, a practice the Austrians did not want to support.

The Strategic Initiative _____

In a manner not at all customary under a Socialist system, the company motto has for some time been "the customer is the king." This typically "Western" philosophy is the pride of the Hungarian General Manager Mr. Csabai, as he seeks to develop the operation to prove the excellence of Hungarian workers and products. He mentioned,

> We can not defeat the Communist system through war, but through the development of the economy. Under the Communist system people traveled or ate, but were not focused on investment and technology. The company would go to bankruptcy.

The General Manager aims to make Roofex the premier supplier of roof tiles in the Hungarian marketplace. He outlined that the strategy of placing the customer first began at a time when "this kind of thinking was not natural." Further,

> Perhaps success lies in these things. Our system changed in thinking and we began six years earlier than other companies. It is not simple. People can understand and have a positive attitude because they can hear another motto. And they are surprised how such things can occur here in Hungary. Of course, there were mistakes.

The General Manager's adoption of a quality and customer-oriented focus might be partially explained by his broad and international experience. Mr. Csabai trained at the technical university as an electrician, also playing on the basketball team. Due to his sports involvement he had the opportunity to travel to France, Germany, Italy and Austria. He mentioned he made numerous contacts in the West over these years, as well as studied economics. In 1980, Mr. Csabai became the "chief for investments" in a large company of 20,000 employees. He joined Roofex in 1984 at the joint venture start-up, and made a conscious decision to take the company in a new direction. Mr. Csabai's strategy for the joint venture was two pronged: (1) reduce hierarchical levels in the organization and implement more of a team approach, and (2) emphasize training.

Reducing the Hierarchy

To realize strategic objectives, employees are encouraged to use their own ideas and to operate more independently. Although there is a union in the plant, union support is weak. Generally, the union works to support management directives. Employees work in informal "teams," and although the General Manager noted he has the final decision, employees have considerable autonomy. Mr. Csabai noted that at first it was difficult for workers to accept a system of greater worker independence. He added,

> They [the workers] are glad to make the changes and people would like to realize themselves. If you order or demand, they don't like it. Then you need a closed hierarchy. And if mistakes are not allowed, they say it was the other [who made the mistake]. If mistakes are O.K. then they learn from the mistakes and do better the next time. There were some small problems in creating this change, and there were some people who couldn't understand. But the majority understand. Workers don't think about this, but they understand the philosophy.

Asked about where his own philosophy was derived, Mr. Csabai said that he got these ideas from playing basketball. "Everyone needs to decide once in his life how groups can best play to be successful and win. And then it's very simple. I need the support of others." Concerning his own performance, he contrasted the old system of government orders with the current system in which profit and competitiveness are key words. Returning to the sports analogy, Mr. Csabai remarked,

> I am now in training myself to spring to a high height. Before I only jumped to a smaller height. Before I jumped 120 centimeters, now it's 130 centimeters. In the West, they are jumping 200 centimeters. We would like to be in the world championships. Before we were told 120 centimeters was enough. Now they [the workers] need to train themselves. And they want to be the world champions.

The philosophy for teamwork and equality that Mr. Csabai advocates appears to be implemented at managerial and supervisory levels in practice. The Director of Production mentioned,

> I am able to determine how things are done in my area. If something is important I go to my team for how to solve problems. Information is the key word.

A foreman reinforces the operation of a team approach,

> Everybody has to feel they have a working place, and security. We work as a group and have worked together a long time. And it took a while to create the group. My slogan is "If someone has problems with another, don't hit, solve the problem together rather than come to the foreman. We are trying to get to where we are laughing together."

When asked about the style of management in the plant, a second foreman describes how during his time at Roofex there had been two directors of production. He perceived two distinct styles between the directors,

> The former director was very strict. The advantage is you can't say anything back to the leader. The disadvantage is that some ideas can't get to the managers. Since Mr. V. is here, he listens to the people and he's less strict. But time will determine which style is better.

When prompted, the foreman added he prefers the second style, because if he makes a mistake he has the responsibility. The next time he can correct his error. In the first case, it is the leader who decides, and the worker has his or her responsibility taken away.

An Emphasis on Training

A major thrust for the realization of strategic goals at Roofex is training for workers at all levels of the operation. Training is provided on the job in the plant in Hungary, at outside courses locally, or in the Austrian facility. There is also a roofing school that serves to enhance the vocational abilities of those persons who will be using the tiles from the venture in roofing projects. The various forms of training available are outlined following.

Training in Austria

In the early days of the joint venture, a large number of Hungarian workers (about 70) went to Austria for training. This approximately included:

- Directors—4 months
- Production Directors—6 months
- Foreman—2 months
- Advertising—6 weeks
- Marketing Manager—6 weeks
- Production Workers—6 weeks

Managers in the joint venture felt the training was worthwhile, and fulfilled the objective of learning not only technical skills, but also how to think in more market-oriented terms. The costs for training were paid from the joint venture rather than from the Austrian parent. More recently, as profits at Roofex have dwindled, one manager mentioned there is less interest on the part of the Austrians to provide ongoing training. On the employee questionnaire as well, overall employees felt sufficient training was not provided by the foreign partner.

A System of Job Rotation

Although job rotation is considered in the West to be a progressive and effective form of work organization, the rotation of workers to various jobs and broad skill training also existed for some positions at Roofex. The Production Director describes that it is important to have workers trained to do each other's jobs in order to fill positions if someone is ill. Workers are asked if they would like to rotate to different positions on the line, and employees have the option to decline if they wish. About 25 percent of 85 workers in one factory have decided to participate in job rotation. In addition, workers on the production line work as teams, with about 13 workers and one foreman on each team.

In contrast, the training of Austrian workers was viewed by some of the Hungarian staff as too narrow and limiting. This impression was gained during training of Hungarians in the Austrian plant. In the book on Roofex titled "The Customer is King" the following excerpt describes this perception:

> Our Austrian colleagues have lower qualifications than we have. It was surprising that there [in Austria] every worker had his own little field (the mechanic, the foreman, etc...). Let's talk about the labor work now. We were responsible for a 10-15 meter long section. Our colleague knew all the parts of that section from the last nail to the last screw. It was his responsibility that this section had to work perfectly...They were all very competent in their own field, but in other fields, with which they also should be familiar they don't know a thing.

Other Forms of Training

At the local level, staff is eligible for training as needed. For instance, courses are provided in electrical skills or computers. Employees are required to attend training programs on their own time. Managers are able to attend training provided through a Hungarian consulting company. The Finance Manager attended a course in time management through this company. Although one manager indicated German language training is desirable, people found they did not have sufficient time (e.g. personal time) to attend the classes. A large number of respondents (33%) on the survey questionnaire indicated they would benefit from training related to production.

Finally, the roofing school that was a joint project between Roofex staff and representatives in Hungary and Austria was opened in 1992. The three year course which accommodates 320 students is aimed to provide classroom training, combined with on-the-job experience for roofers. The vocational training is suitable for the Hungarian market and based on Austrian practices. The syllabus includes a German language course, business administration, computer training, carpentry, metalwork and physical education.

The Communication System

Communication occurs on at least three levels: (1) between the Austrian partner and the joint venture, (2) in the joint venture at all levels, and (3) in the plants related to production requirements.

Partner Meetings

Monthly meetings are held in Austria for a period of two days. Mr. Csabai, the General Manager is in attendance. In addition, after the seven person management team was established (in 1992), the General Manager and the Controller from Tiling International would attend meetings at Roofex in Hungary in order to ensure the management team was working effectively together. The meetings between the Austrians and the Hungarians have sometimes been problematic due to language differences.

Communication in the Joint Venture

Within the JV the senior management team meets on a weekly basis. In general, managers think these meetings are useful and they feel well informed. Directors also meet weekly for production meetings. Other meetings are held as needed. For example, building advisors who work with the suppliers meet every two months. In addition, sales meetings are held every two months for three days during which issues related to the economy are discussed. A newsletter produced for the Austrian parent company is distributed in Roofex. In keeping with the strategy of reduced hierarchy, Mr. Csabai has an "open door" policy. He describes he hopes employees can come and talk to him about problems as they arise, in order to create solutions.

Information Exchange at the Production Level

In one of the Roofex plants a production manager is responsible for 92 workers. This manager describes that communication occurs between workers and himself in many ways. For instance, each morning he meets with the foremen for approximately thirty minutes. Foremen are responsible for bringing forth needs or ideas presented by the workers. In addition, the production manager spends about fifteen percent of his time walking around on the production floor in order that he is directly accessible to workers. Discussions encompass both technical and personal matters. Production meetings are held as needed with the foremen and workers.

A comprehensive range of information is exchanged. This may include: plant quantities and amounts of production; quantities of tiles sold; the market situation in Hungary; the economic situation in Hungary (living standards, inflation, unemployment) in order that workers can understand the situation at the Roofex factory relative to other operations in the country; the financial situation in the factory; planned investments; or numbers of personnel.

When the production manager was asked whether or not workers appreciated and understood the breadth of information provided he replied,

> Workers are very interested and this comes out from the questions. At first I thought they would relate to how much money people would have. But questions weren't in this direction. If I give detailed information about the market or financial standards, then they [the workers] have a better chance of understanding and don't fear about the future. And they belong better emotionally to the company.

In turn, both production workers and foremen indicate they receive sufficient information. This sentiment was confirmed by the employee questionnaire survey as well. The personalized management style of the production manager is extended to "entry and exit interviews" for all those who either come into or leave the factory. He informs new workers of what they can expect. For personnel who leave, these meetings are intended to determine problems that exist in the factory and how they might be solved. A spirit of camaraderie in the venture is enhanced by providing "perks" for workers when production goes well. When staff succeed in meeting a goal, the company buys beer for everyone. On manager "name days" (a designated day for individual celebration), managers in the plant cook and eat together. On occasion, workers invite the production manager to join them for breakfast.

Human Resource Management Policy and Practice ———————

There is no formal human resources department or representative at Roofex. Mr. Csabai described that the joint venture is small and that human resource policies are handled by line staff.

Recruitment

Most staff selected into Roofex have worked previously with a company related to the Austrian partner located in the local area. The General Manager for Roofex (Mr. Csabai) was chosen by the Austrian owners. Mr. Csabai had been the technical manager at the Austrian partner's company for 20 years, and as an additional asset he was able to speak German. Other staff from the Austrian company were selected into the joint venture by a committee. In addition, new people are recruited through newspaper advertisements. All employees have an interview before being hired to the JV. According to Mr. Csabai, decisions about whom to hire are based more on personal skills than technical capabilities.

The production manager noted that when hiring in his area he consults with workers to determine if they know of someone who would be suitable to bring into the venture. That person would then receive an interview, and "first impressions are very important." People are hired on various criteria, ranked in the following order: (1) experience (2) ambition and (3) education. Production workers are first interviewed by the foreman, and second interviews are conducted by the Production Supervisor. If a candidate is selected, a plan for his future career is outlined. The production manager mentioned the importance that workers feel when they have the opportunity to advance.

Reward Systems

Salaries are based on (1) a fixed portion and (2) a variable portion (the "premium") that can be withheld from workers for substandard performance. The variable portion differs depending on the job. For example, in marketing or finance the variable amount is 20%; in production this amount may be up to 60% of the fixed salary. Wage scales are kept secret.

In production the foremen decide the percentage of variable salary to be held back based on individual performance, which is then reviewed by the Production Director. The amount of the premium is decided based on four factors: level of production; machine usage; defects; the quality number (based on a quality control system).

In theory approximately fifteen percent of the premium is based on each factor. However, in practice, few distinctions are made between workers unless there are large problems with performance. As one production worker described, the foremen prefer not to create distinctions between the workers who are supposed to function as a group. Another production employee suggested the tendency to make few wage distinctions among workers related to the old Socialist philosophies. He mentioned,

> In Austria, salaries are based on individual performance. The system is "Hungarized" here. If there were unequal bonuses they [workers] would leave. They want equal bonuses because it is more like the thinking in the old system. They want the same bonus for everyone so they all share the same standard of living.

A production manager suggested that although he liked the premium system as it is, he would prefer different forms of the premium related to the requirements that are most relevant for different work areas (e.g. maintenance, storage). For example, in the storage area premiums should be available for reduced breakage. This manager continued that if quality is important, then the volume of production (which may detract from quality) should be a secondary consideration.

Overall, workers would like to see an increase of wages due to inflation and the cost of living. In the previous year there had been no wage increases at Roofex, and salaries are the main reason why employees leave the company. Some employees describe that their salaries actually declined. A foreman described the impact of no salary increase in the following way,

> It is hard to make the people work harder and morale is not so good. This was not the problem before. Before people did overtime for no payment.

> Now they want to know how much they'll be paid. I think salaries should be matched to inflation like it is in other countries.

A bonus for superior performance additional to the base salary (e.g. fixed plus variable portions) does not exist. However, on the questionnaire survey, employees strongly supported the initiation of a bonus system. Further, nonmonetary recognition for special work contributions is absent. Managers and supervisors may receive company tokens such as caps, calendars or umbrellas but not specifically linked to work excellence. Overall, employees feel there should be more company benefits available.

Past Successes and Future Challenges ————————————

Roofex is a strategically oriented company with an emphasis on customer service and quality accomplished through a team approach. In the Hungarian context, and following closely on the heels of a post-socialist regime, this strategic emphasis is both progressive and unique. Despite existing strengths, the General Manager Mr. Csabai was continually probing to see what they could still do better. More specifically he knew that how responsibility was shared between the Austrian and Hungarian partners was not ideal. There were hints the Austrians were stifling innovation and not paying enough attention to the local context. How might this be improved? Further, how could the corporate culture at Roofex be sustained, especially if the leader who had led the charge for change retired? How could the team focus identified as important for workers be retained or even augmented?

In the training area, training budgets had been reduced and workers didn't think the foreign partner provided enough training. Some workers questioned the competence of foreign trainers, and the fact workers didn't have enough time to take courses. Finally, there was some concern that rewards did not provide an adequate incentive to workers. Mr. Csabai had heard some other joint ventures in Central/Eastern Europe were adopting performance bonuses for workers. On the questionnaire, employees strongly advocated the use of a bonus arrangement. Should he consider this option at Roofex? Mr. Csabai was lost in a myriad of thoughts as he gazed toward the future.

Appendix 1. Questionnaire Results[3]

Item	Score
1. Local/foreign managers have similar goals	3.5
2. Foreign managers have primary responsibilities	2.5
3. Local managers have primary responsibilities	3.3
4. Better understanding of competitiveness	3.8
5. Company has long-term benefits	3.9
6. More concern for production than people	3.8
7. More emphasis on individuals than groups	2.7
8. Change is positive	3.5
9. Important to avoid mistakes	4.5
10. Control on the job	3.8
11. More concern for present than future	3.1
12. Need to go through supervisor	2.9
13. Good personal connections are important	4.1
14. Cultural differences are respected	3.8
15. Employees selected for technical skills	3.1
16. Fair chance for promotion	3.0
17. Concern about layoffs	3.2
18. Employees feel loyal	3.9
19. Have information to do the job	3.9
20. Have information about company policies	2.5
21. Managers listen to employees' ideas	3.4
22. Managers don't always share information	3.0
23. Communication problems due to language	2.7
24. Enough training for the job	3.9
25. Learning new skills on the job	4.2
26. Learning new skills in class	2.6
27. Sufficient training by the foreign partner	2.7
28. Satisfied with salary	2.3
29. Salary based on ability/performance	2.8
30. Salaries depend on who you know	2.1
31. Should be bonuses	4.1
32. Enough company benefits	2.6
33. Rewards are fairly distributed	2.9
34. Understand job goals	4.2
35. Know what to do to get rewards	3.9
36. Receive feedback for performance	3.5
37. Future of company is positive	4.2

Endnotes

1. This project was generously funded through a competitive research grant from INSEAD. At the request of managers in the joint venture, company names are fictitious and are not meant to represent real companies.

2. At the time the case was written, $1 U.S. equals approximately 110 Forints.

3. Scores presented are mean scores based on a scale of 1 (low) to 5 (high). Eighty-nine employees responded to the questionnaire and represented a wide range and level of jobs. Eighty-two percent of the respondents were male, with an average age of 38.4 years. Average number of years employed in the venture is 6.5 years.

Part 9

MANAGING EXPATRIATE ASSIGNMENTS

A Practical but Theory-based Framework for Selecting Cross-Cultural Training Methods

Reading 9.1
J. Stewart Black
Mark Mendenhall

> Global citizenship is no longer just a nice phrase in the lexicon of rosy futurologists. It is every bit as real and concrete as measurable changes in GNP or trade flows (Ohmae, 1989, p. 154).

There is little debate that for executives in large multinational corporations (MNCs) today globalization is a daily reality. But what exactly is unique about the international environment that MNCs face compared to non-MNCs, what skills do executives need to successfully lead firms in this emerging global village, and how can appropriate training be designed to facilitate the acquisition of these new skills? These are not trivial questions.

One of the first issues that MNCs face that non-MNCs do not is the fact that if a firm operates in multiple countries, it must deal with multiple sources of sovereign authority. This involves working with different laws and legal systems or, in some cases, the lack of systematic legal structures and processes. Executives in positions at headquarters or at foreign subsidiaries must have the skills to understand the impact of various laws, tariffs, taxes, enforcement practices, and overarching legal systems and be able to work with host government officials in enacting and maintaining reasonable legislation across a wide variety of countries and cultures.

Second, MNCs must also operate in different markets with different cultures, histories, values, social systems, and languages, which often require not only product diversification but intraproduct differentiation by country. This requires managers who have a "sensitivity to local conditions" (Doz and Prahalad, 1986) and who can understand, work with,

Source: J. Stewart Black and Mark Mendenhall. "A Practical but Theory-based Framework for Selecting Cross-Cultural Training Methods." *Human Resource Management*, 1989, 28 (4), pp. 511-539. Copyright © 1989 John Wiley & Sons, Inc. Reprinted by permission of John Wiley & Sons, Inc.

and direct people from various cultures. Third, different "countries offer different strategic opportunities for MNCs. . . . Differences in size, resource endowment, economic development, political regime, national development and industrial policies . . . play roles in differentiating the opportunities offered to MNCs by individual countries" (Doz and Prahalad, 1986, p. 56).

Despite the need for cross-cultural skills and the shortage of managers who possess these skills, most human resource decision makers do nothing in terms of cross-cultural training (CCT) for employees in general or for selected employees embarking on international assignments (Baker and Ivancevich, 1971; Black, 1988; Runzheimer, 1984; Tung, 1981). For example, 70 percent of U.S. expatriates and 90 percent of their families are sent overseas without any cross-cultural training (Baker and Ivancevich, 1971; Black, 1988; Black and Stephens, 1989; Runzheimer, 1984; Tung, 1981).

This is significant given that studies have found between 16 and 40 percent of all expatriate managers sent on foreign assignments return before they are supposed to because of poor performance or the inability of the employee and/or the family to effectively adjust to the foreign environment (Baker and Ivancevich, 1971; Black, 1988; Dunbar and Ehrlich, 1986; Tung, 1981). Other studies have found that negotiations between businesspeople of different cultures often fail because of problems related to cross-cultural differences (Black, 1987; Graham, 1984; Tung, 1984). The costs of failed cross-cultural encounters are high; for example, studies have estimated the cost of a failed expatriate assignment to be $50,000 to $150,000 (Copeland and Griggs, 1985; Harris and Moran 1979; Misa and Fabricatore, 1979). For a firm with hundreds of expatriate employees worldwide, the costs can easily reach into the tens of millions of dollars per year. In fact, Copeland and Griggs (1985) have estimated that the direct costs of failed expatriate assignments for U.S. corporations is over $2 billion a year, and this does not include unmeasured losses such as damaged corporate reputations or lost business opportunities. In addition, Lanier (1979) estimates that up to 50 percent of American expatriates who do not return early are nonetheless ineffective in their overseas jobs, or what she terms "brownouts." Given that the average compensation package for a U.S. expatriate is between $200,000 and $250,000 (Black, 1988; Copeland and Griggs, 1985), the costs of brownouts are staggering.

Cross-cultural training has long been advocated as a means of facilitating effective cross-cultural interactions (Brislin, 1981; Landis and Brislin, 1983; Bochner, 1982; Harris and Moran, 1979; Mendenhall, Dunbar, and Oddou, 1987; Tung, 1981). However, its use in American business organizations is not widespread. Various reasons have been cited by business organizations for the low use of cross-cultural training; the most prevalent being that such training is not thought to be necessary or effective, and thus, top management sees no need for the training (Baker and Ivancevich, 1971; Mendenhall and Oddou, 1985; Runzheimer, 1984; Schwind, 1985; Tung, 1981; Zeira, 1975). However, the fundamental reason behind the lack of training seems to lie in the same assumption that causes American corporations to look only at domestic track records and to ignore cross-cultural-related skills when selecting expatriate candidates. The assumption is that good management is good management, and therefore, an effective manager in New York or Los Angeles will do fine in Hong Kong or Tokyo (Miller, 1973). Consequently, based on this assumption, it is logical for HR decision makers to conclude that CCT would not be needed or justified.

An extensive review of the cross-cultural training literature, however, suggests that HR managers are mistaken in their assumptions that good management is good management, that a firm can simply select employees who have been successful in the U.S. for overseas assignments, and that cross-cultural training is not necessary or effective. Harvey (1982) argued that domestic track record is not a good predictor of whether or not an expatriate will return early from an overseas assignment. A simple example can illustrate the reason for this finding. Generally in the U.S., setting clear, realistic, and difficult goals with specific time lines and then rewarding individuals who achieve the goals on time would be considered a good management practice (see Locke and Latham, 1984, for a detailed review). People will be motivated if they believe they know what is expected, believe they can achieve the goal, and believe they will be rewarded for their efforts. However, in Japan such goal specificity would be contrary to cultural norms, and the rewarding of an individual for personal achievement can often result in decreased motivation on the part of the rewarded individual because he or she would not want to stand out from or above the group (Mendenhall and Oddou, 1986a). This is a work-related norm that would be counterintuitive to an American expatriate manager with no training regarding Japanese culture or management practices.

A review of the CCT literature and its effectiveness also strongly indicates that American managers are mistaken in their belief that CCT is not necessary or effective. In a recent review of the empirical literature, Black and Mendenhall (1990) examined the effectiveness of CCT relative to three outcomes: (1) cross-cultural skill development, (2) cross-cultural adjustment, and (3) job performance. Of the ten studies that examined the relationship between CCT and self-confidence concerning one's ability to function effectively in cross-cultural situations, nine found a positive relationship. Nineteen out of nineteen studies found a positive relationship between CCT and increased cross-cultural relational skills. Sixteen out of sixteen studies found a positive relationship between CCT and more accurate cross-cultural perceptions. Nine out of nine studies found a positive relationship between CCT and cross-cultural adjustment. Finally, eleven out of fifteen studies found a positive relationship between CCT and job performance in the cross-cultural situation. However, the review also found that most of the empirical work was not founded on a theoretical framework per se and that the literature lacked a systematic approach to the study of CCT effectiveness. It is possible that the lack of a systematic stream of research has allowed the belief that CCT is not effective enough to persist. Additionally, the lack of a theoretical framework has left managers with little means of deciding who would benefit most from training, or what training method would be most effective, or how to best design such training programs. Perhaps until managers are presented with a systematic yet practical means of addressing these questions, they will continue to resist the prescriptions from academics (or consultants) that CCT is necessary and effective.

The purpose of this paper is to begin to shed some light on a framework for CCT that would be both theoretically sound and useful in practice. Recently, scholars have argued that social learning theory (SLT) provides a solid theoretical basis for understanding cross-cultural learning, training, and adjustment (Black and Mendenhall, 1990; Church, 1982; David, 1976). This paper explores the utility of SLT as a framework for systematically examining four important questions: (1) how can the level of training rigor of specific cross-cultural training methods be determined, (2) who would benefit most from cross-cultural training, (3) what CCT methods are most appropriate in specific situations, and (4) what level of CCT rigor is needed for maximum positive results? A brief review of past typologies and frameworks of CCT is followed by a discussion of the major components of SLT. Finally, a new framework of cross-cultural training based on SLT is delineated and practical implications are explored.

Review of Past Frameworks

Most of the writing in the cross-cultural training literature has focused on the discussion of different methods of training and general classifications of these methodologies, while less attention has been focused on the development of frameworks that would determine which training methods to utilize or the important contingency factors to consider in such determinations. The first part of this section summarizes a generally accepted typology of CCT methods, and the second part of the section reviews two recent frameworks that try to help managers determine which cross-cultural training methods to use in organizations.

Landis and Brislin (1983) have proposed a typology of cross-cultural training methods that has largely been accepted as a broad and integrative classification scheme of cross-cultural training methods. They developed the typology based on a broad review of the cross-cultural training literature. Their classification scheme is summarized in Exhibit 1.

Exhibit 1. Fundamental Cross-Cultural Training Methodologies

Information or Fact-Oriented Training: Trainees are presented with various facts about the country in which they are about to live via lectures, videotapes, and reading materials.

Attribution Training: The attribution approach focuses on explanations of behavior from the point of view of the native. The goal is to learn the cognitive standards by which the host-nationals process behavioral input so that the trainee can understand why the host-nationals behave as they do and adapt his or her own behavior to match the standards of behavior in the host country.

Cultural Awareness Training: The aim is to study the values, attitudes, and behaviors that are common in one's own culture so that the trainee better understands how culture impacts his or her own behavior. Once this is understood, it is assumed that he or she can better understand how culture affects human behavior in other countries.

Cognitive-Behavior Modification: The focus here is to assist trainees in linking what they find to be rewarding and punishing in their own subcultures (work, family, religion, etc.) and then to examine the reward and punishment structure in the host culture. Through an examination of the differences and similarities, strategies are developed to assist the trainee to obtain rewards—and avoid punishments—in the host culture.

Experiential Learning: The goal of this approach is to involve the trainees as active participants, to introduce the nature of life in another culture by actively experiencing that culture via field trips, complex role-plays, and cultural simulations.

Interaction Training: Here trainees interact with natives or returned expatriates in order to become more comfortable with host-nationals and to learn from the first-hand experience of the returned expatriates. The methods utilized can range from in-depth role plays to casual, informal discussions.

Source: Adapted from Landis and Brislin (1983).

Given the fragmented state of the literature, the development of a classification scheme for various cross-cultural training methodologies was an important step in improving an understanding of the area. However, managers responsible for training within corporations were often left without a means of determining which of the methodologies were most appropriate for specific training situations or which methods were more or less rigorous and effective. Recently, scholars have attempted to present means of making some of these determinations.

Tung's Framework of Training Method Selection

Tung (1982) presented a contingency framework for choosing an appropriate CCT method and its level of rigor. She argued that the two determining factors were the degree of interaction required in the host culture and the similarity between the individual's native culture and the new culture. The related training elements involved the content of the training and the rigor of the training. Essentially, Tung argued that if the expected interaction between the individual and members of the target or host culture was low, and the degree of dissimilarity between the individual's native culture and the host culture was low, then the content of the training should focus on task- and job-related issues as opposed to culture-related issues, and the level of rigor necessary for effective training should be relatively low. If there was a high level of expected interaction with host nationals and a large dissimilarity between the cultures, then the content of the training should focus on the new culture and on cross-cultural skill development, as well as on the new task, and the level of rigor of such training should be moderate to high.

While this framework does specify some criteria (i.e., degree of expected interaction and cultural similarity) for choosing CCT methods, the conclusions that the framework allows the user to make are rather general. Essentially, the framework suggests that the user emphasize task issues by utilizing training methods with relatively low levels of rigor and to emphasize culture learning, skill development, and task issues by utilizing a relatively high level of rigor. However, the framework does not help the user determine which specific training methods to use. In addition, the framework does not define what training "rigor" is and, therefore, does not help the user determine which specific training methods are more or less rigorous.

Mendenhall and Oddou's Framework for Selecting Training Methods

A more recent framework presented by Mendenhall and Oddou (1986b) moves beyond Tung's framework and provides more specificity. Like Tung, Mendenhall and Oddou acknowledge the importance of degree of expected interaction and similarity between the native and host cultures in determining the cross-cultural training method. In addition, Mendenhall and Oddou propose three key elements related to training. The first is the training method. Based on cross-cultural training typologies such as the one by Landis and Brislin (1983), Mendenhall and Oddou propose a three-part classification system and group specific training methods into low, medium, and high levels of rigor.

The framework presented by Mendenhall and Oddou is a significant improvement over the more general framework offered by Tung (1982). It provides a grouping of specific methods by level of rigor and also discusses the duration of training relative to the criteria of interaction and culture similarity. Despite these important improvements, the framework does not explain how the level of rigor of a specific CCT method or group of methods was determined and tells us little about the training and learning processes and, therefore, why the particular determinations are made. Also, the content of the training all seems to be "cultural" in nature and little integration of the individual's new job-related tasks and the new host culture is made. Finally, while both frameworks make intuitive sense, their theoretical grounding is never made explicit, and therefore, in the absence of empirical data to support the frameworks, it is difficult to evaluate their soundness for use and success in the real world.

The Need for a Theoretical Framework ━━━━━━━━━━━━━━━━━

Despite the plethora of work advocating the use of cross-cultural training in organizations, the empirical research in this area and even the conceptual work have been almost totally devoid of a theoretical framework (Adler, 1986; Black and Mendenhall, 1990; Roberts and Boyacigiller, 1982; Schollhammer, 1975). Bochner states that cross-cultural "research cannot be said to have been conducted with a great deal of theoretical sophistication. The tendency has been to use lengthy and diffuse questionnaires and/or interviews that generate masses of unrelated information" (1982, p. 16). A previous review of the empirical literature in cross-cultural training indicates that, in general, cross-cultural training seems to have a positive impact on skill development, adjustment, and performance (Black and Mendenhall, 1990); however, the lack of a theoretical framework leaves questions like why cross-cultural training is effective and which situations are best served by which specific training methods essentially unanswered. The purpose of this next section is to examine social learning theory as a theoretical framework that would begin to shed light on these questions.

Social Learning Theory

The potential of SLT to facilitate an understanding of the theoretical relationship between cross-cultural training and cross-cultural performance is significant (Church, 1982; David, 1976). Before discussing the particular relevance of SLT to cross-cultural training and its effectiveness, it is perhaps useful to briefly summarize the main points of the theory. SLT, as described by one of its leading authors (Bandura, 1977), argues that learning takes place both by the effect reinforcement has on behavior and by imitating or modeling the behavior of others and symbolically or vicariously making associations between behavior and consequence without direct, actual experience. As described by Bandura, SLT has four central elements: attention, retention, reproduction, and incentives (see Exhibit 2).

Attention. Before someone or something can be modeled, it must be noticed by the learner. Several factors have been found to influence the attention process of the subject or observer, including: (1) the status of the model, (2) the attractiveness of the model, (3) the similarity of the model,

Exhibit 2. Model of Social Learning Theory Process

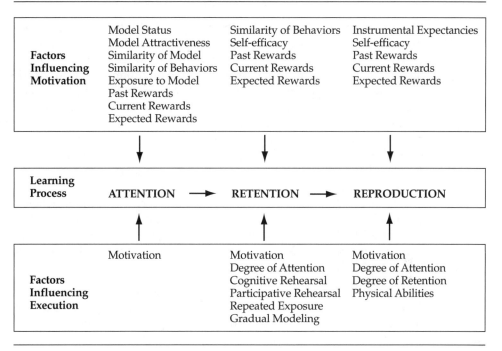

Factors Influencing Motivation	Model Status Model Attractiveness Similarity of Model Similarity of Behaviors Exposure to Model Past Rewards Current Rewards Expected Rewards	Similarity of Behaviors Self-efficacy Past Rewards Current Rewards Expected Rewards	Instrumental Expectancies Self-efficacy Past Rewards Current Rewards Expected Rewards
Learning Process	ATTENTION →	RETENTION →	REPRODUCTION
Factors Influencing Execution	Motivation	Motivation Degree of Attention Cognitive Rehearsal Participative Rehearsal Repeated Exposure Gradual Modeling	Motivation Degree of Attention Degree of Retention Physical Abilities

(4) the repeated availability of the model, and (5) past reinforcement for paying attention to the model (either actual or vicarious rewards).

Retention. Retention is the process by which the modeled behavior becomes encoded as a memory by the observer. Two representational systems are involved. The imaginal system is utilized during exposure to the framework. During exposure, images are associated on the basis of physical contiguity. These images are stored as "cognitive maps" which can later guide the observer in imitation. The second system is the verbal system. It represents the coded information in abbreviated verbal systems and groups similar patterns of behavior into larger integrated units. It should be noted that both the repeated modeling of a behavior and the repeated cognitive rehearsal of the modeled behavior serve to solidify the retention process.

Reproduction. The third major component of the modeling process involves the translation of the symbolic representations of the modeled stimuli into overt actions. As individuals try to imitate the modeled behavior, they check their performance against their memory of what was modeled. Actual reproduction of the modeled behavior, of course, can be inhibited by physical differences between the model and the person imitating the model, how well the model is observed, and how well the modeled behavior is retained.

Incentives and the Motivational Processes. The fourth major component of SLT involves the influence of incentives on the motivational processes of modeling behavior. Incentives have three primary sources. Incentives can come from the direct external environment, from vicarious association, and from the individual him- or herself. In turn, each of these different sources of incentives can affect several aspects of the learning process. Incentives can affect which models are observed and how much attention is paid to observed models. Incentives can influence the degree to which the modeled behavior is retained and rehearsed. Also, incentives can influence which learned behaviors are emitted. It is important to note that Bandura (1977) argued on the basis of empirical work that incentives play a much larger role in influencing what behavior is emitted as opposed to what behavior is learned. He concluded that individuals learn numerous behaviors which are not usually emitted because they are not positively rewarded. However, if the reward structure is changed, the behaviors are performed.

Expectancies. In relation to the motivational processes of learning, Bandura (1977) distinguishes between two types of expectancies. The first type of expectations Bandura calls "efficacy expectations." The individual's self-efficacy is the degree to which the individual believes he or she can successfully execute a particular behavior. This expectation is similar to the "effort to performance" expectancy proposed by Vroom (1964). In his view of the literature, Bandura (1977) found that higher levels of self-efficacy led individuals to persist at imitating modeled behavior longer and to be more willing to try to imitate novel behavior. The sources for increasing self-efficacy, in order of importance, includes past experience ("I've done it or something like it before"), vicarious experience ("other people have done it"), and verbal persuasion ("people say I can do it").

In addition to efficacy expectations, Bandura (1977) argues that outcome expectations influence the modeling process. Outcome expectations are people's beliefs that the execution of certain behaviors will lead to desired outcomes. These expectations are similar to the "expectancy-of-performance-to-outcome" (instrumentality expectancies) proposed by Vroom (1964). Bandura concluded that in addition to the modeling processes of attention, retention, and reproduction, incentives influence what people learn and incentives and efficacy and outcome expectancies influence what learned behaviors are emitted.

Important Empirical Findings. Although a number of empirical findings are reviewed by Bandura (1977), several are important to summarize because of the insight they provide about fundamental elements in the learning process. The first finding is that gradual modeling is more effective than "one-shot" modeling, especially if the modeled behaviors are novel to the observer. Gradual modeling involves providing successive approximations of the final behavior to be modeled. This modeling process is more effective than modeling only the final behavior for several reasons: (1) observers pay more attention to models and modeled behaviors which are more familiar, (2) observers can more easily retain models which are more similar to cognitive maps already possessed, (3) observers have higher expectations of efficacy and outcome of behaviors which are more familiar, and (4) observers are more likely to be able to reproduce more familiar behaviors.

Second, Bandura argues that individuals can learn completely through symbolic modeling, that is, just by watching and rehearsing mentally. This symbolic learning process can be facilitated by the other variables discussed (attractiveness of the model, similarity of the model, etc.) and by having multiple models. Also, Bandura found that participative modeling is generally more effective than symbolic processes alone. Participative reproduction simply means that the observer actually practices (as opposed to only cognitive rehearsals) the modeled behavior. The external, and especially the internal, feedback processes serve to refine the observer's ability to reproduce the modeled behavior at a later time in the appropriate situation.

Social Learning Theory and Cross-Cultural Training ——————————

Social learning theory provides a theoretical framework for systematically examining the level of rigor that specific CCT methods generally contain and for determining the appropriate cross-cultural training approach for specific training cases and situations. Based on the central variable of "modeling process" in SLT, the first part of this section explores a means of ranking specific cross-cultural training methods by the degree of rigor generally contained in the methods and examining two other factors that are related to the total rigor a training program might have. The second part of this section examines how SLT processes can provide a heuristic framework for deciding which CCT methods would be appropriate in specific situations. Throughout the second part of this section, we examine the practical implications of the framework for Mel Stephen's dilemma.

SLT and CCT Rigor

As was mentioned earlier, many of the past attempts to provide a means of choosing CCT methods have included the concept of training rigor but have not attempted to define what the term meant. Within the framework of SLT, rigor is essentially the degree of cognitive involvement of the learner or trainee. The modeling processes in SLT provide a useful means of not only defining rigor but also determining the relative degree of rigor that specific training methods generally have.

Within SLT, there are basically two modeling processes—symbolic and participative. Symbolic modeling simply involves observing modeled behaviors. However, this observation can have two forms. The first form consists of the learner or trainee hearing about the behavior and then translating those verbal messages into imagined images. Thus, the learner or trainee observes the behaviors in his or her mind. Cross-cultural training methods that generally exhibit this type of modeling process include verbal factual briefings, lectures, and books. The second form of symbolic modeling involves the trainee actually seeing visually the behavior being modeled. In this case, the trainee both sees and retains a cognitive image of the behavior and is more cognitively involved than when the symbolic modeling process only involves translating verbal messages into cognitive images. Specific CCT methods that generally exhibit this type of modeling include films, role modeling, demonstrations, and nonparticipative language training.

The second basic form of modeling is termed participative modeling. Participative modeling essentially means that in addition to observing the modeled behavior, the trainee also participates in modeling the behavior. This participation can take two forms. The first form involves "verbal" participation. In other words, the trainee participates in modeling the behavior by describing verbally what he or she would do. Cross-cultural training methods that generally exhibit this type of participative modeling include case studies and culture assimilators. The second form of participative modeling involves more physical participation in modeling the behaviors being learned. Cross-cultural training methods that generally require this type of participative modeling include role plays, interactive language training, field trips, and interactive simulations. Trainees are more cognitively involved when they must physically, as opposed to only verbally, participate in modeling the behaviors being taught.

In addition, rehearsal increases the level of cognitive involvement during symbolic or participative modeling. Rehearsal also has two basic forms. Cognitive rehearsal involves the mental rehearsal or practice of the modeled behavior (e.g., practicing eating with chop sticks in one's mind). Behavioral rehearsal involves actual physical practice of the modeled behavior. Because behavioral rehearsal involves both mental and physical processes, it is more cognitively engaging than cognitive rehearsal alone and, therefore, is more rigorous. By definition, symbolic modeling can utilize only cognitive rehearsal, while participative modeling can utilize either cognitive or behavioral rehearsal or both. Thus, the rigor of any specific CCT method could be enhanced through cognitive or behavioral rehearsal. Thus, by examining the modeling and rehearsal processes involved, the relative rigor of a specific CCT method can be approximated. Exhibit 3 provides an illustration of the relative ranking in terms of rigor for a set of specific and common CCT methods.

Exhibit 3. Modeling Processes, Rigor, & Training Methods

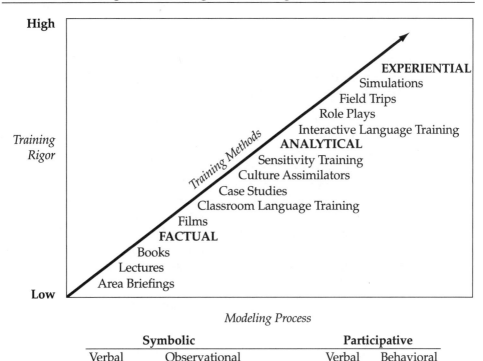

Modeling Process

	Symbolic		**Participative**	
Verbal	Observational		Verbal	Behavioral

In determining the rigor of a CCT program, one would need to consider the rigor of the specific CCT method(s) utilized and the duration and intensity of the total CCT program. The duration and intensity of a CCT program is a function of the total hours of training and the time frame within which the training is conducted. Thus, all other things being equal, a training program that involved a total of 25 training hours over five days would be less rigorous than a program that involved 100 total hours over three weeks.

In general, the SLT literature and the CCT literature provide evidence to strongly suggest that the more rigorous the training the more effective the training will be in terms of the trainee being able to actually and appropriately execute the learned behaviors (Bandura, 1977; Black and Mendenhall, 1990; Tung, 1981). The basic explanation for this relationship is that rigor (i.e., cognitive involvement) increases the level of attention and retention, which in turn increases reproduction proficiency. As an example, Gudykunst, Hammer, and Wiseman (1977) found that a more rigorous CCT training program involving the "Contrast American" role play, "BaFa BaFa" cross-cultural training simulation, and field trips was significantly more effective for a sample of Navy personnel on overseas assignments in Japan than was CCT involving lectures on Japanese values and culture alone.

Important Situational Factors

In addition to providing a means of determining the general level of rigor of specific CCT methods, SLT also provides a framework for identifying situational factors that are important to consider in choosing appropriate CCT methods in specific situations. Social learning theory argues that the more novel the behaviors are that must be learned, the more difficult it is to attend to, retain, and reproduce them. In addition, SLT argues that the more frequently or accurately the learned behaviors are required to be reproduced in actual situations (as opposed to training situations), the greater the importance of the attention and retention processes during training. Thus, the greater the novelty of the behaviors to be learned and the greater the required level of reproduction, the higher the requisite levels of attention and retention needed, and the higher the level of the rigor of the training needed. These specific situational factors that are relevant to CCT are briefly discussed below.

Culture Novelty. Based on SLT and the arguments just made, the more novel the host culture is, the more difficult it will be for the individual to attend to and retain the various models of appropriate behavior (in the training situation as well as in the actual host culture). Thus, the more novel the host culture, the more assistance through rigorous training the individual will need in order to be aware of, retain, and appropriately reproduce the new behaviors appropriate in the foreign culture.

An important practical question is "How does one determine the degree of novelty in the host culture?" Once this question is answered, then the HR decision maker can begin to determine what the appropriate levels of CCT rigor and corresponding specific CCT methods are. While definitive decision rules are perhaps impossible to create, past cross-cultural research presents some rough guidelines (Haire, Ghiselli, and Porter, 1966; England and Lee, 1974; Hofstede, 1980). Information provided in Hofstede (1980) presents perhaps the most comprehensive yet simple means of estimating cultural novelty. Hofstede (1980) examined native employees in a U.S. multinational firm in 48 countries along four different scales (power distance, uncertainty avoidance, individualism, masculinity). A rough estimate of culture novelty can be obtained by calculating the absolute difference in scores on each one of the four scales between the employees of the target country and the American employees and then summing these differences. The larger the final number, the greater the culture novelty relative to the American culture. The work of Torbiorn (1982) also gives insight into the degree of cultural novelty. Torbiorn (1982) found that for Scandinavians the most difficult regions of the world to live and work in were: (1) Africa, (2) Middle East, (3) Far East, (4) South America, (5) Eastern Bloc, (6) Europe, (7) North America, and (8) Australia and New Zealand.

In addition to using Hofstede's (1980) results, one might estimate culture novelty by simply assessing whether the language of the host culture is different from that of the individual's home culture and whether learning the language will be a necessity for living and working in the host country. For example, even though Cantonese Chinese is the most common language of use in Hong Kong, English is still an official language and one can survive without Chinese language skills; however, survival would be more difficult without Spanish language skills in a country such as Chile (Kepler, Kepler, Gaither, and Gaither, 1983).

The next step in assessing the novelty of the target country and culture is to examine the previous experience of the specific individual candidate. Social learning theory would argue that the more experience the individual has had with a specific culture, even if that experience was in the distant past, the more the individual is able to recall and utilize those past experiences in coping with the present situation in the host culture. It should be mentioned that both the duration and intensity of the past experience serve to deepen what was retained from the experience and to facilitate later recall (Bandura, 1977). Thus, all things being equal, the Indonesian culture would be less novel for the candidate who lived there before than the candidate who had not. Likewise, all other things being equal, the candidate who had frequent and involved interactions with Indonesians during a three-year stay would find the culture less novel in a later visit than an individual who had infrequent and superficial interactions with Indonesians during a similar three-year stay. Thus, both the "quantity" and "quality" of an individual's previous experience must be examined. In addition, there is some empirical support that suggests that previous international experience, even if it is not in the host country's culture, reduces the novelty of the culture (Black, 1988). Based on SLT, one would expect that a candidate with previous experience in a country or region similar to the host country and culture would perceive less culture novelty, have an easier adjustment, and need less training than a candidate with previous experience in a totally different country or region, and that a candidate with frequent and involved previous interactions would need less training than a candidate with infrequent and superficial interactions. The following simple equation represents the basic assessment process: Net Culture Novelty = Objective Culture Novelty – (Quality + Quantity of an Individual's Previous Experience).

Degree of Interaction. The second situational factor in determining the degree of CCT rigor needed is the degree of expected interpersonal interaction between the individual and members of the host culture. The degree of interaction can be viewed in three ways. First, one can assess the degree of interaction through the relative frequency of inter-action expected between the individual and members of the host cul-ture. Also, one can assess the degree through the importance of the interactions. If one expects relatively few and mostly trivial interac-tions between the individual and members of the host culture, then the individual's ability to reproduce appropriate behaviors in the host cul-ture is less important (and therefore, so would be the individual's attention and retention needs and the individual's need to get help to enhance attention, retention, and reproduction through rigorous train-ing). If, on the other hand, one expects many and primarily important interactions between the individual and members of the host culture, then the individual's ability to reproduce appropriate behaviors is more important (and therefore, so would be the individual's need in getting help to enhance that ability).

In addition to the frequency and importance of the interactions, the nature of the interactions should also be assessed. Specific aspects of the nature of the interactions with host country nationals include the following:

1. how familiar or novel the interaction is;
2. the directionality of the interaction (one-way vs. two-way);
3. the type of the interaction (routine vs. unique);
4. the form of the interaction (face-to-face vs. other forms like mail);
5. the total duration of the cross-cultural interaction (e.g., one vs. five years); and
6. the format of the interaction (formal vs. informal).

Based on the communication literature (Jablin, Putnam, Roberts, and Porter, 1987), one would expect that novel, two-way, unique, face-to-face, long-term, and informal cross-cultural interactions would be more difficult than the opposite. The following equation represents the basic assessment of degree of interaction: Degree of Interaction = (Frequency of Interactions with Host Nationals) x (Importance of Interactions) x (Nature of Interactions).

Job Novelty. The third important situational factor involves the novel-ty of the new job and its related tasks. Based on precisely the same the-oretical arguments that were presented concerning culture novelty, the more novel the tasks of the new job in the new culture, the more assis-tance the individual will need through rigorous training to produce the desired and necessary behaviors to be effective in the new job. Some scholars may reason that it is difficult to separate culture novelty from job novelty, arguing that if the culture is novel then to some degree the job will also be novel. Although culture novelty and job novelty are not independent of each other, there is both logical and empirical basis for separating the two issues. First, if there is little interaction between ele-ments of the new culture and the job, and if the new job is very similar to the previous job, then it is quite possible to have a situation involving a novel culture but a nonnovel job. Likewise, it is possible to have a situation in which the new job is very different from the previous job but the host culture is similar to the individual's home culture. Recent empirical evidence suggests that individuals in international assignments adjust differentially to the culture and the job (Black, 1988; Black and Stephens, 1989), which suggests that while the novelty of the new job and culture can be linked they are not necessarily intertwined.

The question the HR decision maker must ask is "How novel is the new job and its tasks and responsibilities?" Although it is perhaps impossible to draw a definitive line between what would and would not be a novel job, Stewart's (1982) framework of job characteristics provides a useful means of determining where "job novelties" might occur. Based on Stewart's (1982) framework, the HR decision maker should first try to determine if the new *job demands* are similar to or different from those of previous jobs held by the candidate.

- Are performance standards the same?
- Is the degree of personal involvement required in the work unit the same?
- Are the types of tasks to be done similar?
- Are the bureaucratic procedures that must be followed similar?

Next the HR decision maker must determine how similar the new *job constraints* are.

- Are resource limitations the same?
- Are the legal restrictions similar?
- Are the technological limitations familiar?

Finally, the HR decision maker must determine the novelty of the new *job choices*.

- Is the freedom to decide how work gets done the same?
- Is the discretion about what work gets done similar?
- Is the freedom to decide who does which tasks the same?
- Are the choices about what work gets delegated similar?

If the HR decision maker examines the three job characteristics proposed by Stewart (1982), he or she should be able to make a rough estimate of the extent to which the new job is novel relative to a specific candidate. According to SLT, the more novel the new responsibilities and tasks, the more help the individual will need through rigorous training to learn and execute the desired and necessary behaviors.

The Family and CCT

The previous discussion has been presented as though the only person the HR decision maker needed to consider was the employee; however, research provides strong evidence to suggest that the candidate's family, especially the spouse, is also important to consider (Black, 1988; Black and Stephens, 1989; Harvey, 1986; Tung, 1981).

Culture Novelty. The process of determining the extent of training the family needs also begins with an assessment of culture novelty. The process of assessing the novelty of the culture obtained in relation to the candidate can be used for the family with two important qualifications. First, the final assessment of the host country's culture novelty must be made relative to the family's previous experience. Second, children under the age of about thirteen may need much less preparation than older children because they seem to have less difficulty adjusting to foreign cultures (Tung, 1984), and spouses must be given nearly as much consideration as the candidate is given because their adjustment or lack of adjustment can be a critical determinant of the candidate's success or failure in the foreign culture (Black, 1988; Black and Stephens, 1989; Tung, 1981).

Degree of Interaction. The spouse should also be given considerable attention concerning the degree of expected interaction in determining the level of CCT rigor needed to prepare him or her for living and functioning effectively in the foreign culture. The degree of expected interaction can be assessed in much the same manner as was suggested for the candidate (i.e., frequency and intensity). However, some important differences between candidates and spouses need to be considered. First, most spouses do not work in the host culture even if they worked before the foreign assignment (Stephens and Black, in press). Second, even if spouses are not required to interact with host country nationals, lack of the ability to interact can lead to feelings of isolation and loneliness, which in turn can be the primary cause of inadequate adjustment to the host culture and an early or premature return on the part of the entire family (Harvey, 1986; Tung, 1984; 1988). Consequently, even if the required degree of interaction between the spouse and host country nationals is low, the spouse will be better adjusted if he or she has the ability to interact effectively (Black and Stephens, 1989). Thus, it may be important to facilitate this ability through rigorous CCT even if the required degree of interaction does not seem to merit it.

Integrating Culture Novelty, Interaction, Job Novelty, and CCT Rigor

The theoretical reasoning behind the integration of culture novelty, interaction, and job novelty is relatively straightforward. The greater the culture novelty, required interaction, and job novelty, the greater the need for rigorous CCT. However, each of these three conditions is not "created equally." Research shows that adjusting to the culture and interacting with host country nationals is more difficult than doing the job (Black, 1988; Black and Stephens, 1989). This can be represented pictorially by a three-dimensional cube with a line running through the cube diagonally from the front left corner to the back right corner (see Exhibit 4).

**Exhibit 4. Integration of Cross-Cultural
Training Rigor and Main Contingency Factors**

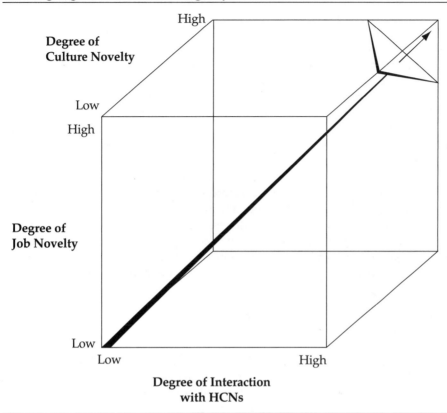

The vertical axis represents the dimension of job novelty, ranging from low to high novelty. The bottom horizontal axis represents the dimension of interaction, ranging from low to high required interaction. The top horizontal axis represents relative culture novelty, ranging from low to high novelty. The diagonal line, which runs from the front left corner to the back right corner, represents training methods and rigor, ranging from low to high rigor. Thus, a point can be plotted in the three-dimensional space by estimating the culture novelty, degree of required interaction, and job novelty of a specific impending cross-cultural assignment. The intersection of the plotted point and the diagonal line, and therefore the determination of the requisite level of rigor, can be determined by imagining a plane at a right angle to, and traveling on the same diagonal as the CCT rigor line. When the plane intersects the point plotted based on estimates relative to each of the three dimensions, it also intersects with a point on the diagonal line representing CCT rigor. That intersection provides a rough estimation of the CCT rigor required.

The plane is placed at a right angle because research has demonstrated that adjusting to a novel job in the work situation of an overseas assignment is easier than adjusting to the general culture or interacting with host nationals (Black, 1988; Black and Stephens, 1989). Thus, even in the case of a highly novel job but low culture novelty and low required interaction with host nationals, the highest level of CCT rigor is not required. By contrast, even if the level of job novelty is moderate, a high level of culture novelty and required interaction necessitates a high level of CCT rigor.

The content of the training would, of course, be a direct function of the three dimensions discussed. If the assessment indicates that there will be a high level of job novelty, then the CCT program should include content relative to the new behaviors that need to be learned to effectively perform the job. If there is a high degree of interaction required, then the CCT program should include in its content such topics as cross-cultural communication, interpersonal skills, perception, and ethnocentricity. If there is a high degree of culture novelty, then topics such as the host country's values, religious systems, political systems, social customs, and business practices should be included. The relative emphasis of the content would be a direct reflection of the relative low or high scores on each of the three dimensions.

Two Case Illustrations

Wave, one of the market leaders in the computer software industry, had just sealed a joint venture pact with one of Japan's largest designers and manufacturers of computers, Nippon Kankei. Wave, a Seattle-based company, agreed to send six Americans to work in Tokyo with fifteen of Nippon Kankei's best "high potential" software designers. The purpose of this effort was to train the Japanese designers in state-of-the-art software design while working on software applications for Nippon Kankei's products. Also, Nippon Kankei, through its distribution network, would market any products created by the joint venture research and development team to other computer manufacturers, distributers, and retailers as well. Wave would retain the copyright and share significantly in profits generated by the joint venture.

Wave retained complete managerial and creative control of the R & D team. The project manager was to be designated by Wave, and John Selby was selected and had agreed to go. John had vast experience in all aspects of the industry and had overseen four projects in the U.S. from the idea to the final product. The other five designers had limited managerial experience—they were pure designers. Nippon Kankei's management hoped that by rubbing shoulders and working jointly with these American designers their own staff would get "up to speed" in software design.

All of the designers agreed to relocate to Japan after feeling that their families' financial position and standard of living would not suffer because of the move. All of the designers were married. None of the designers indicated any reluctance on the part of their spouse concerning the three-year assignment; however, there were rumors that at least three of the wives were "less than thrilled" about disrupting their childrens' education and creating a new life in Japan.

What practical guidance concerning the cross-cultural training of this team of expatriates who are about to be sent to Japan can the framework we have discussed provide? The first step is to assess the culture novelty of the host country to which the team is being sent.

If Wave generalized Hofstede's (1980) research of Japanese who worked for an American multinational corporation to those Japanese who will be working with Wave's people in the joint venture, it would find the following: (1) Japanese have a much higher power distance (the degree workers accept power difference between managers and subordinates) of about 20 index points, (2) Americans are much more risk taking (53 index points on uncertainty avoidance), (3) Americans are much more individual and less group oriented than the Japanese (45 index points), and (4) Japanese accept traditional sex roles and have a higher work ethic than Americans (35 point differential). Hofstede's results suggest that not only does Japan have a culture quite different from American culture but it is one of the most different. The main language of Japan is also different. But to what degree will the expatriates from Wave need to speak Japanese? The ability of the Japanese assigned to the joint venture to read English is quite high, but their speaking and listening comprehension skills are marginal. Also, the American expatriates are likely to find it difficult to function effectively without Japanese language ability outside the workplace.

Next, Wave must assess the previous experience of the candidates. Unfortunately, though many had vacationed a time or two overseas, none of the candidates have lived or worked in Japan or have lived and worked outside the U.S. Thus, their previous experience would not reduce the culture novelty or the need for CCT. Based on all this information, it seems clear that the level of "culture novelty" that the Wave expatriates will experience will be quite high.

At first the degree of required interaction with Japanese workers for the American software designers would be fairly low, but would be much higher for John Selby, the project manager. However, the group-oriented nature of Japanese work organizations and the practice of consensus decision making increases the likelihood that all of Wave's expatriates will be interacting frequently with the Japanese. Additionally, the interactions are likely to be face-to-face, two-way, informal, and both routine and unique in nature over several years. Thus, while the degree of required interaction is likely to be higher for John Selby, it is still likely to be high for the other expatriates as well.

For Wave, on the surface it does not appear that the job novelty for the group of expatriates is very high. John Selby has managed four "start-up" projects before, and all the designers have had considerable experience in new product design. There are no new technical skills needed by the designers, and coming up with programs for new hard-ware systems is what they do for a living. Upon closer examination of the job demands, it seems that there is a high potential for performance standards, the tasks concerning training or working with Japanese, the way in which decisions get made, and the bureaucratic procedures that must be followed to all be different compared to their old jobs back in Seattle. Wave must also consider the novelty of job constraints. There is a high probability that resource limitations (e.g., communicating with colleagues and experts back at Wave), budgets, and legal restrictions are significantly different in Japan compared to Seattle. Finally, Wave needs to examine the novelty of job choices or discretion. Will the American designers be free to decide how to get work done (e.g., working hours) as they were in Seattle? Will John Selby be able to assign tasks and man-age the team the same way he did back home? It is quite likely that all the members of the Wave team will need to make adjustments in order to work effectively with the Japanese. Wave's answers to these ques-tions suggest that job choice novelty will be moderately high as well.

While there may be limits to Wave's budget, if it can, spouses should be included in the CCT program. This is because the novelty of the culture is high, and the ability to interact with shopkeepers, neigh-bors, banks, etc. greatly facilitates the spouse's ability to adjust to the new culture. As mentioned earlier, the spouse's adjustment is impor-tant because of the significance it has on expatriate adjustment (Black, 1988; Black and Stephens, 1989).

Thus, based on Exhibit 4, Wave needs to design or purchase a CCT program of fairly high rigor. The program should include some ele-ments of symbolic modeling (both symbolic and observational) such as lectures, articles, books, and films on Japanese culture and business. But the CCT program should also include training methods that involve participative modeling as well. Specific methods might include case studies, culture assimilator exercises, interactive language study, role plays, and perhaps a premove visit to Japan. Additionally, the con-tent of the training should include job, business, and general culture issues given the novelty of both task and culture. Obviously, a training program that includes all of these specific training methods will take time to execute. A reasonable estimate is that at least sixty hours of training will be needed. If time and scheduling constraints prevent all the training from occurring before departure to Japan, some follow-up training might be useful once the expatriates were settled in Japan.

A second case may provide further illustration of the practical implications of the framework presented. An academic association of management educators, primarily university and college business pro-fessors, was planning to hold a joint conference in Japan with Japanese business and business education leaders. The American professors were asked to submit professional papers on a wide range of business topics, and sixty were selected to participate in the international conference. The conference organizers decided to provide some type of CCT for the selected participants.

The designers of the training program had to first determine the culture novelty of Japan relative to the U.S. As has already been described, the work by Hofstede suggests that Japan is one of the most novel countries in relationship to America. However, the previous international experience of the selected participants in general or specifically in Japan were not known. Because participation in the training session could not be required, it was assumed that those who had the least amount of previous experience with Japan would be most likely to attend the training session. This, in fact, turned out to be the case. Thus, the degree of culture novelty was high.

Next the degree of interaction with host nationals had to be assessed. The design of the conference was such that there would be a mixture of formal, one-way interaction and informal, two-way interaction. The conference was scheduled to last only four days, so the duration of the interaction would be quite short but would involve frequent interactions during the four days. Although one of the purposes of the conference was to create better ties between the American and Japanese business scholars, the importance of the interactions was considered moderate. Also, the degree that the American scholars would need to know and utilize Japanese was small. It was expected that the Japanese participants would have a reasonable command of English since the entire program was to be conducted in English with very few sessions providing translators. Thus, the overall degree of interaction between the Americans and Japanese was expected to be low to moderate.

Finally, the job novelty for the American scholars had to be assessed. At first glance, the job novelty would seem quite low. In terms of presenting and listening to papers at an academic conference, this conference on paper looked quite similar to conferences held in the U.S. However, the demands of presenting research results to a culturally mixed audience (Japanese and Americans) were somewhat different from those of presenting to just an audience of American scholars. Overall, however, the job novelty for the American scholars was considered to be low to moderate.

Based on these assessments, Exhibit 4 would suggest the use of moderately rigorous training methods. Exhibit 3 indicates that moderate levels of training rigor consist of primarily symbolic modeling processes. Consequently, the training program was scheduled for a single day and included symbolic verbal modeling via (1) short lectures on specific aspects of Japan and Japanese culture that the American professors would likely encounter in their four-day stay, (2) a short video on the specific location of the conference, and (3) classroom language training focused on simple Japanese greetings and phrases. The training program also included some symbolic observational modeling via (1) demonstrations of such things as greetings and the exchanging of business cards and (2) role plays done for the training participants on presenting to a culturally mixed audience and on presenting using a translator.

Conclusion ————————————————————————————

A variety of implications can be derived from an SLT-based approach to CCT. The first three implications are related specifically to international or expatriate assignments. The next two implications are related to broader issues of good global development practices.

CCT Is a Necessity Not a Luxury

It is very clear from the research literature that the vast majority of senior executives do not support CCT programs for their employees who must work with foreign business people. The research literature is equally clear that American expatriates who work with foreigners without the benefit of CCT are less effective than those who have been trained. With so much at stake, from the success of business negotiations to the effective operation of overseas subsidiaries or joint ventures, there seems to be little reason not to invest time and money into training one's people who must work internationally. The training costs are small compared to the potential costs of early returns or business losses due to the lack of cross-cultural competency. As with any training intervention, unless top management support exists, the potential of a successful CCT program is low. HRM staff generally do not try to push through programs that are not sanctioned from on high; American senior executives need to start blessing the utilization of CCT programs—it's as simple as that.

It's a Family Affair

Of the few firms in the U.S. that do offer CCT to their expatriates, few offer such training to their spouses or other family members, despite the fact that research has demonstrated the impact that spouse and family adjustment can have on premature expatriate returns. A simple way to counteract this problem is to simply send spouses to the training sessions and to give them the same CCT the employee receives. While large portions of the training may be business related, much of it will be applicable to the nonworking spouse because cultural values and norms that affect business behavior also affect social behavior outside of the workplace. Also, knowing the challenges the employee will face at work may assist the spouse in offering support to the employee during the assignment. A more substantial effort would be to tailor a program that deals with the specific daily and cultural challenges that the spouse will face overseas. In some aspects, the spouse faces more challenges than does the employee. While the employee has his or her job and people at work, the spouse often has an empty house, no friends, and isolation with which to contend. Although much of the focus of this paper has centered on the employee and determining appropriate CCT methods for the employee, we have argued that these same assessment processes could be used to determine when it would be more or less critical to provide CCT for the spouse as well.

Avoid "Dog and Pony" Shows

Since many firms do not have the in-house expertise to design CCT programs, the use of external consultants and trainers is common. The lack of internal CCT expertise means that the ability of the HR staff to evaluate the quality and suitability of external CCT programs may be less than desired.

The framework presented in this paper provides HR decision makers with at least a rough template by which they can evaluate the quality, rigor, and appropriateness of training programs offered by consultants or universities. The decision maker could use the framework to evaluate consultants' bids or university programs in a more analytical fashion by comparing the training methodology to the various methods described in the paper. Next, by examining the various dimensions discussed, the decision maker could determine if he or she were buying more than was needed or whether the proposed training program would be inadequate and not sufficiently rigorous to meet the needs of the trainees in order to be more effective in their cross-cultural assignments.

CCT Is Not Just for Expatriates

Throughout this paper, much of the focus has been on expatriate employees; however, CCT is necessary for repatriated employees, for employees who go on short-term assignments, for good succession planning, and for general managerial development.

Just as the framework can be a guide for selecting or designing CCT for expatriates being sent overseas, it can also be used for selecting or designing training programs for employees returning to their home country after an international assignment. Although many managers would think that "coming home" would be "no big deal," Adler (1986) found that most managers found returning to the U.S. more difficult than adjusting to the foreign country.

In addition to CCT for employees being sent on or returning from long-term international assignments, the framework and theory presented suggests that employees sent on short-term assignments need CCT as well. The content of the training may need to be more focused and topic specific than for those headed for two-to-four-year assignments, as illustrated in the case of the American professors going to Japan for a four-day conference, but it is still necessary. Companies often send managers overseas for important tasks that take a relatively shorter period of time, yet fail to train these individuals as well. Sending someone to Korea to "explore business opportunities" or "work through the details of a joint venture agreement" require cross-cultural knowledge and skills. For example, Graham (1985) has demonstrated that Americans who do not understand Japanese negotiation tactics and their underlying values often utilize negotiation tactics and strategies that are counterproductive. The framework outlined in this paper regarding CCT methodology provides a means of determining the level of CCT rigor that is needed and specific methods that are appropriate.

The lack of CCT for international assignments can have a rather significant impact on succession planning for American firms. Consider the following scenario. U.S.A. MNC, Inc. does not provide CCT before international assignments. As a consequence, many good employees fail in their international assignments because they were not adequately prepared. Also, the firm does not provide CCT for returning expatriates or managers sent on short-term assignments. Some of these employees also fail because of inadequate preparation. Other bright employees notice this. Not wanting the same fate to befall them, the best and the brightest decline to accept international assignments. These best and brightest, who lack any in-depth international experience, then continue to move to the top of the firm. Once they make it to the top, one has to wonder how capable they will be at dealing with foreign competitors, with global markets, with international suppliers, with multicultural workforces, and so on.

In the introduction, we cited scholars who argue that corporations need to develop managers with the new skills, such as global visioning skills, multicultural relation skills, and so on, to effectively lead firms in the 1990s and into the twenty-first century. Consequently, developing these skills is a critical element of succession planning. At a macro level, the framework presented suggests that if managers in the future must deal with cultures different from their own, must tackle tasks quite novel from those in which they currently engage, and must be proficient in interacting with people from other cultures, then they must receive over the course of their career and development quite rigorous cross-cultural training. Thus, the framework can provide guidance concerning the level of CCT rigor and specific training methods, such as culture assimilators, necessary for a specific international assignment, but it can also suggest the level of CCT rigor and training methods, such as international assignments, needed to prepare individuals for general positions and responsibilities in the future.

Ethics and CCT

In addition to the "utilitarian" functions that CCT may serve, firms may want to consider the issue from a social responsibility or ethical perspective. The military trains its soldiers before sending them into battle, churches educate and train their missionaries before sending them out to proselytize, and governments train secret agents before they go under "deep" cover, but U.S. firms send employees overseas cold. Such a "sink-or-swim" approach would seem irresponsible and unreasonable to the military, clergy, or government, why then does it seem logical to the industrial sector? One must wonder if it is ethical to uproot an individual or a family, send them across the Pacific or Atlantic Oceans, and expect them to make their way skillfully through an alien business and social culture on their own. Perhaps American executives reason that the extraordinary compensation packages expatriates receive make the exchange a fair and ethical one. Living and working overseas involves adjustments and stress of a high magnitude. Placing individuals in such conditions without giving them the tools to manage these conditions seems not only economically costly to the firm, and personally costly to the individuals, but simply wrong. Ignorance is not held to be justifiable for failure domestically—why then should it be a justification for failure regarding international assignments? If U.S. firms are to successfully compete in what is becoming a global battleground, they must provide their soldiers with the weapons and ammunition necessary to wage effective and victorious campaigns.

References ————————————————————————————

Adler, N. *International dimensions of organizational behavior.* Boston, Mass.: Kent, 1986.

Baker, J. C. and Ivancevich, J. M. "The assignment of American executives abroad: systematic, haphazard, or chaotic?" *California Management Review,* 1971, 13, 39- 44.

Bandura, A. *Social learning theory.* Englewood Cliffs, N.J.: Prentice-Hall, 1977.

Black, J. S. "Japanese/American negotiations: The Japanese perspective." *Business and Economic Review,* 1987, 6 (1), 27-30.

Black, J. S. "Work role transitions: a study of American expatriate managers in Japan." *Journal of International Business Studies,* 1988, 19, 277-294.

Black, J. S. and Mendenhall, M. "Cross-culture training effectiveness: a review and theoretical framework for future research." *Academy of Management Review,* 1990, 15, 113-136.

Black, J. S. and Stephens, G. K. "The influence of the spouse on American expatriate adjustment and intent to stay in Pacific Rim assignments." *Journal of Management,* 1989, 15, 529-544.

Bouchner, S. *Culture in contact: Studies in cross-cultural interaction.* New York: Pergamon Press, 1982.

Brein, M. and David, K. H. "Intercultural communication and adjustment of the sojourner." *Psychology Bulletin,* 1971, 76, 215-230.

Brislin, R. W. *Cross-cultural encounters.* New York: Pergamon Press, 1981.

Church, A. T. "Sojourn adjustment." *Psychological Bulletin,* 1982, 91, 540-571.

Copeland, L. and Griggs, L. *Going international.* New York: Random House, 1985.

David, K. H. "The use of social learning theory in preventing intercultural adjustment problems." In Pedersen, P., Lonner, W. J., and Draguns, J. (eds.), *Counseling across cultures.* Honolulu, Hawaii: University of Hawaii Press, 1976.

Doz, Y. and Prahalad, C. K. "Controlled variety: a challenge for human resource management in the MNC." *Human Resource Management,* 1986, 25(1), 55-71.

Dunbar, E. and Ehrlich, M. "International practices, selection, training, and managing the international staff: a survey report." *The Project on International Human Resource.* Columbia University, Teachers College, 1986.

Early, P. C. "Intercultural training for managers: a comparison of documentary and interpersonal methods." *Academy of Management Journal,* 1987, 30, 685-698.

England, G. and Lee, R. "The relationship between managerial values and managerial success in the U.S., Japan, India, and Australia." *Journal of Applied Psychology,* 1974, 59, 411-419.

Graham, J. "The influence of culture on the process of business negotiations: an exploratory study." *Journal of International Business Studies,* Spring, 1985, 81-95.

Gudykunst, W. B., Hammer, M. R., and Wiseman, R. L. "An analysis of an integrated approach to cross-cultural training." *International Journal of Intercultural Relations,* 1977, 1, 99-110.

Haire, M., Ghiselli, E. E., and Porter, L. W. *Managerial thinking: An international study.* New York: Wiley, 1966.

Harris, P. and Morgan, R. T. *Managing cultural differences.* Houston: Gulf, 1979.

Harvey, M. C. "The other side of the foreign assignment: dealing with repatriation problems." *Columbia Journal of World Business,* Spring 1982, 53-59.

Harvey, M. C. "The executive family: an overlooked variable in international assignments." *Columbia Journal of World Business,* Spring 1985, 84-92.

Hofstede, G. *Culture's consequences: International differences in work related values.* Beverly Hills, Calif.: Sage.

Jablin, F. M., Putnam, L. L., Roberts, K. H., and Porter, L. W. *Handbook of organizational communication.* Beverly Hills, Calif.: Sage, 1987.

Kepler, J. Z., Kepler, P. J., Gaither, O. D., and Gaither, M. C. *Americans abroad.* New York: Praeger, 1983.

Latham, C. "Human resource training and development." *Annual Review of Psychology,* 1988, 39, 545-582.

Landis D. and Brislin, R. *Handbook on intercultural training.* Vol. 1. New York: Pergamon Press, 1983.

Lanier, A. R. "Selection and preparation for overseas transfers." *Personnel Journal,* 1979, 58, 160-163.

Locke, E. and Latham, G. *Goal setting: A motivational technique that works.* Englewood Cliffs, N.J.: Prentice-Hall, 1984.

Mendenhall, M. and Oddou, G. "The cognitive, psychological, and social contexts of Japanese management." *Asia Pacific Journal of Management,* 1986a, 4(1), 24-37.

Mendenhall, M. and Oddou, G. "Acculturation profiles of expatriate managers: implications for cross-cultural training programs." *Columbia Journal of World Business,* 1986b, 21, 73-79.

Mendenhall, M., Dunbar, E., and Oddou, G. "Expatriate selection, training, and career-pathing: a review and critique." *Human Resource Management,* 1987, 26, 331-345.

Mendenhall, M. and Oddou, G. "The dimensions of expatriate acculturation." *Academy of Management Review,* 1985, 10:39-47.

Miller, E. "The international selection decision: A study of managerial behavior in the selection decision process." *Academy of Management Journal,* 1973, 16, 234-252.

Misa, K. F. and Fabricatore, J.M. "Return on investment of overseas personnel." *Financial Executive,* April 1979, 42-46.

Ohmae, K. "Managing in a borderless world." *Harvard Business Review,* May-June, 1989, 152-161.

Roberts, K. H. and Boyacigiller, N. "Issues in cross national management research: the state of the art." Paper presented at the National Meeting of the Academy of Management, New York, 1982.

Runzheimer Executive Report 1984. "Expatriation/repatriation survey." No. 31. Rochester, Wisconsin.

Schollhammer, H. "Current research on international and comparative management issues." *Management International Review,* 1975, 15, 29-45.

Schwind, H.F. "The state of the art in cross-cultural management training." In Doktor, Robert (ed.), *International Human Resource Development Annual* (Vol. 1), 7-15, Alexandria, Va.: ASTD, 1985.

Stephens, G. K. and Black, J. S. "The impact of the spouse's career orientation on managers during international transfers." Forthcoming in *Journal of Management Studies.*

Stewart, R. *Choices for managers.* Englewood Cliffs, N.J.: Prentice-Hall, 1982.

Sundaram, A. "Unique aspects of MNCs: a top-down perspective." Working paper series. Amos Tuck School of Business Administration, Dartmouth College, 1990.

Torbion, I. *Living abroad.* New York: Wiley, 1982.

Tung, R. "Selecting and training of personnel for overseas assignments." *Columbia Journal of World Business,* 1981, 16:68-78.

Tung, R. *Key to Japan's economic strength: Human power.* Lexington, Mass.: Lexington Books, 1984.

Vroom, V. *Work and motivation.* New York: Wiley, 1964.

Zeira, Y. "Overlooked personnel problems in multinational corporations." *Columbia Journal of World Business,* 1975, 10(2), 96-103.

The Contemporary International Assignment: A Look at the Options

Reading 9.2
Glenn M. McEvoy
Barbara Parker

Three Expatriates

Gerald Borenstein's selection for Bandag's Hong Kong office seemed a perfect fit for company needs. Not only had Borenstein authored a marketing plan for China, but he had lived in another country before and had years of experience at Bandag—the leading U.S. maker of retread tires. Borenstein himself had good reasons to accept an overseas assignment: the job offered strategic opportunities and an increase in rank, Bandag's international revenues were growing, and the perquisites far exceeded those usual for the home office in Muscatine, Iowa (e.g., a fully paid three-bedroom apartment, a full-time housekeeper, private school for the children, and a travel allowance). Soon after Borenstein arrived in Hong Kong in 1997, however, Bandag's Asian sales began to slow and domestic competitive pressures increased. Borenstein found it difficult to cut costs fast enough to satisfy headquarters, and those who had selected Borenstein for the Hong Kong job retired or were reassigned. Within only 18 months, the Hong Kong job evaporated, and Bandag was unable to find a new job for Borenstein. Borenstein and his wife packed their belongings and, with their two small children, returned to the United States to launch his career anew (Kaufman, 1999).

Stephanie Thompson's route to expatriation began in a different way. Born in a rural U.S. town, Thompson was scarcely aware of the outside world until a dynamic university class revealed new options. After completing an international studies degree, she explored those options by teaching English in Ecuador. Her family welcomed her return at the end of a year and watched with pride as one success followed another: budding career, completion of a part-time MBA program, and a series of promotions. But Thompson felt that something was missing in her life,

Source: Glenn M. McEvoy and Barbara Parker. "The Contemporary International Assignment: A Look at the Options." Reprinted by permission of the author.

and after some years she decided to return to Latin America. It took time for her family to accept the decision and even more time for her to liquidate her belongings. But in 1998 Thompson returned to Ecuador with high hopes. Her personal network helped her secure a job she had first seen posted on the Internet—a job that drew on both her Spanish-language skills and her business acumen.

On the evening of the day he'd been offered an assignment in London, Robert Nathan returned home with a map. Unfolding it on the kitchen table, he announced "we have some decisions to make." Nathan explained that the job represented an important promotion for him, but he asked his family to consider how the assignment could change their lives. He described opportunities he'd experienced in an overseas posting before he had a family: to travel worldwide, make new friends, learn more about how other people live. Further, he outlined some of the costs: leaving old friends at home, adjusting to a new country, learning new habits. For his wife, it would mean postponing her career for a few more years. For the children, it would mean new schools and an unfamiliar educational system. He described the job he'd been offered and laid out the possibilities he saw for his career and the family. The company expected to provide pre-departure training to help Nathan and his family adjust to their new life, but Nathan cautioned that some cross-cultural challenges cannot be anticipated. Acknowledging this, Nathan asked: Should we take this international assignment?

Gerald Borenstein, Stephanie Thompson, and Robert Nathan are all expatriates—people who leave their home to live in another country. As theirs and other stories would illustrate, expatriates can follow various routes to an overseas assignment, including education, company selection, personal choice, and even chance. Additionally, although these experiences may seem unique, in fact almost all expatriate experiences differ according to variables that can be classified as personal, organizational, and contextual characteristics (such as where one works abroad). For example, Gerald Borenstein's expatriate experience might have turned out quite differently had he been located somewhere other than Asia during the 1997 economic downturn. In combination, personal, organizational, and contextual characteristics motivate decisions to create or take overseas jobs. And, as the three experiences described above show, the expatriate experience contributes to career opportunities, affects self-esteem, and influences relationships with family, friends, and colleagues. For some, an assignment abroad can be and often is more than a job; it is a life-changing experience that affects all dimensions of one's life.

The U.S. Expatriate Experience

The expatriate experience has not always been viewed as involving personal, organizational, and contextual factors. In the early 1950s, when significant numbers of U.S. expatriates first began to work abroad, an overseas assignment usually was viewed only in terms of its job characteristics. Accordingly, the majority of U.S. firms selected expatriate employees based on their technical skills alone. For example, if overseas expansion strategies called for increased production abroad, the likely personnel choice would have been someone with outstanding experience and success in domestic production. For many firms, yet another reason for selecting expatriate home-country managers was that with them in place, headquarters could exert more control over the foreign operation. Further, like Gerald Borenstein, the expatriate could expect to be better compensated abroad in salary or benefits. For example, perceived "hardship posts" were sometimes compensated at one-and-a-half to two times domestic salary. Additionally, most expatriate assignments from the United States were of relatively short duration—a few months to two years at most. Finally, unlike today, few women or minority group members were considered for overseas assignments, and it was very unusual for U.S. citizens to become "voluntary" expatriates like Stephanie Thompson.

By the late 1970s and early 1980s these practices had begun to change, as international competition affected U.S. firms in two ways. First, cost reduction efforts led firms to send fewer expatriates abroad from headquarters. Second, the growing need for employees who were both technically qualified and culturally adaptive could not easily be satisfied by U.S. employees. Many companies attempted to satisfy these dual job/cultural needs by hiring host- or third-country nationals familiar with the culture of the host country, but this practice turned out to have three principal disadvantages: (1) hiring host- and third-country managers with no company experience made it more difficult to transmit company values to employees abroad; (2) competition for host- and third-country managers made it difficult to retain good ones; and (3) managers at headquarters were gaining too little international experience even as international growth became more important to many firms. As a result, many U.S. firms have begun to develop more managers from home and abroad who know their jobs well, are personally adaptive to life and work abroad, and are knowledgeable about other countries and cultures.

For Gerald Borenstein, Stephanie Thompson, Robert Nathan, and the many thousands of U.S. expatriates who work abroad each year, success depends not only on personal and organizational attributes but also on contextual variables beyond the control of the individual and the organization. Expatriate jobs provide opportunities but also carry risks. Although some people control the decision to work abroad and have ample time to balance opportunities and risks (as Stephanie Thompson did), for others the offer of an overseas assignment arises almost overnight (as it did for Robert Nathan). By describing these opportunities and risks, this essay will help you assess your own interest in, and suitability for, working in another country and will prepare you to answer the question: Should you take or seek an overseas assignment?

Success and Failure in International Assignments _____

Early research on U.S. expatriates suggested high "failure rates," which could easily derail or delay an expatriate's career trajectory. Someone is typically considered to have "failed" in an international assignment when he or she returns home before the anticipated end of the assignment. Using this definition, it has been suggested that from 10 to 45% of all expatriates "fail" by returning home early, though the higher failure rates were associated with assignments to developing countries. Also, European and Japanese companies report lower levels of expatriate failure rates than do U.S. companies. Problems in personal adjustment, family accommodation, and worries over career derailment can all contribute to an early return (Black, Gregersen, Mendenhall, & Stroh, 1999; Swaak, 1995).

Given that failure is a distinct possibility, you must carefully consider the pros and cons of an international assignment before accepting or seeking it. On the upside, an international assignment represents an opportunity to expand your personal horizons, experience other cultures, and enhance your creativity and problem-solving skills. It requires that you learn to live with—and capitalize on—diversity. Expatriates who overcome the innumerable obstacles of an international assignment are like athletes or Outward Bound participants who enjoy the self-confidence of one who has experienced success outside one's comfort zone. An international assignment puts you in close contact with a different set of stakeholders, including customers and suppliers, and therefore provides you with first-hand knowledge of how to contribute to the success of the business. It can be a wonderful learning opportunity for your partner and children, and, with the right organization, can be an essential stepping-stone to further career advancement. Finally, many international assignments carry with them an excellent package of perquisites, including enhanced salary, home leave arrangements, and educational and housing allowances. Because of the higher cost of hiring expatriates, firms usually send only one or a few people abroad, and those sent abroad can therefore develop generalist skills to supplement the specialist skills that may have led to the overseas assignment.

On the downside, an international assignment can derail a career. Some companies tend to forget about their expatriates—out of sight is out of mind. There may or may not be a promotion waiting for you when you return. You may lose track of valuable mentors or insider information critical for career success as Gerald Borenstein did. Companies sometimes suggest that international postings are critical to career advancement, but the backgrounds of senior executives reflect the opposite. The position itself can be uncomfortable if the expatriate is viewed as the home country "spy" or the person charged with telling host-country nationals how the work is done back home. You may learn skills or styles that actually hurt you in your career back home (e.g., learning to be accommodating and to value harmony in an Asian posting), you may find a specialist job less challenging after a generalist position abroad, or you may become so enamored with the host-country culture that you "go native" and either do not want to return home or arouse loyalty concerns among sponsors back home. Your partner may have to give up her or his job to accompany you, and getting back on a career track for either of you may be difficult upon return. If you are going to a less developed economy where the technology in use is out of date, you may be unable to keep your technical skills on the cutting edge. A posting to a country where you must learn another language requires time and commitment. The financial perquisites, as good as they sound, may not cover the additional costs of living in some expensive cities abroad. Finally, family safety, health, living standards, and education may require compromises in some parts of the world. For example, the educational system in smaller, less developed economies may not be appropriate for college-bound teens, so students may have to be sent home to finish their high school education.

Of course, "success" or "failure" in an international assignment involves a lot more than simply sticking out the posting until the designated return date. Expatriates may finish out their assignments and yet perform poorly in the assigned tasks, may behave in ways that alienate the host-country nationals with whom they work, or may be so maladjusted that they quit the organization upon repatriation or avoid international assignments throughout the remainder of their careers.

One way to think about the issue of success or failure is to view it as a two-by-two matrix, as in Figure 1. The two general dimensions of success are adjustment and performance. Adjustment is more internally and personally focused and refers to the general degree of psychological comfort the individual has with various aspects of the host country, including working in the country, interacting with the locals, and accepting critical features of the country such as education, food, climate, and medical facilities (Black & Gregersen, 1991). Performance is more externally and organizationally focused; though it may include premature returns, it is more indicative of achievement relative to established organizational objectives (e.g., the development of host- or third-country nationals to assume greater responsibility) or subsidiary or joint venture performance indicators (e.g., market share, revenue, costs, cash flow, turnover). Viewed this way, performance incorporates the possibility that the expatriate may return early because the assignment was finished ahead of schedule and thus was a success rather than a failure. Overall, this model incorporates the notions of both employee satisfaction and employee satisfactoriness with the assignment.

Figure 1. Possible International Assignment Outcomes

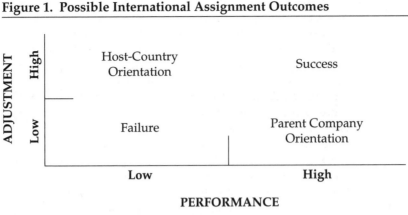

Using the model in Figure 1, success and failure can be related to the combined effects of performance and adjustment. Intermediate levels of success may be achieved in either the Parent Company Orientation cell or the Host-Country Orientation cell. Persons in the former may be expected to exhibit substantially more commitment to the parent firm than to the local operation, substantially more organizational commitment than career commitment, and a greater intent to return early but stay with the parent company upon return. Persons in the Host-Country Orientation cell are likely to exhibit opposite outcomes: higher commitment to the local operation and to their personal careers, less likelihood of returning early, but greater likelihood of quitting the parent company upon return (Takeuchi, 1997).

Of course, the optimum outcome in the model in Figure 1 is to be high in both performance and adjustment. Once you've decided that the potential rewards of an international assignment outweigh the potential risks for you, your next concern should be to identify situations that increase the likelihood of a fully successful international assignment in your case. This requires examination of the three interrelated sets of factors we identified earlier: personal, organizational, and contextual (Parker & McEvoy, 1993).

Personal and Professional Skills and Attitudes _____

The first questions to answer before accepting an international assignment revolve around the skills and temperament you need to be successful in another culture. First, what is your motivation for wanting to go abroad? Did you study or live abroad as a student? Do you take the opportunity to interact with foreigners in your home country when you have a chance? Do you enjoy the opportunity to get to know people who are different than you?

Extensive interviews with returned American expatriates suggest that important prerequisites for a successful international experience are a willingness to go, a sense of adventure, and a desire for challenge and learning (Osland, 1995). Of course, if you've gotten this far in the process, you apparently have the willingness to go. This is important because expatriates forced to go abroad against their will are likely to be poorly adjusted. A sense of adventure is also critical. Do you feel more "alive" when experiencing something new and completely different? Successful expatriates sometimes feel something akin to a "mission" in their international work, a sense that they are doing good work not only for their company, but also for their country and the world. Lastly, most international assignments require that expatriates confront challenges and be open to learning new ways of doing things. A narrow-minded, ethnocentric view of the world ("my way is the best") is a setup for failure.

Next, what is your temperament? Are you willing to accept a "cultural mentor," someone who will show you the ropes and "break the code" (i.e., explain how things work) in a different country? Do you get frustrated and impatient when you can't figure things out on your own? Are you willing to ask for help without feeling that you have diminished your personal power base?

Other personal attributes that tend to predict success in an international assignment include a certain amount of extroversion or gregariousness, cultural empathy, perceptual accuracy, tolerance for ambiguity and stress, a sense of humor, and some ability to laugh at oneself (Parker & McEvoy, 1993). At the same time, the expatriate who is able to enjoy his or her own company may find it easier to weather feelings of isolation and loneliness that sometimes arise during an overseas assignment. Each of these characteristics is important in fostering both personal adjustment to a different culture and high performance in an environment much different from the one at home.

Research suggests three general categories of skills that are critical to successful adaptation to an international assignment: personal, people, and perceptual (Mendenhall & Oddou, 1985). Personal skills include mental and emotional well-being and stress reduction techniques such as effective delegation, time management, meditation, prayer, or physical exercise. People skills include capabilities in effective interaction with others, including communication, listening, conflict resolution, influence, and leadership. Depending on the country of assignment, they also include the willingness to attempt to learn another language and the confidence to try to use it. Perceptual skills assist you in understanding why foreigners do things the way they do. Those skills allow you to be conscious of social cues and behaviors. It is important to resist the tendency to jump to conclusions in an international setting because the cues and meanings are often quite different from the ones you learned at home.

There is also evidence that both maturity and pre-departure knowledge of a country can assist the expatriate in successful acculturation (Parker & McEvoy, 1993). Of course, the two are interrelated, assuming that older expatriates have had the opportunity to travel more and gain more international experience, both directly and indirectly (reading, self-study, discussions with returned expatriates, etc.). Some organizations invest in training or orientation programs for expatriates in the belief that such preparation helps the expatriate to "hit the ground" running upon arrival in the host country. Training can vary from introductions to the history and geography of the country to cultural orientations, language training, or sensitivity to cultural differences (Tung, 1982). But as only about 5% of U.S. firms train employees for overseas assignments, much of your training will have to be self-initiated. If you are unwilling to make this investment, you should seriously reconsider your decision to seek an international position.

One expatriate summed up his experience by saying: "For me the most important thing was to understand that I was in a continual adjustment phase. I would go through many periods of hating it and loving it, happiness and depression. It was realizing that my current emotions would only be temporary; understanding and grasping the fact that the first one-and-a-half to two years will not be easy is also very important. You won't fit, you won't be one of them, so just be yourself. The grass is not as green as you thought it would be but it is still a nice yard, just different. I am not sure if I have been "successful" as an expat but I am still living abroad after nearly two years and have started calling my new country of residence 'home'" (Kidd, 1997).

The Organization's Philosophy and Practices_____

Organizational factors must also be considered in predicting success in an international assignment. What is the organization's general philosophy toward expatriation and repatriation? What specific policies and practices are in place to facilitate expatriate success? A good deal of research suggests that organizational practices can make or break an assignment, and this research is relatively unambiguous in suggesting what it takes to be successful.

The Strategic Importance of International Assignments

The first question you should explore is the strategic importance of international assignments in general (and the specific assignment you are considering in particular) to building your career. Strategic importance in general can be assessed by the degree to which your firm values international experience when making promotion decisions. Do senior executives have multicultural backgrounds and international exposure? If so, you can assume that this experience is valued. A few years ago, only 20% of U.S. CEOs had any real first-hand international experience (Adler, 1991). And although that percentage has increased in recent years, the level of senior executive international expertise is still a key indicator you should consider. Caution is advisable because executives who have not worked overseas will not really understand the difficulties and challenges involved, nor will they appreciate the personal growth and skill development that take place in such an assignment.

Of course, some organizations have a commitment to international expansion but are in transition from a domestic to a global orientation. They may have few internationally seasoned managers currently on board, and it will take time to build such a corps. In cases like this, you might ask questions such as the following. Does there appear to be a logical career path for you upon repatriation that builds directly on the experience you will gain in the potential international assignment? Have recently returned expatriates obtained desirable positions with growth potential? Is there a long-term strategic commitment to develop an internationally experienced corps of senior managers?

As an indicator of genuine upper management commitment to internationalization, ask about the support and communication system in place to facilitate expatriate success. The research is clear that such support and communication systems are vital to successful expatriation and repatriation (Black, Gregersen, & Mendenhall, 1992). One overseas subsidiary has a support system whereby the highest-ranking expatriate, as part of her or his job, is expected to help other expatriates adjust to the country of assignment. Duties include informal counseling and the sponsorship of monthly social gatherings to discuss successes and problems of expatriation. In addition, the spouse of this senior expatriate serves as a mentor for other spouses before they depart and after they arrive in the country of assignment (Mendenhall & Oddou, 1988).

Such efforts are exemplary. It is common, however, for a single expatriate to be assigned to a particular overseas site. How do firms support their expatriates under such circumstances? The better ones provide regular telephone and e-mail contact, including counseling with both work and family problems. Frequent trips back to headquarters for the expatriate (and home leave for spouse and family) are helpful. A committed firm also provides advice on how to gain the support needed in the local community. For example, the organization may provide information about nearby groups for those who are active in an organized religion or service clubs such as Rotary or Lions for those who participate in such organizations. In larger international cities, there are frequently organizations of expatriates from a single country, or related countries (e.g., Hash House Harriers), working for different international firms that share information on how to ease the transition into the local culture. Such organizations can provide a local support network for an expatriate and his or her spouse.

If you intend to stay with the same firm over a long period of time, be leery of firms that practice the "out of sight, out of mind" philosophy of managing expatriates. This approach reflects the lack of a genuine strategic commitment to international work. In one company an expatriate complained that calls to headquarters were routinely ignored and that there were no organized social systems for either him or his spouse. Mentors were unavailable for advice and no counseling was provided either before departure or within the country. The total experience put extreme pressure on his marriage, and he eventually sent his family home early and then remained overseas just a short time longer alone (Mendenhall & Oddou, 1988).

Don't leave home without knowing what kinds of support systems will be in place to help you once you reach the country of assignment. These support systems should not only include the features mentioned above, but should also provide you with a clear link to the job you will have upon repatriation. The stronger the support system, and the more it is directed not only to you but also to your spouse and family, the greater the likelihood of success.

The specifics of the assignment under consideration are also important. Is the assignment with a strategically critical subsidiary or highly visible international joint venture? For example, you may be offered a position as vice president for marketing in the Caribbean region. This position may be considerably less desirable than vice president for marketing in the rapidly expanding Far East region. Even within the same region, some business ventures will be rapidly expanding and therefore of more strategic significance than others. Ask to see past financial statements and future performance predictions for any business you are considering. It's much easier to be "successful" in some emerging markets than others.

The Human Resource Management System for International Assignments

Other critical success factors for an international assignment pertain to the human resource (HR) management system the organization has to facilitate successful expatriation. How sophisticated is the expatriate selection system? How much lead time is typically provided for expatriates to decide on an assignment? How extensive is the pre-departure training and orientation for the expatriate and family, and what type of relocation assistance is provided? How clear are the job responsibilities and the amount of authority inherent in the position? How will performance be measured and rewarded overseas? What is the compensation and benefits package, and how is it tailored to the country of assignment? How tightly is the international assignment tied to career development, and what arrangements are made in advance for eventual repatriation?

Expatriate selection systems are critical. How were you chosen? Did someone simply say, "Hey, do you want to go abroad?" Or was an in-depth, competitive screening process used to identify not only the willing but the qualified? The vast majority of organizations select their expatriates on the basis of technical or managerial expertise. Of course, this is only the foundation for success. Critical traits and skills such as those mentioned earlier (openness to others, perceptual skills, cultural empathy, comfort with ambiguity, self-deprecating sense of humor, and so forth), should also be considered in a competent selection system. It is a vast simplification to believe that managerial and technical skills alone can ensure success in an international assignment. If this assumption exists in your organization, it is a sign that either upper management or HR—or both—has little firsthand experience with international work.

Further, sophisticated selection systems take into account the needs and interests of the potential expatriate's spouse and family. Inability of a spouse and/or family to adapt to an assignment is a frequent cause of premature returns (Black & Gregersen, 1991). As a result, the better organizations interview family members during the screening process and treat their concerns as part of the placement and orientation process. A critical challenge today is how to deal with dual-career families. Assistance in finding appropriate employment for a trailing spouse overseas and/or similar support upon repatriation is often critical to getting the best qualified expatriate to accept the assignment.

Training and orientation for expatriate assignments range from nonexistent to barely adequate. Few organizations spare much time for formal training either pre-departure or post-arrival. Considerable experience with cross-cultural training exists in academic, religious, and diplomatic communities, but few firms avail themselves of this expertise. Churches have been sending missionaries abroad for years, schools have been sending students, and the State Department diplomats. Many of these organizations have developed relatively sophisticated approaches to training "sojourners." For example, the Peace Corps started in the early 1960s with extensive pre-departure training programs that included language and cross-cultural training. With experience, they learned that a shorter pre-departure training regimen, followed by a more extensive in-country curriculum, was more effective (McEvoy & Aven, 1991).

When you are assigned to a country where the culture and language are quite different, a substantial amount of pre-departure training, reinforced by occasional in-country refreshers, can be useful. Techniques such as case analysis, role-playing, culture confrontation, and behavior modeling can be effective. Returned expatriates often make good trainers because they have the credibility that comes with personal experience. An extensive language and cross-cultural training program reflects a firm's commitment to you and your success in an international assignment. The odds are good that such a firm will also forecast worldwide HR needs well in advance and provide you with a career-enhancing position suitable to both your and its needs. On the other hand, if you are are handed a brochure on your way to the plane as the only form of pre-departure training, watch out. Other critical pieces of the HR support system are probably missing as well!

An important part of the HR package is the performance measurement and appraisal system. Valid performance assessment is difficult enough in domestic operations. Thousands of miles away in a foreign country, you may rightly wonder how your boss can evaluate your performance in a fair and unbiased way. Unable to observe you directly, your boss will be forced to assess your performance using some combination of indirect and objective measures. What does the boss hear through the grapevine about your performance? How will she or he interpret your phone calls or e-mails asking for advice—as weakness or as willingness to keep the boss "in the loop"? Realistically, you can expect that your boss will likely rely more on objective, organizational indicators of performance. What is the ROI for the business? The cash flow? Revenue growth? Costs? Quality improvement? Market share? These are indicators over which you do not have complete control. This realization reinforces the advice given earlier to pick your assignments carefully. It is easier to succeed in a favorable economic climate than a difficult one, and although stability is not perfectly predictable, it can be estimated based on historical patterns. Finally, your performance appraisal is likely to rest more heavily on the success or failure of the business than on your individual behaviors and attitudes.

Another critical piece of the HR support system is the repatriation process. Studies have shown that many organizations pay little attention to repatriation; consequently, turnover among returned expatriates is very high, possibly as much as 55% within three years of repatriation (Black, Gregersen, & Mendenhall, 1992). This has been a serious concern for expatriates in recent years. Possibly as a result, more firms are now paying attention to this problem. For example, Prudential Relocation International, a firm that assists organizations in overseas placements, reports that over 50% of companies with expatriates now guarantee them a position upon returning home (Coming home, 1998). This marks a significant improvement over the past when returning expatriates frequently had to scramble to find jobs after returning. One American expatriate even lost his "identity" during repatriation. Apparently, he did not exist on company records for the first three months after his return. He did not learn of the problem until he was denied two loans (car and home) because he was "unemployed" (Black, Gregersen, & Mendenhall, 1992).

"Reverse culture shock" can also complicate the return. Expatriates frequently report that the shock of reentering their old home culture is every bit as severe—sometimes more so—as the shock they received on their outbound sojourn. Family members are likely to experience the same shock, although children may have difficulty describing their concerns. The problem here is likely one of expectations. When going abroad, you expect to be confronted with a different culture and lifestyle, so you prepare for it mentally. Most people, however, are unprepared for the culture shock that comes with the return home. Only if you realize that you are now a different person because of your international experience will you appreciate that the return is likely to be a problem. If your organization has a program and support system to help returning expatriates and their families readjust to their home country, you can take this as a sign that your firm understands the issues and wants to help. Firms offering family adjustment and readjustment programs find that they ease entry and reentry transition and encourage other employees to accept overseas assignments. For example, Motorola employees abroad are reimbursed for personal computers that improve telecommunications between family and their friends at home, and John Deere has developed youth programs to help teens make friends and fit in at school (Lublin, 1999).

Clearly, the advice given so far is contingent on the nature of the assignment as well as other contextual variables. Some expatriate assignments are of long duration, two to four years, and attention to many of these suggestions is warranted. However, contemporary organizations use a variety of types of international assignments depending on their goals and needs (Roberts, Kossek, & Ozeki, 1998). For example, firms sometimes use short-term "awareness-building" assignments that last only three months to a year. If you are considering such an assignment, issues such as repatriation and career advancement may be of much less concern. In other instances, you may be asked to join a "SWAT team" for an even shorter time period, just long enough to complete a major assignment such as the installation of a computer information system. Under such circumstances, your family will probably not accompany you, so issues of spouse adjustment and children's education become moot. Lastly, given the advances in telecommunications, e-mail, and videoconferencing, you may be asked to join a global team without ever leaving home, a so-called virtual team. Under these circumstances, even fewer of the concerns discussed here are an issue.

The point is that the nature of the assignment and the organization determine what is important. But you should attend to other contextual variables as well. These are covered in the next section.

The Context for the International Assignment _____

Contextual variables usually are outside the control of both the individual expatriate and the organization. Two types of contextual variables are particularly relevant to the success of an international assignment: family and spouse adjustment and cultural novelty.

Family and Spouse Adjustment

Many expatriates return early from an overseas posting due to adjustment issues for a spouse or children. Those can play out in many ways. For example, following a spouse or partner overseas may mean giving up a rewarding job or career opportunities at home, with a resulting loss in self-esteem or income for the "trailing" spouse or partner. Companies can sometimes alleviate this risk by arranging for spousal employment abroad, but local laws and customs may be a barrier to this option. Engaging in satisfying cultural, volunteer, or family activities is another way partners can develop fulfilling lives during an overseas assignment, and these pursuits are often important when the expatriate works long hours or travels in the job. The general management role typical of many overseas assignments may also call for an active social life that will be a perfect fit for partners who enjoy planning and hosting social events. Finally, partners often enjoy travel in and outside the assigned country. Although these examples show that a "trailing" spouse can find fulfillment abroad, much depends on the individual's personal characteristics. Like the expatriate, the accompanying spouse and children should complete a self-assessment of the personal and professional characteristics described earlier. Doing so will help all members of the family rate their potential for success abroad.

Children create special challenges for the parent contemplating life abroad. Young adults and teens may be reluctant to leave their friends at home, and it is important to consider how schools abroad will help them achieve educational goals. In settings where there are international schools, the costs of leaving a known educational system may be offset by cross-cultural learning that comes from making deep friendships with peers from many nations. Other family issues may arise as well. For example, laws and customs in other nations may conflict with family values. For example, many countries do not have a "drinking age." Others do not allow 16-year-olds to drive automobiles. For young adults, there may be dating issues that motivate an early return home. Younger children generally present less of a challenge abroad than do teens, but there are issues to consider here as well. For example, an active social life for the expatriate family may mean leaving infants with full-time nannies who become central to the child's life. Because most expatriate postings are for only a few years, the child is almost certain to lose an important adult presence upon repatriation. Additionally, special needs for any child can be difficult to satisfy in some nations.

Culture Novelty

Assumptions and habits acquired in one's country of origin often make it difficult to adjust to countries where cultural habits and assumptions differ from—or even conflict with—one's own. This phenomenon is known variously as cultural "distance" or "toughness" (Mendenhall & Oddou, 1985). Research generally shows that the greater the difference between the home and host country, the more difficult the expatriate adjustment is. These differences are likely to include behavioral ones, such as punctuality, and more value-based ones, such as the role of family and friends in one's work life. A U.S. expatriate who believes that "time is money" may be disturbed by late arrivals at meetings in nations where time and work are less highly valued than in the United States. For example, when a Brazilian says "work is not a rabbit, it will not run away," he or she is suggesting that work is less central in Brazil than in the United States. Although it is possible for the expatriate to acquire cognitive knowledge of cultural differences like these, often the manager learns how these differences really work only through failed interactions. For instance, the motivational systems so reasonable for U.S. individualism often fail in collectivist cultures where the opinion of friends or family is far more important than individual productivity. This can be frustrating for the American manager whose only experience is in motivating employees from individualistic cultures like the United States.

Although cultural distance can increase managerial difficulties and delay adjustment, it often is not a problem when the sojourner's net benefits are perceived to increase. For example, many expatriates to advanced economies—particularly those from developing economies—enjoy the greater social mobility and material goods offered in these consumer cultures. Similarly, U.S. expatriates sometimes prefer host cultures, either because they offer a good fit with the expatriate's own value system or because the expatriate can live a better life abroad than in the United States. Managerial assignments abroad can include interactions with high government officials, visiting dignitaries, and others the expatriate is unlikely to meet at home. All this suggests that the degree to which a nation is "tough" for the expatriate depends in part on national conditions (e.g., health care systems, economic climate, product offerings) and in part on the expatriate's own aspirations and perceptions. Both point to the importance of advance preparation for any assignment abroad.

Conclusion

If you've decided you want to go abroad, how do you prepare/position yourself to be selected and successful? First, review the section on Personal and Professional Skills and Attitudes to assess your current suitability for living and working abroad. If you have a life partner, ask your partner to engage in a similar assessment. Talk honestly with each other and reflect earnestly on your personal suitability for seeking an international assignment. If you can't predict how you'd feel in a new culture, find local opportunities to cross cultures. Depending on your community, you can find these opportunities by visiting a Chinese New Year's celebration, tutoring refugees at the Somalia Relief Center, or attending cultural events on your university campus. Even visiting neighborhoods where you've never traveled is a way to assess your comfort in new situations.

Also assess your current knowledge of geography, as well as cultural, social, and political events in other nations. Are there parts of the world about which you know very little? Other areas where your knowledge is deep? Answering these questions may lead you to focus on a particular region of the world, as Stephanie Thompson did, and perhaps acquire language fluency. If, like Gerald Borenstein and Robert Nathan, you need to be open to whatever posting your company offers, limited regional knowledge may call for a self-study program so that you become more of a generalist.

Weigh your current strengths and weaknesses for an expatriate assignment, set clear and measurable objectives for addressing them, and then follow through. Take a university class that moves you outside your comfort zone; attend an event that introduces you to a new culture; make friends with people who are not just like you. Crossing cultures—even within your own town—often is difficult to do, but if you begin today, you are on your way to preparing for an international sojourn. Enjoy the adventure!

References

Adler, N. J. (1991). *International dimensions of organizational behavior.* (2d ed.). Boston: PWS-Kent.

Black, J. S., and Gregersen, H. B. (1991). The other half of the picture: Antecedents of spouse cross-cultural adjustment. *Journal of International Business Studies, 22,* 461-477.

Black, J. S., Gregersen, H. B., and Mendenhall, M. E. (1992). *Global assignments: Successfully expatriating and repatriating international managers.* San Francisco: Jossey-Bass.

Black, J. S., Gregersen, H. B., Mendenhall, M. E., and Stroh, L. K. (1999). *Globalizing people through international assignments.* Reading, MA: Addison-Wesley.

Borstorff, P. C., Harris, S. G., Feild, H. S., and Giles, W. F. (1997). Who'll go? A review of factors associated with employee willingness to work overseas. *Human Resource Planning, 20:* 29-40.

Coming home: Companies prepare warmer welcome for returning expatriates. (1998). *The Wall Street Journal,* October 27, A-1.

Kaufman, J. (1999). The castaways: An American expatriate finds Hong Kong post a fast boat to nowhere. *Wall Street Journal,* January 21, A1, A6.

Kidd, G. K. (1997). From "Expat Chat." {GOTOBUTTON BM 1 www.expat-forum.com/msgboard/webx.cgi?13,} September 2.

Lublin, J. S. (1999). To smooth a transfer abroad, a new focus on kids. *Wall Street Journal*, January 26, B1, B14.

McEvoy, G. M., and Aven, F. F. (1991). What multinational corporations should know about Peace Corps expatriate training. Paper presented at the western regional meeting of the Academy of International Business, April 4, Pomona, CA.

Mendenhall, M., and Oddou, G. (1985). The dimensions of expatriate acculturation: A review. *Academy of Management Review*, 10, 39-47.

Mendenhall, M.E. , and Oddou, G. (1988). The overseas assignment: A practical look. *Business Horizons*, September/October, 78-84.

Osland, J. S. (1995). *The adventure of working abroad: Hero tales from the global frontier*. San Francisco: Jossey-Bass.

Parker, B., and McEvoy, G. M. (1993). Initial examination of a model of intercultural adjustment. *International Journal of Intercultural Relations*, 17, 355-379.

Roberts, K., Kossek, E. E., and Ozeki, C. (1998). Managing the global workforce: Challenges and strategies. *Academy of Management Executive*, 12(4), 93-106.

Swaak, R. A. (1995). Expatriate failures: Too many, too much cost, too little planning. *Compensation and Benefits Review*, 27 (6), November/December, 47-55.

Takeuchi, R. (1997). Expatriate success and failure revisited: A taxonomy and consequences of international assignment outcomes. Paper presented at the annual meeting of the Academy of Management, August 8-13, Boston, MA.

Tung, R. (1982). Selection and training procedures of U.S., European, and Japanese multinationals. *California Management Review*, 25(2), 57-71.

American Expatriates Abroad: From Neophytes to Cosmopolitans

Reading 9.3
Rosalie L. Tung

For some time now, politicians, practitioners and academicians alike have been talking about the globalization of the world economy. The Asian financial crisis, for example, highlights the extent to which the economic fates of nations around the world are inextricably interwined. What began as currency devaluation in a relatively small economy, Indonesia, has triggered a seismic reaction in financial markets around the world. To deal effectively with the challenges in the new economic world order, it is imperative that managers of the Twenty-first century possess a global perspective. Kanter (1995), for example, has posited that in order to become "world class, organizations must not only meet the highest standards anywhere in the world," but must also develop a new breed of managers, cosmopolitans, who are rich in three intangible assets: concepts, competence, and connections. An effective way for developing cosmopolitans is to send them on international assignments where they can assume a broader range of duties and responsibilities, and thus hone and further develop these three intangible assets.

To date, much of the published literature on expatriation has focused on the selection, training, and adjustment of expatriates in international assignments. Little is known, however, about whether expatriates perceive international assignments as having a positive or negative impact on their subsequent career advancement, the modes of interaction between expatriates and host country nationals, and the processes and mechanisms that expatriates find most useful in adjusting to living and working in a foreign environment. This paper seeks to redress this deficiency by focusing on expatriates' attitudes toward international assignments and their experience abroad, including the acculturation process.

Acculturation refers to "the process by which group members from one cultural background adapt to the culture of a different group" (Rieger & Wong-Rieger, 1991). Berry and Kalin (1995) identified two dimensions of acculturation: Cultural preservation, i.e., the extent to

Source: Rosalie L. Tung. "American Expatriates Abroad: From Neophytes to Cosmopolitans." Journal of World Business, 33(2), 1998, pp. 125-144. Reprinted by permission of JAI Press Inc.

which members of a cultural sub-group need to preserve their own cultural norms; and partner attractiveness, i.e., the extent to which members of a cultural sub-group are attracted to the norms of the larger society in which they operate. Based on these two dimensions, four basic orientations to cultural group relations are possible:

- Integration (attraction to partner's culture and preservation of own cultural norms)

- Assimilation (attraction to partner's culture but non-preservation of own cultural norms)

- Separation/segregation (preservation of own cultural norms but non-attraction to partner's culture)

- Marginalization (non-preservation of own cultural norms and non-attraction to partner's culture.

These four orientations run the gamut from "highly functional" to "highly dysfunctional" patterns of interaction between peoples of two national cultures. Based on studies of immigrant and sojourner populations, Berry and Kalin (1995) showed that integration was the most optimal form of interaction between peoples from two cultures, while marginalization was the most dysfunctional mode. Between these two extremes lay assimilation and separation.

This typology can be applied to the process of interaction/acculturation between expatriates and host country nationals in an international context. Under integration, the better elements of the host and home country cultures are "preserved, combined, and expanded upon to create a new whole . . . (T)he whole is greater than the sum of the parts" (Tung, 1993). Under marginalization, the expatriate either rejects or is rejected by both the host and home country cultures. In the case of assimilation, the expatriate unilaterally adapts to the norms and behavioral patterns of the host country. While promoting local responsiveness, this strategy is not conducive to global integration. Under separation, the expatriate retains his/her distinct set of norms and behavior. While less dysfunctional than marginalization, this mode of interaction cannot facilitate organizational performance.

This paper presents the findings of a questionnaire survey of the attitudes and experience of expatriates toward international assignments. Specifically, it examined:

(a) expatriates' perceptions of the importance of international assignments to their overall career development;

(b) the modes of acculturation they used in interacting with host country nationals in target countries;

(c) the mechanisms they have found most useful in coping with the stress and strains associated with international assignments;

(d) attributes that facilitate interaction abroad; and

  (e) the relationship between performance abroad and country difficulty.

The Expatriates Surveyed

Based on literature review and interviews with expatriates from three multinationals headquartered either in the U.S. and Canada, a 14-page questionnaire was developed to examine the attitudes and experience of expatriates on international assignments, including their modes of acculturation abroad and repatriation.

  The questionnaire was distributed by Arthur Andersen's International Executive Services (now known as Human Capital Services) to 800 expatriates who were currently on assignment or who had returned from an international assignment within the past two years (Tung & Arthur Andersen, 1997). Foreign nationals (inpatriates) who were then on assignment to the United States were also included in this study. The questionnaires were sent to the corporate head offices of 49 U.S. multinationals. The head office then forwarded the questionnaires to their expatriates abroad. The completed questionnaires were returned directly to the author. In this way, the respondents were guaranteed anonymity and confidentiality of responses. After two follow-up mailings, 409 completed questionnaires were received for a response rate of 51.13%

Countries of Assignment

The expatriates came from a diversity of functional backgrounds and were assigned to 51 different countries in west Europe, Australia/New Zealand, east and southeast Asia, Canada, Middle East, Latin and South America, eastern Europe and Africa. Sixty-one of the respondents were currently on assignment to the U.S. These came from western Europe, Australia/New Zealand, east and southeast Asia, Canada, Puerto Rico, and Latin and South America.

Demographic Profile of Expatriates Surveyed The demographic profile of the respondents in this sample suggests several interesting trends in international human resource management practices.

1. There appears to be a slow but steady increase in the use of women in international assignments. In the early 1980s, Adler (1984) reported that about three percent of expatriates in U.S. multinationals were women. This figure increased to five percent in the late 1980s (Moran, Stahl, & Boyer Inc., 1988), and 11% in the early 1990s (Florkowski & Fogel, 1995).

2. Contrary to popular perception that Americans are insular, the American expatriates in this study are quite cosmopolitan. A vast majority of them have lived and/or worked for an extended number of years abroad and over one-half are bilingual or multi-lingual. Previous research has shown that there is a posi-

tive correlation between foreign language skills and successful performance abroad.

3. Despite the growing number of dual-career couples in the United States and the increased participation of women in the domestic workforce, it is somewhat surprising that the vast majority of spouses in the study (wives, in most cases) did not work outside of home. However, this finding may be attributed to the problem that spouses might encounter in securing suitable employment abroad as some expatriates could have misinterpreted the question, "Does your spouse/partner work outside of the home," to mean the spouse's employment status during the course of the international assignment.

Importance of International Assignments

Consistent with the beliefs that, one, possession of a global perspective is crucial to survival in the Twenty-first century and, two, international

---

Table 1. Demographic Profile of Respondents

- Gender   male (86.1%); female (13.9%)

- Management level: senior (33.7%); middle (41.8%)

- Functional areas: General management/administration (28.3%); marketing/ sales (14.2%); engineering (10.6%); production/operations (7.4%); accounting (6.4%); manufacturing (4.6%); finance (4.6%); research (3.9%); information systems (3.4%); human resources (2.2%); legal (1.7%); public relations (0.2%)

- Organizational tenure: over 10 years (61.1%); 6-10 years (23.5%)

- Average # of int'l assignments of > 1 year: 1.7

- Average years abroad (both personal and career):   6.64 years

- Age: 36-45 (43.9%); 46-55 (25.8%)

- Ethnicity: white (83.7%); Asian/Pacific Islander (7.7%); Hispanic (6.9%); African-American (1.5%)

- Marital status: first marriage (67.1%)

- Spouse's employment: not employed outside of home (63.65%)

- Children: with children (72.7%); average of 1.55 children living with respondent

- Languages: speak one or more west European languages (50.1%); speak an east or southeast Asian language (6.6%)

- Annual income: >$150,000 (30.1%)

---

assignments are an expedient means to acquire such expertise, the majority of respondents perceived that an international assignment is essential for their career development. Table 2 presents the means of the three items used to gauge the significance of international assignments.

In general, expatriates who were younger (under 35 years of age) perceived an international assignment as very important as compared to those who were older, i.e., those over 60 years of age. This is logical as younger expatriates still have a long career ahead of them; hence, they can expect to benefit most from the broader range of duties and responsibilities usually associated with working abroad.

Similarly, a vast majority of the expatriates believed that successful completion of an international assignment will have a positive impact upon their subsequent career advancement either in their current organization or elsewhere. Again this perception was stronger among expatriates who were younger and for those who had served on multiple international assignments. The latter finding could be explained by the fact that if those expatriates who had served abroad on multiple occasions had not perceived an international assignment as a positive, they would have turned down subsequent offers to serve abroad.

Despite this belief, however, an overwhelming majority of the expatriates was not guaranteed career advancement opportunities upon repatriation—almost 60% of the respondents were not guaranteed a position in the home organization upon successful completion of the international assignment, while another 33% were only promised a position at the same organizational level at which they were expatriated. Only 7 percent of the respondents were promised a promotion upon return. Thus, there appears to be a contradiction—on the one hand, most expatriates were concerned about repatriation, yet the vast majority still perceived an international assignment as essential to their overall career development.

A possible explanation for this apparent paradox can be found in the evolving nature of employment. Under this new perspective, careers are seen as "boundaryless" and "repositories of knowledge"

Table 2. Attitude toward International Assignments

Item	Mean
• Essential for career development	4.0
• Positive impact upon subsequent career advancement either in their current organization or elsewhere	4.2
• Opportunity to acquire skills and experience usually not available at home	4.52

Note: *Mean scores are based on 5-point scale, 5 = strongly agree

(Bird, 1994; Arthur & Rousseau, 1996). Schein (1996), for example, distinguished between "internally-perceived" (i.e., subjective) versus "externally prescribed" (i.e., objective) careers. The former "involves a subjective sense of where one is going in one's work life," whereas the external career refers to advancement within the organizational hierarchy. There is increasing evidence that for many people, the internal career appears to take precedence over the external career. For these people, one's career may no longer be perceived as a progression of jobs within a single firm or industry. Rather, the skills that can be acquired abroad are viewed as contributing to the repertoire of core competencies essential to the development of cosmopolitans. Hence the premium attached to international assignments.

The linkage between international assignments and the enhancement of one's "internal" career is supported by the finding that the vast majority of expatriates in this study viewed overseas positions as an opportunity to acquire skills and experience that are not usually available at home. Again, this attitude was more prevalent among those who had served abroad on multiple occasions. This belief was also more salient among those with university education and may be attributed to their greater expectations of upward career mobility.

This highly positive disposition toward an international assignment constitutes a very significant departure from the attitude prevalent a decade ago. In a 1987 survey conducted by Moran, Stahl and Boyer, a consulting firm in Colorado, only four percent of American expatriates surveyed considered overseas assignments as having a "positive effect on career advancement" (*Wall Street Journal*, June 30, 1987).

Acculturation Mode

Expatriates' perception toward the efficacy of different modes of interaction with host country nationals to performance abroad is presented in Table 3.

Consistent with Berry and Kalin's (1995) finding among immigrants and sojourners, the vast majority of expatriates in this study believed that an integration mode, which entails selecting the best from both home and host country cultures, is crucial to effective performance abroad. Similarly, many felt that in order to be effective abroad, they have to be both attracted to and knowledgeable about the host country's culture. Without such attraction and knowledge, the expatriate either has no desire or the wherewithal to relate effectively with host country nationals.

The assimilation mode, whereby the expatriate adapts unilaterally to the norms of the host country most of the time, was also perceived to be very important to effective performance abroad. Furthermore, more than one-half of the expatriates felt that they should attempt to do things the local way even if such behavior/practices were inconsistent with the norms of the home country. However, the percentage of

Table 3. Modes of Acculturation

Item	Mean
• Important to select and choose from better elements of both home and host countries	4.20
• Conform and adapt to norms of host country most of the time	4.02
• Keep certain distance between self and host country nationals	1.76
• Conform to norms of corporate headquarters even if inconsistent with that of host country	2.93
• Important to be attracted to culture of host country	3.95
• Important to be knowledgeable about host country's culture	3.85
• Socialize more with others from similar cultural backgrounds	3.07

Note: Mean scores are based on 5-point scale, 5 = strongly agree

people who subscribed to the assimilation mode was slightly smaller than those who advocated an integration mode. This finding suggests that expatriates realize that in a global economy, they have to balance the conflicting demands between global integration, on the one hand, and local responsiveness, on the other. Consequently, over-adaptation (i.e., being too locally responsive) may lead to difficulties in relating back to corporate headquarters. Most respondents believed that the separation mode was dysfunctional abroad.

There were significant differences among the expatriates based on demographic profile, however. Those with children were more prone to favor a separation mode. This tendency may be due to the expatriates' desire to create an environment for their children in the foreign country as close to home as possible. Somewhat surprisingly, in comparison to their female counterparts, male respondents in the study tended to favor the separation mode. A possible explanation for this finding may be attributed to the fact that since women are still a relative minority in professional and managerial ranks at home, particularly at the senior management level, to function effectively they have to either assimilate or integrate with the majority mainstream culture. Under these circumstances, from a woman's perspective, separation is not a viable option either at home or abroad.

Despite the overwhelming rejection of separation mode as an effective means of interacting with host country nationals, slightly over one-half of the expatriates confessed that while abroad, they tended to socialize more with others who come from similar cultural backgrounds. This apparent inconsistency may be attributed to Ibarra's (1993) concept of "homophily" which describes the extent to which people tend to associate with those who are like themselves. The tendency to form such homophilious relationships stems from greater ease of communication, increased trust and a common perspective toward life and the world in general. Again, expatriates with children and male assignees resorted to this socialization pattern more than those without children and female expatriates.

Time to Feel Comfortable

Table 4 presents a breakdown of the length of time it takes expatriates to feel comfortable in a foreign environment.

Fortunately, only a very small percentage of the respondents "never felt completely comfortable" in the foreign setting. One-third of the respondents took six to twelve months to feel completely comfortable (i.e., adjust) in an international assignment. Another one-fourth of the sample took four to six months, while the balance took one to three months.

The management level and marital status of the expatriate appeared to affect the amount of time it takes to adjust. In general, those who were in non-supervisory positions took the least amount of time to adjust while those in senior management took the longest period of time to feel comfortable. This finding lends support to Tung's (1981) contingency paradigm of selection and training of expatriates which called for the use of more rigorous selection criteria and the provision of more comprehensive cross-cultural training programs to those who fill positions in the chief executive officer and functional head categories, i.e., senior management. This stems from the fact that jobs at that level usually require more extensive contacts with people in the host country. Furthermore, the duration of assignments at the senior management level is typically longer. Consequently, it is imperative that assignees at senior management be better suited (through proper selection) and trained for living and working abroad. Previous research has also shown that if expatriates could be exempted from active administrative duty in the first six months of the assignment, that will facilitate adjustment abroad.

Expatriates who were divorced or separated also took longer periods of time to adjust. Consistent with spillover theory, this finding suggests that non-work related issues do affect adjustment on the job. Consequently, people who seek an international assignment with the

Table 4. Time to Adjust

Time	Percent
• 1–3 months	22.3
• 4–6 months	25.3
• 6–12 months	33.7
• Never	5.2

primary intention of escaping from personal problems at home are most probably not suitable as non-work issues could further compound to their difficulties of adjusting abroad.

Coping Mechanisms

Expatriates resort to a variety of mechanisms to help them cope with the stress and strains associated with the isolation of living and work abroad and the foreignness of the local environment. Table 5 presents the methods expatriates have found most useful in helping them adjust to the foreign environmental setting.

Socializing with Host Nationals versus Other Expatriates In general, more respondents resorted to socializing primarily with host country nationals over fraternization with other expatriates. However, consistent with the findings on mode of acculturation discussed earlier, expatriates with children were more prone to socialize with other expatriates. Furthermore, people who were assigned to Asia and the less developed countries were more inclined to fraternize with other expatriates; while assignees to industrialized countries and other Euro-Anglo nations were more likely to socialize with local nationals. This finding could be explained by "homophily"—since most respondents in this study are white, there is a greater likelihood that they would want to associate more with host country nationals in other Euro-Anglo societies.

Engaging in Sports/Athletic Activities Some expatriates sought to cope with the stress and strains associated with living abroad by keeping themselves occupied with sports/athletic activities. In general, more men than women relied upon this mechanism. This appears to be consistent with the trend in the U.S. In addition, those who were single were more inclined to resort to this mechanism because they have

Table 5 Coping Mechanisms

Item	Mean
• Socializing with host nationals	3.67
• Socializing with other expatriates	3.25
• Occupied with sports and athletic activities	3.16
• Communicating with family and friends back home	3.37
• Learning more about host country including language, sightseeing	4.16
• Spending more time with one's family	3.47
• Keeping busy with work all of the time	3.14
• Engaging in stress-relieving activities, such as consume alcohol, etc.	1.90

Note: Mean scores are based on 5-point scale, 5 = strongly agree more leisure time at their disposal whereas those who were living with someone most probably were more occupied with other commitments to their partner and/or family. This mechanism was also used to a larger extent by assignees to less developed nations. Since the separation mode is more common in less developed countries due to the more limited social circles that expatriates feel comfortable in, many of them may find physical workout as an effective way to cope with the isolation of living and working in such communities.

Communicating with Family and Friends at Home Yet some expatriates resorted to communicating with family and friends back home via phone, fax, etc as a means of coping with the isolation abroad. In general, women tended to use this mechanism more than men. This may be consistent with the trend in the U.S. Expatriates who were single were also more likely to engage in this activity. An inverse relationship was found between the number of international assignments and the use of this mechanism, i.e., the more times one has served abroad, the less likely one will utilize this mechanism. This finding supports contact theory which asserts that there is a steep learning curve associated with international assignments. Expatriates who have served abroad on multiple occasions tend to experience less isolation in the foreign environmental setting; hence the lower need for them to be in touch with people back home. This may serve to explain why they were willing to accept and undertake subsequent international assignments in the first place.

Learning More about Host Country Culture and Language As noted earlier in the paper, the majority of respondents in this study was quite cosmopolitan in their background and orientation, such as speaking another language and having lived for an extended period of time abroad. This cosmopolitan outlook may serve to explain why so many of them chose to spend their leisure time to learn more about the language, history and/or culture of the host country while abroad. In general, those with post-graduate education were more prone to engage in these activities. This finding may be attributed to the need for cognition, i.e., the greater intellectual curiosity among those who were highly educated. Consistent with the need for cognition, respondents with spouses who worked full-time were more likely to engage in this pursuit over those whose spouses did not work outside of home or who worked part-time. In addition, women expatriates were more prone to resort to this mechanism. Expatriates with children were also more inclined to pursue such activities. This latter finding may stem from the greater desire of expatriates to engage in activities the entire family can participate, sightseeing and visits to museums being some such pursuits.

Spending More Time with Family Another frequently used mechanism for coping with the isolation experienced in living and working abroad is to spend more time with one's family. In general, those who were living with someone tended to use this mechanism more than those who were single. As expected, those who have children naturally wanted to spend more time at home. A positive relationship was also found between income level of the respondent and the extent to which this mechanism was used, i.e., the higher the income level, the greater the desire to spend more time with one's family. Somewhat surprisingly, men tended to select this mechanism more than women, while controlling for marital status. A possible explanation for this finding may be that since women, as compared to men, typically spend more time with their families in their home countries, they would continue to spend as much time with their families while abroad. Hence, many women expatriates might not perceive a noticeable difference in the amount of time spent with their families whether at home or abroad. In addition, a positive relationship was found between age of the respondents and use of this mechanism. This is consistent with the trend where older people are more likely to resort to the comforts of home and family.

Keeping Busy with Work To cope with the isolation associated with living and working abroad, some expatriates kept busy with work all the time. There was no significant difference across sub-groups.

Engaging in Stress-Relieving Activities Some expatriates sought to cope with the isolation of living and working abroad by engaging in stress-relieving activities such as alcohol consumption. In general, respondents who were single and those who did not have children at home were more likely to engage in these activities. Furthermore, assignees to less developed countries were more prone to such devices as compared to those posted to the industrialized countries. This could be attributed to the higher level of stress experienced by those who were on assignment to the less developed countries. Typically, operations in the developing countries may be in the start-up phase and/or encounter more problems attributable to the less developed nature of market conditions. Furthermore, such countries may lack the amenities that expatriates from an industrialized nation may be accustomed to. These work and non-work situations may contribute to the higher level of stress.

Attributes Facilitating Interactions _____

Previous studies on interactions between expatriates and host country nationals have sought to examine either the efficacy of different management styles in cross-cultural settings, such as authoritarian versus democratic approaches or personality traits that facilitate adjustment, such as openness and ability to handle ambiguity. In this study, the focus was on what specific behavioral characteristics or traits were perceived by the expatriates to be conducive to effective performance abroad. The expatriates were presented with a list of attributes and asked the extent to which they perceived each of these traits as facilitating interaction with host country nationals. Host country nationals included superiors, subordinates and clients in the host society. The list of attributes and mean scores are presented in Table 6.

There were some significant differences across sub-groups. For example,

- There was a positive relationship between age and adoption of a nurturing mode. This is consistent with the phenomenon in the U.S.

- Those who were more highly educated and who were in higher income brackets tended to espouse a compromising style.

- Similarly, those who were highly educated favored a more compassionate and understanding mode.

- Female expatriates and those who were highly educated emphasized co-operation over excessive competition

- Respondents with children and those who were living with someone tended to stress harmony. This may result from practice at home.

- Expatriates who were older and those who were assigned to the industrialized countries were more likely to espouse an inclusive leadership style.

- Assignees to Asia were least likely to favor an inclusive leadership style. This finding may be attributed to the greater power distance in many Asian societies where subordinates typically defer to the superiors' opinions and decisions.

Table 6. Attributes Facilitating Interaction with Host Nationals

Item	Mean
• Nurturing	3.33
• Compromising rather than domineering	3.91
• Greater sensitivity to needs of others	4.02
• More compassionate and understanding	3.79
• Cooperative as opposed to overly competitive	4.02
• Engage in rapport talk	3.81
• Espouse an inclusive leadership style	3.95
• Adopt a listening mode	4.13
• Emphasize harmony by avoiding conflict	3.38
• Indirectness in communication	2.54

Note: Mean scores are based on 5-point scale; 5 = to a large extent

- Consistent with Hall and Hall's (1987) distinction of high- versus low-context cultures, assignees to Asia and the less developed countries emphasized indirectness in communication while such style was least likely to be adopted in assignments to Euro-Anglo societies.

It is interesting to note that the above behavioral attributes were identified by Tannen (1990) as distinctly feminine, as opposed to masculine, traits. For some time now, however, the popular press has speculated about the "feminization" of American society. This finding lends support to Tung's (1995) assertion that certain feminine traits (such as emphasizing harmony and heightened sensitivity) that might have held women back in organizational advancement at home may actually make them better suited for success in international assignments, particularly in Asia and the less developed countries. Both Adler (1987) and Taylor and Napier (1996) have posited that women can be equally as successful as their male counterparts in assignments to Asia.

Satisfaction with International Assignments

Most of the expatriates included in this study were satisfied with their current or last international assignment (mean = 4.1). However, when overall satisfaction was decomposed into two dimensions, namely satisfaction with expatriation programs and policies and satisfaction with repatriation, a different picture emerged. While the majority of people was satisfied with expatriation (mean = 3.37), most were unhappy with repatriation (mean = 2.61).

Satisfaction with Expatriation

- Consistent with the general and expatriate literature on job satisfaction, there was a positive correlation between organizational tenure and satisfaction with expatriation.

- In line with findings of other studies, those who were promised a promotion and/or position at home upon successful completion of the international assignment (i.e., career advancement) were also more satisfied than those who did not receive such a warranty.

- In this study, it was found that expatriates could be very satisfied with "overall expatriation" while being dissatisfied with repatriation at the same time. This could be attributed to the growing emphasis on one's internal career discussed earlier.

- Furthermore, expatriates who felt less pressured to conform to the norms of the host society, despite their strong attraction to the culture of the host society, were more likely to be very satisfied with expatriation.

The last finding suggests that satisfaction in itself is a multi-faceted construct. Where expatriates felt less pressured to conform to the norms of the host society, they were less stressed since forced compliance can often lead to higher anxiety. On the other hand, however, in order to be satisfied with expatriation, they must find the host society attractive in order to make the experience abroad worthwhile.

Satisfaction with Repatriation

- A positive relationship was found between repatriation and organizational tenure.

- As expected, those who were guaranteed a promotion and/or position at home upon return were also more satisfied.

- Expatriates who felt a greater need to conform to the norms of corporate headquarters while abroad were usually more satisfied with repatriation. This latter finding may be attributed to the greater ease that these individuals will have upon re-entry. Expatriates who adhered to corporate norms while abroad may experience less of a reverse culture shock upon repatriation.

- In contrast, assignees that adapt too well to the host society may experience a more severe culture shock upon re-entry.

The last finding again highlights how difficult it may be for expatriates to maintain that delicate balance between not adapting to the host culture, on the one hand, and overly adapting, on the other. The latter situation can generate concerns in corporate head office that the expatriate has "gone native" and possibly lead to problems of re-absorption upon return. In other words, the expatriate has to adapt just enough (i.e., not too much nor too little) to perform effectively abroad.

Turnover upon Return The high level of dissatisfaction with repatriation can pose problems for the multinationals that dispatched these people in the first place. High levels of dissatisfaction can lead to high turnover. Black, Gregersen, and Mendenhall (1992) found that 74% of American repatriates expected to leave their employers within a year of repatriation and 26% of them were actively seeking alternative employment. In this study, no data was available on turnover upon return. However, if high levels of dissatisfaction were to result in high turnover, then it could have disastrous long-term consequences on multinationals. Since multinationals are increasingly using international assignments for overall career development purposes as opposed to merely filling a position abroad, multinationals can lose out on such investments. A principal contributing factor to the high level of dissatisfaction with repatriation is job insecurity or inadequate advancement opportunities upon return. As presented earlier in the paper, only 7 percent of the expatriates were guaranteed a promotion at home upon successful completion of an international assignment.

Discrepancy Between Overall Satisfaction and Satisfaction with Expatriation While the discrepancy between "overall satisfaction with current/last international assignment" and "satisfaction with expatriation program and policies" is less than that between "overall satisfaction" and "satisfaction with repatriation," a gap still exists between the two former variables. This discrepancy may be explained by the fact that most respondents appeared to place an intrinsic value on international assignments per se, i.e., they value an overseas posting for the experience and the opportunities it brings for personal development and career enhancement, even though it may not be with the same company. This provides further support for the concept of "boundaryless" careers and the increasing significance that "internal" careers can play in motivating people to accept relocations, including undertaking international assignments. Despite their positive attitude toward an international assignment, some respondents are still dissatisfied with the following aspects of their company's expatriation policies and program:

- Many expatriates felt that their company did not provide them with a realistic job preview of what to expect in their current/last international assignment.

- An even larger number of expatriates felt that their company failed to furnish them with adequate cross-cultural training to deal with the realities of living and working with people in the host society. In other words, expatriates often had to rely on their resources to survive and thrive in the international assignment.

The finding that many multinationals apparently failed to provide adequate cross-cultural training and a realistic job preview is disturbing. Fortunately, from the corporate perspective, this deficiency did not appear to affect success abroad, discussed in the subsequent section. This finding contradicts earlier research results which showed that unrealistic job previews can be detrimental to cross-cultural adjustment and effective performance abroad, and the provision of cross-cultural training could minimize the incidence of failure abroad. The finding here may be attributed to the more cosmopolitan background of the expatriates surveyed. As noted at the beginning of the paper, many of them are bilingual or multilingual and have several years of prior experience in living and working abroad.

Success Abroad _____

While Caligiuri (1997) suggested that success in international assignments may be a multi-faceted construct (premature termination, cross-cultural adjustment, and actual performance on the assignment), this study has focused on the third dimension only. Even though cross-cultural adjustment is important, it is believed that many expatriates who fail to adjust may yet remain abroad to serve out the full term of the assignment.

In this study, success was defined as ability to "accomplish corporate goals/objectives." Self-reported measures of success were used. While it would be best to gauge performance through superior, peer and subordinate evaluations, given the method of distribution of the questionnaires described earlier, it was logistically impossible to obtain such assessments. The self-reported measures of success were considered as acceptable substitutes for three reasons:

1. Over one-half of the respondents had been with their companies for ten years or more. If they had been dismal failures, they would most probably have been dismissed from their respective companies a long time ago.

2. Another item in the questionnaire asked the respondents whether they had ever failed in a previous assignment, domestic and international. Following Tung (1981), "failure" was defined as "an inability to perform in the position and therefore the person had to be fired and/or recalled before the completion of the regular term of the assignment." Because the questionnaires were returned directly to the author and the responses were guaranteed confidentiality, the respondents appeared to be comfortable in disclosing these statistics. This lends support to the argument that success and failure cannot be used interchangeably, i.e., success is not simply the obverse of failure.

3. There was a very low correlation between success and satisfaction. This suggests that these are indeed two separate and distinct constructs and respondents did not simply report that they were successful because they were satisfied nor vice versa.

The mean score for success was 4.23. This implies that the vast majority of respondents perceived themselves to be successful in attaining corporate goals and objectives in their current/last international assignment. While this success rate may appear very high in comparison to previous published research, the findings are plausible for the five following reasons:

1. In a meta-analysis of published literature on expatriate failure, Harzing (1995) found that "the persistent myth of high expatriate failure rates seems to have been created by massive (mis)quotation of three articles," only one of which (Tung, 1981) contained empirical evidence that even in U.S. multinationals, 93 percent of the firms had recall rates of 20% or lower.

2. With the growing incidence of cross-cultural encounters arising from the globalization of the world's economy throughout the 1980s and 1990s, Americans apparently have become more adept at interacting with peoples from other countries. Adler (1987), for example, found that 97% of the female expatriates in her study reported that they were successful in assignments to Asia Pacific. Self-reported measures of success were used in Adler's study. In a replication of her 1981 study, Tung (1989) found that none of the 163 U.S. multinationals had failure rates in excess of 7 percent, even in assignments to culturally distant countries, such as the Middle East. While one-on-one tracking of the performance of U.S. multinationals included in her 1981 study was not possible since the respondents were not required to provide their company's name, Tung's 1989 study utilized essentially the same questionnaire and the surveys were sent to

the same population of multinationals included in her original study. The substantial decrease in incidence of failure suggested that, indeed, American expatriates appeared to have improved significantly their intercultural skills over time.

3. As noted earlier, the respondents in this study appeared to be very cosmopolitan as evidenced by the fact that over one-half of the respondents were bilingual or multi-lingual and many had lived for extended periods of time abroad.

4. The overwhelming majority of respondents perceived an international assignment as having a very positive impact on their overall career development. This supports other research findings that the perceived connection between expatriate assignment and long-term career plans was positively related to overall performance.

5. Even though the response rate in this study was very high, 48.87% of the expatriates did not return the questionnaire. Consequently, there may have been some self-selection bias.

Success and Country Difficulty

The study then examined the relationship between success and country difficulty. Previous research has suggested that the greater the cultural gap between the home and host country cultures (i.e., large cultural distance), the more problems of adjustment, hence adversely affecting performance. Conversely, the more similar the cultures (i.e., low cultural distance), the easier it is to adjust. This should improve performance. Similarly, one would expect that expatriates from industrialized countries who are assigned to less developed countries would experience greater problems of adjustment in comparison to those sent to other industrialized economies. In this study, country difficulty was calculated along two dimensions: cultural distance and difference in levels of economic development. Cultural distance was calculated using the technique advanced by Kogut and Singh (1988). No significant relationship was found between cultural distance and difference in level of economic development, on the one hand, and success, on the other. This suggests that American expatriates can be successful anywhere in the world, regardless of how similar or dissimilar the host country culture is and how economically advanced or underdeveloped the host society is.

This is a happy finding because in the era of globalization where market opportunities can arise in any corner of the world, regardless of level of economic development and cultural proximity, U.S. multinationals can no longer be selective about where they will invest and, consequently, to which countries they will send their expatriates. In fact, the countries which have experienced the fastest economic growth rates in the world in the past ten to fifteen years have come from societies which are culturally dissimilar and economically less developed, such as China.

Conclusion and Future Directions _____

This study sheds light on some very significant developments in the area of expatriate assignments in the past decade and a half. These were alluded to throughout the paper and will be summarized below:

First, as compared to Tung (1981), the expatriates (primarily Americans) in this sample appeared to be very successful in their international assignments. This may stem from the more cosmopolitan outlook of the majority of respondents included in this study—many were bilingual or multilingual and many have lived and/or worked for extended periods of time abroad, both personal and career-related. Furthermore, country difficulty did not appear to affect performance abroad, the measure of success used in this study. This is an encouraging finding because in this era of globalization where business opportunities can arise in any part of the world, regardless of cultural diversity and disparity in economic levels, American expatriates included in this study were apparently able to perform effectively anywhere to meet corporate goals and objectives. This is an important requisite to becoming "world class," to use Kanter's (1995) terminology.

Second, the majority of expatriates were favorably disposed toward an international assignment because they perceived the positive impact it has upon their subsequent career advancement. This is a significant improvement from the situation a decade ago where most high flyers were reluctant to accept international postings. Unwillingness to undertake such assignments could, of course, hamper the development of cosmopolitans.

Third, similar to the findings in the area of managing intra-national diversity, most expatriates believed that integration (which involves combining the best of both the home and host country cultures) and assimilation, to a lesser extent, can facilitate effective performance abroad. With the growing popularity of network organizations which require people of different companies, industries and countries to work together in projects and/or teams, it is increasingly imperative that executives of the future be able to combine, choose and select from a diversity of approaches. Most expatriates believed that separation, as exemplified by expatriate enclaves commonplace one or two decades ago, was not conducive to effective performance abroad.

Fourth, contrary to previous research which usually portray the family situation as a liability, in this study, the family was found to have a stabilizing effect on the international assignment. Expatriates who are living with someone or who have children often resorted to the comforts of home to cope with the stress and strains of working abroad.

Despite these positive developments, certain problems appear to persist, primary of which is repatriation. In this study, while most expatriates were satisfied with international assignments, in general, they were very dissatisfied with the fact that most multinationals still did not devote adequate attention to their repatriation policies or programs. This can have disastrous consequences for the multinationals in the long-term. Other problem areas pertain to the failure of many multinationals to provide adequate cross-cultural training programs and realistic job previews of the nature of the international assignment. Another persistent problem is the need for expatriates to maintain a delicate balance between overly adapting to the host society, on the one hand, and inability to adjust, on the other. That is, the expatriate has to adapt just enough to perform effectively abroad—the "Goldilocks" syndrome. This "dual allegiance" subjects the expatriate to even more strains in an already high-stress situation characteristic of many international assignments.

Besides the practical implications identified above, the findings of this study point to the need for future research in the following areas:

1. The finding of the positive attitude that many expatriates have toward international assignments, despite nagging problems with repatriation support the emerging notion of "boundaryless" careers. Future research should examine how this evolving notion of careers could affect the theory and practice of international human resource management.

2. The findings on satisfaction show that "satisfaction" is indeed a multi-faceted construct. Future research should seek to obtain a more comprehensive understanding of what contributes to overall satisfaction, satisfaction with expatriation, and satisfaction with repatriation. Furthermore, longitudinal research should be undertaken to determine the relationship between these different aspects of satisfaction and turnover.

3. The findings on effective performance abroad despite admissions of previous failures in domestic and international assignments suggest that success and failure are not interchangeable concepts. Rather, success appears to be a multidimensional construct. Future research should focus on what specific variables can affect different aspects of the "success" construct.

In conclusion, while there has been an explosion of research in the field of expatriate assignments in the past decade and a half, there is still a need to examine some less understood aspects of international assignments. The findings of such research can assist multinationals to better meet the challenges of the Twenty-first century, namely to recruit and develop "people for all seasons," or cosmopolitans, in short.

References

Adler, N. J. (1984). Do MBAs want international careers. *International Journal of Intercultural Relations*, 10(3): 277-300.

Adler, N. J. (1987). Pacific basin managers: A *gaijin*, not a woman. *Human Resource Management*, 26(2): 169-192.

Arthur, M. B. & Rousseau, D. M. (1996). *The boundaryless career: A new employment principle for a new organizational era*. New York: Oxford University Press.

Berry, J. W., & Kalin, R. (1995). Multicultural and ethnic attitudes in Canada: An overview of the 1991 national survey. *Canadian Journal of Behavioral Sciences, 27*: 301-320.

Bird, A. (1994). Careers as repositories of knowledge: A new perspective on boundaryless careers. *Journal of Organizational behavior, 15*: 295-306.

Black, J. S., Gregersen, H. B., & Mendenhall, M. E. (1992). *Global assignments: Successfully expatriating and repatriating international managers*. San Francisco, CA: Jossey Bass.

Caligiuri, P. M. (1997). Assessing expatriate success: Beyond just 'being there.' In D. M. Saunders & Z. Aycan (Eds.), *New approaches to employee management*, Vol. 4 (pp. 117-140). Greewich, CT: JAI Press.

Florkowski, G. W., & Fogel, D. S. (1995). *Perceived host ethnocentrism as a determinant of expatriate adjustment and organizational commitment*. Paper presented at the national meetings of the Academy of Management, Vancouver.

Hall, E. T., & Hall, M. R. (1987). *Hidden differences: Doing business with the Japanese*. Garden City, NY: Anchor Press/Doubleday.

Harzing, A. K, (1995). The persistent myth of high expatriate failure rates. *International Journal of Human Resource Management, 6*(2): 457-474.

Ibarra, H. (1993). Personal networks of women and minorities in women: A conceptual framework, *Academy of Management Review, 18*(1): 56-87.

Kanter, R. M. (1995). *World class: Thriving locally in the global economy*. New York: Simon and Schuster.

Kogut, B., & Singh, H. (1998). The effect of national culture on the choice of entry mode. *Journal of International Business Studies 19*: 411-428.

Moran, Stahl and Boyer, Inc. (1998). *Status of American female expatriate employees: Survey results*. Boulder, CO: International Division.

Rieger, F., & Wong-Rieger, D. (1991). *The application of acculturation theory to structuring and strategy formulation in the international firm*. Paper presented at the Strategy Management Society Annual Meeting, Toronto, October.

Schein, E. H. (1996). Career anchors revisited: Implications for career development in the 21st century. *Academy of Management Executive, 10*(4): 80-88.

Tannen, D. (1990). *You just don't understand: Men and women in conversation*. New York, NY: Ballatine.

Taylor, S., & Napier, N. K. (1996). Working in Japan: Lessons from western expatriates. *Sloan Management Review, 37*(3): 76-84.

Tung, R. L. (1981). Selection and training of personnel for overseas assignments. *Columbia Journal of World Business, 16*: 21-25.

Tung, R. L. (1989). *International assignments: Strategic challenges in the twenty-first century*. Paper presented at the 49th Annual Meetings of the Academy of Management, Washington D.C., August 14-16.

Tung, R. L. (1993). Managing cross-national and intra-national diversity. *Human Resource Management, 32*(4): 461-477.

Tung, R. L. (1995). *Women in a changing global economy*. Paper presented at the Tenth Annual Conference of the Society for Industrial and Organizational Psychology, Orlando, Florida, May 17-20.

Tung, R. L. & Arthur Andersen Inc. (1997). *Exploring international assignees' viewpoints: A study of the expatriation/repatriation process*. Chicago, IL: Arthur Andersen Human Capital Services.

Wall Street Journal, June 30, 1987, p. 1.

Fred Bailey: An Innocent Abroad—A Case Study in Cross-Cultural Management

Case 9.1
J. Stewart Black

Fred gazed out the window of his twenty-fourth floor office at the tranquil beauty of the Imperial Palace amidst the hustle and bustle of downtown Tokyo. It had been only six months since Fred Bailey had arrived with his wife and two children for this three-year assignment as the director of Kline & Associates' Tokyo office. Kline & Associates was a large multinational consulting firm with offices in nineteen countries worldwide. Fred was now trying to decide if he should simply pack up and tell the home office that he was coming home or if he should try to somehow convince his wife and himself that they should stay and finish the assignment. Given how excited they all were about the assignment to begin with, it was a mystery to Fred how things had gotten to this point. As he watched the swans glide across the water in the moat that surrounds the Imperial Palace, Fred reflected on the past seven months.

Seven months ago, Dave Steiner, the managing partner of the main office in Boston, asked Fred to lunch to discuss business. To Fred's surprise, the business they discussed was not about the major project that he and his team had just finished, instead, it was about a very big promotion and career move. Fred was offered the position of managing director of the firm's relatively new Tokyo office, which had a staff of forty, including seven Americans. Most of the Americans in the Tokyo office were either associate consultants or research analysts. Fred would be in charge of the whole office and would report to a senior partner. Steiner implied to Fred that if this assignment went as well as his past projects, it would be the last step before becoming a partner in the firm.

When Fred told his wife about the unbelievable opportunity, he was shocked at her less than enthusiastic response. His wife Jennifer (or Jenny as Fred called her) thought that it would be rather difficult to have

---

Source: J. Stewart Black. "Fred Bailey: An Innocent Abroad—A Case Study in Cross-Cultural Management." Reprinted by permission of the author.

the children live and go to school in a foreign country for three years, especially when Christine, the oldest, would be starting middle school next year. Besides, now that the kids were in school, Jenny was thinking about going back to work, at least part time. Jenny had a degree in fashion merchandising from a well-known private university and had worked as an assistant buyer for a large women's clothing store before having the two girls.

Fred explained that the career opportunity was just too good to pass up and that the company's overseas package would make living overseas terrific. The company would pay all the expenses to move whatever the Baileys wanted to take with them. The company had a very nice house in an expensive district of Tokyo that would be provided rent free, and the company would rent their house in Boston during their absence. Moreover, the firm would provide a car and driver, education expenses for the children to attend private schools, and a cost-of-living adjustment and overseas compensation that would nearly triple Fred's gross annual salary. After two days of consideration and discussion, Fred told Mr. Steiner he would accept the assignment.

The current Tokyo office managing director was a partner in the firm but had been in the new Tokyo office for less than a year when he was transferred to head up a long-established office in England. Because the transfer to England was taking place right away, Fred and his family had about three weeks to prepare for the move. Between transferring things at the office to Bob Newcome, who was being promoted to Fred's position, and getting furniture and the like ready to be moved, neither Fred nor his family had much time to really find out much about Japan, other than what was in the encyclopedia.

When the Baileys arrived in Japan, they were greeted at the airport by one of the young Japanese associate consultants and the senior American expatriate. Fred and his family were quite tired from the long trip, and the two-hour ride to Tokyo was a rather quiet one. After a few days of just settling in, Fred spent his first full day at the office.

Fred's first order of business was to have a general meeting with all the employees of associate consultant rank and higher. Although Fred didn't notice it at the time, all the Japanese staff sat together and all the Americans sat together. After Fred introduced himself and his general idea about the potential and future directions of the Tokyo office, he called on a few individuals to get their ideas about how the things for which they were responsible would likely fit into his overall plan. From the Americans, Fred got a mixture of opinions with specific reasons about why certain things might or might not fit well. From the Japanese, he got very vague answers. When Fred pushed to get more specific information, he was surprised to find that a couple of the Japanese simply made a sucking sound as they breathed and said that it was "difficult to say." Fred sensed the meeting was not achieving his objectives, so he thanked everyone for coming and said he looked forward to their all working together to make the Tokyo office the fastest growing office in the company.

After they had been in Japan about a month, Fred's wife complained to him about the difficulty she had getting certain everyday products like maple syrup, peanut butter, and good-quality beef. She said that when she could get it at one of the specialty stores it cost three and four times what it would cost in the States. She also complained that since the washer and dryer were much too small, she had to spend extra money by sending things out to be dry cleaned. On top of all that, unless she went to the American Club in downtown Tokyo, she never had anyone to talk to. After all, Fred was gone ten to 16 hours a day. Unfortunately, at the time Fred was preoccupied, thinking about a big upcoming meeting between his firm and a significant prospective client, a top 100 Japanese multinational company.

The next day, Fred, along with the lead American consultant for the potential contract, Ralph Webster, and one of the Japanese associate consultants, Kenichi Kurokawa, who spoke perfect English, met with a team from the Japanese firm. The Japanese team consisted of four members: the VP of administration, the director of international personnel, and two staff specialists. After shaking hands and a few awkward bows, Fred said that he knew the Japanese gentlemen were busy and he didn't want to waste their time so he would get right to the point. Fred then had the other American lay out their firm's proposal for the project and what the project would cost. After the presentation, Fred asked the Japanese what their reaction to the proposal was. The Japanese did not respond immediately, so Fred launched into his summary version of the proposal thinking that the translation might have been insufficient. But again the Japanese had only the vaguest of responses to his direct questions.

The recollection of the frustration of that meeting was enough to shake Fred back to reality. The reality was that in the five months since that first meeting little progress had been made and the contract between the firms was yet to be signed. "I can never seem to get a direct response from Japanese," he thought to himself. This feeling of frustration led him to remember a related incident that happened about a month after this first meeting with this client.

Fred had decided that the reason not much progress was being made with the client was that Fred and his group just didn't know enough about the client to package the proposal in a way that was appealing to the client. Consequently, he called in the senior American associated with the proposal, Ralph Webster, and asked him to develop a report on the client so that the proposal could be reevaluated and changed where necessary. Jointly, they decided that one of the more promising Japanese research associates, Tashiro Watanabe, would be the best person to take the lead on this report. To impress upon Tashiro the importance of this task and the great potential they saw in him, they decided to have the young Japanese associate meet with both Fred and Ralph. In the meeting, Fred had Ralph lay out the nature and importance of the task, at which point Fred leaned forward in his chair and said to Tashiro, "You can see that this is an important assignment and that we are placing a lot of confidence in you by giving it to you. We need the report by this time next week so that we can revise and represent our proposal. Can you do it?" After a somewhat pregnant pause, the Japanese responded hesitantly, "I'm not sure what to say." At that point, Fred smiled, got up from his chair and walked over to the young Japanese associate, extended his hand, and said, "Hey, there's nothing to say. We're just giving you the opportunity you deserve."

The day before the report was due, Fred asked Ralph how the report was coming. Ralph said that since he had heard nothing from Tashiro that everything was under control, but that he would double-check. Ralph later ran into one of the American research associates, John Maynard. Ralph knew that John was hired for Japan because of his language ability in Japanese and that, unlike any of the other Americans, John often went out after work with some of the Japanese research associates, including Tashiro. So, Ralph asked John if he knew how Tashiro was coming on the report. John then recounted that last night at the office Tashiro had asked if Americans sometimes fired employees for being late with reports. John had sensed that this was more than a hypothetical question and asked Tashiro why he wanted to know. Tashiro did not respond immediately, and since it was 8:30 in the evening, John suggested they go out for a drink. At first Tashiro resisted, but then John assured him that they would grab a drink at a nearby bar and come right back. At the bar, John got Tashiro to open up.

Tashiro explained the nature of the report that he had been requested to produce. Tashiro continued to explain that even though he had worked long into the night every night to complete the report it was just impossible and that he had doubted from the beginning whether he could complete the report in a week.

At this point, Ralph asked John, "Why didn't he say something in the first place?" Ralph didn't wait to hear whether or not John had an answer to his question. He headed straight to Tashiro's desk.

Ralph chewed Tashiro out and then went to Fred explaining that the report would not be ready and that Tashiro, from the start, didn't think it could be. "Then why didn't he say something?" Fred asked. No one had any answers, and the whole thing just left everyone more suspect and uncomfortable with one another.

There were other incidents, big and small, that had made especially the last two months frustrating, but Fred was too tired to remember them all. To Fred it seemed that working with Japanese both inside and outside the firm was like working with people from another planet. Fred felt he just couldn't communicate with them, and he could never figure out what they were thinking. It drove him crazy.

Then on top of all this, Jennifer laid a bombshell on him. She wanted to go home, and yesterday was not soon enough. Even though the kids seemed to be doing all right, Jennifer was tired of Japan—tired of being stared at, of not understanding anybody or being understood, of not being able to find what she wanted at the store, of not being able to drive and read the road signs, of not having anything to watch on television, of not being involved in anything. She wanted to go home and could not think of any reason why they shouldn't. After all, she reasoned they owed nothing to the company because the company had led them to believe this was just another assignment, like the two years they spent in San Francisco, and it was anything but that!

Fred looked out the window once more, wishing that somehow everything could be fixed, or turned back, or something. Down below the traffic was backed up. Though the traffic lights changed, the cars and trucks didn't seem to be moving. Fortunately, beneath the ground, one of the world's most advanced, efficient, and clean subway systems moved hundreds of thousands of people about the city and to their homes.

Catskill Roads

Case 9.2
J.B. Ritchie
Alan Hawkins

Introduction

Autumn had come early to the Catskills this year, and a fresh coating of leaves covered the floor of the yellow woods. Kathryn Hill-Baker rolled down her van window and the fresh, cool, mountain air that poured in seemed to ease the tension that had mounted over the past two hours. Kathryn's husband, Brian, was driving slower now as he looked for the turn-off to the lodge where they planned to stay for the weekend. As they left the crowded highways of metropolitan New York City two hours ago, they talked intensely about the future. But discussion slowed as they approached the mountains, and now Kathryn was lost in her own thoughts.

A few weeks ago four senior partners from Kathryn's New York City law firm had announced their plans to leave the firm and form their own. One of those partners was Kathryn's mentor, and he asked Kathryn to come with them and to assume the lucrative litigation practice with the new firm. If she accepted the offer, it would mean a substantial increase in salary and a tremendous career boost. However, she was currently involved with an enjoyable and challenging project with her present firm's largest client, a multinational pharmaceutical company that was establishing a new operation in Argentina.

But what was an important career decision for Kathryn became a critical family problem two days ago when Jim Collins called Brian into his office. Collins is an executive vice president at Universal Bank. He wanted Brian to go to Mexico City to pull Universal Bank (UB) through the coming crisis. During the oil boom years, UB's Mexico City office was one of its most profitable units. No one anticipated the severity of the economic collapse in Mexico, which sent banks with big Mexican loan portfolios reeling. UB was among the hardest hit—over four-hundred million dollars in loans outstanding to Mexico. A few smaller loans had already come due and were renegotiated to avoid default. But the next eighteen months would be

Source: J. Bonner Ritchie and Alan Hawkins. "Catskill Roads." Reprinted by permission of the authors.

critical as many big loans would come due and would almost certainly need to be refinanced. With domestic profits already squeezed by deregulated competition, UB couldn't afford losses in Mexico. Top management wanted a savvy manager to go to Mexico City to take the reins and they were personally involved in the selection process. Brian Baker, with his familiarity with the Mexican loan operations, his technical competence, his international experience, and his fluent Spanish, was the obvious choice.

Kathryn Hill-Baker _____

Kathryn, her husband Brian, and their two children currently live in an old but quaint house in a quiet New Jersey suburb. She was born while her family was abroad. Her father was a commissioned officer in the U.S. Marines. She was the fifth of six children in her family, the second one born in Japan. However, she was the only girl, and the family lavished her with affection. The Hills were very religious. Every morning the family would gather and read a brief passage from the Bible before breakfast. And every Sunday the family attended church services on the base.

Kathryn's family lived on a military base near Tokyo until she was eight when her father was transferred to West Germany. They were only there two years. Her father retired from the military and took a management position with a large firm in Detroit that did a lot of contract work for the Defense Department. Through junior and senior high school, Kathryn excelled in both athletics and academics. She was a National Merit finalist and received a full-tuition scholarship to the University of Michigan where she was an English composition major. She also played on the junior varsity tennis team until her senior year. She graduated in the top five percent of the class.

Kathryn was initially attracted to Brian when they met during her senior year in an English literature class in which they studied Robert Frost poems. Over the summer, she gradually fell in love with a sensitive and warm man. He was different from her macho brothers and the guys she had usually dated in high school and college. Kathryn's family attended the wedding but her parents were upset that she was marrying outside her religious faith.

Brian Baker _____

Brian was born in Panama City where his father was a diplomat for the U.S. government. When he was five his family moved to Mexico City where his father became the head of the U.S. Consulate there. His father was a decorated World War II fighter pilot and his mother had been an army nurse.

After the war, Brian's father finished up his degree in Public Administration and International Relations at American University, while his mother worked for a VA hospital in Virginia. His father graduated summa cum laude and was offered a diplomatic position in Panama City. Brian was born two weeks after their arrival there. Despite the demands of a young baby, his mother was actively involved in UN efforts to upgrade health care in Panama. Brian's earliest memories were tagging along with his mother as she inspected hospitals in the more rural areas of Panama.

The family moved to Mexico City when Brian's father was promoted to an important consulate position there. Brian attended a private Catholic school and most of his companions were children of wealthy Mexican industrialists and government officials. Over the years he learned to speak Spanish as fluently as he spoke English.

Summers were the source of Brian's richest memories. When summer vacation began, Brian and his mother would fly to Vermont where his maternal grandparents lived. They usually spent about a month there. Then they would fly to Michigan and meet Brian's dad and spend another month or two at a summer cabin in northern Michigan owned by Brian's paternal grandparents. The cabin was right on a lake and Brian probably spent three-fourths of his waking hours in or on the water, swimming, sailing, water skiing, and fishing. In the evenings they barbequed on the beach, ate and watched the sun sink into the lake, painting the sky with streaks of warm colors.

When Brian was 16, his father suffered a mild stroke and decided to ease up and take a "cushy, state-side desk job." They moved to New York where Brian finished his senior year of high school. He was accepted to the honors program at the University of Michigan and decided to go there and live with his grandparents. He studied political science and journalism, planning to eventually go to law school. After graduating he worked for a year at a local insurance company before beginning his graduate work. He was disappointed when he was not admitted to the University of Michigan Law School. But he enjoyed his work at the insurance company and decided to apply to the business school and was accepted.

The summer before he began in the MBA program at Michigan, he took a couple of evening classes to sharpen his math skills. Just for fun he also took an English literature class, something he never seemed to have time for as an undergraduate. There he met an attractive English major, Kathryn Hill, who was attending summer school in order to graduate by fall. They often studied together at night in the library and then went to an ice cream parlor where they talked until it closed. They were married in August.

Work and Graduate School ⎯⎯⎯⎯⎯⎯⎯⎯⎯⎯⎯⎯⎯⎯⎯⎯⎯⎯⎯

After a honeymoon, Kathryn worked as a staff reporter for a Detroit newspaper and edited and typed student papers to earn extra income. Brian started the MBA Program at Michigan and although busy, they enjoyed their marriage and looked forward to starting their own family when Brian graduated. The only significant friction between them was a result of Kathryn's desire to attend Sunday services each week. Busy schedules didn't allow them much time together during the week, and they felt it was important to spend weekends together. Eventually, Kathryn decided to curtail her church attendance to every other week, and would spend the other weekends with Brian up at his grandparents' cabin.

Brian did well in school although he didn't "set the world on fire." His writing ability and hard work put him in the top third of his class. He received two good job offers, one with a small but respected brokerage firm, the second with a large multinational bank. Both offers would put the Bakers in New York City where Brian's parents lived. The brokerage firm offered more money, but the bank offered more exciting career opportunities. Brian hoped to go abroad in the future. Universal Bank had branch operations all over the world with many internationally assigned managers. Kathryn liked the idea of living in New York with its endless cultural opportunities. And there would be ample opportunities in the future to continue her career in journalism, if she wanted. They accepted UB's offer and moved to New York.

Universal Bank

Universal Bank was an established, somewhat conservative bank with a large portion of their business overseas. In an average year, UB earned nearly sixty percent of their revenues abroad. The year Brian began working the bank had revenues of nearly four billion dollars. The International Banking Division was run almost like a separate subsidiary and was the glamour division of the bank. However, they seldom hired entry level managers, preferring to take promising managers with good track records from the various domestic divisions. UB had strong footholds in most of the big cities in Europe and England. In recent years, they had gained ground in an increasingly competitive Far East market, where U.S. multinationals brought their capital and built many manufacturing facilities to escape the high labor cost in the U.S. During the start-up phase of a foreign operation, UB catered mostly to U.S. and other English-speaking industrialists doing business in a particular country. As they got to know the countries better and how local businesses operated, they would do more business with national firms.

The deregulation of the banking industry had strained UB's conservative management. Past strategy had been to put a UB branch "within two miles of nearly every resident and business in New York." As a result, UB owned the largest share of the deposit market in New York. However, recently several of UB's competitors had gone to an automated teller machine strategy with its significantly lower transaction costs. In addition, UB's competitors were rapidly expanding their product lines and services to attract the upper scale customers who were willing to pay a little more for what they really wanted. UB's philosophy had been to move deliberately and carefully into new product lines and services so as not to "overburden the standard customer who just wants a dependable bank in a convenient location." This strategy seemed now to have hurt UB. Profit margins slipped the last two years and their fixed assets-to-sales ratio was now, by a wide margin, the highest among New York banks.

Not surprisingly, a new top management team was installed in the late 1970s. They were young, brash and aggressive and determined to turn UB's domestic operations into a market-driven organization. They were depending on UB's healthy international operations to provide them the cash flow to put the domestic bank back up on its feet and in the race again.

New York _____

Brian began at UB as a loan officer in a branch handling mostly small corporate loans from steady customers with revolving accounts. Although the job did not really push his skills, he enjoyed the regular, close contact with his clients and took pride in the growth of their small businesses. He spent a lot of time out of the office with his clients trying to get a better feel for their unique needs and problems.

His track record after two years was good, and he was transferred to the central office downtown and asked to handle the accounts of some large multinational companies. But these big companies were just after the best prices and personal contact was lacking in the job. After a year he took a third position with a branch that did a good deal of loan business with Mexican and South American multinationals operating in New York City. Personal contact was more available in the job, and he enjoyed using his fluent Spanish again.

Kathryn had given birth to their first child shortly after they arrived in New York, and a second child followed only 18 months later. Homemaking was challenging to Kathryn. She had always been so active before, but now taking care of two small children kept her at home almost constantly. After the second child was born, Kathryn suffered a depression. She tried to hide it from Brian, hoping it would go away soon. But it only got worse and Brian started asking questions. Brian suggested some counseling but Kathryn did not like the idea. She tried to find part-time work as a journalist, but no one seemed interested. Instead, she applied to law school and was accepted at Columbia University. Although Brian was a little jealous, he encouraged Kathryn to go. They arranged for a babysitter in the afternoons and Kathryn studied at night and on weekends. Brian would get home about five o'clock and take care of the children and do the housework. Kathryn's mood improved, and Brian gained an appreciation for the rigors of domestic life.

However, leaving work at four o'clock every day did not help Brian's career. Although he got to work early and kept a fair client load, he was unable to drink with his colleagues after work, a regular activity in his unit. Brian's performance evaluations were still excellent but he did not have inclusion in the strong social network of the bank that was valuable for career progress. And because "he couldn't be counted on after four o'clock," he was seldom given the "plum accounts." But Kathryn was happier, and Brian sincerely liked his "daddy" role and the daily counterpoint it provided to the kinetic pace of work. In a few years the kids would be in school, and he could get back on track at work. The drawbacks were that money was tighter because of Kathryn's tuition, and quality time for Brian and Kathryn was limited.

Kathryn's grades her first year were good enough to get her on the law review. She graduated in the top ten percent of her class and accepted an offer to work for a medium-sized law firm that serviced many of the pharmaceutical companies in New York City. The children began school, so with Kathryn's extra income they purchased a small home in a suburb with an excellent school system. Kathryn worked 60-hour weeks and Brian took on some extra work and tried to get back into the social network now that he didn't need to be home at five o'clock every night. However, after about a year of both Kathryn and Brian working, Brian began to feel restless. He had been in the same unit almost five years and was risking career stagnation. He began to look at other positions. Although he was attracted to a possible international assignment, he didn't see quite how it could be managed with his current family situation.

It wasn't long after this, though, that a chance for an international assignment surfaced. UB was opening a branch in Buenos Aires, Argentina. Brian had done some loan work with several small Argentine firms operating in New York and had a pretty good feel for how they did business. With his fluent Spanish, he would be a good candidate to manage that new branch. When he casually mentioned the opening to Kathryn one night at dinner, she was concerned.

"How can we manage that? My work is going so well now, and with the house and all, it just doesn't seem to be the right time, Brian," she remarked.

"My chances are pretty slim, anyway," Brian replied. "They've been cutting back their international managers the last few years because they're just too expensive. It takes $100,000 just to move them, and maybe $300,000 a year for salary, bonus, benefits, and perks. It can be twice that much in some places where the cost of decent housing is so high, or where there's high inflation. Competition for these positions is stiff. And with all the money involved now, an executive-vice president has to make the selection decision. I doubt that they would search low enough in the ranks of the company to find me."

But Brian underestimated his credentials. When Bob Jasper, the Executive Vice-president for UB-International pulled Brian's name out of the computerized personnel planning system in the bank, he was interested and asked Brian to come talk to him. Their thirty-minute chat turned into a two hour lunch as they discussed Brian's background, his work experience, and plans for the new Buenos Aires unit. The British banks dominated among foreign banks in Argentina. Research had shown that times might be right to challenge the "stodgy British banks down there." Brian was honest about his family situation but he could hardly conceal his excitement about the prospects of such an assignment. He would have almost complete autonomy to formulate and implement a strategy for breaking into the Argentina market, as well as responsibility for getting the branch up and running.

Two weeks later Brian was back in Jasper's office.

"You're the man, Brian. We want you down there as soon as you can tie things up here—no more than six weeks. This is the break you need. You'll be in the limelight. This assignment can turn you into top management material."

Brian was nervous when he recounted his conservation with Jasper to Kathryn. He restrained his enthusiasm but still tried to highlight the positive aspects of the assignment.

"This kind of thing is really good for kids," he argued. "It gives them a better perspective of the world. We'll find them a good private school, and the bank said that they'd help in finding you a job somewhere. The bank pays for high class housing and maids. They'll fly us back once a year for a month-long vacation, and they pay for a two-week R&R leave every year as well. Jasper said that he'll bring us back in three years. This is a once-in-a-lifetime shot, Kathryn. I know it comes at a bad time for you with your work and all, but when we get back, I promise you that we'll settle in and you can pursue your career full steam!"

Kathryn wanted time to think. They continued to talk about it, usually until two or three in the morning. Kathryn wondered what she would do. Despite Brian's assurances, she was uncertain about the prospects of employment down there. She couldn't speak the language and knew little about the culture. Kathryn's firm told her that she could have her job back at any time, which made things easier, but still, the uncertainty was almost overwhelming. One night she phoned her parents to talk about it. Relations between Kathryn and her parents had become strained over the past few years. Although her parents would not actually come right out and say it, she knew that they felt she had "abandoned" Brian and the children when she went to law school and began working. Still, she wanted their input. They both encouraged Kathryn to go.

"Believe me, Kate," her father's voice boomed over the phone, "these kinds of opportunities come along only once. If you don't jump now, Brian may never get another chance."

That night, Kathryn informed Brian that she was willing to go. They had only four weeks to get their affairs settled and Brian was so busy at work that Kathryn had to do most of it herself while trying to wrap things up at work. The bank offered to pay for a week-long language and culture training program for Brian and Kathryn, but they simply didn't have the time to go. They stored the furniture, left the selling of the house to a real estate agent, packed their bags and were gone.

Argentina

For the first 18 months in Buenos Aires Brian put in 16-hour days and traveled frequently. But it was just what he wanted: autonomy, challenge, responsibility, and excitement. The first few months he concentrated on putting together a good staff. Rather than bring down some Americans though, he hired away from other banks some local professionals who knew how business was done in Argentina and who had extensive contacts. And rather than target the big foreign multinationals, and compete head-on with the established British banks' bread and butter, he went after some middle- to large-sized domestic firms. Whereas English was usually the international language in business, Brian conducted all his business in Spanish. This meant he could usually deal directly with the president of the company rather than the designated English-speaking finance officer. His strategy was successful. The branch was soon profitable and growing rapidly.

His only major disappointment was that, contrary to Bob Jasper's "limelight" predictions, no one back in New York seemed to take notice of his accomplishments. Anonymity could be tolerated, but headquarters was painfully slow responding to any special requests. Of course, if his reports were late, he would get a call from some "knucklehead in the accounting department who thought Buenos Aires was another socialist state in the Caribbean."

Kathryn had a more difficult time adjusting to the move. The family spent the first two months in a hotel unable to find suitable housing within the bank's allotted housing allowances. Brian finally got someone in International Compensation back at headquarters to raise the allowance enough so they could afford a decent place to live. The children were sick much of the time the first few weeks.

Eventually they found a nice home to rent in a suburb of the city in a price range the bank would accept. But Kathryn hardly left the house the first few months. A maid did all the shopping and most of the housework. With the children in a private British school most of the day, Kathryn had more free time than ever before in her life. Much of it was consumed by Dickens' novels, which were enjoyable, but the loneliness grew more intense. Brian was concerned and hired a private Spanish tutor to come every day and help Kathryn learn the language, which the bank paid for. He also kept his eyes open for some kind of work for her. But women professionals were not well accepted in Argentina. After about a year there, he was able to pull some strings with a man who worked at the U.S. Embassy who had known Brian's father many years ago, and got her a position working with immigration cases, visas, and some sticky international licensing problems. Although apprehensive of her ability to speak the language, she was happy to be working and using some of her legal skills again. She quickly made some new friends.

At that point, things began to go well for the Bakers. Even though Brian still wasn't around much, Kathryn and the children took advantage of long school holidays to travel to scenic spots along Argentina's vast and beautiful coastline. Kathryn made close friends with some American women at work, and often they would travel together. Five years passed and no one seemed anxious to return to the United States.

Unfortunately, Brian's father's health had been deteriorating while Brian was in Argentina. Nevertheless, his death of a sudden stroke came as a shock to Brian. The family returned to New York for the funeral. While there, Brian dropped in to Jim Collins' office who had replaced Bob Jasper as Executive Vice President of UB International upon Jasper's retirement.

"It's good to get to meet you, Brian," Collins said. "You've done an outstanding job down there. You've put UB on the map in South America. As a matter of fact, we're thinking about opening a couple more branches in Chile and Brazil. If we do, I want you to move up and be a regional director for South America. I'll make you a senior vice president. You can still live in Buenos Aires if you want. Give it some thought, Brian."

Brian was flattered to finally be getting some recognition. Regional Director would be another exciting position. More importantly, Brian thought it was a signal from top management that he was being groomed for bigger things to come. Collins was a regional director in Europe prior to his promotion to Executive Vice-President at UB-International.

In addition, his family seemed genuinely happy. The children were receiving a superior education to what they would have received in the States. They had friends, and could speak the language. But they would soon be entering their teenage years and Kathryn was concerned that they might miss a crucial socialization period if they stayed abroad too much longer. If Brian took the Regional Director position, it would likely entail another five years of hard work. And Brian was concerned about the effect his long hours of work had on his marriage and his relationship with his children. He was also concerned about his mother, who was alone for the first time in her life. As her only child, Brian felt a responsibility to be closer to her now and help her adjust to his father's absence. It seemed clear to Brian and Kathryn that it was time to return to the States. Brian contacted Jim Collins and informed him of his plans to return in a few months when school let out for the summer. Collins was disappointed but said he would try to find a slot for him somewhere by the time he got back. With a feeling of pride for what they had accomplished during the last five and a half years, and anticipation for the future, the Bakers packed their bags and returned home to New York.

The Repatriation

Coming home wasn't easy. They left the warmth of Argentina and returned to the cold of winter in New York. There were no "Welcome Home" banners for Brian when he returned to work. In fact, he wondered if he was even in the right place. He hardly recognized anyone. Some major restructuring of the organization left Brian confused about strategic directions of the bank. The new (to Brian) top management team had replaced the old "knife-and-fork" banking culture with a lean, market-driven organization. But there were more serious problems. No clear position was available for Brian when he returned. Brian felt that he needed to get back into domestic operations if he was going to become top management material. But it soon became clear that no one was all that interested in taking him on board.

"These repatriates are out of touch with domestic operations now," was a frequently expressed opinion at the bank. "They walk around dazed for six months and when they finally come out of shock, they want to run the whole show. Overseas they had it all to themselves, but back here they forget we're a team."

Brian was assigned to work on a few projects at UB-International while he waited for some position to open up for him. He got involved with some of the sticky negotiations going on with refinancing some of the Mexican loans the bank had outstanding. But he felt more like a translator than a decision-maker. These projects hardly used the management skills he developed while abroad.

Meanwhile, the Baker children were having serious difficulties readjusting to American life. In terms of their education, they were well ahead of their peers in junior high. Socially though, they were perceived as odd, even stuffy, and had difficulty making friends. Brian felt responsible for the problems they were having and tried to compensate for it by taking the children to movies and spending a lot of time with them at night and on weekends. Although tired from work, Kathryn spent a good deal of time in the evenings talking with the children and helping them deal with their problems.

Kathryn was the only family member who seemed to be readjusting well. She went back to work full-time for the firm that she had worked for before they left for Argentina. They were delighted to have her back, and even paid for some legal update sessions at a nearby university. The firm had grown as some of their client companies had grown. One client company was now in the planning stages for a new manufacturing facility in Argentina. Kathryn become valuable in that process with her language ability, familiarity with local legal systems, and contacts. She traveled several times to Argentina on business and was very busy.

Brian was hoping that their return to the U.S. would give the family more time to spend with each other. He did spend more time with the children, but Kathryn's work didn't allow them to spend much time together as a couple. The five and a half years in Buenos Aires with Brian working 70-hour weeks had left their marriage strained. Their ability to communicate with each other, which played an important part of the happiness of their early years together, was rusty. But more importantly, they felt as if they were two separate persons traveling the same road, but in different directions, loosely coupled only by a son and a daughter. Brian and Kathryn were spending some time now with a marriage counselor, trying to repair some of the damage before it was too late.

After eight months of project work, Brian was still unable to find a suitable position at the bank. He was angry, frustrated, and wanted to quit. But the financial shock that accompanied their return to the States militated against that action right now. With the economy down, jobs were not easy to come by. Despite Kathryn's income, they were still struggling to meet their financial obligations. Real estate prices and interest rates had soared while they were gone and their new home required both incomes. Brian hung on, hoping that something would soon open up.

Then Brian ran across a friend he had gone to school with at Michigan. His friend mentioned an opening in the small New Jersey bank at which he had a revolving account. The vice-president of the bank was retiring next month. Although promotion opportunities were limited because the president was only a few years older than Brian and likely to remain in the number one slot for a long time, this kind of position would allow Brian to use his management skills again, and he would only have to work forty- to fifty-hour weeks. It was a stable position, and he could drive to work in ten minutes rather than commute two hours a day. He seriously considered applying for the position.

That's when Jim Collins called and asked Brian to go to Mexico City for eighteen months to handle the crucial negotiations coming up.

"You draw up the ticket," Collins told Brian, "and I'll sign it. Any guarantees you need, you name them, we'll do it. You've got my word that I'll bring you back in eighteen months as a senior vice-president anywhere you want to be. We're counting on you, Brian."

When Brian mentioned the offer to Kathryn, she was visibly shaken. Kathryn was still trying to decide whether she wanted to go with the new law firm or stay with the old one. And now this.

Brian called his mother and asked her to come stay with the kids for the weekend. Then he and Kathryn jumped in the van and headed for the Catskills to do some hard choosing.